LATITUDE
36.50

*Warming recipes
from the mountains*

LATITUDE 36.50

Warming recipes from the mountains

JEAN-MICHEL GERST

First published in 2012 by
New Holland Publishers Pty Ltd
London • Sydney • Cape Town • Auckland

www.newhollandpublishers.com • www.newholland.com.au

Garfield House 86–88 Edgware Road London W2 2EA United Kingdom
1/66 Gibbes Street Chatswood NSW 2067 Australia
Wembly Square First Floor Solan Street Gardens Cape Town 8000 South Africa
218 Lake Road Northcote Auckland New Zealand

National Library of Australia Cataloguing-in-Publication entry:

Gerst, Jean-Michel.

    Latitude 36.50 / Jean-Michel Gerst ; landscape photography
    by Ron Molnar ; food photography by
    Graeme Gillies.

ISBN: 9781742572123 (hbk.)

    Includes index.
    Subjects: Cooking, French. Cooking, German. Comfort food.

Other Authors/Contributors: Molnar, Ron. Gilles, Graeme.

641.5

Publisher: Linda Williams
Publishing manager: Lliane Clarke
Project editor: Jodi De Vantier
Designer: Celeste Vlok
Cover designer: Celeste Vlok
Food photography: Graeme Gillies
Production manager: Olga Dementiev
Printer: Toppan Leefung Printing Ltd (China)

10 9 8 7 6 5 4 3 2 1

Follow New Holland Publishers on Facebook:
www.facebook.com/NewHollandPublishers

Dedication

To my mum Monique, my dad Roland
and to all those beautiful people who have helped my fantastic career.

Acknowledgements

First, I would like to thank my friend Ron Molnar, for his amazing alpine photography and for the lengths he went to in capturing some of these images. It was so great to work with someone with a similar vision and who understood my concept.

To my (maître d'apprentissage) Charles Ritter, who is up there with the other stars of French cuisine, for having faith in me and showing me the way.

To all my teachers, for their patience when imparting their knowledge to me.

To all the farmers in the world, who put all their effort and love into providing us with their produce.

To all the fishermen, who risk their lives every day to bring us the fruits of the sea.

To my team at the Thredbo Alpine Hotel, both past and present, you, too, have contributed to my success. I will forgive your absences after big nights out, but I will not forget your efforts and your hard work.

And a special thanks to my tasting team for gaining a few kilos for me while we tested the recipes.

To Jhaney Kusar, for her valued opinion and friendship. Thank you so much for allowing us to use all the beautiful items from your shop for the photo shoot.

To my publisher Linda Williams, publishing manager Lliane Clarke, editor Jodi De Vantier and designer Celeste Vlok, thank you very much.

To all my chef friends for sharing their knowledge, their time and their friendship.

To all my friends in Thredbo for their help with ideas and suggestions for the book. A big thanks to Jade Guttridge for her help with marketing ideas and information on local producers.

To my beautiful wife, for all her hard work and patience and for coping with not having a husband for a year.

To my beautiful children, Dean, Yannick and Xavier.

And finally to my Maman and Papa (Monique and Roland) for all the sacrifices they have made for me so that I could become the chef I am today.

Sauce Vanille

1 ltr de lait
200 grs de sucre
50. grs de poudre vanille (ou farine)
2 œufs

Génoire au chocolat

1 ltr d'œufs ⎫ chaud-froid
500 grs de sucre ⎭
450 grs de farine
150 grs de poudre de cacao
1 cuillère au soupe de poudre à lever

Pâte brisée

1 kgrs ½ de farine
500 grs de saint doux
500 grs de Margarine
7 à 8 dl d'eau
50 grs de sel

Contents

Introduction   10

Hit the Slopes: Breakfast   14

Mountain Refuel: Light lunchtime meals   34

Après Ski: Evening snacks and canapés   94

Hearty Meals With Friends   122

Winter Warmers: Soups, stews and oven dishes   164

Sugar Hit   198

Extra Bits & Pieces   238

Index   270

Introduction

My childhood was an institution for my future.

In summer, we would gather blackberries in the woods. There was only one strict rule—never take all the berries, always leave some to share with the animals.

In autumn, when I was off school, my mother would prepare a basket for me with some snacks and I would leave for the woods in search of mushrooms. In the afternoon, with a full basket I would go to the pharmacy to check that the mushrooms were safe. And in the evening I would be enchanted by my mother's knowledge as she cooked up my pickings. I still remember the smell...

The kitchen was the heart of our home. My mum was always cooking something and all our meals were shared together. I would always be in the kitchen talking to my mum while she prepared the day's meals so I was constantly surrounded by food.

My father's vegetable garden was always full of produce. We had more than enough to live on and my father would store lots of the harvest in our cellar for use in the winter months. Having grown up just after the war, my parents were also very frugal and never wasted anything. They taught me to respect food and the people that produce it. All these things nurtured my desire to become a chef.

I was thirteen when my grandmother took me with her to a friend's restaurant in a small village in the Jura. It was there I first learnt to wash dishes but what I really wanted to do was to help the chef. The chef made a deal with me and let me peel and cut the vegetables. When she realised my interest and desire to learn, she suggested I start an apprenticeship at one of the best restaurants in the area. I seized on this opportunity and two months later what would become my lifelong passion began.

At the restaurant, we made everything ourselves. There was nothing kept in the storeroom, everything was fresh. It was seasonal and nose-to-tail eating at its best. The restaurant even reared its own pigs, ducks and chickens, the animals being fed any scraps from the kitchen. The hunters would come with their catch and we would hang the beasts and butcher them ourselves, using every

part of the animal. It was the best start a chef could ask for, and after three years I was ready to take on the world.

Certain that I wanted to be a chef, I left to work in Basel, Switzerland. I came out of my shell and into a big city with so many restaurants making so many different types of cuisine. I was amazed and passionate about my trade.

I travelled far and wide, learning as much as I could from every culture I encountered. From London and Gstaad, to Bangkok and Hong Kong, my influences were diverse. Coming to Australia gave me the opportunity to draw on all this inspiration and make my own path.

This path eventually led me to the beautiful Snowy Mountains. In many ways it feels like home: the climate, the European influences and the snow. Whatever it is, the mountains here have captivated me for some time now—I just can't seem to bring myself to leave.

Winter is our busiest time of year and after action-packed days on the slopes, the visitors are always looking forward to a wholesome and comforting meal. Snow food is comfort food. It warms you up and gives you all the energy you need for a big day out on the slopes.

Inspired by the traditions and recipes of my family, the region of Alsace and other winter destinations around the world, I hope these recipes bring to you all the warmth and comfort that they bring to me. They are sometimes a nostalgic memory of my childhood or a reminder of great times with friends. And I hope that these recipes will also create great memories for you too.

Hit the Slopes

Breakfast

Eggs with Piperade

Serves 4

Easy—a good start to the day.

1 small white onion, finely
  chopped
2 cloves garlic, finely chopped
olive oil
½ red capsicum (bell pepper),
  deseeded and cut into strips
½ green capsicum (bell pepper),
  deseeded and cut into strips
½ yellow capsicum (bell pepper),
  deseeded and cut into strips
salt
pinch cayenne pepper
2 roma tomatoes, cut into large
  chunks
4 large eggs
butter
1 large slice sourdough, cut into
  fingers
6 slices chorizo, cut into fine strips

Stir-fry the onion and garlic in a pan with some olive oil, until nicely caramelized. Add the capsicum, some salt and a pinch of cayenne pepper.

Gently simmer for 20 minutes, then add the tomatoes and simmer for a further 10 minutes to make the piperade.

In four small gratin dishes, evenly distribute the piperade.

Separate the egg yolk from the white and place the egg white on top of the piperade. Place the gratin dishes into a bain-marie with hot water three-quarters of the way up the sides of the dishes.

Bake in a 150°C (300°F) degree oven for 10 minutes or until the whites are set.

In a pan, heat some butter and cook the chorizo until crisp. Add the bread sticks and toss until golden.

Put the egg yolks on top of the baked whites, top with the chorizo and place under a grill for a few minutes. Serve with the crispy bread sticks.

Toast with Caramelized Apples and Double Cream

Serves 4

3 apples, peeled and quartered

100g (3½oz) brown sugar

2 knobs butter

2 large eggs

300ml (10¼fl oz) milk

1 splash vanilla extract

4 slices brioche

double cream, to serve

icing (confectioners') sugar,
    to serve

Classic, warm, easy and delicious. Breakfast in my home was as much of an occasion as any other meal. My family would always eat together, whether it was for a simple tartine and coffee or something as special as this dish. I love you, Mum, for all those beautiful meals.

Sprinkle the apples with half the sugar and cook in a pan with the butter until caramelized.

In a bowl, mix together the eggs, milk and vanilla extract. Soak the brioche slices in the milk mixture.

Heat a non-stick pan, sprayed with a little oil. Sprinkle the bread slices with a little sugar and fry gently on each side until golden brown.

Serve on a plate with the apples, a good dollop of double cream and a dusting of icing sugar.

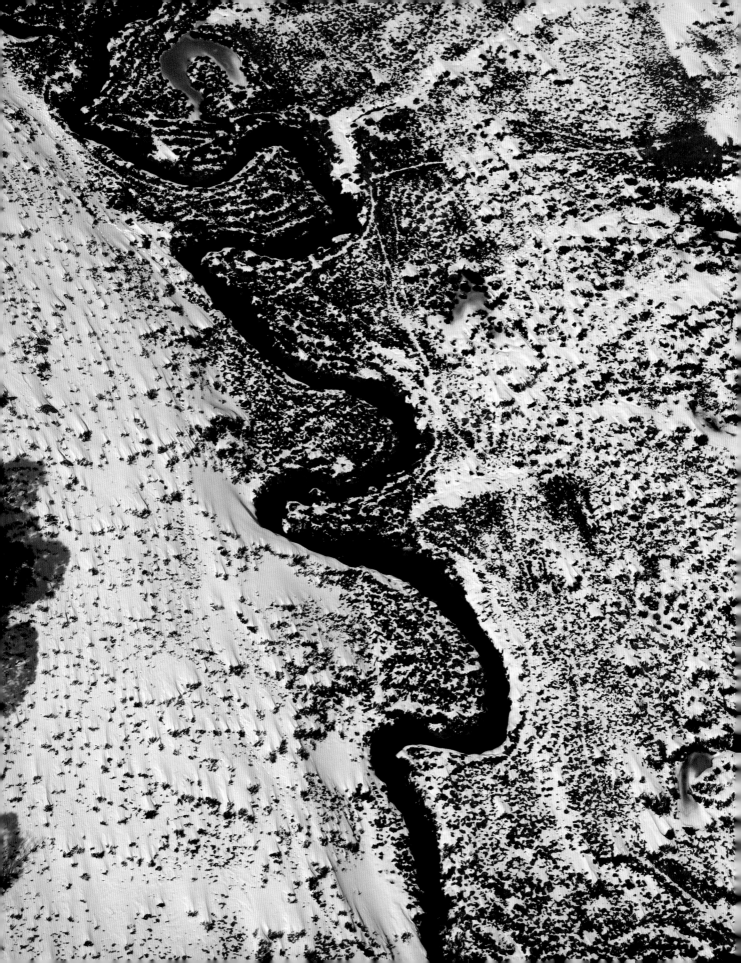

Mountain

Omelette Soufflé

Serves 4

90g (3oz) red (Spanish) onions, finely sliced

1 clove garlic, chopped

butter, for frying

200g (7oz) smoked bacon or any good-quality bacon

3 large field mushrooms, stem removed and finely sliced

1 beef tomato, peeled and diced

½ cup parsley, chopped

10 eggs, separated

100ml (2¾fl oz) cream

salt and pepper

200g (7oz) Emmenthaler cheese, grated

So light and so delicious. We used to eat something similar to this when I was working in Gstaad, Switzerland, just before heading up onto the slopes.

Preheat the oven to 170°C (335°F).

In a frying pan, sauté the onions and garlic in some butter until soft. Add the bacon and mushrooms and cook for a couple of minutes (do not colour). Stir in the tomatoes and parsley and set aside for 30 minutes or until cool.

Whisk the egg yolks with the cream and season.

Whisk the egg whites to soft peaks (not too stiff—just so they stick to the whisk without falling off). Fold gently in with the egg and cream mixture.

In an ovenproof, non-stick pan, melt a little knob of butter. Pour half the egg mixture in the pan, then the cooled bacon mixture. Top with the rest of the egg mixture and the grated cheese.

Put the pan in the oven for about 30 minutes.

Barley Porridge

Serves 4

200g (7oz) pearl barley, soaked overnight in cold water

600ml (21fl oz) milk

pinch salt

8 teaspoons honey

4 teaspoons walnuts, roasted and roughly chopped

fruit compote, to garnish

I love barley. It has such a beautiful texture and keeps your belly nice and warm in the morning. It does take a bit more time than your standard porridge but the result is well worth the wait.

Soak the pearl barley in cold water overnight.

Drain the pearl barley and place the barley and 1.5L (52fl oz) of water in a saucepan. Bring to the boil, then reduce heat and simmer for 30 to 45 minutes or until tender, then drain.

In the saucepan, mix the barley, milk, salt and honey and simmer for another 10 to 15 minutes.

Place in serving bowls and top with the walnuts and fruit compote.

Muesli

Serves 4

200g (7oz) rolled oats

2 pinches salt

4 tablespoons milk powder

4 tablespoons brown sugar

1 teaspoon cinnamon

1 pinch ground ginger

150g (5oz) dried apples, coarsely chopped

100g (3½oz) mixed nuts, coarsely chopped

150g (5oz) mixed grains (linseed, sunflower seeds, pepitas)

In Switzerland, this was always a bestseller. We used to fold whipped cream through it as well to make it even more luscious.

Mix all ingredients together and serve with yoghurt or milk. If desired, add some fruit compote as well.

For a warm breakfast, heat some milk with a cinnamon stick. Once hot, pour the milk over the muesli.

Date

and Apricot Compote

Serves 6

300g (10½oz) dried apricots

200g (7oz) dates, cut into small
strips

40g (1½oz) pistachio nuts,
de-shelled, coarsely chopped

3 tablespoons honey

In the autumn, my mother's kitchen always smelled of the sugary goodness of jams cooking away on the stove. So many jars of jam and compote—I think she used to make them for the whole street!

Put the apricots, dates, pistachio nuts and honey in a pan. Pour over 500ml (17fl oz) of boiling water and leave overnight.

This is ideal served with yoghurt, on top of muesli or stirred into porridge and does not require refrigeration.

Grapefruit
and Orange Compote

Serves 4

5 organic oranges
3 organic grapefruit
100g (3½oz) honey

My mother always used to say that if you eat plenty of this compote you will not get sick in the winter. It is best to find organic fruit for this recipe as you need to use the rind.

Zest one orange and one grapefruit and set aside.

Peel and segment the citrus fruit. Drain the juice from the cut segments and put into a pan together with the zest and the honey.

Bring to the boil then reduce the heat and simmer until you achieve a syrupy consistency.

Pour the syrup over the segments and allow to cool before storing in the fridge.

Pear

and Cardamom Compote

Serves 6

1kg (36oz) pears, juicy, not hard,
    peeled and de-seeded
juice of 1 lemon
400g (14oz) caster (superfine)
    sugar
14 cardamom pods
3 star anise

Pear and cardamom—what a marriage. It is just made for the cold winter months.
Serve it just on toast with butter or stirred through some hot porridge.

Cut the pears into large chunks and place in a bowl with the lemon juice and the sugar.

Crack the cardamom pods open and remove the seeds. Using a mortar and pestle, crush the seeds into a powder. Mix in with the fruit and cover the bowl for 30 minutes to marinate.

Put the fruit mixture in a pot, add the star anise and simmer over a low heat for 30 to 40 minutes. To check if the compote is ready, place a pea-sized amount on a cold plate. Turn the plate on its side. If the compote runs all the way down, it is not ready—cooking time varies depending on the water content of the fruit you have used. Continue to simmer on a low heat until the compote is done.

Rhubarb

Compote

Serves 4

600g (21oz) rhubarb
80g (2½oz) brown sugar

My parents have a big garden and 20 per cent of it is rhubarb. So you can imagine whose job it was to clean the stalks and peel them. But it was also me that was eating the most of it!

Preheat the oven to 180°C (350°F).

Cut the rhubarb into 5cm (2in) pieces. Wash them and place in a sieve to drain.

Line a baking tray with baking paper. Mix the rhubarb and the sugar and place on the tray. Cook in the oven for 25 to 30 minutes or until the rhubarb is tender.

Once cool, place in a container and store in the fridge.

Mountain
Refuel

Light lunchtime meals

Rainbow Trout Roulade with Citrus Salad and Maple Syrup Dressing

Serves 4

1 small witlof (chicory), cut into
    quarters

4 rainbow trout fillets, skin off and
    de-boned (can be substituted
    with Atlantic salmon)

4 slices prosciutto

4 heaped tablespoons butter

pinch sage, chopped

salt and pepper

2 large oranges, peeled and
    segmented

4 cups well-packed baby spinach
    leaves

Maple Syrup Dressing
    (see Index)

Welcome to the Snowy Mountains, home of the trout.

Preheat the oven to 180°C (350°F). Cut the witlof into quarters and remove the core, taking care to keep the leaves intact.

Place the trout fillets on a chopping board, flesh side up, and top with a slice of prosciutto. Place the witlof quarter on top and roll the fillet around the witlof. Tie the roll with string and place the roulades in an ovenproof dish.

Add some butter to the dish and a knob of butter on top of each roulade. Top also with a pinch of freshly chopped sage and season with salt and pepper.

Bake in the oven for 8 to 10 minutes or until the trout is cooked.

Serve on a plate with a salad of orange segments, baby spinach leaves and dressed with Maple Syrup Dressing.

Fillet Cooked in Almond Salt Crust

Serves 4

1kg (36oz) almond meal
500g (17½oz) salt
500g (17½oz) plain
    (all-purpose) flour
6 egg whites, beaten
pepper, for seasoning
few sprigs thyme
600g (21oz) leeks, white only
knob butter
olive oil
2 cloves garlic, finely chopped
⅓ cup white wine
salt and pepper
1 bass fillet, about 800g (28oz),
    de-boned (can be substituted
    for barramundi)

This can be made when you want to have a big day on the hill and the Joneses are coming over for dinner. Prepare, refrigerate and then bake when you're ready! To impress them just put it on the side of the hearth and serve drinks.

In a bowl, mix together the almond meal, the salt and the flour. Add the beaten egg whites and some pepper. Remove the thyme leaves from the stalks and add to the bowl.

Mix well and knead to get a dough-like consistency. If the dough is too dry, add some water. Wrap the pastry in cling film and allow to rest for 12 hours.

Preheat the oven to 200°C (400°F).

Cut the leeks in half, wash them and then cut them into 3cm (1in) pieces. In a pan, add a knob of butter with a splash of olive oil. Cook the garlic and leek and then add the white wine. Cook over a low heat until the wine has evaporated. Season with salt and pepper and allow to cool.

Roll out the pastry to 3mm (⅛in) thick and cut into two pieces, large enough to fit the fish fillet. Place the cold leek on one piece of the pastry, rest the fish on top and season with salt and pepper. Baste around the edge of the pastry with water and place the other piece of pastry over the fish to form a parcel. Pinch the edges around the fish to seal. Bake in the oven for 15–20 minutes.

Once cooked, remove and discard the pastry and serve the fish with a salad or some boiled potatoes.

Quenelles

Serves 6

500g (17½oz) bass meat, skinned and de-boned (can be substituted with barramundi)
4 whole eggs
300ml (10½fl oz) cream
50g (1¾oz) butter, melted
salt and pepper, to season
pinch of nutmeg
3L (105fl oz) fish stock
200g (7oz) button mushrooms, sliced
100g (3½oz) oyster mushrooms, sliced
knob butter
1 clove garlic, finely chopped
1 tablespoon chives, chopped
200ml (7fl oz) cream

Another dish that is just as easy to prepare in advance so you can enjoy your day on the slopes. All you have to do when you get home is bake it in the oven and open a bottle of white wine.

Cut the bass flesh into small pieces and pulse in a food processor until you achieve a smooth consistency. Add the eggs, cream and the melted butter. Season with salt and pepper and a pinch of nutmeg. Place in the fridge for 10 hours.

Bring the fish stock to the boil and then reduce to a simmer. Form quenelles with the bass mixture using two spoons and drop into the stock for about 5 minutes or until they float.

Place the cooked quenelles in a gratin dish. Preheat the oven to 180°C (350°F).

Sauté the mushrooms in the butter and garlic, add the chives and cream and reduce by half or until thickened. Season with salt and pepper.

Pour the mushroom sauce over the quenelles.

Bake for 10 minutes.

Gnocchi

Serves 4

1.8kg (62oz) raw beetroot
260g (9oz) désirée potatoes
50g (1¾oz) plain (all-purpose)
    flour
½ egg, beaten
sea salt flakes and pepper
olive oil
100g (3½oz) unsalted butter
400g (14oz) spinach, chopped

This dish is best eaten with confit duck and goat's cheese.

Peel the beetroot and juice them.

Peel the potatoes, cut them into a large dice and place into a saucepan. Pour the beetroot juice over the potatoes and cook on a medium heat until they are tender.

Drain the potatoes and push them through a sieve. Mix the potato with the flour and egg, then season. Knead the dough and roll out into sausage shapes.

Cut the dough sausages into 2cm (¾in) gnocchi pieces and poach them in boiling salted water. When the gnocchi come to the surface of the boiling water, remove from the pan and place in iced water for 5 minutes or until cold. Drain and toss in olive oil and set aside.

Heat a pan and toss the gnocchi with some butter, then add the fresh spinach. Serve topped with the Alsace Duck Confit or Goat's Cheese Baked with Alpine Honey and Granny Smith Apple Salad (see Index).

Cabbage

Rolls

Serves 6

250g (9oz) pearl barley
1 small Savoy cabbage
olive oil
salt and pepper
2 smoked trout fillets

TOMATO SALSA
15g (½oz) preserved lemons,
    diced
60g (2oz) tomatoes, flesh only,
    finely diced
12 basil leaves, torn
100ml (3½fl oz) extra virgin
    olive oil
10ml (⅓fl oz) rice wine vinegar
salt and pepper

HORSERADISH MAYONNAISE
1 tablespoon fresh horseradish,
    grated
50g (1¾oz) mayonnaise

This is my European nori roll.

Soak the pearl barley in water overnight.

Discard the green outer leaves of the cabbage as they are too hard. Use only the tender inner leaves. Blanch these leaves in hot water, drain and dry them and set aside. They need to be soft enough to be folded and rolled without tearing.

Drain the barley and place it and 500ml (17fl oz) of water into a pan. Bring to the boil and then reduce to a simmer and cook for about 1½ hours. The barley should still have some crunch to it.

Lay the cabbage leaf on a sheet of plastic film, brush with a little olive oil and sprinkle with salt and pepper. Spread just enough barley onto the cabbage leaf to cover it, with a thickness of between ½ and 1cm (¼–½in). Add the smoked trout fillets along the front edge. Roll as you would for a nori roll, using the plastic film to aid in the rolling process. Take the far edge of the plastic film and roll back again, wrapping the plastic film tightly around the cabbage roll. Twist the plastic film at each end to tighten and store in the fridge until set hard like a sushi roll.

To make the tomato salsa, combine the ingredients in a bowl and set aside.

To make the horseradish mayonnaise, combine the horseradish with the mayonnaise and stir together. Serve both sides with the rolls.

Veal Schnitzels

4 veal steaks, from the backstrap

100g (3½oz) flour

salt and pepper

6 eggs, beaten

200g (7oz) panko crumbs
(Japanese breadcrumbs)

2 small knobs butter

2 tablespoons olive oil

lemon wedges, to serve

SAUCE

6 anchovy fillets, finely chopped

100g (3½oz) capers, finely
chopped

6 small gherkins (cornichons),
finely chopped

2 shallots, finely chopped

¼ cup parsley, chopped

1 tablespoon Dijon mustard

1 cup mayonnaise

The quality of the meat will make all the difference in this dish. It is a dish served in nearly every ski resort in the world.

Beat the veal schnitzels out to about 2cm (¾in) thick. Dip in the flour that has been seasoned with salt and pepper. Shake off any excess and then dip in the egg. Again, shake off any excess and crumb, making sure you push the crumbs into the schnitzels so the crumbs stick properly.

Heat the butter and the oil in a non-stick pan. When hot, place the veal in the pan and fry for about 3 minutes on each side. Place on absorbent paper towel to drain.

For the sauce, put all the ingredients in a bowl and fold in the mayonnaise. Serve with some lemon wedges.

Eggplant

(Aubergine) Meunière

Serves 3

1 eggplant (aubergine), cut into 6
    slices about 3cm (¾in) thick

sea salt flakes

100g (3½oz) chickpea (besan/
    garbanzo) flour

salt and pepper

olive oil, for frying

100g (3½oz) unsalted butter

½ cup rye bread, diced into small
    pieces

60g (2oz) slithered or flaked
    almonds

2 tablespoons capers

¼ cup chopped flat leaf parsley

sherry vinegar

100g (3½oz) fresh goat's cheese

A simple dish that is ideal for an easy lunch. I like using our local fresh goat's cheese (chèvre) and you can get goat's cheese from most good providores. Serve with some watercress or rocket (arugula) leaves.

Cut the eggplant and sprinkle the slices with some sea salt flakes.

Put on a rack and refrigerate for about 45 minutes. This will get some moisture out of the eggplant and make it crispier when frying.

Dry the eggplant with some paper towels, dip them in the flour, season with salt and pepper and fry in some olive oil in a non-stick pan until crispy on both sides. Remove from the pan and place the eggplant on serving plates.

Wipe out the pan and add the butter. When it starts frothing, add the bread and the almonds and cook until nicely coloured. Add the capers and stir for 1 minute. Make sure you don't burn the butter—take the pan away from the heat and stir. Then add the chopped parsley and pour over the eggplants. Add a couple of splashes of sherry vinegar and a sprinkling of goat's cheese to the top of the eggplant before serving.

Farcon

de Chamonix

Serves 8

1 onion, thinly sliced

30g (1oz) butter

100g (3½oz) bacon, cut into thin
strips

1kg (36oz) désirée potatoes,
peeled and grated

200g (7oz) prunes, cut into
quarters

50g (1¾oz) raisins

100ml (3½fl oz) cream

2 eggs

salt and pepper

10 slices speck

A typical mountain heavy-weight from the Savoie region of France. It was traditionally a poor-man's dish that was cooked in a special tall mould with a central chimney. It is full of wonderful rich flavours and can be served with pork or sausages.

Preheat the oven to 150°C (300°F).

In a saucepan, sweat off the onions with the butter and bacon.

In a bowl, add the grated potatoes, the cooked onions and bacon, prunes, raisins, cream, eggs and salt and pepper.

Using a meatloaf pan or terrine mould, place the speck slices in a layer to cover the mould. Place the potato mixture inside. If there is any excess speck, fold the slices over to cover the mixture inside.

Place the pan inside a bain-marie and fill with hot water to halfway up the sides of the terrine. Cover with tin foil and cook in the oven for 3–4 hours.

Tarte

Flambée
(Flame Cake)

Serves 8

BREAD DOUGH

40g (1½oz) dried yeast

1 teaspoon caster (superfine) sugar

1kg (36oz) plain (all-purpose) flour

2 teaspoons salt

I have had such memorable evenings with my friend Serge, cooking and eating tarte flambée *(French for flame cake). He has a shed at the back of his house with a fabulous old bread oven that is ideal for cooking this dish. The tart can be topped with a variety of toppings just like a pizza but the most important thing is to have the dough as thin as possible.*

To make the bread dough, mix the yeast with the sugar and 1 cup tepid water.

Make a well in the centre of the flour and when the yeast mixture is bubbly, pour in the yeast.

Dissolve another 2 cups of tepid water with the salt and mix it into the flour. Work the dough until fairly stiff.

Turn the dough out onto a lightly floured surface and knead for about 10 minutes. Return it to the bowl and sprinkle with a little flour. Cover with a cloth and put in a warm place, around 40°C (104°F) for about 2 hours or until the dough has doubled in size.

After 2 hours, punch the dough down and turn it out onto a lightly floured bench. Cut the dough into eight pieces and knead each piece until smooth. Roll them into 2mm (⅛in) thin circles.

TOPPING

2 onions, finely sliced

40g (1½oz) butter

150g (5oz) speck, very finely
    sliced

250g (9oz) sour cream

salt and pepper

olive oil

Sauté the onions in the butter. Add the speck and cook over a low heat for 3–4 minutes so that the onions don't have any colour. Set aside.

Spread some sour cream on each of the eight thin circles of dough you have prepared. Sprinkle over the onion and speck mixture. Season with salt and pepper.

Ideally, the tarts should be cooked in a wood-fired oven but you can also bake them in a normal oven which has been preheated to 250°C (485°F). Bake in the preheated oven for about 5 to 10 minutes.

When they come out of the oven, splash some olive oil over the top and serve immediately.

Cheese Baked with Alpine Honey and Tart Apple Salad

Serves 4

320g (11oz) fresh goat's chèvre
4 tablespoons alpine honey
20 half walnuts, toasted
2 tart apples, cut into thin strips
couple handfuls watercress
1 small lemon, juiced
4 tablespoons olive oil
salt flakes
freshly ground pepper

This has been on the menu at my restaurant for the last two years. It walks out the door! It is fresh and clean in taste and the cheese and the honey are from local producers.

Divide the goat's cheese into four small ramekins or other small dishes.

Grill for about 2 to 3 minutes to slightly warm the cheese. Pour 1 tablespoon of honey into each ramekin and add five toasted walnuts per dish.

In a bowl, mix the apple and the watercress and season with the lemon, olive oil and salt and pepper. Serve.

Moricettes

and Bretzels

Serves 8 to 10

BREAD DOUGH

500g (17½oz) plain
(all-purpose) flour
10g (⅓oz) dried yeast
8g (⅓oz) salt
150ml (5fl oz) milk
30g (1oz) butter, softened

The first thing that comes to mind when I think of bretzels is beer. Bretzels are great served with an aperitif but can be eaten at anytime of the day. Where I come from, bretzels are sold on almost every street corner. The moricette is a roll that is made with the same dough. They are usually served all through the day as a snack with all different types of fillings. It is a speciality of the east of France.

To make the dough, put the flour in a bowl and place the salt on one side of the flour and on the other side, the yeast. Mix the milk and and 150ml (5fl oz) water together in a jug and warm slightly (not too hot as it will kill the yeast). Add to the flour and mix. Add the softened butter and mix.

Put the dough onto a floured bench and knead for about 5 minutes or until the dough has formed into a ball. Put the dough in a bowl, cover with a cloth and put in a warm place next to your oven, around 40°C (104°F).

Leave to rise for about 1½ hours or until the dough has doubled in volume. Once the dough has risen, cut it into twelve pieces, about 70g (2¼oz) each. Knead six of the balls for about 3 minutes and form into little loaves. These will be the moricettes.

Knead the other six pieces of dough and roll them out into 25cm (10in) long rolls. Take each end and bring them together and cross over into a knot to form the shape of a pretzel.

WATER BATH

2 teaspoons salt

240g (9oz) bicarbonate of soda
(baking soda)

1 egg white, beaten

caraway or sesame seeds,
for sprinkling

Preheat the oven to 200°C (400°F).

In a pan, make a water bath with 3L (105fl oz) water, salt and bicarbonate soda and bring to the boil.

Plunge the moricettes and the bretzels, one by one, into the boiling water for 2 seconds each. Take them out and put them on a tray lined with a cloth to drain.

Place the blanched items on a tray lined with baking paper and brush with the egg white. With a sharp knife, cut a couple of incisions on the loaves only and sprinkle with some caraway seeds or sesame seeds. For the bretzels, you can sprinkle the same, but I recommend sea salt.

Bake them in the oven for about 15 minutes.

Mushrooms

with Anchovy Sauce

Serves 4 to 6

Enjoyed most of the time as a tapas-like dish with a nice glass of wine, sharing your day on the hill with a friend.

ANCHOVY SAUCE

200g (7oz) anchovy fillets

1 tablespoon red wine vinegar

200ml (7fl oz) olive oil

1 clove garlic, crushed

50g (1¾oz) sourdough
    breadcrumbs

1 tablespoon thyme, chopped

pepper

½ lemon, juiced

MUSHROOMS

2 small eggs, lightly beaten and
    seasoned

pinch nutmeg

salt and pepper

2 tablespoons cream

400g (14oz) mushrooms, stem
    removed and skin removed

2 cups panko crumbs (Japanese
    breadcrumbs)

To make the anchovy sauce, drain the anchovies and put in a food processor with the rest of the sauce ingredients and pulse into a paste.

Put the paste in a bowl and set aside.

To make the mushrooms, combine the eggs and nutmeg in a bowl and season with salt and pepper to taste. Add the cream and mix well.

Dip the mushrooms into the egg mixture, then in the panko crumbs. Make sure you press the crumbs onto the mushrooms by squeezing them between your hands.

Fry the mushrooms in batches in hot oil heated to 195°C (380°F) for about 2 to 3 minutes or until golden brown. Drain on paper towels and keep warm.

Serve with the anchovy sauce.

Pan-fried

Flank Steak, Potato and Truffle Chaussons and Shallots Sauce

Serves 4

3 knobs butter
6 eschalots (shallots), finely
    chopped
2 small carrots, finely diced
2 sprigs thyme, finely chopped
1 bay leaf
2 tablespoons tomato paste
    (purée)
280ml (10fl oz) red wine
30ml (1fl oz) brandy
20ml (⅔fl oz) red wine vinegar
400ml (14fl oz) beef stock
olive oil, for frying
4 flank steaks, 250g (9oz) each
salt
1 tablespoon coarse pepper
¼ cup parsley, chopped, for
    garnish

Beef flank is also known as skirt steak. It has an amazing taste and should be on more menus. A chausson is simply a turnover. You will see chausson aux pommes *(apple turnovers) sold all over France but this is a savoury version that goes beautifully with this steak and a nice salad.*

In a pan, melt one knob of butter and add the eschalots and the carrots and cook until soft.

Add the herbs, the tomato paste and the wine and reduce by one-third. Add the brandy and the vinegar, bring to the boil and pour in the beef stock. Reduce by half and keep warm.

In a frying pan, melt some butter and some oil. Add the steaks and cook for about 3 minutes on each side. Season with salt and pepper.

When the steaks are cooked to your liking, pour over the sauce and serve with the potato and truffle chaussons. Sprinkle with parsley, to serve.

POTATO AND TRUFFLE
CHAUSSONS

500ml (17fl oz) cream

4 sprigs thyme

50ml (1½fl oz) white wine

2 cloves garlic, crushed

1kg (36oz) désirée potatoes,
peeled and cut into
3mm (⅛in) slices

2 pinches nutmeg

100ml (2¾fl oz) milk

4 sheets good-quality store-
bought puff pastry

50g (1¾oz) truffle paste or
½ fresh truffle, thinly
sliced (substitute porcini
mushrooms for truffles)

salt and pepper

3 egg yolks, lightly beaten

For the chaussons, first heat the cream with the thyme, white wine and garlic for 5 minutes. Remove from the heat and infuse overnight. The next day, strain the cream.

Put the potato slices in a pot and pour over the cream mixture, nutmeg and milk. Cook the potatoes for about 10 minutes. They have to stay slightly firm. Cool them in the cream on a tray.

Preheat the oven to 180°C (350°F).

Cut out four circles of puff pastry about 20cm (8in) in diameter. With a pastry brush, paint some egg wash around half the circle. Place the potato mixture on one side, add the truffles and fold the pastry on itself. Pinch the pastry together with your fingers, ensuring the pie is airtight.

Brush the top of each pie with the egg wash and place on a lined tray and bake for 20 minutes in the oven.

Croquette

Potatoes with Truffles and Goat's Curd

Serves 4

600g (21oz) kipfler potatoes, peeled and cut into 3cm (1¼in) square pieces

60g (2oz) eschalots (shallots), finely diced

1 clove garlic, finely chopped

2 knobs butter

15g (½oz) truffle paste or truffles, finely diced

65g (2¼oz) goat's curd

1 pinch nutmeg

1 tablespoon plain (all-purpose) flour

salt and pepper

2L (70fl oz) peanut oil

The first time I ate this dish it was at a friend of mine in Chamonix. The truffles came from Italy and the curd from the farm down the road—there is nothing better than local produce. But this is also one of those meals you don't eat often because it's something special.

Cook the potatoes in a pot three-quarters full with cold water and 1 tablespoon of salt.

Simmer for about 30 minutes or until tender. Make sure the potatoes are dry and not watery. When ready, strain and crush with a fork.

Sauté the eschalots and garlic in two knobs of butter for 10 minutes over a low heat. Add to the potatoes together with the truffle paste or fresh truffles, the goat's curd, nutmeg and the flour and season to taste.

Mix all ingredients well and shape the mixture into little oval shapes about 5cm (2in) long and 2cm (¾in) thick.

Heat the peanut oil in a large pot with about a 3L (105fl oz) capacity to 180°C (350°F) and fry the croquettes until golden. It should take about 2 minutes to cook the croquettes so that they are crispy on the outside and gooey in the middle.

Serve with a green salad or with grilled meat.

Rabbit Terrine

Serves 8 to 10

1 whole rabbit (about 1.5 kg/3lb 5oz), cut into 10 pieces

½ pig's trotter, cut in half and then length ways

1 teaspoon mustard powder

250ml (9fl oz) white wine

5 cloves garlic, crushed

½ small bunch thyme

1 tablespoon tarragon, chopped

2 bay leaves

300g (10¼oz) carrots, cut into slices

1 leek, washed and cut into 2cm (¾in) circles (white only)

8 small eschalots (shallots), cut in half

1 good pinch saffron

salt and pepper

1L (36fl oz) chicken stock

This jellied terrine is a recipe I had for years in one of my notebooks. Rabbit is a real staple in France so I was really shocked when I first arrived in Australia to find that no one was eating this delicious meat. But times have changed—three years ago my supplier ran out of rabbit and I had to take it off the menu!

Put the rabbit pieces, trotter, mustard powder, wine, garlic, thyme, tarragon, bay leaves, carrots, leek, eschalots and the saffron in a large bowl and mix together. Season with salt and pepper and cover and refrigerate for one day.

The next day, preheat the oven to 170°C (335°F).

Pour the rabbit mixture into a casserole dish, which has a lid, add the stock and put in the oven in a water bath for about 2 to 2½ hours.

When the rabbit is cooked, cool and remove the pieces out of the dish. Remove the trotter. Strain the liquid, keeping the carrots and leek in one bowl and the broth in another.

Peel the meat off the bones and cut into small pieces. Place the meat into a terrine mould or a similar dish and add the carrots and leeks.

Taste the broth and check if it needs seasoning. Add salt and pepper if necessary. Check if the stock will set by pouring a small ladleful into a bowl and placing it in the refrigerator for 5 minutes. If the jelly does not set, you can always add a little gelatine (one sheet of geleatine per 1 cup of stock). Pour over the rabbit mixture and refrigerate for 24 hours.

Slice the terrine and serve.

Trout Fillet in Toasted Sesame Seed Crust

Serves 4

100g (3½oz) pancetta, thinly
    sliced

3 egg whites

4 rainbow trout fillets, bones and
    skin removed

70g (2¼oz) sesame seeds,
    toasted

knob butter

olive oil

1 bunch chives, chopped

salt and pepper

This way of pan-frying the trout is similar in taste to the traditional trout and almond butter. It is very fresh and crisp.

Place the pancetta slices on a tray lined with baking paper. Top with another layer of baking paper and place another tray on top so that the pancetta slices are sandwiched between the trays to stay flat.

Cook in a 120°C (250°F) oven for approximately 20 minutes or until crispy.

Whisk the egg whites in a bowl. Brush the trout fillets on one side only with the egg whites and sprinkle with the toasted sesame seeds.

Heat some butter and olive oil in a non-stick pan over a moderate heat. Pan-fry the fillets in the pan for about 2 to 3 minutes each side, taking care not to burn the side with the sesame seeds.

Sprinkle the trout fillets with chopped chives and serve with the crispy pancetta and a fresh garden salad, dressed with Maple Syrup Dressing (see Index).

Trout with Bass

Serves 4

4 rainbow trout, 250g (9oz) each

200g (7oz) sea bass meat, cut
　　into small pieces (can be
　　substituted with barramundi)

1 egg

300ml (10fl oz) cream

50g (1¾oz) spring onions
　　(scallions)

200ml (7fl oz) Muscat wine

500ml (17fl oz) fish stock

2 knobs butter

salt and pepper

chervil or dill, to garnish

Open the trout from the back and remove bones.

In a food processor, pulse the bass meat until it becomes smooth. Add one egg and 100ml (2¾oz) of the cream and season to taste.

Preheat the oven to 170°C (335°F).

Place the trout in a gratin dish. Put the bass mixture into a piping bag and pipe into each of the trout. Top with the shallots. Pour the Muscat and fish stock into the dish and add a knob of butter. Cook in a preheated oven for 15 minutes, basting regularly with the Muscat and fish stock.

Meanwhile, in a small pan on a low heat, reduce the remaining cream by half. Add a knob of butter and season.

Place the trout on a plate, with some of the cooking juices spooned around the plate. Spoon some of the reduced cream onto the plate and garnish with chervil or dill.

Fillet Gravalax-Style, Warm Potato Salad

Serves 4

Marinade
100g (3½oz) salt
80g (2½oz) caster (superfine) sugar
400g (14oz) salmon fillets
200ml (7fl oz) olive oil

Potato salad
400g (28oz) désirée or kipfler potatoes
250ml (9fl oz) olive oil
1 clove garlic, crushed
few sprigs thyme
1 bay leaf
8 small eschalots (shallots)
pinch salt
2 tablespoons chives, chopped

Easy, simple and so delicious—the perfect lunch on the mountain. The sauce ravigote is a classic French sauce that adds a nice acidity and texture to this dish.

For the marinade, mix the salt and sugar together and then place the salmon fillets flesh side down on the salt mixture. Put in the fridge for 10 hours.

Then wash the salmon under cold water and marinate in the olive oil for a further 3 hours.

Make potato salad by peeling the potatoes and then, with a slicer, slice into 3mm (⅛in) thick slices. Blanch them in hot water until tender but still firm—the potatoes must not fall apart. Drain and dry them and place them in a bowl with the olive oil, garlic, thyme and bay leaf. Peel the eschalots and slice as thinly as possible using a mandolin. Add to the potatoes, along with a pinch of salt.

SAUCE RAVIGOTE

3 hard-boiled eggs, chopped

3 shallots (spring onions/
     scallions), finely chopped

½ cup parsley, chopped

2 tablespoons sage, chopped

4 small gherkins (cornichons),
     finely diced

2 tablespoons mustard

¼ cup olive oil

salt and pepper

2 tablespoons capers, chopped

1 tablespoon cider vinegar

For the sauce ravigote, mix all the ingredients in a bowl and season.

Cut the salmon into very thin slices (as thin as you possibly can).

Warm the potato mixture on the stove then, with a slotted spoon, remove the potatoes from the oil. Place on a serving dish, topped with the salmon slices. Strain some of the shallots from the oil and add on top of the salmon. Top with a spoonful of sauce ravigote. Serve with a couple of slices of toasted bread and sprinkle the potato salad with the chopped chives.

Sandwiches

of Swede Confit, Pork Kassler and Horseradish Mayonnaise

Serves 4

SWEDE CONFIT

1 large swede, peeled and cut into juliennes (strips of 6mm (¼ in) thick)

50g (1¾oz) sea salt flakes

olive oil

½ onion, thinly sliced

1 clove garlic, thinly sliced

½ cup white wine

2 bay leaves

2 pinches cumin seeds, roasted

100g (3½oz) smoked bacon, sliced

780ml (26¼fl oz) chicken stock

pepper

A beautiful sandwich—I guess you could call it my version of the Reuben sandwich. The sweetness of the swede and the saltiness of the Kassler go so very well together.

Put the strips of swede in a bowl and sprinkle them with the salt. Cover and refrigerate for three days.

On the third day, squeeze the excess liquid out of the swedes.

In a small pot, heat some oil, add the onions and the garlic and sauté. Add the swede and stir for about 1 minute. Pour in the wine and let it evaporate then add the aromatic herbs, bay leaf and cumin, the bacon and the stock. Simmer for about 30 minutes.

Sprinkle with some pepper and serve (the swedes should still have some crunch to them).

SANDWICHES

4 moricettes (rolls) or 8 slices
    walnut bread

butter

4 slices pork kassler, about 150g
    (5oz) each

4 tablespoons chicken stock

200g (7oz) swede confit (see
    recipe opposite)

¼ cup mayonnaise

1 teaspoon grated horseradish
    (or good-quality, bottled
    horseradish)

¼ cup capers, fried

1 cup watercress

salt and pepper

Slice the moricettes in half and butter each slice. If using walnut bread, toast each slice before spreading with butter.

Place the kassler slices in a pan with a little butter and chicken stock and heat for a couple of minutes.

In another pan, heat the confit.

To put the sandwich together, divide the confit onto four halves of the rolls or four slices of the bread. Top with the kassler.

Mix the mayonnaise and horseradish together and spread on top of the kassler. Sprinkle with the capers, top with the watercress and then the other half of the roll or slice of bread.

Enjoy with a salad or some gherkins (cornichons).

Salmon and Dill Cake

Serves 6

1 tablespoon butter, melted
200g (7oz) flour
10g (⅓oz) dried yeast
200g (7oz) egg, shells removed
100ml (3½fl oz) white wine
100g (3½oz) olive oil
salt and pepper
50g (1¾oz) parmesan, grated
30g (1oz) cheddar cheese, grated
260g (9oz) smoked salmon,
    diced small
1 bunch dill, finely chopped

My mother used to put this one in our lunchbox as kids when we were on the way to the slopes. Delicious with some cornichons (gherkins) and a creamy cucumber salad.

Preheat the oven to 180°C (350°F). Grease a loaf mould with the melted butter. Dust with some flour and shake off the excess.

In a large bowl, sift the flour and mix in the yeast. In a separate bowl, whisk the egg, white wine and oil together. Season with salt and pepper.

Combine the egg mixture with the flour, then add the cheese, salmon and chopped dill.

Add the mixture to the mould and bake for 40 minutes until firm to the touch and golden. If a skewer pushed into the centre comes out clean, it is cooked.

Trout Brandade

Serves 4

300g (10½oz) starchy potatoes, peeled and chopped
100ml (2¾fl oz) extra virgin olive oil
salt and pepper
4 tablespoons parsley, chopped
200g (7oz) smoked trout, torn into small pieces or crushed with a fork

Perfect for tapas in the afternoon, watching the sun go down on the hill with a glass or two of wine.

Cook the potatoes in salted water until tender. Once cooked, drain and crush them with a fork.

Add the oil, salt and pepper. Mix in the parsley and the trout. If the mix is too thick, just add a little more olive oil.

Serve with char-grilled sourdough, rubbed with garlic.

Soufflé
of Potato and Smoked Trout

Serves 6

300g (10½oz) potatoes, peeled
and diced
50g (1¾oz) cream
40g (1½oz) butter
ground pepper
pinch cayenne pepper
pinch nutmeg
2 large eggs, separated
300g (10½oz) smoked trout
1 large egg white
butter, to grease the ramekins

Preheat the oven to 180°C (350°F).

Cook the potatoes in salted water until tender. When the potatoes are cooked, drain well to remove any excess moisture. You don't want the mashed potatoes to be sloppy. Mash the potatoes. Ideally, puree the potatoes using a mouli, but if mashing make sure they are mashed really well. While the potatoes are still hot, add the cream, butter, pepper, cayenne pepper, nutmeg and the two egg yolks. Mix well.

Break up the smoked trout really well using your fingers. The smaller the pieces, the better the soufflé will rise. Then fold the smoked trout into the potato mixture.

Whisk the three egg whites to firm peaks and fold into the potato mixture very gently.

Melt some butter and, using a brush, finely coat the inside of six 1-cup ramekins or one large 6-cup dish. Sift some flour over the ramekins to coat the butter and shake off any excess. Do not touch the inside of the ramekins as any marks will prevent the soufflé from rising.

Fill the ramekins with the potato mixture to three-quarters full. Place the ramekins on a tray and bake for 20 minutes.

Terrine

of Duck Liver in a Jar

Makes 5 x 250ml jars

10 bread slices

1 cup milk

800g (28oz) duck liver, cleaned
and cut in half

800g (28oz) duck meat, cut in
large dices

1 cup caramelized onions

200g (7oz) bacon

½ cup curly parsley

2 tablespoons thyme, chopped

¼ cup brandy

salt and pepper

10 bay leaves

*In most charcuterie in France you will find this method of preserving pâté.
You can buy it in the jar and go and get yourself a loaf of fresh bread, a good bottle of
wine, a relaxing spot in the sun and the rest I let you imagine.*

Soak the bread in the cup of milk.

Put the duck meat and the liver through a mincer using a fine blade or ask
your butcher to do this. Mix together the onions, bacon, parsley, thyme and the
bread that has now soaked up the milk in a bowl. Mix in the brandy, add the
meat mixture and season.

Pour the mixture into prepared parfait jars with rubber rings. Add two bay
leaves on top of each pot, seal them and place in a steamer for 2 hours at 90°C
(195°F).

If you don't have a steamer you can put them in a pot and cover them with
water on a low heat. Make sure there are no bubbles forming from the boiling
water as it may crack the glasses from the vibrations. Place a round rack on the
bottom of the pot to stop the bubbles from rocking the jars.

Serve with some char-grilled sourdough.

Tourtons

des Alpes
(Fried Potato and Truffle Ravioli)

Serves 8

FILLING

1kg (36oz) potatoes, peeled and
    cut into pieces

2 knobs of butter

4 eschalots (shallots), finely sliced

salt

2 heaped tablespoons truffle
    paste

PASTRY

1kg (36oz) flour

150g (5oz) butter, softened

100g (3½oz) cream

3 eggs

pinch salt

Many years ago the tourton *was mostly eaten on special occasions such as Christmas Day (it was also known as a 'Jesus pillow'). Marvellous as a lunch with a little green or witlof (chicory) salad—you can also add some beautiful goat's cheese to the filling.*

To make the filling, cook the potatoes in salted water. Heat the butter in a pan and cook the eschalots until softened and don't have any colour. Once the potatoes are tender, mash with a fork and add some butter and salt. Add the cooked eschalots and truffle paste and mix well. Set aside.

To make the pastry, place the flour on a bench and make a well in the middle. In a bowl, whisk the butter, cream, two eggs and salt. Pour the mixture into the well and combine to form a dough. Rest the dough for about one hour in a bowl with a cloth over it—do not refrigerate. Roll out the dough with a pasta machine, or by hand with a roller, making it very thin.

To make the ravioli, use a glass or cookie cutter and cut circles about 8–10cm (3¼–4in) diameter from the pastry. In the centre of each circle, place a teaspoon of filling, or as much as possible while still being able to close the ravioli. Beat the remaining egg and use your finger to spread some around the outside of the pasta circle. Fold the pasta circle over the filling and press the top down into the bottom, crimping with your fingers to fuse the dough and form a seal. Squeeze out the air as you go, making sure there are no air bubbles.

Heat some oil in a pan. Cook the ravioli in the oil, a few at a time, for about 5 minutes or until crispy and golden. Drain on absorbent paper.

Après Ski

Evening snacks and canapés

Camembert

and Pear Char-grilled Baguette

Serves 4

1 ciabatta baguette

4 tablespoons Dijon mustard

20ml (⅔fl oz) honey

4 tablespoons toasted walnuts,
    chopped

4 pears, washed, cored and cut
    into thick slices

400g (14oz) camembert, cut into
    slices

rocket (arugula) leaves

extra virgin olive oil

This can be a quick lunchtime snack in the middle of a ski session or served as an easy meal after a fabulous day cruising the slopes.

Preheat the barbecue or char-grill. Cut the baguette lengthways, brush with a little olive oil and mark on the char-grill.

Spread the baguette with the mustard and the honey. Sprinkle with walnuts, arrange the pear slices and the camembert slices on top. Place under a grill until the cheese melts and serve with rocket leaves and a splash of extra virgin olive oil.

Croque-monsieur

From My Childhood

Serves 2

5 tablespoons cream

4 heaped tablespoons Gruyère or Emmenthal cheese, grated

1 tablespoon raspberry vinegar

salt and pepper

4 bread slices

2 leg ham slices

2 knobs salted butter

2 slices, Gruyère or Emmenthal cheese, ½cm (¼in) thick

My mother used to make this dish for me when I was coming back from skiing—I just love the way it warms you up. Now I make it for my boys.

Preheat the oven to 180°C (350°F).

Mix the cream, grated cheese, vinegar and salt and pepper together.

Place two slices of the bread on a baking tray. Top with the ham slices, folding the ham if necessary, and then the cheese slices. Place a knob of butter on top, followed by the remaining two slices of bread. Spread the cream mixture on top of the bread leaving a 1cm (½in) border of bread so that the cream mixture does not overflow the edges too much.

Cook in the oven for 10 minutes or until the sandwich has a nice golden colour.

Fondue

Serves 4

400ml (13½fl oz) dry white wine

1kg (36oz) cheese (Emmenthal, Beaufort, Comté, Gruyère), cut into pieces or grated

½ teaspoon cornflour

1 tablespoon kirsch

cracked pepper

pinch nutmeg

sourdough bread, chopped into bite-sized pieces

kipfler potatoes, chopped into largish chunks, boiled till tender

Now this is a fantastic combination of food, friends, warmth, joy and conversation. As a young chef in Switzerland, I used to go every Wednesday night to a restaurant in Gstaad for a fondue party, an event that sometimes lasted the whole night. And of course it involved skiing back down under the starlight, usually at about one in the morning. Ah, the memories...

Some other tips for making a fondue: The less fat in the cheese, the better the fondue; Crush a garlic clove and rub it around the pot before you start to infuse the fondue with garlic.

Put the white wine in a fondue pot. As it starts to boil, add the cheese and mix until well combined. Mix together the cornflour and kirsch and add to the cheese mixture. Stir well.

Before serving, add some cracked pepper and a pinch of nutmeg. Serve with sourdough bread or, for something different, cooked pieces of potatoes.

Raclette

Serves 4

14 medium-sized potatoes
800g (28oz) raclette (hard)
    cheese, sliced

SLICED CHARCUTERIE TO SERVE
    FOUR
sliced prosciutto, sliced pancetta,
    sliced leg ham, sliced coppa
cornichons (gherkins)
pepper grinder, for the table

Nothing more simple and convivial than a raclette. Raclette is a semi-hard cheese,
mostly used for melting. It is very popular in France in the Rhône Alpes region and,
of course, in Switzerland. It is mostly served with hot drinks, like tea or schnapps, as
it is believed that serving with other colder beverages will cause the cheese to harden
in your stomach and give you indigestion.
This is a fantastic meal where cheese is heated and the melted cheese is served with meat,
cornichons (gherkins) or potatoes. Share with family or friends as it is a very social way
to eat.

Cook the potatoes with skin on in salted water.

Meanwhile, heat up your raclette stove. Place platters of the sliced cheese and charcuterie on the table, together with a bowl of cornichons and a pepper grinder.

When the potatoes are cooked, place them in a heat-proof dish with a little water inside and place the dish on top of the raclette stove to keep the potatoes warm.

Each person serves themselves, using the raclette trays to melt the cheese or heat up any combination of sliced meat and pour the melted cheese over the top—whatever combination you desire. Once melted, pour over the potatoes and enjoy!

Mountain

Toast

Makes 4 toasts

This toast represents life in the mountains—hearty and warm.

4 large slices of sourdough bread,
    from a big loaf

¼ cup butter

4 teaspoons wholegrain mustard

4 teaspoons white wine

400g (14oz) caramelized onions

200g (7oz) raclette cheese, sliced

4 eggs

salt and pepper

1 tablespoon sage, chopped

Preheat the oven to 180°C (350°F).

On a char-grill, grill the bread and place on a tray lined with baking paper. Brush the bread with butter then spread each slice with mustard and one teaspoon of wine. Top with the onions and the cheese and bake in the oven for about 10 minutes.

When the toasts are ready, fry the four eggs and place one on each slice of toast.

Season and sprinkle with the sage and serve.

Poêlade

with Raclette Cheese

Serves 4

1 small onion, finely sliced

600g (21oz) potatoes, diced and cooked

50ml (1¾fl oz) white wine

100g (3½oz) smoked bacon pieces

250ml (9fl oz) cream

250g (9oz) raclette (hard) cheese, sliced and rind-on

This is a traditional dish served straight from the hearth. Fun to make with kids as they watch the cheese melt and get mesmerised by the flames of the fire.

Preheat the oven to 200°C (400°F).

In an ovenrpoof pan, sauté the onion and potatoes till the onions are soft. Add the white wine, the bacon and the cream and bring to the boil.

In the same pan, spread the slices of cheese to cover the onion mixture. Bake for 20 minutes till the cheese has melted. If your pan is not oven-proof, you can transfer the ingredients to a gratin dish instead.

Quiche

with Jensen's Red

Serves 8

SAVOURY SHORTCRUST PASTRY
250g (9oz) plain (all-purpose)
  flour
100g (3½oz) butter, softened
75ml (2½fl oz) cold water
2 pinches salt

FILLING
4 potatoes
½ onion
butter
400g (14oz) Jensen's Red cheese,
  cut into slices
5 eggs
400ml (14fl oz) cream
10g (⅓oz) cumin seeds, roasted
salt and pepper

Not your average quiche! My mother makes this one with Munster cheese. It is purely Alsatian and just the smell of it would empty a restaurant. But the taste is unforgettable, creamy and rich, similar in a way to the Jensen's Red. Please try this recipe on a cold winter's night.

Preheat the oven to 210°C (410°F).

To make the pastry, mix the flour and butter together by rubbing them between your fingers. Add the water and salt and form into a ball.

Rest the dough for 20 minutes before rolling out. Then line a large tart mould, 24cm (10in) in diameter. Prick the base and the sides with a fork and set aside.

Wash the potatoes and cook them in water with the skin on, till just tender. Once cooked, peel them and slice thinly.

Chop the onion and fry in a little butter.

Spread a layer of the potatoes over the bottom of the tart dish, followed by the onions and the cheese. Continue layering until all ingredients are used up.

Mix together the eggs, cream and cumin. Season with salt and pepper. Pour into the tart mould and bake in the oven for 35 minutes.

Serve warm with a fresh seasonal salad.

Raclette-style

Potatoes

Serves 5

5 large potatoes
sprigs thyme, leaves picked and
    chopped
10 slices raclette (hard) cheese
10 slices speck or smoked bacon
salt, to taste
butter, to taste

This recipe is for people who don't have a raclette oven and still want to enjoy the taste of this amazing cheese.

Preheat the oven to 180°C (350°F).

Peel the potatoes and cook them whole in salted water for about 40 minutes, or until tender.

Let them cool, then cut each potato into three pieces.

Sprinkle the potatoes with chopped thyme leaves. In between each potato piece, insert slices of cheese until you have re-created the potato—so you have potato, cheese, potato, cheese, potato. Then wrap the potato in two slices of speck.

Lay on a buttered gratin dish, season and place in the oven for 20 minutes until cheese has melted and the bacon is crispy.

(fiserie).   # Truffes au Chocolat

125 g de chocolat
75 g de beurre
(2 cuillères d'eau pour fondre)
1 jaune d'œuf
25 gr de chocolat rapé ou granulé
ou cacao ou amande.
Extrêt de café - ou Krek.

Couper le chocolat en morceaux
ou le raper
Ajouter le jaune d'œuf essence
et le beurre ramolli en crême.
Laisser raffermir. former les
truffes et rouler dans le
chocolat rapé - ou granulé.
Servir à volonté dans des petits
caissettes en papiers.
            Pour truffes Pralinés :
On ajoute à la préparation 50
gr. d'amandes emondées et hachées

Tartiflette

Serves 4

1kg (2lb 4oz) starchy potatoes
2 large onions
olive oil
300g (10½oz) pork lardons, cut into strips
pepper
⅓ cup cream
800g (28oz) Reblochon or King River Gold (semi-soft) cheese

Every two years I go back to France and visit my friend, who has a hotel up in Saint-Pierre-de-Chartreuse in south-east France in the Isère region. We eat this dish and talk for hours—it has become a tradition.
This dish is native to the Savoie, a heavenly combination of flavours and texture.

Preheat oven to 220°C (430°F).

Wash and cook the potatoes, skin on, in salted water.

Cut the onions in half and then thinly slice. In a pan, heat the oil, add the onions and lardons and stir for 3 to 4 minutes until the onion is softened. Set aside.

Peel the potatoes while still warm and cut them into 3cm (1¼in) slices. In a buttered gratin dish, put half the potatoes, followed by half of the onion and lardon mix. Season with pepper. Repeat once, then spread the cream over the top. Cut the cheese into thick slices and spread evenly on top.

Cook for about 15 to 20 minutes until the cheese has melted and started to brown on top.

Serve with a salad and some sliced bread.

Elixir

Serves 6

CARDAMOM AND VANILLA SYRUP
300g (10½oz) brown sugar
½ vanilla pod
6 cardamom pods, roasted

4 egg yolks
100g (3½oz) brown sugar
2 cups milk, heated
2 cups strong green tea, heated
1 cup cardamom and vanilla
    syrup (see below)
150ml (5fl oz) kirsch

A perfect drink to share among friends after a hard day on the slopes. Warming, comforting and ideal to sip by the fireplace.

To make the syrup, put 500ml (17fl oz) of water and the sugar in a pot and bring to the boil. Reduce to a low heat, add the vanilla and cardamom pods and simmer for 20 to 30 minutes.

Strain the syrup and set aside.

Whisk together the eggs and the sugar in a saucepan big enough to hold about 2L (70fl oz) of liquid.

Add the hot milk, hot tea and the syrup. Whisk everything together vigorously for 4 minutes over a moderate heat or until liquid is hot (do not boil as it will split the mixture). Just before you pour the drink into the mugs, add the kirsch.

Chaud

Serves 6

300g (10½oz) brown sugar
zest of 3 oranges
2 cinnamon sticks
4 whole cloves
3 bay leaves
1.5L (52fl oz) red wine
orange slices

Also known as glühwein *and yet another mountain tradition around the word. I remember, as a kid, at every winter event that happened in the village, people used to make* vin chaud *and keep warm by holding the cup in their hands. But most importantly, it brought everyone together.*

Dissolve the sugar with 200ml (7fl oz) of water. Add the orange zest, cinnamon stick, cloves and bay leaves. Infuse for 20 minutes.

Pour in the wine and strain the liquid. Heat up the wine and keep warm. Serve with orange slices.

Hot and Spiced Chocolate

For 4 mugs

500ml (17fl oz) milk
500ml (17fl oz) coconut milk
1 vanilla pod, cut in half and
    scraped
pinch hot chilli powder
1 cinnamon stick
pinch nutmeg powder
40g (1½oz) brown sugar
5 tablespoons dark (semisweet)
    chocolate, 70 % cocoa, grated
2 egg yolks
100g (3½oz) flaked almonds,
    toasted

Chocolate and chilli, a match made in heaven that really warms you up! Hot chocolate is always a favourite in the mountains—winter in a mug.

In a saucepan, simmer the milk and coconut milk for about 5 minutes, stirring in the vanilla pod, chilli powder, cinnamon stick, nutmeg and the sugar.

In a separate bowl, mix the chocolate and the egg yolks. Pour the hot milk into the chocolate and eggs and stir to a smooth consistency. Return to the saucepan and stir over a low heat until the liquid thickens a little bit. Be careful not to boil it or you will scramble the egg.

Take out the vanilla pod and the cinnamon stick.

Serve in a mug and sprinkle with some toasted almond flakes.

Coffee

Makes 4 coffees

4 double-shot coffees
80ml (2fl oz) grappa
50ml (1¾fl oz) Chantilly cream
caster (superfine) sugar, to taste
chocolate, shaved

*Coffee and grappa or any schnapps is on every menu in any mountain in the world.
Why? Just try it!*

In each cup add the coffee and equal amounts of grappa and sugar, to taste.
Whip the cream and top each cup with a dollop of cream and some shaved
chocolate. Enjoy.

Coffee

Makes 1 glass

1 scoop vanilla ice-cream
1 scoop chocolate ice-cream
1 teaspoon Williams pear
    schnapps
1 teaspoon chocolate liqueur
1 espresso coffee
2 tablespoons thickened cream

Coffee, chocolate, schnapps and cream. What more can you want?

Put the ice-creams, schnapps and the liqueur in a tall glass. Pour the coffee over
the ingredients and add the cream and stir.

Warmer

Serves 2

6 apples, peeled
1 black tea bag
1 cinnamon stick
2 tablespoons brown sugar
½ vanilla bean, scraped
2 cardamom pods, crushed

This recipe uses the skin from the snow apple recipe; you can drink it hot or cold or even with a shot of Williams pear schnapps.

Wash the apple peel well and place in a pot. Add all the other ingredients and cover with 500ml (17fl oz) boiling water.

After 5 minutes of infusion take out the tea bag and strain into two glasses.

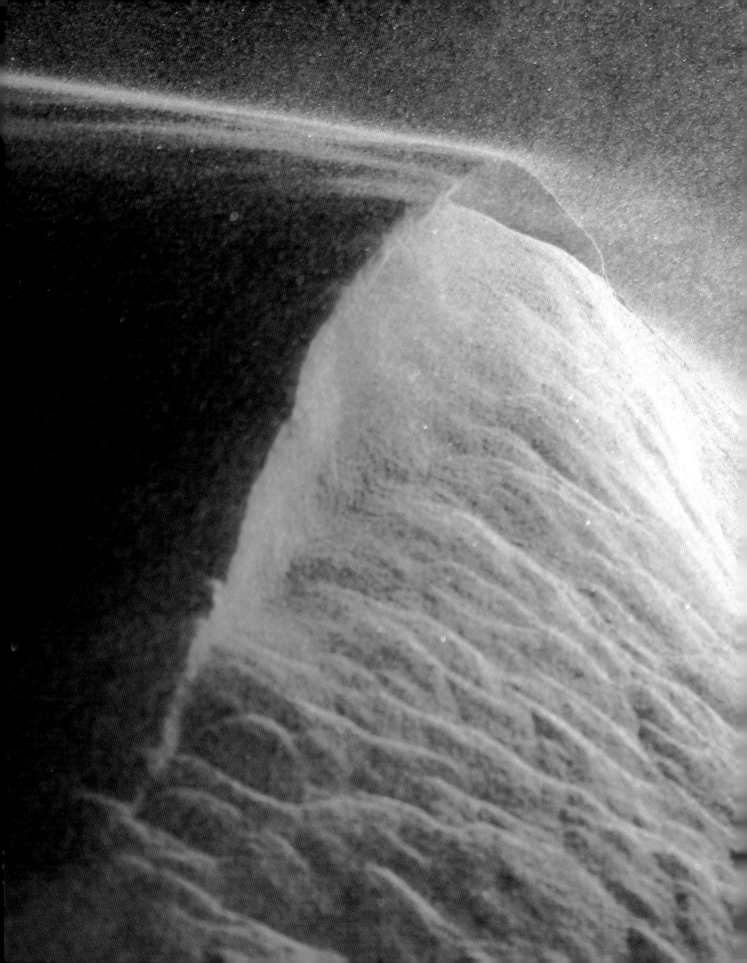

Hearty
Meals With
Friends

aux Cuisses de Canard
(Duck Legs Baked in the Oven)

Serves 4

4 duck legs

4 potatoes, peeled and sliced

4 carrots, peeled and sliced

2 small fennel bulbs, sliced

2 cloves garlic, finely chopped

2 onions, sliced

2 leeks, washed and sliced

salt and pepper

bay leaf

8 cloves

8 juniper berries

2L (70fl oz) chicken stock

Translated baeckeoffe *means 'baked in the oven'. It is the ultimate dish to share and it is so easy to prepare. Put it in the oven and go and carve up the slopes for a few hours while it cooks.*

Preheat the oven to 160°C (325°F).

Seal the duck legs in a frying pan at a moderate–high heat for about 5 minutes. The duck legs should be nicely caramelized.

In a casserole dish, put all the vegetables, seasoning and aromatics. Place the duck legs on top and cover the vegetables with the chicken stock. Only the vegetables should be submerged, not the duck legs.

Place the lid on the casserole dish and place the dish in the oven. Cook for 3 hours. Once cooked, remove from the oven and allow to stand for a further 30 minutes.

Serve with a fresh salsa verde or a little Dijon mustard.

Beef Cheeks

Serves 6

1.4kg (3lb 1oz) beef cheeks
salt and pepper
olive oil
1 onion, cut into eighths
4 cloves garlic, smashed
300g (10½oz) carrots, roughly
    chopped
200g (7oz) leek, roughly
    chopped
90g (3oz) shallots, roughly
    chopped
30g (1oz) tomato paste (purée)
1L (36fl oz) red wine
1 small bunch thyme
1 juniper berry
4 whole cloves
1 cup port wine

Before starting with this dish make sure you trim all fat and sinew from the cheeks.
And it is always important to use a good-quality wine.

Preheat the oven to 180°C (350°F).

Season the beef cheeks with salt and pepper. Heat some oil in an ovenproof pan and brown the beef cheeks on both sides until nice and crispy. Add the vegetables and sauté until softened. Skim any excess fat from the pot, and then add the tomato paste. Deglaze with the red wine. Once this starts to boil, add the thyme, juniper berries, cloves, port wine and 1L (36fl oz) water.

Cover with a lid and cook at 150°C (300°F) for 3 hours. Once cooked, remove the beef cheeks and place on a plate. Strain the sauce through a sieve, pushing through some of the vegetables, pour oven the beef cheeks and serve with some pasta or potato or vegetable purée.

Lamb Shanks in Orange Juice and Star Anise

Serves 4

2 tablespoons olive oil

8 lamb shanks, french trimmed

400g (14oz) carrots, peeled and
   roughly diced

1 onion, thinly sliced

3 cloves garlic, crushed

60g (2oz) tomato paste (purée)

salt and pepper

500ml (17fl oz) fresh orange
   juice

3 star anise

1L (36fl oz) beef stock

2 bay leaves

2 tablespoons thyme leaves

Ask your butcher to french the shanks as it will present better on the plate.

Heat the oil in a pot and brown the lamb shanks until they are nicely caramelized.

Add the carrots, onion and garlic and cook until the onion has softened.

Add the tomato paste and cook for a few minutes.

Season with salt and pepper, and then add the orange juice, star anise, beef stock, bay leaves and thyme.

Cook, covered, on a very low heat for 2 to 3 hours until the shanks start to come away from the bone. Serve with couscous, mashed potato or potato gratin.

Pork Cheeks Shepherd's Pie Gratinated with Parmesan

Serves 4

olive oil

2 cloves garlic, finely sliced

5 large eschalots (shallots)

2 punnets oyster mushrooms, about 200g (7oz), just torn in half

15 truss cherry tomatoes, quartered

2 tablespoons thyme, chopped

1 tablespoon sage, chopped

1 cup jus

6 braised pork cheeks, torn into pieces (refer to Braised Pork Cheeks in Index on how to prepare)

1kg (2lb 4oz) potatoes, peeled

300ml (10½fl oz) cream

300g (10½oz) butter

200g (7oz) parmesan, freshly shaved

salt and pepper

When I was an apprentice back in France, we used to make this dish on cold winter days using wild boar. It is such a comforting dish.

In a frying pan, heat some olive oil and sauté the garlic and the shallots till brown. Add the mushrooms and stir for a couple of minutes. Add the tomatoes and the herbs and stir again for 2 minutes. Pour in the jus and simmer for 10 minutes. Add the pork cheeks and set aside.

Cut the potatoes and put in a pot with cold water to level. Add some salt and cook for about 25 minutes or until tender. Drain the potatoes and push through a vegetable mill or a ricer. Add the cream and the butter and season with salt and pepper.

Preheat the oven at 170°C (335°F).

Pour the pork mixture into a gratin or baking dish, top with the potatoes and sprinkle the parmesan on top. Bake for 15 minutes.

Serve with a leafy salad.

Pork Belly

Serves 4

1kg (2lb 4oz) Berkshire pork
    bellies, skin on

salt and pepper

1 head garlic, cut in half

4 eschalots (shallots), peeled and
    halved

1 teaspoon Chinese five spice

¼ cup soy sauce

¼ cup golden syrup

4 kaffir lime leaves

3 star anise

*This recipe is from an old friend of mine. It is absolutely delicious and allows for lots
of ski time while it cooks. This dish is also made to be cooked in the hearth.*

Preheat the oven to 120°C (250°F).

Place the pork belly on a rack in a deep roasting tray. Add the garlic and the
eschalots. In a jug, mix together the Chinese five spice, soy sauce, golden syrup,
kaffir lime leaves and star anise. Rub the five spice mixture over the pork, then
add 1.5L (52fl oz) of water. Wrap the tray with tin foil and place in the oven for
4 to 4½ hours.

Once cooked, allow the pork to cool until just warm and then wrap them
individually in plastic wrap. Place between two trays and put in the fridge over
night. Place something on top of the tray—nothing too heavy but just enough
to flatten the pork but still retain its shape.

Cut the pork belly to desired shape and heat in a non-stick pan to crisp up
before serving.

Pork Cheeks

For 6 cheeks

butter

olive oil

6 pork cheeks, cleaned and skin
    removed

1 onion, roughly chopped

2 cloves garlic, crushed

2 carrots, cut into chunks

1 large tomato, peeled and
    chopped

½ cup tomato paste (purée)

2 pinches Chinese five spice

200ml (7fl oz) red wine

60ml (2fl oz) cider vinegar

1L (36fl oz) veal or beef stock

BOUQUET GARNI
   (IN A CLOTH BAG)

5 coriander seeds

3 star anise

3 sprigs thyme

1 sprig rosemary

3 bay leaves

Heat some butter and oil in a casserole dish. Season the cheeks with salt and pepper and seal the cheeks until they are nicely caramelized. Add the vegetables, spoon out the excess fat and stir in the tomato paste and the five spice.

Pour in the wine and the vinegar and allow the liquid to reduce by half. Add the stock and the herb bag, cover with a lid and cook for 2 hours over a low heat.

When the cheeks are cooked, remove them from the pot and reduce the sauce down by half. Strain the sauce, pushing some of the vegetables through the sieve.

Pour the sauce over the meat and serve with mashed potatoes and kale or with some Spätzle (see Index).

in Riesling Sauce

Serves 4

1 x 1.5kg (3lb 5oz) free-range
  chicken
salt and pepper
100g (3½oz) flour
150g (5oz) butter
1 brown onion, thinly sliced
4 spring onions (scallions), thinly
  sliced
750ml (24fl oz) Riesling
3 bay leaves
300ml (10½fl oz) thickened
  cream
1 teaspoon thyme, chopped
400g (14oz) button mushrooms,
  quartered
knob butter
¼ cup parsley, chopped

This recipe for me evokes Sunday lunch at my grandmother's place. It was a family tradition and she used to make her own noodles. I can remember walking into the kitchen and there were strings of pasta hanging all over the place. It is so delicious.

Cut the chicken into eight portions, season and roll them in the flour.

Heat the butter in a casserole dish, then brown the chicken pieces, being careful not to burn the flour. Add the onion and shallots, stir for two minutes, then add the Riesling and bay leaves. Cover and simmer for 1 to 1½ hours or until the chicken is cooked.

Remove the chicken pieces from the pot. Then add the cream and the thyme to the pot and reduce until the sauce thickens.

In another pan, sauté off the mushrooms with a knob of butter.

To serve, place the chicken on a dish, cover with the sauce and top with the mushrooms and sprinkle with some freshly chopped parsley.

Serve with noodles or homemade Spätzle (see Index) and a green salad.

Confit

of Monaro Lamb Leg
with New Potatoes

Serves 6

1 leg of lamb, about 2kg
    (4lb 6oz), bone-in
salt and pepper
oil
10 eschalots (shallots), quartered
6 cloves garlic, skin-on
5 small carrots, peeled and cut
    into 4 pieces
200ml (7fl oz) white wine
400ml (13½fl oz) lamb stock
600g (21oz) new potatoes,
    washed
1 celeriac, peeled and chopped
½ fennel bulb, sliced

This is a one-pot meal—easy to make and even easier to eat. It is rich and full of flavours, a good one to share with friends.

Preheat the oven to a very low temperature such as 100–130°C (210–265°F). Season the lamb leg with salt and pepper.

In a large casserole dish, brown the lamb in oil on all sides. Add the shallots, garlic and the carrots and colour all ingredients. Pour the wine and the stock over the mixture.

Place the potatoes, celeriac and the fennel on top and cook in an oven at a very low temperature for 2 to 3 hours, making sure you check there is enough liquid in the dish. The meat is ready when it falls off the bone.

This dish could also be cooked in a hearth.

# of Veal Shanks

Serves 4

4 veal shanks, french trimmed

800ml (28fl oz) red wine

3 sprigs thyme

250g (9oz) bacon, diced

½ bunch parsley stalks

2 small onions, quartered

½ celeriac, cut into large chunks

1 leek, white only, sliced

4 cloves garlic, skin-on and
    crushed

2 bay leaves

4 whole cloves

2 star anise

2 cups veal stock

salt and pepper

¼ cup oil

A daube is a stew, traditionally made in a daubière, which is a pot made out of clay. It is also a dish you can cook and eat the next day so all the flavours have gone through the meat.

Put the shanks in a bowl. Cover with the wine, thyme, 100g (3½oz) bacon, parsley stalks, onions, celeriac, leek, garlic, bay leaves, cloves and star anise and marinate for 24 hours.

Preheat oven to 180°C (350°F).

Drain the marinade off into a bowl and fry the meat in the oil, browning the shanks on all sides. Remove the whole cloves from the marinade and cover the shanks with the marinade, the stock and the rest of the bacon.

Cook, covered, for 2 hours in the oven or until cooked. Check after 1½ hours—the shanks will be cooked when you can push a knife into the shanks very easily, like pushing a knife into butter.

Drain the sauce and put through sieve. Pour the sauce over the shanks and serve with some swede and parsnip purée.

If the sauce is too thin, just reduce a bit more on the stove top.

Duck Confit

Serves 6

1 x 1.6kg (3lb 8oz) whole duck or
    6 x 240g (8½oz) duck legs

80g (2½oz) salt flakes

4 fresh bay leaves

½ bunch thyme

3 cloves garlic, crushed

3 juniper berries, crushed

3 whole cloves, bruised

¼ teaspoon cracked pepper

1kg (2lb 4oz) duck fat, melted

One piece of advice for this dish—follow the recipe! The result will be rewarding.

Cut the duck into bite-sized pieces and place in a tub or a terrine.

Rub the duck pieces with the salt, bay leaves, thyme, garlic, juniper berries, cloves and pepper. Cover with a lid or some plastic wrap. Refrigerate for 24 hours.

The next day, wipe the pieces of duck and sear them in a casserole dish with a little duck fat. Cover with the rest of the melted fat. Simmer, covered, on a very low heat for 3 hours, depending on the size of the pieces. Cool and put the meat in a tub, pouring the fat over it and refrigerate.

Cooked in Pinot Noir

Serves 6

50g (1¾oz) butter

1 x 1.8kg (3lb 15oz) duck, cut
    into 6 pieces

150g (5oz) bacon pieces

4 cloves garlic, finely chopped

6 small pickling onions, quartered

4 small eschalots (shallots),
    quartered

1 medium carrot, cut into large
    dice

¼ cup tomato paste (purée)

2 teaspoons thyme, chopped

4 fresh bay leaves

50ml (1¾fl oz) brandy

500ml (17fl oz) pinot noir

1.25L (44fl oz) chicken or duck
    stock

salt and pepper

I have been serving this dish for the last ten years so I can almost do it in my sleep. My best advice to you, when cooking this dish, is to buy a good wine and you are already halfway towards a great meal.

Preheat the oven to 180°C (350°F).

In a casserole dish, melt the butter. Season the pieces of duck and sear until golden. Discard some of the fat and add the bacon pieces, garlic, onions, eschalots and the carrots. Stir well and then add the tomato paste. Stir until well coated and add the thyme and bay leaves.

Flambé with brandy then pour in the pinot noir. Bring the pot to the boil and add the stock.

Cover the pot with a lid and bake in the oven for about 45 minutes or until the duck is cooked. Season with salt and pepper.

Fleischschnaka

(Meat Snail)

Serves 4

NOODLE DOUGH

30g (1oz) butter, softened

2 egg yolks

2 eggs

250g (9oz) flour

pinch salt

600g (1lb 5oz) braised beef cheeks, cooked and cold

1 cup mixed vegetables, cut into strips and cooked in some butter

2 small onions, finely sliced and browned in butter

1 egg

120g (4oz) smoked bacon, cut into small pieces and fried

½ cup parsley, finely chopped

salt and pepper

1 pinch nutmeg

150ml (5fl oz) beef stock

This is a traditional Alsace dish made from leftover stewed meats and noodle dough. It is rolled into a snail-like shape and mostly served in the cold months.

To make the dough, whisk together all the wet ingredients.

On a benchtop, place the flour and salt and create a well in the middle. Add the wet ingredients and mix together by hand to form a dough. Knead until all ingredients are well incorporated.

Place dough in a bowl, cover and put in the fridge to rest for a couple of hours before use.

Preheat oven to 170°C (335°F).

Cut the beef cheeks into thin strips. Add the vegetables, onions, egg, fried bacon and parsley. Season with the salt, pepper and the nutmeg.

Cut the noodle dough into two pieces and then roll out in a pasta machine or with a rolling pin until it is 2mm (⅛in) thick. Spread the meat mixture onto the pastry and roll into sausage-like shapes then roll the sausages into a snail shape.

Fry the snails in some butter till they are golden brown on both sides. Use a wide spatula to turn them over and be careful you don't break them. Add the stock and place the pan in the oven for about 25 minutes, adding more stock if necessary.

When cooked, you can cut the snails or just leave them whole and put them on a platter in the middle of the table, served with a bowl of fresh salad.

Green

Pawpaw (Papaya) Sauerkraut, Smoked Quail and Parsley Potatoes

Serves 4

PAWPAW SAUERKRAUT

400g (14oz) green pawpaw
(papaya)
1 teaspoon salt
olive oil
2 large eschalots (shallots), finely
sliced
½ clove garlic, finely chopped
100g (3½oz) speck, cut into
lardons
¼ cup dry white wine
1 cup strong chicken stock
1 pinch roasted cumin powder
2 bay leaves

This is my take on the traditional Alsatian Sauerkraut. The smokiness of the quail and the crunchy, salty texture of the pawpaw go so well together.

If you can't find smoked quails, it is possible to smoke them yourself. Place 30g (1oz) black leaf tea and 30g (1oz) caster (superfine) sugar in the bottom of a wok. Place a rack on top (like a round cake rack). Season the quails and place on the rack. Put the wok on the flame and wait until the tea and sugar starts to smoke. Cover with a lid or tin foil, turn the flame off and leave to smoke for 10 to 15 minutes.

To make the sauerkraut, grate the pawpaw, using a mandolin, not a cheese grater, into julienne-like strips.

Mix the pawpaw with salt, cover and leave in the fridge for 1 to 2 days. This will tenderise the pawpaw and remove excess moisture.

Once the excess moisture has been removed, take the pawpaw out of the fridge, place in a strainer and wash it. Let the pawpaw drain and use your hand to press out some of the excess moisture.

In a pan, put a good splash of olive oil, the eschalots, garlic and speck and sauté. Add the pawpaw. Deglaze with the white wine. Add the chicken stock, cumin and the bay leaves and simmer gently for about 10 to 15 minutes. When it is ready, the pawpaw should still have some crunch.

4 désirée potatoes, peeled and
    cut into 3cm (1¼in) pieces
knob of butter
2 tablespoons coriander,
    chopped
salt and pepper
butter
4 smoked quails, de-boned

For the potatoes, place in salted water and cook until tender. Strain the potatoes, add a good knob of butter to the cooked potatoes, together with the coriander. Season with salt and pepper and toss.

Preheat the oven to 180°C (350°F).

For the quails, place some butter in a pan and crisp up the seasoned quails. Then roast in the oven for about 10 minutes.

To serve, place the sauerkraut in the middle of the plate. Place the quail on top and arrange the potatoes around the quail. If desired, add some of the juices from the sauerkraut.

Inverted

Cordon Bleu

Serves 4

4 veal cutlets

butter

oil

3 spring onions (scallions), finely
    chopped

400g (14oz) mixed mushrooms
    (oyster, swiss brown, field),
    sliced

1 tablespoon sage, chopped

100g (3½oz) fresh breadcrumbs

salt and pepper

3 knobs salted butter

4 slices pork speck

4 skewers

My mother used to make this dish with pommes sarladaise *(potatoes cooked in duck fat) and a salad.*

With a sharp knife, make an incision in the side of the cutlets creating a pocket large enough to hold stuffing.

Heat some butter and oil in a pan and sauté the shallots and the mushroom mixture for 3 minutes. Add the sage, breadcrumbs and seasoning. Stir in the 3 knobs of butter and set aside.

When the mixture is cold, form into little parcels with your hands. Wrap the speck around each parcel and insert into the cutlet.

Close the cutlet by weaving a skewer through it.

Season the meat and pan-fry with some butter and oil for 5 minutes on each side.

and Porcini Stew

Serves 4

50g (1¾oz) butter

olive oil

salt and pepper

1 whole rabbit (1.5kg/3lb 5oz),
    cut into pieces (ask your
    butcher to do this for you)

150g (5oz) celeriac, cut into 2cm
    (¾in) dice

150g (5oz) carrots, cut into 2cm
    (¾in) dice

60g (2oz) shallots (scallions),
    sliced

1 clove garlic, crushed

20g (⅔oz) dried porcini
    mushrooms, soaked in
    hot water

6 large button mushrooms,
    quartered

½ cup white wine

1.5L (52fl oz) chicken stock

1 tablespoon thyme, chopped

When I was growing up in France nearly everyone had rabbits in their backyard. So when my mother did not know what to cook for dinner, Dad would go and kill a rabbit. No need for a trip to the supermarket in those days!

Preheat oven to 160°C (325°F).

Heat the butter and olive oil in an ovenproof pan and season the rabbit pieces with salt and pepper. Brown the rabbit pieces in the pan then add the celeriac, carrots, shallots and garlic.

Strain the porcini mushrooms, reserving the liquid.

Once sweated off, add the button mushrooms, porcini mushrooms and then deglaze with ½ cup of the strained mushroom water and the white wine. Add the chicken stock and the thyme.

Cover the pan and bake in the oven for 1 hour and 40 minutes or until rabbit pieces are tender.

Pheasant My Way

Serves 4

300g (10½oz) butter, softened
80g (2½oz) truffle paste
3 tablespoons parsley, chopped
3 pheasants
salt and pepper
6 sprigs thyme
3 cloves garlic, crushed
3 slices sourdough bread
salt and pepper
olive oil

I like how easy this dish is to make and it tastes like heaven.
Truffle paste is versatile—you can add it to mashed potatoes, risotto, butter and
sauces and the good thing about it is you don't need much. It is a handy alternative
when you can't find fresh truffles.

Preheat the oven to 200°C (400°F).

Mix the butter with the truffle paste and chopped parsley.

With your fingers very gently lift the skin of the pheasant from the flesh.

Put the butter in under the skin as evenly and as far as you can. Fold back the skin and season the birds with salt and pepper.

In the cavity, put two sprigs of thyme in each pheasant together with one clove of garlic and one slice of bread.

Season the pheasants with salt and pepper and place on a roasting tray with some olive oil and put in the oven for 15 minutes. Then reduce the temperature to 170°C (335°F).

Roast the birds for about 40 to 50 minutes and baste the birds frequently with the cooking liquid.

When the birds are ready, rest on a cooling rack for 15 minutes in a warm place.

Sauerkraut

Serves 8

2.5kg (5lb 8oz) sauerkraut

2kg (4lb 6oz) hot-smoked pork
neck

8 eschalots (shallots), chopped

4 cloves garlic

¼ cup oil

3 small smoked pork hocks,
cooked in water for 1 hour

400g (14oz) smoked bacon

750ml (26fl oz) white wine

salt and pepper

8 frankfurters

4 smoked pork sausages

BOUQUET GARNI
(IN A CLOTH BAG)

2 bay leaves

4 whole cloves

4 sprigs thyme

8 juniper berries

*This is a recipe for Alsace sauerkraut (choucroute in French). This dish makes
a perfect Sunday lunch among friends and good wine. As a child, the smell of
sauerkraut meant it was not long for the snow to arrive and the skis to come out. My
dad used to buy the cabbages and slice them with a massive slicer. He would then put
the cabbage in big sandstone barrels, salt them and store them for 2 months in the
cellar. We eat sauerkraut in the cold months only.*

Wash the sauerkraut in a large amount of cold water for about 5 minutes and
strain.

Soak the pork neck in cold water for 2 hours.

In a large pan or ovenproof casserole dish, sauté the eschalots and the garlic
in oil until translucent. Add the pork meats and cover with the sauerkraut. Add
the wine, 2 cups of water, the bouquet garni and a little salt and pepper (but not
too much salt).

Cover and cook gently on a low heat for 2 hours. You can also cook it in the
oven at 180°C (350°F) for the same amount of time.

Thirty minutes before it's cooked, add the sausages and check that you still
have some cooking liquid. If not, add some water.

When the sauerkraut is ready, place on a large platter and surround with the
meats and sausages. You can also serve with boiled potatoes and lots of French
mustard.

Pork Hocks Glazed
with Honey and Citrus Juice

Serves 4

2 smoked pork hocks

1 carrot, peeled and chopped into
   big chunks

½ celeriac, peeled and chopped
   into big chunks

1 small leek, sliced thickly

1 small bunch of curly parsley
   stalks

2 whole cloves

2 bay leaves

2 juniper berries

6 black peppercorns

GLAZE

2 oranges, washed

1 pink grapefruit, washed

60g (2oz) honey

This is a great winter dish—the smokiness of the pork and the sweetness of the citrus glaze go so well together.

Put the two pork hocks in a pot and fill with enough water so that the hocks are completely submerged. Cut all the vegetables into big chunks and add to the pot with the herbs. Simmer for about 3 to 3½ hours making sure you regularly skim the impurities from the stock.

Preheat the oven to 160°C (325°F).

To make the glaze, zest one orange and then juice both the oranges and the grapefruit. Put the zest, the juices and the honey in a roasting pan.

Put the pork hocks on top (you can take the bones out and discard the fat) and put in the oven for about 20 minutes, regularly basting them.

Serve with mashed potatoes or just boiled potatoes tossed in a little butter with chopped parsley.

Venison

and Dark Chocolate Stew

Serves 4

1kg (2lb 4oz) venison, cut into 5cm (2in) dice

1 large carrot, cut into thick slices

1 small celeriac, cut into 2cm (¾in) dice

3 cloves garlic, crushed

5 eschalots (shallots), cut into quarters

4 bay leaves

3 juniper berries

salt and pepper

1L (36fl oz) red wine

½ cup tomato paste (purée)

1.5L (52fl oz) veal stock

100g (3½oz) dark chocolate, grated

2 tablespoons caster (superfine) sugar

1 large knob butter

2 large apples, peeled, cored and quartered

150g (5oz) speck, finely diced

300g (10½oz) oyster mushrooms

How much better can it get? Beautiful venison and chocolate, so hearty and warm. Best cooked on the side of a fireplace with a lid on, nice and gentle.

Marinate the meat in a large bowl with the carrots, celeriac, garlic, eschalots, bay leaves, juniper berries, salt, pepper and red wine. Cover and refrigerate for 2 days.

Preheat the oven to 170°C (335°F).

Drain the meat, straining out the vegetables and reserving the marinade liquid.

In a large saucepan, sauté the meat pieces until they are golden. Remove the meat and sauté the marinated vegetables in the same pot. Add back in the meat and stir in the tomato paste, stirring well to coat. Add the veal stock.

Pour in the marinade liquid, place a lid on the pot and cook for 2 hours in the oven or until the meat is tender. Make sure you skim the stew from time to time.

When ready, pick out the meat pieces and strain the sauce into another pot, pushing some of the vegetables through the sieve. Add the chocolate and if the sauce is too thin, it can be reduced a little. Put the meat back into the sauce and keep warm.

Put the sugar and the butter in a saucepan. Add the apple quarters and add ½ cup of water. Cook for 5 minutes and set aside.

In another pan, melt some butter and sauté the speck until brown. Add the mushrooms, season and stir-fry for 5 minutes.

To serve, put the stew in a large serving dish, top with the apples and the speck and mushroom mixtures. Serve with some noodles.

Duck Stuffed with Sweetbread and King Brown Mushrooms

Serves 6

1 x 1.6kg (3lb 8½oz) duck

STUFFING
400g (14oz) chicken breast, cut into small pieces
200g (7oz) cream
2 eggs
butter
olive oil
1 small onion, finely chopped
2 cloves garlic, finely chopped
250g (9oz) king brown mushrooms, sliced
300g (10½oz) veal sweetbread, soaked in cold water and cut into 2cm (¾in) pieces

Ask your butcher to de-bone the duck for you. On the other hand, if you want to have a go at it—good on you! You can also cook the duck on the bottom of your fireplace or your barbecue with the lid down. We don't use barbecues enough through the winter months but we should, especially if there isn't a fireplace available.

De-bone the duck.

To prepare the stuffing, blend the chicken meat in a food processor until smooth. Add the cream and eggs and season. Make sure the mixture is well mixed (also make sure all the ingredients are kept cold).

In a frying pan, melt some butter and a little oil. Add the chopped onion and the garlic and cook without any colour. Add the mushrooms and the sweetbread, stir and cook for about 3 minutes. Set aside and cool.

When cold, fold in the chicken mix and place the mixture in the cavity of the duck. Roll the duck and wrap in plastic wrap twice. Tie both ends and refrigerate for 2 hours.

Steam the duck in a steamer tray or in a bamboo steamer over a pot of boiling water for 30 minutes at 90°C (195°F), then refrigerate for 1 hour. This will set the stuffing.

SAUCE

5 eschalots (shallots), chopped

2 knobs butter

3 juniper berries

150ml (5fl oz) port wine

cracked pepper

2 bay leaves

4 sprigs thyme

1L (36fl oz) veal or beef stock

15ml (½fl oz) brandy

40g (1½oz) butter

To warm the duck for serving, preheat the oven to 180°C (350°F). Take the duck out of the plastic wrap and tie with some butcher's twine like you would a roast. Do not tie too tightly. Season with salt and pepper, spread with butter and wrap in tin foil, folding from left to right and right to left forming a loaf-like shape. Repeat a second time, put on a tray and bake for about 1½ hours. Rest for 15 minutes before carving.

To make the sauce, sauté the eschalots with the two knobs butter and juniper berries, add the port wine and reduce by three-quarters.

Add the cracked pepper, the bay leaves and the thyme. Pour in the stock and reduce by half. Strain the sauce, add the brandy and whisk in the butter.

Serve this dish with homemade spätzle (see Index) or just some buttery mashed potato.

Winter

Warmers

Soups, stews and oven dishes

Marrow Bread and Butter Pudding

Makes 4 x 9cm (3½in) diameter ramekins

75g (2½oz) butter, melted

400g (14oz) brioche

100g (3½oz) bone marrow, sliced

40g (1½oz) Confit Eschalots (see Index)

150ml (5fl oz) cream

2 eggs

1 egg white

salt and ground pepper

This is a little teaser, one of those dishes that when you have some, you want more. Best eaten with a salad in-between skis.

Preheat the oven to 180°C (350°F). Grease four ramekin moulds with butter.

Slice the brioche into 1cm (½in) slices and cut 12 x 8cm (3¼in) diameter circles. Place one circle in the bottom of each ramekin, then place a layer of bone marrow, shallots and salt and pepper. Repeat with another layer of brioche, followed by the bone marrow and shallots and top with one final layer of brioche.

Whisk the cream and the eggs together and pour the mixture into each mould. Place the ramekins in a bain-marie, fill with hot water halfway up the side of the ramekins and cover the tray with tin foil.

Cook in the oven for 30 to 35 minutes. Once removed from the oven, be careful when opening the foil so that you do not get burned from the steam.

Witlof (Endive)

Serves 4 as a side or as an entrée

I always look forward to returning home to France to eat my mother's version of this dish. She always makes it in the winter and the kitchen becomes full of this most wonderful aroma.

2 knobs butter

12 witlof (endive) halves, stalk removed

40g (1½oz) brown sugar

100g (3½oz) spring onions (scallions), sliced

1 clove garlic, finely sliced

200g (7oz) bacon, diced

3 bay leaves

10 juniper berries

salt and pepper

150ml (5fl oz) blonde or pale ale beer

50ml (1¾fl oz) chicken stock

100g (3½oz) butter

Preheat the oven to 170°C (335°F).

Heat the two knobs of butter in a pan and gently sauté the witlof for a couple of minutes to soften. Turn them and sprinkle with the brown sugar. Turn them over again and cook for a few minutes so the witlof become nicely caramelized.

Add the shallots, garlic and bacon and cook for another couple of minutes.

Place the witlof mixture into a gratin dish, add the herbs and seasoning and cover with the beer and chicken stock. Break up the butter into knobs and scatter around the gratin dish. Cover the dish with tin foil and bake in the oven for 1 hour.

Remove the tin foil and cook for a further 5 minutes to allow the dish to dry out a little on top.

Gratinated

Witlof (Endive) Soup with Toast

Serves 4

6 large witlof (endive)

butter

2 large onions, finely chopped

1 clove garlic, finely chopped

80g (2½oz) caster (superfine) sugar

¼ cup tomato paste (purée)

250ml (9fl oz) red wine

2.5L (88fl oz) chicken stock

4 sprigs thyme

3 bay leaves

salt and pepper

4 slices of bread

300g (10½oz) Gruyère cheese, grated

chives, chopped

Wash the witlof, cut it lengthways and remove the stalk to reduce the bitterness. Chop the witlof into slices.

Heat a saucepan over medium heat with some butter. Add the onions, garlic and the witlof and sauté them until softened.

Add the sugar and stir for about 2 minutes. Add the tomato paste and stir again for 2 minutes, making sure it coats the mixture well. Add the wine and cook for 5 minutes. Add the stock and the herbs. Season and simmer for 20 minutes.

Just before the soup is ready, place the bread slices on a tray and sprinkle with the grated cheese. Place under a grill or broiler until the cheese has melted and gratinated.

Taste and, if required, season the soup and pour into four bowls. Top with the Gruyère toast and sprinkle with chopped chives.

Cotechino

and Puy Lentils

Serves 10

1 cotechino
3L (105fl oz) good-quality
    chicken stock
good knob of butter
200g (7oz) bacon, diced
2 cloves garlic, crushed
50g (1¾oz) shallots, finely
    chopped
300g (10½oz) carrots, small
    diced
200g (7oz) celeriac, small diced
200g (7oz) leek, small diced
200g (7oz) Savoy cabbage, diced
800g (1lb 12oz) Puy lentils
4 bay leaves, fresh

Wow, this brings back memories! Chamonix, France, 1986—my friend's mum is Italian and she made this dish for us and I have been hooked on it ever since. Her dish was with cabbage and polenta, but this is my version. Cotechino is a mild, fatty pork sausage.

Cook the cotechino in plain water for 30 minutes. Throw out the water and start again with cold water and cook for another 30 minutes. Repeat this process once more. The water should be starting to become clear by this time.

The next day, place the cotechino in 2L (70fl oz) of the chicken stock and cook for another hour.

Heat the butter in a large pot and sauté the bacon, garlic and all the vegetables. Add the lentils and bay leaves. Add the rest of the chicken stock to cover and simmer for 45 minutes or until cooked.

Slice the cotechino, place on top of the lentils and serve.

Serve with mustard or salsa verde.

Wild Rabbit Soup

Serves 4

butter
oil
1 x 1.5kg (3lb 5oz) rabbit, cut into
    12 pieces
1 knob butter
1 large onion, finely sliced
1 clove garlic, crushed
3.5L (122fl oz) chicken stock
2 pinches saffron
300g (10½oz) field mushrooms,
    finely chopped
1 cup pearl barley, cooked
salt and pepper
200ml (7oz) cream

BOUQUET GARNI
    (IN A CLOTH BAG)
3 sprigs thyme
1 small stick rosemary
4 parsley stalks
6 basil leaves
4 coriander seeds
2 juniper berries

I can still see my uncle, rifle on his back, coming home from the hunt with rabbits hanging from his bag. This recipe is another heart warmer, full of rich flavours—the perfect refuel.

In a saucepan, heat some butter and oil and seal the rabbit pieces. Remove the rabbit from the pan and wipe out any excess liquid with some paper towel.

Add a little knob of butter and sauté the onions and the garlic for 3 minutes. Return the rabbit pieces to the pot together with the stock, saffron and the bouquet garni and simmer at a low temperature for 1½ hours.

Remove the pieces of rabbit and strain the stock, returning the strained stock to the pot.

Add the mushrooms and the barley to the stock and simmer for 10 minutes. Season with salt and pepper. Add the cream and simmer for another 10 minutes.

Pull the rabbit meat from the bones, and divide the meat into four plates. Top with the soup and serve with a salsa verde or a basil pesto.

Mushroom

Tarte Tatin

Serves 4

30g (1oz) butter

50g (1¾oz) shallots, finely chopped

2 cloves garlic, crushed

300g (10½oz) swiss brown mushrooms, sliced

200g (7oz) oyster mushrooms, hand-torn

200g (7oz) button mushrooms, sliced

1 packet enoki mushrooms, separated

3 tablespoons white wine

½ cup cream

2 tablespoons chopped thyme

1 teaspoon chopped rosemary

½ cup chopped parsley

salt and pepper

4 sheets puff pastry

1 egg yolk

When I was an apprentice, my old chef told me that during the war, when food was scarce, they would make do with what they could find. In the colder months, there were always a lot of mushrooms (and they were free if you went and picked them) and enough butter to make puff pastry. A dish similar to this was the result.

Melt the butter in a large pan, then add the shallots and garlic and cook until softened.

Add all the mushrooms and sauté until they have cooked down. Add the white wine and cream and reduce until the mixture thickens.

Add the herbs and toss. By this stage, there should not be too much liquid left. Basically, the liquid should just coat the mushrooms. Cool the mixture. Line 4 x 15cm (6in) tart moulds (non-fluted) with silicone paper. Add some of the mushroom mixture to each mould.

Cut 4 x 15cm (6in) rounds of puff pastry. Place on top of the mushroom mixture and tuck in around the edges.

Beat the egg yolk with a little bit of water and brush the puff pastry with the egg wash.

Refrigerate for one hour and then bake for 20 minutes at 180°C (350°F).

Once cooked, turn the tarts over onto a plate and remove the mould and baking paper.

Serve with some fresh goat's cheese crumbled over the tart and fresh rocket (arugula) or spinach leaves.

Spelt Flour Soup

Serves 4

120g (4oz) spelt flour
2L (70fl oz) good-quality chicken
    stock
30g (1oz) butter
300ml (10½fl oz) cream
salt and pepper
2 cups rye bread croutons, toasted
100g (3½oz) parmesan, shaved
    or grated
olive oil
parsley, chopped, to garnish

This soup is a tradition from near where I come from. Every February, when we celebrate carnival, it is extremely cold outside so to warm up there is nothing better than a roasted flour soup

In a pot with a 4L (140fl oz) capacity, roast the flour on a medium heat. Make sure the pot is dry and roast for about 5 to 10 minutes, stirring constantly.

When the flour is brown in colour, add the chicken stock, being very careful not to burn yourself with the steam coming from the hot pot.

Simmer for about 5 to 10 minutes or until the soup starts to thicken. Add the butter and cream and season.

Pour into four bowls. Add the croutons and the parmesan.

Garnish with a little olive oil and some chopped parsley.

Soup

Serves 4

This is not made with rocks! This soup used to be very popular hundreds of years ago.
It is simply a vegetable soup, which has been cooked by the hearth for a long time.
The rocks are in there to crush the vegetables as it bubbles.
You need one river rock, smooth and convex like a small rugby ball in shape and
about 10cm (4in) long.

250g (9oz) leeks, white part only
250g (9oz) carrots
250g (9oz) celeriac
500g (17½oz) potatoes
250g (9oz) parsnips
200g (7oz) smoked bacon
80g (2½oz) butter
3L (105fl oz) chicken stock
2 bay leaves
1 tablespoon sage, chopped
200ml (7fl oz) cream

Peel and wash all vegetables, then cut them into a large dice.

In a large pot or casserole, sauté all the vegetables and bacon with the butter.

Stir for 4 minutes and reduce the heat to medium.

Cover with the stock and add the rock. The rock will be in constant motion during cooking and will act as a pestle, crushing the ingredients.

Season, add the herbs and simmer for about 1½ hours.

When the soup is ready, take out the rock and add the cream.

Serve with some crusty bread.

Cabbage, Pearl Barley and Smoked Bacon Soup

Serves 6

50g (1¾oz) butter

2 tablespoons olive oil

3 small eschalots (shallots), finely sliced

2 cloves garlic, finely chopped

200g (7oz) smoked bacon, diced

500g (17½oz) Savoy cabbage, finely sliced

500g (17½oz) starchy potatoes, cut into 2cm (¾in) dice

200ml (7fl oz) white wine

400g (14oz) pearl barley, soaked overnight

1L (36fl oz) chicken stock

salt and pepper

Cabbage, barley and bacon are staple foods in the winter as they are very filling and tasty. This soup is a substantial meal on its own or you could add some confit duck meat to beef it up even more.

In a large pan, heat the butter and the olive oil over medium heat. Add the sliced shallots, garlic and bacon and caramelise the mixture for 3 minutes.

Add the cabbage, the potatoes and the wine and cook for 10 minutes.

Add the pearl barley and the stock. Let it simmer for about 1 hour and if necessary, add more stock.

Salmon

and Prawn (Shrimp) Pie

Serves 6

2 knobs butter

2 sheets puff pastry to cover a 24cm (9½in) diameter pie dish

500g (17½oz) salmon fillet

5 egg whites

380ml (13fl oz) cream

1 splash of pastis (an anise-flavoured liqueur) or Pernod

salt and pepper

1 tablespoon tarragon, chopped

1 tablespoon dill, chopped

1 tablespoon flat-leaf parsley, chopped

500g (17½oz) prawn (shrimp) meat

1 egg, beaten

This is the perfect light lunch on the balcony, as you watch everyone having a great time. A nice glass of white wine and a crisp salad complement this dish perfectly.

Butter a pie dish and place the first sheet of pastry in the dish, prick the bottom with a fork and refrigerate while you prepare the filling.

Cut the salmon into small pieces and blend in a food processor. Take out of the bowl and put the salmon in a bowl on a bed of ice.

Whisk the egg whites until stiff. Then whisk the cream to soft peaks. Mix egg and cream together gently and fold in the salmon pureé, followed by the pastis and herbs, then season.

Stir-fry the prawns in a little oil, just for 30 seconds, and then cool.

Arrange one-third of the mousse in the bottom of the mould and top with some prawns then another layer of salmon mousse and the rest of the prawns and finish with the rest of the mousse.

Cover the pie with the remaining piece of pastry. Brush with the beaten egg and refrigerate for 1 hour.

Preheat the oven to 170°C (335°F). Bake the pie for 40 to 45 minutes or until golden brown.

Salsify

Beignets

Serves 4

PASTRY

100g (3½oz) plain (all-purpose) flour

2 eggs, separated

70ml (2¼fl oz) blonde beer or pale ale

2 pinches dry yeast

salt and pepper

SALSIFY

2 lemons, juiced

4 bunches salsify, about 800g (1lb 12oz)

500ml (17fl oz) milk

50g (1¾oz) plain (all-purpose) flour

salt and pepper

Salsify is a winter vegetable full of vitamins and minerals. Make sure when choosing that the roots are firm. They are delicious when cooked and have a creamy taste. As an apprentice I used to peel up to five crates of salsify a day, it was so popular.

To make the pastry, in a bowl, mix the flour with the egg yolks and the beer and whisk well. Add the yeast, cover with plastic wrap and set aside.

To make the salsify, mix 200ml (7fl oz) cold water with the juice of one lemon. Peel the salsify and put them in the lemon water.

In a pot, mix the flour with 1.3L (44fl oz) of water and the milk. Add some salt and the juice of the remaining lemon. Bring this mixture to the boil, stirring with a whisk and making sure the mixture does not stick to the pan.

Remove the salsify from the lemon water and add to the milk mixture. Simmer for about 25 minutes or until tender, then strain.

Heat a pot half-filled with oil to a temperature of 180°C (350°F). Whisk the two egg whites until stiff and fold them into the egg and beer mixture to make a batter.

Dip the salsify into the batter and then fry for 3 to 4 minutes.

Season them with salt and pepper and serve them with mayonnaise or as an accompaniment to a roast dish.

Rösti

Serves 4

1kg (2lb 4oz) starchy potatoes, peeled

300g (10½oz) speck, cut into small pieces

1 large onion, finely sliced

40ml (1½fl oz) oil

½ cup of chopped parsley

salt and pepper

¼ teaspoon cumin powder

How many of these have I made over the last twenty years? But it is still one of the best cold weather meals and something that we can all make. Crunchy, warm and filling, rosti are a favourite of the Swiss and you can get as creative as you like with your toppings. I would suggest some beautiful goat's cheese just sprinkled over the top.

Grate the potatoes and strain to get as much moisture out as you can.

Sauté the speck and the onions in the oil in a large frying pan until golden in colour.

Add the potatoes, mix well and spread the potatoes evenly in the pan. Flatten with a wooden spoon, cover and reduce the flame to low heat. Cook for 15 minutes on each side.

To turn the rosti over, put a plate on top of the pan and, in a rotating motion, flip the pan over and then slide the potato cake back into the pan.

When the rosti are ready, serve them with salad or with a stew or casserole.

Onion and Bacon Tart

Serves 4

340g (12oz) plain (all-purpose)
    flour
¼ teaspoon salt
120g (4oz) butter, cut into small
    pieces
1 egg
6 tablespoons water
20g (⅔oz) butter
350g (12oz) onions, sliced
25g (¾oz) flour
100ml (2¾fl oz) full-cream milk
100ml (2¾fl oz) cream
salt and pepper
¼ teaspoon thyme, chopped
¼ teaspoon nutmeg
2 egg yolks
100g (3½oz) smoked bacon
    (speck)

A winter favourite from my native Alsace, this tart is true comfort food. This dish can be served as a light lunch with a salad or as a more substantial meal with a slice of braised pork belly and fresh lettuce leaves.

Preheat the oven to 200°C (400°F).

Sift the flour with the salt. Rub the butter into the flour with your fingers until the mixture looks like coarse meal. Sprinkle with the water and mix together to form a ball. Add more water if necessary to hold the dough together. Knead for about 3 minutes.

Put in a bowl, dust with a little flour, cover and put in the refrigerator for one hour before using.

Roll out the pastry and line a 24cm (9½in) tart mould. Blind bake the tart in the oven and set aside.

In a pan, melt the butter. Add the onions and cook them for a couple of minutes or until they are translucent. Dust with the flour and mix well.

With a wooden spoon, stir in the milk and the cream. Season and add the thyme and the nutmeg. Stir constantly for a couple of minutes.

Remove from the heat and let the mixture cool down. Add the two egg yolks and mix well. In another pan, fry the bacon until crispy then place on absorbent paper to drain.

Put the bacon pieces on the bottom of the tart shell and cover with the onion mixture. Bake in the oven for about 30 minutes.

Goulash

Serves 6

1.5kg (3lb 5oz) venison meat, diced
salt and pepper
olive oil
2 small onions, finely chopped
3 cloves garlic, finely chopped
2 tablespoons plain (all-purpose) flour
60g (2oz) tomato paste (purée)
3 tablespoons smoked paprika powder
300ml (10fl oz) white wine
800ml (28fl oz) beef stock
200ml (7fl oz) cream

This is a really rich hearty, wintry dish that can be served with rice, mashed potatoes or, even better, potato dumplings.

Season the meat and sear in a large casserole pan with some oil.

Colour the meat then add the onions and the garlic and stir for a couple of minutes until the onions are translucent.

Dust with the flour, add the tomato paste and the paprika; stir and cook for 3 minutes.

Add the white wine and the stock and simmer for 1½ to 2 hours. When ready, stir through the cream and serve.

Lasagne

Serves 6

NOODLE DOUGH

5 whole eggs

2 tablespoons olive oil

2 tablespoons vinegar

10g (⅓oz) salt

pepper, to taste

nutmeg, to taste

550g (19oz) plain
(all-purpose) flour

LASAGNE

olive oil

2 eschalots (shallots), finely
chopped

3 cloves garlic, finely chopped

1 small onion, finely chopped

900g (1lb 15¾oz) venison meat,
minced

300g (10½oz) button
mushrooms, quartered

2 pinch ground cloves

3 bay leaves

1 teaspoon marjoram, chopped

1 teaspoon thyme, chopped

*Use leg or shoulder when you buy your meat and you can always ask your butcher
to mince it for you. It is always better to eat stewed meat the next day as it will have
even more flavour.*

To make the noodle dough for the lasagne sheets, whisk together the eggs, olive
oil, vinegar and 3 tablespoons of water. On a bench top, place the flour, salt,
pepper and nutmeg and create a well in the middle. Add the wet ingredients
and mix together by hand to form a dough. Knead until all ingredients are well
incorporated. Wrap the dough in a tea towel and allow to rest for one hour.

Heat the oil in a large pan. Add the eschalots, garlic and the onions and
cook for a couple of minutes. Add the meat, mushrooms and all the spices and
herbs and colour for 10 minutes.

Add the tomato paste and the flour and mix well. Add the red wine and the
stock and simmer for 1 hour.

100g (3½oz) tomato paste
 (purée)
2 tablespoons plain (all-purpose)
 flour
400ml (14fl oz) red wine
1L (36fl oz) beef stock
150g (5oz) Gruyère cheese,
 grated

BÉCHAMEL SAUCE
40g (1½oz) butter
40g (1½oz) plain (all-purpose)
 flour
500ml (17fl oz) milk
2 egg yolks
salt and pepper
pinch of nutmeg

To make the béchamel sauce, melt the butter in a pot, add the flour and stir for about 4 minutes.

Add the milk and stir the mixture until it starts to boil. Cook for about 4 minutes until the sauce thickens, making sure it does not stick to the pot or burn. Season with the salt, pepper and nutmeg, add the egg yolks and stir until combined.

Now it is time to assemble the lasagne. Preheat the oven to 180°C (350°F).

Cut the dough into eight balls. Roll out the lasagne sheets as thin as possible using a pasta machine and cut to the desired size. Cook the sheets in salted boiling water for 8 to10 minutes. Refresh the sheets in cold water, drain and use immediately.

In a baking dish, place a layer of pasta, followed by a layer of the meat mixture and a layer of béchamel. Repeat once through and finish with a final layer of pasta followed by the meat mixture. Sprinkle the grated cheese over the top and bake in the oven for 20 minutes.

Spiced

Pork Sausages
with Onion, Beer and Currant Jam

Makes 40 sausages at about 100g (3½oz) each. Jam makes enough for one small jar

2.5kg (5lb 8oz) pork neck
500g (17½oz) pork fat
500g (17½oz) caramelized onions
20g (⅔oz) sage, chopped
3 cloves garlic, finely chopped
5 tablespoons tomato paste
    (purée)
300ml (10½fl oz) red wine
1 tablespoon cayenne pepper
2 tablespoons Cajun spice
3 fresh chillies, finely chopped
4m (13ft) hog casing
Onion, Beer and Currant Jam
750g (1lb 10oz) red (Spanish)
    onions, finely sliced
100g (3½oz) dried currants
500ml (17fl oz) white wine vinegar
120g (4oz) brown sugar
330ml (11½fl oz) blonde beer
3 bay leaves
3 sprigs of thyme
salt and pepper

Serve these with crunchy bread, some caramelized onions and some shredded lettuce. Mmm, might need a cold beer with that too! Ask your butcher for hog casings.

Prepare the sausage filling by mincing the pork neck, the pork fat and the onions. Combine with all the other ingredients and mix well.

Using a sausage maker, stuff the mixture into a hog casing. Sausages should be about 10cm (4in) in length. Try not to over-stuff them as they will split when you cook them later. If you do not have a sausage maker, you could try using a piping bag with a very large nozzle attached. Also, make sure that you check that there are no holes in the casings.

For the jam, mix all ingredients in a heavy-based pan.

Simmer for 1 hour until the onions are translucent and there is hardly any liquid left.

This jam goes well with chorizo sausages or any homemade sausages.

Semolina

Serves 4

1L (36fl oz) milk
2 eschalots (shallots), cut in half
2 cloves garlic, crushed
4 sprigs thyme
90g (3oz) semolina
¼ cup cream
20g (⅔oz) parmesan, shaved
salt and pepper

So smooth and creamy and a perfect meal for people who don't like polenta. It is not as heavy as polenta and can be served with any topping. My favourite variation is a wild mushroom ragout, and my mother always used to serve it with rabbit stew. You can even make semolina for breakfast—serve it with some stewed apple or Rhubarb Compote (see Index).

In a saucepan, boil the milk with the shallots, garlic and the thyme. Turn the heat off and infuse for 5 minutes.

Strain the milk and pour the semolina into the liquid. Simmer for 5 minutes or until the mixture thickens. Add the cream and stir. Put the mixture in a bowl, add the parmesan and top with a mushroom ragout, duck confit or, my favourite, braised pork cheeks.

You can also do a sweet version of this recipe by adding 100g (3½oz) sugar and removing the shallots, garlic and thyme from the milk infusion.

Sugar

Hit

Beignets

Serves 4

On our first trip to France together, my wife and I went to a local apple festival where they were serving these delicious treats. My wife enjoyed them so much that she didn't want to stop eating them.

Perfect with ice-cream or just some whipped cream and a lovely little apple schnapps.

BATTER

5 eggs, separated
80g (2½oz) caster (superfine) sugar
1½ cup beer
80g (2½oz) olive oil
300g (10½oz) wholemeal flour
2 pinches ground cinnamon
1 pinch salt

6 large apples, peeled and cored
20ml (⅔fl oz) kirsch (or any other schnapps)
caster (superfine) sugar, for sprinkling

Start the batter by whisking the egg yolks with the sugar, add the beer, oil and the flour little by little with the cinnamon. Keep cool for 1 hour.

Cut the apples into 1cm (½in) thick slices and marinate them in the schnapps.

Whisk the egg whites with the pinch of salt until stiff and fold into the batter.

Dip the slices of apple into the batter and fry in a pot with 2L (70fl oz) oil heated at 180°C (350°F) for 4 to 5 minutes. To test if your oil is ready, dip a wooden spoon into the oil. If bubbles form around the spoon and start to float, your oil is hot enough.

Drain the apple pieces on absorbent paper and sprinkle with sugar.

Tea Cake

Makes one cake

150g (5oz) butter, softened

150g (5oz) caster (superfine) sugar

3 eggs

pinch salt

110g (3¾oz) plain (all-purpose) flour

110g (3¾oz) almond meal

2 drops vanilla extract

zest of 1 lemon

½ lemon, juiced

4 apples, peeled, cored and cut into 12 pieces each

icing (confectioners') sugar, for dusting

The apples in this cake are still crunchy and warm in the gooey almond cake. Very tasty with a little schnapps.

Preheat the oven to 180°C (350°F). Grease one 24cm (9½in) spring-form cake tin and dust with a little flour. If you have a non-stick mould just use butter.

Firstly, whisk the butter and the sugar for 3 to 4 minutes then add the eggs one at a time.

Add the salt and fold in the flour, almond meal, vanilla extract, the lemon zest and the juice. Do not over-work this dough or it will split.

Pour the mixture into the spring-form tin and place the apples all over the mixture. Bake in the oven for about 20 to 25 minutes.

Let the cake cool for 30 minutes before dusting with icing sugar and serving.

Snow Ball

Serves 6

6 tart apples
6 small knobs butter
6 tablespoons brown sugar
600ml (21fl oz) water
6 walnut halves, toasted

RHUBARB COMPOTE
2 small knobs butter
¼ cup brown sugar
200g (7oz) rhubarb, peeled and
    cut into small pieces
3 drops vanilla extract

My grandfather always used to make this dessert by using apples that had been stored in September in the cellar. We would then eat them in December or even January. Some of the apples used to shrink by half but the flavours were amazing. From memory, the type of apples were Benedictin. We would eat the fruit and make tea from the skins.

Preheat the oven to 180°C (350°F).

Peel and core the apples, using a large corer. Take care not to core the apple all the way through.

Place the apples in a gratin dish. Top with the butter and the brown sugar.

Add the water and cover the dish with tin foil. Bake for about 20 minutes. The apples should still be a little firm when cooked.

For the rhubarb compote, melt the butter in a saucepan, add the sugar and mix until well combined.

Add the rhubarb pieces and vanilla and simmer until the mixture is cooked and has a thick consistency.

ITALIAN MERINGUE
300g (10½oz) caster (superfine)
    sugar
4 egg whites

For the Italian meringue, add 120ml (4fl oz) of water to the sugar and boil until the mixture reaches a temperature of 120°C (240°F), also called the 'soft ball' stage. If you don't have a candy thermometer, drop some of the sugar syrup into cold water. It should form a soft, flexible ball, which will flatten when pressed.

Whisk the egg whites to soft peaks, then add the sugar syrup and beat until stiff.

Take the apples out of the liquid and stuff with the rhubarb compote.

Top each apple with some toasted walnuts and cover with the meringue. You can pipe it on or just spread it with a small spatula.

Place on a plate and serve with some custard, cream or fruit coulis. You can also torch the meringue with a gas burner.

Nicole's Kougelhopf

200ml (7fl oz) milk

37g (1⅓oz) fresh yeast

560g (19½oz) plain
  (all-purpose) flour

100g (3½oz) caster (superfine)
  sugar

3 pinches salt

1 large egg or 2 small ones

70g (2¼oz) raisins, soaked in
  20ml (⅔fl oz) kirsch

100g (3½oz) butter, softened

This makes enough dough for 1 kougelhopf mould

In Alsace this cake is eaten as a morning or afternoon tea.
When I was a child, my Aunty Nicole used to make this (and still does) every
Saturday afternoon. We used to go and get this wonderful cake from her house,
where it had been baked in the oven located on the side of the barn. My uncle would
sometimes bake bread in this oven too. You don't eat the kougelhopf the same day it
is baked. It is always eaten the next day. In my home, we had it for breakfast with my
mother's homemade jams. If you ever go to Alsace, try it and tell them I sent you.

First, you need to make a starter dough.

Take 100ml (3½fl oz) milk (it should be tepid) and dissolve the yeast in it.
Add 75g (2½oz) flour and mix. You should obtain a smooth dough.

Put the rest of the flour in a bowl and in the centre form a well. Place the
starter dough in the centre and cover with a cloth and store in a warm place,
around 40°C (105°F) and let the dough rise for 30 minutes.

Mix the starter dough with the rest of the flour and knead until you have a rough dough. Put the dough in a bowl with an electric mixer attachment and add the sugar, the remaining milk and the salt. Mix for 3 minutes then add the eggs and the soaked raisins.

Stir in the butter and mix on medium speed for another 2 minutes or until the dough does not stick to the sides of the bowl anymore. Cover the bowl with a cloth and rest in a warm place for 2 hours.

Butter your mould or moulds depending on what type you are using.

After 2 hours, the dough should have doubled in size. Place the dough in the mould and cover and rest for another hour.

Bake the kougelhopf for 45 minutes in a preheated oven at 180°C (350°F). If you are making mini kougelhopfs, like the ones pictured on the next page, they take 15 minutes at 180°C (350°F). If you like, you can dust them with icing (confectioners') sugar before serving.

Beignets

with Cinnamon Sugar

Serves 6

500g (17½oz) plain
  (all-purpose) flour
10g (⅓oz) dried yeast
30g (1oz) caster (superfine)
  sugar
2 eggs
1 egg yolk
½ teaspoon salt
125ml (4fl oz) tepid milk
100g (3½oz) butter, melted
oil, for frying
cinnamon sugar or caster
  (superfine) sugar, for
  sprinkling

Once cooked, allow them to cool before filling with your own jams. Or eat them just as they are. However you eat them they are a real treat!

In a bowl, sift the flour and the yeast. Add the sugar, eggs and the egg yolk. Dissolve the salt in the milk and add to the mixture with the melted butter. Mix in a bowl with an electric beater hook attachment at medium speed for about 5 minutes. Put the dough on a bench and knead into a ball.

Put the dough in a bowl, cover with a tea towel, leave in a warm place for 1 hour until the dough doubles in size.

Now the dough is ready, knead it again for about 3 minutes. Roll out the dough to 2cm (¾in) thick.

With a water glass or a pastry cutter, cut circles out of the dough. Knead the leftover dough again and re-roll and cut until you have used up all the pastry.

Put all the circles on a tray and cover again with the cloth and stand in a warm place for 1 hour.

Half-fill a large pot with oil and heat to 180°C (350°F).

Fry the beignets, four at a time, making sure you fry both sides for a couple of minutes. With a strainer, remove the beignets from the oil and drain on absorbent paper. Repeat until all the beignets are cooked.

Put on a plate and sprinkle with sugar or cinnamon sugar. You can also serve them with homemade jams or cream.

Cookies

Makes about 30 to 40 cookies

5 eggs
250g (9oz) caster (superfine)
    sugar
125g (4oz) almond meal
125g (4oz) butter, melted
15ml (½fl oz) schnapps
600g (21oz) plain (all-purpose)
    flour
oil, for frying
icing (confectioners') or caster
    (superfine) sugar, for
    sprinkling
cinnamon, for sprinkling

My mother has shared this recipe with me. This is a delicacy from Alsace and is usually served during the Christmas period and the month of February during the carnival season. The taste is in between a beignet and a cookie and is best served with a nice café au lait.

In a bowl or electric mixer, beat the eggs and the sugar until pale.

Add to this mixture the almond meal, the butter and the schnapps, folding gently.

Add the flour bit by bit, and knead the dough into a ball.

Cut the ball of dough into little pieces and form into little fingers.

In a pot, heat some oil at 180°C (350°F) (only half-fill the pot with oil) and fry until they are golden. Drain onto absorbent paper and sprinkle with icing sugar or a mixture of cinnamon and sugar.

Serve when cool.

Chestnut

Truffles

Serves 10

500g (17½oz) sweet chestnut
    purée
100g (3½oz) unsalted butter
100g (3½oz) good-quality dark
    (semisweet) chocolate,
    70% cocoa, crushed
¼ teaspoon vanilla extract
2 drops brandy
cocoa powder, for dusting

I found this recipe in my grandfather's cooking notes.

Warm the chestnut puree slightly in a double boiler or on the stove top.

In another bowl, melt the butter and the chocolate together. Stir in the chestnut puree, vanilla extract and brandy and pour into a mould or a dip dish lined with plastic wrap.

Chill for 24 hours.

The next day roll little balls in the palm of your hand, then roll them in cocoa powder and serve with coffee or as a wonderful treat.

Chocolate
and Hazelnut Cake

Makes one cake

250g (9oz) caster (superfine) sugar

4 eggs, separated

250g (9oz) dark (semisweet) chocolate

125g (4oz) butter, softened

75g (2½oz) plain (all-purpose) flour

125g (4oz) hazelnut meal

I guarantee that you will be popular after serving up this cake. Just serve it with a little cream and strawberry coulis.

Preheat the oven to 180°C (350°F). Grease one 24cm (9½oz) spring-form tin with butter and dust with a little flour.

In a bowl with an electric mixer attached, mix the sugar, the egg yolks and 5 tablespoons of water until pale and the consistency of whipped cream.

Melt chocolate in a double boiler, add the butter and whisk well.

In another bowl, whisk the egg whites to soft peaks

Fold the chocolate mix into the egg yolk mix then fold in the flour and the hazelnuts. Finally, very gently fold in the egg whites.

Pour the cake mixture into the tin and bake in the oven for 25 to 30 minutes. You can check if the cake is cooked by inserting a skewer into the cake. If it comes out clean, the cake is ready.

Let the cake cool for 20 minutes before removing from the tin. Dust with icing sugar before serving.

Galette

of Pear and Dark Chocolate

Serves 6

For this cake, make sure you choose juicy pears and use a good-quality dark chocolate. You can shape the galette however you want, there is no real rule, the only one is to enjoy it.

FRANGIPANE

100g (3½oz) butter, softened

100g (3½oz) caster (superfine) sugar

70g (2¼oz) eggs, shells removed

120g (4oz) almond meal

40g (1½oz) plain (all-purpose) flour

10ml (⅓oz) Williams pear schnapps

600g (1lb 5oz) puff pastry, pre-rolled

1 egg, lightly beaten

2 pears, peeled and thinly sliced

100g (3½oz) dark chocolate (semisweet) bits

2 tablespoons milk

For the frangipane, whip the butter until it is smooth, then add the sugar and mix together until well combined and pale in colour. Add the eggs, almond meal, flour and the schnapps and mix until combined.

Cut out two discs of puff pastry, 20cm (8in) in diameter. Place one disc onto a lined baking tray. With a pastry brush, paint around the edge of the pastry with a beaten egg. Spread the frangipane mix in the centre of the pastry with a palette knife. Place the sliced pears on top of the frangipane and sprinkle with the chocolate bits.

Place the other disc of pastry on top and press down around the edge, marking with a fork. Brush the pastry with beaten egg and milk. Put in the fridge for 30 minutes. Remove from the fridge and egg wash again to make it more shiny. At this stage, you could make some designs on the pastry with a knife, if desired.

Place back in the fridge for a further 30 minutes and then bake in a preheated oven at 220°C (420°F) for 30 minutes.

de Loup
(Wolf's Teeth)

Serves 10

250g (9oz) caster (superfine) sugar
100g (3½oz) butter, softened
3 eggs
250g (9oz) plain (all-purpose) flour
splash of Williams pear schnapps
2 drops vanilla extract

If you don't have one of these moulds just make a similar one by folding silicone paper on itself like an accordion to a 2cm (¾in) height. You can also flavour the 'teeth' in different ways by substituting the schnapps for other flavours or essences such as apple, almond or cinnamon.
Enjoy with a hot chocolate or coffee.

Preheat the oven to 180°C (350°F).

Mix the sugar and the butter until creamy. Add the eggs, one by one, until the mix is homogenised. Slowly add the flour, finishing with the schnapps and the vanilla.

Butter the wolf's teeth mould and put a dollop of the dough in each indentation and bake for 10 minutes.

Store in an airtight container.

Gratin

of Pear with Williams Pear Sabayon

Serves 6

6 pears, peeled and cored
850g (1lb 13oz) caster
    (superfine) sugar
3 vanilla beans, scraped

SABAYON
5 egg yolks
70g (2¼oz) caster (superfine)
    sugar
1½ tablespoons Williams pear
    schnapps
100ml (3½fl oz) whipped cream
icing (confectioners') sugar, to
    dust

As apprentice chefs, we used to make a dessert a bit like this one. It used to walk out the door and it is so simple and fast. The quality of the fruit is very important with this dish—always check that your fruit is not too hard.

Preheat the oven to 180°C (350°F).

Poach the pears in 1.2L (52fl oz) of water, sugar and vanilla pods and the scraped seeds for about 15 to 20 minutes or until tender. Slice the pears so that the pear fans out when placed in a heat-proof dish or soup bowl.

For the sabayon, place the egg yolks and sugar into a bowl over simmering water. Whisk vigorously for about 5 to 10 minutes, making sure that the eggs do not scramble. Once well blended and starting to thicken, add the schnapps.

Take it off the heat and continue to whisk for about 1 minute. Fold in the whipped cream (do not over-whip the cream).

Pour the mixture onto the pear so that the dish is about three-quarters full. Dust with icing sugar and bake in the oven for about 5 minutes. The sabayon should start to rise a little and turn golden brown on top.

Serve with vanilla ice-cream.

Gingerbread

(*Pain d'épices*)

Serves 4

140g (5oz) honey

250g (9oz) plain (all-purpose) flour

130g (5oz) muscovado or dark brown sugar

1 teaspoon star anise powder

½ teaspoon Chinese five spices

½ teaspoon ground ginger

¼ teaspoon ground cloves

1 tablespoon bicarbonate of soda (baking soda)

250ml (9fl oz) milk

30ml (1fl oz) kirsch

This is one to eat in the afternoon with coffee or tea. You can also use it as a substitute for the plain bread used in French toast in the morning. Use a small loaf tin, about 20cm (8in) long.

Preheat the oven to 200°C (400°F).

Mix all ingredients together until well combined. Pour the mixture into a buttered loaf tin.

Bake in the oven for 40 minutes. Check that the top is not burning. If it looks a bit dark, place a sheet of greaseproof paper over the top.

The cake is ready when a skewer comes out clean.

La Bamboulene

Savoyard

Serves 4

1kg (2lb 4oz) tart apples, peeled

90g (3oz) caster (superfine) sugar

40g (1½oz) plain (all-purpose) flour

1 egg yolk

40g (1½oz) almond meal

20ml (⅔fl oz) Calvados (apple brandy)

750ml (26fl oz) milk

20g (⅔oz) butter

¼ teaspoon vanilla extract

This is a kind of clafoutis traditionally made with apples called Golden Reinette. They are quite tart in flavour so I suggest that you use Granny Smith, Cortland or Pippin apples for this recipe. Serve warm with some vanilla or cinnamon ice-cream.

Preheat the oven to 170°C (340°F).

Cut the apples into 5mm (¼in) thick slices.

Simmer the apples with a cup of water and 40g (1½oz) of the sugar. The apples should still be firm and not falling apart.

In a bowl, mix the flour, the rest of the sugar, egg yolk, almond meal, vanilla, Calvados and one cup of the milk and mix well.

In a pot, heat the rest of the milk. Pour into the flour mixture and mix well. Butter a gratin dish and place the apple slices into it. Pour the milk mixture over the top. Bake in the oven for 20 minutes or until the top has caramelized.

Mousse

au Chocolat

Serves 4

40g (1½oz) icing
   (confectioners') sugar
5 egg yolks
30ml (1fl oz) Calvados or apple
   brandy
250g (9oz) dark (semisweet),
   chocolate, 60% cocoa
3 egg whites
1.5L (52fl oz) cream

This is definitely an adults-only chocolate mousse. Send the kids to bed first, then enjoy with some fruit or just some Chantilly cream.

First, mix the sugar, egg yolks and the Calvados in a double boiler and whisk for 4 to 5 minutes until you reach the consistency of a lightly whipped cream.

Melt the chocolate in a double boiler until all melted.

Whisk the egg whites until just a bit more than soft peaks.

Whisk the cream to soft peaks.

In a bowl, mix the egg and sugar mixture with the chocolate, stirring vigorously. Add the cream and when well mixed fold in the egg whites.

Pipe into individual serving glasses or bowls and refrigerate for 3 hours before serving.

Meringue Tart

Makes one 24-cm (9¾ in) tart

1 quantity Sweet Pastry (see
    Index)
1kg (2lb 4oz) rhubarb
300g (10½oz) caster (superfine)
    sugar
4 eggs, separated
150ml (5fl oz) cream

I just love rhubarb and meringue. The tartness of the rhubarb contrasts with the sweetness of the meringue so well. This is my grandmother's recipe—she was the queen of meringue!

Prepare the mould with Sweet Pastry (see Index).

Wash and peel the rhubarb and cut into 5cm (2in) pieces.

Put them in a bowl and sprinkle with 100g (3½oz) of the sugar. Cover and leave in a cool place for 6 hours. This is to extract as much of the water as possible so that the tart does not get soggy.

Preheat the oven at 180°C (350°F).

Drain the rhubarb and place them in the pastry casing.

Whisk the egg yolks with 100g (3½oz) of sugar and the cream. Pour over the tart and bake for 25 minutes.

Now you can do the meringue. Whisk the eggs whites with rest of the sugar until stiff. Once the tart has been in the oven for 25 minutes take it out and top with all of the meringue, using either a palette knife or a piping bag.

Increase the heat to 200°C (400°F) and put the tart back in the oven for another 10 to 15 minutes or until the meringue has coloured.

Serve warm.

Soufflé

Glacé au Chocolat
(Iced Chocolate Soufflé)

For 8 ramekins

6 eggs, separated
75g (2½oz) caster (superfine)
    sugar
150g (5oz) dark (semisweet)
    chocolate, 60% cocoa
12g (⅓oz) cocoa powder
625ml (21½fl oz) cream
250g (9oz) caster (superfine)
    sugar

This is the bee's knees, so rich and yet so light. All this beautiful dessert needs is some fresh fruit or some toasted nuts.

Using electric beaters, whisk the six yolks, 75ml (2½fl oz) water and the sugar until the mixture turns pale and has the consistency of whipped cream.

Melt the chocolate in a double boiler, making sure it does not get too hot as this will make the chocolate very grainy. Add the 50ml (1¾oz) of water and the cocoa powder and stir well. The finished product should look silky smooth.

Whisk the cream to a little more than soft peaks.

Whisk the egg whites with the sugar on high speed until they are stiff.

Then combine the egg yolk mixture with the chocolate mixture. Add the cream and gently fold in the egg whites.

Wrap the outside of the ramekins with a strip of baking paper (higher than the ramekins) and attach with a strip of sticky tape. Pipe the mixture into each ramekin and freeze for about 2 hours before serving.

Sweet

Pastry

200g (7oz) plain (all-purpose) flour

3 tablespoon caster (superfine) sugar

½ teaspoon dried yeast

pinch salt

100g (3½oz) butter, melted

1 egg yolk

1 tablespoon kirsch

As long as I can remember this has been the pastry my mum has used for her fabulous tarts. Everyone loves to eat the crust of her tarts, just as much as the filling. This pastry is very short so use your fingers to distribute the dough into the tart mould.

Mix the dry ingredients together and make a well in the centre.

Mix the wet ingredients together and pour into the well. Blend everything together by hand to form a dough. Roughly roll out the dough and push into a tart mould.

There is no need to blind bake this pastry. Simply add your chosen filling and bake.

Coulis

300g (10½oz) strawberries
250g (9oz) caster (superfine)
    sugar

Wash the strawberries and remove the hull.

Blend the strawberries in a blender and pass through a sieve. Mix with the sugar until the sugar has dissolved.

Anglaise

250ml (9fl oz) full-cream milk
1 vanilla stick, cut and scraped
100g (3½oz) caster (superfine)
    sugar
5 egg yolks

In a saucepan, heat the milk with the vanilla stick.

Mix the sugar and the egg yolks in another saucepan and gradually pour in the milk as you stir.

Transfer to a low heat and stir continuously until the mixture coats the back of a spoon. Be very careful that the milk does not boil. Pour through a sieve and serve.

Brioche

Serves 6

30g (1oz) fresh yeast
300ml (10½fl oz) milk, tepid
40g (1½oz) caster (superfine) sugar
645g (22½oz) plain (all-purpose) flour
pinch salt
zest of 1 lemon
1 pinch star anise powder
80g (2½oz) eggs, beaten
60g (2oz) butter
150ml (5fl oz) oil, for frying

In French, this is pain soufflé. *It is an Alsatian dessert that should be served immediately with some stewed apples, Milk Jam (see Index) or dried fruit paste. You can also serve them with ice-cream. Just beware of the steam when you pour the water in the hot oil.*

In a bowl, place the yeast and milk. Add the sugar and stir gently.

In another bowl, mix together the flour, salt, lemon zest, star anise, eggs and the butter. Make a well then pour the milk into the centre of this mixture.

Knead until the dough does not stick to your hands anymore. If needed, add some more flour. Form dough into a ball, place in a bowl, cover with a tea towel and leave in a warm place for about 45 minutes to 1 hour. The dough needs to rise by double the volume.

Once your dough is ready, roll it out on a floured bench to about 3cm (1¼in) thick. Cut circles with a 6cm (2½in) diameter cutter and place on a floured tray. Cover and let them rise again for 45 minutes in a warm place.

When they are ready, heat the oil in a large pot and place the little circles in the pot, quickly pour 150ml (5fl oz) water over it and cover with a lid and hold on to it (make sure you use a lid that fits the pot). Keep the lid on for a couple of minutes or until they are golden.

Tart

Makes one tart

PASTRY

250g (9oz) caster (superfine)
   sugar
2½ eggs
1 teaspoon orange zest
1 teaspoon lemon zest
250g (9oz) butter, softened
½ teaspoon salt
500g (17½oz) plain
   (all-purpose) flour
1 pinch baking powder

FILLING

300ml (10½fl oz) cream
125g (4oz) caster (superfine)
   sugar
300g (10½oz) ground walnuts
3 tablespoons vanilla extract
250g (9oz) walnuts, halved
   without shell
icing (confectioners') sugar, to
   dust

Whisk the sugar and the eggs. Add the zests, butter and salt.

On a clean bench top, make a well in the flour and the baking powder. Slowly mix the wet ingredients into the dry ingredients and knead until the dough does not stick to the bench anymore. You can also put all the ingredients into a food processor and mix together.

Place dough in a bowl, cover with a tea towel and rest in a warm place for 2 hours before using.

Preheat the oven to 200°C (400°F). Grease and flour a 24cm round tart tin. Roll out the pastry and line the tart case. Blind bake for about 15 minutes until done. Leave the tart in a cool place for 1 hour.

When ready to make the filling, preheat the oven to 210°C (410°F). In a bowl, mix together the cream, sugar, ground walnuts and the vanilla extract. Pour the mixture into the pastry shell and bake for 15 to 20 minutes or until set.

Cool and garnish with the walnut halves and a dusting of icing sugar.

Jam

Makes two to three jars, about 250–375ml (9–13fl oz) each

3L (105fl oz) milk

2kg (70oz) caster (superfine) sugar

2 vanilla pods, cut in half and scraped

This jam tastes like caramel. Serve it just on bread with some fleur de sel flakes or as an accompaniment for desserts. Make sure you keep a close eye on this jam while it is cooking as it can burn easily.

Mix the milk, sugar and the vanilla in a saucepan.

Bring to the boil, then turn the heat down as low as possible (barely a simmer) and skim any foam on the surface. Simmer, uncovered, for around 2 to 2½ hours, stirring every 10 minutes or so, skimming the foam when necessary.

Check the consistency at about 2 hours. Stop the cooking now if you want a runnier caramel to use in other recipes or cook it a little longer if you want a thicker jam to use as a spread. The jam will also thicken up when it cools so keep this in mind when deciding how long to cook the jam. At this stage, you also need to keep an eye on it to prevent it from burning on the bottom of the pan.

When you have the desired consistency, take it off the heat and whisk the jam until it is glossy and smooth.

Pour into a clean jar and allow to cool uncovered. Once completely cool, place the lid on it and put it in the fridge.

The jam should keep for around 1 to 3 weeks.

Extra
Bits & Pieces

Stock

Makes 7.5L (15.85 pt)

3 carrots, chopped

2 onions, chopped

2 cups chopped celery

2 tomatoes

1 small leek, chopped

butter

salt

4kg (8lb 14oz) beef bones, with
lots of marrow, meaty

BOUQUET GARNI
(IN A CLOTH BAG)

½ bunch thyme

2 cloves garlic, crushed

½ bunch parsley

2 bay leaves

3 whole cloves

10 white peppercorns

Sauté the vegetables in some butter in a large pot and season with some salt. Add the bones and the herb bag, top with about 15L (about 31pt) water and bring to the boil. Simmer on low heat for 5 hours, constantly skimming the stock of impurities. If the liquid evaporates while cooking just add more water to keep the level up.

Season and gently strain the stock. Chill and remove the excess fat, which should have risen to the surface and set on top.

You can also freeze this stock in small containers. It will keep for three to six months.

Stock
with Roasted Chicken Bones

Makes 3.5L (122fl oz)

1.5kg (3lb 5oz) chicken wings, roasted

1.5kg (3lb 5oz) chicken bones, roasted

1 large carrot, chopped

1 large onion, chopped

2 cups celery, chopped

1 leek, washed and sliced

BOUQUET GARNI

(IN A CLOTH BAG)

5 sprigs thyme

2 bay leaves

5 celery leaves

2 sprigs rosemary

2 juniper berries

2 whole cloves

3 cloves garlic, crushed

Put the chicken pieces in a large pot and top with 7L (14.8pt) of water. Bring to the boil and skim the foam that is forming on top.

Add all the vegetables and the herb bag and simmer for about 3½ hours, making sure you skim the stock frequently.

Season with salt and pepper and strain gently so that the stock does not get cloudy.

Cool and remove the remaining fat that has formed on top.

You can then freeze into small containers.

Stock

Makes 3.5L (122fl oz)

3kg (6lb 10oz) lamb bones,
    roasted
1 large carrot, chopped
1 large onion, chopped
2 cups celery, chopped
1 leek, washed and sliced

BOUQUET GARNI
    (IN A CLOTH BAG)
5 sprigs thyme
2 bay leaves
5 celery leaves
2 sprigs rosemary
2 juniper berries
2 whole cloves
3 cloves garlic, crushed

Put the lamb bones in a large pot and top with enough water to cover. Bring to the boil and skim the foam that is forming on top.

Add all the vegetables and the herb bag and simmer for about 3½ hours, making sure you skim the stock frequently.

Season with salt and pepper and strain gently so that the stock does not get cloudy.

Cool and remove the remaining fat that has formed on top. You can then freeze the stock into small containers.

Stock

Makes 3.5L (122fl oz)

3 carrots, chopped

2 onions, chopped

2 cups chopped celery

2 tomatoes

1 small leek, chopped

butter

salt

5kg (10lb 16oz) veal bones, cut into small pieces and roasted

2kg (4lb 6oz) veal trimmings, cut into small pieces and roasted

BOUQUET GARNI
(IN A CLOTH BAG)

½ bunch thyme

2 cloves garlic, crushed

½ bunch parsley

2 bay leaves

3 whole cloves

10 white peppercorns

In a large pot, sauté the vegetables in some butter and season with salt.

Add the bones, the meat and the herb bag, top with 10L (21pt) of water and bring to the boil. Simmer on low heat for 5 hours, constantly skimming the stock of impurities. If the liquid goes down while cooking, just add more water to keep the level up.

Season and gently strain the stock. Chill and remove the excess fat.

You can also freeze this stock in small containers.

Confit

Shallots

Serves 6

30 medium-sized eschalots
  (shallots)
½ head garlic, left whole with the
  skin on
100g (3½oz) duck fat
100g (3½oz) butter
2 tablespoons thyme leaves
2 bay leaves
40g (1½oz) salt flakes

Preheat oven to 140°C (285°F).

Put all ingredients in a gratin dish and mix. Cover with tin foil and bake for 1½ hours.

When the eschalots are cooked just pinch them away from the skin and serve.

Gratin

Savoyard

Serves 4

1kg (36oz) potatoes

300g (10½oz) Emmenthal
cheese, grated

500ml (17fl oz) beef stock

50g (1¾oz) butter

salt and pepper

Butter a gratin dish and preheat oven to 180°C (350°F).

Wash, peel and slice the potatoes into ½cm (¼in) thick slices.

Place a layer of potatoes in the gratin dish, followed by a layer of cheese, alternating each layer and finishing with a layer of cheese. Season with salt and pepper.

Place a few knobs of butter on top and then add the beef stock.

Place the gratin dish on the stovetop to start. Heat until the stock starts to bubble and then place in the oven for 45 minutes.

Maple Syrup Dressing

Serves 8

40g (1½oz) balsamic vinegar
30g (1oz) maple syrup
90ml (3fl oz) olive oil
10g (⅓oz) lemon juice
salt and pepper

Whisk all ingredients together.

2 egg yolks
15g (½oz) Dijon mustard
200ml (7fl oz) olive oil
½ lemon, juiced
salt and pepper

In a bowl, beat together the egg yolks and mustard.

Slowly add the olive oil, whisking continuously. Stir in the lemon juice and season with salt and pepper.

Gratin

Serves 4

250g (9oz) macaroni
150g (5oz) speck, diced
⅓ cup cream
100g (3½oz) duck liver pâté
½ cup milk
salt and pepper
100g (3½oz) grated Emmenthal
   or good-quality parmesan
40g (1½oz) butter

Cook the pasta in a pan of boiling water till al dente.

Butter a gratin dish and preheat the oven to 220°C (420°F). Lightly sauté the speck.

In a bowl, mix the cooked macaroni, speck, cream, pâté and milk and season with salt and pepper. Pour into the gratin dish and sprinkle with the cheese. Flake the butter over the gratin dish.

Bake for 20 to 30 minutes or until the top is melted and golden.

Beignets

Serves 4

1kg (2lb 4oz) potatoes, peeled
1 onion, finely chopped
1 teaspoon thyme, chopped
3 tablespoons plain (all-purpose) flour
3 whole eggs, lightly beaten
¼ tablespoon parsley, chopped
salt and pepper
200ml (7fl oz) cream
pinch nutmeg

Grate the potatoes and put them into a kitchen cloth and squeeze out as much liquid as possible.

Sauté the onions in some butter and add the thyme.

Place the potatoes in a bowl and mix in the flour, onions, eggs, the parsley, salt and pepper, cream and nutmeg.

Heat a non-stick pan and add a splash of oil. Add individual spoonfuls of the potato mixture to the pan, pushing them down slightly to form a patty. Cook for about 4 minutes on each side, taking care not to burn them.

Drain on absorbent paper and serve.

Dumplings

Serves 4

900g (32oz) désirée potatoes

200g (7oz) plain (all-purpose) flour

pinch nutmeg

3 eggs

1 onion, finely diced

30g (1oz) butter

1 cup cream

bunch chives, chopped

100g (3½oz) Gruyère cheese, grated

salt and pepper

Preheat the oven to 180°C (350°F).

Wash the potatoes, put them in a pan, cover with water, add salt and cook for 25 minutes. When the potatoes are cooked, put them through a mouli. Add the flour, nutmeg and the eggs to the potatoes and mix everything together. Sauté the finely diced onion and add to the mix.

In another pan, bring some water and salt to the boil, then reduce to a simmer. Using two spoons, form little dumplings from the potato mixture, and place in the water for about 8 minutes. When the dumplings are cooked, remove from the water and place on absorbent paper to drain.

Grease the gratin dish with the butter and place the dumplings inside.

In a bowl, mix together the cream and the chives. Pour over the dumplings and sprinkle with the gruyere. Cook for 20 minutes and serve with a fresh salad.

Potatoes

with Crispy Duck Skin

Serves 4

1kg (36oz) potatoes, peeled and cut into thin slices

80g (2½oz) goose fat

300g (10½oz) duck skin, cut into thin slices

salt and pepper

2 cloves garlic, finely chopped

3 tablespoons parsley, chopped

Dry the potato slices well.

In a large pan, melt the goose fat, add the duck skin and fry until crispy.

Add the potatoes and cook for about 15 minutes, stirring constantly. When the potatoes start to become golden brown, add the salt and pepper. Cover and cook over medium heat for a further 15 minutes.

Add the chopped garlic and parsley, stir to mix and cook, uncovered, for a further 10 minutes over medium heat or until the potatoes are cooked.

Red Cabbage with Apple and Chestnuts

Serves 4

3 tablespoons duck fat

2 eschalots (shallots), finely diced

800g (28oz) red cabbage, thinly sliced

salt and pepper

1 tablespoon red wine vinegar

2 tart apples, peeled and cut into small dices

2 tablespoons light brown sugar

200g (7oz) chestnuts, cooked

In a large heavy-based pot, melt the duck fat and sauté the shallots. Add the cabbage, salt, pepper, vinegar, apples, sugar and ½ cup of water.

Simmer very gently for 1 to 1½ hours, stirring occasionally. There will not be much liquid, but continue to stir and the end result will be like a confit. It is very important to keep the cooking temperature as low as possible.

Add the chestnuts 30 minutes before the end of the cooking time. This dish goes well with pork or sausages on a cold winter day.

Spätzle

(Alsace Pasta)

Serves 4

500g (17½oz) plain
(all-purpose) flour
1 teaspoon salt
6 large eggs, beaten
200ml (7fl oz) milk

Boil a large pan of salted water.

Meanwhile, place the flour and salt in a bowl. Make a well, add the eggs and stir with a wooden spoon. Add the milk and stir until well combined. The consistency of the pastry should be elastic but still slightly runny.

Place the pastry inside the spätzle machine. Then place it over the pot and push the pastry through the machine so that the noodles fall off into the water below. If you don't have a spätzle machine, then you can use a knife and a chopping board to cut noodle shapes into the pot of boiling water (see photo opposite).

The spätzle are ready when they rise to the surface. Drain well.

You can serve them as is, seasoned and with a knob of butter.

Or, for a crunchier texture, you can pan-fry the spätzle in some butter.

Porcini *Spätzles*

Serves 4

50g (1¾oz) dried porcini
    mushrooms
2 knobs butter
⅓ cup onions, finely diced
1 clove garlic, finely chopped
4 eggs
250ml (9fl oz) milk
350g (12oz) flour
pinch nutmeg
salt and pepper

Soak the mushrooms in hot water and boil for about 10 minutes. When the porcini are tender, drain and reserve some of the cooking liquid. Make sure you strain the liquid through a cloth.

Melt the butter in a pan and add the onions and the garlic. When they are translucent, add the mushrooms and some of the cooking liquid and cook for about 5 to 10 minutes or until the liquid is reduced.

Put the mushroom mixture in a food processor and blend to a paste.

Put the eggs, milk and the puree in a bowl and whisk.

Add the flour, mix well and season with nutmeg, salt and pepper. Whisk to a smooth batter—if needed add some more milk.

Put a pot of water on the stove, salt the water and bring to the boil. Put the batter in a spätzle machine and push the batter through the holes. They will sink to the bottom but will rise to the surface when they are ready. Remove and put in some cold water to refresh.

Drain the noodles and when they are dry, fry in a pan with a good knob of butter until they are golden brown.

Serve them with any stew.

Wine Jus

Makes 500ml (17fl oz)

350ml (12fl oz) red wine

250ml (9fl oz) Madeira wine

3 small eschalots (shallots), finely
    diced

2 star anise

2 juniper berries

1 cinnamon stick

3 peppercorns

salt and pepper

350ml (12fl oz) veal stock

BOUQUET GARNI
   (IN A CLOTH BAG)

3 sprigs of thyme

2 bay leaves

2 sage leaves

2 parsley stalks

In a large pot, add the wines, eschalots, star anise, juniper berries, cinnamon stick and peppercorns and salt and pepper.

Simmer until the liquid is reduced by half. Add the stock and reduce by half.

When ready, strain through a fine sieve and serve.

Fruit Paste

Serves 10

125g (4oz) dried apples
125g (4oz) dried dates
125g (4oz) dried figs
125g (4oz) dried pears
15g (½oz) cinnamon
2 pinches white pepper
1 pinch star anise powder

Soak all the fruit in 1L (36fl oz) of warm water for about 3 hours.

Add the cinnamon, pepper and star anise powder to the fruit, transfer everything to a food processor or blender and mix to a smooth paste.

This recipe goes well with Terrine of Duck Liver in a Jar or Steamed Brioche (see Index).

Serves 6

salt
50ml (1¾fl oz) lemon juice
50ml (1¾fl oz) sherry vinegar
300ml (10½fl oz) olive oil
pepper

Mix the salt and the lemon juice. Add the vinegar and slowly stir in the olive oil. Season with pepper.

Bread

Makes two loaves

14g (½oz) dried yeast

1 teaspoon caster (superfine) sugar

1½ cups tepid water

750g (24oz) rye flour

250g (9oz) plain (all-purpose) flour

250g (9oz) walnuts, chopped

2 teaspoons salt

First mix the yeast with the sugar and a ½ cup of lukewarm water.

In a large bowl, mix the two flours. When the yeast mixture is bubbly, make a well in the centre of the flour and pour in the yeast.

Dissolve the salt with the remaining cup of water and mix it into the flour. Work the dough until fairly stiff.

Turn the dough out on a lightly floured surface and knead for about 10 minutes. Return it to the bowl, sprinkle with a little flour. Cover with a cloth and put in a warm place, around 40°C (104°F) for about 2 hours until the dough has doubled in size.

After 2 hours, punch the dough down and turn it out on a lightly floured bench. Cut in half and knead each piece until smooth or for about 4 minutes. Work ½ cup of walnuts into each piece. Shape each ball into a 20cm (8in) loaf. With a sharp knife, make three to four incisions on top of each loaf.

Put the loaves on baking paper, cover and put in a warm place to rise for another hour.

Once risen, preheat the oven to 210°C (410°F).

Bake loaves in the oven for about 30 minutes. To test if the bread is ready, tap it a few times—it should sound hollow when cooked.

Index

alpine coffee, 119
alpine elixir 112
Alsace duck confit 140
Alsatian porcini *spätzles* 264
Alsatian sauerkraut 156
apple, see fruit
apple *beignets* 200
apple snow ball 202
apple tea cake 201
Aunty Nicole's kougelhopf 206

baeckeoffe aux cuisses de canard 125
baked eggs with piperade 17
baked rainbow trout roulade with
    citrus salad and maple syrup
    dressing 37
bass fillet cooked in almond salt crust
    38
bass quenelles 43
beef
    beef stock 240
    bone marrow bread and butter
        pudding 167
    braised beef cheeks 126
    fleischschnaka 144
    meat snail 144
    pan-fried flank steak, potato and
        truffle chaussons, shallots
        sauce 66
beef stock 240
beetroot gnocchi 44
beignets with cinnamon sugar 210
bone marrow bread and butter
    pudding 167
braised beef cheeks 126
braised lamb shanks in orange juice
    and star anise 128
braised pork belly 132
braised pork cheeks 133
braised pork cheeks shepherd's pie
    gratinated with parmesan 129
braised witlof (endive) 168
bretzels, see moricettes and bretzels

cabbage rolls 47

camembert and pear char-grilled
    baguette 97
carnival cookies 213
cheese
    camembert and pear char-grilled
        baguette 97
    cheese fondue 101
    croque-monsieur from my
        childhood 98
    croquette potatoes with truffles
        and goat's curd 70
    goat's cheese baked with alpine
        honey and tart apple
        salad 58
    gratin savoyard 248
    macaroni gratin 252
    poêlade with raclette cheese 105
    potato dumplings 255
    quiche with Jensen's red 106
    raclette 102
    raclette-style potatoes 107
    tartiflette 111
cheese fondue 101
chestnut truffles 214
chocolate and hazelnut cake 215
compote
    date and apricot compote 26
    grapefruit and orange compote 29
    pear and cardamom compote 30
    rhubarb compote 33
confit of monaro lamb leg with new
    potatoes 136
confit shallots 247
cotechino and puy lentils 171
crème anglaise 231
croque-monsieur from my childhood 98
croquette potatoes with truffles and
    goat's curd 70
crumbed veal schnitzels 48

date and apricot compote 26
daube of veal shanks 139
dents de loup 218
drinks
    alpine coffee 119
    alpine elixir 112
    hot and spiced chocolate 116
    vin chaud 115
    winter coffee 119
    winter warmer 120

duck, see poultry
duck cooked in pinot noir 143
duck legs baked in the oven 125

eggplant (aubergine) meunière 51

farcon de chamonix 52
fish
    baked rainbow trout roulade
        with citrus salad and maple
        syrup dressing 37
    bass fillet cooked in almond salt
        crust 38
    bass quenelles 43
    mushroom with anchovy sauce 64
    rainbow trout fillet in toasted
        sesame seed crust 74
    rainbow trout with bass 75
    salmon and prawn (shrimp)
        pie 181
    salmon fillet gravalax-style,
        warm potato salad 78
    smoked salmon and dill cake 86
    smoked trout brandade 87
    soufflé of potato and smoked
        trout 88
flame cake 54
fleishschnaka 144
French toast with caramelized apples
    and double cream 18
fried potato and truffle ravioli 92
fruit
    apple *beignets* 200
    apple snow ball 202
    apple tea cake 201
    baked rainbow trout roulade
        with citrus salad and maple
        syrup dressing 37
    braised lamb shanks in orange
        juice and star anise 128
    camembert and pear char-grilled
        baguette 97
    date and apricot compote 26
    French toast with caramelized
        apples and double cream 18
    galette of pear and dark
        chocolate 217
    goat's cheese baked with alpine
        honey and tart apple
        salad 58

grapefruit and orange compote 29
gratin of pear with williams pear
    sabayon 221
la bamboulene savoyard 225
pear and cardamom compote 30
red cabbage with apple and
    chestnuts 258
rhubarb compote 33
rhubarb meringue tart 227
strawberry coulis 231
winter fruit paste 267
winter warmer 120

galette of pear and dark chocolate 217
gingerbread 222
goat's cheese baked with alpine
    honey and tart apple salad 58
grapefruit and orange compote 29
gratin of pear with williams pear
    sabayon 221
gratin savoyard 248
gratinated witlof (endive) soup with
    toast 169
green pawpaw (papaya) sauerkraut,
    smoked quail and parsley
    potatoes 146

hearty wild rabbit soup 172
hot and spiced chocolate 116

iced chocolate soufflé 229
inverted *cordon bleu* 151

la bamboulene savoyard 225
lamb
    braised lamb shanks in orange
        juice and star anise 128
    confit of monaro lamb leg with
        new potatoes 136
    lamb stock 244
lamb stock 244

macaroni gratin 252
maple syrup dressing 251
mayonnaise 251
meat snail 144
milk jam 236
moricettes and bretzels 60
mountain omelette soufflé 21
mountain toast 103

mousse au chocolat 226
mushroom tarte tatin 175
mushroom with anchovy sauce 64

pain d'epices 222
pan-fried flank steak, potato and
    truffle chaussons, shallots sauce 66
pasta
    Alsatian porcini *spätzles* 264
    beetroot gnocchi 44
    fried potato and truffle ravioli 92
    macaroni gratin 252
    spätzle (Alsace pasta) 263
    tourtons des alpes 92
pastry
    savoury shortcrust pastry 160
pear, see fruit
pear and cardamom compote 30
pearl barley porridge 22
pheasant, see poultry
poêlade with raclette cheese 105
pork
    braised pork belly 132
    braised pork cheeks 133
    braised pork cheeks shepherd's
        pie gratinated with
        parmesan 129
    cotechino and puy lentils 171
    croque-monsieur from my
        childhood 98
    farcon de chamonix 52
    flame cake 54
    rock soup 179
    sandwiches of swede confit,
    pork kassler and horseradish
    mayonnaise 82
    savoy cabbage, pearl barley and
        smoked bacon soup 180
    smoked pork hocks glazed with
        honey and citrus juice 159
    snowy onion and bacon tart 188
    speck rösti 187
    spiced pork sausages with onion,
        beer and currant jam 196
    tarte flambée 54
poultry
    Alsace duck confit 140
    baeckeoffe aux cuisses de canard 125
    chicken in riesling sauce 135
    chicken stock with roasted

chicken bones 243
duck cooked in pinot noir 143
duck legs baked in the oven 125
green pawpaw (papaya)
    sauerkraut, smoked quail and
    parsley potatoes 146
roast pheasant my way 155
terrine of duck liver in a jar 91
whole duck stuffed with sweet
    bread and king brown
    mushrooms 162
potato
    confit of monaro lamb leg with
        new potatoes
    croquette potatoes with truffles
        and goat's curd 70
    flame cake 54
    fried potato and truffle ravioli 92
    gratin savoyard 248
    green pawpaw (papaya)
        sauerkraut, smoked quail and
        parsley potatoes 146
    pan-fried flank steak, potato and
        truffle chaussons, shallots
        sauce 66
    potato *beignets* 254
    potato dumplings 255
    potatoes with crispy duck skin 257
    rock soup 179
    salmon fillet gravalax-style, warm
        potato salad 78
    soufflé of potato and smoked
        trout 88
    speck rösti 187
    tarte flambée 54
    tourtons des alpes 92
pheasant, see poultry
potato *beignets* 254
potato dumplings 255
potatoes with crispy duck skin 257
potted rabbit terrine 73

quiche with Jensen's red 106

rabbit
    rabbit and porcini stew 152
    hearty wild rabbit soup 172
    potted rabbit terrine 73
rabbit and porcini stew 152
raclette 102

raclette-style potatoes 107
rainbow trout fillet in toasted sesame
    seed crust 74
rainbow trout with bass 75
red cabbage with apple and
    chestnuts 258
red wine jus 266
rhubarb compote 33
rhubarb meringue tart 227
roast pheasant my way 155
roasted spelt flour soup 176
rock soup 179

salmon and prawn (shrimp) pie 181
salmon fillet gravalax-style, warm
    potato salad 78
salsify *beignets* 182
sandwiches of swede confit, pork
    kassler and horseradish
    mayonnaise 82
savoy cabbage, pearl barley and
    smoked bacon soup 180
smoked pork hocks glazed with
    honey and citrus juice 159

smoked salmon and dill cake 86
smoked trout brandade 87
snowy onion and bacon tart 188
soufflé glacé au chocolat 229
soufflé of potato and smoked trout 88
spätzle (Alsace pasta) 263
speck rösti 187
spiced pork sausages with onion, beer
    and currant jam 196
steamed brioche 232
strawberry coulis 231
sweet pastry 230

tarte flambée 54
tartiflette 111
terrine of duck liver in a jar 91
tourtons des alpes 92

veal
    crumbed veal schnitzels 48
    daube of veal shanks 139
    veal stock 245
    whole duck stuffed with sweet
        bread and king brown

    mushrooms 162
    veal stock 245
venison
    venison and dark chocolate
        stew 160
    venison goulash 191
    venison lasagne 192
venison and dark chocolate stew 160
venison goulash 191
venison lasagne 192
vin chaud 115
vinaigrette 267

walnut bread 269
walnut tart 235
wet semolina 197
whole duck stuffed with sweet bread
    and king brown mushrooms 162
winter coffee 119
winter fruit paste 267
winter muesli 25
winter warmer 120
wolf's teeth 218

Australia's Yesterdays

Australia's Yesterdays was edited and
designed by Reader's Digest Services
Pty Ltd, Sydney
Cyril Pearl provided historical guidance
and contributed most of the text.

Third edition

© 1974, 1979, 1986 Reader's Digest
Services Pty Limited (inc. in NSW)
26-32 Waterloo Street, Surry Hills, NSW
2010.
© 1986 The Reader's Digest Association
Far East Ltd
Philippines copyright 1986 Reader's
Digest Association Far East Ltd

National Library of Australia cataloguing-
in-publication data
Australia's Yesterdays
  3rd ed.
  Includes index
  ISBN 0 949819 98 0
  1. Australia – Social life and customs –
  20th century
  I. Reader's Digest Services.
  994.04

Australia's Yesterdays

A look at our recent past

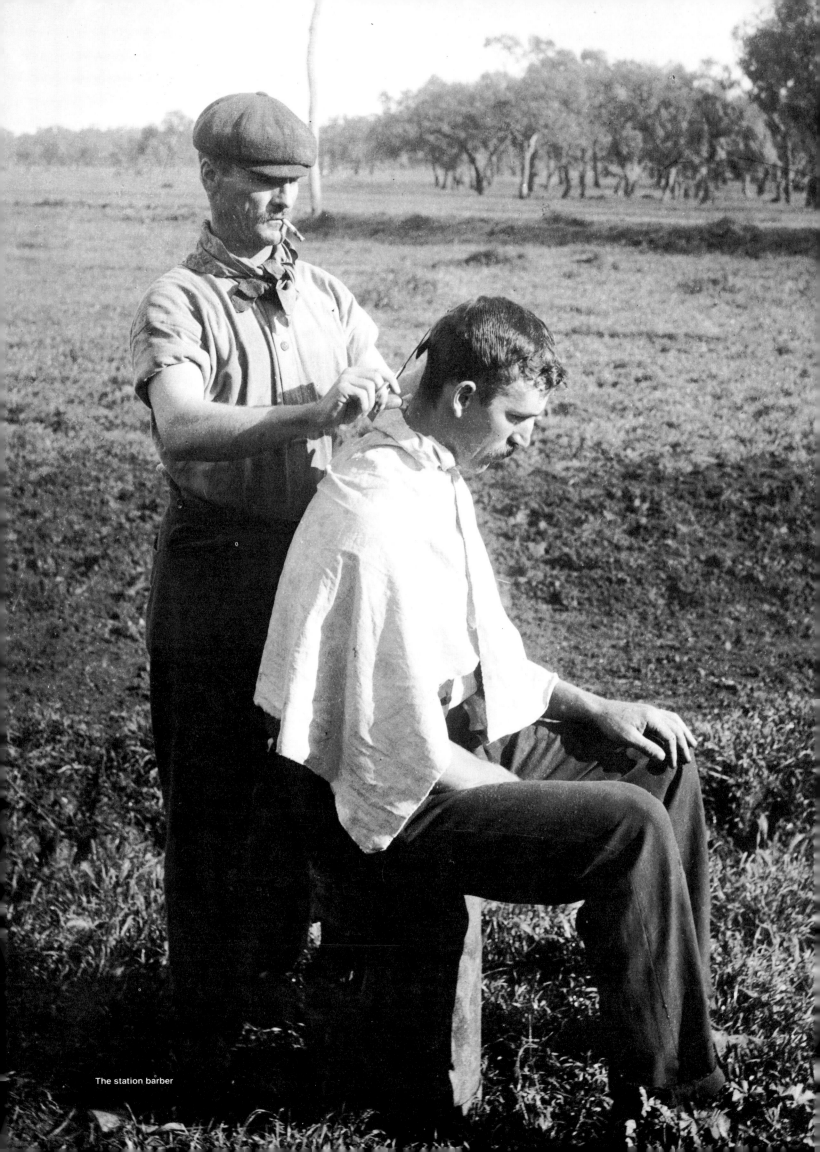

The station barber

Contents

Part one: **Australia in the 20th century**   7

Birth of the Commonwealth 9
The Australian people 25
Cities and towns 47
House and home 79
Leisure and pleasure 103
The performing arts 137
The printed page 149
Sporting life 173
Going places 205
Fashion parade 243
Earning and spending 259
Health and education 279
Wartime life 297

Part two: **The passing years 1901-1985**   321

Historic events charted year by year

Part three: **Makers of modern Australia**   341

A biographical dictionary of Australians who
made news in the 20th century

Index   354

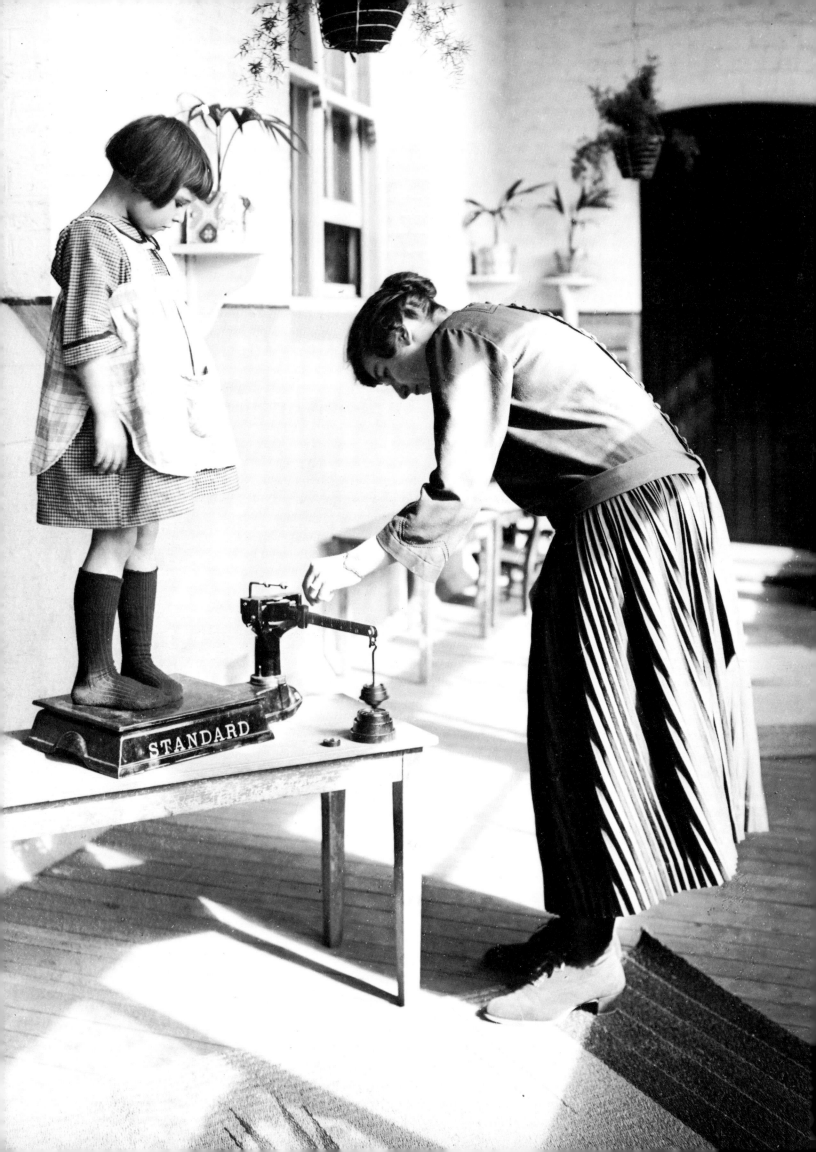

Part one: Australia in the 20th century

Australia in 1901, when it became one nation, was a huge, empty land, populated by only 3.8 million people. Nearly all were of British stock, living in cities isolated by long distances and poor roads.

Victorian buildings dominated the cities, though Sydney and Hobart retained many gracious Georgian survivals. The cities were compact, as most residents lived in closely-packed terrace or semi-detached houses.

Every kind of tram clanked through city streets, and trains pulled by steam engines carried people and goods from town to town.

Cars were expensive and few could dream of owning one. The majority were lucky if their wages paid for more than a bare subsistence. Women also toiled all day, for there were few labour-saving devices.

Most families lived on a dreary and nutritionally unsound diet based on meat, bread, potatoes and tea. Hygiene was poor, and the threat of illness hung over every family.

But there was a brighter side to life. Theatres flourished and moving picture shows were becoming popular. Talking machines were bringing tinny facsimiles of European and American voices into Australian homes. There were circuses and shows, football and cricket matches, races and picnics.

This was Australia when the Commonwealth was born. *Australia's Yesterdays* looks back at life in 20th century Australia, its distinctive flavour, and some of the people and events behind the changes.

It was also an Australia which would undergo vast economic pressures and developments, part of a century of turbulence and strain.

MONEY EQUIVALENTS
In this book, where amounts of money are stated, equivalents in dollars and cents are printed in square brackets afterwards. These equivalents allow for inflation and therefore represent the purchasing power of the money quoted.

A teacher weighs a small girl at a progressive school in Sydney in 1922

Birth of the Commonwealth

Six sovereign states federate for the common good

In January 1901, a new nation was born and an old Queen died. The Commonwealth of Australia was proclaimed on January 1, and 82-year-old Queen Victoria died on January 22. When she had come to the throne in 1837, Australia consisted of four separate colonies: New South Wales (which included what are now Victoria, Queensland, and the eastern part of the Northern Territory); South Australia; Western Australia; and Van Diemen's Land (now Tasmania). Much of the continent was unexplored, and the total white population was fewer than 160,000. When the Queen died, Australia was a federation of six sovereign states, with a population of nearly three and three-quarter million people.

Why did Australian people decide to federate in 1901? Many factors contributed to the decision. Australia was emerging from the colonial and pioneering era. Improved transport and communications had brought the colonies into closer contact with one another. By 1872, the main towns were in telegraphic communication with each other and with Great Britain.

The last British imperial troops had left Australia in 1870, and there was obviously a need for a unified national defence scheme. Federation would also abolish the irritating customs barriers between the colonies. A federal government was needed to deal with postal services, immigration, and with foreign powers—particularly Germany and France, which both had interests in the Pacific. And despite intercolonial jealousies, there was a burgeoning spirit of nationalism which found expression in the federal movement.

So, in Sydney's Centennial Park, on the first day of the new century, with pomp, prayer and ceremony, the Commonwealth of Australia came into being.

Australia's first Governor-General, Lord Hopetoun, takes the oath of allegiance in Centennial Park, Sydney, on 1 January 1901

Life in the colonies

Even in 1900 most people lived in the cities

By 1900 two long-standing myths about the character of the Australian people had become widely accepted. According to the myths, the average Australian was a bushman and he lived in a classless society.

But, despite the prolific warblings of 'bush bards' such as Henry Lawson and 'Banjo' Paterson, the typical Australian was a town dweller. Comparatively few had shared Paterson's 'vision splendid of the sunlit plains extended'. They were more familiar with the not-so-splendid vision of miles of huddled houses and shabby slums.

The drift to the cities

When the first Commonwealth census was taken on 31 March 1901, the population of Australia was 3,773,801. Of these 1,342,675, or 71 persons out of every 200, lived in the six capital cities.

The drift to the cities has continued. It accelerated after 1911 when the census showed that 38 per cent of the population lived in the capitals. By 1921 the figure was 43 per cent, by 1953, 50 per cent and by 1983 about 63 per cent. Today Australia is one of the world's most urban nations.

At the turn of the century, employment in primary industries, including mining, was declining—and increasing in secondary industries, building, the professions and in occupations such as transport and communications. There were still more than 200,000 domestics, but the figure was diminishing rapidly as families grew smaller and the substantial middle class, which for generations had employed an eighth or more of workers in domestic service, lost in importance.

Out of the total workforce of about 1,616,000, 26 per cent was employed in manufacturing, building or construction. To put it another way, out of every 100 breadwinners, only 20 earned a living on the land.

The myth of a classless society

Even the 'bush bards' did not pretend that class distinction did not exist. Henry Lawson wrote a bitter poem about it in 1893, after travelling as a steerage passenger to Australia from New Zealand. The last verse began:

But the curse of class distinction from our shoulders
shall be hurled,
An' the sense of Human Kinship revolutionise the
world;
There'll be higher education for the toilin', starvin'
clown,
An' the rich an' educated shall be educated down.

Australians are still divided to some extent by wealth, education and occupation. But the borders between the different social groups are not clearly defined. There is overlapping and mobility. In 1900 Australia had a much more rigid class system, derived from England's traditional social structure.

At the top, in the 'Government House' set, were wealthy graziers, who spent some of their time on their properties and some in their city mansions, high-ranking officers of the armed services, the judiciary,

wealthy businessmen, eminent professional men and politicians and clergy—preferably Anglican—above a certain rank. Wives, of course, acquired the status of their husbands and assumed many airs and graces.

A male member of this upper crust probably belonged to an exclusive club, had a town house, employed many servants, rode in an elegant carriage, sat in the Legislative Council and, when he felt like it, took a leisurely sea trip 'home' to England.

The middle class, always a less distinct group, included professional men of lesser standing, small businessmen and a variety of salary earners, as distinct from wage earners. They lived in villas in outer suburbs, travelling to work by train, bus, tram or ferry.

The working class, skilled and unskilled, comprised the great majority of the city

dwellers. Most of them lived in the inner suburbs, perhaps within walking distance of work. They lived in terraces built in the 1880s, or cottages built even earlier, paying from 6s to 10s [$15.15 to $25.20] a week in rent.

In the country, class distinctions were—and still are—more clearly defined. At the top of the social pyramid was the grazier in his comfortable station homestead where he perhaps dressed for dinner. The more land he owned and the longer it had been in the family, the greater was his prestige. Below him, in the country town, was an upper middle-class, which included the bank manager, the doctor, the lawyer and the clergyman. Lower down the scale were the school teacher, the chemist, the estate agent and the small shop-keeper. At the bottom came the artisan and unskilled worker.

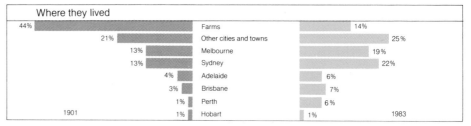

In 1901, nearly half of Australia's 3,773,801 people lived on the land. By 1966 this figure had dropped to only about 1 in 5. Over the next 20 years, the drift to the cities continued, although at a slower rate. New South Wales is at one end of the scale with 73% of the population in urban areas, Tasmania at the other with only 51%

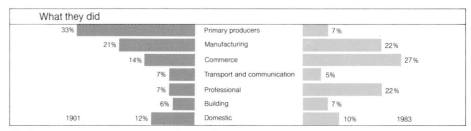

The Australian workforce in 1901 was 1,616,000. One in three earned their living in primary industries. By 1983 this figure had dropped to 1 in 14. As forms of employment changed during the period, so did the categories, and now all clerical workers are included in 'commerce', and all service industries in 'domestic'

Although emigrants saw Australia as a land of unlimited space, the true picture was far removed from this romantic vision. Most Australians were city dwellers, and many lived in appalling conditions. This picture shows Wexford Street, Sydney, near the present Campbell Street, in 1900

A day in the life of a respectable Australian

Let us look at a typical Sydney white collar worker of 1900. He is an experienced highly-paid chief clerk in an insurance company, earning £300 [$15,130] a year. Junior clerks are paid as little as £100 [$5045] a year, less than a skilled artisan. But clerks consider themselves members of the middle-class, and emulate its way of life. Income-tax in New South Wales is at the flat rate of 6d in the pound [2.5c to the dollar] on incomes in excess of £200 [$10,085], so his tax-bill is £7 10s [$380] a year. In Victoria, where the rate is 4d in the pound [1.67c to the dollar] on incomes up to £1000 [$50,425], he would pay only £5 [$250] a year. There is no federal income-tax. Not until 1915 will the Federal Government dip into the taxpayer's pocket.

Our chief clerk lives in a new brick six-roomed Queen Anne villa, about eight kilometres from his office in the city, to which he travels by train. The villa is roofed in red Marseilles tiles, with a terracotta griffin, also imported from Marseilles, perched incongruously on top of a tiled spire.

The walls above the floral leadlights in the casement windows are covered in roughcast, and the interior is fussy with inglenooks, angle bays, window seats, and mirrored overmantels towering high above the tiled fireplaces. The metal ceilings are ornately embossed. A well-clipped pittosporum hedge borders the wooden picket fence, and from the gate a gravel path winds across the buffalo-grass lawn to the front door.

The bathroom has a heavy, roll-rimmed cast-iron bath standing on four claw feet, and a chip bath-heater. Waiting for the bath to fill, our chief clerk strops his hollow-ground 'cut-throat' razor and dips his beaver-hair brush ('Guaranteed Free From Anthrax') into an embossed silver-plated mug.

Chops and Worcestershire sauce

His wife, meanwhile, is grilling his breakfast chops and sausages in the kitchen, a lean-to extension to the back of the house. The gas-stove stands in the fireplace, as the old wood-stove used to, and there is a zinc-lined oak ice-chest. Ice is delivered three times a week in four and a half kilogram blocks costing 6d [$1.25]each. Next to the kitchen is the wash-house, a separate structure housing a copper heated by wood fire, a cast-iron tub with only a cold water tap, and ponderous mangle. From the light fitting above the breakfast-table hangs a flypaper, a curling strip of paper impregnated with melted resin and golden syrup. It is studded with flies.

Our chief clerk deluges his chops, sausages and eggs in Worcestershire sauce and washes them down with two cups of strong, sugary tea. Promising to ring his wife if he has to work late—he is one of the 10,119 Sydney citizens who enjoy the luxury of a telephone—he takes his round-crowned hard hat from the hall-stand and sets out for the office. He is wearing a blue serge three-piece suit with tight narrow trousers, a shirt with detachable starched cuffs, a high, stiff, winged collar, and tight glace-leather nine-buttoned boots. A gold watch-chain known as an Albert spans his

All the trappings of smug middle-class family life are present in this picture taken about the turn of the century. Father is the unchallenged head of the household, his wife knows her place and the children are no doubt familiar with the instruction that they should be seen but not heard

waistcoat; from one end hangs his gold watch. The waistcoat is an indispensable badge of respectability. Even in the privacy of his office, on a sweltering summer day, when he might be tempted to shed his coat, his waistcoat must stay on.

If you moved several notches up the social scale to, say, the manager of the insurance company, you would probably have found a portly man who each Sunday unfailingly led his family to its own pew in church, wearing a long black coat and silk top hat and carrying gloves and a gold-mounted walking stick. His two-storey house, set in spacious grounds, had a panelled billiard-room, a conservatory, and a coach-house for his sulky and dog-cart. His children, five or six, called him 'Pater', and his staff and tradesmen, 'Sir'. The household maintained two servants—a cook, earning 17s 6d [$44.10] a week and a general servant, or 'slavey', earning 6s [$15.15] a week.

His wife, 'Mater' to the children, was a 'lady', not a mere woman. One afternoon each month she was 'at home'. On that important day—the first Monday or the second Thursday, as announced on her engraved copperplate visiting card—she received in her immaculate but uncomfortable drawing-room, dispensing tea from a silver pot, cakes from a three-tier silver stand, and genteel conversation to her genteel callers—ladies, of course. Calling was an essential and rigid

social ritual. The visitor seldom stayed more than an hour and on departing left *her* card, with its implied invitation, on the embossed silver salver in the hall. It was a sort of social chain-letter system.

Correct behaviour for young ladies

Neither 'Mater' nor her grown-up daughter used lipstick or face powder, except perhaps for a discreet application to a shiny nose. None of them smoked, though no doubt they knew that there were Fast girls who did. None ever used such words as 'sex', 'contraception' or 'pregnancy', although they talked (in lowered voices) of 'expecting', and being 'confined'. They knew more about the workings of a sewing machine than about their own bodies. The daughters, even in their twenties, were not allowed to go out at night without an escort.

Looking into his crystal ball, a versifier in the Melbourne *Argus* foresaw a greater freedom for the girl of the future:

Oh, the twentieth century girl!
What a wonderful thing she will be,
She'll emerge from a mystical whirl,
A woman unfettered and free.
No corset to crampen her waist,
No crimps to encumber her brain,
Unafraid, bifurcated, unlaced,
Like a goddess of old she will reign.

Towards an Australian federation

Free traders fight protectionists to delay national unity

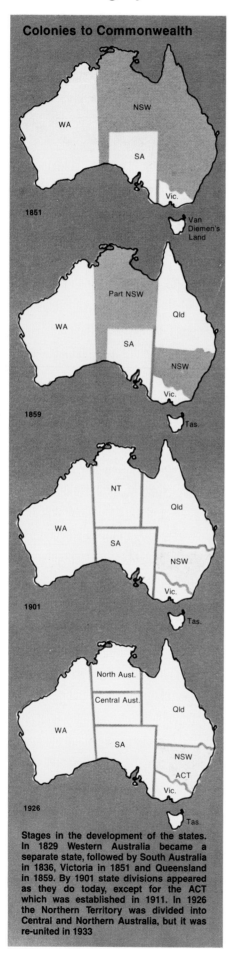

Colonies to Commonwealth

1851

1859

1901

1926

Stages in the development of the states. In 1829 Western Australia became a separate state, followed by South Australia in 1836, Victoria in 1851 and Queensland in 1859. By 1901 state divisions appeared as they do today, except for the ACT which was established in 1911. In 1926 the Northern Territory was divided into Central and Northern Australia, but it was re-united in 1933

In 1856 Charles Gavan Duffy, an Irish lawyer, former journalist and patriot, emigrated to Australia. Gavan Duffy, a member of the House of Commons, had stood trial for treason four times in Ireland, and made it clear where his real sympathies lay as soon as he arrived in Melbourne. 'Let me not be misunderstood,' he said at a welcoming dinner, 'I'm an Irish rebel to the backbone and the spinal marrow.'

A few weeks later he spoke at an enthusiastic public reception in Sydney, urging the federation of the Australian colonies with remarkable foresight. 'If you want speedy communication with Europe, if you want uniform administration of justice, if you want cheap and registered postage, you must have some assembly competent to act for all of Australia,' he said.

'I call myself an Irishman and rejoice to be so called. But how can any man venture to call himself a New South Welshman? He may be proud indeed of the name Australian which, I trust, will be a memorable name in history—but you are not Australians till there is some federal connection between the separate members of Australia. What matters on which side of the imaginary line that separates you from the neighbouring colony. I believe your interests are identical and that all Australia will rise or fall together.'

When Duffy became a member of Victoria's Legislative Assembly in November 1856, one of his first acts was to advocate federation, but New South Wales would not consider it. He continued his unsuccessful efforts until 1870 when—a year before he became Victoria's Premier—he sponsored an ineffectual Royal Commission on federation. But

he lived long enough to see his dream of a united Australia realised. When he died at Nice in February 1903, as Sir Charles Gavan Duffy, having retired on a pension of £1000 [$48,365] a year, the Commonwealth he had foreseen nearly half a century before was already two years old.

Duffy was not the first man to advocate federal union. As early as 1847, Earl Grey, the Secretary of State for the Colonies, suggested a 'central legislative authority'.

At that time New South Wales still included most of eastern Australia: areas which are now Queensland, Victoria, and part of South Australia. Western Australia had been claimed by the British Government in 1836. Tasmania, then Van Diemen's Land, had separated from the parent colony in 1825. Victoria became a separate state in 1851 and Queensland in 1859. Towards the end of the century, Australia—which had begun as a political unity—was groping its way back to unification and nationhood.

Distance had been an important reason for decentralisation. For example, the 900 kilometre journey from Sydney to Melbourne took 60 hours before 1883, when the time was cut to 18 hours by the completion of the rail link between the two cities. 'We want federation and we want it now,' James Service, the Victorian Premier, told the 1016 guests who celebrated the link at a banquet in an Albury locomotive shed. But the guests seemed more interested in food than federation.

Before the completion of the rail connection the traveller left Melbourne by train at 3 p.m. and reached Wodonga, on the border, eight hours later. A coach took him to Albury, five kilometres away, where he spent the night

The first Home Guards

Although Australia was protected by a British Garrison until its withdrawal in 1870, volunteer militia units also played a part in defence. They were first officially formed in 1854 following the Crimean War, although some small bodies had been raised earlier. Although these groups were intended mainly for domestic defence, some Australians served in irregular militia units in the Sudan in 1885 and in South Africa at the turn of the century. In 1903, the newly-formed Commonwealth took control of the military and the various state units disappeared entirely

Queensland Permanent Artillery

South Australian Infantry

Victorian Mounted Rifles

Adelaide Lancers

New South Wales Naval Brigade

Tasmanian Infantry

West Australian Infantry

New South Wales Lancers

Tasmanian Infantry, Derwent Regiment

before catching another coach to Wagga Wagga at 5.30 a.m. The 128-kilometre journey took him 12 hours in 16 kilometre stages. He spent the night at Wagga Wagga, and left at noon the following day for Bethungra, a 70 kilometre coach journey that took six hours. At Bethungra he caught the train at 6.30 p.m., and arrived in Sydney at 7 a.m. the following morning.

Six years later when the Hawkesbury River, 48 kilometres north of Sydney, was bridged, one could travel by rail from Adelaide to Brisbane. In the same year Major-General Sir J. Bevan Edwards, sent out by the British Government to inspect Australia's military forces, urged the colonies to federate for their common defence.

Cheating the customs

After the separation of New South Wales from Victoria in 1851, the haphazard lifting and reimposition of customs duties bedevilled people travelling from one state to the other. There were customs houses on each side of the border and customs officers examined every article taken across and collected the appropriate duty. Workmen crossing and recrossing the river had to pay duty on their tea and tobacco two or three times.

Whenever the duties were lifted there was great rejoicing in the border towns. On the first occasion, in December 1855, half of Albury's population of 400 celebrated with a stupendous banquet. The guests, who had paid the then enormous sum of £5 [$300 approximately], attacked a whole roast bullock, ten sheep, ten turkeys, a plum pudding weighing 100 kg and a mountain of tarts, jellies and custards. 'Carving knives of scythe-like proportions are ordered from a Melbourne foundry,' reported the Sydney *Empire* before the great event. In 1867 when duties were again lifted, 400 children were entertained at a monster picnic, and a huge ball was held and a bonfire kept alight on a hilltop for two days.

New South Wales became a free trade state in 1873 while Victoria remained protectionist. Clothing imported from overseas was cheaper in New South Wales than in the southern state, where a duty of 35 per cent was imposed. Thrifty citizens in the Victorian border town of Wodonga would walk across the border to Albury, fit themselves out with new clothes and return carrying their old ones—used clothing being exempt from duty.

The border duties were greatly resented by New South Wales stock-raisers, for whom Victoria was an important market. With a duty of 30s [$76] a head on cattle, 10s [$25] a head on pigs and 2s [$5] a head on sheep, it was not surprising that herds of animals were sometimes swum across the river at a quiet spot, remote from customs surveillance.

The irritations caused by customs duties did much to promote the federal movement in the border towns. 'All customs are anomalies serving simply to divide people who are really one in race, sentiment and interest,' said Echuca's newspaper the *Riverina Herald* in July 1896. 'The true relief can only be obtained by complete federation.'

A contemporary cartoon pokes gentle fun at the inconvenience suffered mainly by female travellers between states. Tariffs were levied on a wide variety of goods to protect local industry—and women's clothing, if new, was a prime target for snooping customs officers. A person who regularly crossed a state border on business often had to pay duty on the same possessions two or three times

The customs house at the NSW border town of Jingellic on the Murray, east of Albury, was one of many such posts on state boundaries. Duties collected at these posts were a constant source of anger to travellers and did much to bring about popular support for federation

Interstate jealousy blocks federation

Sir Henry Parkes makes his stand at Tenterfield

In 1889 the movement towards federation among liberal-minded and far-seeing politicians was accelerating so rapidly that it attracted the attention of Sir Henry Parkes, Premier of New South Wales, a venerable and cunning opportunist.

Parkes, 74, had spoken in favour of federation at an intercolonial conference in Melbourne in 1867, but he made his major step into the federation arena in a speech at Tenterfield, NSW, on 24 October 1889.

Parkes had arrived in the northern tablelands border town, 774 kilometres from Sydney, from Brisbane, where he had discussed federation with Queensland's political leaders. His arrival in Tenterfield was a memorable event. Shops were closed, flags were flying and Parkes was met at the station by a band, an escort of soldiers and most of the town's citizens. In the evening, the inevitable banquet was held in the School of Arts.

A contemporary writer, describing Parkes on the night, said: 'The voice was a little veiled by fatigue and age. The massive shoulders were a little bowed, but the huge head, with its streaming wave of silver hair and beard was held as erect as ever.'

In his speech, Parkes stressed the necessity for federal defence and for a uniform railway gauge. Australia, he said, had a population of three-and-a-half million. Australians were nearly equal to Americans when they formed the 'great commonwealth of the United States'. The time was close at hand when they ought to set about creating a great and historic national government.

This speech gained for Parkes the scarcely deserved title of the 'Father of Federation'. Although it was seen by some merely as an attempt to build a new political base, it did lead to the representative federation conferences of 1890 and 1891.

A *Bulletin* cartoon of 1890 showing Sir Henry Parkes setting out for Melbourne and the Federal Convention. With Parkes (lower left) are the NSW Treasurer William McMillan (upper right) and two of the Premier's closest parliamentary cronies, Sir J. P. Abbott next to Parkes, and J. P. Garvan facing him. Parkes' long political career was almost at an end. He resigned as leader of the Free Trade Party in 1891 and, after some years of domestic trials, died in 1896

Colonial politicians, including two from New Zealand who held a 'watching brief', in Melbourne during the 1890 Federation Conference. Victorian's Premier Duncan Gillies (12) remained in profile and kept his hat on because he believed he looked at his best this way. In the picture are: 1. Inglis Clark (Tas. Attorney General); 2. Captain William Russell (NZ Colonial Secretary); 3. Sir Samuel Griffith (Qld Opposition Leader); 4. Sir Henry Parkes (NSW Premier); 5. Thomas Playford (SA Opposition Leader); 6. Alfred Deakin (Vic. Chief Secretary); 7. Stafford Bird (Tas. Treasurer); 8. G. H. Jenkins (Secretary to the Conference); 9. William McMillan (NSW Treasurer); 10. Sir John Hall (NZ Former Premier); 11. John Macrossan (Qld Colonial Secretary); 12. Duncan Gillies (Vic. Premier); 13. Sir John Cockburn (SA Premier); 14. Sir James Lee Steere (WA Speaker). Despite much oratory, the only outcome of the meeting was an agreement to meet to draft a federal constitution

NSW drops objections to joining the 'cabbage garden'

Despite the impact made by Parkes' speech there were still many obstacles to federation. One of the most formidable was the tariff question. New South Wales was a free trade state, but in Victoria heavy duties protected expanding local industries.

Federation would mean free trade between the states and the introduction of a uniform tariff on overseas imports. New South Wales feared this might be unacceptably high.

In 1890 when an informal conference arranged by Parkes was held in Melbourne to discuss federation, James Service, a former Victorian Premier, described the tariff question as 'the lion in the path' which federalists would have to slay. Not to be outdone in rhet-

oric, Parkes replied: 'The crimson thread of kinship runs through us all.' But despite much oratory, the conference achieved nothing.

It passed several resolutions which pledged the participants to persuade the legislators of their colonies to appoint delegates to a National Australasian Convention. When it met on 2 March 1891, the convention passed more resolutions in favour of federation, but the initial impetus soon petered out. In New South Wales, Parkes' retirement in 1891 forced a temporary halt to plans to federate.

Jealousy between New South Wales and Victoria was a cause of bitter disagreement. 'We cannot stand that progressive colony; they are rather too insolent,' Sir John Robert-

son, five times Premier of NSW, said in 1887. Sir John, who was a bitter opponent of federation, always referred to Victoria as 'the cabbage garden'. Though a vigorous speaker, he had a limited range of adjectives. Once he asked: 'Why should we bloody well close our gates to all the world in order to trade with those bloody fellows across the Murray, who produce just the same as we do; and all they can send us is bloody cabbages?'

It was a Victorian journalist and barrister, Dr Quick, who in 1893 devised the mechanism that broke the deadlock. He proposed that a national convention, representing the six states, should draw up a constitution and submit it to a referendum of the people.

The state premiers met in Hobart in January 1895, agreed to a draft Enabling Bill and elected 10 representatives from each state to the convention. It held its first session in Adelaide on 22 March 1897.

Under the leadership of Edmund Barton, who was to become Australia's first prime minister, a constitution was drafted. In 1898 Alfred Deakin, one of Australia's most eminent statesmen, wrote in his diary: 'Today . . . after an all-night sitting and under conditions of great nervous exhaustion and irritability, we have practically completed the draft Bill for the Constitution . . .'

In June 1898, referendums were held in Victoria, New South Wales, South Australia and Tasmania. Victoria cast 100,520 votes for the bill and only 22,099 against. The patterns were similar for South Australia and Tasmania. But in New South Wales there were 71,595 votes in favour and 66,228 against. As the New South Wales Government had insisted on at least 80,000 affirmative votes, the bill was 'deemed to be rejected'.

After the referendum an Adelaide citizen, Hubert Hancock, wrote to Rudyard Kipling, who had visited Australia briefly in 1891, and told him that before the vote thousands of people had worn a federation badge on which a verse of Kipling's was inscribed. In his reply, Kipling said: 'I fancy her very safeness from external attack is one of the reasons why Australia has taken her time over federation. However, as the Pacific fills up with other powers, that safeness will decrease; if you want to hurry up federation, you ought to make a syndicate to hire a few German cruisers to bombard Sydney, Melbourne and Brisbane for twenty minutes; there'd be a federated Australia in 24 hours.'

Apart from the tariff question and its dislike of Victoria, New South Wales was also worried that the federal capital might be established in the southern state. To counter this, the premiers, led by Victorian Premier Sir George Gurner, agreed that the capital would be in New South Wales, but not within 160 kilometres of Sydney. The *Victorian Year Book*, commenting smugly on the issue, said: 'In this state it was considered that the federal cause was greater than any local matter of pride or jealousy.'

At a second referendum in June 1899, the bill was carried in New South Wales by 107,420 votes to 82,741. The Victorian figures

An anti-federation referendum poster issued by New South Wales free traders. NSW politicians were the most bitter opponents of federation

Results posted on the *Sydney Morning Herald's* special board outside its offices during the second decisive vote on the federation issue

were: Yes, 152,653; No, 9805. Queensland took part in this referendum, recording 38,488 votes for federation and 30,996 against. Again no referendum was taken in Western Australia and the men of the goldfields, who strongly supported the federal movement,

petitioned Queen Victoria to allow them to set up a separate state and join the Commonwealth. Ultimately, having been promised a railway link with the east, plus other concessions, Western Australia was joined with the other states on 31 July 1900.

The Constitution Act received the Royal Assent from Queen Victoria on 9 July 1900. The Queen signed her assent to the Bill in duplicate and gave one copy, as well as the pen, inkstand and table she used, to the new Federal Parliament. They are preserved in Parliament House, Canberra

Cole's funny prizes

At the height of the debate on federation Mr. E. W. Cole, the enterprising proprietor of Cole's Book Arcade in Melbourne, offered a prize of £100 [$5000] for the best essay in favour of federation and a similar prize for the best essay opposing it. James Edmond, who was then associate editor of *The Bulletin*, won both prizes; one under his own name for the pro-federation essay and the other under a pseudonym. But Cole refused to hand over the second prize, claiming that Edmond's whimsy was 'contrary to the spirit of the competition'.

The birthday of a nation

Bad health mars arrival of first Governor-General

On the morning of 15 December 1900, HMS *Royal Arthur* steamed through Sydney Heads carrying John Louis Hope, Earl of Hopetoun and Australia's first Governor-General.

Lord Hopetoun arrived in Australia a sick man. The combination of a rough voyage and an attack of typhoid caught in India on the way out left him weak and pale. A planned landing at Fremantle had already been cancelled, and it was with some difficulty that he stepped ashore from the naval pinnace on to the pavilion anchored on the eastern side of Farm Cove. His illness did not, however, save him from the inevitable welcoming speeches made by NSW Premier Sir William Lyne and others, nor the ordeal of a three kilometre tour of Sydney in an open carriage in the broiling summer sun.

The naval pinnace carrying Australia's first Governor-General, Lord Hopetoun, nears the east-ern side of Farm Cove. Hopetoun's arrival was greeted with enthusiasm, as he had become a popu-lar figure during his term as Governor of Victoria between 1889 and 1895

Commonwealth born amid political wrangles

Lord Hopetoun's first and most important task was to select the first Prime Minister of Australia. The obvious choice was Edmund Barton, the leader of the federal movement. But Hopetoun, for some obscure reason, amazed everyone by choosing Sir William Lyne, an acknowledged opponent of federation.

The blunder was soon corrected, for determined opposition led by Alfred Deakin, a Victorian parliamentarian, resulted in Lyne being unable to form a government.

The next day, Christmas Day, Lord Hopetoun invited Barton to form a government, and he did so with little difficulty. One of the ministers he chose was Deakin, as Australia's first Attorney-General. Deakin had recently been appointed special Australian correspondent to the London *Morning Post*, but he apparently saw no conflict between this job and his Cabinet responsibilities. Indeed, he contributed his anonymous reports to the paper for 14 years—even during his three short terms as Prime Minister of Australia between 1903 and 1910.

One of Deakin's early despatches described the noisy enthusiasm with which Sydney bade farewell to the 19th century and welcomed the 20th century and Federation.

'Never was a moonlit midnight in Sydney marked by a wilder, more prolonged, or generally more discordant welcome than was December 31, 1900,' Deakin wrote. 'Hymns in the churches, patriotic songs in the theatres, glees in the homes, and convivial choruses at the clubs were extensively sung. Outside these places, however, all music was lost in the tremendous uproar of the streets, where whistles, bells, gongs, accordions, rattles and clanging cutlery utensils yielded unearthly sounds.'

The place chosen for the proclamation of the Commonwealth was Centennial Park in Sydney's eastern suburbs. A vast procession was to leave the Domain and snake through the city streets to the park. Privately owned grandstands were erected along the route, with seats priced from 5s to 25s [$13 to $63], according to their situation, safety and comfort. The amenities of some, such as the Martin Place Elite Grandstand opposite the Post Office, included carpets, refreshments and bands to entertain the watchers.

Dawn broke on 1 January 1901 with overcast skies and steady drizzle but the clouds soon cleared away and by midmorning it was already oppressively hot and sticky. The procession moved off at 10.30 a.m. through streets lavishly decorated with triumphal arches, Venetian poles, Japanese lanterns, festoons, flags, crowns, bannerets, plaster statues and oil paintings. Precedence was judged by proximity to the Governor-General, who came last, so the procession was headed by representatives of the 22 trade unions. Next came the fire brigades, making a brilliant show with their gleaming brass helmets, shining engines and well-groomed horses. They were followed by floats, troops and triumphal cars crammed with mayors, aldermen, judges and state premiers—many looking uncomfortable in hired belltoppers—and Australia's first Prime Minister, Edmund Barton. Finally came the Governor-General in his splendid carriage, with postillions and outriders, and an escort of lancers.

More than 150,000 people had gathered at Centennial Park, and as the boom of the one o'clock gun died away Lord Hopetoun entered the white swearing-in pavilion. The Queen's proclamation was read, Hopetoun took the oath of allegiance, a 21-gun salute boomed out and 10,000 children burst into the 'Federal Anthem'. The Commonwealth of Australia was born.

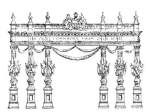

Some of the many arches that decorated Sydney streets during the Commonwealth celebrations

Electric lights decorated buildings in Sydney for the first time during the celebrations

Invitations such as this caused much heartburning. Some visiting dignitaries did not receive any, and left in a huff, while others would receive half-a-dozen for the one event

The wife and children of a NSW selector, dressed in their Sunday best to celebrate Commonwealth Day, pose outside the shack they live in

The gleaming, horse-drawn engines of the fire brigade on their way to Centennial Park

'One people, one destiny'—Norman Lindsay's wry comment on the festivities in a *Bulletin* cartoon

The Commonwealth of Australia was officially born with the publication of this royal proclamation

This children's carnival was one of the entertainments that followed the swearing-in on January 1. There were also highland concerts, banquets, fireworks and even theatre matinees for the poor

Lavish start for first parliament

Melbourne spares no expense to impress royal visitors

Just over four months after the last echoes of Sydney's lavish celebrations to mark the proclamation of the Commonwealth had died away, Melbourne citizens were preparing themselves for their part in the federal junketings—the visit of the Duke and Duchess of Cornwall and York and the opening of the first Commonwealth Parliament.

An interim government had been formed in December 1900, with Edmund Barton as Prime Minister to prepare the business of the new Parliament. The first Federal elections were held in March 1901 and Barton continued in his post as Prime Minister. The first Parliament was made up of three distinct groups, divided principally on one issue, that of tariffs. Barton's team was protectionist and mainly liberal and the opposition was divided into the free-traders led by George Reid,

Premier of NSW until 1899, and the Labor Party. Of the three groups, only the Labor Party formed an organised body.

The Duke and Duchess—irreverently dubbed 'corned beef and pork' by Sydney school children—arrived in Melbourne on the Orient liner *Ophir* on 4 May 1901. The royal party was greeted at Port Melbourne by Lord Hopetoun and immediately set off on a procession through streets lined with enthusiastically cheering crowds.

The ceremony to open the first Parliament was to take place in Melbourne's Exhibition Building before an invited crowd of 14,000 people. At noon, the Duke of York—a little bearded man dressed as an admiral—the Earl of Hopetoun, the British High Commissioner, and a glittering escort of officers, entered the hall and took their places on the dais. The

grand orchestra struck up the National Anthem and the Usher of the Black Rod, through the Clerk of the Parliaments, let the honourable members know that His Royal Highness desired their immediate attendance at that honourable house. The honourable members duly trooped in and took their places.

Hymns were sung and the Earl of Hopetoun read prayers beseeching the Almighty to endue King Edward VII plenteously with heavenly gifts. The Duke, in a clear, well-pitched voice, then declared Parliament open in the name of His Majesty. The Royal proclamation was followed by a fanfare of trumpets, and the members of Australia's first Federal Parliament were sworn in.

Excitement overwhelms ministers

That evening, the Duke and Duchess attended a grand concert in the Exhibition Building where Nellie Stewart, recently returned from triumphs at Drury Lane, sang the ode *Australia*, specially written for her by Charles Kenningham. In the excitement, the cabinet ministers forgot to bow when passing the Duke and Duchess, a gaffe that the observant Governor of South Australia, Lord Tennyson, duly noted in his diary.

Melbourne, although officially still in mourning for the death of Queen Victoria on January 22, tried to outdo Sydney in the splendour and extravagance of its celebrations. Streets were lined with arches. Flags and banners were everywhere, and all the major buildings in the city were strung with electric lights. The *Bulletin* was less than enthusiastic about the decorations. 'The opening of the first parliament of Australia was a large enough event to stand alone,' it said. 'It wanted no tawdry trappings, no small accidental prince, no lank, flapping frills and gaily-coloured rags to make it memorable. The people who hung out their cheap and shoddy decorations—their calico banners, their pine porticos, and their lath-and-whitewash arches round an occasion like this would hang a string of glass beads on the tomb of Paul the Apostle, and tie a sixpenny red handkerchief on the Parthenon.'

Farrier's noble gesture

There was a monster procession on May 11 in which the principal trades were represented by elaborate tableaux, showing men at work. The *Argus* reported a picturesque incident:

'The farriers, in their leather aprons, presented the most sturdy appearance of all in the march. They were accompanied by a lorry carrying a forge, in which two blackened smiths worked with might and main. As the procession halted at the royal pavilion, a bar of iron was speedily cut and hammered into a horseshoe, which the proud craftsman held out in his pincers at arm's length. An idea seemed to strike him suddenly. Pushing to the front of the lorry, he reached to a crimson shield on which were six polished horseshoes, and tore one from its fastenings. Then, leaning from the lorry, he swung his brawny arm like the Discobolus and the horseshoe flew through the air, clanging on Parliament

The Duke of Cornwall and York, later King George V, opens the first Federal Parliament in Melbourne's Exhibition Building on 9 May 1901. A painting of this scene was done by Australian artist Tom Roberts on a 1000 guinea [$30,000] commission. The huge 5.5 x 3.3 m canvas took two years to complete

Alfred Lee, the recipient of these invitations to the opening of Federal Parliament and the reception that followed, was a notable collector of Australiana. He was also one of the first car and telephone owners in Australia and claimed to have introduced the first typewriter into a Sydney office

House steps at the foot of the royal pavilion. It was picked up and carried to the Duchess, who held it high and bowed her thanks to the dusky smith.'

When the royal visitors left Australia on June 7, the final reckoning of the vast sums spent on the celebrations proved that it had been an expensive visit for the Australian taxpayer. An official who was called upon to justify each item on a colossal liquor bill for one reception wrote opposite the entry for one case of dry gin the unchivalrous annotation 'For the Duchess'. It was also an expensive visit for Lord Hopetoun. He had spent large sums of his own money to entertain the royal visitors in an effort to make the tour a success. He applied to Barton for an official entertainment allowance but, although Barton agreed to the proposal, it was rejected by the House of Representatives who decided instead to grant Hopetoun a lump sum of £10,000 [$474,000]. This came nowhere near covering Hopetoun's expenses, and it was a dispirited man who asked to be recalled to England later that year. Hopetoun left Australia in 1902, still about £15,000 [$711,000] out of pocket, and died six years later.

Ten thousand electric lights decorate Melbourne's Exhibition Building, scene of the opening of the first Federal Parliament. A Melbourne journalist, describing a city 'scribbled over with electric fires', said: 'The illuminations of the exhibition comprised the most gigantic scheme of pyrotechnics ever attempted in the Southern Hemisphere. The immense cupola, to a height of 174 feet from the ground, bristled with incandescent bulbs set 12 inches apart.' It made a great impression

Melbourne's Chinese citizens welcome the Duke of York. There were 5000 Chinese in Melbourne

The first Federal Parliament sitting in Parliament House in Melbourne. Parliament met here until the new parliament buildings were completed in Canberra in 1927

A group of imperial army officers who accompanied the Duke of York on his visit to Australia

The first federal ministry late in its term of office. Prime Minister Edmund Barton is seated second from the left with Australia's second Governor-General, Lord Tennyson, in the centre

Ballarat citizens await the arrival of the Duke of York during his tour of Australia in 1901

19

Australians search for national symbols

Huge response to Australia-wide flag quest

On 1 January 1901, Australia had a federation but no capital city and no flag. The Union Jack took pride of place at the celebrations, but another flag was much in evidence—the Australian ensign, flag of the Australian Federation League. The league's flag had become the unofficial flag of the newly-formed Commonwealth, but it was soon to be replaced by an official flag.

Two competitions seeking a design for a Commonwealth flag had been started by Melbourne journals. The first was conducted by the Melbourne *Herald* and the second by the magazine *Review of Reviews for Australia*. In 1901 the Commonwealth joined the quest with an additional offer of £75 [$3780], bringing total prize money to £200 [$10,085]. From the 32,823 designs submitted, the judges selected five that were almost identical, and divided the prize among the five competitors. One was a 14-year-old Melbourne schoolboy, Ivor Evans. The winning designs incorporated a Union Jack on a blue ground, a large six-pointed star, representing the six federated states, and five stars of nine, eight, seven, six and five points respectively, representing the Southern Cross. 'The experts are to be complimented for steering clear of weird shapes and conventional stripes,' commented the *Australasian*, a Melbourne weekly.

Some of the rejected designs were more picturesque than practical. One depicted a monstrous kangaroo with six tails; another, six boomerangs in full flight; another, a circle of hands with six index fingers pointing reproachfully at a scantily-dressed Britannia; and another, the symbolism of which was obscure, a fat kangaroo aiming an ancient flintlock at the Southern Cross.

The Australian flag—a huge ensign measuring 11 m by 5.5 m—was flown for the first time on 3 September 1901, when it was raised over the dome of Melbourne's Exhibition Building.

Prime Minister Barton announced on 11 February 1903 that His Majesty the King had approved of the flag, as published in the Government Gazette on 20 February 1903.

In 1912, at the request of the Admiralty, the design was amended to improve its appearance and to reduce the cost of manufacture. The large star now has seven points; the Southern Cross has four seven-pointed stars and one with five points.

The flag is curiously similar to one unfurled by the Anti-Transportation League at its inaugural meeting in Melbourne in 1851. The League was formed to unite the various state organisations which opposed the dumping of convicts in Australia. Its original silk flag, measuring 3.6 m by 2.7 m, is preserved in Launceston's Queen Victoria Museum.

These cigarette cards with drawings of the flags and coats of arms of the states date from about 1900. Some of the designs are fanciful, as some of the states did not have official flags or coats of arms until well into this century

One of the entries submitted to the *Review of Reviews for Australia* flag contest in 1900. All but one of the five identical winning entries in the final competition were submitted to this contest

The official (top) and unofficial (centre) Australian ensigns. The official flag resembles the Anti-Transportation League flag of 1851 (bottom)

The first of these three designs submitted in the 1901 flag contest was chosen by a disgruntled Melbourne *Herald* as its winning entry

Three entries in privately run flag contests in 1971 (top and centre) and 1986 (bottom). The Government made no plans for change

Anthem quests end on notes of discord

Despite 150 years of searching, Australia in the early 1970s did not have its own national anthem, but retained the British national anthem, 'God Save The Queen'.

The reasons were not hard to find. From the time ardent nationalist Dr John Dunmore Lang wrote an *Australian Anthem* and an *Australian Hymn* in 1826, successive attempts to produce an anthem that met with lasting popular approval all failed.

In a competition conducted in 1908 by *The Bulletin*, the prize was shared by two entries. One of them, *Battle Hymn* by J. Alex Allen, held a warning:

Watch eyes, where your lazy vineyards shine,
And your white wives smile and weave,
Lest an Orient foot crush down your vine
And a Western robber reive!

A similar contest conducted in 1971 by the Australian National Anthem and Flag Quests Committee, formed by the Fellowship of First Fleeters, fared little better despite the large number of entries received.

One entry had the words:

Where cookabarrows build their nests
Where oceans flow and come to rest.

And another the lines:

Koalas bark, and the platypus quack
Jackasses laugh their loud Ha Ha's.
Should I depart, I must soon come back.
Yirra, Yirra, Yirra—Ka La. Ka La, Ka La.
KaLa.

Over the years, the only 'anthem' that received any praise was one submitted to *The Bulletin* by C. J. Dennis as a joke during that publication's 1908 quest.

Its chorus went:

Git a . . . . move on
Have some . . . . sense
Learn the . . . . art of
Self de-. . . . . -fence

The Bulletin commented: 'In a class of its own stands Den's blankey Australaise. This is really the only satisfactory battle-song submitted and it is quite Australian.'

There was another competition in 1913 conducted by the Musical Association of New South Wales. Mr Arthur Adams won with his entry *'Fling Out the Flag'*. However, the song was attacked on grammatical grounds and was soon forgotten. Another contender, the *Song of Australia*, then enjoyed a brief vogue, but moves to have it made the official anthem in 1929 failed.

Apart from *Waltzing Matilda*, one song—*Advance Australia Fair*—received some acceptance. It was first performed at a St Andrew's Day ceremony in Sydney in 1878. It was written by a Scot, Peter Dods McCormick, who also claimed to have composed the music. This was questioned in 1943 when the Minister for Information, Arthur Calwell, persuaded

theatre proprietors to play the song as well as the English and American national anthems.

In the public outcry that followed it was claimed that the tune was either *God Bless the Prince of Wales*, or a German drinking song. Newspapers all over Australia condemned it and *The Sydney Morning Herald* summed up the general feeling at the time when it said *Advance Australia Fair* was of 'distressingly low standard' and composed for 'school children's entertainment'.

Despite this, Mr Calwell succeeded in having it played before ABC news sessions. In a referendum held in 1977 to choose a national song from *Advance, Australia Fair*, *Waltzing Matilda, God Save the Queen*, and *Song of Australia, the final result gave 2,353,617 votes to Waltzing Matilda, and 4,415,642 to Advance, Australia Fair* – though few people know the words. *God Save the Queen* is now played only before a member of the Royal Family.

Some of the proposed national anthems enjoyed passing popularity, and many were published. One

of them, *Awake! Awake! Australia*, was composed by the author of *Advance, Australia Fair*

Stamps and notes of the new nation

The forlorn kangaroo in an empty land

On 1 March 1901, the Commonwealth took over control of all postal, telegraph and telephone services, but not until January 1913 did it issue its own stamps. Soon after Federation it was suggested that the stamps of each state should be overprinted with the initials AC, but this was not done. A clause in the Constitution provided that the accounts of the six States should be kept separate for ten years, so until 1910 every Commonwealth post office in Australia sold only stamps of the state in which it stood. A stamp was valid only in the state that issued it. When the ten years were up, stamps of any state could be used anywhere in the Commonwealth.

Design competition

On 1 May 1911, uniform postal rates were introduced and at the end of the same month entries closed in a competition for designs for the first Australian stamps. The Government had invited 'skilled artists' to submit designs for a uniform postage stamp, offering two premiums, one of £100 [$4470], the other of £50 [$2235] for the two best entries. 'The designs must contain features characteristic of Australia,' said the announcement. And the treatment 'should not be too photographic or realistic'. A counsel observed only too well!

The judges were Bernard Hall, director of Victoria's National Gallery, J. B. Cooke, the government stamp printer, and A. S. A. Whelan, representing the Philatelic Society of Victoria. There were 533 entrants, who submitted 1051 designs. The first prize was awarded to a Victorian, Herman Altmann

of St Kilda. His design had the head of King George V in the centre, a kangaroo and emu facing each other in the bottom corners, and three shields in each of the two top corners, each shield displaying the arms of a state.

It was a fussy, crowded composition, and the Postmaster-General, C. E. Frazer, who was not bound to accept any of the submitted designs, rejected it. In December 1911, Frazer asked the Victorian Artists' Association to nominate one of its members to submit further designs. The association chose Blamire Young, a Yorkshire-born artist who, after years of struggle, had recently been acclaimed for his decorative, romantic watercolours. But there was little of romance or decoration in the bleak design that was approved by the Postmaster-General. It depicted a kangaroo standing forlornly on an empty map of Australia.

The stamp was not popular. For days, Sydney newspapers published letters from indignant citizens denouncing it. Typical comments were:

● 'Every artistic sense revolts at it. I can only conceive it to be the result of some abnormal vicious two-year-old's precocity.'

● 'Is the kangaroo . . . supposed to represent Australian feeling? If so, the person responsible for the poor dejected animal . . . overlooked the temperament of the average Australian, especially after a successful cricket match or win on the turf.'

● 'It is certainly emblematic of the present position of the Commonwealth and different States, in showing by the expression of the

poor beast that it is suffering from what cannot be other than "financial constipation".'

● 'The design is delightfully truthful—an empty land with nothing but kangaroos in it.'

● 'A rubbishy label advertising some particular brand of kangaroo tail soup.'

Australia's 'mournful monstrosity'

A writer in *Art in Australia* summed up the criticism succinctly. The stamp, instead of suggesting the spirit of the Australian people, was both incongruous and unedifying, and was certain to do Australia damage abroad. 'What the new stamp does is to present Australia as a barren continent, inhabited by a mournful monstrosity, intended for the representation of a kangaroo,' the writer said.

'The colour contrast is woeful, the drawing bad, and the setting execrable. Cheapness and poverty are the distinguishing features, whereas health, wealth and happiness should be depicted,' he added.

The architect W. Hardy Wilson wrote to say that Blamire Young, who was then on his way to London, did not approve of the design that was attributed to him. 'The crude and commonplace idea of decoration could not possibly have been produced by an artist,' he said. Blamire Young, he added, had asked him to say he was not responsible for the design 'in any way'. Blamire Young himself made no further comment, nor did the Postmaster-General. The press credited them as being either singly or jointly responsible for the unhappy kangaroo, but all the Post Office ever said was that 'the approved design

The search for an Australian stamp

The first Commonwealth stamps went on sale in 1913, after much debate over a suitable design. In 1911 the PMG held a design competition and selected a stamp by Herman Altmann from Victoria as the winner, and designs by Edwin Arnold and Donald Mackay as equal second. None of them were used. Instead the PMG issued a stamp designed in collaboration with the artist Blamire Young—the kangaroo stamp. Late in 1913 an adapted version of the Altmann design was issued, and this was followed by the kookaburra stamp in 1914

Altmann design, 1911 competition

Arnold design, 1911 competition

Mackay design, 1911 competition

Blamire Young/PMG design, 1913

Adapted Altmann design, 1913

Harrison kookaburra design, 1914

First commemorative—opening of Parliament House, 1927

was a combination of ideas, and not the work of any one person in particular.'

In a statement to the press, at the time he invited Blamire Young to submit designs, the Postmaster-General had said: 'If a picturesque stamp can be provided in which an outline of Australia is a feature, I am certainly favourably inclined towards it.' Most of Blamire Young's designs are believed to have shown scenes within an outline map of Australia, but none of his designs were accepted. One of them, however, showed two kangaroos within an outline map. This, together with a similar Post Office design showing one kangaroo and some of the designs from the competition, then became the basis of a new model design, from which the approved design was developed.

The kangaroo stamp went on sale in January 1913, in colours ranging from green, worth a ½d to black and rose, worth £2. Some values remained on sale up to 1950. The kangaroo was joined in December 1913 by a pale red penny stamp, adapted from the rejected prize-winner of 1911. It depicted the head of King George V in an oval surmounted by a crown, with a kangaroo at one side, an emu at the other, and a wattle-blossom in the top corners.

In August 1914, a sixpenny stamp was issued, showing a fat kookaburra on a branch of a gum tree. The colour was described officially as 'claret', but few wine-lovers would accept the description. The stamp was designed by R. A. Harrison, an engraver employed by the Victorian Note and Stamp Printing Office, and the son of the Commonwealth note printer, T. S. Harrison.

First commemorative

The Commonwealth issued its first commemorative stamp in 1927, to celebrate the opening of Parliament House, Canberra. Again a competition was held with Bernard Hall as one of the judges. The winner was R. A. Harrison. His design depicted a seated female figure, representing Australia, holding in one hand a shield bearing the Southern Cross, and in the other a palm branch with which she greets Parliament House, the central motif. If the palm branch were intended to symbolise political peace and harmony in Canberra, it was an unfortunate choice.

Since 1929, commemorative stamps have appeared frequently—to the great satisfaction of stamp collectors, and even greater satisfaction of the Treasury. Distinguished Australians who have appeared on commemorative issues include Sir Charles Kingsford Smith (1931 and 1958), Ferdinand von Mueller (1948), Lord Forrest of Bunbury (1949), Henry Lawson (1949), Sir Edmund Barton (1951), Nellie Melba (1961), Lawrence Hargrave (1961), Sir John Monash (1965), 'Banjo' Paterson (1968), and Albert Namatjira (1968). Archer, the first Melbourne Cup winner, appeared in 1960, and a prize Hereford bull in 1948.

In February 1966, Australia adopted decimal currency, and all stamps then current were withdrawn from sale on 12 February.

When banks issued their own notes

From the 1850s until 1911 most Australian banks issued their own notes. With ten or more banks issuing notes in perhaps five denominations, this meant that there were dozens of different types and sizes of notes in circulation—a delight to forgers. The £5 note at the top was issued by the Union Bank in 1905. The Union Bank merged with the Bank of Australasia in 1951 to become the Australia and New Zealand Bank. The £50 note in the centre was issued by the National Bank of Australasia in the late 1880s. The newly formed Commonwealth had no notes of its own ready for circulation so it bought unissued notes from the trading banks and overprinted them with the words 'Australian Note' and the signatures of two Treasury officials. The Treasury sold the notes to the banks in exchange for sovereigns. By 1912 the Commonwealth was only issuing National Bank notes, and it continued to circulate them until the first Commonwealth designed and printed notes became available in 1913. Among the new notes was the first 10s note (bottom) which was considered to be too small, and was boycotted by bank managers in Perth

The Australian people

An urban nation that came together from many sources

Once, it might have been possible to find the 'typical Australian' of fiction—the lean, rangy, long-jawed, laconic, happy-go-lucky, sun-bronzed Man from Snowy River or the Never-Never. But this type was never more than a small minority of the country's population, which even in 1901 was predominantly urban. At the inception of the Commonwealth, nearly half of Australia's 3,750,000 people lived in the six capital cities, and today more than three-quarters of 16 million are town-dwellers.

The 'typical Australian' of today is city born and bred. He has substituted the status snobbery of the suburbs for the 'mateship' of the bush legend. He is more interested in swimming pools than billabongs, in station-wagons than station horses. He knows what a smorgasbord is but has never seen a damper.

The men who founded the Commonwealth of Australia were determined to maintain its racial homogeneity. In 1901, the population was 95 per cent British and 99 per cent white. 'The unity of Australia is nothing if it does not imply a united race,' said our second Prime Minister, Alfred Deakin. And by a united race Deakin meant 'a people possessing the same general cast of character, tone of thought, the same constitutional training and traditions'.

Today we think differently. The Anglo-Saxon and Celtic traditions of the past are being enriched by a flow of immigrants from other countries. Since 1947, more than a million non-British immigrants from dozens of different countries have settled in Australia, bringing with them their historical and cultural memories, their religious beliefs, their eating and drinking habits.

But we can still acclaim the men and women who pioneered this brave new Australia. As the historian Brian Fitzpatrick wrote: 'The Australian people made heroes of none, and raised no idols, except perhaps an outlaw, Ned Kelly, and Carbine, a horse. But generation of them after generation, they fought with beasts at Ephesus—blight and drought, fire and flood; their own taskmasters and covetous alien—and, suffering their setbacks, still made Australia a home good enough for men of modest report to live in, calling their souls their own.'

This elderly swagman, his swag of blankets over his shoulder, posed warily for the camera in 1901. Swagmen, once a common sight on outback roads, have almost disappeared since the Depression

The changing patterns of immigration

A basically British nation becomes a European melting pot

European immigrants have altered the lifestyle of Australians more than any other single cause this century. But, until the end of World War II, Australia was basically a British nation. After transportation to the eastern states ended in the 1850s, most immigrants came from England, Scotland and Ireland, together with a few Germans and Scandinavians.

Immigrants from Europe were a novelty in 1902, when the Melbourne magazine *Table Talk* greeted 38 Greeks and five Italians with the hope that the new arrivals would not turn into 'fruit hawkers and flower sellers'. 'If, on the contrary, they are of the farming or peasant class, then their arrival may be welcomed as a distinct gain,' the magazine said. 'We want to encourage here a peasant population used to old-world methods of thrift and the Greek and the Italian of the right sort would be eminently welcome.'

Some immigrants came from Italy in the 1920s, but Queensland fears of a southern European takeover in the canefields led to the policy being discouraged in 1925.

In 1933 only 92,448 people out of the total population of 6,629,839 were classified as Europeans. Italians, with 26,693 were the largest foreign group followed by Germans (16,829) and Scandinavians (11,042).

In 1938 Australia started to take a trickle of refugee immigrants who had fled Europe after Hitler rose to power in Germany. The outbreak of war interrupted this programme, but in September 1940 the *Dunera* steamed into Sydney Harbour with more than 2000 victims of Nazism who had been rounded up and transported by the British authorities on the grounds that they were possible fifth columnists. It was a unique cargo of European talent.

After a nightmare voyage of nearly two months during which they were robbed and brutally treated by their guards, they were interned in Australia. At the end of the war 915 of them decided to remain. Among those who have contributed greatly to Australian life have been Professor Hugo Wolfsohn, Dean of the School of Social Science, La Trobe University; Franz Stampfl, adviser on

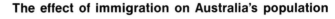

The effect of immigration on Australia's population

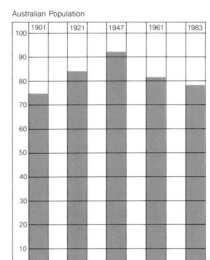

Australian Population

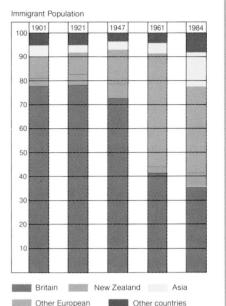

Immigrant Population

These graphs show the way in which the make-up of the Australian population has changed since Federation. The left-hand graph shows the percentage of native-born Australians in the total population. The drop from 90.8% in 1947 to 78.8% in 1983 reflects the post-war boom in immigration. The right-hand graph shows the changing proportions of im-

Britain   New Zealand   Asia

Other European   Other countries

migrants from various countries. There has been a steady decline in the proportion of British as against other European immigrants since 1921 and a rise in Asian entries

athletics, Melbourne University; Felix Werder, composer and music critic; Uwe Radok, head of the department of meteorology, Melbourne University; and Hans Buchdahl, professor of theoretical physics at the Australian National University.

At the end of World War II, the Labor Government realised the population was scarcely increasing naturally. The Labor Party had never been enthusiastic about assisted immigration because it believed immigrants would reduce standards of living and compete for jobs. But the war had exposed Australia's vulnerability in defence and there was a severe shortage of workers for industry, so Arthur Calwell, Minister for Immigration, introduced assisted immigration.

It was agreed by all political parties that about half the immmigrants could be non-British, although Mr. Calwell somewhat wistfully hoped that for 'every foreign migrant there will be ten people from the United Kingdom'. This was not fulfilled.

Between 1945 and 1965 Australia received more than 2 million migrants and the population rose from 7.5 million to 11 million. By 1971, when the population had reached 13 million, 2.7 million had been born overseas and another 1.2 million were Australians born of immigrant parents. Then in 1972, a new Labor Government decided to slow down the scheme because the huge inflow was thought to be severely straining housing, schools and social services.

Successive Australian Governments, whatever their political colour, firmly believed that British immigrants were the best. Here, a British yeoman, who migrated to Western Australia in 1910, poses proudly with his family

Many immigrants, despite some unofficial disapproval, continued to keep up the customs and national dress styles of their homelands, as is shown in this German wedding group in South Australia

Dagos, Balts, Skis and the mysterious Yellow Peril

Until the immigration boom after World War II, Australians were highly suspicious of immigrants who appeared to be either strange or different. They were expected to become 'true Australians' and to abandon the customs of their former homelands.

This suspicion was shown in one of the first acts of the Commonwealth Parliament after Federation, when it passed the Immigration Restriction Bill, creating the 'White Australia policy'. At the same time, the Government also introduced a hypocritical 'dictation test' which gave it the power to exclude any immigrant who could not pass an examination in *any* European language chosen by the immigration officer.

This test was aimed primarily at excluding Asians, who were lumped together under the chilling title of the 'Yellow Peril'. To Australians 'yellow' meant Chinese or Japanese indiscriminately and 'peril' applied to the presence of a few Chinese living in Australia who were suspected of nameless debaucheries and lustful designs on Australian virgins.

Influential newspapers and obscure journals alike attacked Asians as sub-human at every opportunity. In 1903, when three Japanese warships visited Sydney, *The Opal Miner*, published in White Cliffs, NSW, stated: 'Sydney is yaller . . . with the slant-eyed, cat-haired, blob-nosed, monkey-faced . . . ape-like Asiatics.'

The Asians were not the only race to be jeered at. Australians have always shown their dislike of foreigners by labelling them with contemptuous names. 'In my youth,' wrote John Hetherington in 1965, 'Dago was a term meaning Italian first of all, but vaguely denoting other southern Europeans also. Dagos were all inferior people who ate spaghetti instead of good honest steak, fought with knives instead of bashing their enemies, cleanly and straightforwardly, with beer

The widespread Australian fear of the possible results of unchecked black and Asian immigration is shown in this *Bulletin* cartoon. It purports to show the Christmas party of an Australian family of the future, and demonstrates how other races were regarded as either sub-human or savages

bottles . . .' Eastern Europeans were known as Balts; German and Austrian refugees were called 'Reffos'; and in Western Australia Yugoslavs and Albanians alike were given the name of 'Skis'.

In 1949, in an attempt to stop immigrant baiting, Mr Calwell appealed to press and radio not to use such terms as Balt, displaced person or DP, and to describe post-war immigrants as New Australians—a phrase that itself has been used disparagingly.

Xenophobia continued to thrive into the 1970s. When pupils at a Sydney school were asked in 1971 whether they would like their sister to marry a Greek or Italian immigrant the class, with one dissenter, voted 'No!'

The Bulletin for many years was anti-Asian in character, carrying the slogan 'Australia for the White Man', underneath its masthead. Writers for the magazine in its early days supported this stand with enthusiasm, and often contributed articles bitterly attacking Asian habits and customs. *Bulletin* cartoonists also made fun of Asians and other coloured races

A Czechoslovakian writer fails the Gaelic test for entry into Australia

'Tisn't the colour I object to: that's nothin' —it's the spellin'.'

The dictation test meant that any immigrant could be tested in any European language. It was introduced to keep Asians out, but it could also be used to exclude anyone the Government disliked politically. This was done when the anti-fascist Czechoslovakian writer Egon Kisch came to Australia in 1934 to speak at the invitation of the Australian Anti-War Council.

The Government, claiming it was acting on information received from British authorities, tried to have Kisch barred as an 'undesirable visitor'. When he attempted to land in Melbourne he was arrested and returned to his ship, but while the ship was travelling to Sydney friends took his case to court. The Government was unable to produce its information, so he was allowed to land in Sydney.

On landing, Kisch was taken to a police station and given a dictation test. He could speak several European languages, but a test in an official's version of Scottish Gaelic was beyond him. He was arrested, prosecuted as an illegal immigrant and sentenced to six months' gaol.

On appeal, the High Court ruled that Gaelic was not a European language within the meaning of the act. Kisch was freed, given a second test. He failed and was again declared an illegal immigrant. He left Australia voluntarily

KISCH'S CENSORED SPEECH

What They Prevented
KISCH
From Saying

Photo taken on board "Strathaird" immediately preceding his jump to the wharf at Melbourne

ALSO
A COLLECTION OF FACTS ON THE KISCH CASE

The unlucky Australians

Aborigines begin to struggle for basic rights

Section 127 of the Constitution of the Commonwealth, proclaimed on 1 January 1901, read: 'In reckoning the numbers of the people of the Commonwealth, or of a State or other part of the Commonwealth, Aboriginal natives shall not be counted.'

Thus, according to the founding fathers, the new-born Commonwealth did not recognise the existence of the original Australians. It would not make laws for them, give them a vote, or even count their heads.

When white settlement began in 1788, there may have been as many as 300,000 Aborigines scattered over the continent, divided into hundreds of tribes. But throughout the 19th century, their numbers decreased catastrophically. Deprived of their hunting grounds, they starved, or perished from the diseases of the white man. Many were killed in clashes with the settlers, who also on occasions poisoned their waterholes or fed them poisoned wheat cakes.

The Aborigines' resistance and their attempts at retaliation were regarded as criminal acts to be punished ruthlessly and indiscriminately. The full-blood Tasmanian Aborigines were hounded to extinction. European diseases also took their toll to such an extent that it was believed Aborigines would eventually die out. In 1921 a census showed merely 33,558 full-blood Aborigines, including 26,000 who were patronisingly described as 'wild and wandering'.

No votes in welfare

Not till the 1860s were attempts made by any of the self-governing colonies to set aside reserves for Aborigines, and to give them some protection. Aboriginal welfare was of little concern to politicians. There were no votes in it. Missions, rather than governments, tried to provide Aborigines with food, clothing, medical care, education, and, of course, religion.

When the overlander Francis Birtles returned from Darwin to Adelaide in 1924, he wrote: 'The blacks of central Australia are being starved to death. Their state in some areas is appalling and a national scandal.'

Their traditional way of life largely lost to them, many Aborigines chose the protection of the station camp, where they could live in a semi-tribal state. While they were there, and worked, they were given paternalistic security; when they went on walkabout, the boss accepted it. In many cases this relationship was satisfying to both parties, generating strong bonds of affection and loyalty. Many Aborigines became an indispensable and valued part of station life, and it sometimes seemed that these circumstances offered the best chance for the survival of Aboriginal cultural identity.

But many of the black farmhands lived in virtual serfdom, with their traditions discarded and their freedom of movement curtailed. It was not uncommon for the native labourer to be regarded as his master's property, and for absconders to be brought back by force and with police help.

As late as 1949, Aboriginal hands on West-

Fanny Cochrane Smith claimed to be the last full-blood Tasmanian Aborigine. Some disputed her claim to purely Aboriginal ancestry, but the Tasmanian Parliament accepted it and in 1884 granted her 80 hectares of land. She was a popular figure and used to entertain visitors to her property by singing native songs, using her barn as a makeshift concert hall. In 1899 and again in 1903, when this photograph was taken, she recorded several of her songs on wax cylinders. These are preserved in the Tasmanian Museum as unique documents of the language. She died in 1905

ern Australian cattle-runs received no wages, and five years later, the Commissioner of Native Affairs in Perth reported that in most cases they were receiving 'little better than pocket-money and keep', a state of affairs he described as traditional and time-honoured.

In the country, many continued to occupy squalid shacks on the fringe of townships. In the cities, they were often huddled in shabby, over-crowded tenements in rundown inner suburbs. Not surprisingly, the Aboriginal infant mortality rate was ten times that of whites, and respiratory infections, gastrointestinal diseases, and leprosy, were rife.

By the 1950s there was general agreement that Aborigines should be equipped for equal citizenship. The goal, however, was assimilation, which meant Europeanisation. Many Aborigines believed that their culture should remain intact while discrimination was removed. In 1965, Charles Perkins, who was to become the University of New South Wales' first Aboriginal graduate, led fellow students on a 'freedom ride' to towns where Aborigines suffered from blatant prejudice at swimming pools, cinemas, hotels and clubs.

A turning point was the referendum held in 1967, when the people of Australia voted by a 10-1 majority to amend the outworn constitution by giving power to the Commonwealth to make laws and plans for the Aboriginal people, and to include them in the national census. The census of 1971 showed an Aboriginal population of about 106,000; in 1985 it was about 170,000.

Demands for land rights

The 1960s also saw demands for land rights becoming strident. In May 1963, 362 square kilometres of the 519 square kilometre Yirrkala Mission at Gove on Cape York Peninsula was revoked by the Commonwealth Government to make way for the activities of a bauxite mining company.

The 500 Aborigines at Yirrkala presented a petition to Parliament, written on bark, stating their grievances. In 1971 their case was taken before the Northern Territory Supreme Court, which ruled that Aboriginal people could not own any land, and that the company could begin mining.

Since then, however, there has been some progress in meeting Aboriginal aspirations. One step was to establish a federal Department of Aboriginal Affairs, which took over what used to be the responsibility of the States, except Queensland, thus giving some unified action for Aboriginal welfare. Aborigines have gained title to some lands: in 1981 the Pitjantjatjara people of South Australia were given 184,738 square kilometres, or nearly 19 per cent, of that State. But the greatest change has been in the Northern Territory where under the Aboriginal Land Rights Act of 1976, Aboriginal people have gained 'inalienable' title to many traditional areas. By 1985, about 34 per cent of the Northern Territory had been handed over.

Despite these advances, there are still voices being raised to express dissatisfaction with the continuing apathy of many Australians toward the tragedy of the country's original inhabitants.

When a *Newsweek* correspondent, Australian-born Tony Clifton, revisited his native land in December 1972, to cover the federal elections, he reported scathingly on the general plight of the Aborigines. 'I've watched people die in a cholera hospital in Bengal and witnessed starving children fight for food in Biafra,' he wrote. 'I have seen people killed and mistreated in Vietnam. But the most emotionally wearing experience of my life has come just in the last few days—among the Aboriginal population of my native land. Now I have seen how we Australians are condemning a whole race of our fellow citizens to short, brutish and miserable lives.'

Until the early 20th century police who arrested an Aboriginal offender against white laws often arrested 'witnesses' as well and took them all, chained together, to court

Many Aborigines who rejected the European way of life were removed from their tribal lands and fed on handouts. Here South Australian Aborigines receive flour rations in 1913

This Aboriginal woman was posed in a studio to record a vanishing mode of dress

New South Wales officials distribute blankets. The Aboriginal question was seen as a need for sparse charity—the occasional issue of clothing and rations, which rarely included meat

The typical Australian

What observers saw behind the facade

The casual, independent swagman seemed to typify the 'real Australian'. These two local graziers dressed the part in Gundagai in 1905

In 1877, the novelist and journalist Marcus Clarke predicted that the typical Australian of 1977 would be 'a tall, coarse, strong jawed, greedy, pushing, talented man, excelling in swimming and horsemanship' and 'freed from the highest burden of intellectual development'. He would suffer from bad teeth, liver disease and premature baldness, and his expectation of life would be 59 years if unmarried, and 65 and a bit if married. (Why married men should live longer than bachelors was not explained.) And Australia would be a republic with Sydney its 'fashionable and luxurious capital'.

Clarke's predictions may have been facetious, though some have been fulfilled, but three years later, James Hogan, a Victorian teacher and historian, made a serious attempt at prophecy. 'The three main characteristics of the native Australian,' he wrote, were 'an inordinate love of field sports, a very decided disinclination to recognise the authority of parents and teachers and a grievous dislike to mental effort.'

And by 1900, 'the coming Australian will spend most of his time out-of-doors . . . He will be distinguished by independence of character . . . Ambition is a vice with which he will never be charged. He will daily move on a circle bounded by his own little horizon, taking but little interest in the proceedings of the great world outside . . . In fine, the coming inhabitant will be peaceably disposed and sportively inclined . . . contented and easygoing, but non-intellectual and tasteless,' wrote Hogan.

In 1891, Rudyard Kipling, after spending 10 days in Melbourne and one day in Sydney, described Australia as 'a hard land . . . made harder for itself by the action of its inhabitants, who—it may have been the climate—always seemed a bit on edge'. He found Sydney—on that day—'populated by leisure multitudes all in their shirt-sleeves and all picnicking all the day. They volunteered that they were new and young, but would do wonderful things some day, which promise they more than kept.'

Kipling was impressed by the Americanism of Melbourne. 'But remember it is secondhand America,' he said.

When the English sociologists Beatrice and Sidney Webb visited Australia in 1898, Mrs Webb wrote that Australian society was 'just a slice of Great Britain and differs only slightly from Glasgow, Manchester, Liverpool and the *suburbs* of London . . . Bad manners, ugly clothes, vigour and shrewdness characterise the settlements of Sydney, Melbourne and the bush stations, exactly as they characterise the lower and upper middle-class folk of the old country. If anything, the manners are worse, the dress more pretentious and glaring and lacking in taste, than with us,' she wrote. 'The well-to-do women especially lack culture, charm and any kind of grace; and the richer they are the more objectionable they become.'

On the other hand, there was 'more enjoyment of life, a greater measure of high spirits among the young people of all classes'. Australians were 'obviously and even blatantly a young race proud of their youth'.

In 1906, Edward Dyson published a series of sketches titled *Fact'ry 'Ands*. His characters, he wrote in a foreword, were 'true types of a pronounced Australian class' not previously written about—men and women 'earning honorable if humble subsistence in jam, pickle, lollie and biscuit factories, in tobacco factories, box factories, shirt factories, rope works and paper mills'.

In the first Commonwealth Year Book, published in 1909, the Commonwealth Statistician, G. H. Knibbs, discussed the changes that were likely to take place in the 'physical characteristics and the social instincts' of the Australian people. 'At present,' he wrote, 'the characteristics . . . are only in the making, and probably it will not be possible to point to a distinct Australian type until three or four generations more have passed. The Australian at present is little other than a transplanted Briton, with the essential characteristic of his British forebears, the desire for freedom from restraint, however, being perhaps more strongly accentuated.'

When a contributor wrote in *The Lone Hand* in 1910 that Australians abroad were disliked because they were 'provincial' and 'unreliable', and had an 'irrepressible tendency' to blow, brag, or skite, the author J. H. M. Abbott in reply asked indignantly: 'Did

Lean, bronzed, with a 'devil-may-care contempt for physical danger'—two successful show-business realisations of the Australian myth, Chips Rafferty and the former Harbour Bridge painter, Paul Hogan

Melba, or Ada Crossley, or Amy Castles prove "unreliable" when their voices were taken in hand? . . . Is Brennan's torpedo and mono-rail any the worse for having been invented by an Australian? And what of Norman Brookes, who recently won the world's championship at lawn tennis . . . And in cricket and football have Australians proved their unreliability against England's best teams? . . . Did Lord Kitchener suppose them to be "unreliable" in the war, when he had every troop of them in the fighting line, whilst 90,000 British regulars, militia and South African volunteers defended the lines of communications? . . . It almost seems,' Abbott concluded modestly, 'that the Australian has a pretty fair right to an "irrepressible tendency" towards brag.'

L. A. Adamson, headmaster of Wesley College, Melbourne, in an address to the mental science and education section of the Science Congress in 1913, said: 'The sense of the wide free open spaces came easy to the Australian boy. He had no class consciousness and was not afraid . . . how he spoke to his elders. In alertness, self-reliance and power of initiative, he had no equal . . .

'On the other hand the Australian boy was often brusque in manner—perhaps a defect his home must bear the responsibility for. Nor could it be denied that the average Australian boy was lacking in chivalrous respect for girls of his own age; nor was he wholly to blame in that matter . . . There had taken place a gradual and even a rapid breaking down of the old formalities of intercourse between the sexes. The life of the camp and beaches was only symptomatic of the change that had been going on in the social system. Whichever sex might be at fault later . . . in adolescence it was almost always the girl who commanded the casual acquaintanceships made in public places . . .'

In December 1922, *The Triad* addressed a poem to *The Girl of the Period*:

She formerly talked of the weather,
The popular book, or the play:
Her old line of chat,
Was of this thing or that
In the fashions and fads of the day.

But now she discusses eugenics,
And things that pundits perplex:
She knocks you quite flat
With her new line of chat,
And her 'What do you think about Sex?'

But according to Nellie Stewart, this new emancipated Australian girl had lost one of her former charms—attractive legs. 'I do not think the Australian leg has improved during my time,' Miss Stewart wrote. 'Female legs were more charming five and thirty years ago than they are now. That was largely because ankles were more slender in the late eighties than they are in 1923.'

George Johnston in 1953 pointed out that the familiar picture of the suntanned, adventurous Australian 'against a background of billabongs, coolibah trees, salt-pans, sheep on a dry hillside, great herds of cattle droving lustily across eroded plains . . .' was just as false as the other picture of a 'ubiquitous and apparently unending sequence of attractive sun-tanned girls in white satin swimsuits' against a background of 'wide white beaches and surf-boats tossing on the swing of the Pacific breakers'.

In fact, wrote Johnston '. . . to most of the country's inhabitants, Australia is anything but an eternal playground for sun-lovers, or, alternatively, some milder equivalent of America's romantic Wild West. Four out of five Australians live an urban life which . . . is not greatly to be distinguished from the

In cartoons with themes like this, in short stories, poetry and articles, *The Bulletin* fostered Australian nationalism. The typical Australian of *The Bulletin* was a tough, goodhearted individual who felt himself to be the equal of anyone and who had the same frank, open manner with everyone

urban forms of life practised by millions of other people in other countries.'

Another Australian writer, Craig McGregor, in 1966 described the typical Australian as 'a youngish clerk or businessman, with nice button-down shirts, sincere tie, last year's Holden, a cheque account, and a wife in the suburbs'. And he added ungallantly: 'The men tend to run to beer guts and the women to flabby upper arms.'

Australians in black and white

Cartoon and comic strip characters depict the stereotypes of 'Australian character'. Saltbush Bill, drawn by Eric Jolliffe for many years, is the bushman, sometimes irascible, sometimes laconic, but always independent. Bluey and Curly, the World War II diggers created by Alex Gurney and later drawn by Les Dixon, are in the city larrikin tradition. Barry McKenzie is the 1960s version of the innocent abroad. His adventures were drawn by a New Zealander, Nicholas Garland, but written by an Australian, Barry Humphries. *Private Eye*, the English magazine in which 'Bazza' McKenzie appeared, was long banned in Australia, but Australians recognised him as one of their own in 1973, when they saw a film of his adventures

A nation of meat-eaters

Monotonous food before the culinary revolution

An anonymous 19th century ballad about the Kelly gang has this verse:

They spent the day most pleasantly,
Had plenty of good cheer,
Fried beefsteak and onions,
Tomato sauce and beer.

In 1897, Dr Phillip Muskett, a distinguished Sydney physician and dietician, summed up Australia's eating habits thus: 'We eat meat and drink tea. Meat eating in Australia is almost a religion.'

The Australian's breakfast, said Muskett, was 'the eternal trio' of chops, steak and sausages, and, when he was not drinking beer, he was drinking tea. 'The gentler sex are greatly given to extravagant tea-drinking, exceeding all bounds of moderation. Many of them, however, live absolutely on nothing else but tea and bread and butter. No wonder, then, that they grow pale and bloodless.'

Western Australians were the greatest tea-drinkers, with a yearly consumption of 4.8 kg a head, compared with 3.5 kg in New South Wales. (Today, the average Australian consumption is about 1.4kg per head.)

Muskett found much else to deplore. Australians ate little fish or fruit. There was an endless recurrence of boiled potatoes and boiled cabbage. Salads were almost unknown. So were many vegetables, including artichokes, brussels sprouts, asparagus, celeriac, egg plant, Jerusalem artichokes, salsify, capsicum and sweet corn.

Muskett would get a pleasant surprise were he alive today. A great gastronomic revolution has taken place in Australia, largely because of the great influx of European immigrants since the end of World War II—more than a million arrived between 1952

Tomato sauce has long occupied an honoured place in Australian cuisine. Legend says it was enjoyed by the Kelly gang

and 1972. Another reason is that more and more Australians now go abroad and discover the cuisines of other lands.

A curious fact about the eating habits of Australians is that they do not seem to be affected by climatic or seasonal variations. An investigation made during World War II found that there was more demand for cold salad in an industrial cafeteria in temperate Hobart than in a similar cafeteria in tropical Townsville, where, no matter how hot the weather, the large majority of workers demanded hot meals.

If Australians ate dreary food in the 1900s, it was not for the want of expert instruction or interesting ingredients. In 1898, Mrs Hannah Maclurcan, proprietress of the Queen's Hotel, Townsville—Australia's finest hotel, outside Melbourne and Sydney—produced a comprehensive cookbook that quickly ran to three editions. 'A copy of this book in a house is better than a dozen cures for indigestion,' said the *Armidale Chronicle*. And the *Towers Evening Herald* commented: 'The work treats only how to cook Australian products, so there is no waste space given to the unattainable.'

Among Mrs Maclurcan's typically Australian dishes were jugged wallaby, roast scrub turkey, kangaroo-tail soup, *bêche-de-mer* (a kind of sea slug) soup, baked paw-paw, roast wonga pigeon, turtle fins on toast, curried green bananas, and prickly pear jelly.

Mrs Maclurcan's cuisine was not all chauvinistically Australian. Her repertoire

In 1906 a rural magazine proudly demonstrated that an Australian ate more meat than an American and a Briton together. Australians now eat less meat: from the 119 kg per head in 1906 it has dropped to 97 kg. People of the other countries eat a good deal more than they did at the turn of the century. In 1983, Americans consumed an average of 109.9 kg of meat per person, Britons 71.6 kg and West Germans 81.8 kg. In Japan, consumption has doubled since 1977 to 31 kg per person included classic English, French, Spanish and Indian dishes, and one of the advertisers in her book, Mr B. Skinner, 'turtle, meat, and fruit preserver' of O'Connell Town, Brisbane, had a range of products that could not be matched in Australia today. It included *bêche-de-mer* soùp ('specially ordered with Skinner's Turtle Soup by the Queensland Clubs and the leading Clubs and Hotels in the Southern Colonies'), potted dugong and guavas in syrup.

Another advertiser proclaimed the excellence of his Mount Graham coffee, grown on his plantation on the Russell River, north of Innisfail, and processed in Cairns.

Coffee had been grown around Cairns since the early 1890s, and by 1900, Queensland growers were supplying about 40 per cent of the state's requirements. One of the biggest plantations on the Russell River was established by two aristocratic brothers of Lady Hopetoun, wife of Australia's first Governor-General. They were named de Moleyns, but three generations before in County Kerry, Ireland, the family name had been Mullins.

At first coffee was harvested by coloured workers, Ceylonese and then Aboriginal, but towards the turn of the century, Europeans were employed—men, women and even school-children on holiday. Ultimately, the industry was unable to compete with imports from countries where labour was cheaper, though as late as 1913 Queensland produced more than 68,000 kg of coffee.

Today, Australia consumes about 30,357 tonnes of coffee a year, nearly all of it imported.

Mrs Maclurcan sent a copy of her cookbook to Lady Lamington, wife of Baron Lamington, Governor of Queensland. Lady Lamington, in a gracious acknowledgement, wrote 'I think my Household will be the better of having a copy,' but the book seems to have had little influence on Australian households.

The cuisine of meat, potatoes and cabbage, zested with tomato or Worcestershire sauce, and washed down with tea or beer, remained standard Australian fare for generations.

A classic story, which has passed into folklore, tells of a hungry and hopeful American traveller who sits down to dinner in an Australian country pub, and is given a plate of cold meat and potatoes. Timorously, he asks the reluctant waitress: 'Do you think I could have a little salad to go with this?' She glares at him in astonishment, and turning to the other guests, announces loudly: 'This bastard thinks it's Christmas!'

The Australian hotel, with a few honourable exceptions, has maintained a proud tradition of execrable food. When the Cambridge professor D. W. Brogan visited Australia in 1947, he reported in the London *Spectator*: 'The food in public places in Australia would shock the traveller used to Ireland or the Deep South. Even dealing with a potato is beyond the culinary resources of an Australian hotel.'

And he suggested that Australia, 'a great country rightly proud of its achievements in plant and animal genetics, should devote a little research into the cooking of a potato, and cooking meat without hiding the burnt offering under a horrible congealing axle-grease gravy'.

Another English visitor who took away poignant memories of Australian country cooking was Dr. Thomas Wood, author of *Cobbers*, who visited Australia in 1931.

'Meals at small hotels in Western Australia are usually square,' he wrote. 'Tea always is; and one menu card could be used throughout the State. It would say soup, fried steak with two veg., corned beef or cold mutton, sweets. Everyone knows so well what is coming next that speculation is a waste of time until the second course is cleared. Then you are free to wonder which of the two traditional sweets will appeal.' The traditional sweets were port-wine jelly and apple pie. But sometimes a more adventurous pub-keeper would serve college pudding or jam tart.

Wood had an equally memorable meal in Queensland, in a railway 'refreshment room'. It was a tin shed—'an oven in which flies buzzed and butter ran'—and the menu read: *Mutton broth—roast mutton, boiled mutton, mutton pie—mashed potatoes—college pudding, preserves—tea, coffee.* A culinary challenge!

Bert Sachse shows the true pavlova. He first made it in 1935

Dishes that Australians claim as their own

Has Australia made any contribution to the noble art of cooking?

The carpetbag steak—a thick piece of rump or fillet steak stuffed with oysters and grilled—is often regarded as an Australian dish, but it originated in the United States.

The pavlova is generally regarded as an Australian invention but recent research shows that the honour may have to be shared with New Zealand. The pavlova—a shell baked from egg whites, sugar, cornflour, vinegar, vanilla essence and cream of tartar and filled with whipped cream and topped with passionfruit pulp—was first made in Australia by Bert Sachse, chef of Perth's Esplanade Hotel, in 1935. The hotel named it for one of its most distinguished guests, the Russian dancer, Anna Pavlova. It is not known whether she ever tasted the confection.

The lamington, a square piece of sponge cake, coated with chocolate, cocoa and desiccated coconut is unquestionably Australian. It was named for Baron Lamington, Governor of Queensland from 1895 to 1901, after he had left for England.

Victorians claim that the Victoria sponge, a light sponge cake, originated in their state. No-one has disputed the claim. And South Australia is undeniably the home of the 'floater', an exotic dish that consists of a meat pie immersed in pea mush and topped with lashings of tomato sauce.

Seventy years of eating out

How a gastronomic desert came to bloom

'The average Australian takes no aesthetic pleasure in food . . .' wrote the Melbourne playwright Louis Esson in 1918. 'This country was pioneered on corned beef and damper . . . That is why the Australian in general takes plain and heavy food, looking askance on anything exotic, and why the general run of our restaurants lack enterprise and variety.'

If Australia as a whole was a gastronomic desert there were a few pleasant oases. Perhaps the most famous was Paris House, in Phillip Street, Sydney. There for a quarter of a century—until his death in 1920—Gaston Lievain, a small, genial, rotund Frenchman with a bald head and a walrus moustache, presided over a restaurant of international standard patronised by artists, writers, musicians, men-about-town—and their lady friends as well.

Writing in *The Triad* in 1928, G. F. Everett recalled Saturday lunches at Paris House in Edwardian times: 'Gaston Lievain . . . welcoming one into the intimate little rooms . . . Soup served steaming in silver tureens; wine, red or white; lobster Newburg; *poulet en casserole*; turtle steak (the shell displayed in the hall, as a guarantee of good faith) . . .'

Memories of real dining

Everett evoked other 'ghosts of gastronomia'—'Walkers in Park Street, with its menu of 50 cooked dishes . . . Pfahlert's Grill, with its be-napkined rounds of Stilton; its crystal bowls of clean, crisp celery, its porterhouse steaks, its pewters of foaming ale . . . The old Metropolitan, where host Usher . . . would have hanging from his rafters an appetising display of game . . . Hares, black duck, kangaroo tails, venison, pigeons, quail, wild turkeys . . . One does not dine in Sydney now-a-days,' Everett lamented. 'One merely pays to eat.'

Sydney's artists, writers and talkers of the 1920s had two other regular haunts—Amendola's and Pelligrini's. Amendola's in Wilmot Street was a wine bar with a back room where a group met every Saturday afternoon. It later became the Café de Bohème, and finally the site was swallowed up by the Regent Theatre. Pelligrini's was a basement wine bar in Hunter Street, run by a fat jovial Italian named Truda.

Coffee and dominoes

Equally popular with Sydney bohemians were the Mockbell coffee shops. Most of these were in cellars, with dim electric lights, marble-topped tables, comfortable chairs, and upholstered leather seats around the walls. For fourpence [25c] you got a tin jug which yielded two or, if you were lucky, two and a half cups of coffee. You could also call for a set of dominoes, and sit as long as you liked over a game.

The headquarters of Sydney's Bohemia in the 1930s was Pakie's Club, a small upstairs room in Elizabeth Street, opposite Hyde Park, curtainless, carpetless and plasterless. Paintings by Roland Wakelin, Roy de Maistre, Bernard Hesling and other members of the Australian *avant-garde* hung on its bare brick walls, and the decor included an orange-and-red screen, and chairs painted yellow, red, purple and blue.

The proprietress was a genial middle-aged woman named Pakie Macdougall. In her blue smock, she dispensed tea, coffee, macaroni cheese and talk, and turned an indulgent eye on patrons who arrived with a discreet bottle. 'Most Sydney creative people of my age owe a debt to Pakie,' wrote Hesling.

In those days, too, you could sip tea in the walled garden of Burdekin House in Macquarie Street, sitting at green tables under great overhanging trees. Burdekin House, the most beautiful building in Sydney, was demolished in 1934 to make way for the erection of St Stephen's Church.

Melbourne bohemians in the early years of the century met at the Pension Suisse, or Fasoli's, a café behind a little wine shop in Lonsdale Street, just east of Wesley Church. The site was later occupied by the Ritz Café, now also vanished.

The proprietor, Vincent Fasoli, did his cooking in heavy copper pots, and served only one main course—*osso buco, spezzatino di vitello* or some other stewed, braised or pot-cooked

Paris House was the most famous restaurant in Sydney in the first two decades of this century. As these 1907 menu covers suggest, it was a place where well-heeled bohemians met and where couples could dine discreetly; private rooms were among its attractions. Its proprietor was a Frenchman, Gaston Lievain

Hotel dining rooms often used to be austere places. Here the chef and dining room staff of the Imperial Hotel in Hobart pose in a room whose austerity triumphs over the array of food—including ham, turkey, crayfish and sucking pig—and the festive paper hats on the table

dish. Sometimes quail appeared on the menu; sceptical gourmets suspected it was cockatoo or rosella cunningly disguised. Fasoli made his own *spaghetti*, *ravioli*, *gnocchi*, *tagliatelle* and *salami*.

You entered through a door over which an artistic customer had painted the device 'Light Hearts and Empty Pockets', with symbolic decorations, and sat at a long bare table, about 20 on each side. In the back yard was a spreading willow tree under which on fine days you could sit, drink and talk the Melbourne sun to sleep.

Menu for 1s 3d
In 1907, Fasoli moved to ampler premises in King Street, and the Lonsdale Street café, renamed the Café Bohemia, was taken over by a compatriot, Lorenzo Camusso. Signora Camusso was the hostess. For an inclusive charge of 1s 3d [$1.85] you could talk your way through a home-made *salame*, a choice of half a dozen salads, a piled plate of *spaghetti* or *maccheroni*, a meat dish, sweets, cheese and fresh fruit, washed down with black coffee, and red or white wine from pot-bellied flagons, and accompanied by soothing music from piano and guitar.

'It is the only bit of the Continent in Melbourne,' wrote the art historian William Moore. 'Travellers will tell you there is no other place like it in the Commonwealth.'

Meeting place of politicians
The Café Bohemia was also patronised by members of the Victorian Socialist Society, among them a future Prime Minister, John Curtin, a future Premier of South Australia, Jack Gunn, and a future Labor Premier of Victoria, Jack Cain.

The Café Bohemia advertised regularly in the *Socialist*, the weekly organ of the Victorian Socialist Society. An advertisement in 1909 read: 'The only place in Melbourne where you can enjoy a good meal and feel at home with the many good folk that frequent the café. And if you like to amuse yourself, come along on Wednesday night—you have a chance to see the Melbourne bohemians enjoy themselves à la Continentale.'

Intimate and elegant
On a higher social—or economic—level was the Café Denat in Exhibition Street, founded in 1910 by a French Swiss, Calexte Denat, and patronised by politicians, businessmen, and men-about-town. It was an intimate, elegant place, lushly carpeted and curtained, with walls lined from floor to ceiling with ornate gilt-framed mirrors. Like Paris House, it had a slightly raffish reputation.

Denat, like Lievain, was short and rotund, with the pointed beard of the stage Frenchman. He was trained in the opulent Edwardian tradition of *la grande cuisine*, and claimed to have cooked for Kaiser Wilhelm II and the European aristocracy.

Dinner cost one guinea [$12.20], an enormous sum in the days of sixpenny [55c] meals. The menu proclaimed the motto: *Honi Soit Qui Mal Y Mange*. Music was provided by an

Buckley and Nunn's tea rooms were a popular meeting place for Melbourne women. In 1921 the store advertised that its tea rooms were second to none for tasteful surroundings and 'would compare favourably with any tea room in any capital city in the world'

unusual combination of violin and harp. Denat presided in the kitchen, sustaining himself with a bottle of cognac a day. Ernesto Molina, one of his cooks, later opened his own restaurant in Melbourne.

In 1920, Denat sold out to Samuel Wynn, a small wine merchant who later founded S. Wynn and Company. Soon after his retirement, Denat went to sleep on the dummy of a cable tram, fell off, and was killed.

Change of name
In 1928, the Café Denat moved to Bourke Street, and its name was changed to the Florentino when it was taken over by Rinaldo Massoni, a former instrument maker, and a friend of Fasoli. The first chef at the Florentino was a handsome Roman, Salvatore, who had been sweet cook to King Victor Emanuel, and was brought to Australia by the South Australia Hotel. He too, later opened his own restaurant.

These men, with Camillo Triaca of the Latin Cafe, Mario Vigano of Mario's and Beppi Codognotto of the Italian Society—later the Society Restaurant—introduced Melbourne to good Italian cooking long before the gastronomic explosion that began in the 1960s and has continued.

Before the restaurant boom, Sydney in 1948, for example, had at the most four good restaurants and hundreds of steak-and-egg, pies-and-peas cafés and milk bars. There were very few places where you could drink wine with your meals.

In 1983, Sydney had nearly 3000 restaurants, of which over 1000 were licensed. There has been a similar growth in other states. In 1985, Brisbane, a city once not noted for gastronomy, had over 130 licensed restaurants and in Canberra the number increased from 36 to 190 in just over 10 years.

'Ethnic' restaurants have also proliferated. The first Lebanese restaurant in Australia opened in Sydney in 1953. Vietnamese refugees introduce Australians to another exotic cuisine in the late 1970s and Japanese, Korean and Thai restaurants are now common in the major cities.

In earlier years, almost the only alternative to 'meat-and-two-veg' meals in cities and towns all over Australia was Chinese food in a pseudo-Cantonese cuisine devised for Western tastes. Standard dishes were chop suey, chow mein and sweet-and-sour-pork. There were few properly qualified Chinese chefs available to educate Australian palates. In the 1980s, an influx of true Chinese chefs brought to Sydney and Melbourne some of the best Chinese food in the world.

Restaurants for the Chinese
Few white Australians knew any Chinese food at the beginning of the century. In 1908, a contributor to Melbourne *Punch* wrote that the Chinese were the only foreign citizens of Melbourne who had formed 'a real colony of their own—with their own special shops and their own special restaurants'.

He described the curious cuisine of these restaurants: 'You get "long soup" which has a sort of macaroni in ropes that you could trail across the room . . . It is a satisfying dish. After only one long soup—three-penn'orth—the ordinary stomach will feel it can go without refilling for a week. "Short soup" has the macaroni in smaller hunks. There are little pies, reputed to contain "duck and fowl" and queer celestial sweetmeats. If the proprietor wishes, however, he can give you a cup of rare tea; pale China tea of delicate flavour which you may not like if you are used to the India and Ceylon teas which are served in most Australian households.'

Changing standards and tastes

Victoria outlaws the food adulterators

Victoria was the first Australian state to enact pure food regulations. An international conference held in Paris in 1908 passed a resolution applauding Victoria for its Pure Food Act of 1905. According to *The Lone Hand* this would never have come into being but for the overwhelming pressure of public opinion brought to bear as the result of exposures made by the Victorian Government Analyst, W. Percy Wilkinson.

The most popular temperance drinks of the 1900s—mostly consumed by women and children—were raspberry vinegar and raspberry syrup. The many manufacturers of these drinks adorned their bottles with mouth-watering labels suggesting that the principal ingredient was the juice of fresh raspberries. But in November 1902, Wilkinson analysed 44 representative samples and found that 43 of them were blends of coal-tar dye, cochineal, salicylic acid and saccharin. There was no trace of raspberry juice.

'A pound of coal-tar dye costing a few shillings could colour a volume of water equal to that of the pure juice of at least two tons of raspberries,' he reported. 'The raspberry-growers of this state may be said to be labouring in vain; by honest toil they produce pure fruit for which they find scant demand.' Wilkinson urged that the 'knavish practices' of the soft drink manufacturers should be extinguished by law, but it was not until 1913 that legislation was passed in all the States, to ensure that raspberry vinegar and raspberry syrup should contain at least 20 per cent by weight of raspberry juice.

Wilkinson also examined other beverages sold in Victoria, and found that of 266 samples of Australian wine, 167 were adulterated—either with salicylic acid (a chemical then widely used for burning out corns) or saccharin, or both. Of several hundred samples of Australian beer, 40 per cent were adulterated, and many were unfit for safe human consumption.

The indefatigable Wilkinson then turned his attention to sausages, and reported that most of Melbourne's pork sausages contained considerable quantities of starch, bread, flour and water, with chemical preservatives, but no pig meat. A sample of Sydney sausages contained over 50 per cent of water.

In 1908, *The Lone Hand* published a comprehensive list of foods that were adulterated in New South Wales:

Flour—mixed with other cereals, alum and mineral substances.

Confectionery—glucose, saccharin, alcohol, caramel, artificial colouring substances.

Milk and cream—water, boric acid, boron compounds, formaldehyde (formalin), carbonate of lime, peroxide of hydrogen, annatto and coal-tar colours.

Butter and cheese—boric acid, formaldehyde, salicylic acid, fluorine compounds, coal-tar dyes.

Meat and poultry—injected with preparations of sulphurous acid to keep the bright red colour in the meat, and as a preservative.

Pickled vegetables—verdigris, and sulphate of copper.

Jams and jellies—vegetable pulps, salicylic acid, glucose, fluorine compounds.

Potted meats—benzoic acid, salicylic acid, coal-tar dyes, sulphurous acid and sulphites.

Hams—alum for whitening and hardening.

Tea—old tea leaves, collected from restaurants and treated with gum and chemicals; excessive mineral matter.

Coffee—chicory, roasted wheat, barley, burnt refuse and toast.

Tomato sauce—yellow pumpkin, apple pulp coloured and flavoured to deceive the consumer.

Pepper—ground olive stones and ground rice.

Olive oil—peanut oil from China; cottonseed, maize and other cheap oils.

Cream of tartar—'terra alba' (pipe clay), and gypsum. As a substitute, acid phosphate of lime was frequently used.

Baking powder—part of the bicarbonate was replaced by carbonate of ammonia; the whole was then mixed with a quarter of its weight of starch and flour, and sold as the genuine article.

Not what they seemed

'With a little less sugar, these liquids might be used as red ink,' reported the NSW Government Analyst after examining samples of raspberry syrup. Hop beer, another popular temperance drink of the 1900s, was found in Victoria to contain up to 4 per cent alcohol

Learning to eat unfamiliar seafoods

Australians, despite their 19,300 kilometre coastline, are not great fish eaters. Their average yearly consumption is only about 7 kg per head—about 8 per cent of their meat consumption. Sydneysiders are the biggest fish-eaters, averaging 11.69 kg per head but this is trifling compared with Hong Kong's 49 kg a head, Iceland's 43 kg and Japan's 36 kg.

European immigrants are slowly pushing up the Australian average by their taste for seafoods, especially unfamiliar varieties that Australians have long neglected—such as octopus, squid, and cuttlefish.

T. C. Roughley, for many years Superintendent of New South Wales Fisheries, in his classic *Fish and Fisheries of Australia* (1951) gave his selection of 'the best half-dozen fish in Australia': the pearl perch, john dory, Tasmanian trumpeter, Westralian jewfish, Murray cod and barramundi.

The barramundi, he pointed out, was also a favourite food of the north Queensland aborigines, who wrapped it in the leaves of the wild ginger plant and baked it in hot ashes—an indigenous Australian recipe which white people in Queensland sometimes copy today.

In 1954, a visiting team of American spearfishermen were surprised to find that the abalone, though abundant in our coastal waters, was despised as food. It was collected only for its pretty iridescent shell.

Australians who knew it by such unappetising names as mutton-fish, sea ear or warty ear shell, found it too tough to eat. This was because it was cooked according to the bush recipe for cooking galah—'boil with a brick till the brick becomes soft, and then throw the galah away'.

The Americans explained that the tough flesh of the abalone becomes even tougher with prolonged cooking. Abalone should be cooked in bubbling oil for no more than 45 seconds with batter, or 30 seconds without.

Now that Australians have learned how to cook abalone, they like it so much and seek it so eagerly that some beds are in danger of being wiped out.

New foods introduced by immigrants

The great revolution in Australian eating began about 1937, when thousands of Europeans—Germans, Austrians and Czechs—fled their homelands to escape Nazi persecution. Among them were men with experience of food processing. There were also professional men who, knowing they would be unable to practise in Australia without further qualifications, had taken brief trade courses or brought with them recipes for sausages, pickled cucumbers, sauerkraut, breads and confectionery.

For example, Hans Otto Stern, a former German film comedian, arrived in Australia in 1938 with a recipe in his pocket for pumpernickel, a dense black bread made from rye and molasses. Before long, Stern had set up a pumpernickel factory in Sydney, and his products were selling widely.

'Their supremacy will soon be challenged,' wrote Gerald Stewart in the Sydney magazine *A.M.* in June 1952. And Stewart, himself a refugee from Germany, reported on the changing gastronomic scene: 'Liverwurst is spreading itself over thousands of Australian sandwiches each day, and a growing number of Viennese and knackwursts take the plunge into Australian saucepans. Hostesses serve pretzels, pumpernickel, and Continental cucumbers for supper, and food-processing plants work hard to satisfy Australian's newly-acquired appetite for sauerkraut.'

The traditional Australian 'ham-and-beef' shop became transformed into a well-stocked delicatessen, and Australians who had known only two or three varieties of sausage, including the ubiquitous 'pork fritz' or Devon, and the saveloy or 'sav', now titillated their taste-buds with such exotics as *cabanossi, clobacki, debriciner, knackwurst, mettwurst, mortadella* and *salame, coppa* and *prosciutto*.

They discovered too, that there were many other kinds of cheese besides the inevitable mild or tasty of the old ham-and-beef shop.

In the 1920s, all these foods—even fresh pineapple—were unfamiliar to many Australians. Now all are readily obtainable if not commonplace. Wine, once a novelty, now often appears on suburban dinner tables

When paw-paws, grapefruit and avocados were novelties

'The Australian is not a gourmet where food is concerned,' said a writer in the Sydney *Sun* in 1921. 'Beyond fruit salads and such things he has not evolved a national menu. But there is time yet. Fruit for breakfast is growing as a habit, though thousands can still get out of bed on a hot morning and face eggs and bacon without a qualm.'

About ten years later tropical fruits from Queensland were appearing shyly in the more exclusive Melbourne fruit shops. 'The celebrated paw-paw (pronounced p-pyah) are now obtainable at one shilling each,' reported *Table Talk* in September 1930. 'And the citizen who has had a large slice of it flavoured with lemon for breakfast is prepared to swear that it is the queen of fruits. The mango is coming south, too, and also the grenadilla (passion-fruit) and cape strawberries, and as for pineapples, they can be had in perfect condition for a shilling.'

About the same time, the grapefruit made its Australian debut. 'Grapefruit is an acquired taste, like olives and oysters, but once you have got to like it, you will want to eat it whenever it is in season,' said *Table Talk* in July 1931.

The avocado, a native of Central America and the West Indies, was also slow to win acceptance in Australia. In 1883, an avocado tree in Brisbane's Botanic Gardens bore fruit, and in 1914 a few trees were cultivated in Sydney—but in tubs and purely as decorative plants.

But as late as November 1932, H. Jenkyns was writing in the Sydney magazine *The Home* that the avocado—then sometimes wrongly termed the alligator pear—was unknown in Australia, except to a few gastronomes dotted about the cities and to a small number of growers in Queensland. 'It may be seen sometimes in one or two fruit shops . . . taking its slender chance of being seized upon by its devotees, but its humble form is rarely distinguished from among that glittering and tropical concourse of pineapples, bananas, custard apples and mangoes that are its climatic brethren . . .

'It may be eaten like a boiled egg with pepper and salt or in a dessert with sugar and lemon juice. In America, it is used principally as a salad food with French dressing, and as it grows in popularity it will undoubtedly take its place as one of the world's greatest fruits,' he wrote confidently.

Queensland farmers in the Nambour-Tamborine area grew avocados mainly as shade trees, or windbreaks. Many did not bother to pick the fruit. During World War II, roving GI's were astonished to find avocados rotting on the ground. They bought them eagerly, enthused over them, and taught Australians how to eat them.

In 1943, avocados, still often called 'alligator pears', were selling in Sydney for 1s [$1.17] each, and New South Wales was growing them at experimental stations in Grafton and Wollongbar. 'When it becomes widely known this attractive fruit will be cultivated as a fine payable crop for tropical areas,' prophesied the Melbourne magazine *Walkabout* in August 1943.

Eating without formality

Australia's own meat pie

Sydney's Lord Mayor, Alderman David Griffin, made a memorable pronouncement in 1972. 'Australia,' he said, 'is built on meat pies, sausages and galvanised iron.'

The origin of the Australian pie is lost in the mists of history, but more than a century ago—in the 1850s—the Melbourne Argus reported a debate in the Melbourne City Council on the quality of the food served in the council chambers. One disgruntled councillor declared that rather than eat the awful council food, he would go across to the Bull and Mouth for one of their marvellous beefsteak pies. (The Bull and Mouth, a famous Bourke Street hotel dating back to the Gold Rush, was demolished in 1935.)

By the 1930s the meat pie was so well established it began to be enshrined as the 'national dish'—which as Richard Beckett points out in his book *Convicted Tastes* like judging Italian food tastes on the consumption of pizza alone.

In the 1960s, Sydney pie magnate Peter Scott said that his firm catered for Parliament House, royal visits and VIP functions. Thousands of pies were sent overseas for Australian Government entertainments. 'Internationally,' he said, 'people think of Australia in terms of beer, pies, boomerangs and sometimes wool.'

Australian pies were a feature of an Australian Night dinner given in Tokyo in 1971 by the chairman of the Australian Tourist Commission, Mr C.A. Greenway. The 2579 guests consumed 200 dozen pies lubricated with 192 bottles of tomato sauce, as well as 100 dozen oysters and 150 dozen saveloys. Mr Greenway was surprised that they ate their pies with forks.

On its Christmas dinner menu in 1972, the Bali Beach Hotel offered a 'meat pie, Australian style'. The writer Max Harris nostalgically tried one, but found that the Indonesian chef had been unable to capture 'the soggy, thin, meatless sophistication' and the 'mass of agglutinous pastry' of the dinkum Aussie pie.

Despite occasionally being the food of mockery in some circles and despite the onslaughts of other take-away foods, the meat pie holds its own. In 1982 a Melbourne

Pie carts drawn by ponies tinkling bells on their harness were once a feature of Toowoomba, Queensland. To the right of the pieman, in a special holder, is the essential tomato sauce bottle. To the connoisseur a meat pie without tomato sauce is like corned beef without carrots

manufacturer opened a pie factory capable of producing 100,000 in an hour. The firm generally sells one pie to every 2 or 3 people at a football match; about half the crowd watching an Australian Rules final will down a pie each. Half a million pies a day leave the factory to be sold fresh, refrigerated in supermarkets, or frozen for transport over long distances, whether to the north and west of Australia or exported to such countries as Saudi Arabia, Japan, the United States and Britain.

In 1984 in New South Wales, the State Rail Authority resurrected the 'railway pie', once synonymous with the blandness of Railway Refreshment Room catering. The railways catering service, which received a bronze plaque of appreciation for supplying six dozen railway pies a week to a sergeant's mess during the Vietnam war, recreated the delicacy born in the 1920s. It then cost threepence with sauce or fourpence with peas and gravy (32c or 46c); in 1964 it was voted by a Sydney newspaper 'the State's best pie'. As a handy snack, the pie is perpetual.

What's in a pie

Fat	32 grams
Water	70 grams
Protein	13.4 grams
Vitamin A	327 micrograms
Carbohydrate	44.9 grams
Riboflavin	2.3 milligrams
Thiamin	0.174 milligrams
Niacin	2.4 milligrams
Calcium	58 milligrams
Iron	2.1 milligrams

Here is a nutritionist's analysis of a typical pie, which weighed 163 grams. It also contained 2170 kilojoules. In New South Wales, government regulations say a pie must weigh 140-155 g with at least 25 per cent meat filling, and the meat must be no more than one-third fat. Nearly half of this pie was made up of water

Memories of the free counter lunch

Before World War II, free counter lunches were an essential part of drinking in every Australian hotel. They varied in quality from the humble snags-and-mash—with tomato sauce—to satisfying repasts of roast meats, poultry, curries, salads, and even oysters.

In Sydney, at Adam's famous Marble Bar—which was reconstructed in the Hilton Hotel—a special counter lunch was served on Saturday mornings before the races. The food was displayed on a long trestle table and a white-coated, white-hatted chef sliced turkey and ham and distributed the accompaniments with skill and decorum. In Melbourne, the Bull and Mouth specialised in hot roast rabbit, and Hadleys in Hobart was famous for its curried scallops.

Curried and spiced, fried in batter, or served with hot gravy, scallops were served during the season in most Tasmanian hotels. It was the accepted thing to drop in for a plate at 11 in the morning, or between 5 and 6 in the early evening.

'Hobart hotel patrons fare pretty well so far as counter lunches are concerned, as there is always a good stack of cold meats, salads, sandwiches, from which to choose at any time,' wrote a contributor to *Walkabout* in January 1942. 'But it is the hot scallop...that fills the bar room at the scheduled hours.'

'This pub-habit of freely feeding the beerhound was an Australian thing,' Jack Lindsay wrote nostalgically in 1960, when the habit was only a dim memory.

A counter lunch of oysters in 1940

Soda fountains and milk bars

The 1920s ushered in Australia's Soda Fountain and Sundae Age. Elaborate soda fountains, copied from American models, flourished in all the big cities. The first, The Golden Gate, was opened in Sydney in 1921 by a Californian, S. M. McKimmin, and become the best-known soda fountain in Australia.

When it closed its doors in 1933, *The Australian Confectioner* lamented: 'It's a business tragedy.' But it could not be helped. 'It was the inevitable effect of the "depression", and the ever-growing competition of cheap-jack places.' There were many of them.

In 1923, the Wattle Path Palais de Danse in St Kilda, Melbourne, claimed to have installed the biggest soda fountain in the Southern Hemisphere. It was a gaudy complex of marble, onyx, leadlights and mirrors, 8.8 m long, with 16 syrup pumps gushing forth the ingredients for a dazzling variety of drinks.

The soda fountains also served sundaes—the word originated in America in 1904—and the recipes for these became more and more extravagant as competition increased. Here are a couple from a Melbourne trade magazine of the 1930s:

DELMONICO BANANA SUNDAE Lay on lettuce leaves on a platter a split banana, and on this put two dishers of ice cream. Pour crushed maraschino cherries over one and crushed raspberries over the other, with a ladle of whipped cream in the centre, sprinkle with chopped nuts and a whole cherry.

BOMB SUNDAE Put a round disher of vanilla ice cream round side down in a sundae dish. Make a small depression in the centre of the flat top with a spoon and put into it a red and a green cherry and two pineapple cubes. Cover with another disher of ice cream, of some other flavour if possible, flat side down, so as to make a ball. Dress with whipped cream to look like smoke.

In 1923, the Eskimo Pie reached Australia. It was an ice cream and chocolate confection, made under licence in Sydney and sold in a foil wrapper imported from the USA.

Milk bars appeared in Sydney, Melbourne and Brisbane in 1933. The pioneer Sydney establishment in Martin Place had an electric cow in the window. This was copied in Brisbane. The standard price of drinks at milk bars was 4d [57c], except when eggs were used. Ice-cream sodas cost 6d [83c] and sundaes 9d [$1.24]

The first milk bar in London was opened in 1935 by an Australian, the boxing promoter, theatrical entrepreneur and newspaper proprietor Hugh D. McIntosh, who began his career in the mines at Broken Hill, made many fortunes, and died a pauper.

Soda fountains, fitted with ornate pumps like these, were the rage in the 1920s. By 1937, when the photograph below was taken, milk bars had gained wide popularity in Australia

New kinds of fast food challenge the traditional

'The hunger for standardised American-style fast-foods is shattering old tradition and cooking up a global future-shock orgy of fried chicken, block-buster hamburgers, steaming pizzas, crispy French fries, and thick milkshakes,' reported the American magazine *Newsweek* in October 1972.

The Australian 'orgy' began when 'Colonel' Sanders, the benign Kentuckian who claimed to hold an honorary commission in the Kentucky National Guard, opened his first fried chicken dispensary in Australia. That was at Guildford, NSW, in 1968. Today, there are 236 of them, each with its standard red-and-white striped roof and picture of the smiling colonel.

According to *Newsweek* the recipe for his chickens consists of 'one part food, one part packaging, and one part mythology'. But it sells 1.5 million meals a day. The fingerlickin' flavouring is a closely guarded secret.

The flamboyant colonel's invasion of Australia's fast food or take-away food market was soon challenged by other outlets. About 20 chicken, hamburger and fish-and-chips chains and three ice-cream chains sprang up after 1968. Some were Australian-owned, others subsidiaries of overseas firms. Many, to use a gastronomic idiom, bit off more than they could chew.

Kentucky Fried Chicken was followed in 1969 by Red Barn; in 1970, by Beef Ranch, Mr Chips, Henny Penny Chicken, Cap'n Abe's Fish and Chips, and Burger Chef; and in 1971, by Clancy's (a subsidiary of H. J. Heinz), Pizza Hut, Wimpy Hamburger Bars, Church's Fried Chicken, Hartee's and the giant McDonald's. Only Kentucky, Pizza Hut and McDonald have a big share of the market today; the rest were taken over, went bankrupt, or failed to expand. As an American expert Howard Bellin puts it: 'Fast food does not mean a fast buck. The food business has the highest failure rate of all retail businesses.'

The universally standardised Big Mac burger can be bought at 156 McDonald's restaurants in Australia. Australians apparently like to know what they are getting on their plates: equally regulated pizzas can be eaten at 130 Pizza Huts.

The pioneer of pizzas (the correct plural of *pizza*, which means 'pie', is *pizze*) in Australia was an Italian, John Battista. He came to Australia in 1949, as chef on an Italian liner, and stayed to cook for Italian diplomatic missions, first in Sydney, then in Canberra.

Then he launched the pizza on the Australian public, convinced that the food most Australians did not know how to pronounce would become as popular as in America. By 1966, although the *Australian Women's Weekly* and even the *Australian Confectioners' and Restaurant Journal* both still found it necessary to explain to their readers what a pizza was, Battista was selling 12,000 pizzas every week. The number doubled in the next five years.

The first pizza shop in Melbourne, Toto's, in Lygon Street, Carlton, opened in 1966. Three years later the pizza boom was under way. Today there are pizza restaurants in country towns such as Boulder, Cobar and Bordertown; Sydney alone has 140 take-away pizza shops.

In 1969 there were 3468 take-away food outlets Australia-wide. In 1980, 25 cents of each dollar spent on food was for food eaten away from home. By 1988 Australians are likely to be spending $5000 million a year on eating and drinking in restaurants, clubs and take-away outlets. The choice has expanded vastly from meat pies, hamburgers, pizzas and the spaghetti sandwiches that appalled and amazed the distinguished food writer and restaurateur Robert Carrier. It is now possible to eat a Mexican meal in Darwin, an Indian meal in Launceston and a Mauritian meal in Sydney.

Australia has still a long way to go to rival the United States, where it is estimated that fast foods account for one-fifth of the $30 billion the nation spends annually on food in all its hotels and restaurants.

Deep-frozen foods—poultry, fish, fruits and vegetables—appeared on the Australian market in 1957 to almost universal acceptance. 'There is little doubt that this most recent development is here to stay and that it will eventually have an influence on the Australian food consumption pattern', wrote R. C. Hutchison in 1958. 'The great selling point...is that they bring to the home kitchen essentially fresh fruits and vegetables out of season, and maybe thousands of miles from where they are harvested.'

Today, with refrigerators in 97 per cent of Australian homes, frozen foods have certainly changed the pattern of Australian eating. In 1965, Australia produced 35 million kg of frozen vegetables. By 1983, the figure had risen to 178.9 million kg.

Changing tastes in drink

Australians discover their own wine

At the turn of the century, when France was annually consuming 136 litres of wine a head and Italy 109 litres, the average Australian consumption was just over 4.5 litres a head, a figure which remained constant for decades.

Consumption of wine in the early 1900s varied greatly from state to state. South Australia drank 15 litres—nearly 20 bottles—a head, followed by Victoria with 6 litres, and Western Australia with 4.5 litres. At the bottom of the list came Tasmania, with consumption of only 0.68 litres a head.

Australia had been making good wine almost from the first days of settlement, but not drinking it, a fact which often puzzled observers from abroad. In this, as in most of their living habits, Australians inherited the Englishman's preference for beer and spirits.

'Why is it that the Australian, who has now learned to make wine, has not yet learned to drink it?' asked *The Lone Hand* in 1909. It blamed the system of distribution. Hotels did not serve Australian wine. Most of it was drunk in squalid wine bars, the haunts of prostitutes and thieves. And these places only stocked cheap and potent fortified wines, indiscriminately labelled port, muscat or sweet sherry. Light table wines were unknown.

The New South Wales Director of Health, Dr W. G. Armstrong, interviewed in 1921 said: 'If you must drink alcohol, drink Australian wines or light beers. But I think Australian wines are better than anything.'

The New South Wales Premier, Mr James Dooley, was also an advocate of Australian wine. But few Australians followed their example, and 10 years later, a writer in *Table Talk* observed: 'Australians have a singularly

deep-rooted suspicion of wine. Beer, whisky, rum, brandy—any of them is a hearty fellow without a stain on his character. But wine is treated as circumspectly as a tawdry lady of questionable morals at a church bazaar.'

Wine was little more respectable in 1951, when a writer in the Sydney magazine *A.M.* said: 'The typical Australian wine saloon is like a hangover from Hogarth—a dingy rendezvous for the disreputable, dedicated to the sale of cheap ports and sherries. Ask in one of these chambers of horrors for a glass of light wine, an iced refreshing hock, a soft caressing claret—and you're likely to evoke a menacing grunt or a contemptuous guffaw. Take your girl-friend in for an amiable drink and she'll probably slap your face and walk out on you...

'The bewildered visitor to Australia, when he learns, if by accident he ever does, of the excellence of our wines, looks in vain for somewhere where he can sample them in comfort, for the inviting, tree-shaded café table on the footpath or in the park. He returns to the Old World, wondering at the eccentricity of us wild colonial boys, who with an incomparable climate, and with vistas as lovely as those of Alexandra Avenue, the Swan River, or Sydney Harbour, do our drinking in the hogswill foetor of hotel bars, and who, with the cheapest, good wines in the world, do little or nothing to encourage their general use.'

Between 1961 and 1983 there have been many changes in the eating and drinking habits of Australians. They have consumed less meat and butter, and more fish, vegetables, fruit and coffee, beer and wine.

Beer consumption has risen from 102.7 litres a year a person to nearly 122 in recent

years. But the most remarkable change has been in wine consumption which was nine litres a person a year in 1961, but had risen to almost 20 litres by 1983.

The increasing popularity of wine was undoubtedly influenced by the growth of national and ethnic restaurants, where wine was considered a natural accompaniment to food. The easier availability of wine in casks and flagons also assisted the change, and in 1984 34.5 million litres of dry red was sold, and 175.3 million litres of dry white wine. In the same year Australians bought no less than 17.5 million litres of port.

Australian wines were slow to win recognition in the United Kingdom for many reasons. Most of the exports were cheap fortified wines, and Australian table wines have been sold in England under misleading or ridiculous labels. To call an Australian wine burgundy, hock, or sauternes is to misrepresent it. And some of the other names given to Australian wines in England seem to have been devised by practical jokers.

The 1907 catalogue of London's Army and Navy Stores lists a number of Australian wines including '"Melbonia"—Burgundy type', at 19s [$47] a dozen, and '"Perthonia"—Hermitage type', at 27s [$66] a dozen. Other enticing Australian wine names are 'Emu Cabernet', 16s [$39] a dozen and 'Harvest Burgundy', 13s [$32] a dozen. Things were slow to change but by 1985 Australian wines—with proper varietal labels—had become so accepted by the British consumer that a sales increase of almost half in that year made wine the fastest growing export to Britain.

"Ah! my PENFOLD'S!

Thanks Nurse."

Bottling Emu wine for the British market. The name Emu was no advantage, but neither is the practice of using European wine names. '... I'm inclined to think the practice is something of a hindrance to the advancement of sales in the British quality market,' mused a writer in the London *Times* in 1971

The founder of Penfolds, Dr Christopher Rawson Penfold, a general practitioner, believed strongly in the therapeutic properties of port, and in 1844 he planted a vineyard to make wine for anaemic patients. Port especially used to be valued for anaemic people. In this century it was a recognised prescription item and even sold by chemists. Some ports are still labelled 'invalid port'. In 1984 Australians bought more than 17.4 million litres of port, a remarkable quantity

The six o'clock swill

For many years after World War I, the six o'clock swill in Australian hotels was a unique phenomenon that wide-eyed tourists talked about, wrote about, and recorded in movies to show sceptics back home. Feature writers described it in such dissimilar publications as *The Saturday Evening Post* and *Pravda*.

'The average Englishman, accustomed to his friendly and civilized inns and pubs, possesses an almost pathological interest in the riotous wildness of Australian drinking,' wrote George Johnston in *The Sunburnt Country*, a symposium presented to Queen Elizabeth II in 1953. So had the average American. 'Your five to six o'clock swill hit some American Olympic Games visitors between the eyes ... It is a most interesting sight,' said J. Lyngham Bingham, of the US Games committee, in 1956.

Early closing as patriotism

Before World War I, Australian hotels were open until 11.30 p.m. Temperance organisations had campaigned vigorously for decades to reduce trading hours, in the fallacious belief that this would reduce drunkenness. The war enabled them to make a patriotic issue of early closing. They had the inspiring example of King George V, who in April 1915 had banned all alcoholic drinks from the Royal Household for the duration of the war. So one by one, New South Wales, Victoria, South Australia and Tasmania introduced six o'clock closing, also for the duration of the war. But the war ended, and early closing remained, and with it, the famous six o'clock swill.

Jack Lindsay gives a vivid picture of the Sydney scene in *The Roaring Twenties*: 'All around the bar a heaving mass of men elbowing, pushing, trampling on each other's feet, and shouting their orders. Reaching over shoulders, waving pound-notes, dropping irretrievable coins. The one time when even the most pugnacious of Australians had no time to pick a quarrel, intent only on attracting the attention of those floating goddesses, the pink-bosomed pneumatic barmaids...'

The Melbourne swill is evoked equally vividly by Keith Dunstan, in *Wowsers*: 'Like the last moments before an execution, time ticks away, tension mounts and mounts... It is ten to six, now five to six, the bar is ten deep with pushing bodies, all thrusting handfuls of glasses towards the barmaids... But now it is two minutes to six, the mob is getting desperate, like the last few fighting for the lifeboats on a sinking ship.' Afterwards the crowd would stagger out to the footpath, some clutching bottles desperately, others reeling.

The typical Australian bar in the bad old days of the swill was starkly functional, with brown linoleum on the floor and bar, and tiled walls. There was no furniture to slow down the process of dispensing as much beer as possible to as many men as possible. Tasmania changed to 10 o'clock closing in 1937, New South Wales in 1955, Victoria in 1966, and South Australia in 1967. Once the most restrictive state, South Australia now has drinking hours as long as any other state in Australia. And the six o'clock swill has passed into legend.

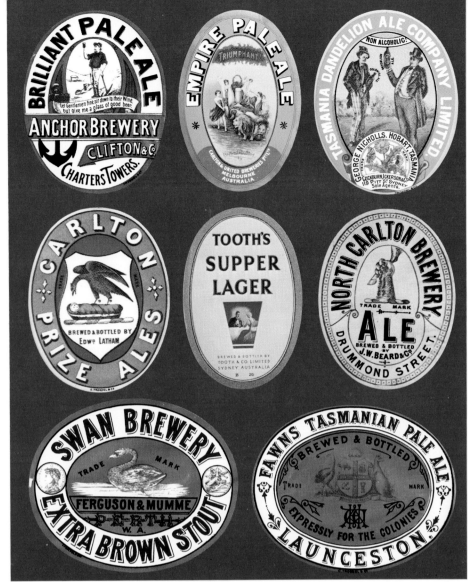

Many old beer bottle labels were rich and colourful. Some even bore messages. 'Let Gentlemen fine sit down to their Wine, but give me a glass of good beer', proclaims the Anchor Brewery's miner. The prosperous drinker of Dandelion Ale is contrasted with the deadbeat who drinks 'colonial aie'

Sydney breweries once liked to suggest that beer was the choice of elegant sophisticates in evening dress. This poster dates from 1939

Vanished breweries

The loyal Australian who wished to toast the newborn Commonwealth in nut-brown ale had an astonishing variety of brews to choose from. There were 21 breweries in Sydney alone, and beer was brewed in at least 35 country towns in New South Wales. Victoria had 50 breweries.

Some of this multitude of breweries were small family-owned establishments, with an output of as little as 1000 hogsheads a year (a hogshead is 209 litres, or 276 bottles). You could buy one as a going concern for as little as a few thousand pounds [$40,000 to $50,000].

Many of these breweries disappeared soon after Federation, when the Commonwealth Beer Excise Act of 1901 imposed stringent regulations on brewers. Sixteen Sydney breweries closed down in 1901, and one by one, in Victoria as well as in New South Wales, the survivors were taken and amalgamated into giant companies.

In 1907, when the number of breweries in Victoria had dwindled to 37, Carlton and United Breweries Ltd was formed to take over six of the State's biggest breweries— Carlton Brewery, McCracken's City Brewery and the Victoria, Castlemaine, Shamrock and Foster Breweries.

At the start of the second decade of the Commonwealth, Australian beer consumption stood at 125 litres a person a year. In 1978 it was 137 litres, but it had known a sharp decline in the Depression years when it dropped to 33.81 litres.

The smoking habit

Pipes give way to ready-made cigarettes

Australians at the turn of the century were—as they remain—heavy smokers. The amount of tobacco smoked in a year equalled nearly 1.3 kg a head, more than double the annual consumption of the United Kingdom.

Men who could afford them smoked cigars, but the popular smoke was a pipe. 'Anyone detected smoking a cigarette was suspected of habits obnoxious to an exclusively male earth,' Norman Lindsay recalled. 'Tobacco in those days was a cult and the pipe its holy symbol. Religious frenzy was exploded over the virtues of briars, clays, meerschaums, cherry-woods, corn-cobs, or even German porcelain bowls with a yard of cherry-wood stem. Friendships barely survived conflict of opinion over whether dry or damp tobacco smokes best, and brands of tobacco were discussed as gourmets acclaim rare vintages.'

Pipes for 3d each

In July 1908 the tobacco department of Grace Brothers' store in Sydney offered a wide range of products for the smoker. The most elaborate pipe cost 13s [$30.20], while Vienna-made cherry-woods were offered at 3d, 6d and 8d each [65c, $1.16, $1.53]. The most expensive pipe tobacco cost 6s 3d [$14.50] a half kilo—the equivalent nowadays of about 87 cents per 30 grams. Pipes strengthened with a silver band were particularly popular in the bush, where a broken pipe-stem could be a tragedy.

'Respectable' women, of course, did not smoke at all. And the few 'advanced' women who occasionally puffed a cigarette did not dare to do so in public. (In 1896, the Duchess de Clermont Tonnerre had shocked London society by smoking a cigarette in the dining-room of the Savoy Hotel.)

'Whether or not it is correct for ladies to smoke, or whether or not men like to see them smoking, are much mooted questions at the present time,' wrote 'Minetta', in Melbourne *Punch*, in March 1904. 'In the poorer classes old women take to smoking as a solace and a comfort. In their case it is a less evil than drinking. In the upper classes, it seems to me it is more a fad and fashion than a desire . . .' But four years later, another woman columnist in *Punch* wrote: 'Fragrance of lavender, scent of rose-leaves, are not the only perfumes which cling to ladies' boudoirs. The cigarette habit has apparently come to stay. Little smoking is done in public. Our women have not attained the Continental disregard for worn-out conventions. In Paris and London it is "the thing" to smoke unabashed, provided you have got over the splutter and choking stage.

'A Melbourne tobacconist who has made a speciality in dainty cigarettes to suit the feminine palate, assures me that quite fifty percent of the "Best People" are now smoking in this city . . . The Railway Commissioners are said to have ordered designs for ladies' smoking carriages, out of respect for the prejudices of men, who do not like the company of ladies when smoking.'

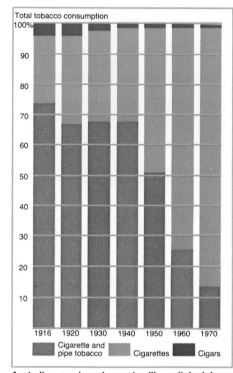

Total tobacco consumption

Australian smokers have steadily switched from pipes and hand-rolled cigarettes to ready-made cigarettes since World War II. This graph shows changing proportions in smoking of cigars, ready-made cigarettes and pipe and cigarette tobacco. Overall tobacco consumption in 1982 was 2.8 kg per person, but smoking is less popular. Forty per cent of the population smoked in 1968; 34% in 1983

"Milo" Cigarettes.

A daring Sydney show girl, Pansy Montagu, gave her stage name, 'La Milo', to a popular brand of cigarettes sold early this century

The Cameo cigarette was popular in Australia before World War I. It is not recorded whether this visual pun helped to increase its sales

Ally Sloper was the hero of the world's first regular comic strip, which appeared from 1884 to 1920 in a British weekly paper bearing his name

Popular brands of the past

1934-47

1911-24

COSMOS

TORTOISESHELL CIGARETTES

1909-36

1942-45

LUCY HINTON TOBACCO.

MANUFACTURED BY
W.D.& H.O.WILLS (AUSTRALIA) LTD
SYDNEY.

1909-42

"LOG CABIN"
FLAKED GOLD LEAF
CAVENDISH

2 OZ. NET WEIGHT WHEN PACKED

1919-74

"CAPSTAN" PLUG
Highest Grade Tobacco

W.D.& H.O.WILLS. (AUSTRALIA) LTD
SYDNEY.

1919-27

CROSS-CUT
CROSS-CUT
SMOKING TOBACCO

1909-19

GOLD FLAKE
HONEY DEW

1922-42

Cigarette card craze

In the heyday of cigarette cards, many series depicting Australian subjects were issued. These wildflowers date from 1912

Any man walking home from his train or tram in the earlier decades of this century was likely to be bailed up by a small boy with the cry: 'Got any cigarette cards, mister?' The first Australian cigarette cards appeared about 1904. They were a series depicting Australian footballers, issued by the Melbourne firm of Sniders and Abrahams, who marketed Standard, Peter Pan, King's Own and Milo Cigarettes. ('La Milo' was the stage name of a Sydney show-girl named Pansy Montagu who shocked or delighted Edwardian audiences with her scantily-clothed impersonations of Greek goddesses or nymphs. Having given her name to a popular cigarette in Australia, she became a success in England, where she was said to have earned £10,000 [$227,800] a year.)

The Australian footballers were followed by actresses (31 photographs, including two of Miss Montagu), admirals and warships of USA (coinciding with the visit of the Great White Fleet in 1908), animals, cricketers, jockeys, racehorses and racing scenes.

During World War I, there were series of Australian VCs and officers, crests of British warships, and great war leaders. Other subjects included Melbourne buildings, S. T. Gill's views of Victoria and stereoscope views of the world, for which a small folding viewer was available. Later series presented film stars and caricatures of well-known Australians, chiefly sporting heroes. Cards were still being issued with Standard and Turf cigarettes in 1934.

Almost all matches used in Australia were imported until 1909, when Bryant and May started a factory. In 1913 the Federal Match Company started. Australian-made matches came in boxes bearing Australian-inspired labels. Some foreign match companies then produced special Australian labels such as the English Kookaburra

THE KOOKABURRA
OR LAUGHING-JACKASS
IMPRECNATED
DAMP PROOF
AVERAGE CONTENTS 60 MATCHES
SAFETY MATCH
MADE IN ENGLAND

The wail of the wowser

Saving Australians from themselves

Australia has a rich and colourful slang, as the 6000 or more words in Sidney J. Baker's *The Australian Language* show, and at least one has gained international currency—the magnificent word 'wowser'. The great American lexicographer, H. L. Mencken, described it as an 'excellent noun' and himself used it. The sleuths of the big *Oxford English Dictionary* found it in the London *Daily News* in 1909, and next year, it even crept into the staid London *Morning Post*.

What is a wowser? The closest approximation in English is 'kill-joy' and in American, 'blue nose'. The Oxford Dictionary definition is 'a Puritanical enthusiast or fanatic'.

Australian definitions

In 1910, when Sydney's liberal-minded Cardinal Moran used the word three times in a speech, a newspaper held an enquiry into its meaning. William Holman, New South Wales Attorney-General, said a wowser was 'a man who, being entirely destitute of the greater virtues, makes up for their lack by a continuous denunciation of little vices'.

In 1912 the Premier of Western Australia, John Scaddan, gave a more succinct definition: 'a person who is more shocked at seeing two inches of underskirt than he would be at seeing a mountain of misery'.

Wowsers have exercised a dank and melancholy influence on Australian life, with their clamant objections to almost anything that made other people happy, from Sunday sport to dancing, from 'mixed bathing'—as it used to be called—to having a drink after 6 p.m.

Dancing has always been a prime target for the shock troops of wowserism. In 1903 the Rev. Dr Torrey, a Melbourne divine, announced that dancing was productive of all sorts of iniquities. 'If the girl knows what a man thinks when he is dancing with her, she would never dance again,' he declared.

In 1907 Lionel Lindsay wistfully imagined this open-air restaurant at Mrs Macquarie's Chair on the foreshore of Sydney Harbour. The people in the sketch enjoying a quiet drink would no doubt have scandalised the wowsers, who regarded drink as the cause of much evil and made every effort to have it banned

At the Methodist Conference in 1907, a suggestion was made that dancing was being taught at the Methodist Ladies' College in Melbourne. The founder and headmaster, the Rev. W. H. Fitchett, published a stern disclaimer in the Methodist church paper, *The Spectator*: 'Let me say that at the Methodist Ladies' College we do not teach dancing. A boarder, whose parents wish her to take this subject, is sent outside to learn it. We have no entertainments capable of being described as theatrical at the College. Once or twice a year, at social evenings, we have such innocent charades as girls may fitly play, and they are played only to an audience of other girls.'

In 1914 Sydney and Melbourne were introduced to the dance sensation from Argentina, the tango. The entrepreneur Hugh McIntosh, copying the current London craze, put on 'tango teas' at which the dance was demonstrated to eager learners who could then take the floor and practise it between their tea and cakes. To the scandalised wowsers there was something specially wicked about dancing in the afternoon, and the costume of Mr McIntosh's demonstrators was an additional outrage. 'The shock came when six lovely girls in silken bloomer-cum-petticoat array, over which they wore corsets—suspenders loose and all a-jingle—calmly walked before the audience with the complete self-possession of a woman in the privacy of her boudoir,' reported Melbourne *Punch*. 'A coat of black ninon, and boudoir cap, completed each one of these undress toilettes, that created more sensation than the tango.'

An antipodean Sodom

To many Melburnians, Sydney was an antipodean Sodom. 'Sydney has enjoyed two or three years of uninterrupted hedonism,' said Melbourne *Punch* in March 1914. 'It has been pleasure and liberty all the time, with a good deal of licence. It has seized on the tango and the jauntiest of music; its saloons intoxicate with a generous gaiety; its surf frolics have become world famous; it sports the X-ray skirt and the scantiest of fashionable modes.'

But a few months later, when the New South Wales Presbyterian Assembly denounced Sydney for its 'wicked dramas, shameful dresses, and naughty new dances', *Punch* commented philosophically: 'We remember that the bustle and the crinoline were just as hotly condemned in their day.' About the same time a clergyman in Ballarat denounced the 'disgusting improprieties' of women's dress, which he thought was designed 'for the purpose of arousing the lascivious instincts of men's minds'.

When the Palais de Danse was about to open on the bayside at St Kilda, Melbourne, with an announcement that the tango would be a nightly attraction, a clergyman named McNab predicted Melbourne's imminent 'moral downfall', and declared: 'Promiscuous dancing influences passions and will introduce a new element into St Kilda . . . It is easy to know what the result will be.'

A protest meeting of more than 700 citizens, chaired by the sombre McNab, perhaps

These Adelaide women gathered outside their State Parliament in 1938 to protest against a proposal to extend hotel closing hours. They won their case, and South Australia became the last state to abolish 6 o'clock closing, in 1967. The first state to abolish it was Tasmania, in 1937

influenced the Palais management to keep a watchful eye on its patrons. 'Be careful that you don't "rag",' warned a *Punch* writer. 'The authorities at the Palais de Danse are no respecters of persons . . . and if you so much as "wobble" or show the least tendency to a "two-step" a fierce attendant will approach you and order you off the floor like winking.'

In his 1917 Lenten pastoral letter, Dr Michael Kelly, Roman Catholic Archbishop of Sydney, denounced collectively 'the feast, the dance, the theatre, the racecourse, the stadium, the field sports, etc. . . .' and warned that those who spent their days 'in good cheer . . . in a moment go down to hell'.

When the Presbyterian Assembly in Perth in 1926 banned dancing at church functions, the Rev. Hugh Morris said: 'The first steps of a life of shame can be traced to the dance hall.' Delegates who feared that this might stop the highland fling being performed in a church hall were reassured that the highland fling was not a dance but a pastime. In 1935 the Rev. H. E. Wallis addressed the Methodist Mission in Fitzroy, Melbourne, on 'the Deadly Dance—a Draught of Poisoned Wine',

and quoted approvingly an anonymous doctor who, in a mess of metaphors, had said, 'the dance hall is the nursery of the Divorce Court, the training ship of prostitution and a modern ulcer that is threatening morality'.

Wowsers fought long and bitterly to make Sunday a day of gloom, often invoking archaic laws to serve their purpose. In 1900, a Melbourne barber was fined 5s [$12] for shaving a man on Sunday, under an act dating back to Charles II. And in 1908 a citizen of Scottsdale, Tasmania, was fined 20s [$46] because 'on the Lord's Day, commonly called Sunday, he did unlawfully travel with waggon and seven horses on the open King's highway' in violation of another 17th century statute.

Melbourne was the last city in the British Empire to allow its art gallery, public library and museum to open on Sundays. It was not until 1904 that, despite bitter protests from the wowsers, this ungodly step was taken. A law of 1889 prohibiting Sunday papers in Victoria was in force until 1969. Melbourne's wowser Sunday did not end officially until 1968, when an Act was passed permitting commercial sport on the Lord's Day.

Sydney Long's painting *The Flamingoes* shocked Dr Michael Kelly, Roman Catholic Archbishop of Sydney in 1914. 'The tendency of modern art is to reproduce things which it is a shame to look at,' he said

Norman Lindsay, who loathed wowsers, drew this acid pair, alert for something to disapprove of, for *Smith's Weekly* in 1930

45

Cities and towns

Ever-growing capitals of an urban nation

'I am not a believer in dumping people into any of the great cities,' declared Billy Hughes, then Prime Minister, in 1920. 'That will not help us. What has enabled France to bear a burden many many times greater than that which we have had to bear? It is the fact that 70 or 80 per cent of her population are on the land. Until we are able to so adjust matters that we can say that at least 60 per cent of the people of Australia are on the land we are living in a paradise of fools.' He hoped people would listen.

But the Prime Minister's warning was not heeded. Around the time that he spoke, 40 per cent of Australia's population lived in the six State capitals; 19 per cent lived in other cities and towns, and 37 per cent lived on the land. Today, according to United Nations figures, Australia ranks as the fourth most urbanised country in the world, coming below only Singapore, the United Kingdom and Israel. A mere 14 per cent of Australians live in rural areas.

More than 70 of every 100 Australians live in one or other of the twelve major cities – the capital cities and Newcastle, Wollongong, Geelong and the Gold Coast conurbation. Darwin, with a population increase of 369 per cent – to 63,300 – over the last 20 years, is easily the fastest growing city in the Commonwealth. Canberra comes next, with 262 per cent growth, to 255,900.

Sydney is Australia's biggest city, with a population in June 1983 of 3,335,000 – an increase by 48 per cent, 1,078,900 people, over the preceding 20 years. Melbourne and Hobart grew at the lowest rate, 43 per cent, to 2,865,700 and 173,700 respectively. Brisbane grew by 63 per cent to 1,138,400, while Perth boomed by 118 per cent to 969,100.

Outside the capital cities, Newcastle in 1983 had 414,700 people, and Wollongong 235,000, while Geelong had about 143,000. The Gold Coast, though lacking some features of a normal city, can certainly claim to be an intensive centre of population, with no less than 189,100 permanent residents.

Satellite towns have also widened the horizons of Australia's cities. With some as long established as Adelaide's Elizabeth and Brisbane's Inala, or as recent as Melbourne's Sunbury and Darwin's Palmerston. What were once sleepy townships now found themselves transformed into respectable residential areas, with dwellings in manicured groves earnestly named after aldermen's wives or the native shrubs and trees that were uprooted for the sake of progress and subdivision.

Thousands of eager Sydneysiders inspected their new bridge after the official opening on 19 March 1932. The ceremony was disrupted by Captain de Groot, whose sabre cut the ribbon before the Premier, Jack Lang, could snip it with his scissors

City life early in the century

When sparrow-starvers tended the streets

Even in 1912 city streets could be crowded, especially Bourke Street, then the main shopping centre of Melbourne, in front of the department store of Buckley and Nunn. The building is the same today, though an awning has been added and the facade has been altered at street level. In 1917, Sidney Myer opened his store next door, though the present gigantic Myer Emporium was not completed until 1937

Contrasts of fashion at the corner of Collins and Swanston Streets, Melbourne, in 1912: the old woman with the basket wears the style of 1890

At the turn of the century, most city streets were still lit by gas. At night a lamplighter came round with a narrow pole which had a protected kerosene flame at the top. He poked this through an opening at the bottom of the lamp, turning on the gas jet and igniting it at the same time. In the morning, he used the pole to extinguish the light. Later, streets were lit by the new-fangled electric arc lamps, which were lowered by a pulley and rope when the carbon sticks that operated them had to be changed. Butcher shops often used arc lamps with special carbons that produced a red glow, flattering to the meat. Shoe blacks plied their trade in city streets; crossing-sweepers, known as 'sparrow-starvers', were busy disposing of the horse-droppings. In dingy offices, often still called 'counting-houses', clerks sat on hard stools at high desks under the watchful eye of the chief clerk, writing in a copperplate script, as they had done in Charles Dickens' day.

Dancing bear in Bohemia

In Sydney, the centre of bohemian life was picturesque Rowe Street, only 4.8 metres wide and 109 metres long and connecting Castlereagh and Pitt Streets. Artists, writers and musicians were among the residents—Lionel Lindsay, Dattilo Rubbo and Sydney Ure Smith among the artists, A. G. Stephens among the writers. A bearded Russian street singer with a big voice and a big brown dancing bear used to serenade the passers-by. At the end of his performance he would remove the bear's muzzle and stand it a pint of beer—costing 3d [60c]. On the corner of Rowe and Castlereagh Streets—now dominated by the M.L.C. Centre—was the Hotel Australia, where single rooms cost 12s 6d [$31.31] a day. It advertised 'Hotel Porters in Attendance to all Steamers and Trains'. Many women booked in with their maids, and men arrived with their valets. At a shop called Tost and Rohus—a place with a stock as curious as its name—Sydney-siders could purchase a lyre-bird tail, a musket, a suit of armour, a stuffed tiger or a live snake; and any jeweller would sell you a gold toothpick to carry in your pocket for about 7s 6d [$16.39].

Before World War I, Melbourne's Bourke Street from Swanston to Spring Street was a rather raffish collection of theatres, brass bands, pedlars, eating houses, cheapjack shops and pubs. Shopkeepers displayed their goods on the footpath, and employed dog-wallopers to keep dogs from misbehaving on them. The Eastern Market, where the Southern Cross Hotel now stands, was a rowdy jumble of stalls. There you could buy anything from live poultry to glass-enclosed wreaths of artificial flowers. Across the street, a waxworks displayed effigies of notables from criminals to kings. On the other side of Swanston Street, Bourke Street was slightly more sedate, for there was the elegant department store of Buckley and Nunn. But also there was that incredible edifice Cole's Book Arcade. This ran right through to Collins Street and hundreds of painted rainbows shone on its three storeys, inside and out.

Bulletin cartoonist Ted Scorfield satirised 1920s 'improvement' of the cities in these drawings entitled 'The March of Progress in Our Suburb'

Doing the Block

When life in the big cities was leisurely, certain streets in Melbourne and Sydney became known as 'the Block'; it was fashionable, especially on Saturdays, to 'do the Block'—that is, to saunter along them, displaying one's latest clothes, looking languidly in shop windows or chatting with friends.

The practice started in Melbourne about the 1860s, and later spread to Sydney. Rose Lindsay remembers how in Sydney the parade began about three o'clock. The ladies in their 'finery of feathers, laces and silk, daintily holding up befrilled and beribboned skirts . . . bowed under shady hats perched on rolls of padded hair to passing friends.'

In Melbourne, 'the Block' was the northern side of Collins Street, from Elizabeth Street to Swanston Street. In Sydney, it was bounded by King, George, Hunter and Pitt Streets. 'Doing the Block' continued in Melbourne up to World War I.

Cast-iron urinals added a Parisian touch to city streets in the 1900s. An Adelaide ironfounder offered this elegant model with optional lamp

Sydney, 'a sailor-town city'

A nineteenth century city disappears

At the time of Federation, 488,968 people—35 per cent of the population of New South Wales—lived in Sydney, the largest city in the Commonwealth.

Circular Quay, which had been constructed in the 1840s, was surrounded by bond-stores, factories and hotels; the wool clippers no longer berthed

there, but it was a thriving commercial centre. This view up George Street North shows that the city already had an impressive skyline

In 1901, the artist Norman Lindsay, then 22, came to Sydney to take a job on *The Bulletin*. Fifty-six years later he recalled that time and wrote: 'I am not yielding to a nostalgic illusion of charm over that Sydney . . . When I arrived there it was at its best, a city that will never again be seen on earth—a sailor-town city, a free-trade city, a pre-mechanised city, in which one jostled in lower George Street and the Quay sailors from all the earth, and glimpsed over wharves and roofs of harbourside houses the tall spars of sailing ships. The Sydney of today is a cosmopolitan replica of any other city.'

Something of this had been predicted by Sir Henry Parkes in 1889, when he was laying the foundation stone for the Australia Hotel in Sydney. 'Changes will take place in Australia which will arrest the attention of the whole world and among those changes will be a complete change in the character of this great city of Sydney,' he declared.

The Australia Hotel was opened in July 1891. Sarah Bernhardt was the first to sign its register. 'The first visitor to the Australia Hotel will probably be the most distinguished that will ever sleep beneath the roof,' commented *The Sydney Morning Herald*.

By the 1970s, the character of Sydney had

changed beyond anything Sir Henry could have imagined. Not only had the Australian Hotel disappeared, but with it every other historic Sydney hotel—Petty's, Usher's Metropolitan, Aaron's Exchange, Adams' Tattersalls, Pfahlert's, the Grosvenor and the Metropole. And splendid colonial buildings such as Burdekin House in Macquarie Street and Dr Lang's Auld Kirk in Jamison Street had been sacrificed to 'progress'.

Sydney's sylvan suburbs

In 1915, Arthur Rickard and Company, Sydney 'Realty Specialists', were advertising building blocks on terms of 'Only £1 [$34] down and 10s [$17] monthly payments (including interest at 5 per cent per annum) for every £25 [$850] purchased':

'**Hurstville.** Marine view, bright, breezy, cheerful situate at Connell's Point, overlooking the finest stretches of George's River, including Como, etc.—an ideal spot for a home site, special feature being the natural facilities for outdoor and aquatic pleasure. Lots from 60 × 200 ft (18 × 60 m), from 6/- [$10.15] foot (per 30 cm).

'**Lindfield.** Heart of Lindfield Estate, high class home sites, right at the station, at prices to suit all. Lots level and ready to build on.

Just the place for a business man's home. Only 20 minutes from Milsons Point. 60 × 150 feet (18 × 45m) allotments from 45/- [$76] foot.'

'**Bellevue Hill.** Cooper's Estate. A high class property in a most select locality, commanding magnificent ocean and harbour views and overlooking Rose Bay, Golf Links, Bellevue Hill, and Bondi Beach. Lots 66 × 226 feet (20 × 68 metres), to be sold at 50 feet (15 metre) frontage, at 70/- [$118] foot.'

The prices were in shillings per running foot of frontage, not per square foot. This means that a block of land in Bellevue Hill with a 50 ft frontage would have cost about £175 in 1915—the equivalent today of about $5,925. Of course, Bellevue Hill was not such a desirable address in those days.

At the same time, H. W. Horning and Company were advertising 'Kurnell, Famous as the Landing Place of the Greatest of Navigators, Captain Cook.' Now an industrial suburb on the shores of Botany Bay, Kurnell was described as 'one of the most lovely spots in Australia' while Como, on the Georges River was advertised as 'Sydney's New Riverside Suburb—only 35 minutes by train from Sydney'. Como was then served by 25 trains a day, and a theatre service at night.

Completed in 1888 and demolished in 1928 to make way for the new Harbour Bridge, the Grosvenor Hotel was only one of the many large residential hotels built in Sydney in the late 19th century

Old houses in Surry Hills at the turn of the century. Many of the older houses in Sydney were demolished as part of measures to control the plague epidemic which broke out in 1900. Nevertheless, Surry Hills and other inner suburbs still have many small houses much like these

In April 1919, a Sydney writer, W. F. Bayal, described a vision he had of Sydney as it would be in the year 1971: 'Towering buildings, Babylonish in style, ten to twenty storeys high, lined both sides of the street. Between each pile and the next was an open garden, or lawn, or fountain court . . . The pavement was of some kind of concrete, pale green in colour, most soothing to the eye . . . Not a single wire, telephone pole or spar marred the splendid effect of the vista.' The magazine *Sea, Land and Air* showed its readers how Macleay Street, Potts Point, might have looked if Bayal's vision were realised. Other marvels envisaged by the writer included an aerial passenger service across the harbour and trams that run without jolting

Electric trams first came to Sydney in 1898. By the time this photograph was taken in 1912, the city had a comprehensive tramway system. Horse-drawn vehicles were still common in the streets, for motor cars were not yet very popular. In the centre of this view down George Street towards Circular Quay looms the elaborate bulk of Anthony Hordern's department store, built in 1905. The building was demolished in 1986

Sydney grows upwards

Early skyscrapers provoke height restrictions

Growth of a metropolis

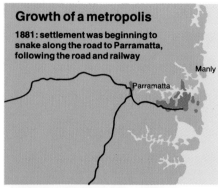

1881: settlement was beginning to snake along the road to Parramatta, following the road and railway

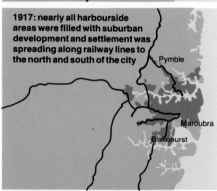

1917: nearly all harbourside areas were filled with suburban development and settlement was spreading along railway lines to the north and south of the city

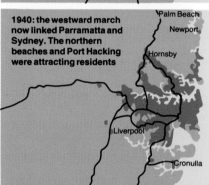

1940: the westward march now linked Parramatta and Sydney. The northern beaches and Port Hacking were attracting residents

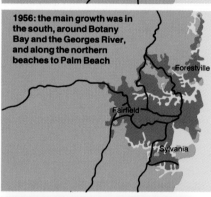

1956: the main growth was in the south, around Botany Bay and the Georges River, and along the northern beaches to Palm Beach

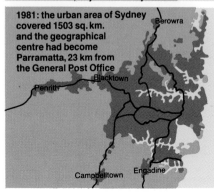

1981: the urban area of Sydney covered 1503 sq. km. and the geographical centre had become Parramatta, 23 km from the General Post Office

In 1889, just as Victoria's land boom was busting, the Australian Building, at the corner of Elizabeth Street and Flinders Lane, was completed. It was then the tallest office building in the world, rising 46 m. It remained Melbourne's tallest building for more than 60 years. It was demolished in 1980, its uniqueness commemorated by a plaque on the building which replaced it.

It was originally planned to rise even higher, but the Melbourne City Council limited it to 11 storeys. In 1910, the council, perhaps alarmed at the prospect of steel-framed skyscrapers spreading from the United States to Melbourne, decreed that no building in the city should be higher than one and one-third times the width of the street it faced. This meant that in the widest street the height limit was 40 m.

This ruling was eventually adopted by other capitals, except Sydney. In that city, in 1910, the first self-supporting steel-framed building appeared. It was nine-storey Nelson House, built on a 6 m wide site in Clarence Street where it still stands.

Sydney's first skyscraper

Sydney got its first steel-framed skyscraper in 1913, when Culwulla Chambers, in Castlereagh Street, was completed. It was 52 m high and clad in red brick. Its cost was about £100,000 [$4,017,000].

Even before Culwulla Chambers was completed, its height appalled the authorities—for its upper floors were far beyond the reach of fire-fighting equipment—and in 1912 the Sydney City Council imposed a 46 m limit on the height of buildings. The council was apparently too late to curb the Castlereagh Street skyscraper, for in October 1912 a reporter noted rapturously that the 'huge red pile' had already climbed 14 storeys high and that its elevation facing King Street rose 50 m from the pavement.

Culwulla Chambers remained Sydney's tallest building for many years until, in 1917, the Sydney City Council lifted the building limit from 46 to 60 m, but the New South Wales Government legislated to revert to the 46 m limit. Not until 1956 were buildings in Melbourne and Sydney released from these regressive restrictions.

Breaking the height barrier

The first building to break the 40 m barrier in Melbourne was the 20-storey ICI House, begun in 1956. In Sydney, in 1962, the AMP Building at Circular Quay rose to a height of 117.3 m. The permissible limit in Sydney continued to rise and in 1967, after five years of planning, the circular tower of Australia Square, with its 50 floors of 41 m diameter, attained a height of 183 m.

This was surpassed in 1978, by the completion of the MLC Centre, the tower block of which rises to 250 m above sea level, and is 228 m above the street. But Sydney's most arresting sight is the Centrepoint Tower, 280 m above sea level, and 262 m above the street. Not classified as a building, it crowns a busy shopping complex in the heart of the city.

Culwulla Chambers, 52 m high and completed in 1913, was for many years the tallest building in Sydney. The old Surrey Hotel, at the corner of King and Castlereagh Streets, still huddles doggedly in the angle of the skyscraper, surviving in the form of a children's clothing store

The poet Kenneth Slessor, who went to live in King's Cross in 1922, when he was 21, wrote: 'I have lived in or on the margin of King's Cross for more than 40 years. During that time I have watched hundreds of houses decay and vanish, streets change their name as well as their geometry, rows of buildings topple and become holes in the ground, and other buildings rise almost instantly like the mango-trees of Oriental conjurors. I have seen the swishing trolley buses come and go and I have watched horses change to station waggons. I have watched the old William Street eating places (21 meal-tickets for £1 [$27]) turn into bistros, niteries, wine-and-dine cafes, steak houses, spaghetti bars and espresso lounges.'

A free and easy city

The novelist D. H. Lawrence was another who arrived in Sydney in 1922. He was impressed with how Australians appeared to 'run their city very well...Everything was very easy, and there was no fuss...Nobody seemed to bother, there seemed to be no policemen and no authority, the whole thing went by itself, loose and easy, without any bossing.' A disarming picture!

By 1927, however, things seemed to have speeded up. 'Sydney now enjoys the inestimable benefits of one-way traffic, an underground railway, Sunday shops, speed racing-tracks for motor-cars, jazz cabarets, and sudden death; all institutions very necessary to an up-to-date city,' wrote W. F. Jackson that year in *By-Ways of Romance*.

In 1931 the Melbourne magazine *Table Talk* summed up Sydney less enthusiastically. 'A more apathetic, indifferent, pleasure-loving populace it would be hard to find,' it said. 'No doubt the warm, caressing sun of the tropical city has a lot to do with it.'

By 1938 Sydney was starting to look like a big city, with numerous office blocks built up to the 46 m height limit. At Circular Quay, the old half-timbered ferry wharves were starting to be rebuilt. Most were rebuilt by 1942, but the outermost pair remained until 1960, when they were demolished and not replaced

In 1931, the right-hand side of Sydney's Bridge Street, looking down from George Street, was much as it is today. But the palms and the median strips (removed in 1946), the elegant lamp posts and most of the buildings on the left have gone. The pavements are now lined with Lombardy poplars

Peaceful Wynyard Park (above) was dug up during the 1920s (below) in the building of Sydney's underground railway. The Central to St James line was opened in 1926 and Central to Wynyard in 1932, but the lines were not linked until 1956

The trees and palms that now shade Sydney's Hyde Park were infants when the Manchester Unity Building began to rise in Elizabeth Street in 1923. Completed the next year, the 11-storey building was the highest in the street. It still stands; next door is the Great Synagogue built in 1878

How Sydney got its harbour bridge

Early dreams and schemes came to nothing

Sydneysiders dreamed of bridging their harbour for more than a century before the dream came true. In 1815, when Sydney was only 27 years old, the colony's most gifted architect, the convict Francis Greenway, first proposed a harbour bridge. 'In the event of the bridge being thrown across from Dawes Battery to the North Shore, a town would be built on that shore,' he prophesied. His plans, however, were never clearly defined and nothing came of them. The earliest existing drawing for a North Shore bridge dates from 1857; it was the work of Peter Henderson, a Sydney engineer who had been apprenticed to George Stephenson, the railway pioneer.

The first practical plan was one for a floating bridge, drawn up in 1878 by the New South Wales Commissioner for Railways, W. C. Bennett. The following year a seven-span truss bridge was designed, and in 1880 the New South Wales Government negotiated with an engineering firm for a high-level bridge to cost £850,000 [over $50 million today].

Plan after plan followed. In 1901 the Union Bridge Co. of New York offered to build a cantilever bridge for £645,845 [$32,567,380], and the following year another tender costing £1,940,050 [about $92 million] was recommended by an advisory board. In 1908 a committee of inquiry proposed two tunnels beneath the harbour—one for trains, the other for road traffic. Again nothing came of either of these projects.

All the while the need for a bridge became more and more pressing. Ferries and punts carried people, horses and vehicles across the harbour, but the shortest road route from downtown Sydney to the expanding suburbs on the northern shore involved a 19 kilometre detour around the head of the harbour. It was known as the 'five bridges road' because it crossed bridges at Pyrmont, Glebe Island, Iron Cove, Gladesville and Fig Tree.

Finally in 1912 the New South Wales Government appointed Dr J. J. C. Bradfield, a Queensland-born engineer in the Public Works Department, to design an electric railway system, including a bridge across the harbour. In 1913 the Public Works Committee accepted Bradfield's proposal for a cantilever bridge from Dawes Point to Milson's Point.

World War I interfered with the plans which had to be shelved until 1922, when legislation authorising construction was at last passed. Six companies put forward 20 tenders for various designs, including suspension bridges not covered by Bradfield's specifications. The English firm of Dorman Long and Co. Ltd. won the contract with a tender costing £5,217,721 [about $142 million] which kept substantially to Bradfield's proposed cantilever bridge.

High arch grew from each shore

The Sydney Harbour Bridge consists of a steel arch span and an approach span on each side made up of five truss spans. The arch span covers 503 m and the total length of the bridge is 1149 m. The deck which carries the roadway, railway and footways is 49 m wide and is hung from the lower chords.

The harbour bridge under construction in 1931. The steelwork was erected from each shore by a huge creeper crane moving on top of the half arch. The cranes placed the steelwork in position panel by panel and, after it was fixed, moved out onto it and built another section

Huge loops of 7 cm diameter cable supported the arches as they grew out from the shores on either side. The cables passed through horseshoe shaped tunnels bored into the sandstone

When the two halves of the arch were completed they were closely aligned, but they still had to be joined. This was done by slackening off the cables so that the half-arches dropped

The abutment towers which carry the pylons at each end do not support the arch. Its entire weight rests on four steel bearings set into massive concrete foundations embedded 12 m into the solid sandstone rock of the harbour shores on either side.

Construction work began in April 1923 with the approaches. The Rocks district on the southern shore—Sydney's oldest suburb, notorious in the 19th century as a haunt of drunken sailors—was completely transformed as old cottages and many fine colonial buildings were demolished to make way for the southern approaches of the bridge.

For the erection of the steelwork, special workshops were built on Milsons Point. The main steel members forming each joint were fabricated and fitted in the workshops to make sure that a perfect joint would result when the steelwork was finally in position. To support the bridge until the arch was joined and became self-supporting, the half arches had to be anchored by cables to the rocks of the harbour shores because the construction could not be supported from below.

When the two halves of the arch were completed they were closely aligned—but they still had to be joined. This was done by slackening the anchorage cables so that the half arches dropped until the lower chords

The bridge was completed in 1931 at a final cost of £9,577,507 [$291 million]. The steelwork weighs 52,834 tonnes and the total length is 1150 m. Ships passing under the bridge have a clearance of 52.5 m at mean sea level. The original tramway on the eastern side was converted to roadway in 1959

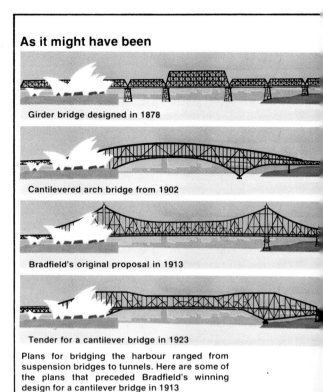

As it might have been

Girder bridge designed in 1878

Cantilevered arch bridge from 1902

Bradfield's original proposal in 1913

Tender for a cantilever bridge in 1923

Plans for bridging the harbour ranged from suspension bridges to tunnels. Here are some of the plans that preceded Bradfield's winning design for a cantilever bridge in 1913

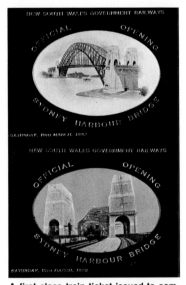

A first class train ticket issued to commemorate the opening of the bridge on 19 March 1932. The return fare from Wynyard to North Sydney was 10s [$16]

Captain de Groot, a member of the New Guard, dramatically interrupted the official opening ceremonies by slashing the ribbon with his sword. The incident was a right-wing plot to upstage the Labor Premier of NSW, Jack Lang

Another notable structure among Sydney's bridges is the Gladesville Bridge over the Parramatta River, completed in 1964. The concrete arch spans 305 m and has a clearance of 41 m

nearly met. Then 25-tonne jacks drove locking pins on one side into recesses on the other. Finally four 1000-tonne hydraulic jacks prised the top chords apart to allow steel packing pieces to be inserted, making the arch into a complete continuous structure resting on the bearing pins at each end.

The arch was closed in March 1930, after 22 months' work. Hanging the steel deck from the arch took another eight months. Finally the deck was covered with two railway tracks and a footway on the western side of the roadway and two tramway tracks and a footway on the eastern side.

The bridge was officially opened by the New South Wales Premier, Jack Lang, on 19 March 1932. The ceremony of cutting the ribbon resembled a scene from a comic opera. Eric Campbell, head of the New Guard—a private, semi-military organisation opposed to Lang's radical politics—announced publicly that a member of the New Guard would beat Lang to the cutting.

While the public speculated on how this could possibly be done in full view of hordes of policemen and Lang's military escort, a Captain Francis de Groot, calmly riding as part of that official escort, dashed forward on horse-back and cut the ribbon with his sword. The police rushed at him, and he was dragged

to the ground, with nearly every policeman in sight on top of him, while the crowd cheered enthusiastically.

All approved of the bridge, including the poet C. J. Dennis, who wrote of a dream in which Governor Phillip ('a queer old cock, wif lace an' wig on 'ead') talks to the Sentimental Bloke about Sydney's wondrous growth, symbolised by the 'mighty span' of the new harbour bridge:

Then both of us, like some queer
*   instinct bids*
Stands up, serloots the Bridge,
*   an' dips our lids.*

55

Inter-city rivalry

'Melbourne for the indoor life and Sydney for the open air'

When the traveller H. M. Vaughan wrote *An Australasian Wander-Year* in 1914, he reported that the 'improved manners and reasonable courtesy to be found everywhere in Melbourne streets and shops were a refreshing change from the gratuitous rudeness one so often encounters in Sydney, where the labouring classes are apt (so it is sarcastically said) to consider civility identical with servility'. Vaughan found it difficult to decide why this was so. Some declared it was the result of the sub-tropical climate in Sydney, others ascribed it to the attitude of the Labor Government in New South Wales.

Vaughan found the intense rivalry between Sydney and Melbourne a wearying and profitless discussion, and summed up: 'Melbourne for the indoor life and Sydney for the open air', while Adelaide 'in its exquisite setting between blue sea and green hills can hold its own against the boasting beauties of Sydney and Brisbane'.

The absurd Melbourne-Sydney rivalry has been going on for more than a century. 'There is great jealousy between the two colonies', wrote Ellen Kean, wife of the Shakespearean actor Charles Kean, in 1863. And in 1964,

when there was a squabble over where an international airport should be situated, Alderman F. P. Moran announced in the Sydney City Council: 'Sydney is the premier city of Australia. It was the first place in Australia to be settled. Sydney built the first railway in the Commonwealth. It is the finest seat of learning and the academic centre of the nation.' To which the Melbourne *Age* replied witheringly: 'It is only a matter of time before Alderman Moran calls for the formation of a New South Wales Air Force, with fighters ready to buzz any aircraft rash enough to head south across the Murray, instead of forcing their way through the sea-gulls over Sydney.'

In July 1920, C. N. Bayertz, the music critic of *The Triad*, spent two weeks in Melbourne, the city where he had been born. He found it a dull place. 'During the whole of my stay I never once saw the sun, and the tintinnabulation of the tram bells was almost as exasperating as the weather,' he wrote. 'In Melbourne, there is no restaurant open on Sunday. There is not one Sunday newspaper. There are no Sunday morning trams or trains. Trains may come on Sunday, but they may not go to the other unregenerate capitals.'

However, the Melbourne electrified train service was 'quite one of the best anywhere' and there was more 'civic dignity and aesthetic enterprise in Melbourne than in Sydney'.

About the same time, R. Keith Harris, a Sydney architect who had been abroad for several years, also complained of the lack of civic pride in Sydney. 'When people extol Sydney it is the natural surroundings rather than the city to which they refer,' he said. And he recommended that the whole of the block from the Post Office to King Street should be resumed and made into an open piazza similar to Trafalgar Square, the Place de l'Opera, Paris, or the Piazza San Marco in Venice. More than half a century later, his suggestion was partly carried out, when Martin Place, was closed to all but cross-traffic.

When Jeanne MacKenzie came to Australia in 1959 with her husband Norman MacKenzie, then on the staff of the British review, *New Statesman and Nation*, she thought that Perth was 'the most isolated capital city in the world'. But she liked the way Perth people enjoyed the attractions it offered them—'perfect climate, lovely beaches, strolling in a delightful park in the centre of the town . . .'

Magnificent High Victorian buildings once lined Collins Street, Melbourne, between King and William Streets, contributing greatly to the air of 'civic dignity and aesthetic enterprise' noted by visitors to the city in the early years of the century. These ornate facades were photographed in the 1950s; the scene is much changed today. Most of the buildings have been torn down and replaced by plain, rectilinear concrete and glass boxes

Melbourne, on first sight, gave her a shock. Walking down Collins Street on a chilly evening in spring reminded her of 'a Manchester of thirty years ago'. The train that brought her to the city, and the station, were uncannily English, 'old, dirty, and all built in the Victorian age', and the workpeople wore English raincoats and English suits, but 'old fashioned in cut and design'. It was a sharp contrast to 'the relaxed, sunny, happy Australia' she had heard about.

Sydney, too, surprised her, but pleasantly. She found the harbour 'more beautiful and spectacular' than she had ever dreamed it to be, and King's Cross had 'the lively sophistication of a metropolis'. But the suburbs were a different world. 'We drove out of town for miles, over ill-paved streets in tatty districts. The contrast between the harbour and the western suburbs was too great . . .' she wrote. 'The detached bungalows repeated themselves with a dreary monotony. Some were weatherboard, some were brick, some roofs were corrugated iron, some of tile; some were neat and tidy, some scruffy and shabby . . .'

Inside the half-brick, half-fibro bungalow that her friends were renting, the rooms were 'dark and dingy, the furniture old and nondescript. Pottery birds in flight adorned the plasterboard wall. There was an ancient geyser in the kitchen and no hot water . . . The windows at the front of the house were inlaid with stained-glass panels . . . It was the Australian equivalent of a jerry-built bungalow on the fringes of East London.'

Two faces of Australia

Later, she found that her first reaction to Melbourne had been 'distorted and unfair . . .' She also discovered that Sydney and Melbourne dramatised the contradictions of Australia. 'These two cities,' she wrote, 'are utterly different in character and between them they reveal two faces of the country. Sydney—rough, brash, materialist, and Irish Catholic. Although there are some rich families who have been established in Sydney for sometime, its wealth is largely a new wealth from which is emerging a new business rich caught up in the acquisitive society. Melbourne, serious, demure, genteel; Protestant and English; its rich are long established, deriving their status from tradition as well as money. "Wowserism" probably has its headquarters in Melbourne. On Sunday Melbourne has no newspapers, no cinemas and no pubs.'

In 1962, James Morris reported on Australia for the London *Guardian*. He was not flattering about Sydney: 'The origins of Sydney are unsavoury,' he wrote. 'Her history is disagreeable to read, her temper is coarse, her organisation seems to be slipshod, her suburbs are hideous, and her politics often crooked, her buildings are most plain, her voices rasp on the ear, her trumpeted Art Movement is, I suspect, half spurious, her newspapers are either dull or distasteful . . .' Only the harbour and the racing commentaries pleased him. But he thought Melbourne's Collins Street was 'recognisably one of the great streets of the world'.

As in other Australian cities, the old residential inner suburbs of Melbourne are gradually being absorbed into the city as it expands. Elaborate and substantial terrace houses like these are products of the boom of the 1880s. 'Marvellous Melbourne' led Sydney in population and spread over 250 square kilometres until the collapse came in the 1890s. Victoria was 'tainting the Continent with its foulness' and should be declared an infected province, said a Sydney magazine in 1900

The 'Paris end of Collins Street' in the 1960s suffered from an un-Parisian wowserism; no alcohol could be consumed at its sidewalk tables. However, Collins Street did once have grace and charm unique in Australia. It has even been called one of the great streets of the world

Contrasts in Melbourne

Festering slums and broad avenues

In the years before World War I, Melbourne *Punch* repeatedly condemned Melbourne's slums, and advocated the building of municipal or state tenements to replace them.

A typical editorial published in December 1908, during a heat wave, described the plight of the 'hovel-inhabitants of Melbourne' who lived in tiny, unsewered two or three-roomed houses; families of seven, ten or even 12 'crammed into one dirty little squalid hut, fronting on a steaming, malodorous lane', breathing tainted, poisonous air. 'Perhaps they groan in their misery occasionally,' said the editorial, 'but the whir of the electric fan or the tinkle of the ice in the glass prevents us from hearing them.'

In January 1914, the Housing of the People Committee of the Victorian Parliament reported that Melbourne had worse slums than London. *Punch* commented: 'The owners of the slums deserve no sympathy. Some are among the city's most prominent men. One is, according to the Committee, the most lavish entertainer in Melbourne.'

A property-owner in Fitzroy, an inner working-class suburb, charged 10s [$19] a week for each of six houses huddled together on a 16.5 m frontage, *Punch* said. And in Collingwood, a suburb of the same type, as many as six people lived in each room of some houses.

Slum dwellings in inner Melbourne in the 1940s. Norman Lindsay lived near here in 1900, paying 6s 6d [$16.40] a week for a two-and-a-half-room house 4.2 m wide, with a hawker of rabbits on one side and a brothel on the other

Victorian Melbourne was a city of wealth and solid respectability, symbolised in the massive proportions of hotels such as the Grand and Menzies (right). There the city's 'establishment' held receptions and dinners, and the rich graziers stayed. The Grand was renamed the Windsor in 1920; Menzies has been demolished

In the early 1920s, Collins Street was a pleasant thoroughfare lined with sober Victorian buildings—

banks, churches and the Town Hall (centre). Melbourne's main streets were planned from the first,

unlike Sydney's, and the best of them are still wide and leafy boulevards

Elizabeth Street, Melbourne, about 1900, looking from Flinders Street, where the tramline still ends.

The shops have the elegant verandah awnings, with cast-iron posts, that were universal then.

Within a few years these began to be replaced by awnings suspended from steel tension rods

Bourke Street has always been Melbourne's main shopping street. This 1950s view includes the old

Eastern Markets building (on the left past the first intersection), where stalls sold everything from

poultry to paintings. The Southern Cross Hotel now stands on this site

Brisbane

Relaxed in the sun

In 1970, a visiting English writer, Jonathan Aitken, found Brisbane 'torpid, tranquil and tropical', symbolised by 'shorts, singlets and swallows of ice-cold beer'. He disliked it for air pollution, lack of response to new ideas, and puritanism 'unequalled anywhere outside the Bible Belt of America's mid-west'. But its people were 'exceptionally hospitable and friendly. . . not crazy for money like those galahs down south in Sinny'. And given 'a paw-paw on every breakfast table and a few tubes of beer in the ice-box every evening', Brisbane would keep on relaxing.

The American writer John Gunther found Brisbane 'a happily helter-skelter city'. Its architecture was rather dreary, apart from some filigreed balcony railing and some quaint old buildings on stilts, and its citizens were good trenchermen with enormous appetites. But they were more acutely preoccupied with puritanism and drinking habits than with bigger issues.

And what does an Australian writer find in Brisbane? To Craig McGregor it is 'a ragged, dissonant conglomeration of shops and houses on stilts sprawled beneath a subtropical sun . . . an informal easygoing city, the strict bonds of its Anglo-Saxon nature loosened by the rigours of the climate'.

None of these experienced observers found Brisbane physically attractive, in spite of the river winding intimately through the city, and the occasional vivid glimpses of colour from tropical trees and shrubs.

Brisbane, the third largest city in Australia, has never been as dominant in Queensland as Sydney, Melbourne, Adelaide and Perth have been in their states. In 1901, only 24 per cent of Queensland's population lived in Brisbane, whereas in other capitals the percentage of the state's population was: Sydney, 36; Melbourne, 41; Adelaide, 45 and Perth, 37.

Reasons for Brisbane's less dominant pos-

ition and its comparatively sluggish growth include its location in the extreme south-east corner of the state; the long coastline with its string of regional ports; a decentralised transport system; and government policies that have consistently promoted the development of rural industries at the expense of urban industries, particularly manufacturing.

Nevertheless, Brisbane has grown enormously since 1901, when its population was 96,000 and the furthest suburb was less than eight kilometres from the centre. Eighty-two years later, the population was 1,138,400 and new suburbs were being formed up to 40

kilometres from the centre. The urban sprawl that was just beginning to creep along the transport corridors in 1901 has progressed along highway and railway to convert Ipswich from a separate town into a suburb.

By the turn of the century the citizens of Brisbane had already begun to question their fragmented system of local government, consisting of more than 20 local authorities and more than a dozen joint local authorities and special statutory authorities. Pressure grew until the 1915 elections brought to power a Labor Government committed to create a greater Brisbane with a council to match.

An embarrassing moment for the Brisbane Fire Brigade in 1937. A fire engine, immaculately polished for a procession celebrating the coronation of King George VI, stalled and had to be restarted by cranking

The Victoria Bridge about 1918, with the Treasury Building behind it at right. This steel structure replaced the original wooden bridge in 1897, the year electric trams came to Brisbane. A new bridge was opened in 1969

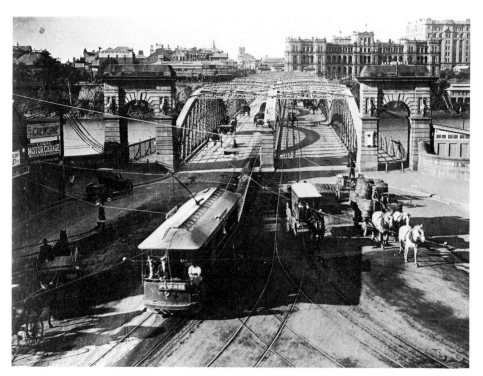

Brisbane at the turn of the century, seen from near where the Story Bridge now crosses the river. The National Hotel, at right, and the domed Customs House are still landmarks on the north bank

It had expansive ideas, and when the Greater Brisbane City Council was set up in 1924 it was an all-purpose authority which governed an area of 970 square kilometres and was responsible for street transport, water supply and sewerage, electricity generation and supply, and town planning, as well as the normal functions of local authorities.

The council improved and expanded services in most of these fields, in spite of the restraints imposed by the Depression and World War II, but it has been criticised for not producing a proper town plan and for allowing indiscriminate high-rise building.

Umbigumbi grows up

Ninety-six kilometres south of Brisbane is a city that is quite different not only from Brisbane but from anywhere else in Australia—that 1950s boom phenomenon, the Gold Coast and its environs.

Eastern Australia's favourite holiday resort began back in 1917, when an estate agent was trying to sell mudflat land at a place called Umbigumbi on the Nerang River. He decided to change the name of the area to something more evocative and chose 'Surfers Paradise'.

By the 1920s a hotel had been built there and the area was gaining mild popularity. Development was still slow in 1950, when the travel writer Colin Simpson paid a visit to Surfers Paradise. He was not impressed. He agreed with the Brisbane journalist who wrote that only the rich could afford to pay such prices for mudflats and mangroves. The journalist had sarcastically named the area 'the Gold Coast'.

Simpson did not buy land at Surfers Paradise in 1950 and therefore, as he ruefully remarks, he did not become a rich man. Because two years later Surfers Paradise began to boom and the boom has not stopped even yet.

Many of the buildings in these two 1930s photographs of Queen Street, Brisbane's busiest thoroughfare, have been replaced by modern office blocks. The central business area was largely built in the 1880s and met the city's needs until after World War II. The lower picture, looking southwest, also shows the old-established department store of Finney Isles and Co., which was taken over by the Sydney firm David Jones. The upper picture looks the other way

The planned city

The 'new, noisy, pleasure-loving Adelaide'

Adelaide, once dismissed as complacent, parochial and dull, has changed astonishingly in recent years. When the historian Russel Ward, who was born in Adelaide, published his book *Australia* in 1965, he wrote:
'Adelaide is still praised by many of its own citizens as the "City of Churches" and still occasionally referred to ironically by non-South Australians as "The Holy City".

'Within a hundred miles of the capital are produced some of the best grapes in Australia and some of the best wine in the world; yet South Australian hotels still cease serving liquor at 6 p.m. sharp and even in daylight hours women may have nothing to do with the sinful business. Strong waters are sold by men usually dressed like undertakers in black alpaca coats.'

Professor Ward would not be able to say this of Adelaide today. In March 1967, South Australia's unconventional Premier, Don Dunstan, introduced a new licensing bill which gave Adelaide and the rest of the state the longest drinking hours in Australia at that time—from 9 a.m. to 10 p.m. During the Adelaide Festival of 1972, strong waters were served in an open-air cafe on North Terrace until 1 a.m.—and not by sombre men in black coats, but by smiling girls in mini-skirts.

The late John Gunther, who visited Adelaide in 1970, wrote: 'Industry, technology and immigration are forming a new, noisy, pleasure-loving Adelaide. It is easier to drink, dine, dance and watch a floor show in Adelaide nowadays than it is in Melbourne.'

Decentralisation plan

One of the things that combine to make Adelaide different from other Australian cities is that it has always had a plan. The first one—drawn up by the founder Colonel William Light in 1837—gave the city its five central parks and its famous green belt, which have no counterpart anywhere in the world. And in the 1970s, Adelaide was the first of the state capitals to develop long-range plans for satellite cities and decentralisation.

When Adelaide was gazetted a city in 1919, the population of the whole State of South Australia was less than half a million. Today Adelaide's own population is nearly one million. The first satellite town, Elizabeth, 27 kilometres north of the city, was proclaimed in 1955, when Adelaide's population had reached 506,000. Elizabeth is designed on modern town-planning principles, with many walkways instead of streets and 150,000 trees; it covers an area of about 26 square kilometres, including 566 hectares of parkland and a common of 26 hectares. Most of Elizabeth's original residents were immigrants, with Britons predominating.

Another satellite development, at Christie's Beach, 26 kilometres south of Adelaide, was begun in 1961, and a further major development project at Golden Grove, 16 kilometres to the north, was commenced in 1985.

Saving the city centre

The South Australian Government has also commissioned a strategic study in order to suggest ways in which population of the city centre can be prevented from dwindling at its present rate. For the first 25 years of this century, the city itself was the most densely populated part of Adelaide's metropolitan area. At its peak it was more than 45,000, but by 1930 the usual Australian tendency for city people to move to the suburbs became apparent. The city lost a quarter of its population in less than 40 years. Now the permanent population of the city is believed to be little more than 14,000. But efforts are being made to prevent Adelaide from becoming a dead-after-dark city. Land zoning is being enforced to prevent the residential areas from being further destroyed by commercial development, and some old, industrial, inner suburbs are being rezoned as residential.

In 1901, as today, John Martin's store was a focal point for Christmas shoppers in Adelaide. John Martin's is still on the same site but it is now a large department store. The hitching posts, and their descendants, the parking meters, have long since gone and the street is now a pedestrian mall

The South Australian Hotel in North Terrace, built in 1894, was given a new and imposing facade shortly before this photograph was taken in 1902. 'The South' was a vital centre of Adelaide's social life, with particular appeal to visiting graziers, until its demolition in 1971

Rundle Street, which became a pedestrian mall in the 1970s, has always been Adelaide's busiest street, lined with fashionable shops and cafes. By the 1920s, as this view eastwards from King William Street shows, it had taken on the bustle of a city—Adelaide was gazetted a city in 1919. The picture shows the profusion of double-storied verandahs, wide streets and substantial freestone buildings that characterise the city

In the year this photograph was taken, 1904, the Eagle Hotel, on the corner of Hindley and Bank Streets, was rebuilt with a second storey. In 1984 it was converted to a fast food restaurant

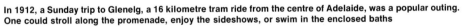

In 1912, a Sunday trip to Glenelg, a 16 kilometre tram ride from the centre of Adelaide, was a popular outing. One could stroll along the promenade, enjoy the sideshows, or swim in the enclosed baths

Adelaide shoppers of the 1930s nearly all wore hats, in the fashion of the day. Many women carried fibre suitcases for shopping

63

Booming away in the west

The fastest-growing state capital in Australia

In 1929, on the centenary of the foundation of Perth, the *Western Mail* published this vision (left) of what the city would look like in 2029. Some of it is now reality: the bridge across the Narrows was completed in 1959, and some Perth buildings are even taller than the artist imagined

Hay Street, Perth's main shopping centre, in 1949. Buses replaced trams in Hay Street in 1958, and then in 1970 this part of central Hay Street, between William Street and the Town Hall on the corner of Barrack Street (background), became a pedestrian mall

'Perth is where the Australian dream comes true. Now, like a suddenly created beauty outshining her ugly sisters, Perth is surging ahead of all rivals. The informal friendliness of Brisbane; the surf-soaked leisure of Sydney; the financial enterprise of Melbourne; the horticultural beauty of Canberra; the environmental and cultural grace of Adelaide; all are distilled in the capital of Western Australia.' So wrote the English journalist Jonathan Aitken in 1971. Some will think him over-enthusiastic, but certainly Perth has experienced an astonishing boom since the great mineral discoveries in Western Australia in the 1960s.

Perth has grown faster in the 20th century than any other state capital in Australia. In 1976 its population was 22 times what it was in 1901 and in 1983 it topped the 1,000,000 mark. In 1901, the city was in the middle of a boom. Its population was about 36,000 and growing fast. Only ten years before Perth had been a sleepy overgrown village of scarcely 10,000 people. There were only 46,000 people in the whole colony of Western Australia.

Gold and wheat

The boom that changed everything started with the discovery of the Coolgardie-Kalgoorlie goldfields in 1890. The gold boom continued until 1905, and then slowly began to decline. But Perth continued to prosper because the city shared in the riches brought to the state by the development of a large wheat export trade, and wool production also increased in importance. The tempo of government, business and professional activities

Murray Street, one of Perth's main thoroughfares, in 1922. By the 1920s the city had a proper water supply and drainage system, a tramways system, and was phasing out the bucket method of sanitation. Streets were lit by electricity—the first street lights had been installed in 1912

Perth's boom has had its casualties; among them was the magnificent red-brick, Dutch-gabled Esplanade Hotel, pulled down in 1973 to make way for an office block. The drawing above shows the hotel as it was built in 1898; the photograph at right shows it shortly before it was demolished

quickened until World War I broke out. Then one person in every ten enlisted for service overseas, and Perth slowed down.

By 1930 Western Australia was producing nearly a quarter of the national wheat crop, but the state was almost entirely dependent on primary products, so it suffered severely during the Depression. Perth's development also suffered, because only a little manufacturing industry existed around the city and the falling wheat and wool prices affected everyone. Hundreds of unemployed camped on the Perth Esplanade. Prosperity did not really return to the city until 1935.

Perth's latest boom began with post-war immigration and it has continued with the discoveries of nickel, iron ore, oil and gas in

Western Australia. Sandy scrubland north and south of the Swan River has filled up with thousands of homes. In the city centre old landmarks have come down to make way for towers of steel, concrete and glass.

A preference for Sydney

Whether all this makes Perth a better place to live may be questionable, but one who would prefer the new Perth is Richard Bowers, a Perth journalist who became a successful television scriptwriter in London. In 1951 he explained in a Sydney magazine why he preferred Sydney to Perth. He liked the 'fierce and incessant competition of hurry and go-get'. The cost of living was higher in Sydney, but the reason was a good one—you

could 'live higher, eat better, dress better, be better entertained'.

Perth in 1951 had only two cafes, both Italian, that could offer good cooking and menus off the 'soup-grill-sweet track'. Which, Bowers asked, was better value—'an ample, alluring Chinese or Dutch or whatnot dish in Sydney for 5s [$3.50], or soup, water-proofed chops and hackneyed sweets for 6s [$4.25] in Perth?' But the over-riding reason why Bowers liked Sydney was because it was too busy to waste his time, and 'too hard-boiled to let him become soft'. 'Perth,' he concluded, 'is a dose of chloroform, Sydney a shot of benzedrine. I would rather risk over-excitement than oversleep.' He would not suffer from over-sleep in Perth today.

A policeman stands on point duty at an intersection on Barrack Street—named for the place where the soldiers camped in the early days of settlement—

in the early 1920s. This photograph does not indicate much motor traffic, but there were then over 2000 motor vehicles in Perth, and it had been

considered necessary to introduce an efficient system of traffic control for the protection of pedestrians—and of horses

The second city

Bridging the Derwent with floating concrete

From the earliest days of settlement, Hobart lacked room for expansion until a bridge was built across the wide Derwent River. The first Derwent Bridge, seen above shortly after its completion in 1943, was unique — a floating arc of concrete. The arc was made in two halves, each consisting of 12 pontoons. The pontoons were rigidly connected, then the halves were towed out into the river and joined in midstream (right). Traction engines on the bridge winched the halves together as small ships nudged them into alignment. The floating bridge, designed by A. W. Knight of the Tasmanian Public Works Department, provided a roadway 12 m wide and cost about £500,000 [$11,700,000]

By the mid-1950s the floating bridge could no longer cope with the increasing traffic generated by Hobart's expansion on the eastern bank of the Derwent. In 1964 the new viaduct bridge came into use. The length of the river crossing is 1025 m—about twice the distance that is spanned by the Sydney Harbour Bridge. In 1975 the bridge was partly demolished when an 11,000 tonne freighter ran into one of the pylons (below). Restoration took over two years and cost $20 million.

Hobart, Australia's second oldest city, made Australian history in 1973, when Australia's first casino opened at Wrest Point, on Sandy Bay. (In its first three weeks of operation the casino paid $62,855 in gambling tax, representing 30 per cent of its gross profit.)

Hobart has other claims to distinction. No other Australian city has so many beautiful, well-preserved colonial buildings. Its Theatre Royal—originally called the Royal Victoria—which dates from 1837, is the oldest theatre in Australia to have given performances continuously. And, until 1964, Hobart had a unique floating bridge.

'The Hobart Bridge, now under construction, is more than just a bridge,' said a writer in *Walkabout* in February 1941. It was certainly a most unusual bridge—the only one of its type in the world. It was a floating arc, consisting of two sections, each a curved concrete structure 480 m long, connected by a lifting span which allowed 45 m of head room for ships to pass through.

Plans for a bridge across the Derwent River date back to 1832, only 28 years after the settlement began on the western bank, where the land suitable for settlement is little more than a narrow strip between the river and the foothills of Mount Wellington.

Construction of the floating bridge began in 1938, and the bridge was completed in 1943. Suburbs on the eastern bank of the Derwent, formerly dependent on ferries, grew rapidly. By 1955, the bridge could not cope with the traffic, and when a violent storm damaged one of the floating sections, it was decided to replace the floating bridge with a high-level viaduct structure. Construction of this began in May 1960, and the new four-lane 1025 m bridge became fully operational in December 1964.

In January 1975, however, the bridge was partially destroyed when a freighter, the *Lake Illawarra*, ran into it. The ship sank, along with several cars, and twelve people died in the mishap. Disruption to Hobart's life continued until October 1977 when the $20 million restoration was complete.

No ardour for Federation

One reason why Hobart has retained so many of its colonial buildings is that it has grown slowly. At Federation there were only 34,000 people in Hobart—about the same as Bundaberg today—and most of them had better things to do on New Year's Day 1901 than watch the ceremony of proclaiming the Commonwealth and swearing in the Chief Justice as Administrator of the new State of Tasmania on the Supreme Court steps. The Hobart *Mercury* reported: 'It was an eventful occasion, being the first official act performed in connection with the new Commonwealth; but the crowd was not a large one, nor was it very demonstrative. The best that may be said of it was that it was a representative gathering of citizens . . . Mr Barton having ignored our strong claim to have a Tasmanian minister included in his Cabinet is being keenly felt by all classes, and this seemed to have completely dampened the ardour of all who assembled . . . giving rise to feelings that prompted such remarks as; "We would have stood out of it if we could; but unfortunately we could not afford to".'

But the weather was pleasant, and it must have been easy to forget political disappointments. 'The summer heat was nicely tempered by cooling breezes . . . as usual the great majority of Hobart people were out of town either picnicking on in sylvan retreats, or away on the river . . .' said the *Mercury*.

Switched-on city

The resurgence in Hobart's importance in the 20th century owed much to the connection of the city to the Great Lake hydro-electric power system in May 1916. The Governor-General, Sir Ronald Munro Ferguson, said when he threw the switch that he felt he was switching Tasmania on to 'the main current of the industrial life of Australia'.

Sir Ronald became quite lyrical about Tasmania's future: 'When the good fairy passed over Australia, she scattered all her choicest gifts, but the water sprite established herself in Tasmania alone. And her cup in the central hills is filled to overflowing, and man has shown that he can keep it full to the brim . . . a bright day is dawning for Tasmania.'

In the same year the Electrolytic Zinc Company of Australasia began operations on a waterfront site in Hobart. This was the foundation of the city's growth.

Early in the 20th century Hobart was the smallest of the state capitals. Its growth had been slow and it retained many Georgian buildings. One, on the corner of Elizabeth and Collins Streets, was the All Nations Hotel, which in the 1830s was known as the Hobart Town Bazaar

By 1935, when this photograph was taken at the corner of Elizabeth and Liverpool Streets, Hobart was well out of its period of stagnation. Cheap hydro-electric power had permitted establishment of industries, and the population had almost doubled since 1901

The quest for the capital site

Through NSW on sandwiches and bottled ale

Jealousy between Victoria and New South Wales, which had long delayed federation, flared up again when the site for a federal capital was being debated. The Premier of New South Wales, Sir John See, declared that the capital should be Sydney. 'Of course Victoria will growl,' he said. 'That is only to be expected.' Victoria did growl, and years of wrangling followed.

The New South Wales Government appointed a Royal Commissioner in 1899 to report on the 41 capital sites nominated in response to advertisements in major country newspapers. The Federal Capital Committee was asked to present the case for each site in terms of climatic conditions, accessibility, physical features, ownership and value. After studying all these submissions, the Commissioner, Alexander Oliver, recommended Bombala in southern New South Wales, a full 532 kilometres distant from Sydney. His second choice was Orange or Yass.

In 1902, groups of federal members of both houses inspected a number of contending sites. Melbourne papers sneered at these 'silly picnic excursions'. *Table Talk*, a social and political weekly, satirised them in verse:

The Representatives on Tour

We're off—it is a special train
For Capitals we're looking
For many days, through devious ways,
And variegated cooking.

The populace turn out in crowds
And give us greeting hearty
Not every day there comes their way
A Parliamentary party.

Each hill and dale, each stream and lake
Seems all the more alluring,
When sandwiches and bottled ale
Alleviate our touring.

On one of these jaunts, William Morris Hughes, then the federal member for West

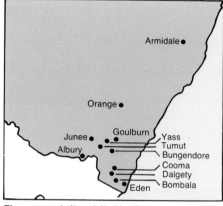

The proposed sites visited by the senators in 1902. The search for a capital city site took eight years between 1899 and 1908

Sydney, became Grand Master of a 'weird secret society', the Order of the Blue-Legged Pelicans. His party was visiting Dalgety, described by Hughes as 'a place where the highest flights of Nature's beauty are associated with her lowest temperatures'. It was midwinter and a cutting wind was blowing straight off Mt Kosciusko.

The party shivered as their four-horse char-a-bancs clattered along the frozen road on the way to a hostel by the Snowy River. In the parlour, as they thawed out in front of a huge log fire, standing first on one leg and then on the other, King O'Malley remarked that they looked like 'pelicans of the wilderness'. 'I'm jolly well *blue* with cold,' said another, and thus the order was born.

As the evening wore on, a system was adopted whereby each man had to queue for a place in front of the fire. To speed up the process, a cold man at the end of the queue would shift one at the front by the somewhat alarming method of pushing a red-hot poker between his parted knees from behind.

As more coaches arrived and more frozen senators stepped inside, each man was ceremoniously led to the fire and given a pickled onion and a bit of cheese speared on two forks—and while he patiently awaited instructions for his initiation, the poker would take him by surprise, making him jump aside and give way to a new arrival. Hughes was particularly skilful in manipulating the poker, and for this reason he was unanimously elected Grand Master.

A tragedy nearly occurred when one of the members, greedy for warmth in his frozen state, stayed in front of the fireplace for so long a time that his trousers caught fire. So did his wooden leg.

In 1903, a Commonwealth Royal Commission rejected all the proposed sites and chose Dalgety, that tiny, cold township in the far south-east of New South Wales. To add to the confusion Federal Parliament, which had to make the decision, could not agree. The Senate voted for Bombala and the House of Representatives for Tumut.

The debates on the capital site were enlivened by the unconventional oratory of the member for Tasmania, King O'Malley, who ardently championed the cause for Bombala.

Inspecting the capital sites was an enjoyable junket for the parliamentarians. At each township they were entertained lavishly and briefed on the unique advantages of the neighbourhood. This photograph was taken at a fruit luncheon at Orange, a small town in the foothills of the Blue Mountains

The tours, satirised by newspapermen for their undeniably 'picnicky' overtones, afforded the senators some pleasant leisure hours. Here members relax in the waters of the Snowy River in summer

'The full-blooded horse Bombala, with distended nostrils, high withers, and long neck, drinking in the sweetness of his own breath as he flies along, cares nothing for the billy-goats behind him,' he said during one session. On another occasion, when Tumut was mentioned, he said: 'If we select a site at less than an altitude of 450 metres, we had better start a parliamentary boiling-down works, or a cemetery. I have visited Tumut, and if I owned that town and Hades, I should let Tumut and live in Hades, because there is no scientific evidence to show that it is hotter in Hades than it is in Tumut.'

O'Malley's colourful eloquence added its characteristic flavour to a *Hansard* report on the Seat of Government debate in 1903: 'If ever there was a spot set apart by the Creator to be the Capital of this great Australia—the pivot around which Australian civilisation should evolve—it is Bombala . . . It will be a black crime against posterity if we select any place but Bombala. A number of honourable members . . . have asked how honourable members will reach the seat of Government, if it be fixed at Bombala. Why, the Leader of the Opposition, for instance, could step on a steamer in Melbourne, and next morning be at Twofold Bay, whence he might be wafted to the scene of his legislative labours in the buckets of an aerial railway . . .

'Take the sons of some of the greatest men in the world, and put them in a hot climate like Tumut or Albury, and in three generations their lineal descendants will be degenerate. I found them in San Domingo on a Sabbath morning going to a cock-fight with a rooster under each arm, and a sombrero on their heads. I want to have a cold climate chosen for the capital of this Commonwealth.' But O'Malley's wishes failed.

The dispute went on until 1908 when, as a compromise, the present site of Canberra, in the Molonglo Valley, was agreed upon. A little closer to Sydney than Melbourne, all it could boast then were a few grazing properties, and a distant view of the mountains.

Members await their turn as Sir William Lyne, Premier of New South Wales, clambers over a fence at Albury. It was generally thought that this would be the selected site, but on the party's arrival the town was smothered in dust—a rare and untimely occurrence which spoiled Albury's chances

Where railway lines were not available, the senators were conveyed to the suggested sites in four-horse carriages, with diversions such as lunches in the open and stops at idyllic spots like this one in the rain forest on the way to Bega on the south coast of New South Wales

Capital cities that were never built

Plans for the new national capital started as a mixture of designs and utopian visions of the 'ideal federal city' for Australia. Before the site was agreed upon in 1908 some designs were put forward for a city located on the shores of Lake George. This rather Indian-looking design was proposed in about 1900 but failed to gain favour

In 1901 Robert Coulter, who worked in the Government Architect's Office, drew this rather grandiose view of a possible capital on Lake George. Coulter later toured the proposed capital sites with the Government Architect and sketched the surrounding country. His panorama of the Canberra site was sent to all the entrants in the design competition

The artist versus the bureaucrat

Griffin's plan replaced by 'a third rate Luna Park'

'Londoners may be all too aware of the disadvantages of living in a city without a plan,' quipped a *Punch* journalist, 'but these cannot be compared with the rival disadvantages of living in a plan without a city.'

For many years after the boundaries of the Capital Territory had been fixed this was the fate of the national capital of Australia, and some present-day critics of Canberra suggest that it has never really overcome this deficiency. Be that as it may, those who had dreamed of a federal capital were theoretically free to realize it entirely according to rational and aesthetic principles.

'The finest capital in the world'

Andrew Fisher's Labor Government announced a world-wide competition for the design of the capital, offering first, second and third prizes of £1750, £750 and £500, about $70,000, $30,000 and $20,000 in 1984. Entries were to close on 31 January 1912.

The Minister for Home Affairs, who was in charge of the contest, was the flamboyant Canadian-born King O'Malley. 'This must be the finest capital in the world,' he declared.

But not everyone approved of O'Malley's control of the project, nor indeed of the composition of the adjudicating board. The eminent Sydney architect Hardy Wilson declined to enter, and there was a general boycott of the competition by members of the Royal Institute of British Architects, the Institute of Civil Engineers and affiliated bodies in the British Empire. Nevertheless 137 entrants submitted their plans, and on 23 May 1912 the winners were announced.

Griffin's winning plan

First prize went to Walter Burley Griffin, a 35-year-old American architect and associate of Frank Lloyd Wright. He had submitted plans and drawings of a city to be laid out in a series of circles and rectangles grouped around radiating roads and so conceived as to harmonise with the amphitheatre formed by Mt Ainslie, Black Mountain and Pleasant Hill. 'I have planned the city,' he explained, 'so that the three mountain peaks will close its principal vistas and form a splendid background for its architectural beauty.'

There was a general professional enthusiasm for Burley Griffin's plan, but an undercurrent of complaints against its extravagance from the bureaucratic sector grew sufficiently strong to cause O'Malley to refer the question to a specially constituted departmental board for further consideration. The board rejected the plans of all three place-getters, and offered instead a fourth of its own contrivance. Thus when on February 20 King O'Malley drove in the first peg to mark the commencement of construction, it was according to the board's plan, and not Griffin's, that work was to proceed.

Sydmeladperbrisho

The capital was still nameless—although a good many inventive suggestions had been received from members of the public. Among them were 'Auralia', 'Australopis', 'Cooee-ton', 'Caucus City', 'Engirscot' (a combination of England, Ireland and Scotland), 'Kookaburra', 'Laborall', 'Sydmeladper-brisho' (ensuring that none of the state capitals could feel slighted), 'Woolgold', and—anticipating Sinclair Lewis by nine years—'Zenith'. Another was 'Myola', a popular favorite until an alert newspaper correspondent claimed that it was a cunning anagram for 'O'Malley', although O'Malley denied it.

However the final choice was kept a closely-guarded secret until, on March 12, 1913 the Governor-General, Lord Denman, arrived for the founding ceremony on Capital Hill. The Governor-General, the Prime Minister and King O'Malley declared the foundation stones well and truly laid and Lady Denman formally named the city 'Canberra'; the area was already known by that name.

Had events followed the course set by O'Malley, Griffin's design might have been shelved forever in favor of what an eminent British townplanner described as 'a third rate Luna Park'. However, by mid-1913 the Fisher Government was out of office and the new Prime Minister, Joseph Cook, took over the portfolio for Home Affairs, with W. H. Kelly as Acting Minister.

The plan in danger

The architects and engineers, whose anger had for so long smouldered against the Government's compromise, seized their opportunity. Eight hundred of them presented a petition to Cook urging him to 'review the present built up design, to which so much exception has been taken'. Griffin meanwhile had written from America in defence of his plan, and in August 1913 was invited to Canberra for discussions. Two months later Kelly dismissed the Board, and Griffin was appointed Federal Capital Director of Design. It now looked as if his plan would be preserved in its entirety.

But the struggle between artist and bureaucrat was not over. P. T. Owen's complaint that 'Mr Griffin desired to take control of all engineering works, a principle which, as Director General of Works, I resent' was typical. Then, when the Fisher Government was returned again in September 1914, a dismayed Griffin found that his plan appeared to be in danger after all. Requesting clarification of his position, he pointed out that 'it was only because of the acceptance of my design that I entered into my agreement with the Commonwealth, and it would be unfair and unreasonable to require me to continue my services on any other basis'.

At the moment of crisis the political kaleidoscope shifted again. Billy Hughes replaced the retiring Prime Minister, and King O'Malley returned to the post of Minister for Home Affairs. Whatever O'Malley's original

Two visions and the final reality

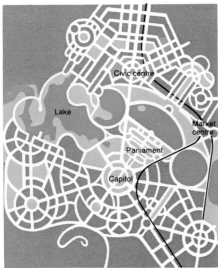

Walter Burley Griffin's prize-winning design for an Australian capital. It was only after a long and bitter struggle that it was finally accepted

The alternative plan suggested by a departmental board in response to allegations that Griffin's plan was unduly extravagant

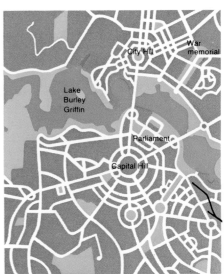

Canberra today substantially follows Griffin's concept, particularly since the central lake was formed by damming the Molonglo River in 1964

position, he now threw his weight behind what was after all still the officially endorsed plan and supported Griffin's full authority over its execution. In April 1916 the architect's contract was extended for another three years. Soon after, a Royal Commission found that if Griffin had not proceeded properly with his duties between October 1913 and November 1915, it was largely because of the obstructionism of Archibald, then Minister for Home Affairs, and officials of the departmental board. J. S. Murdoch, the Department's chief architect said that he would 'like to see the Federal Capital strangled for 100 years'. Griffin and his plan were vindicated.

But by then the war was on, and the drain of military expenditure crippled the progress of the city's construction. Nevertheless, within the limits of his budget, Griffin pressed on. He built Commonwealth and Adelaide Avenues, the main arteries running north and south-west from Capital Hill, as well as part of the National Circuit and a temporary railway. Griffin had always been convinced of the need for the city to develop both north and south of the Molonglo River to prevent one side from expanding at the expense of the other. Thus, with funds short, the construction of north-south communications became his first priority.

'A good sheep paddock spoiled'

Quite remarkably anticipating the views of today's town planners, he looked forward to the time when fast modern transport would 'mean a very different distribution of trade than where walking range has been the determining factor'. And if the spaciousness in which early Canberra developed provoked doubters to such sardonic jibes as 'a good sheep paddock spoiled', time appears to have vindicated Griffin's vision. Canberra may have started its life as 'a plan without a city', but it was a plan into which a modern city could gracefully and comfortably expand.

The Governor-General, Lord Denman, and an escort of Lancers canter towards Capital Hill for the founding ceremony at which Lady Denman formally named the city Canberra. The meaning of the aboriginal word Canberra is in doubt; it may mean either 'meeting place' or 'woman's breasts'

King O'Malley, Minister for Home Affairs, drives the first peg on a survey line running from the proposed site of Parliament House to Mount Ainslie on 20 February 1913. At this stage Griffin's plan had been rejected and work was to proceed on an alternative design by the Department of Home Affairs

Canberra as it might have been

Australia's national capital as it was envisaged by a Frenchman, Professor D. A. Agache, winner of the third prize in the 1912 competition

This design, submitted by Eliel Saarinen of Finland, took second prize in the competition. Eliel Saarinen is now regarded as one of the great architects of his time, although his son, Eero, a leader of the modernist movement in the 1950s, is perhaps better known

The plan becomes a reality

A city of foundation stones becomes a national capital

The official opening of Federal Parliament House on 9 May 1927—26 years to the day after the opening of Federal Parliament in Melbourne. By the time the new Parliament House on Capital Hill opens in 1988, this building will have had 61 years of 'temporary' use. It may become a museum

The Duke of York reads the King's commission establishing the new seat of government at the first session of Federal Parliament in Canberra

The opening of Canberra's Civic Centre by Prime Minister Stanley Bruce on 3 December 1927 was a step towards providing the newly transplanted community with facilities that it badly needed. Bruce disliked Griffin's name 'Civic Centre' and refused to use it when he opened the building

After the end of World War I, interest in the growth of the national capital revived. But funds remained short—from 1917 to 1920 total expenditure on construction was a mere £8744 [$201,000]; politicians and public servants continued their squabbling delays; and press and public often displayed a disillusioned scepticism about the whole project. Construction proceeded slowly. When the Prince of Wales visited Canberra in 1920, he remarked as he added yet another stone to those already dotting Capital Hill, that the city appeared to consist chiefly of numerous foundation stones.

When, soon after, Prime Minister Billy Hughes decided that the time was ripe to move the Federal Administration from Melbourne to Canberra, the need for speed became paramount, and a Federal Capital Advisory Committee was appointed.

Since October 1919, Walter Burley Griffin's contract had been under review. Now it was decided not to renew it, although he was invited to sit on the committee. Reluctantly he relinquished control, bitterly concluding that 'the essence of the matter is that

the design and construction of the city is . . . to be transferred from me to the Works Department, which has on the evidence of oath in open court before a Royal Commission . . . been adjudged hostile to myself, my plan and to my procedures.'

The establishment of Parliament House was clearly the first step in turning Canberra into a workable administrative capital and the first sod for the temporary building, below Capital Hill, was turned by the Minister for Works in August 1923. Used ever since, this building will be overshadowed in 1988— the year of Australia's Bicentenary—by a new Parliament House crowning Capital Hill itself, its design chosen from the entrants to a competition among architects registered in Australia.

A. P. Herbert, visiting Australia in September 1925 with a press delegation, wrote of his visit to the still incomplete Parliament House: '. . . I crawled under a ladder, put my foot in some cement, and entered the great Parliament House . . . We heard a noise like a battle. Our guide peered through a forest of beams into a space floored with corrugated

iron, in the middle of which a cement mixer was noisily at work.

' "That is the Senate", he shouted . . . He took us to look at a crowd of men hard at work in a cloud of dust.

' "The Lower House", he said with a proud gesture . . .

Finally they took us out to a grand terrace . . . Our friend pointed to an empty field and said: "That is the National Library."

' "Remarkable", we said; and so it was, for at that moment there was passing through the National Library a real Australian cow.'

Work on Parliament House was completed by 1927, and although the parliamentary session had already begun in Melbourne, a ceremony to open the new Parliament House was held on 9 May 1927. Dame Nellie Melba led the crowd in singing the National Anthem; then the Duke of York (later George VI) formally opened the door of Parliament House. Later he read a message from his father in the Senate chamber. And Canberra, with a population of about 7000, became the official seat of Federal Government.

The spectacle of the distinguished visitors

Canberra grew in area from 39 km² in 1939 to 605 km² in 1985. Planned housing, like this in Curtin, accounted for much of it

A view of Canberra from Mt. Ainslie in 1937 shows a few buildings scattered over a large area, and explains why the capital called forth such descriptions as 'a good sheep paddock spoiled' and 'six suburbs in search of a city'. However, after World War II the city expanded rapidly

gathered for the occasion in the still embryonic capital must have been a strange one, with the royal coaches, the uniformed cavalry escorts, the glittering gold braid, the orders and the decorations all resplendent among rural surroundings where sheep could be seen cropping the nearby pastures. As there were few hotels in the area, many of the important guests were invited to camp out overnight. With the Canberra winter approaching they did not accept the offer.

The authorities expected a crowd of at least 30,000 and had, in true Australian fashion, ordered 60,000 meat pies to feed them. But the supply, as it turned out, greatly exceeded the demand, and more than 10,000 luscious pies were quietly committed to a mass grave.

One of the curious circumstances of life in the early days of the new capital was that prohibition was imposed. King O'Malley, during his term as Minister for Home Affairs in the second Fisher Ministry, had seen fit to forbid the sale of liquor in the Capital Territory.

Explaining later how the legislation came to be passed, he wrote: 'I found three men carrying a paling, and when I suggested that a fourth should help with the job, they wanted to fight me . . . Whisky and rum were planted about the job. There were numerous intervals, for a draw on the tonic.

'I said to myself "King, this will have to be stopped." I had to be canny about it. The cabinet was by no means "dry". I went to a meeting with the ordinance in my pocket and, when towards the end, Andy Fisher called me and said 'Well, King, what have you today?' I brought out the document. George Pearce was busy raising the "screws" of his admirals; other ministers were not very interested, so the ordinance slipped through.'

Canberra remained 'dry' until 1928—and neighbouring Queanbeyan's five pubs reaped a glorious profit. Every Saturday afternoon saw a huge exodus from Canberra. Taxi-drivers charged 16s [$21] to take a car-load of thirsty citizens the 11 kilometres across the NSW border to Queanbeyan and back, and not only the town's publicans but all its tradespeople profited handsomely.

'During prohibition, there was,' in one historian's cautious words, 'a certain amount of public and private celebration.' But then in accordance with the results of a poll of 1 September 1928, the prohibition laws were rescinded. Only Queanbeyan felt regret.

Canberra's population grew slowly, as more and more public servants were uprooted from Melbourne and replanted in the capital city. 'By car and train they came,' wrote journalist Warren Denning, an eyewitness of the exodus, 'their household effects packed into rail-waggons, their families, servants, dogs, canaries and cats. The transfer was no respecter of persons. Heads of departments and messenger boys, all grades between, participated in this unique colonisation—almost all with loathing and regret. The real martyrs of the transfer were the women-folk. Some that were ailing, and some that were not brave, remained behind in Melbourne. But in most cases there was no option, for the lower paid public servant cannot keep two homes.' Those earning more than £336

a year (equivalent to a Clerk, Class 2/3, earning $16,417 in 1985), were given first class sleeping berths on the train to Canberra. Those with lesser salaries had no sleepers.

However the Depression of the 1930s and World War Two slowed growth again. In 1939 the population was about 13,000; by 1945 it had risen by only 2000. Canberra's rapid growth began after the war and accelerated noticeably after the mid-1950s as more and more Government departments moved there. By 1954, the population had risen to 28,000; by 1963, on its fiftieth birthday, to 70,775, and in June 1983 to 255,900, of whom 61,300 were employed as public servants.

Canberra today, for all its fine, natural setting, its broad, curving avenues, its parks, gardens and fountains, its well-designed buildings, its well-equipped schools and thriving population is still for some people a city without a soul. For many it lacks an inner core, a sense of having been lived in. 'A good place to work in but not to retire in', in the words of Professor C. P. FitzGerald.

The 140 m water jet in Lake Burley Griffin keeps six tonnes of water in the air at any one time

Modern Canberra with the War Memorial in the foreground and Parliament House across the lake

73

Life in country towns

Vigorous business and social activity

Cairns, with its broad main street, unhurried cyclists and shady verandahs, was the epitome of a country town in the early 1920s. The town, basking in the tropical sunshine 1600 kilometres from the nearest big city—Brisbane—then had a population of fewer than 8000

Country towns, with your willows and squares,
And farmers bouncing on barrel mares
To public-houses of yellow wood
With '1860' over their doors,
And that mysterious race of Hogans
Which always keeps General Stores . . .

—Kenneth Slessor

By 1907 Australia had 11 towns of 20,000 to 30,000 people, 21 of 5000–10,000 and 33 of 3000–5000. Many more towns had fewer than 3000 people. Many settlements that had begun as no more than centres of rural districts were growing into sturdy business communities in their own right. Some were

recovering from the depression of the 1890s. In New South Wales in particular, old towns flourished anew and new towns grew up as wheat production boomed in the 1900s.

One such town was Moree, 686 kilometres north-west of Sydney. In 1901, Moree, with a population of 2298, had four solicitors, three physicians, a dentist, four stock and station agents, eight stores, seven tobacconists, a photographer, a millwright, a coachbuilder and a number of other businesses. There were two daily newspapers.

Bathurst, NSW, with a population of 9223, at that time had three daily papers, and so did dozens of other towns before improved

transport allowed the big city dailies to be distributed quickly far into the country. The telegraph permitted a country paper to carry international and national news no more than two days old alongside news of the rich and vigorous social life of the town.

The newspapers were a good pennyworth. They gave details of mail closing times and river steamer services; they carried notices of parcels arrived by train and awaiting collection. They announced forthcoming visits of dentists, chiropodists and herbalists. They devoted entire columns to lists of ladies present at functions, the lady's name being followed by a note of her attire—'Mrs C. Campbell, vieux rose voile, Mrs T. Head, white silk; Mrs H. Prudy, blue ninon . . .'

A Toowoomba local historian, Mr K. Donges, born in 1889, vividly recalls the social life of Queensland country towns when he was a young man: 'The older folk often visited each other on Sundays after church or on special occasions such as picnics, ploughing matches . . . annual shows, and parties in the homes. For the younger generation, there were concerts in town, dances in barns, cornhusking parties, and various games, cricket, horseshoe quoits, and even horse-racing on the back roads.'

In a town of 4000 people there might have been a musical society, a band and a lyric club which presented comic opera. Even Queanbeyan, NSW, which had only 1200 inhabitants in 1910, could muster 15 instrumentalists for an orchestra supporting a chorus of 25, a fairly notable achievement.

Most towns had cricket, football and tennis clubs, several church organisations and three or four lodges, such as the Foresters, the Star of the East Oddfellows or the Ancient Order

Late on a hot afternoon in January 1916, the people of Mudgee, NSW, welcome a dusty column of volunteers who have reached the town during a 388 kilometres recruiting march from Tooraweenah to Bathurst. Here the local brass band leads the volunteers, who called themselves the 'Kookaburras', past the Town Hall. Mudgee, administrative and trading centre of a rich grazing and farming district, then had about 3000 people

Congregational Church services at Boulder, on the Western Australian goldfields were held in this corrugated iron chapel at the turn of the century. Boulder, named after the famous Great Boulder Lode, was laid out, 11 kilometres from Kalgoorlie, in 1897. In 1903 water was piped in from near Perth. In 1905 the twin towns, together with Coolgardie, 38 kilometres to the west, had a combined population of over 200,000. But the gold became harder to mine and the population of the area declined rapidly. In 1981 the combined population of Kalgoorlie and Boulder was 19,848 and that of Coolgardie 891, a notable fall in numbers

In 1916 these children and their teacher posed outside their school at Myrtle Bank, in Gippsland, Victoria. The population of the settlement then is not recorded, but in 1921 it was 31. It may have been no more in 1916, when the school also served as the post office as the sign indicates

In leisurely Bathurst, NSW, in the early 1920s townspeople could chat in the middle of the street or in wide-verandahed hotels while their horses drank from a trough combined with a gas lamp. Bathurst's street gas lamps, which were replaced by electric lights in 1924, were not lit during the week around full moon

This dusty township was photographed in 1933, the year its name changed from Stuart to Alice Springs. The population was 526. In 1985, the 'Alice' had 22,000 people, its first set of traffic lights, and a prosperous tourist industry thanks to a standard-gauge rail link with Adelaide and Sydney

of Buffaloes. There might also have been a Burns Society and a May Day committee; a sparrow club for shooting at clay birds, and a poultry club for showing real ones.

Town councils did little to organise outdoor recreation beyond providing a park where townspeople could stroll. Tennis tournaments were played on private lawns. Swimming was for boys only, and confined to secluded parts of rivers after dark. On sports days most competitions were for boys and men, although women could try their skill at dancing the hornpipe or the Irish jig or at bowling a hoop.

There were regattas and shows and picnic races, and besides all these there were visits from travelling dramatic and vaudeville companies, circuses and occasionally renowned singers such as Dame Nellie Melba, Dame Clara Butt or Ada Crossley. To hear Melba at the height of her career, the citizens of Bathurst paid up to 15s a seat [$29].

Cinemas became popular during the early 1900s; Bathurst had four by 1910. Some country town picture palaces had the screen at the street end, and the audience passed beneath it to get to their seats in the galvanised iron auditorium. On hot summer nights the walls and roof would be removed and the audience would sit under the stars.

If the town were prosperous, or had been prosperous during the boom period of the 1880s, the main street would be lined with substantial buildings. The courthouse, the police station, the town hall and the banks were usually solidly built of brick. The big hotels might also be of brick—at least the facades. Leading hotels had their own one-horse cabs which met all mail and passenger trains and conveyed guests from the station.

The lamplighter was a familiar figure until electricity arrived. At dusk each day he came around in his sulky to trim the street lamps and fill them with enough kerosene to last until about 9 p.m. Toowoomba's streets were lit by gas and the lamplighter did his rounds

on a tricycle. Publicans were required by law to keep a light burning in front of their premises all night—a welcoming beacon for thirsty and weary travellers.

Toowoomba, like many country towns, had a bellman, or town crier, who walked along the streets swinging his bell and lustily announcing coming events—social functions, entertainments, sales, and auctions. There was also a sandwichman.

The Chinese market gardener would also be seen daily, trudging behind the cart bringing produce from his garden into town. 'Afghan' hawkers with wagons full of haberdashery, sewing-machine agents, piano-tuners, book-canvassers, saddlers and wood-carvers were frequent visitors. Another familiar figure in country towns was the tinker, who mended billycans, quart-pots, pannikins, buckets and dishes, an indispensable tradesman.

Australia's front door

A city devastated by man and nature

Darwin has always had something of the frontier town about it. With its mixed racial composition, its situation in the remote north-west and its sultry climate, it is, perhaps, more like some flourishing colonial outpost than an Australian city.

Port Darwin was discovered in 1839 by Captain Wickham of HMS *Beagle*. He named the port after the famous naturalist, Charles Darwin, who had sailed with the *Beagle* on a previous voyage between 1831 and 1836. The township began life as Palmerston, after the British Prime Minister at the time of its founding in 1869, but the name was changed in 1911. In that year, the Northern Territory was transferred from South Australian to Commonwealth administration, and Darwin, a ragged settlement of just over a thousand people, became the administrative capital of the Northern Territory, an area of some 1,346,200 sq. km.

At the time of Federation, there were fewer than 50,000 people in the whole north of Australia. The population of the Northern Territory was 4096. In 1911 Darwin's population was 1082; in 1947 it was 2538; in 1972 it was 36,000; and in 1985 it was 65,000. A long-range plan for the city envisages 200,000 people in two decades. Darwin is Australia's fastest-growing city, with a high proportion of people under 40. With comparatively little industry and agriculture in the region, about 45 per cent of the workforce are public servants. It has one of the most racially diverse populations in the country—it is home to some 45 nationalities. Among builders, electricians and the businessmen who control much of the city's real estate are many descendants of Greeks who came as sponge divers. The forefathers of many professionals, public servants and successful merchants of Chinese origin came to Darwin after the gold-rush of 1873 as labourers, cooks and laundrymen. The population also includes Aborigines, Malays, Timorese, Italians, Central Europeans and people of mixed race.

But Darwin was not always such a flourishing city. Dr Mervyn Holmes, appointed Palmerston's Chief Medical Officer in 1869, condemned the whole town roundly, but the hovels of Chinatown in particular.

'The conditions were simply shocking. Not more than 20 percent of the hotels had a privy at all. Disease was rampant. Conditions at the hospital were little better. The sanitary pans were kerosene tins. The roof leaked, and in the wards nurses were often ankle deep in water. Aborigine girls were sold openly, and there was widespread opium addiction . . .'

Things had not improved much in 1917 apparently, when the Member for Brisbane, W. F. Finlayson, gave Federal Parliament a sombre report on Darwin's three Government-run hotels. 'No matter what time of the day or night, one can find idlers sitting in and around the Darwin hotels, spitting or blaspheming,' he said. 'On . . . pay day there are scenes of orgies that would bring despair to the heart of the bravest temperance reformer. No writer but one with the gift of Charles

The sparse scattering of houses that was Darwin in 1911, just 43 years after it was founded. The harbour was named after Charles Darwin

Darwin in 1970 still bore a superficial resemblance to the tiny settlement of 1911, but in this time the population had grown from 1082 to over 25,000. On Christmas Day 1974 a cyclone struck the city, killing over 50 people and destroying most buildings. It was Australia's worst natural disaster

A Chinese Buddhist temple on the outskirts of Darwin, photographed in 1911. The inscription above the door reads 'Northernmost temple'

Darwin's Chinatown in 1911; the shanties were destroyed in World War II. The Chinese form an important part of Darwin's racial mix

Darwin in 1911 was still very much a shanty town that had grown up out of the gold rushes of the 1870s and 1880s. The population was little more than 1000, and improvised shacks like these lined the dusty streets. The head of a mine shaft can be seen rising above the shack at the end of the street

Dickens could adequately describe the wholesale abandonment of human dignity.'

Hudson Fysh, the founder of Qantas, who lived in Darwin for nine months in 1919, preparing the landing ground for Ross and Keith Smith, wrote that Darwin was 'a strange, tough town, not at all like other Australian settlements in the south . . . There were pearlers, buffalo hunters, prospectors, trepangers [gatherers of *bêche de mer*],

sandalwood-getters, and a miscellaneous mixture of cattlemen and overlanders.'

During World War II, Darwin became an important military and air-force base. Then came repeated Japanese air raids. Between 19 February 1942 and 12 November 1943, Darwin was bombed, more or less heavily, 59 times. Much of the town was devastated and most of its population fled south.

Reconstruction was slow but the discovery

of uranium ore at Rum Jungle in the 1950s brought a prosperity. Modern Darwin became a city in 1959, but on Christmas Day 1974, it was almost completely destroyed by a cyclone. More than 30,000 people were evacuated to the south. Three years and $700 million later the city had been rebuilt. It now has the dignity of being the capital of a territory with full self-government, this being proclaimed on 1 July 1978.

The Northern Territory was transferred from South Australian to Commonwealth administration on 1 January 1912. Here Mr Justice Mitchell, acting

Administrator, reads the proclamation in the grounds of the government residence. Some extreme White Australia faddists objected to the fact

that the new flag for the ceremony had been made by local Chinese tradesmen; to avoid trouble an old and tattered—non-Chinese—one was used instead

House and home

Dwellings influenced by local needs and foreign styles

Robin Boyd, one of the most perceptive students of Australian architecture, thought three national influences had acted on it. One was the English tradition, 'the fountainhead of nearly all building ideas throughout the nineteenth century,' which gave us the beautiful neo-Georgian houses of the early days of settlement and the Victorian exuberance of later years. Another more recent influence was American. Boyd saw two manifestations of this—'Hollywood and serious'. The third influence was Australian and it included the use of native materials and 'the psychology of isolation'.

Boyd associated these three influences with three men who were active about the time of World War I—Robert Haddon, an Englishman; Walter Burley Griffin, an American; and Harold Desbrowe Annear, an Australian.

After World War II, when the five-roomed red brick villa with an orange-tiled roof was still the archetypal Australian dwelling, architects like Roy Grounds, Sydney Ancher and Harry Seidler turned to Europe and America for inspiration. Despite the obstruction of bumbling aldermen and councillors, they gradually introduced Australians to the clean-cut 'international' style.

Suburban development in Australia's big cities has followed a familiar pattern. Once-fashionable areas close to the city centres decay as their inhabitants move out to newer suburbs. Spacious mansions become institutions or boarding houses, or are subdivided into flats. Iron lacework on terrace houses is sold for scrap, their balconies are closed in to make shabby sleep-outs and kitchenettes. Factories and workshops creep into former residential areas.

Years later, the process is reversed. As new suburbs stretch out farther and farther, the neglected suburbs revive, battered terraces are restored, and towering blocks of 'home units' replace villas in suburban streets.

It belongs to no recognised style, but this house, with its keyhole arch and faintly *art nouveau* verandah posts, is unmistakably Australian. It was built about 1901

The mansions of yesteryear

Some castles crumble, others are converted

One of the few great Australian mansions that is still privately owned and has not been converted into flats is *Mona Vale*, near Ross in the rich pastoral midlands of Tasmania. Built in 1867, it is often called the 'Calendar House' because of a popular misconception that it was designed with 365 windows to represent the days of the year, 52 rooms to represent the weeks of the year, 12 chimneys to represent the months, seven entrances to represent the days of the week and four staircases to represent the seasons. The truth is that there are only 300 windows and 50 rooms and the rest of the numerical symbolism is quite accidental. Another adjunct to this grand house was the large glassed-in conservatory

Australians first began to build mansions in the 1850s, when gold brought sudden wealth, but most of Australia's large houses were built in the 1870s and 1880s. In the country, the wool kings competed to construct lavish homes. In the cities, the mansions were built by merchants who wanted to entertain their new-rich friends on an extravagant scale. In Melbourne, a motto on the front door of *Norwood*, at Brighton read 'Welcome is the best cheer'; more than 600 people could be seated in the ballroom of *Studley*, at Kew.

Often only three or four servants were employed to run these large houses. But after the boom of the 1870s and 1880s burst and servants became hard to get, many owners were forced to sell or subdivide. One was James Grice, who in March 1904 offered for sale his mansion *Oma*, in Albany Road, Toorak, Melbourne. Its ground floor comprised a wide hall, opening into a spacious vestibule; drawing room; library; morning room, ballroom; breakfast room with folding doors opening on to an enclosed 15 by 5 m verandah; and 'exceptionally large' dining room 'with servers, fitted with a gas range for heating plates, etc.'; a butler's pantry; a china pantry; lavatory and cloakroom; a large kitchen; scullery and larder; servant's hall, butler's room and 'a large, dry and commodious cellar'.

On the first floor there was a best bedroom (6 by 8 m), with a dressing room and bathroom-suite, and ten other bedrooms. There were also a linen-room, box-room and three more 'completely fitted' bathrooms. Out-buildings included a laundry 'fitted with troughs, copper and ironing-room' and an extensive two-storey brick stables, with stabling for six horses, two coach houses accommodating 10 vehicles, harness room, hay loft and two men's rooms.

Grice bought the house in 1889 for £27,000 [$1.5 million] and spent £3000 [$168,000] on improvements. In 1904 all he could get for it was £11,000 [$567,000]. In 1954, when the property was subdivided and sold for £350,000 [$4 million], the house was still in its original state, and was still lit by gas.

A deliberate mixture of architectural styles was *Norwood* in Brighton, Melbourne, demolished in 1955. Built in 1891, it had stained glass windows which depicted Shakespearean characters

Tranmere House, Adelaide, an elaborately-turreted Edwardian pile, in its full glory about 1910. Once divided into flats, it is now a single dwelling again

Oma, in Melbourne stood in 2.2 hectares of grounds laid out in lawns, shrubberies, flower gardens, a horse paddock, a fowl run and a vegetable and fruit garden. The plants included palms and many rare ornamental shrubs brought from other states, especially Queensland

Fads and fashions

The reign of red Queen Anne in the suburbs

In 1911, Ernest Newman, Vice-President of the Royal Institute of British Architects, commented on the confusions of domestic architecture in Australia. 'We were asked 40 years ago to invent a new style and we have invented a dozen,' he wrote. 'We have had houses recalling the buildings of the 17th and 18th centuries, and of earlier periods; we have made full play with building materials, concrete, stone, tiles, pebbles, rough-cast, in all sorts of skilful and playful combinations of colour, form and texture; we have used all motifs, from adzed beams to painted ceilings and marble floors.'

At the time he wrote, the fashionable style for houses was 'Queen Anne'. The term was used at the time in both Britain and the United States to describe different styles of red-brick architecture, but Australian Queen Anne houses had unique features.

The only characteristic they shared with houses built in the time of Queen Anne (1702-14) was a structure of unplastered red-brick. They had roofs of terra-cotta tiles. The main impression they gave was of a dominant orange-redness and an exuberant roof-line—towers and turrets pushed upwards, gables flew outwards and bays bulged, while terra-cotta frills bounded along the roof ridges at irregular levels to terminate in terra-cotta finials shaped like dragons, griffins or even kangaroos.

Cast-iron was discarded, and elaborately turned or fretsawn wood became the only acceptable material for verandah railings, columns and decoration. Wooden shingles—a fashion imported from the United States—appeared as facings for houses or as roofing for turrets which looked as if they had been taken direct from a French chateau. Casement windows, which opened outwards replaced double-hung sashes, and were often made up of small panes of leaded glass. Windows were commonly banked together in threes, fours and fives, or pushed out to form bays. In Melbourne suburbs like Kew and Camberwell, and Sydney suburbs like Burwood and Mosman, Queen Anne houses were built on a large scale, and often with great imagination. In Sydney particularly, the balconied versions of Queen Anne often showed inventive use of ornamented woodwork and shingles. But the decorative characteristics of the style spread throughout the country on houses that were too small to support it—houses of the old 19th century passage-down-the-middle type became 'Queen Anne' by the application of terra-cotta dragons or casement windows.

Between the 1890s and World War I, many suburban houses in Australia were built in the style known as 'Queen Anne'. The grand example above has the wooden shingles and 'candle-snuffer' turret that are peculiarities of the style. The house below was photographed in 1913, shortly after it was built in Mosman, Sydney. It had not suffered the alterations that have diluted the style of most of the suburb's numerous Queen Anne houses

The bungalow arrives from California

In the early 1920s, an architectural fashion called the Californian bungalow was imported from the United States. Houses in this style were originally low single-storey structures built of timber or brick, the latter often coated with stucco, or pebble-dash. The inside effect was rustic, with exposed beams, dark-stained panelling and large fireplaces.

It was not long before it became popular in the middle-class suburbs. In the adaptation developed by Australian builders the bungalow had a high-pitched roof, roughcast walls and two squat columns supporting the flat roof of the front porch. The chimney of the main room was placed on the outside of the front wall as a feature. *Real Property Annual* commented on these bungalow-style cottages in 1921: 'In the newer suburbs . . . streets upon streets of these houses have been built . . . The similarity of these cottages . . . is indeed remarkable . . . To the discriminating eye this resemblance in design is rather monotonous, but it is nevertheless a welcome contrast to the hideous two-storey houses of the late seventies and early eighties which mar so many of the older suburbs.'

Spanish-American influences

In 1922, an English architect, Leslie Wilkinson, came to Sydney University to be the first professor of architecture in Australia. He admired the work of the early colonial architects such as the convict Francis Greenway, and at Vaucluse he built himself a house called *Greenway*. In this he combined some of the simplicity of a Greenway house with Spanish-American elements such as a thick wall pierced by rounded archways. Wilkinson had considerable influence on some of his students and, just before the Depression, they built many simple, faintly Spanish-American houses, well suited to Australia.

But at the same time, popular adaptations of the Californian 'Spanish mission' style began to appear. True Spanish mission houses, with their thick walls and shady terraces, would have been well suited to the Australian climate, but in the Spanish mission houses that sprouted in the suburbs the style was mainly an applied decoration. It showed in rounded arches and window openings, semi-circular roof tiles, wrought-iron window grilles and in the cream stucco finish on the outer walls. A curious aberration of the the late 1930s, especially in Melbourne, was so-called 'Tudor'. It had black-stained boarding over brick walls to give the effect of Elizabethan half-timbering, high roofs with fancy chimney pots, and diamond-paned leadlight windows. The shopping centre of Toorak, known as 'The Village' built between 1934 and 1937, remains as a museum of the mock-Tudor invasion. But the most flagrant example is 'London Court', the shopping lane in Perth designed in 1936.

This early example of a Californian bungalow was built in Cremorne, Sydney, in 1919 and is well attuned to its setting. Its sprawling roof, wide eaves, roughcast walls and wooden detailing show the style at its best

A 'Spanish mission' house in the Sydney suburb of Vaucluse. The arched porch with its barley-sugar columns, the curved tiles and the window grilles are all marks of the style made popular in the 1920s

Leslie Wilkinson, Australia's first professor of architecture, built himself this house, called *Greenway*, in 1923. It combined early colonial simplicity with Spanish-American touches such as the thick arched wall and the curved tiles

Housing the increasing thousands

The wealthy move into flats to make do without servants

Flats were 'doing their share of housing Sydney's increasing thousands', *Real Property Annual* reported in 1911. While the erection of 'huge flat tenements' was too costly for most investors, many large family residences were being converted into flats, especially in the seaside suburbs such as Manly and Coogee in Sydney. A similar process was taking place in Melbourne. In the boom-and-bust days of the 1880s, Victoria had more than 1200 mansions with 20 or more rooms. By 1911, only 862 such dwellings remained in the whole of Australia. The others had been turned into flats, schools, boarding-houses or tenements.

In August 1917, *Real Property Annual* discussed the unsatisfied demand for flats in Melbourne, Sydney and Adelaide, and concluded that the principal causes were 'the interminable question of how to secure, and then how to retain, satisfactory servants'. During the previous few years, the irritation caused by servants had caused dozens of people to move from their large private houses into flats or boarding-houses of the more expensive sort.

In Melbourne, these flats were in Spring and Collins Streets, in the city, and in East Melbourne, South Yarra, St Kilda and Albert Park. One East Melbourne building, *Cliveden*, was particularly fashionable. Built as his town residence by Sir William Clarke, the mansion had been converted to flats before World War I. Rents there in the 1920s for three unfurnished rooms were from £250 to £470 a year—equivalent to $131 to $246 a week these days. Tenants were served their meals in the elegant dining room or in their own luxurious apartments.

Service flats with kitchens

Flats with fully equipped kitchens were in more general demand. 'This class of flat is seen at its best in a new city building where very pretty furnished flats were let at from £4 4s [$133] to £6 6s [$200] a week,' said *Real Property Annual*. 'Each contains from three to four rooms, in addition to a bathroom and lavatory. The housework is done by a staff of 16 servants, employed by the management. Several of the tenants are squatters and other wealthy people who formerly occupied large private houses in the suburbs.'

But the flats most needed were those that could be let from 30s [$47] to £2 [$63] a week. Self-contained flats in big blocks had begun to appear in Sydney before World War I; *The Astor*, in Macquarie Street, perhaps the first block of own-your-own flats in Australia, was built in 1924. During the Depression ugly red-brick flat buildings multiplied rapidly in Sydney, notably around Kings Cross. The population in this area rose to 500 people to the hectare—the highest in Australia. In the late 1930s, flats spread to the eastern suburbs and to the North Shore; the buildings were

usually three or four storeys high, containing 10 or 12 flats of three or four rooms.

Melbourne followed Sydney's example in the years immediately before World War II; most flat buildings there were limited by council regulations to three storeys. *Cairo* in Fitzroy, built in 1935, marked the first appearance of the small bachelor flat.

In the other capitals, few flats were built until after World War II, when flat-building began to boom again in Melbourne too.

Throughout Australia between 1930 and 1939, the ratio of flat and tenement dwellers to dwellers in private houses changed from one to 19 to one to 12. According to the 1947 census, Sydney had 56,820 flats—more than all the other cities combined. By 1966, flats comprised about 19 per cent of all private dwellings in the Sydney metropolitan area but by 1971 this had risen to 25 per cent, and some harbourside municipalities could boast a figure as high as 71 per cent. However, the proportion of flats to other dwellings in the Sydney area has shown a downward trend in recent years, with a ratio of 49 per cent in 1973, and only 26 per cent in 1981.

Nevertheless, Sydney still leads in its number of flat-dwellers. In the other capitals in 1981, the proportion of flats to other dwellings was: Canberra 13 per cent; Melbourne

18 per cent; Hobart 16.23 per cent; Brisbane 13 per cent; Perth 14 per cent; Adelaide 14 per cent and Darwin 19 per cent.

Rising land and building costs, and the ever-widening suburban sprawl, made the young Australian couple's dream of 'our own house on our own land' more and more difficult to realise. An inevitable result was a boom in 'home units'—as own-your-own flats came to be called.

Older couples whose children had grown up, and who preferred looking at a view to looking after a garden and a large family house, were also moving to standardised home-units. When each unit had its own cantilevered balcony, the tall blocks seemed to the architectural historian Professor J. M. Freeland to be like 'expensive human filing cabinets . . . with the drawers open', a felicitous description with which many will agree.

Home units, especially in towering buildings of 22 or more storeys, have many social disadvantages, and in the early 1970s there was a revival of interest in 'town houses', a modern version of the terrace houses of the 1880s. Two or three town houses can be built on the space occupied by one detached house; they offer as much privacy as a detached house, and escape the institutional atmosphere of huge blocks of home units.

The innermost residential areas of Sydney and Melbourne were mainly slums in the early years of the 20th century. These two rows of tiny houses, photographed in 1913, stood in Liverpool Street, which is now in the heart of Sydney's downtown business district

Tale of a terrace

In 1876 a collection of small cottages in the inner Sydney suburb of Surry Hills was pulled down to make way for this terrace of eight houses. In 1878 the entire terrace was sold for £9150, and in 1914, the year after the photograph on the left was taken, it changed hands again for £9000; the terrace had fallen in value—unheard of today. In 1968 one of these houses was sold for $22,000, and two years later for $36,000. The owner of this house refused an offer of $55,000 in the middle of 1973, when the photograph below was taken. Surry Hills was gradually becoming more fashionable and in 1985 one of these large dwellings would fetch about $140,000 and would have a queue of eager prospective renovators vying for possession

The terrace revival

Only some 25 years ago, a publication called *Town and Country Planning* referred to the 'belt of sub-standard housing surrounding the main business area' of Sydney. Obsolete areas in which immediate demolition of buildings was considered necessary included all of Woolloomooloo, Paddington, Surry Hills and Redfern, as well as most of Newtown, Glebe and Balmain.

Even in 1958, the journalist John Douglas Pringle wrote in *Australian Accent* that Paddington and Darlinghurst, with their uniform rows of balconied two-storied terrace houses, were 'working class suburbs whose cheerful slummy life contrasts oddly with their faded charm'.

By the 1960s, however, things were changing rapidly. As Sydney stretched out farther and farther, as public transport and services became less effective and the roads more congested, city-dwellers discovered the advantages of living in the formerly neglected inner suburbs.

The pleas of historians and architects helped too, and today many Sydney houses which seemed doomed for demolition in the 1950s are highly prized and highly priced. So are similar houses in Melbourne's inner suburbs such as Carlton, South Melbourne, Richmond and Fitzroy. Affluent middle-class people have bought the old terrace houses and converted them to suit present-day modes of living. In some places, such as the Rocks in Sydney, terraces have been restored in historically authentic colours and details. The slums of yesterday have become desirable suburbs of architectural interest and great charm.

'A transformation,' said *Real Property Annual* in 1920, when it showed how the eight dignified Melbourne terrace houses in the upper photograph had been converted into the 16 flats of the grotesque Grosvenor Mansions (lower), increasing the total rent from £7 to £24 a week [$161 to $552]

Cheap housing for workers

Government schemes for realising the Australian dream

Before World War I, every State Government in Australia had established some kind of scheme whereby every Australian's dream of his own home on his own block of land could come true. Government-built workers' houses costing between £330 [$14,755] and £550 [$24,595], were sold on terms lasting up to 30 years. Payments were as low as 2s 6d [about $5.60] per week for every £100 [$4470] borrowed. These cheap four-roomed houses were built on the fringes of the cities.

One material which helped to keep down the cost of workers' housing was fibrous plaster. The technique of making plaster sheets reinforced with flax was invented in New Zealand, and was quickly taken up in Australia after it was first introduced in 1916. It was much quicker and cheaper than to plaster walls by the old lath-and-plaster method.

By the 1920s it was being used all over the country for interior walls and ceilings; this extensive use of the material is still peculiar to Australia and New Zealand.

Prefabrication schemes

When World War II ended, there was a shortage of 196,000 dwellings in Australia. One Australian family in three was inadequately housed; one dwelling in every eight was substandard. Many schemes were put forward to prefabricate and mass-produce houses, and several prototypes were built with the encouragement of Labor governments in Canberra and Melbourne but most proposals were abandonded.

By far the best design was the Beaufort house, produced by a division of the Department of Munitions in Melbourne. This was

a practical, five-roomed box 84 m², with steel-framed walls insulated with rockwool. An aircraft factory was re-tooled to begin mass production of the Beaufort and 10,500 houses were ordered by State and Federal Governments for erection in Victoria within three years. But to the Victorian Liberal Government which came to power in 1947, and the Federal Liberal government returned in 1949, the project smelled suspiciously of 'socialism' and it was dropped. The post-war influx of immigrants—from 10,000 to 150,000 a year—worsened the housing problem, and government housing commissions began to tackle it by creating new standardised housing settlements of small villas remote from the city, or by erecting huge, stark blocks of workers' flats on inner-city sites that had been occupied by sub-standard or slum dwellings.

In the 1960s, huge blocks of flats, such as this one built in Melbourne in 1963, seemed to be the answer to the housing shortage

The Department of Munitions planned to mass-produce the Beaufort house in order to solve the tremendous housing shortage after World War II, but governments changed and the scheme was dropped. The house had insulated steel-framed walls enclosing five rooms

Tiles from Marseilles turned the suburbs red

The rash of red tiles that characterises Australia's suburbs began in Melbourne in 1886, and in Sydney six years later. When a house in St Kilda Road, Melbourne, boldly displayed a roof of bright red Marseilles tiles, they quickly became the rage, displacing the once-universal grey slates. Even corrugated iron roofs were painted red to imitate tiling. Marseilles tiles were still being imported to Melbourne in 1910, though local manufacture had started two years before.

In 1892, a cargo of Marseilles tiles reached Sydney. It was consigned to a firm that could not take delivery of it, and the Wunderlich Patent Ceiling and Roofing Company, manufacturers of metal ceilings and building materials, took it over. The tiles were soon in such demand that the company began importing them in large quantities. Between 1892 and 1914, it imported 75 million tiles—enough to roof 40,000 average houses. When

shipments from France were suspended during World War I, Wunderlich began making tiles in Sydney; by 1916 the company was turning out three million a year.

'What the introduction of terracotta meant to the appearance of Sydney is known to those who recalled the drab and grey aspect of Sydney ... Wunderlichs have literally "painted the town red",' says an official history of the company approvingly.

The distinguished architect Hardy Wilson was less approving when he wrote: 'Alas! so far as I know there is not a Roman tile in New South Wales. What sad mischance led to the almost universal Marseilles pattern I am unable to say. It was a calamity for Australia.'

Hardy Wilson's own house had simple shingle tiles, with colours ranging from grey-white, yellow, orange and red to purple-black. In his words, the roof looked like 'a venerable Persian rug of quiet and glowing

colour'. Today Wunderlich makes Marseilles tiles in brindle, buff, chocolate, green and blended colours as well as the traditional red. When concrete tiles appeared in 1920, they were made to resemble the popular terracotta tiles and were used widely.

Roman tiles—the architect Hardy Wilson lamented that this pattern was overlooked when the craze for terracotta tiles swept Australia

Australia's largest housing operation

A typical war service home in the 1920s. Eligible people could obtain durable homes on very easy terms under the War Service Homes Act. In 1924, this sort of house cost about £800 [$21,545]. On a deposit of about £150 [$4040], an applicant could borrow £700 [$18,850], repayable at £3 10s a month [$94]. Under the present Defence Service Homes Corporation scheme, a comparable house costs between $40,000 and $45,000 and the maximum loan offered is $25,000 on monthly repayments of $160.75

Ten weeks after the Armistice ending World War I, an act of the Federal Parliament established the War Service Homes Commission and this Commission then took over all State Government schemes for low-cost housing.

Faced with a great shortage of both building materials and skilled labour, the Commission bought timber mills, tile and joinery works, and even leased a brickworks. Land was also bought on a large scale.

Returned servicemen or their dependants were offered liberal loan facilities, up to a maximum of £700 [$18,230], spread over a period of 37 years for a brick house, and 29 years for a timber one. Between 1919 and 1921 the Commission provided 16,254 houses for low wage-earners, comparing more than favourably with the result after World War II when only 6708 houses were provided between 1945 and 1948. In addition, the maximum loan now offered is only $15,000, a far smaller percentage of the total than was available after World War I.

Three influential architects

Griffin designs a model bushland suburb

Walter Burley Griffin, a gentle, dreamy-eyed man who usually wore a large floppy bow tie, was born near Chicago in 1876. When he was a young man, Chicago was the centre of an architectural movement known as the Chicago School, whose outstanding figure was Frank Lloyd Wright. Both Griffin and the woman who became his wife in 1911, Marion Mahony, worked for many years with Wright and were much influenced by him.

In 1912, Griffin won the competition for the design of an Australian federal capital. So in August 1913, he left his large American practice and came to Australia to be Director of Design for the federal capital. Though he worked full time at the job from 1914 to 1920, he accepted half-time fee of £1000 [$40,170] a year and ran a private practice in what spare time he could find after office hours.

At first Griffin's main office was in Melbourne, and there he designed Newman College at the University of Melbourne, the Capitol Theatre and a number of influential and novel houses in the Melbourne suburbs. The Salter house, in Glyndebourne Avenue, Toorak, built in 1925, was particularly important in the development of Australian domestic architecture. A single-storeyed house with a low-pitched, wide-eaved roof, it is built around a sheltered central courtyard.

In Melbourne, too, Griffin laid out a small estate of three streets at Eaglemont, where he built a house for himself. He also, in 1914, planned the Murrumbidgee Irrigation Area Towns of Griffith and Leeton, but these plans were never carried out. Then in Sydney he came across a neglected pocket of steeply sloping bushland overlooking Middle Harbour. He traced the owner to London and, backed by a group of Melbourne men, including King O'Malley, bought the land. In 1927 he began to create his own model suburb of Castlecrag, at first sight an unlikely prospect.

Originally, all the houses in Castlecrag were designed or approved by Griffin himself. Low, square masses of stone or concrete block, they merge naturally into the terraced bluffs. Their windows are all sizes, from narrow casements to wide unbroken sheets of glass giving stunning views of the harbour. Inside walls were finished in rough plaster, coloured in sunny tints or yellows and buffs. Chimneys are huge affairs of solid stone, and the kitchens had double sinks, then a novelty in Australia though now widely accepted.

However, Griffin's plans for a model suburb were frustrated by the Depression, and for a time he made his living designing Sydney's municipal incinerators. Then in 1935 he was commissioned to design a library for the University of Lucknow, and moved to India. He died of peritonitis in 1937.

Walter Burley and Marion Mahony Griffin in their garden at Castlecrag in 1930. Marion, a forceful and vigorous woman, was bitter about her husband's treatment in Australia

The house Griffin built for himself at Castlecrag (above) has been altered, like most of his other houses in the area, but it remains in harmony with the surrounding bushland. The brochure for the Castlecrag project, from which the drawings at left and right are taken, declared: 'Castlecrag architecture has struck a distinct bold note in Australia. In place of the high peaked tile roofs ... the handsome landscape style, with its stone walls and flat roofs, has been introduced in harmony with the great amphi-theatre of stone and forest'

Apostle of plain surfaces

Robert Joseph Haddon was born in England in 1866. He trained as an architect in London, and came to Australia at the age of 25. At first he worked in Perth as an assistant government architect. In 1900 he moved to Melbourne, where, as head of the school of architecture at the Melbourne Technical College (now the Royal Melbourne Institute of Technology) until 1929, he inspired several generations of architectural students.

'Know the unfailing value of a plain surface,' Haddon said. 'Never be afraid of simplicity.' In his *Australian Architecture*, published in 1908 as a book for architectural students, he advised that 'truth is not confined to an elongated cluster of uprising Gothic shafts or stately classic columns. It may lurk in a kitchen chair'. Elsewhere he advises that ornament should always be applied with restraint, for 'nothing can be more fatal to successful ornamentation than its excess'.

Haddon did not always obey his own precept, however. His home *Anselm* in Caulfield, Melbourne, has sinuous *art nouveau* decoration applied to its brick exterior, while in the bathroom the tiles simulate the waves of the sea. 'Often enough he produced the most disastrous Art Nouveau,' says Robin Boyd, '... but somewhere on every one of his buildings a rare touch may be found.'

Haddon designed churches, schools, houses and facades of great originality—such as the Wharf Labourers' Union building in Flinders Street, Melbourne, since demolished, where the green copper prows of two life-sized 'Viking' ships clung miraculously to an orange terracotta parapet. On another Haddon building, the Fourth Victoria building in Collins Street, two lions' heads in green terracotta used to glower from a white stucco facade. The building still remains but the lions' heads have been removed.

These green lions used to roar from the Fourth Victoria Building in Collins Street, Melbourne. They were placed there by Robert Haddon, an architect who preached plainness, but enjoyed ornament more

Simple buildings of true purpose

Harold Desbrowe Annear, a big, bluff, witty, untidy man with a protruding stomach and ill-fitting dentures, was born in Bendigo, Victoria, in 1866, and never left Australia. He ridiculed tradition, welcomed experiment, and wore a monocle which, in Australia at that time, showed his self-confident independence. He has been described as Australia's 'first functionalist architect'.

'Real architects have always been and must be inventors in mechanics, in form, in tone and colour', Annear told his students. In 1900, he built himself a novel house at Eaglemont, just out of Melbourne. It had no passages, a big living room with a sliding division, counter-balanced sliding windows that disappeared vertically into the cavity walls, and built-in wardrobes, dressing-tables, buffet, bookshelves and cupboards—all features which adventurous architects were discovering more than half a century later.

During World War I, Annear designed a house called *Broceliande* in Orrong Road, Toorak, Melbourne. The architectural historian Robin Boyd described it as 'a white roughcast cube, entirely unornamented, with horizontal gashes of windows ingeniously devised to slip in and out of hollow walls'. The roof was almost flat, with big projecting eaves. The garden was designed to be a 'controlled wilderness of gumtrees'. Both house and gumtrees have now disappeared, but together they embodied Annear's principle that architecture required only 'silence, beautiful form and the pure delicacy of colour'.

Annear thought that the isolation of Australia, in terms both of climate and geography, would help the country to achieve excellence in architectural design; he did not believe that imported ideas would help. Australian architecture, he said, 'must be our own, born of our necessities, our own climates and our own methods of pursuing health and happiness'. He added that those who lived in well-designed homes would 'show that elastic ease of aristocratic well being which should be the true heritage of all good Australians'.

'Simple buildings of true purpose' were Annear's goal, and he designed a number of them in and around Melbourne during the first two decades of the 20th century. He died in Melbourne in 1933.

'A good building trying to be Australian' was Robin Boyd's description of *Broceliande* (later renamed *Troon*), which Harold Desbrowe Annear designed in 1916. The leafy garden full of eucalypts, designed by Annear to complement the house's uncompromisingly plain lines, was replaced early by these ordered rosebeds. The window frames, eaves and porch, originally stained dark to give an effect of recession in the white facade, were soon painted white. However, the house still retained its air of simple dignity until its demolition in the early 1960s

Building for Australian conditions

How flat roofs triumphed over officialdom

Nahum Barnet, writing in the *Victorian Review* in 1882, said that to build a steep-pitched roof 'in a country where snow and sleet are unknown is as incongruous as the adoption of a sou'-wester and ulster as a February costume'. But Australian architects apparently preferred incongruity to innovation. And so did most suburban councillors, who sternly vetoed plans for flat-roofed houses. There was, of course, an occasional exception which always caused comment.

In 1909, when Sydney architect Donald Esplin built a flat-roofed house in North Sydney, *The Bulletin* echoed Mr Barnet's criticism of the high-gabled, steep-pitched roof—

'needlessly steep . . . unnecessarily expensive . . . and with no utilitarian or artistic justification'. But home-builders and councillors remained unconvinced.

In the early 1920s two architects were designing houses with flat roofs—the American Walter Burley Griffin, and a Sydney architect, G. J. Hill. The flat-roofed house, Griffin pointed out in *Real Property Annual*, not only eliminated useless and costly gables but provided 'a terrace for outlook, for secure and airy sleep-outs and for promenade and garden'. Hill, whose house designs were published regularly in the Sydney magazine *The Triad*, expressed similar views. But not until

a quarter of a century later was the battle of the flat roof officially won.

In 1947, the councillors of Warringah Shire, Sydney, ordered the architect Sydney Ancher, 'in the public interest', to put a meaningless 60 cm high parapet above a flat roof he had designed for a house at Curl Curl in their shire. Ancher's client appealed against this arbitrary direction in the Land and Valuation Court.

The council's star witness, its chief health and building inspector, described Ancher's design as 'more like a gun emplacement than a house' and mentioned proudly that in recent years the council had rejected some

In 1921 the Sydney architect G. J. Hill published this design for a two-bedroom house costing £1200 [\$31,600]. Hill and other advocates of flat roofs claimed that steeply pitched roofs were absurd in Australia's climate. In 1914, H. A. Hunt, Director of Melbourne's Weather Bureau, suggested flat roofs and said that in tropical Australia houses should be built in Japanese style, with one wall and the rest framework and screens

Both these houses by Harry Seidler, born and trained in Vienna, aroused obstruction by local councillors who could not stomach their then unusual lines. The battle over the Turramurra house (above) in 1948 lasted three months. The Castlecrag house (right) was built in 1951 after an 18-month battle with a council which had rejected the design as a 'monstrosity'

two dozen flat-roofed designs. But gun-emplacement or not, Mr Justice Sugerman upheld the appeal, declared in an historic judgement that the question was solely an aesthetic one, and that the development of architecture must be impeded if a council closed 'its gates to the unfamiliar . . .'

Unchastened, those councillors next year attacked the 25-year-old Viennese-born architect Harry Seidler, this time for the design of a house at Turramurra with a 'butterfly' roof, pitched slightly inwards to a central pipe. Seidler was informed that the council desired buildings to be 'as pleasant and pleasing as possible and in line with standards commensurate with the development taking place in the shire'.

Seidler prepared a statement which included pictures of eight dilapidated shacks close to his projected house, and described the council's request for conformity to its standards as outrageous. 'I deem it unnecessary to reply to this insolent statement', he wrote. 'Obviously it is a hopeless task . . . since the request itself proves the thorough incompetence regarding matters of aesthetics on the part of the officials concerned'. However, he offered to give the councillors a lantern-slide lecture on modern design, and said his client was prepared to take the matter to court. This must have given the aldermen food for thought. Three months later, the council finally capitulated.

When in 1949, the Willoughby Muncipal Council rejected one of his houses as a 'monstrosity', adding that 'one could spit from the main bedroom into the livingroom', Seidler described the councillors as a 'bunch of grocers, butchers and so on', and threatened legal action. After a battle lasting 18 months, Willoughby yielded. Seidler's next victory was with Ku-ring-gai Council.

In 1952, Keith Newman, writing in *The Sydney Morning Herald*, said that in four years

'More like a gun emplacement than a house', was how a council building inspector described this house by Sydney Ancher in 1947. Ancher's client went to court to challenge the council's order that a parapet must be built above the roof. The judge ruled against the council

Seidler 'had shaken more councils to their foundations than most Australian architects would do in a lifetime'. Fundamentally, wrote Newman, Seidler fought for freedom of expression. He found it intolerable 'that structures should be found guilty or not guilty by municipal councillors who, with few exceptions, knew nothing about the subject'. Australia was the only civilised Western country where they had this power, Newman wrote.

In 1954 Seidler himself wrote of the 'huge and expensive pitched roof structure covered with Marseilles tiles which has absolutely no justification for its existence in this climate . . . Pitched roofs restrict the shape which buildings can take . . . Such roofs put all their weight on to the exterior walls and require

excessive support. They are wasteful in labour and material, not to speak of the horror when we have to look at a whole sea of them from above . . .'

Other architects who have had to struggle against bumbledom include Robert Maclurcan, whose design for his own house at Castlecrag was for a time rejected by the Willoughby Council because the roof was part flat and part skillion; Roy Grounds, for flat roofs in Barwon Heads, Victoria; and the Perth architect Mervyn Parry. When Parry's design for a low-pitched roof was rejected as unsightly, he pointed out that the Parthenon, one of the world's most beautiful buildings, had an even lower pitched roof, and therefore would not have been allowed in Perth's model suburb of Floreat Park.

Queensland's contribution—houses on stilts

One of the few original building styles to evolve in Australia is the typical Brisbane house, perched on heavy tree-trunk stilts 2 or 3 m above the ground. Originally a country style, it dates from about 1860 and is still widespread in the suburbs of Brisbane.

There are many explanations of its origin. One is that the passage of air under the raised floor cools the building in the hot Queensland summer. Another is that destructive termites are deterred, because they do not like the light, and can be detected easily if they do infest the building. Other theories are that houses were initially raised as protection against floods and that the elevation above the ground gave pioneer women a greater sense of security.

The space between the stilts, which is used as a play area, garage or repository for garden equipment or household junk, is often partly screened by a wooden trellis or slats. Apart from the stilts and the slats, however, the typical Brisbane house differs little from the southern Australian cottage.

In Queensland, a housing style suited to the climate developed spontaneously. The typical Queensland house is built of timber and raised high on stilts, allowing air to circulate freely

Victorian hangover

The age of velvet, fenders and fire-irons

The drawing-room of a typical middle-class home at the start of the 20th century was a hotch-potch of Victorian bad taste. There were heavy curtains of velvet, serge or damask, trimmed with fringes of balls or tassels, and floral-papered walls crowded with reproductions of popular pictures, such as Sir Edwin Landseer's *Stag at Bay*, or Lord Leighton's *Wedded*. The *pièce-de-résistance* was the upright cottage piano, with its two curly brass candleholders, its pleated coloured silk above the keyboard, and its round, revolving stool.

The furnishings probably included a *papier-maché* or bamboo occasional table, with a fringed and patterned damask cloth; a set of misshapen and uncomfortable chairs; a horsehair sofa with a heavily carved back; a five-tier corner whatnot displaying a jumble of family portraits in frames of painted fretwork, or green or purple plush; Goss china souvenirs of seaside resorts; a few shells; a pig-shaped silver pincushion; a plaster bust of Queen Victoria; ruby lustre vases, and a silver-mounted emu egg.

The mantelpiece might have had a velvet valance, ruched and fringed with bobbles. On it stood a black, white or green French marble clock, or an American imitation marble clock with gilt decoration, flanked by marble urns or bronze statuettes of knights in armour or silverplated candelabra. Towering above the mantelpiece was a tall, many-mirrored overmantel, its numerous shelves and niches crammed with painted vases, ornaments and assorted bric-a-brac.

In front of the blackleaded fireplace was an ornate brass fender, and near it a coal scuttle of wood, or black japanned metal, and a set of brass fire-irons—shovel, tongs, brush and poker. Poking the fire was a ritual and a pastime, usually reserved for the master.

A Melbourne front room

The writer, Hal Porter, born in 1911, recalls the 'front room' in his parents' house in the Melbourne suburb of Kensington: 'There is the richly fringed saddlebag and Utrecht velvet suite. On its mainly magenta sofa leans a magenta velvet cushion . . . A bebobbled mantel-drape of magenta plush skirts the chimney-shelf . . . There are an eight-sided occasional table on which an antlered buck of fake bronze attitudinises sniffily, two gipsy tables, a bamboo music canterbury, a Renardi upright grand of Italian walnut before which sits a tri-legged revolving piano stool. A dogended nickel fender and a yard-long set of nickel fire-irons, never used, weekly burnished, the shovel pierced almost to filigree, occupy the hearth . . .'

'The wily Celestial'

When much cheap furniture was made by Chinese, Australian manufacturers proudly stamped in purple ink on the inside of wardrobes and chests of drawers: *Manufactured by European Labour Only*.

Chinese labour was always believed to be sweated. 'The awards of wages boards have practically brought the Chinese workers into line with Australian workers,' said *The Advisor* in February 1911. 'But it is admitted by the trade, however, that the wily, plausible, almond-eyed Celestial does not slavishly bow to the dictates of the union-made tribunal. John Chinaman knows full well that if he comes into line with a union rate of wage . . . he will be quickly ousted.'

The Advisor noted that some Chinese furniture-makers had recently installed machinery. 'Not that the Asiatic likes belts, wheels, or revolving cutting tools; he is frightened of them,' it commented patronisingly. 'One Chinese manufacturer, on being asked if he employed machinery, shook his head and said, "Me no likee machinee, him cuttee too muchee quick".'

Old Sir Samuel Davenport, a pioneer South Australian grazier who died, aged 88, in 1906, sits in a room that epitomises Victorian clutter. Specially characteristic are the pictures hung almost to the ceiling, the many-tiered whatnot and the crochet-bordered cloths

The drawing room in Melba's Coombe Cottage, with its odd mixture of Regency and Victorian styles, was hailed as 'modern interior decoration' by the *Real Property Annual* in 1913

The sinuous lines of *art nouveau* decorate this 'artistic and inexpensive bedroom suite in maple,' which was sold by David Jones in 1910. The *art nouveau* influence is not pronounced in the form of the furniture itself except in the tapering columns of the wardrobe

The undulations of *art nouveau*

Art nouveau, a style of decoration based on sinuous flowing lines and formalised flowers and leaves, originated in Europe in the 1880s. About the end of the 19th century it reached Australia and became the rage. It appeared first in a few city offices and suburban houses, and in two Sydney hotels built in 1902, but it had its most enduring and most luxuriant growth in buildings in Melbourne.

The name of the style comes from a shop called *L'Art Nouveau*, which was opened in Paris in 1895 to sell modern art. Staircases, light fittings, friezes, tiles, mantels, lead-lights and fireplace surrounds were all decorated in this style, with its intertwining drawn-out lines and its stylised tulip buds, lilies, leaves and hearts. In Europe the movement produced some work of great distinction, especially in wrought iron—as in the famous entrances to the Paris Metro. The

original impulse was gone by the time the style reached Australia, but it did break with stuffy old traditions.

'Mostly in a spotty or patchy way, it was applied to the most sedate bank, a robust warehouse, a gay shop, a vulgar hotel, or fretted into verandah valances and brackets on frivolous suburban homes . . .,' writes the architectural historian Professor J. M. Freeland. 'The diminishing tendril and heart became the hallmark of the style. They appeared in isolated shyness high on cornices, were worked, green and red, into stained glass windows, pressed into metal ceilings and scattered over verandahs.' Admirers of *art nouveau* saw in its sinuosities the beauty of living plants. But to others, the curving lines suggested 'eels, noodles and tapeworms'. In the 1960s interest in the style was renewed and collectors eagerly sought good examples.

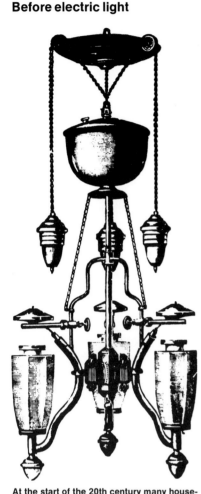
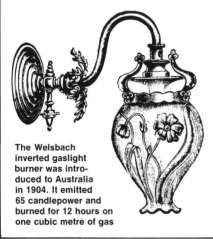
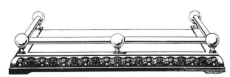

A fender, in brass or cast iron, sometimes both, used to surround every respectable hearth

The "Merrick"

A Dining-room of Distinction

In 1921 the Sydney store of Beard Watson offered this dining room suite—sideboard, extension dining table six small chairs, two carver chairs and dinner wagon, in oak or maple, for £59 10s [$1567]

Pioneers of modern design

The end of 'varicoloured velvet and dusty pink chenille'

Melbourne was introduced to 'modern' furniture by an industrial designer named Frederick Ward, who in 1927, at the age of 27, started manufacturing furniture of his own design. Simplicity, and attractive Australian woods, gave his products great charm.

He opened a shop in Collins Street, where his furniture was displayed with Michael O'Connell's hand-blocked linens, another new contribution to Melbourne interiors. Both pioneers were appreciated only by a discerning few, but in 1931, Ward opened a modern furniture department in the Myer Emporium and these reached a wider public.

Ward made a feature of raspberry jam wood, a close-grained, dark red Western Australian wattle which, when worked, has a distinct smell of raspberry jam. It had long been prized for making fence posts and charcoal. For much of his furniture, Ward used Australian walnut, the name in the timber trade for various trees of the laurel family.

The steel tube chair was being made in Australia in 1933, only four years after its first appearance in Europe. By the late 1930s, chromium had become a symbol of the avant-garde. Associated with it was the cult of cacti as indoor plants. Prickly pear *Opuntia vulgaris*, a widespread pest in Queensland, became a fashionable decoration in 'sophisticated' southern Australian homes. A Melbourne disciple of Ogden Nash wrote in 1934:

> Moonlight and rooses
> No longer attract us,
> Modern taste chooses
> Chromium and cactus
> From Slav to Arunta
> The world acclaims chromium
> And a smiling Opunta
> Decks each happy homium

The typical 'ultra-modern' house would have a tapestry brick fireplace, a chromium-plated reading lamp with a landscape painted on the parchment shade, an apricot-coloured round mirror with a scalloped edge hanging above the brick mantel, a smoker's stand in chromium and black plastic, rows of standard—and often unread—authors in a walnut-veneered glassfronted case, and a nest of glass-topped, wrought-iron tables.

Another Melbourne industrial designer, Grant Featherston, who started making furniture in 1947, evolved a technique for making body-fitting chairs out of curved plywood. By 1953 he was marketing about 20 different types of chairs, including some of upholstered plywood. Two notable Sydney pioneers of modern furniture were George Korody and Douglas Snelling. Korody, an Hungarian professor of architecture, was sent to Australia before World War II to organise an Hungarian exhibition of arts and crafts. He decided to stay in Australia and turned to making furniture for a living. He introduced natural colour wood to a public accustomed to dark-stained furniture, and made chairs from coachwood—a wood never before used except for lining furniture.

Douglas Snelling, a young Sydney architect, studied furniture design in the United States, and returning to Australia in 1941, made a few silver ash and maple chairs for the modern houses he was building. The chairs had webbing backs and seats, which Snelling claimed were more comfortable than stuffed upholstery. The furniture manager of a big Sydney store saw them, and gave Snelling an order for £2000 [$53,260] worth.

The three-piece suite

But despite the contributions of these pioneers, and of others such as Roger McLay, who created cone-shaped plywood chairs with a hole in the back, there was little general improvement in Australian furniture design. Writing in 1960, Robin Boyd referred to the 'suffocating atmosphere of the popular furniture market ... built around a three-piece genoa velvet lounge suite with waterfall back and arms, almost as wide as the seat, inset with little shelves and panels of scalloped, walnut-veneered wood'. However, Boyd detected 'faint stirrings of fresh air' and he welcomed 'the new popular pieces of vynex, laminex, black iron and bright brass' which were a little closer to rational design, and 'lighter and cleaner, figuratively and literally, than the musty, over-stuffed, varicoloured velvet and the dusty pink chenille'. The three-piece lounge suite has survived as basic Australian furniture, though washable vinyl now usually replaces 'genoa velvet'.

Jonathan Aitken, inspired perhaps by Australia's deadliest satirist, Barry Humphries, said the typical Melbourne sitting-room of the 1970s 'might be decorated with lace curtains, a vinyl-covered settee, wallpaper depicting koala bears, four plaster ducks in flight above the piano (which is never played or tuned) and beneath crossed Union Jacks a large reproduction portrait of the Royal Family and their corgis—and make sure you don't trip over the plastic gnome as you go out into the garden'. Australians may not recognise the accuracy of his description!

Sure to get it at Grace Bros

The Stafford

3 PIECE SUITE

This is a Suite of elegant design that will appeal to your artistic taste. It will add to the beauty and cosiness of your Home. As all our Upholstered Furniture is made in our own Factory, we are able to guarantee the workmanship as first-class. The selection we can offer in this department is unequalled in Sydney. The "Stafford" Suite has double spring edge, deep-sprung seat, arm and back upholstered with horse-hair. Covering of best quality Silk Tapestry. Price:

£59 - 10 - 0

GRACE BROS LTD

BROADWAY SYDNEY

This overstuffed three-piece suite was advertised in 1922. Massive furniture like this was then, and for many years afterwards, an essential mark of respectability

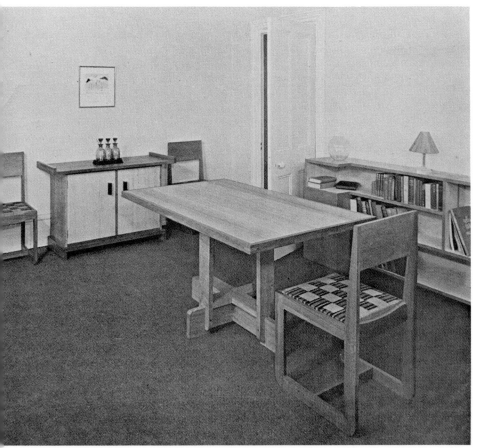

The simple lines and plain wood of this furniture by Frederick Ward were considered to be extremely modern when it appeared in *The Home* in 1932. Ward believed in simplicity and he used Australian timbers whose beauty had not been recognised before

Douglas Snelling was faced with the problem of designing furniture during World War II, when many materials were in short supply. In 1941 he designed and made a few of these chairs in silver ash and maple with webbing backs and seats. The chairs were a success and Snelling joined forces with a manufacturer in 1947 and opened a factory to make the chairs in quantity. The webbing was specially made by a manufacturer who had previously produced only webbing for parachutes and soldiers' uniforms. It proved highly effective

In 1948, Roger McLay, a young Sydney designer, produced these cone-shaped chairs, made from plywood and covered with a variety of materials. They were the first of their kind, and they took advantage of materials that were more readily available after World War II than was solid timber. The conical seat and back was made from thin waterproof coachwood plywood, shaped and then mounted on a steel ring. The legs were attached to the ring. This design was much imitated, and many of the cane chairs now imported from Asian countries are based on the original McLay chair

95

The servant problem

The decline of domestic service

There has been a 'servant problem' just as long as there have been servants. In the 1860s and 1870s, when there were nearly 1,500,000 female domestic servants in England—representing about 11.7 percent of the female population—London *Punch*, under the standing heading of 'Servantgalism', repeatedly made fun of the cheeky or demanding or unreliable servant. Later, publications such as Melbourne *Punch* or the Sydney *Bulletin* found in the Australian servant a similar target for satirical cartoons.

There were constant complaints in Australian papers about the chronic shortage of servants. 'The domestic servant question is now a burning one and is discussed not merely at public meetings and in the press, but forms a staple of conversation in many suburban villas,' said Melbourne *Punch* in June 1901 as it surveyed the scene.

In the 1880s, it had been proposed to import domestics from India, and in 1905, when the National Council of Women in Launceston discussed at length 'the old standing complaint of the scarcity and general inadequacy

of household help', one speaker prophesied that Japanese would be imported.

The Launceston *Weekly Courier* commented: 'A girl is in every way better off in a well-controlled, comfortable household than in a factory, and is, moreover, to a great extent, out of the way of temptation.' But not all households were well-controlled and comfortable, and domestic service involved long hours—perhaps from six in the morning till ten at night—and often sheer drudgery.

The servant, if she did the washing, had to boil it in a wood-fired copper, and iron it with a flat-iron heated on a kitchen range fired by wood or coal. She spent hours blackleading stoves and steps, beating dirty carpets, cleaning ornate silver, dusting hordes of fragile ornaments and polishing fussy furniture. The broom, the dishcloth, the dustpan and the slop-bucket were the symbols of her servitude.

Early in the 1900s, gas coppers were replacing wood-fire coppers in wash-houses, gas heaters replacing chip or kerosene heaters in bathrooms, and gas stoves replacing black iron wood stoves in kitchens. But all were slow to gain acceptance. The early gas stoves, imitating the design of wood stoves, were elaborately ornamented grease traps, almost impossible to keep clean. A housewife advised

readers of the *Home Journal* how to go about it with the least possible labour. You needed 'several paper bags, a pair of men's canvas gloves, a good brush, several large pieces of old flannel, two smaller soft cotton rags, a package of stove polish and a bottle of gum asphaltum, burnt alum, turpentine'. The paper bags, she explained, were to protect the hands, as the mixture hardened the gloves.

The poet Marie E. J. Pitt, in an article contributed to *The Lone Hand* in May 1911, asked 'Is Domestic Service Obsolete?' (A recent Sydney newspaper had devoted 200 cm of advertising space to 'Servants Wanted' and only 12 cm to 'Situations Wanted'.) 'Of the clouds that loom . . . on the social-industrial horizon of today,' wrote Miss Pitt, 'the problem of domestic service looms the largest and blackest.' A problem indeed!

Servants, she said, objected to 'long hours, the piling on of unnecessary burdens, the imposition of extravagant personal service and . . . the constant reminder by work, look, dress and surroundings of social inferiority . . .' Mistresses charged servants with 'their love of pleasure, their ever-growing rebellion against . . . restraint, their lack of respect for employers, and their objection to personal attendance on the wants of the mistress'. Miss

Life for servants such as these was a matter of long hours and dreary work—all that gleaming silver had to be kept polished, for example. In 1901, about one worker in eight was engaged in personal or domestic services, often on very low pay

Pitt's conclusion was that the era of the faithful family servant was past. Girls preferred to work in shops, factories or offices.

Another contributor to *The Lone Hand*, signing herself 'Charmian,' in April 1912 explained how she had solved the servant problem. 'The present "domestic trouble" bears heaviest on the one-servant household. I belonged to that unfortunate class,' she wrote. Her husband was a professional man with a fixed income of £450 [$18,077], and they lived in 'the usual six-roomed villa'.

She had fitted every available inch of floor with a 'handsome linoleum', and then bought every possible invention to lighten labour. 'Among those treasures were an easily worked carpet-sweeper and a divinely inspired instrument for "swabbing" linoleums ... As to the windows—that bugbear of house keepers—I settled that question by once a week hosing the outside of them ... For the insides, I found that by absolute exclusion of flies (through a complete system of wire blinds and doors) ... they needed ... little attention.' Washing and ironing, of course, were 'given out' but that expense, added to the cost of the labour-saving appliances, was 'nothing to the outlay for even one servant in wages alone'.

The domestic staff of a small New South Wales farm pose in the yard for an itinerant photographer in the early 1900s. The maid, who stands at left, was paid £60 [$2845] a year, the housemaid (centre) £40 [$1895] and the parlour maid (right) £50 [$2370]. Each wears a distinctive uniform befitting her station

Labour-saving devices were welcomed by women who could no longer find servants. The contributor to *The Lone Hand* in 1912 who extolled an 'instrument for "swabbing" linoleums' may have been referring to the Patent Mutabor

Black iron stoves like this had to be blackleaded regularly to keep them clean and free from rust

A set of three irons, detachable handle and stand cost 5s 6d [$11] in 1914. Two irons were left heating on the stove while the other was used

POINTS OF VIEW
THE MISSUS: Fancy the butcher-boy taking me for a servant! The impertinence!
THE SERVANT-GIRL: Fancy the butcher-boy taking me for the missus! What an insult!

Cheeky servants were a regular target for cartoonists in *The Bulletin*. This drawing dates from 1901

The servantless house

New devices to replace the unobtainable maid

At the Australasian Science Congress held in Hobart in January 1902, John Sulman, an English architect living in Sydney, read a paper entitled 'A Twentieth Century House with suggestions on the solution of the Servant Problem'. He said: 'It is probable that many middle-class households will, in the future, have to dispense with servants altogether, or depend on lady-helps, or assistance by non-resident servants for a limited time each day. In either case the existing type of house with its arrangements for two classes of inmates is unsuitable.'

Sulman described the essential features of the house of the future. It would have a closed porch for hats and coats, opening into a general living room, like the hall of old English houses. There would be a small dining room close to a compactly planned and well-fitted kitchen. Every bedroom in the house would have a fixed lavatory in a closed but ventilated cupboard and a large built-in wardrobe and a capacious chest of drawers.

'Cooking would be performed by gas or electricity,' said Sulman. 'A continual supply of hot water would be provided by a gas heater, or self-feeding coal boiler in the cellar, and washing up would be performed in a sink without handling, by first steeping in a chemical solution to remove grease, rinsing with clean water, and then drying by a gas heater fixed under the sink.'

All rooms would be heated by gas fires, as coal and wood caused too much dust and labour. Polished parquetry floors laid on solid concrete and impervious cement walls with rounded corners would eliminate constant cleaning; furnishings would be simple, avoiding fluffy carpets and hangings which produced dust. Washing was to be sent out,

and possibly cooking, too. Sulman proposed the establishment of district co-operative kitchens which would deliver ready-cooked meals with table appointments, as in Sweden. His concepts were years ahead of his time; so was another proposal for home-delivered meals made by Mrs Bogue Luffman, a Melbourne literary woman, in June 1902.

She found many supporters for a scheme to establish a Melbourne Distributing Kitchen Company with kitchens in the city and suburbs, to cook and deliver meals. A Melbourne correspondent of the *Sydney Mail* commented that the desire for residential flats and the success of Mrs Luffman's movement showed that the servant problem was not solved.

'Domestic service is often impossible to obtain in Australia,' wrote the correspondent. 'As about half the people of Victoria are crowded in to Melbourne, and a large percentage of the city population think the acme of bliss is to live within a walk of the theatres, and that no bird music equals the melody of tramcar bells, it is surprising that there is not one building in the city suited for residential flats. To live in a flat in Collins Street and have one's meals brought to the door ready-cooked in a motor-car thrice daily is a dream of bliss many women indulge in at the present moment.' But the dream was not realised.

In spite of the novelty of the plan and its many supporters, Mrs Luffman's Melbourne Distributing Kitchen Company never seems to have got past the blueprint stage. By 1918, writing about 'The Architect and the Future', the Queensland architect Robin Dodds was suggesting that the solution to the servant problem was a form of communal living. Twelve separate but similar houses would be grouped around a central building contain-

This lady, who appears to be enjoying a hot bath and shower simultaneously, appeared in *The Bulletin* in 1900. She was advertising the joys of instant hot water from a kerosene-burning heater. You could install it yourself and it emitted neither fumes nor smell, the advertisement said

ing a dining hall, recreation rooms, a kitchen, laundry and accommodation for servants, whose services would be shared.

'Two or three cooks at salaries comparable to those now paid to University professors and with commensurate skill and training, could appear like prima donnas on alternate nights,' Dodds suggested. And a further advantage of this kind of living, he pointed out, would be that 'a four for bridge would be as easy to get as on a P. & O. steamer'.

Machines to help with the washing

Patented in the United States in 1872, this wooden washing machine was being advertised in South Australia as late as 1914

In 1903, the Osmond Little Marvel Washing Machine was said to suck all the dirt out of clothes when placed in the tub and rocked from side to side

Wooden washers often opened at the joints when empty, but there was no timber to shrink in the all-steel tub of the 'Ideal' washer of 1903

The dream kitchen of the housewife without servants in 1920. Advertised as a 'model Kitchen', it had fittings including the 'Gem' dresser, 'embracing almost every conceivable labour saving device known to the culinary art'. The 'Quick Meal' gas stove was 'a great time saver' and the enamel-topped kitchen table at left 'a decided novelty'. For storing food there were the large safe in the left-hand corner of the room and the oak-finish 'Kosciusko' ice chest at right. No sink is shown, but there probably would have been a china one in an adjoining scullery or alcove

Abolishing the long dark corridor and the remote kitchen

The architect W. Hardy Wilson said he had heard many doleful tales of dwelling in the suburbs without a maid. So when he designed his own home, *Purulia*, at Wahroonga, Sydney, in 1912, he omitted accommodation for a maid and placed the kitchen adjoining the living room and the front door.

Purulia's 'four-squareness' so incensed the wealthy gentlemen of Wahroonga that they tried to have the building stopped. They were unsuccessful, for the servantless house was coming to be recognised as the home of the future. When another Australian architect Marcus Barlow, described a modern bungalow in *Real Property Annual* a few years later, he declared that long, dark corridors and dark and dirty kitchens a long distance from the dining room were now a thing of the past.

Barlow described a five-roomed bungalow designed for a site with a frontage of 15 or 18 m. The front doors opened into a wide hall, panelled up to the height of the doors, with a china shelf on little brackets running above the panelling. The ceilings were three metres high, with a heavy wooden cornice, and the plaster was strapped with wooden strips. The floor was of polished Tasmanian hardwood, with carpets and rugs only where there was traffic. Mission furniture—a simple, unornamented style of furniture which originated in the United States — completed the hall.

On each side of the hall were double doors, leading to the dining-room on one side and the living-room on the other. These rooms were treated in exactly the same fashion as the hall. On each side of the dining room fire were seats with cupboards under them. One of the seats, lined with galvanised iron, formed a coal scuttle and wood bin.

A door from the dining room gave access to the kitchen, which was carried out in white enamel, with nickel taps, china sink, gas stove and blue and white linoleum. Two bedrooms, off a smaller hall, were also white enamelled, with built-in wardrobes and linen presses, and polished floors with rugs. The bathroom, again white enamel with nickel, had a porcelain enamel bath, shower screen and shower and basin, and a nickel gas heater. The wash house had a gas copper, and 'needless to say, electricity is throughout the whole house, with light in every room, and on every verandah, and power points for radiators, fans and electric iron in the kitchen'.

Electrical liberation

Machines that vanquished household drudgery

Electricity came slowly to Australian homes. Although electric street lighting was installed in most cities and many towns before the end of the nineteenth century, only a few hundred homes in the capital cities had electricity connected at Federation. Gas reigned supreme for lighting and cooking, and many thought electricity would never rival gas in the home because it was too expensive. Australia lagged behind the rest of the world in realising the potential of electricity. The all-electric home had become a reality in Europe and America by 1911, when an enthusiastic contributor wrote in *Building* magazine of the benefits that Australians were yet to share:

'Perhaps one of its greatest boons will mean the solution of the servant girl problem. It does not signify that because electricity should be installed in a house, "Merely Mary Ann" will be dispensible, but rather that her work will be made much lighter, and the undertaking more pleasant. Instead of laboriously sweeping and dusting, she will merely have to direct the operations of an electrically-worked vacuum cleaner. The duties will become lighter, and the occupation more "lady's helplike," hence Mary Ann will be more inclined to withdraw from the present atmosphere of the factory to the better environment of the private home. The revolution in domestic affairs will be complete with the introduction of the electrical element.' It proved to be so.

The author described the home of Mr S. F. Newlands in the Sydney suburb of Wollstonecraft. Mr Newlands had installed electric machines to help with every conceivable job. Apart from electric lighting and fans and heaters for all rooms, 'all the food is cooked by electricity. There is a process for heating plates—the current which would make them white hot could be regulated to a gentle flow to enable boiling or frying. In some respects the maid's work is made light with a vengeance. In the cleaning of knives and silver, for instance, there is a certain apparatus employed. The pressure of a button sets it whirring. At one end the knives are cleaned, and at the other silver is polished. Even the washing is done with electricity. All that is necessary—with the special apparatus, of course—is to put the clothes into a tub with a quantity of soapsuds, and they are withdrawn beautifully white. The ironing is also done by electricity, and the boots and hats are brushed by the same means. The maid actually becomes a "lady operator". Blistered hands, aching backs, and housemaid's knee are but nightmares in the electric home'.

But for the luxury of his electric home Mr Newlands had to install a generating plant which cost £1500 (the modern equivalent is about $67,000). He estimated that the running costs were about 15s [$33.50] a week.

High cost of installation

Home generating plants were not uncommon at this time, and some experts even advocated them in preference to a central power supply. Most houses were wired only for lighting and the owner had to have additional expensive wiring installed if he wanted power for appliances. In 1915 a member of the Electrical Association of Australia described a house in the Sydney suburb of Double Bay, where 'the whole of the balcony was taken up with meters, appliances and household service leads, and if power leads were brought in, he did not know how the occupants were going to get into the house'.

By that time the future of electricity was assured. The trees that lined the streets of many inner city suburbs were felled and posts and wires marched out to replace them.

The arrival of cheap electric power in the suburbs, however, liberated many women from mechanical tasks. In 1921, Associated General Electric Industries summed up the possible advantages of electricity dramatically in this advertisement:

'Yesterday! The kitchen clock tolls away a woman's life. Toil worn hands, scarred by labor, monotonously dip-dip into a greasy dish pan. A roaring fire, kept burning to heat the water and cook the next meal, smothers the room under a blanket of hot motionless air. Dim, fitful light shadows and multiplies the laboured motions of a drooping figure. Each day is but a repetition of the day before . . . a monotonous routine commanding woman's time, demanding her presence and shutting out all but a brief hour or two that she can call her own. There is little need of a clock in this old-fashioned kitchen for time is not measured here by minutes or hours, but by drab days . . . days that leave the inescapable marks of kitchen toil.

'Today! A youthful hand that defies the years, touches a switch and a brilliant room is flooded with light. Clean, beautiful, efficient . . . every inch of this kitchen is arranged to save woman's steps. Magic electric servants work for her . . . she DIRECTS and they DO. Her days are her own . . . her hours are free! World progress is marked and measured by man's success in lifting the burdens of daily life from his family, and there has been no greater achievement than that of vanquishing the dreary hours of household drudgery. Truly, freedom has come to our womenfolk.'

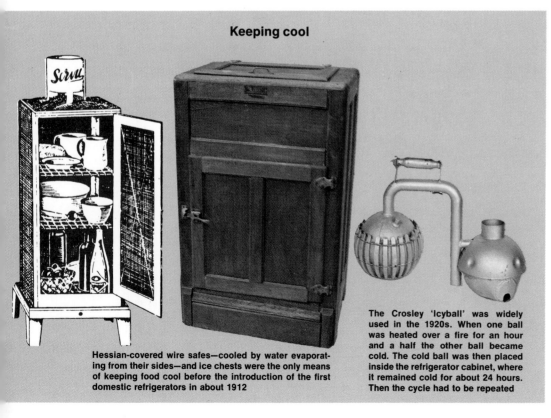

Keeping cool

Hessian-covered wire safes—cooled by water evaporating from their sides—and ice chests were the only means of keeping food cool before the introduction of the first domestic refrigerators in about 1912

The Crosley 'Icyball' was widely used in the 1920s. When one ball was heated over a fire for an hour and a half the other ball became cold. The cold ball was then placed inside the refrigerator cabinet, where it remained cold for about 24 hours. Then the cycle had to be repeated

Sir Edward Hallstrom made this refrigerator —his first—about 1924. He installed the heat-exchange system in an ice-chest

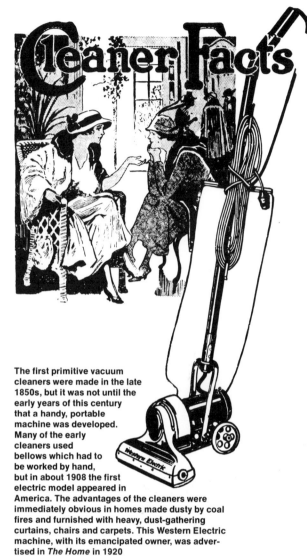

This washing machine, complete with spin dryer, three-armed agitator and water pump, is one of the earliest electrically-driven washing machines. It was made in the United States to a design patented in 1912. The first electric washing machines ap-peared on the market no earlier than 1910. Electric sewing machine motors were available in the late 19th century, but power-driven appliances were un-common until alternating current became available after the turn of the century

The first primitive vacuum cleaners were made in the late 1850s, but it was not until the early years of this century that a handy, portable machine was developed. Many of the early cleaners used bellows which had to be worked by hand, but in about 1908 the first electric model appeared in America. The advantages of the cleaners were immediately obvious in homes made dusty by coal fires and furnished with heavy, dust-gathering curtains, chairs and carpets. This Western Electric machine, with its emancipated owner, was adver-tised in *The Home* in 1920

Developing an Australian refrigerator

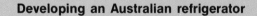

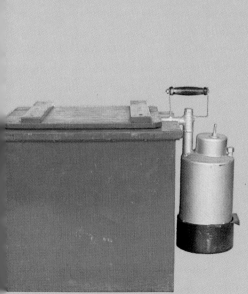

The 1927 model Hallstrom refrigerator was cooled by a device similar to the 'Icyball'. The cold ball is hidden from view inside the chest

It was no longer necessary to remove the cooling device with the Hallstrom model A of 1932. The fin-ned unit was heated by a kerosene flame

By 1936 refrigerators were beginning to resemble their modern counterparts. This upright model still burned kerosene to provide the heat

THE REGENT
...RIS. SCARFE LIMITED.
The £25,000
MIGHTY WURLITZER
for THE REGENT THEATRE
The £25,000
MIGHTY WURLITZER
for THE REGENT THEATRE
The £25,000
MIGHTY WURLITZER
for THE REGENT THEATRE

Leisure and pleasure

From the magic lantern to the television set

When the 20th century was new, Australians took active part in most of their amusements. At home they would play musical instruments, they would play cards or other games, watch magic lantern shows, or read. If they went out it was likely to be to a dance, unless it was for spectator pleasures such as the theatre, a circus or a concert.

At the start of the century too, disc and cylinder recording techniques began to improve, and it was not long before the great singers of the European opera houses, concert halls and music halls could be heard in Australia. Soon the horn of a gramophone or a phonograph sprouted in every up-to-date drawing room.

Motion pictures were another novelty and it was not long before Australians were watching Australian-made-films—two of the world's earliest feature films, *Soldiers of the Cross* and *The Story of the Kelly Gang,* were shot in Melbourne before 1910.

Australian companies continued to produce Australian films for Australian audiences throughout the silent era and into the 1930s but they were unable to withstand the competition—financial as well as artistic—of Hollywood, and the Australian film industry collapsed. But even during the grim Depression years people continued to flock to the cinema for a couple of hours in a flickering world of make-believe. The experience was often made all the more piquant by eating ice-cream or holding hands in the darkened cinema. Many of the picture theatres were marvels of sham opulence and tawdry fantasy. Nowadays most of these plaster palaces have disappeared—vanquished in the struggle against electronic entertainment.

By the late 1930s, one Australian in 16 had a radio set and the next two decades were a golden age of radio stars and everlasting serials. Then in 1956 came television. Technically it offered black-and-white pictures that were likened to electronic corduroy, but it thrust aside movies and the radio alike as it swept into favour. Entertainment was back where it had been at the start of the century—in the home. Despite the resurgence in Australia film making and the opening of multiple cinemas in the mid-70s, the coming of the video cassette recorder meant that for the time being it seemed set to stay there.

The 'Mighty Wurlitzer' arrives at the Regent Theatre, in Rundle Street, Adelaide, in 1928. Cinema organs joined talking pictures in a siren call that lured hundreds of thousands to the flicks every Saturday—kids in the arvo, adults at night

Making their own fun

Home-made music and party games

In the days when collars had to be starched, lisle stockings darned, and the copper scrubbed out after washday, little time was left for amusement at home. Perhaps the scarcity of leisure enhanced even the simplest fun: in the 1920s adults still played hunt-the-thimble and the pencil-and-paper games that were called 'competitions'. But by the end of the 1920s this simplicity had begun to pall. The trend had started with the cinema; it accelerated with the portable gramophone (first made for soldiers in the battlefields of World War I), and then with radio.

In 1901 music was the focus of nearly every gathering. These were sing-songs—called musical evenings in middle-class homes—almost every week. 'Almost everyone had learned to sing in church or at Sunday school, and songs were often sung in parts,' remembers a Sydneysider who lived in Surry Hills, a poor suburb, around 1910. 'We could not afford a piano and anyway the houses were too small, but there was always a fiddle or a harmonium—a small fold-up organ—or a ukelele or a jew's harp. At sing-songs there would inevitably be one show-off with a good voice to give a solo rendition, and the rest of us would mutter about him hogging the attention.'

New popular songs came out infrequently at the start of the century; the current favourite would be whistled by the butcher's boy and hummed over the ironing for as long as two or three months before its place was usurped by a newcomer. Ballads of maudlin sentimentality enjoyed long popularity, and *The Vacant Chair*, *Take the News to Mother* and *Only a Message from Home Sweet Home* were regular features of musical evenings.

The gramophone soon became an important feature of parties. A man from Pyrmont, Sydney, remembers that around 1912 his family used to have visitors in once a week to listen to opera records or they would take the machine to friends' homes, one of the children carrying the great speaker horn and another entrusted with some of the heavy discs. Popular records cost 3s and 5s [$6 and $10]; opera discs usually cost 7s 6d and 10s 6d [$15 and $21]; but records by stars like Caruso or Melba might cost as much as three guineas [$126].

In houses where there was enough space for dancing the furniture was pushed back against the wall, the carpet rolled up and borax sprinkled on the floor. The young people might rather daringly dance some ragtime. In 1910 the sight of a couple dancing close together was shocking to the more old-fashioned, although they did not frown on waltzing. Ragtime was also suspect, since it was American. The acceptance of American popular music came when the foxtrot arrived, at the beginning of the 1920s. It was at this time too that the valeta, the Pride of Erin and the one-step came in.

Fun in the dark

In the 1920s music was still at the centre of all gatherings and adults still played musical chairs. They frequently played blind man's buff, says the man from Surry Hills: 'It was good fun groping around blindfold hoping to grasp another man's wife. The excitement increased considerably in proportion to the amount of beer and port wine consumed. Violence was not far away.'

Radio arrived in 1923 and introduced into many homes an unfamiliar world of sophistication and variety that destroyed the appeal of simple, home-made entertainments. The era of 'turns' and recitations, ballads and poetry readings was soon gone.

Musical elevation

In middle-class homes a piano was a standard piece of furniture. Walking down a suburban street in the morning one would hear scales and exercises coming from nearly every house. 'The piano is the soul of the home,' said a Grace Brothers (Sydney) advertisement in 1913. The copywriter continued eloquently: 'Every parent knows that the home in which a piano is installed and daily used has a far greater chance of elevating and educating the family than a home which has not the advantage of possessing one of these wonderful instruments.'

Beale and Co., the first Australian piano makers, advertised their 'Italian Renaissance style' instrument in 1908 with much veneer and gilt

Two types of pedal-driven player pianos—a Pianola (top) and an Angelus—both from 1910. These machines reproduced music from a perforated paper roll. Rolls were recorded by composers such as Grieg, Strauss, Debussy and Rachmaninov, and by many great pianists who never made gramophone records but whose touch was now preserved

The magic lantern

No lecture at the turn of the century was truly complete unless it was illustrated with magic lantern slides. Many homes had magic lanterns, and in 1901 Messrs Raker and Rouse, advertising in *The Australian Photographic Review*, directed the public's attention to their range of slides illustrating the Paris Exhibition, a Passion Play and the Boer War

Games of skill and chance

Many an evening passed in middle-class households was over a game of five hundred, euchre, piquet or whist. Card-playing, however, was not common in poorer homes, many of which were puritanical; the men would certainly play—and play for money—but they went out to do so, leaving the girls to do fancy work for their glory boxes and the women to do the mending.

People generally kept earlier hours at the turn of the century; musical evenings and parties started at eight and everyone went home about 10.30 to catch the last tram.

Except in grand houses, meals were not a major feature of entertaining. Suppers were mostly sweet: fruit cake, biscuits and scones. Savouries became popular in the 1930s.

Talk, in both upper and lower society, was formal. Often at a gathering people in turn would be prevailed on to retell a favourite story. If your cousins went away for a holiday, they were expected to pay you a visit on returning and tell you about it.

In much wealthier houses, where there were servants, the masters amused themselves with weekend house parties, afternoon teas, tennis afternoons, balls, play readings and less serious theatrical games, such as charades, played in teams.

Mah Jong, a traditional Chinese game

Chinese checkers enjoyed a brief vogue in the 1930s. Here fashionably-dressed visiting American actresses demonstrate the finer points of the game to an enthusiastic Australian student

played with pieces of bamboo and ivory or bone picturesquely engraved in colour, was all the rage in smart houses in the mid 1920s. 'Mah Jong is now the accepted indoor game for social occasions,' David Jones announced in their catalogue for Christmas 1924. 'Since its introduction to Australia, David Jones have sold hundreds of sets.'

Bridge arrived in the late 1920s, becoming a mark of status and almost an obsession with

many of its devotees. One result of the bridge boom was the gradual disappearance of 'at homes' and a decline in the popularity of musical evenings. 'The bridge craze is spreading in Australia and especially in Melbourne,' *Madame Weigel's Journal of Fashion* reported in 1928. 'It is, as a bridge instructor recently put it, more of a social necessity than sandwich cake. . . Every woman recognises she must be able to play bridge'.

Experimenting with colour photography

Photography has been a hobby since its invention in the 1820s, and in the early years of this century the amateur photographer had to be an expert in many fields. Most photographs were still taken on glass plates which were usually processed in a makeshift darkroom constructed in the enthusiast's bathroom—often much to the irritation of other members of the household. The introduction of the cheap, mass-

produced camera and roll film in the late 1880s brought photographs within the reach of everyone—even the most inexpert could manage the simple controls on a box camera. The first colour photographs were taken in the 1860s, but it was not until after World War II that colour photography reached the mass market. However, during the early part of this century enthusiastic amateurs were producing colour photographs. One of the most popular

methods available then was the Lumière Autochrome process—the first commercially successful colour process—introduced in 1907. The Dufaycolour process was also popular when it was introduced shortly afterwards. Both these methods produced transparencies with an obvious dot or grid pattern, and they were dense and difficult to see when projected. There was no method of making colour prints

A Sydney amateur took this Dufaycolour transparency of decorations in Martin Place for Australia's 150th anniversary celebrations in 1938. He processed the film at home

This Lumière Autochrome was taken in a Melbourne back garden in the early 1920s

Bringing the stars into the home

Making records in the early days of the talking machine

It was in 1902, when the great Neapolitan tenor Enrico Caruso made his first records, that the first step was taken towards elevating the talking machine from a mere toy to a means of reproducing serious music. Caruso's records were an immediate success and it was not long before most of the other great singers of the day were recorded. One who was initially reluctant to make records was Melba. But even she was won over when she heard a Caruso record played while she was dining with the composer Saint-Saens, who enthused over it. Melba made her first records in March 1904 at her house in Great Cumberland Place, London. Making records in those days was difficult and often unsatisfactory. In her *Melodies and Memories*, she describes the acoustic recording process:

'Let us suppose that I am making a record with an *obbligato* of flute, and a piano accompaniment. I stand against the wall, in front of a hole which I know to be the thin end of a trumpet leading to the recording apparatus. This apparatus is in the adjoining room, so that all I can see of the work is glimpsed through the tiny hole. In my own room, a tube ending in a trumpet hangs over the piano.

'We get ready to sing, the flautist coming as close to me as possible without actually treading on my toes. A slight whirring noise comes from the other room, the pianist starts to play, the flute blows in my ear, and I begin to sing. There is no audience to cheer me on, only the sight of a little square window. But there is, in my mind's eye, an audience far greater than that of any operatic hall, and I know that if I make the slightest mistake, the faintest error in breathing, there it will remain, mercilessly reproduced, to all eternity.

'What makes the whole thing even worse is the unusual "technique" which it is necessary to observe in making every record. For example, one must lean right back when taking a top note, or the record will jar. And at the end one must stand rigidly still and silent until the signal comes to "stand at ease". I shall never forget that once after making what I believe would have been the most beautiful record, I stumbled backwards over a chair and said "Damn!" in an all too audible tone.'

Melba made more than 100 recordings many by the electrical (microphone) process, which was introduced, with great effect, in 1925, before her frequent farewell concerts.

Some of these acoustic machines were thought to provide high-fidelity reproduction in their day. The best of all were Edison's Diamond Discs, which were recorded with a 'hill-and-dale' groove. Edison made discs and cylinders until 1929

1 Edison 'Fireside' phonograph, 1908
2 Edison phonograph, 1910
3 Edison Diamond Disc reproducer, 1912
4 Columbia graphophone, 1912
5 HMV portable gramophone, 1915
6 Sayola console disc gramophone, 1927
7 Cutter for bamboo needles
8 Sharpener for fibre needles

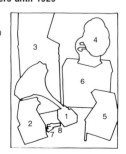

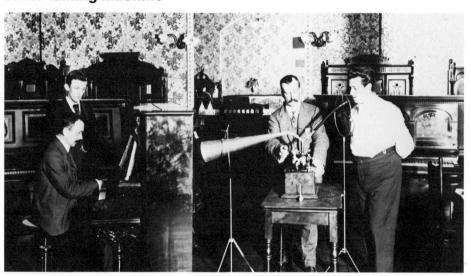

The portly young man in his shirtsleeves is Carlo Dani, a notable Italian tenor who was perhaps the first celebrity to make recordings in Australia. Here he is seen making a cylinder recording in the piano showroom of a Sydney music shop in 1901, when he visited Australia in a touring opera company. He is not making a normal commercial recording but is cutting a cylinder to the order of an individual admirer, who no doubt paid highly for the privilege. The one-off cylinder was no novelty, however; in the earliest days of recording, artists had to perform popular numbers over and over again. Back home in Italy, Dani subsequently recorded commercial discs in a celebrity series

Recording Australians

At least three Australian companies were making cylinder recordings in the first decade of the Commonwealth. A best-seller of the period was a record of Leonard Nelson singing *Goodbye Melbourne Town* (words by Nelson, a professional singer, and music by Frederick Hall, conductor of the orchestra at Rickard's Opera House, Melbourne). Still popular at the beginning of World War I, it was sung by troops of the first AIF contingent as their transports left Australia.

Other companies sprang up after the introduction of electrical recording. Probably the first was the World Record (Aust.) Pty Ltd of Brighton, Victoria, whose 'World Records' played from 10 to 20 minutes ('therefore One World Record contains upon its surface as much music as Five Ordinary Records'). The 20 minute records cost from 5s [$6.75] upwards. Ordinary 'Wocords' records priced from 1s to 1s 6d [$1.35 to $2] were 'unbreakable'; and from 2s to 3s [$2.70 to $4.05], they were 'indestructible'.

The biggest of the new companies was Columbia, which recorded Nellie Stewart, Gladys Moncrieff, Colin and Adele Crane, Stiffy and Mo, Jack Lumsdaine, and the prolific song-writer Jack O'Hagen. Politicians, including Billy Hughes, Stanley Melbourne Bruce, Earle Page and E. G. Theodore, and fliers, including Amy Johnson, Kingsford Smith and Bert Hinkler, all made records.

Topical songs recorded by Columbia in the early 1930s included *Colonel Campbell and Mr Lang* and *Our Don Bradman*. Bradman himself also made a record as a pianist. Gladys Moncrieff's first recording for Columbia, in 1928, was Stephen Foster's *I Wonder If Love Is A Dream*.

Controlling the volume

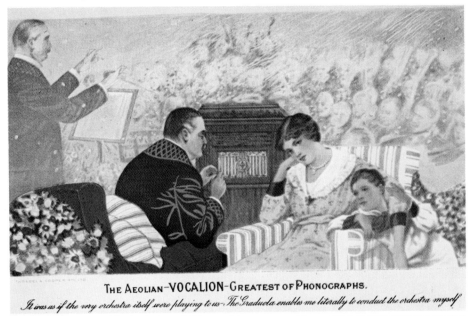

THE AEOLIAN-VOCALION-GREATEST OF PHONOGRAPHS.

It was as if the very orchestra itself were playing to us—The Graduola enables me literally to conduct the orchestra myself

By 1914 many of the original patents on talking machines were expiring, and the market was being flooded with new models. Competition was fierce, and the Aeolian Company in the United States introduced their Vocalion phonographs with a primitive volume control as a selling point

In November 1914 the Aeolian Company in the United States—piano manufacturers—introduced their Vocalion phonographs featuring an Australian invention, the 'Graduola'.

This was a device which was supposed to control the volume of the reproduction. It was described persuasively in advertisements: 'You take up the slender, flexible cable—the "Graduola"—and draw the tip partly out. Instantly the music softens—responds to your touch. Your mind follows the rhythm—an added accent here and there gives a new sprightliness, a novel charm.

'Between music *heard* and music *played* there is a difference as between friendship and love. And with expression music comes a lifting of the spirits, a new and clearer vision, like the clearing of the skies after the cooling, freshening shower.'

But despite the copy-writer's eloquence, the 'Graduola' was not a success, probably because it was merely a shutter device that partly closed off the Vocalion's horn, further muffling the already imperfect sound. A similar effect could be had on many gramophones by closing one of the doors at the front.

Prolific and durable recording artist

Peter Dawson was the only singer whose recording career spanned the years from two-minute wax cylinders to tape. He was the son of an Adelaide plumber and gas-fitter. As an eight-year-old boy soprano he sang in an Adelaide church, and 10 years later took first prize for bass solo at the Ballarat South Street Competitions. He was then working in his father's shop and aimed to be a prize-fighter.

In 1902, however, he went to London to further his musical studies. The young bass-baritone's first professional engagement was singing in an East End church for a fee of 7s 6d [$17.78]. In 1904, he toured the West of England with a concert company led by the great soprano Emma Albani, and the same year made his first record under the name of 'Leonard Dawson'.

In 1906 he signed a contract with the Gramophone and Typewriter Company (later His Master's Voice), receiving £1 1s [$52] for a solo recording and 10s 6d [$26] for a duet or quartet. The association with HMV was lifelong. Dawson made about 3500 records, and by 1940 total sales of his discs had exceeded 12 million. For many years his best-selling title, which he recorded several times, was *The Floral Dance*.

Peter Dawson sings a rousing ballad for the ABC in 1941. He made commercial records under several names besides his own. He sang light songs as Frank Danby, music-hall songs as Will Strong and rivalled Harry Lauder in Scottish songs as Hector Grant. He also wrote songs under eight other names

Shadow-pictures that moved

Silent films and opulent cinemas capture the crowds

Motion pictures as we know them—projected on to a large screen—were invented by two French chemists, Louis and August Lumière. They called their invention *le cinématographe*, and in 1895 in Paris they opened the world's first cinema with a programme of short films of scenery and historic buildings. Less than a year later, motion pictures came to Australia. In August 1896, Carl Hertz, billed as 'The Premier Prestidigateur and Illusionist of the World', presented at the Melbourne Opera House (later the Tivoli) 'The Greatest Wonder of the 19th Century'—the cinematograph. The programme included shots of London streets, waves breaking on a seashore and an English race meeting.

The next month Maurice Sestier, one of the Lumière brothers' roving photographers, arrived in Sydney. He made Australia's first moving pictures—18 m long films, each lasting one and a half minutes on screen—of Sydney Harbour and people boarding ferries, disembarking and walking in the city streets. On September 28 Sestier opened the Salon Lumière in Pitt Street—the first Australian picture house.

'Sydney is going mad over the new inven-tion', said *The Bulletin*. 'What is badly wanted now is some device whereby the machine can be connected with the telegraph and made to represent events while they happen . . .' Sestier could not have been expected to anticipate television, but he did the next best thing—in November 1896 he took his clumsy, hand-cranked camera to Flemington to make a film of the Melbourne Cup. Because his film was too slow, Sestier could not photograph the actual race; but his views showed ladies in lacy hats arriving from Melbourne by puffing steam train, book-makers shouting the odds, the saddling paddock, the crowds and fashion parades. The original of this historic film is in the Cinematheque Francaise in Paris, and a copy is in the National Film and Sound Archive in Canberra.

Professor A. R. Chisholm, who was born in 1888, remembers seeing his first film in the early 1900s. It was projected on to a sheet on the outside wall of a Sydney hotel. Later, he remembers a parlour in Pitt Street where the audience sat in a 'train', looking forward at a railway line along which they appeared to be rushing. 'Presently a mountainous barrier loomed up on the screen; there was a fearful crash, the room was plunged into darkness, and when the lights came on again the walls of the wrecked train lay about in confusion. They were soon reconstructed . . .'

Many Australian short films were shown either in small picture theatres or between variety acts in live theatres. Subjects were usually scenery or everyday events such as passengers leaving Redfern Station. Slightly more exciting were *Breakers at the Bogey Hole, Coogee* (1897, 'the best local picture ever taken') and *The Gallop Past of the Sydney Fire Brigade* (1898 'undoubtedly the most perfect cinematographe picture ever taken in Australia').

City picture houses began to introduce costly mechanical devices to produce sound effects, but suburban and country exhibitors had to be satisfied with a man behind the screen who banged a sheet of galvanised iron for thunder or struck a board with a wooden mallet for revolver shots. And of course there was always the pianist, who sat half-seen in the shadows and matched the mood of the picture with music—soft and sentimental or stirring and dramatic as the action required.

Religious epic made for £600

On 13 September 1900, Melbourne's two morning papers, the *Argus* and the *Age*, both carried this historic advertisement:

*Town Hall
this evening
7.45 o'clock
WONDERFUL LIMELIGHT LECTURE
entitled
'SOLDIERS OF THE CROSS'
by
COMMANDANT BOOTH*

Behind these modest words lay the fact that Australia had produced the world's first religious epic—and possibly the world's first full-length feature film. *Soldiers of the Cross* was a 900 m film with a cast of 600 professional and amateur actors, and it was made three years before America's 240 m film *The Great Train Robbery*, which is generally claimed by historians of the cinema as the first 'real movie'. However, *Soldiers* was not shown continuously—short film sequences were interspersed with slides, hymns and sermons during the evening's programme.

It was a considerable achievement, nevertheless. It was made by Major Joseph Perry, an Englishman then in charge of the Salvation Army's Magic Lantern and Photographic Department in Melbourne. Most of it was filmed on the tennis court of an Army home for girls in the Melbourne suburb of Murrumbeena.

One of the most popular of many silent films made in Australia was *The Kid Stakes*, based on cartoon characters and filmed mainly in Sydney

Cecil B. de Mille would have been proud of Major Perry of the Salvation Army, who in 1900 produced the world's first religious epic, *Soldiers of the Cross*, on a suburban tennis court in Melbourne. It depicted with 'soul-stirring realism' the trials of the Christian Martyrs, and had a cast of 600

A Girl of the Bush, produced by Franklyn Barrett, was typical of the romantic tales of outback life made during Australia's silent film era

Early in the century, an Australian 'western' called *A Maiden's Distress* or *Saved in the Nick of Time* thrilled audiences for a full four minutes

Long before the days of D. W. Griffith and Cecil B. de Mille, and with very limited resources—the film cost about £600 [$30,000]—Perry showed himself a master of crowd scenes and of trick photography. His Christian martyrs were realistically burnt at the stake, stoned to death, forced to jump into a burning lime-kiln, or devoured by a ferocious lion. 'For two hours and a half the Town Hall was almost converted into a chamber of horrors as . . . the sufferings which the early Christians had to endure were vividly brought home to the audience,' wrote the *Argus* reviewer. *Soldiers of the Cross* was taken to America the next year and shown throughout the country. Now an honoured place awaits it in the National Film and Sound Archive, but recent searches by the Salvation Army and other interested organisations have failed to find the film.

The next memorable Australian film was *The Story of the Kelly Gang*, produced by the entrepreneurs J. & N. Tait in 1906 and released the next year. Billed as the 'greatest, most thrilling, and sensational moving picture ever taken', it took six months to make and was 'upwards of three-quarters of a mile'—that is, 1200 m long. Most of the film was shot out of doors, on Charles Tait's property near Heidelberg, Victoria. The four Tait brothers were all involved: Charles directed and wrote the film, and appeared as an extra, as did John, Nevin and Frank. This was the first of five films about the Kellys, the last being the 1970 version with Mick Jagger as Ned, and perhaps the least convincing.

The Victorian Railways obligingly provided a real engine and workmen to re-enact the tearing up of the line near Glenrowan by the Kellys in an attempt to wreck the special police train. The Melbourne *Argus* thought this the best scene in the film. *The Sydney Morning Herald* acclaimed the galloping horses and authentic bush scenes. Anticipating the 'talkies', voices behind the screen 'supplied the realistic dialogue needed to keep the audience in touch with the action'.

The picture show in those days was often run as a family affair. At Sydney's Lyceum

A nasty shock for actress Agness Dobson in *The Face at the Window* (1919)

in 1906, Senora Spencer, 'the only lady projectionist in the world,' cranked the handle of the projector in the dress circle while her husband Cozens Spencer, a pioneer filmmaker, was busy with his cinematograph. Picture theatres became more elaborate in 1910 when a young Canadian entrepreneur, J. D. Williams, opened his 'New Colonial Theatre—home of continuous pictures' in George Street, Sydney. Within a year, Williams had nine theatres in Australia and New Zealand. The *Lone Hand*, a Sydney monthly, explained his success:

'The gay exterior, the lights, and the music all attract people. The splendid vestibules, with marble steps, marble ticket boxes, splendid doors, and vast marble staircases, with railings of burnished brass, make an alluring bait. And when all this splendour is available for sixpence and threepence the places are naturally rushed.' (A mere $1.15 or 57c!)

'In the world of public entertainment nothing in recent years has been so remarkable as the rise and development of the cine-

matograph or moving picture,' said the *Argus* at the beginning of 1911. Many large buildings had been specially built for the purpose of showing these moving pictures, and there were also many open-air picture shows. The *Argus* estimated that there were between 140 and 150 open-air picture theatres functioning in Sydney during the summer months, and that in Melbourne every Saturday night about 15,000 people amused themselves 'by laughing and weeping over "magic shadow-shapes which come and go" upon the cinematograph sheet'. (Sydney's population was then 629,500, Melbourne's 593,237.)

The *Argus* also noted that films were being manufactured in such 'amazing quantities' that they could be sold or hired out very cheaply. The multi-million dollar Hollywood epic was a long way off, but Australia had already developed a flourishing low-budget film industry. More than 250 silent feature films were made in Australia before the coming of the 'talkies' in the 1930s. Of these, only about 30 survive, some only in part.

The Raymond Longford story

From the sea to the docks—via the movies

Raymond Longford, once known as 'Australia's leading scenarist and motion-picture producer', made at least 40 films, including the evergreen silent version of C. J. Dennis's poem *The Sentimental Bloke*. His most imaginative scenario, however, was not more improbable than his own life story.

Longford was born in Sydney in 1875, and when he was a teenager was apprenticed on a windjammer sailing out of Sydney. He was still in his teens when he deserted his ship at the Chilean port of Iquique, where he found himself in the middle of an insurrection, armed with an ancient heavy blunderbuss and wondering what it was all about. The insurrection was put down, and Longford abandoned his weapon and went back to sea.

In London, he sat for his second mate's ticket, and for a while served in the British merchant marine. Then he answered the call of the land again, and became an official of the Indian medical service, with enough Hindustani to qualify for the job of travelling around India distributing pills. In Calcutta, Longford abandoned medicine for melodrama and became a bit player with a theatrical company. Back in Sydney, he trod the boards with such well-known players as Alfred Dampier and Lilian Meyers. He also toured Australia and New Zealand.

Into film-making

In 1908, Longford decided there was a future in films, and commenced his movie career by acting in films produced by the entrepreneur Cozens Spencer. He soon graduated to direction, and his first full-length film, *A Fatal Wedding*, was made in 1911. The leading lady was Lottie Lyall, Australia's first film star. She acted and worked with Longford for many years, until her death in 1925 from tuberculosis at the age of 34.

Longford was one of the first directors to film interior scenes. At first he solved the problem of lighting interior shots by tearing off the roof of a house which he had converted into a studio. Then Cozens Spencer had a studio with a glass roof specially built at Rushcutters Bay, Sydney. There, in 1912, Longford made *The Midnight Wedding*, described as 'a stirring military drama', and featuring the Clarke and Maynell drama company. The film was launched with great ballyhoo. New South Wales' first Labor Premier, 'Big Jim' McGowen, turned the crank of the camera on the opening reel.

In *The Silence of Dean Maitland*, also starring Lottie Lyall and produced in 1914, Longford used the close-up with great effect. When the Dean was confessing his guilt, the camera remained focused on his face while the actor who played the role, Harry Thomas, stood behind the screen and spoke the Dean's lines. It seems that Longford independently developed the close-up in Australia, but the often-repeated claim that he was the first to use the technique is not correct.

Reviewing *The Silence of Dean Maitland*, the Melbourne *Argus* optimistically predicted a great future for Australian films. 'This film drew crowded houses,' it said. 'There is no reason why Australia, with her magnificent climate, wonderful scenery and clever talent should not come right to the front in picture production.' The optimism of the *Argus* was ill-founded. The Australian film industry, despite the work of Longford and other directors, could not meet increasing competition from American and British films.

Raymond Longford, recognised as probably being Australia's most successful director of silent films, spent the last years of his life working as a patrolman on Sydney's wharves (top) after the Australian film industry collapsed in the early 1930s. He is seen below (at left, with pipe) on the set of one of his last films, *Waltzing Matilda*, a talkie

'For upwards of a dozen years Mr Longford has worked and fought to place the motion picture in Australia on a solid footing, and his fights have been many and bitter,' wrote a sympathetic interviewer in *The Lone Hand* in March 1920. 'A less determined man would have given up the game, would have failed utterly long ago.'

By this time Longford had completed and released his film of *The Sentimental Bloke* (1919) and was optimistic about his coming production of Steele Rudd's *On Our Selection*, which he was making for the producer E. J. Carroll in the bush at Baulkham Hills, near Parramatta. 'There I have had Dad stake his claim in the bush, clear his land, and build his little shanty, with Mum and Kate and the boys to help him. No stage atmosphere for me, nothing artificial. I like realism and I think I get it,' he said.

Longford said that the reason for the slow growth of the picture industry in Australia had been the utter lack of support by the Government. 'Not only did they refuse to help me,' he said, 'but they actually opposed me in every possible way; baulked my schemes, prevented me from taking photographs in the most harmful spots, and cut my films to pieces when they were produced.' When he was directing *Mutiny on the Bounty* he was refused permission to shoot scenes of Fort Denison (Pinchgut) in Sydney Harbour. On another occasion, while shooting film in Pitt Street, Longford was arrested for using his camera outside the studio.

Films made in New South Wales could not be released until they had been approved by the Chief Secretary—which meant, in effect, by some policeman seconded from his more important duties at the licensing branch. Longford's film *The Dinkum Bloke*, made in 1922 and starring Arthur Tauchert and Lottie Lyall, famous for their parts in his 1919 *The Sentimental Bloke*, was reported on by an Inspector Young. The report is typical, and reads in part: 'There is a total absence of any objectionable sexual element—the production is most creditable to all concerned.'

Inspector Young therefore recommended the picture for acceptance by the Chief Secretary.

In 1927, Longford was commissioned by the Federal Government to make documentary films about Australia for showing at the big international exhibition at Wembley, England. He spent some time in England, and when he returned gave evidence before a royal commission into the Australian motion picture industry which the Federal Government had set up.

Longford, as an independent producer, bitterly attacked the block booking of American films by distributors in Australia. This system forced Australian distributors who wanted to obtain top attractions to take everything else the American studios wanted to send as well. Australian producers found it almost impossible to get any but minor theatres for their own productions.

However, the Royal Commission achieved nothing to help the independent producers, and before it ended Longford sailed again for England and Europe, where for five years he studied new developments in film-making. He returned to an Australia gripped by the Depression. The film industry was strangled by overseas competition and government indifference. He made his last film in 1934.

In 1950, Longford was a patrolman at the P&O Company's docks at Pyrmont, Sydney. He was still employed on the wharves at the time of his death on 2 April 1959.

The Bloke and his Doreen in an Australian classic

In making *The Sentimental Bloke*, Raymond Longford followed C. J. Dennis's story closely. The picture begins with The Kid, a member of a larrikin push and a two-up addict, coming out of gaol, where he had served a sentence for 'stoushin' the Johns' (translation: assaulting police). He catches sight of Doreen, who works in a pickle factory, pasting on the labels, and falls in love with her.

Later, 'the stror-at coot' makes a bid for Doreen. The Kid hits him and Doreen is angry. But they make it up, and before long are engaged and married.

Soon after the honeymoon, The Kid meets an old cobber, Ginger Mick, a part-time rabbit-o, who talks him into having a few drinks and a flutter at two-up. He comes home stony broke, and Doreen reproaches him. He never plays two-up again.

Doreen's mother dies suddenly, and her old uncle, who lives in the country, installs her and her husband on a fruit farm. The Kid works hard, and the former larrikin, gambler and gaolbird becomes a successful farmer, a devoted husband and a proud father.

Out of this sentimental tale, Longford created an Australian film classic, capturing the mood of Dennis's poem with extraordinary fidelity. His attention to detail and his casting were superb. Though Melbourne is the locale of Dennis's poem, Longford shot the film in Sydney, mainly in Woolloomooloo. The cameraman, Arthur Higgins, developed and printed the entire film at the back of a little shop in Adelaide.

The Sentimental Bloke was first shown at the

Arthur Tauchert (on the left in these three stills from *The Sentimental Bloke*) was a vaudevillian when he was chosen by Longford to play the role of The Bloke. He soon became the most popular Australian screen actor of the 1920s. Lottie Lyell, who played Doreen (above and right), also had a close working relationship with Longford whom she greatly respected. They later formed a company together called Longford-Lyall Productions

Melbourne Town Hall on 4 October 1919, with a full orchestra and a 'songful first part'. It ran for over 100 minutes. Critics were unanimous in their praise. Even the sophisticated Sydney *Triad* acclaimed it: 'It is very easily the best Australian picture yet. And it is a blessed relief and refreshment after much of the twaddlesome picturing and camouflaged lechery we get in so many of the films that come to us from America . . .'

The Sentimental Bloke was shown in England and the United States—where American slang was substituted for the Australian vernacular in the sub-titles.

The screen speaks

Talking pictures come to Australia

A new era in entertainment was ushered in on 6 August 1926, at New York's Manhattan Opera House, when sound came from the screen for the first time. The programme consisted of sound shorts, featuring the violinist Mischa Elman, the tenor Giovanni Martinelli and other well-known musicians, followed by a silent film, John Barrymore's *Don Juan*, which had a recorded musical accompaniment. Less than six months later, in January 1927, a short programme of sound films was shown in Sydney. A critic, Welsa Celott, wrote in *The Triad*: 'The mummers' actions are synchronised with voice production. In the case of the guitar player the act was a success, but in "Opera versus Jazz" ... the metallic reproduction sounded artificial and unconvincing.' However, Miss Celott conceded that 'this addition to the shadow scene has possibilities'.

Some of these possibilities were realised when the Duke and Duchess of York arrived in Sydney on HMS *Renown* on 25 March 1927. The Duke's speech on his arrival and the speech he made when he opened the first session of the Federal Parliament in Canberra on May 9, were both recorded on sound film.

Further possibilities were demonstrated to American audiences the following October when Al Jolson appeared in *The Jazz Singer*. It was a mediocre film, publicised as 'eight powerful reels of vivid talking and singing drama', though the sound consisted only of three Jolson songs and a snatch of dialogue. But the film was enormously successful, and it gradually became apparent to Hollywood's moguls that the 32-year-old silent film was doomed. Not till the middle of 1929, however, did the 'one hundred per cent all-talking film' appear and took the public by storm.

The impact of the 'talkies' on Australian audiences can be judged from a story that appeared on the front page of the Melbourne *Sun* of 4 February 1929 under the heading:

'Mussolini is heckled. Interjections cause row at talkie show.' The heckling took place in The Auditorium, a Collins Street picture theatre, at one of Melbourne's first screenings of the new 'talkie' movies. These were newsreel interviews with King George V, President Coolidge, Beatrice Lillie, and the Italian dictator, Mussolini.

'Shut up!' one indignant filmgoer shouted, when Il Duce appeared on the screen. 'We don't want your ideas here.' And another shouted, 'You're killing your countrymen. What do you have to say about that?' The *Sun* critic considered the new talking pictures showed amazing promise. He noted that King George V, interviewed opening the Tyne Bridge, had a 'quiet, level and cultured voice'; and that President Coolidge had a 'thin, colourless voice with a decided accent'. Discussing Miss Lillie's performance, the critic wrote: 'A certain future for talkies is the recording for people of other lands, stage

May McAvoy comforts a disconsolate Al Jolson in *The Jazz Singer*, the first successful talkie, released in 1927. Jolson played the son of a cantor who preferred singing on the stage to singing in the synagogue. The film was partly silent and the sound was recorded on synchronised discs, but it made history because it contained the first line of dialogue uttered in a full-length motion picture— 'Come on, Ma, listen to this!'

personalities whom they otherwise would never see or hear.'

The newsreel interviews supported the main film, Dolores Del Rio in *Red Dance*, described as a film romance 'made glorious by sound'. At the Athenaeum, just across the street from the Auditorium, Al Jolson was emoting in *The Jazz Singer*. This was preceded by Suppé's *Poet and Peasant* Overture, played by the Vitaphone Orchestra.

In August 1929, Fox Movietone News in Sydney made Australia's first 'talkie' interview, on the mailboat *Sierra*, and in October, Movietone interviewed the newly-elected Labor Prime Minister J. H. Scullin. But much more important was Movietone's newsreel in November of the Melbourne Cup. The film showed the arrival of the Governor-General, Lord Stonehaven (as Sestier's historic film of the 1896 Melbourne Cup had shown the arrival of Lord Brassey), the fashionable crowds, and Nightmarch, carrying 61 kg, flashing past the winning post.

Australian efforts

Apart from newsreels, Australian talking-films had a slow gestation. To encourage producers, the Commonwealth Government in 1929 offered a prize of £5000 [$130,220] for the best Australian-made talkie. Only four films were entered, and the judge decided that none was good enough to take first prize. As a sort of consolation a third prize of £1500 [$39,000] was awarded to *Fellers*, a film directed by Arthur Higgins.

Another entry, *The Cheaters*, had been made as a silent film, and was partly dubbed with sound. It was produced by three sisters, Phyllis, Paulette and Isabel McDonagh.

Arthur Tauchert (right), star of the silent classic *The Sentimental Bloke*, also starred in this 1929 talkie, *Fellers*. The film won third prize of £1500 [$39,000] in government competition which offered £5000 [$130,220] for the best Australian-made talkie. It was the only prize awarded. One critic described *Fellers* as: 'Technique amateurish. Acting forced and stilted. Story absurd and trivial'

The Movietone newsreel of the 1929 Melbourne Cup aroused considerable excitement among cinema audiences. One excited punter was heard to shout 'Wonderful! Oh, wonderful!' The Melbourne Cup of 1896 was the subject of the first film known to have been made in Australia

The Duke of York's speech on his arrival in Sydney in 1927 was one of the first recordings made on sound film in Australia

Australian films of the thirties

The golden days of Cinesound and Efftee

In the 1931, in the middle of the Depression, Frank W. Thring, then Melbourne managing director of the Hoyts chain of picture theatres, and Stuart Doyle, Sydney managing director of the Union Theatres chain, both plunged into talking-film production. Thring leased His Majesty's Theatre in Melbourne—closed as a theatre due to a minor fire and the effects of the Depression—for a studio, and launched Efftee Films; Doyle launched Cinesound Productions in an old skating rink at Bondi Junction in Sydney.

Ken G. Hall, who was Cinesound's producer-director from 1931 to 1956, recalls the conditions under which their first films were made. The equipment was primitive, the 'studios' were inadequately sound-proofed, and the actors and actresses unfamiliar with talkies techniques. The only camera was an old Bell and Howell of the silent era, and Hall had to run this under a canvas cover plus many rugs and blankets in order to suppress its clatter. Hall remembers how over the years the company lost many otherwise good takes because of traffic noise, a dog barking or the rain thundering on the corrugated iron roof of the old rink.

Yet Cinesound was able to make three entire feature films a year on an average overall budget in the mid-thirties of £20,000 [$640,500]—'about the cost', says Ken Hall, 'of a reasonably-sized single set in an overseas equivalent.'

Cinesound's first feature film, and one of its most successful, was a talkie remake of *On Our Selection*, with Bert Bailey playing 'Dad'. It cost only £6000 [$182,300] to make. This film 'founded Cinesound and began an era', says Hall. The popular Bert Bailey appeared again in *Grandad Rudd* (1935) and *Dad and Dave Come To Town* (1938). The cast in this included Alec Kellaway and a young man named Peter Finch. Cinesound's last feature was *Dad Rudd, MP*, which, like its first, starred Bert Bailey as 'Dad'.

Cinesound made 17 feature films between 1931 and 1940, when war stopped production. All of these—with the exception of *Strike Me Lucky*, an unfortunate attempt to translate the idiosyncratic humour of Roy Rene ('Mo') from stage to screen—were box-office successes.

By today's standards they were often crude and amateurish, but they had an Australian atmosphere which Australian audiences appreciated; and two at least, *On Our Selection* and *The Squatter's Daughter*, were successful in England. *The Squatter's Daughter* was sold to Metro-Goldwyn-Mayer for £7500 [$250,000] and shown to English audiences under the title of *Down Under*.

More surprisingly, Thring in 1933 sold the entire output of Efftee studios—seven very stagey feature films, five documentaries on the Barrier Reef, and nine other shorts—in Great Britain. The feature films included a sound version of *The Sentimental Bloke* and the first Australian musical film, *His Royal Highness*, which was written by the comedian George Wallace—who played the leading role—and C. J. Dennis. The film was shown in England under the title of *His Loyal Highness* and was said to have amused the Royal Family; Australian critics, however, found its humour rudimentary and Thring's direction old-fashioned.

A young actor named Peter Finch, born in England but brought up in Australia, made his film debut in Cinesound films directed by Ken Hall

In the 1930s the bewhiskered Bert Bailey starred in a series of Cinesound films about Steele Rudd's characters Dad and Dave. Bailey had made his name through playing the part on the stage and widened his audience when the film appeared

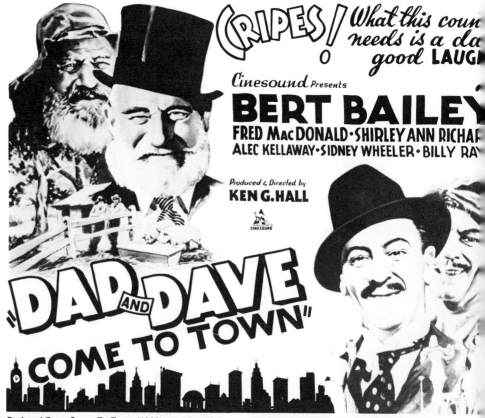

Dad and Dave Come To Town (1938) was the third of the 'Dad and Dave' films made in the 1930s for Cinesound by Ken Hall. The first, and probably the most successful, was *On Our Selection* (1931); the second was *Grandad Rudd* (1935), and the final one was *Dad Rudd, MP* (1939). The cast of *Dad and Dave Come To Town* included, besides Bert Bailey as Dad and Fred MacDonald as Dave, the young Peter Finch. The country humour of these films appealed to Australian audiences

Moth of Moonbi was the first film in the long and interesting career of the Australian film director Charles Chauvel. He also wrote the script for the film, which combines a nationalistic love of the Australian landscape with a somewhat naive storyline of innocence versus evil—here are the innocent maid and the villains of Moth of Moonbi. Chauvel discovered several Australian actors who became international stars. His films include In the Wake of the Bounty (1932), Forty Thousand Horsemen (1940) and Jedda (1954) which included a moving performance by an Aboriginal girl, Ngarla Kunoth

When cavalry charged on Sydney sandhills

The most accomplished film-maker of the 1930s was Charles Chauvel. His first film, Moth of Moonbi was acclaimed for the distinctively Australian atmosphere of the sequences shot on Queensland cattle stations. Chauvel made another silent film with a similar setting, Greenhide, in 1927; then in 1932 he sailed for Pitcairn Island to make a sound film, In the Wake of the Bounty.

When he was looking for a man to play the part of Fletcher Christian in the film, Chauvel saw a picture in a Sydney newspaper of a young man whose schooner had been wrecked off the coast of New Guinea and who had swum ashore with a girl. Chauvel decided this was the man for the part, and ran him to earth in the Long Bar of Sydney's Hotel Australia. When asked if he could act, the man replied with a grin that he would try anything once. His name was Errol Flynn.

Chauvel's next talkie was a historical film, Heritage (1935), which won the first prize of £2500 [$80,000] in a Commonwealth film competition. Then in 1940 he made his most elaborate and successful film, Forty Thousand Horsemen, based on the story of his uncle, General Sir Harry Chauvel, who in the Sinai Desert campaign of World War I had commanded the greatest single cavalry force of modern times. When his board of directors asked Chauvel what the film would cost, he replied, 'A pound a horse—forty thousand pounds.' The highlight of the film, a realistic charge by the Australian Light Horse, was filmed on the sandhills at Cronulla, Sydney.

Forty Thousand Horsemen was enthusiastically reviewed and received. 'There have been some good Australian films before this one,' said the Sydney Morning Herald critic, 'but Forty Thousand Horsemen has every right to be regarded as the first really great Australian film.' Australians queued up to see it, and it was shown in four London West End theatres, in 6000 American theatres, and in most of the world's capitals.

Chauvel made three more feature films: The Rats of Tobruk (1949), with Peter Finch, Grant Taylor and Chips Rafferty; The Sons of Matthew (1949), in which Michael Pate made his film debut; and Australia's first colour feature, Jedda (1954). Much of Jedda was shot in the Northern Territory and it starred a 16-year-old Aboriginal girl, Ngarla Kunoth.

However, the era of wholly Australian-made feature films appeared to have passed. An occasional British or American production took place between 1946 and 1970; but eventually the continued loss of talented Australian film-makers overseas, prompted the Australian Government to establish the Australian Film Commission. Under its aegis and funding as many as 16 films have been made each year.

If Barry McKenzie was a rollicking exposé of a certain Australian type, Picnic at Hanging Rock revealed an Australia of mystery and sensitivity. With nearly $6 million in box office takings, it heralded a list of other notable films like Caddie, Newsfront, My Brilliant Career and Bliss. Such films have been received with enthusiasm, and Australian film-makers, writers and actors, feeling the stimulus of a new curiosity about our continent's varied natural and human landscape, have gained renewed status and confidence in a resurgent industry.

The comedian George Wallace was a star of Efftee films. Harmony Row, made in 1933, and His Royal Highness (1932), Wallace's greatest success for Efftee, were shown in England. He was scriptwriter as well as actor

Palaces of make-believe

Architectural fantasies in plaster and paper

In the early days of the movies, exhibitors often showed films in any hall that was available. In Perth in 1917, Vic's Continuous Pictures—as soon as the programme ended it started again—had their home in the Queen's Hall

The period between the World Wars was the Gilded Age of 'Picture Palaces', architectural horrors where the spirit of make-believe ran riot. 'Everything was make-believe,' says the architect Robin Boyd, 'starting with the pretence that the picture theatre was like a real theatre with the need for a stage and a vast red curtain . . . the audience enjoyed the ceremony of opening and closing curtains, just as they enjoyed being fooled by plaster painted to look like old ivory, or marble, or gold, or wood, or anything else other than plaster.'

In 'atmospheric' theatres, such as the State in Melbourne and the Capitol in Sydney, make-believe reached its most extravagant heights. These pleasure-domes were designed to suggest to enraptured picture-goers that they were sitting in a beautiful park, with classical garden ornaments, plaster gods and goddesses, green paper bushes and trees, paper wistaria on pergolas, immobile wooden doves, and a great blue artificial sky, twinkling with stars lit from behind and passing clouds projected from below. Some also exhibited holy relics of Hollywood, such as the cloak worn by Rudolf Valentino in *Blood and Sand* (1922); it multiplied miraculously, like Lenin's waistcoat in Russian museums.

These rococo monstrosities were inherited from America, together with 'the mighty Wurlitzer organ', with which the organist rose hydraulically, like toothpaste squeezed from a tube, from mysterious depths in the bowels of the building, to disappear discreetly when the show started. Sometimes, the organ was supplemented by a full orchestra, a crooner, and a line of high-kicking ballet girls.

Sydney's State Theatre, with its golden dome, giant chandeliers, statues, paintings and period 'rest rooms', was opened with tremendous ballyhoo in 1929, in the presence of the Governor-General, Lord Stonehaven,

Part of the foyer of Brisbane's Regent Theatre, built in 1929. Florid pattern or texture covers almost every surface

Melbourne's Capitol Theatre (above), built in 1924, was designed by Walter Burley Griffin. It is still in use, unlike the Plaza (below), also in Melbourne and built in 1929. In 1965, however, the lower part of the Capitol was converted into a shopping arcade. The elaborate art-deco curtain was removed and a big screen was installed, but the astonishing prismatic ceiling was not altered. The ceiling is classified by the National Trust as worthy of preservation

the Governor and Premier of New South Wales, and dozens of lesser luminaries. It was described as 'a Gothic palace with an art gallery and interior decoration to take its patrons back to the days of the Court of King Arthur'. What King Arthur would have thought of a men's lavatory labelled 'Empire Builders' Room' was not revealed.

In a different category, though belonging to the same decade of artificial grandeur, was Melbourne's Capitol Theatre, designed in 1925 by Walter Burley Griffin and acclaimed by Robin Boyd as 'the finest picture theatre that was built, anytime, anywhere'. Griffin created an astonishing ceiling of prismatic shapes, lit by concealed lighting from thousands of electric globes, which flooded it in beautiful fantasies of constantly changing colour. His brilliant concept was copied in a New York ballroom two years later, and subsequently in countless other buildings.

The State Theatre in Sydney, opened in 1929, is classified by the National Trust as an essential part of the heritage of Australia that must be preserved

The Regent Theatre in Melbourne was, characteristically, built to look like a real theatre, with boxes, proscenium, stage and curtains. The decoration, equally characteristic of cinema architecture of the time, is derived from many styles, including classic Greek, Islamic and Renaissance. The Regent, which was built in 1929, was rebuilt in 1946-47 after a fire. It was still standing disused and empty in 1985, its future uncertain

117

Radio comes to Australia

Development of wireless telegraphy left to amateurs

After two years of experiment, 22-year-old Guglielmo Marconi was granted the world's first patent for wireless telegraphy in 1896. In 1900, he formed the Marconi Wireless Telegraph Company, which concentrated on installing wireless in ships.

The same year, the chief electrical engineer of Victoria's postal department, H. V. Jenvey, experimented with the Marconi system, with the idea of establishing radio communication between Victoria's Cape Otway lighthouse and passing steamers, but nothing came of his efforts.

Neither the Commonwealth nor the State Governments showed any interest in wireless, but in the middle of 1903, the British Government installed a Marconi plant in Brisbane to communicate with the Cape Moreton lighthouse on the tip of Moreton Island. 'If the system proves successful, it will probably become extended for strategic purposes to other parts of the Australian coast,' said the *Year Book of Australia*. 'As regards the application of the wireless telegraph to business and other purposes, the postal authorities are awaiting the completion of certain improvements projected by the inventor.'

Marconi's man goes home

Marconi continued to make these improvements, and in 1905 his company began a regular service between Queenscliff in Victoria and Devonport in Tasmania. Two years later, a representative spent some months demonstrating that the service could be extended to Hobart. 'But unfortunately for Australia this kind of business is under the control of the Federal Postal Department,' reported *The Storekeeper*, 'and having said that, it is hardly necessary to add that the wretched system of obstruction to anything new ... effectually blocked the way. Consequently the Marconi Company representative packed his bag and departed.'

For many years, the development of wireless telegraph in Australia remained in the hands of amateurs. In 1910, the versatile George Taylor founded the Wireless Institute of Australia, the first association of its kind in the British Commonwealth.

But the man responsible for the development of wireless and broadcasting in Australia on a national scale was a young Englishman named Ernest Fisk.

Became a telegraphist

Fisk, born in 1886, left school at the age of 13. He worked in a factory, a railway station bookstall, and in the clerical section of the Sandhurst Post Office, where he learned Morse code and became a telegraphist.

In 1905, he joined the Marconi Company as a wireless operator. After demonstrating the potentialities of wireless with the Newfoundland sealing fleet off Labrador, he came to Australia in 1910 as wireless operator on the Orient liner *Otranto*. He was then commissioned by the Marconi Company to instal wireless sets on Australian ships.

When Amalgamated Wireless (Austral-

This beam wireless picturegram of Ernest Fisk was received in Australia from London on 12 September 1934, during the first experimental transmission using the new AWA system. Fisk was born in England and trained as an electrical engineer at the Marconi Company's school. He came to Australia in 1910, and three years later was made managing director of the newly formed Amalgamated Wireless (Australasia) Ltd—AWA. In 1918 Fisk picked up the first direct wireless message from England, at his home in the Sydney suburb of Wahroonga. The broadcast was made from the Marconi station at Carnarvon in Wales. Fisk was knighted in 1937. He died in Sydney in 1965

asia) Ltd—better known as AWA—was formed in 1913, Fisk became managing director. At his house at Wahroonga, Sydney, he had an experimental wireless station, which on 22 September 1918, with Marconi's co-operation, received the first direct wireless message from England. 'When I decided to make my first series of tests in an endeavour to reach Australia without the assistance of intermediate stations, I found my friend Fisk in readiness to bring to the experiment the wealth of knowledge and experience that he had accumulated,' said Marconi.

The historic first message was transmitted in Morse code. The sender was the Australian Prime Minister, Billy Hughes, who took the opportunity to make a spirited recruiting speech. It read: 'I have just returned from a visit to the battle-field where the glorious valour and dash of the Australian troops saved Amiens and forced back the legions of the enemy, filled with greater admiration than ever for these glorious men and more convinced than ever that it is the duty of their fellow-citizens to keep these magnificent battalions up to their full strength.'

First public broadcast

The first public demonstration of broadcasting in Australia took place on 13 August 1919, when Ernest Fisk followed an address to the Royal Society of New South Wales with an amplified recording of the National Anthem, transmitted from his office a few blocks away.

A more impressive demonstration, however, was given by Fisk on 13 October 1920 to an audience of politicians and privileged visitors who packed the spacious Queen's Hall in Melbourne's Parliament House.

'Precisely as the last stroke of seven echoed through the great Hall, the vestibule and corridors of the House reverberated with the orchestral strains of *Rule Britannia*,' wrote an awed reporter in the periodical *Sea, Land and Air*. The music came from a gramophone installed in a house at Middle Brighton, 19 kilometres away, and the transmission was so faithful that 'even the gentle grating of the steel needle against the smooth surface of the record' could be heard.

The reporter went on to explain how the transmission was made, from a 'few aerial wires suspended from a mast' in the Middle Brighton garden. 'With these aerial wires as a starting point, so to speak, of their flight, the silent, invisible ether waves, carrying the sound waves on their crests and troughs—precipitated themselves into space at a velocity of 669,660,000 miles an hour [1.078×10^9 km/h] ... Instantaneously they were caught by a similar set of aerials erected above Parliament House, and connected with a highly sensitive and accurate, yet robust and simple, apparatus in the Queen's Hall.'

After some more instrumental pieces, the astonished audience heard 'an actual reproduction of a human voice' singing *Advance Australia Fair*. The first singer in Australia to perform to an invisible audience was Miss L. Walker, who had recently been awarded a Melba scholarship. Only a few months before, Melba herself had made Britain's first broadcast, from the Marconi works.

Fisk told the audience that the object of the demonstration was to show that wireless telephony was real and could play an important part in developing Australia. 'With his own wireless equipment, which is quite as simple to use and maintain as a motor car or machine-shearing apparatus, the man who produces our primary wealth will have a ready means of communicating with his neighbours and with his nearest town,' Fisk said. 'He will be able to transact his business, improve his social life, call for medical assistance and do many other things which to-day are impracticable. He will also be able to receive daily news of the world from the capital cities, and even musical entertainments . . .'

Fisk said that a wireless telephone service between Tasmania and the mainland, or between Australia and New Zealand, was quite a practicable proposition, and that 'within a few years we shall listen to the human voice carried by wireless waves from the United Kingdom'. Less than four years later, his prophecy was fulfilled. On 3 June 1924, Ernest Fisk's voice was transmitted by short-wave wireless from England to Australia.

The oldest radio in this collection, a crystal set, dates from shortly after the beginning of broadcasting in Australia. A crystal set was tuned by moving a tiny piece of wire called a cat's whisker about the surface of a crystal of galena in search of a sensitive spot that detected the signal. Earphones were always used with crystal sets, which were popular until the early 1930s. They required very long aerials, as did most receivers in those days. The paraphernalia over houses in the early days of radio was often very elaborate, while indoors, especially in the 1920s, the sets were dominated by large horn-shaped loudspeakers. The batteries that operated the sets were also large—about the size of a modern car battery—and were usually stored in a cupboard under the set

1 Crystal set, 1924
2 Lady's earphone for crystal set
3 Radiair five-valve set, 1925-26
4 Five-valve radio with horn speaker, 1926
5 Loudspeaker for radio, 1927
6 Telefunken radio, 1928-29
7 Atwater-Kent six-valve set, 1932-33
8 Westinghouse radio, 1937
9 'Fisk' Radiola, 1946
10 Japanese portable valve radio

From amateurs to the ABC

Broadcasting music through the ether

Before World War I, there were about 1000 amateurs in Australia with experimental wireless sets. These were banned during the war, and it was not until 1920 that the restrictions were lifted and enthusiastic amateurs went back to making their own sets. They formed radio clubs, and made successful experimental broadcasts. Early in 1921, AWA gave a series of 'wireless concerts' for Melbourne experimenters, playing records on a hand-wound gramophone with a big carbon microphone in front of the horn.

When the Old Melburnians enlivened their smoke social at the Melbourne Town Hall in June 1921 with a demonstration of broadcasting, the souvenir programme pointed out that it was 'quite unnecessary for any of the windows to be open as the wireless waves are not hindered by obstacles however thick'. In March 1922, AWA arranged for the stage favourites Madge Elliot, Maude Fane, Cyril Ritchard and Alfred Frith to broadcast from Her Majesty's Theatre to convalescent diggers at the Anzac Hostel, Brighton.

Broadcasting was still largely in the hands of amateurs. One of the best-known was Charles Maclurcan, who had been a wireless enthusiast as far back as 1909 when he installed a transmitter on the roof of Sydney's original Wentworth Hotel, which his family owned. In the 1920s he operated a station, 2CM, at his Strathfield (Sydney) home, and published advance programmes of his very popular broadcasts.

Obviously some control of broadcasting was necessary and in May 1923 the Postmaster-General convened a conference to devise 'a workable scheme to provide effective broadcasting services in Australia'. The delegates unanimously recommended a system by which sets were sealed to receive broadcasts from only one of the several licensed stations.

Listeners paid a fee ranging from 10s to £4 4s [$13 to $119] a year to the chosen station, as well as a government licence fee of 10s [$13]. Under this system four stations were licensed: 2SB (later 2BL) and 2FC in Sydney; 3AR in Melbourne and 2FC in Perth.

'The newest magic, wireless music, is about to begin in Australia,' said the *Sydney Mail*. 'The ether will be carrying the strains of orchestras, the voices of singers, the anecdotes of lecturers, and the news of the day for all to hear who care to listen through the wonderful apparatus that receives it from somewhere —perhaps miles away.'

Broadcasting in Australia officially started at 8 p.m. on 13 November, 1923, when 2SB, the first station to operate regularly, broadcast a concert from a roof of *Smith's Weekly*

building in Sydney. A month later, Australia's first wireless exhibition was held in the Sydney Town Hall with the slogan of 'Wireless For All'. Opening it, the acting Prime Minister, Earle Page, said: 'Wireless should be found in the poor man's cottage as well as in the rich man's mansion.' In a burst of prophecy, he added: 'the wonders of the present generation will be the commonplaces of the next.' Congratulatory messages were received from Marconi, and Prime Minister Stanley Bruce, who was in England.

The sealed set system was doomed to failure. It was impossible to police it. Any schoolboy could make a detector with a crystal of galena (native lead sulphide), a wire cat's-whisker to search out its sensitive spots, and a pair of earphones. Unless he flaunted his aerial, he could not be detected. From August 1923 to June 1924, only 1400 licences were taken out. Yet, as *The Australian Motor Owner*, a Sydney monthly, reported in December 1923, broadcasting had 'fascinated and obsessed Australians ... On trains and ferries are heard everywhere remarks bearing on the previous night's broadcasting ... In installing a radio set there is a joyous sense of personal achievement which is lacking, for instance, in a gramophone, and our pride becomes correspondingly greater the larger the

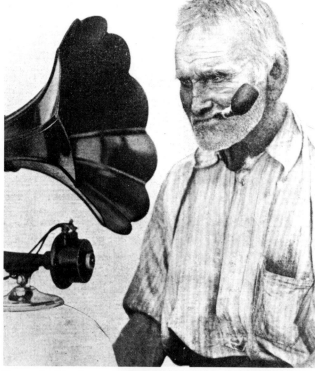

The wonder of radio over a loudspeaker so moved a sub-editor of the *Sun News-Pictorial* in 1925 that he wrote this caption to the picture above: 'Continuous waves of pleasure were generated in the breast of the old man as he eliminated the static from life, and transformed high frequencies of rheumatism into low frequencies of peace and quietude. He is one of the inmates of the Victorian Homes for the Aged and Infirm at Parkville, to which the trustees of the Felton Bequest allotted £100 for the purchase of wireless equipment. Patients are now enabled to keep in touch with the outside world, enjoying to the full the broadcast news and musical programmes.' As the elderly inmate's bemused expression suggests, the clarity of loudspeaker reproduction in those days was not high. Consequently many listeners preferred earphones, which were clearer, and made 'listening-in' a private experience set and the better the results obtained. To listen in to the local broadcasting stations becomes easy and smacks of the commonplace when we have had the pleasure of picking up Perth and Melbourne. These again fade in importance when we can boast, as many can, of having listened to the strains of a waltz from the Palace Hotel, San Francisco.'

A broadcasting boom

In July 1924, the sealed set system was abolished. Existing and new stations were licensed for five years under two categories—'A' (non-advertising) and 'B' (advertising).

By the end of the year, broadcasting was booming in Australia, and sets were much cheaper. A single valve receiver could be bought for £9 [$242], compared with at least £15 [$404] a few months earlier, and crystal sets were less than half the old £5-£7 [$135 to £189]prices. Crystal sets with an aerial and good headphones had a maximum range of no more than 40 kilometres, but gave a purer tone than valve receivers, so they remained popular for many years.

In 1929, the Postmaster-General's Department took over the technical organisation of 'A' stations, with a private organisation, the Australian Broadcasting Company, providing the programmes. In 1932, the Australian Broadcasting Commission, a public body, was formed. It assumed responsibility for 'A' class stations, which were now called national stations, while the 'B' class were all called commercial stations.

On 29 April, 1930, a radio-telephone service between Australia and England began and *The Sydney Morning Herald* reported:

'Your call to Sydney!'

These four words, spoken briskly by a girl operator of the Australian Telephone Service in London, brought the chiefs of the oldest newspapers of Great Britain and Australia into conversation across 12,000 miles [19,000 kilometres] of land and sea yesterday . . . They sounded in the ear of the Editor of the *Morning Post* as he lifted the receiver of the telephone in his room in the *Morning Post* offices in Tudor Street. 'Is that The *Sydney Morning Herald?*' he asked. And a voice from the Antipodes, clear and undistorted, answered: 'Yes, Mr. Williams, the Acting-Editor, speaking.'

An historic conversation had begun. Without form or ceremony oral communications between the peoples of two kindred nations—communications by which business will in future be transacted and friendships strengthened—had opened across the breadth of the earth.

During the controversial cricket tests between Australia and England in 1932-33, a wide interstate hookup for the first time carried broadcasts of the play to every part of the Commonwealth. Loudspeakers and scoreboards outside city shops created so much congestion in Melbourne that police banned them, to the great satisfaction of pubkeepers, who gladly provided a beer-and-scoreboard service in their crowded bars. But this did not deter enthusiasm for the tests.

A poem in the Melbourne *Herald* told of disastrous effects of the cricket broadcasts down on the farm:

I reckon (said Dad) that the country's pests
Is this here wireless an' these here Tests.
Up to the house and around the door,
Stretchin' their ears for to catch the score,
Leavin' the horses down in the crop,
Can you wonder a farmer goes off pop?

There's a standin' crop, an' the rain's not far
An' the price is rotten but there you are:
As soon as these cricketin' games begin
The farm goes dilly on listenin' in,
Not only the boys and the harvester crew
But Mum an' the girls gets dotty too.
An' I reckon (said Dad) that a man's worst pests
Is this here wireless an' these here Tests.

ABC commentators were at Mascot to describe the excitement as Jean Batten came in to land in May 1934, clipping nearly five days off Amy Johnson's England-to-Australia record. On the strengthened roof of the outside broadcast van are Ivor Freshman (left) and Charles Moses, later general manager of the ABC

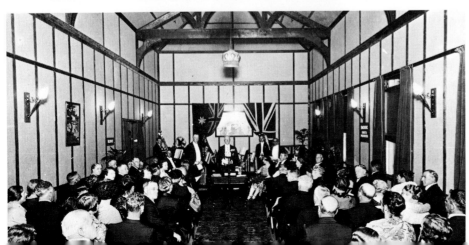

Harry Lauder broadcast from the ABC theatrette in Pitt Street, Sydney, in January 1937. He removed his jacket and used his braces as a belt, but members of the augmented ABC Studio Orchestra decorously kept their dinner jackets on

The panelled room at left was a broadcasting studio. Studio 2FC, Sydney, moved there after it was taken over by a new company in 1927. The station was originally owned by Farmer and Co. Ltd—hence the FC in the call sign—and broadcast from studios on the roof of the company's department store. It began broadcasting on 5 December 1923, 12 days after 2SB, which was the first official radio station in Australia

Sagas of courtship and country life

Radio serials that seemed to run forever

After the establishment of the Australian Broadcasting Commission in 1932, independent commercial radio stations sprang up all over the country. By 1939 more than a million people—one in 16—held radio licences. Only four countries had larger radio audiences, in relation to population, than Australia.

These listeners during the 1930s and 1940s heard mainly romantic serials by day, and in the evenings quiz shows and panel games—

Jack Davey was one emerging personality—and more serials. Many country towns had their own radio stations, with local advertisements and news predominating, and some early serials catered to this important rural audience. *Dad and Dave*, which began in 1936 and ran for 15 years, is one example; *The Lawsons*, which began in 1944 and was the forerunner of *Blue Hills*, is another.

The actors and production teams who

made Australian radio serials in the 1940s gained an international reputation for recording many episodes in a short time. One radio man has recalled that the cast might have arrived at the studio at 9 a.m., read scripts for 15 minutes, rehearsed for 15 minutes and prepared sound effects and props for another 15 minutes. Then they would have recorded four quarter-hour episodes—a week's listening—before they went to lunch.

James Mills (left) was one of three actors who played the hero in *The Air Adventures of Biggles*, based on the novels of W. E. Johns. Walter Sullivan (right) played Algy. *Biggles* began in 1945; one station was rebroadcasting it in 1981

Dr Paul, 'a story of adult love', was the longest-running, most listened-to serial in the world. It began on Australian commercial radio in 1949, and was heard five mornings a week. Production of *Dr Paul* ceased in 1971, after 4634 episodes, but in

1974 the serial was still playing in Singapore, the West Indies, Trinidad, the Bahamas, Bermuda and elsewhere. For most of the serial's life, Alastair Duncan (above) played the dedicated Dr Paul; Lynn Murphy played his wife Virginia

Blue Hills, Australia's longest-running radio serial, was originally centred on the Gordon family. It first went to air in February 1949, when this photograph was taken. In those days Queenie Ashton (centre on sofa) played Mrs Gordon; 25 years later she was still acting in the serial, but as Grannie Bishop, and

Blue Hills had become the saga of the Bishops, Porters and McArthurs. The serial finished, with episode 5795, in September 1976

Recording an early episode of *When a Girl Marries* in the Sydney studios of AWA; the actors are, from left, Queenie Ashton, Alan White, Bob Pollard, Lionel Lunn and Betty McDowell. By the 1940s all radio serials were recorded on acetate discs for broadcasting. No corrections could be made, so it was important for actors not to make mistakes. Tape recording, which came into common use around 1950, made things easier because erasures then became possible

Fred and Maggie Everybody were played by Ted Howell and his real-life wife, Therese Desmond. The first episodes went to air live in the early 1930s. Then in 1937 it became one of the first Australian radio programmes to be recorded

The 3290 episodes of *When a Girl Marries* (1946-65) revolved around the marriage of Joan Davis, née Field. Marie Clarke (right) was one of the first to play the role. This serial, intended for women, was written by an American, Elaine Carrington

Portia Faces Life ran for 3444 episodes from 1952 to 1970. Billed as 'a story taken from the heart of every woman who has ever dared to love . . . completely', it sold well to overseas markets. Its stars included Muriel Steinbeck (standing), Owen Weingott (left) and Leonard Teale (centre)

The George Edwards shows

The best-known of the many radio serials produced for commercial radio by the actor-producer George Edwards (real name Hal Parks) was *Dad and Dave*. It ran for 15 years and 2276 episodes. Listeners became deeply involved with *Dad and Dave*, which featured current events such as droughts and floods. Some listeners even ran sweeps on the Snake Gully Cup, held on the same day as the Melbourne Cup. Another Edwards show with an Australian flavour was *The Search for the Golden Boomerang*, while *Courtship and Marriage* centred on a family of girls and their love affairs

Australia's long wait for television

John Logie Baird sees a bright future for his invention

A distinguished delegate to the World Radio Convention, held at Sydney University in April 1938, was John Logie Baird, who had spent much of his life working on a mechanical television system.

Baird gave the world's first practical demonstration of television before the Royal Society in London in 1926. Three years later, in 1929, the BBC gave him facilities for further experiment, and in 1932 equipped a television studio in Broadcasting House, London, using his system. London had then seen experimental television transmissions using the Baird system for more than a year.

The first Australian broadcast using the Baird system was made in 1929 by Gilbert Miles at Television and Radio Laboratories and radio station 3UZ in Melbourne.

In November 1931, Ernest Fisk, then managing director of AWA, interviewed in Sydney by Fox Movietone on the future of television, said: 'Today we can broadcast a picture but it is only two or three inches square and not as vivid as we are aiming to be . . . I believe that success is just around the corner . . . We shall then look forward to witnessing, in our own homes, the Melbourne

Cup as it is run. Going further, we may expect to sit at home in any part of the world and witness His Majesty the King opening the British Parliament.'

About the same time, the Sydney monthly *Television and Radio Review* (which had just changed its name from *Radio Review*) declared: 'Television is an accomplished fact. It will be in Australia in 1932.' The prediction was over-optimistic, but in 1934, Dr Val McDowall, of Brisbane, with the permission of the Federal Government, made successful telecasts from Brisbane's old Observatory Tower. More experimental transmissions were carried out from the tower next year by another Brisbane pioneer, Tom Elliott, using what was then a high-definition transmission of 180 lines per picture.

Australian amateurs continued their experiments, but little practical progress had been made by 1938, when the World Radio Convention opened in Sydney.

Television had arrived not only technically but commercially, Baird told the convention. He predicted a time when cinema theatres would have television screens showing three dimensional images in natural colour.

'It is true that television has not arrived commercially in Australia, in the United States, or in any country except England,' he said. 'But in England one may go into the shops of any reputable radio dealer and there purchase a television. There is a choice of some 15 different makes. It is estimated that there are at least 8000 televisions in London. Colour is still in the experimental stage but is, I think, certain sooner or later to supersede television in monochrome.' Baird had in fact made the first practical demonstration of colour television in 1928.

Baird demonstrated his television system and Ernest Fisk, congratulating him, said some day television might be operated for profit, but so far, it had meant losses for those who operated it. For example, to install land lines to televise the Melbourne Cup in Sydney would cost about £500,000 [$14.8 m].

Baird's flickering 30-line receivers had enjoyed a vogue in England in 1930s, but his system received its death-blow in February 1937, when the British Broadcasting Corporation, after months of trial, decided on the EMI electronic system that is now universal. Present-day sets have 625 lines.

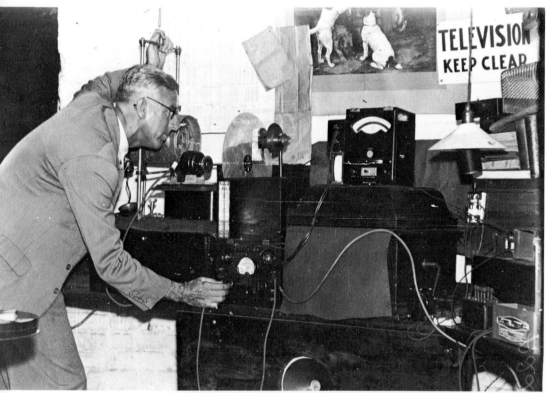

From this makeshift tangle of equipment came Australia's first television transmission using a cathode ray tube. Tom Elliott made the broadcast in Brisbane in 1935. The first Australian television broadcast, made by Gilbert Miles in Melbourne in January 1929, used a mechanical scanning system

John Logie Baird, the Scottish inventor, demonstrated his television equipment at the World Radio Convention held in Sydney in 1938

Television at last

At the 1938 World Radio Convention, Ernest Fisk predicted that Australia would have to wait 10 years for television. It was an optimistic estimate. Next year, Australia was at war, and it was not until 1956, on the eve of the Melbourne Olympic Games, that Australians could excitedly watch their first television programme at home.

TCN Sydney (Channel 9), owned by the

company which then published the Sydney *Daily Telegraph*, televised its first programme on Sunday, 16 September 1956. A 'developmental period' followed and regular programmes began from both TCN Sydney and HSV Melbourne on November 4.

In messages of congratulation which the *Daily Telegraph* whipped up from well-known people all over the world, the American columnist Robert Ruark sounded a lone

dissenting note: 'I think Australia suffers sufficiently without television,' he cabled pessimistically. 'Down with it!'

'We believe our programmes will get better and better,' the *Daily Telegraph* announced on its front page. One of the items on Channel 9's first programme was Lucille Ball in *I Love Lucy*. Twenty-nine years later Channel 9 viewers could still see Lucille Ball, apparently ageless, five times a week.

The vintage years of Australian television

Graham Kennedy, dressed in up-to-the-minute style, signs on *In Melbourne Tonight* in 1958. He was invited to be compère of the long-running (1957-70) variety show after appearing in a telethon

The solemn young man is Barry Crocker, singer and actor of Barry McKenzie, in 1967. With him is Jimmy Hannan, host of Melbourne Channel O's *Tonight*

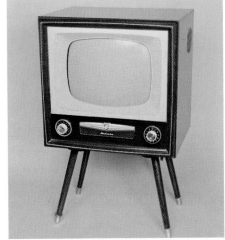

On sets such as this, viewers saw the first offerings of Australian television in 1956

Johnny O'Keefe starred in the ABC's *Six O'Clock Rock*, the most successful pop show of 1959-61

ABC variety shows have gained in polish since this *Café Continental* of 1958, when candles stuck in bottles and funny hats were apparently considered to evoke sophisticated European café society

The pleasures of the picnic

Eating in the open air was a democratic pastime

In 1903, this Tasmanian family gathered together for a picnic in a park and commemorated the day with a photograph. They sat at tables and benches

such as are still set up for picnickers in many Australian parks. The voluminous and stiff clothes that people wore at the beginning of the century must

have made sitting on anything but a bench or a chair rather uncomfortable, but nonetheless many people liked to recline on the ground

Picnicking has been popular from the earliest days of Australian settlement. 'I know no spot in the world better formed for picnic parties than Port Jackson,' said Lieutenant-Colonel Mundy, who arrived in Sydney in 1846. 'Picnics are much in vogue at Christmas time,' wrote Douglas Gane, an English visitor who described life in Sydney in 1885.

Picnicking was a democratic pleasure, enjoyed by all social classes. While the 'artificers and mechanics'—as Gane called them—travelled by ferry, train or drag, the gentry in pre-motoring days drove to remote picnic spots in cavalcades of elegant carriages. One carriage was reserved for the hampers of food and wine, guarded by a team of servants, who also had charge of the portable tables and chairs that allayed the discomfort of eating *al fresco*.

The carriage-builders' picnic

As well as private picnics, annual trade union and company picnics were popular. When the Melbourne carriage-builders held their first annual picnic at the Hampton Tea Gardens in March 1903, the *Australasian Coachbuilder and Wheelwright* was able to report that 'about 1000 persons, a large proportion of whom were ladies, were present', and 'there

was not a dull moment for anybody'. Many people had travelled by special train; others had driven out in carriages.

The most interesting event of the day was the competition in which contestants had to bowl a heavy furniture-van wheel, 1.5 m high, over a given distance. Perhaps next in interest was the 'Hurry Skurry race for Travellers and Ladies, in which the gentleman was required to run fifty yards to where his lady was stationed, the lady being required to adjust his collar, tie, vest and coat before he set out to return to the starting point.' The tug-of-war between the smiths and woodmen led to a 'protracted and exciting struggle, lasting over 15 minutes'. While other stirring events were in progress—including an 'old buffers' race' for men over 45, a single ladies' race, a married ladies' race and an apprentices' handicap—a concert was held with live performers and 'a number of interesting gramophone selections'.

Big Melbourne firms would sometimes organise Moonlight Bay excursions for their employees. A paddle steamer—the *Hygeia* or the *Ozone*—would be chartered for a night trip down Port Phillip Bay. There was dancing on the top and second decks to the music of

string bands, barrels of beer for those who preferred drinking, a programme of songs and recitations in the commodious concert room, and, of course, a hearty supper to round off the lighthearted evening.

Attention to the inner man

Just after 10 o'clock on a fine morning in February 1906, employees of McMurtie and Company, Sydney boot and shoe manufacturers, with their wives, children and friends, boarded the SS *Erina* at a jetty near Circular Quay to embark for their annual picnic at Lane's Gardens, Clontarf. 'The sweet strains of a piano, violin and cornet . . . added zest and enjoyment to the festive occasion,' said the *Advisor*. 'Laughter producers were also in evidence, several of the company wearing comical-looking hats and false noses so that even at the commencement of the day's proceedings hilarity and enjoyment was assured,' the *Advisor* continued.

The enjoyment continued as the party disembarked to the strain of bagpipes, and the sporting programme began. Then came the 'sumptuous luncheon', with handsome souvenir menu cards. 'After full and ample attention had been paid to the wants of the inner man', toasts were drunk with musical honours and responses: 'The King', 'The Firm', 'The Ladies', 'The Day We Celebrate', 'The Visitors', 'The Press', 'The Chairman'.

The 'little ones' were provided with 'toys, spades, balls and lollies.' The shooting gallery was well patronised, and when darkness fell dancing went on in the beautiful dancing hall. Baby Houston danced a Scotch reel to the music of bagpipes. Miss Robinson sang *Underneath the Watermelon Vine*, with a dance, and little Ruth Bailey danced a jig.

At 8 pm, the whistle blew and the homeward journey commenced with 'music up till the last' and a final rendering of *Auld Lang Syne* as the *Erina* arrived at the Quay.

'As long as such reunions are attended with such happy results, one can easily account for the length of years the employees remain at McMurties,' commented the *Advisor*.

Grilled chops and billy tea

In his memoirs of his Australian boyhood, *The Road to Gundagai*, the writer Graham McInnes recalls a typical Australian family picnic in the bush which took place in the early thirties. The menu is likely to be the same today—grilled chops and billy tea. McInnes recalls how he was awarded the 'special and coveted' task of 'swirling the billy' and making the tea:

'When the billy was on the boil, hung by its handle from a pole supported over the fire on two forked sticks, I would throw tea by the handful into the bubbling water, then quickly, before it started to stew, unthread the billy, grab the handle firmly and swirl it about in a vertical circular motion among admiring friends who were amazed, so they said, that when the billy was upside down above my head its contents did not drench me with boiling tea.'

Cleverly posed to demonstrate the appeal of Haywood's biscuits and cakes, the people in this late 1920s picnic scene have a less than casual air. In those days—as now—Australians would drive many miles in their cars in search of a suitable spot to eat lunch or tea out of doors

In the early years of the century, picnicking was a pleasure enjoyed by rich and poor alike. Horse-drawn transport, of course, limited the distance for a day trip—sixteen kilometres there and sixteen kilometres back was probably the most that could be undertaken with any comfort to man and horse

Members of the Launceston Camera Club gather for an informal and apparently copious lunch. Photography was a hobby for the affluent in the early years of the century

For office or group picnics, a programme of the events of the day was often printed in advance

127

All the fun of the fair

When the circus came to town

For the children of many country towns the highlight of the year was the arrival of a circus or a travelling show.

In his book *The Hill End Story*, Harry Hodge tells of a circus that came to the small gold town of Hill End, NSW, about 1912:

A 1914 poster for Wirth Brothers, whose circus was a favourite for many years

'It was a red-letter day in our village when the circus came to town . . . It did not matter to us that the fierce lions and tigers pictured on the bills failed to materialise and that the paint on the waggons was peeling. We passed over the fact that the elephant depicted on the posters was also missing and that the numerous monkeys shown were represented by three rather flea-bitten specimens. There were horses and ponies galore, and on one historic occasion, a sour-looking camel which spent its time scratching its hindquarters against a dead tree and snapping morosely at anyone within range.

'In high excitement we watched the "big top" rise slowly up its central mast, to the accompaniment of much straining and down-to-earth language on the part of the workers, who were also the performers . . . At night, carbide-gas flares lit the entrance and bathed the ring in harsh, white light. It shone on the girl riders in their spangled tights and ballerina skirts, revealing a brassy sort of beauty which often owed more to art than to nature. We queued at the entrance and joined in the scramble for the nearer seats. We all had been saving for some time for the occasion. Some had been out in the creeks that morning with a shovel and fossicking-dish to wash up enough fine colour to pay for their tickets. The more fortunate often staked the luckless in this quest, so that we all got in in the long run, after a last minute appraisal and redistribution of available assets.

'If the ringmaster's tail-coat was a little shiny, his dress shirt a little grimy and frayed at the cuffs and his top-hat dented here and there, these defects were lost in the glamour of the lights and the music of the three-piece band. If the pink tights of the acrobats were darned and faded and the ring ponies lacked the rotund sleekness of our station hacks, we put it down to the rigours of travel and accepted their rib-revealing skinniness without much thought for the austerity of their existence. The box-office returns set the level of chaff in the ponies' nose-bags—often at a very modest level. The drummer beat a prolonged roll on his side-drums, the cornetist blew a thin fanfare and the ringmaster strode in to deliver his stereotyped speech of welcome to the patrons. The show was on!'

As well as the circus there were the travelling shows, with their sideshows, buckjumpers and rough-riders, performing dogs and monkeys and a huge choice of games of chance—or very often games of no-chance.

For a few pence you could see the dancing ducks—they stood on a hot plate while somebody lit a fire underneath; or Phoenix, who invited members of the audience to concoct their own poisons and bring them along for him to drink; or Alf Foster's flea circus—until DDT dried up the supply of performers—or the Artful Dodgers, at whom high-spirited customers threw hard wooden balls.

Life for the showmen was often hard in the pre-war days, as Sam Peasley, who was a showman for 30 years, recalls: 'In the old days, what you made in Bathurst you would spend in Orange, and what you made in

This circus, in 1936, offered its audiences glamour as well as thrills and amusement

Orange you would spend in Wellington. There was very little between receipts and expenses. If you finished the year and could show a few pounds profit it was a year well spent.'

He also remembers that show people were not trusted: 'In the very old days it was a case of "Pull in your doormat; the showmen are in town". This was not always the fault of the showmen, in many cases it was the local crooks who waited until the showmen came to do their nefarious deeds. In those days we were looked on as some sort of scallywag.'

One of Australia's best known showmen was Dave Meekin, who died in 1967. After an early career as a boxer—he once fought Les Darcy—and lion tamer, he discovered and presented amazing acts. Meekin scoured the world, often going on expeditions to Africa himself, looking for acts. Among the many he brought back were a midget stallion from America, fakirs and magicians from India, and Chang the Chinese giant; his best-known discovery was Ubangi Chilliwingi, a woman of the Bushmen people of the Kalahari. After World War II, when customers had more money, the character of the shows changed. But many old showmen who had lived through the Depression could not adapt.

Sam Peasley recalls: 'During the Depression you might only take 30s [$45] in a night and this had to last you a week. After that, when money became more plentiful, a lot of show people did not want to spend it. The younger showmen did not remember the Depression and ploughed their money back into the industry, buying riding devices. We bought houses and kept a few bob in our pockets.'

Latiefa, 'Queen of Reptiles', performs for a crowd that is more interested in the camera than the

snakes. This ramshackle show was at Gladstone, Queensland, in 1912. Its attractions included

Patrick O'Connor, the Irish giant, nearly 214 cm tall but billed here for effect as 246 cm

'Take a glove . . . have a go'

When Sydney's Royal Easter Show opened in 1972, one familiar sideshow was missing—Jimmy Sharman's Boxing Troupe. For nearly half a century, show crowds had gathered round Sharman's tent, listening to the beat of the big drum, the ring of the bell, and the leather-voiced spruiker's shouted invitation: 'Who'll take a glove? Who wants to have a go?' In pre-dollar days the challenge was 'Take a glove and earn a fiver!' There were always plenty who accepted the invitation, especially in country towns. Only drunks were barred. 'Drunks never make fighters' was the Sharman slogan.

The troupe was started by 'Old Jim' Sharman at Ardlethan, NSW, in 1911. Year after year it toured country shows in New South Wales, Victoria, South Australia, Queensland and Tasmania, travelling for as much as ten and a half months in a year.

'Old Jim', one of 13 children, was born on a dairy farm at Narellan, NSW. He took up boxing as a young man, and had the amazing record as a lightweight of 83 knockout wins in 84 fights. He lost the other on a foul.

When he started his tent business, he fought for a time with the troupe, which in its long history, discovered and trained many champions, among them the heavyweight champion George Cook (who had great success in England and America), the triple champion Billy Grime, the Australian featherweight champion Mickey Miller, the Aboriginal lightweight champion Jack Hassen, Frank Burns, Tommy Uren, Frankie Green, 'Bindi Jack', George Fleming, the Sands

brothers, and 'Kid Young'. All learnt their art in the hurly-burly of Sharman's tent fights.

The Sharman troupe varied in size, but averaged eight fighters, a spruiker, a treasurer and a foreman. The equipment consisted of a 'big top'—a tent 15 m wide and 18 m deep—a collection of alluring fight paintings to decorate the front, and the 'bridge', the showman's name for the narrow platform on which the troupe lined up for inspection, and the spruiker barked his challenge.

'Young Jim', who had made a name for himself in Rugby Union and League football, took over the spruiker's job in 1945 and re-

mained with the troupe till he disbanded it in October 1971, after the Shepparton Show in Victoria.

At the Sydney Show the following year, in place of the traditional line-up of Jimmy Sharman's boxers, there were Jimmy Sharman's Scooter Cars and Jimmy Sharman's Jet Ball. 'You can't live in the past,' 58-year-old 'Young Jimmy' Sharman told an interviewer. 'The days of the tent shows are finished. The cost of production—well, with the expenses involved, it just became impossible to show a profit. And the kids of today—they like the thrill-ride life . . .'

Jimmy Sharman (tenth from left) and his boxers await challengers at the Sydney Showground in 1931. Billy Grime, triple champion of Australia and advertised as 'the world famous fistic freak', is 16th from left

Children's games

Australians remember their childhood amusements

In the days when children were neither surrounded by mass-produced toys nor lured indoors by the hypnotic eye of the television set, they had many traditional amusements that have since disappeared. We asked Australians of various ages and backgrounds how they played when they were children. Many recalled making their own toys:

'If you couldn't afford a football you could get some newspaper and fold it and make a package about six inches [15 cm] long and two inches [5 cm] round and tie a string round the middle. It was hard and if it hit you it hurt.'

'You could play humming gum-bubbles. You got new gum leaves in the spring and peeled off the fine rubbery skin, and you put this in your mouth and sucked and blew—like bubblegum—and it would give off a pop. You could get the same gum-leaf skin, a little smaller, and put it behind your front teeth and make it hum loudly, as the Aborigines used to.'

'You could make a notch in the side of a cotton reel and wind a string around, with a loop to hold it at each end, and when you pulled the string you could make the cotton reel go whoop-whoop.'

'You got five knuckle bones from the butcher and got your mum to boil them clean and then they were jacks, to be tossed and caught on your palm or the back of your hand. To be quite fancy you could put on colours with your paint box.'

'You could whittle with your penknife and make little boat hulls, or aeroplane propellers which you fastened to a long stick which you held in your hand as you ran, making it whirr in the wind. You could serrate the rims of a cotton reel and put an elastic band through the middle, with a little wooden peg at one end to hold it and a little stick at the other. You wound it round and round and let it go—a cotton-reel tank. It whizzed over the ground, over obstacles and up and down.'

'You wagered with cherry bobs, a coinage that appeared in one cherry season but somehow was not hoarded until the next. You got your mum to boil all the stones. The condition of the stone was rather important. Some ended up white, some red. You carried them in a little cheesecloth drawstring bag which your mother made.'

'You could go into the bush and find a proper forked branch for a shanghai [catapult]. You had to notch it and con someone for a bit of inner tube and some leather for the little pouch. And you could hardly wait for the lovely scented pittosporum flowers to appear. Their seeds made the best ammunition to shoot at tin cans on a fence—or other boys.'

Small boys put the debris of industrial society to good inventive use:

'You could climb into an old motor car tyre, hunch up your knees and tuck in your head and get someone else to bowl you along the road—down a hill at about 30 miles an hour [50 km/h]. You whirled round and round—thankfully there was little traffic [in the less hectic late 1920s].'

'You could make your own corrugated iron canoe—there was a great deal around. You had to bend your sheet of corrugated iron down the middle, and work and smash at it. And you prised hunks of tar off the edge of the road and melted it down in a billy and poured it over the end to seal it where you had bent it. It usually sank like a stone.'

'You could get a fruit case and pinch a paling from someone's fence and buy iron axles and iron wheels—threepence a pair [55 cents now]—and make a billycart...and scar your arms and legs when you fell off and get splinters in your bottom on the ride.'

Marbles were greatly prized by boys. Each kind had its own value, like coins:

'Aggies [agates] were the best—clear with a

With a perambulator, a tricycle, a rocking horse and lively imaginations, these children produced a carriage and pair. Other children used to harness a couple of their playmates between these shafts of this kind of pram. This photograph was taken in Tasmania before World War I

Children whose parents could afford it were dressed in elaborate and voluminous clothing, especially on holidays, before World War I. The ribbons on boys' straw hats often proclaimed HMS *Indomitable* or some other British warship. The quoits players above were outside the Katoomba Coffee Palace in the Blue Mountains, NSW, and the paddlers at right on a Tasmanian beach

spot of colour in the middle or strips of colour coming from the centre. Connies were coloured glass; some had cats' eyes—which were very rare and valued—and others streaks. Clayies, or clay dabs, made of baked clay were ordinary—commonohs. It was a good trick to get hold of a steelie [ball bearing], which usually broke the others in games like big ring, little ring or threes.'

Boys never played with girls, except at parties. Party games included three-legged, wheelbarrow, egg-and-spoon and sack races, treasure hunts, pinning the tail on the donkey, and a nasty trick:

'Sometimes three or four eggs were put on the floor in a row and a person was blind-folded and had to walk between the eggs. But before they started, the eggs were quietly removed and peanuts put down instead, so the victim went crunching over the peanut shells.'

'It was mostly the girls who skipped—to odd lines and fragments of verse: "Andy Pandy sugary candy. French . . . almond . . . cake (getting slower). Salt . . . mustard . . . vinegar . . . pepper (getting faster)." And, with two others holding the rope, a gaggle of little girls chanted "All in together, this fine weather."'

'In "Queenie, Queenie, who's got the ball?" one girl was "It" and she stood with her back to the others. She threw the ball over her head without looking and then guessed who had caught it. The ball could be tucked in a sleeve or clutched between the knees to hide it.'

The daintily dressed sleeping doll was made in Germany in 1914. It stands about 60 cm, and has real hair in its china head. A dressed, jointed sleeping doll of this size cost 12s 6d [$28.50] or more

This paper doll came with a comprehensive range of afternoon and evening dresses. The tab at the neck of the dress slips into a slit in the doll's neck, and the doll's head slips into a slit in the hat. Paper dolls were inexpensive, as were dolls such as the one at right, made by a travelling toymaker. This one is a dancing doll. You sat on a plank, holding the stick so that the doll's feet just touched the plank. Then you thumped the plank in time to music and the doll danced

Wooden toys of the 1930s and 1940s. The doll's house and the Noah's ark and its fretworked animals may have been home-made, but the Lewis Carroll characters at left were probably bought in a shop. During World War II, most toys were wooden because of shortages of metal and other materials

Australian art

Painters in search of a national identity

In 1918, the Australian Government commissioned the artist Will Ashton to paint the La Perouse Memorial at Botany Bay. On his daily trips by tram out to the site he was usually the only passenger left at the end of the line and the conductor, out of curiosity, asked Ashton what he was doing. 'When I told him I was painting the La Perouse monument,' he wrote, 'he looked at me with admiration and said what a whopping job I'd taken on to paint a big thing like that! Then it dawned on me. He thought I was a house-painter who had been hired to brighten up the monument with a coat or two of paint, and ever so gently I had to disillusion him.'

And for a long time in Australian art such an honest mistake could have been excused. Australian artists showed their skill mainly in landscapes, visited Europe and did not always return, and art was art with a distinctly European flavour.

An Aranda station-hand

Even the original inhabitants, the Aborigines, found it better to copy European styles of painting, at least if they wanted to make a living; and Albert Namatjira proved it could be quite profitable. Born in 1902, he belonged to the Aranda tribe, and worked as a stockman and station-hand. During a stint as a camel-driver, he found he could supplement his earnings by selling hand-made artifacts — Aboriginal weapons like the woomera, and painted and carved panels.

However, it was not until an artist named Rex Battarbee visited the Hermannsburg Mission in 1934, that Namatjira realised his bent for painting in watercolor. With Battarbee's encouragement he made his first attempts at capturing the colours and light of central Australia. He learnt how to use brushes and prepare the paper, and in exhibitions in Adelaide and Melbourne he started to make his name. In a show mounted in Melbourne in 1938, all 41 paintings were sold, and two years later the National Gallery of South Australia became the first gallery to purchase his works.

So popular did his paintings become that an advisory council was formed to protect Namatjira and the other Aranda artists from exploitation. But there were some ironic and tragic twists to Namatjira's life. Until the referendum of 1967, when an overwhelming majority of Australians voted to allow the Federal Government to legislate for Aborigines in all the states, Aborigines did not have citizenship rights in their own land. Citizenship could only be granted on application, and very few had achieved this distinction.

In 1954, Namatjira was presented to the Queen and became a full citizen three years later. His new status gave him the right to drink, but he continued to work amongst tribal Aborigines and not only shared his newly-acquired income with his relatives and fellow-artists, but his access to drink as well.

Whether Namatjira's actions led to some of the violence at Morris Soak, where his family lived, is not clear, but in August 1958 he was charged with supplying liquor to a fellow-tribesman, who was a ward under the Welfare Ordinance and banned from drinking.

Namatjira was convicted and sentenced to six months' imprisonment with hard labour. On appeal this was reduced to three months. He was allowed to serve this 'in the open' and finally returned to his tribal reserve, a citizen denied his own country. Depressed by his experience, his enthusiasm for painting diminished and he died in 1959.

The noble savage

Of course, appreciation of Aboriginal art has only developed in quite recent years. Aborigines infrequently featured in works by Australian artists, except a few of the early colonial painters who saw them as examples of the 'noble savage', named them 'Indians' and did not really believe they had any artistic ability or culture of significance.

As for an expression of nationalism at the time of Federation, the Australian landscape seemed to most artists to speak best for the new-found unity, even if some depictions of the bush were rather fanciful. Sydney Long, a painter of no mean ability, even transformed the bush into a setting for Pan, the Greek god of pastures, and had him dancing along at the head of a flock of native brolgas.

That painting, executed in 1897 and titled

The Spirit of the Plains was accepted as something of a landmark in Australian art, but naturally there was no continuity with the many thousands of years of Aboriginal art which had preceded it and recorded the continent in such a different way. On the other hand, Sydney Long did admit that the day would dawn when the Australian artist would 'bid the Aborigine blossom out in all his manly vigour, when sufficient time has allowed us to forget his failings'.

In the art world itself, however, there was no lack of confidence at Federation. *The Year Book of Australia*, reporting on *'Art Progress in 1901'* had this to say. 'The Australian taste for art is rapidly advancing, and at no previous period in the history of the federated States has the production of Australian artists attained such a high degree of excellence.' Yet it also had to admit that 'the market for high-class artistic work' was limited, and this explained why Australian artists were now so eager to go abroad.

Victorian favourites

In the early years of the Commonwealth, Australian taste in pictures, as in books, was still largely imported from the 'Mother Country'—the United Kingdom. In 1906, the Melbourne *Argus* asked its readers to nominate the 12 best pictures in the National Gallery. Only one by an Australian painter, John Longstaff's *The Sirens*, was chosen. The favourites were mostly Victorian pictures of

Sepia reproductions of *The sea hath its pearls* by W. H. Margetson hung on the walls of many Australian homes at the turn of the century

This august gathering of artistic and literary figures at the Art Gallery of New South Wales in 1940 includes some painters of the old school, many of whom were hostile to so-called modern art. Lionel Lindsay is seventh from left, Julian Ashton is third from right and Sidney Long is sixth from right. When Roy de Maistre showed his *Rhythmic composition in yellow green minor* (left) in 1919, Julian Ashton asked him if he could possibly think the painting 'beautiful' or properly a work of art

the 'every picture tells a story' kind.

In 1918, Sydney's best-selling framed pictures were reproductions of *Cupid Asleep* and *Cupid Awake*, *Penny a Bunch*, and *The Sea Hath Its Pearls*, the original of which still hangs in the Art Gallery of New South Wales.

Sydney leads the way

During 1901, the Art Gallery of New South Wales bought 15 oil paintings, six by Australian artists. *Lady in Black* and *Autumn Showers*, by E. Phillips Fox; *Harbour View*, by Howard Ashton; *Nearing the Township*, by Walter Withers; *Spring Memories*, by Frank Mahony and *Henry Lawson*, by John Longstaff. The Lawson portrait cost £65 [$3280]. But Sydney's example was not followed by Melbourne's National Gallery which bought only one oil painting in the first year of the Commonwealth, and 10 watercolours, none by Australians. Adelaide was a little more patriotic and of four oils, bought one by an Australian, *A Tea-tree Glade*, by Fred McCubbin. Brisbane followed suit, purchasing Julian Ashton's *Jewelled Margin of the Sea*, but Perth and Hobart bought nothing at all.

Laws for the young

In his *Story of Australian Art* (1934) William Moore called the years before 1900 the Genesis, and the years after, the Exodus. Writing in 1962, the art historian Bernard Smith added: 'And he might well have called the 1920s the Leviticus, for it was then that the old men of the tribe, their years of exile over, began to lay down the law for the guidance of the young...

'The air was heavy with the arrogance and respectability of old men, old and tired in spirit and in the handling of paint, if not yet quite old in years.'

The few Australians interested in contemporary art in the 1920s, or even in the 19th century impressionists and post-impressionists, had to be satisfied with reproductions in colour prints or books. During the next decade, a few paintings by modern masters including Matisse, Utrillo, Marquet, Laurençin and Vlaminck were shown in exhibitions, but the work of contemporary Australian painters had little recognition.

Artists take sides on Modern Art

The pioneers of modern art in Australia were Roland Wakelin, Grace Cossington-Smith, Roy de Maistre, and to a lesser extent, Norah Simpson, all pupils of the veteran Italian teacher, Dattilo Rubbo, who opened his art school in Sydney in 1897.

There was, inevitably, opposition to the new movements in Australian painting. In 1927, Lionel Lindsay contributed an article entitled 'Modernism in Art' to *The New Triad*. After two years in Europe, he had come to the conclusion that the 'new movement' in art was finished. 'Historians will regard it as a mad kermesse; a cosmopolitan confusion of white and nigger charlatans; a babel of theory and malpractice...'

But 'modern art' was far from finished, and so was Lindsay's hostility to it. In 1942, he published *Addled Art*, which proved a hilarious though virulent and often ill-informed attack on the modern movement. Lashing about like a latter-day Don Quixote, Lindsay declared that 'Modernism in art is a freak, not a natural, evolutionary growth. Its causes lie in the spirit of the age that separates this century from all others: the age of speed, sensationalism, jazz, and the insensate adoration of money. No great art was created in a hurry, or at the behest of market-rigging dealers. Distasteful to the general public and to all fine taste, it was forced on the world by powerful propaganda, "fixed" critics, and its news value as a novelty. It is the product of Stunt'.

In 1937, Robert Menzies, then Attorney-General, presided over the inaugural meeting of the Australian Academy of Art in Canberra. It soon became apparent that the academy was not sympathetic to modern art, though it included representatives from all the states and diverse schools of painting. Some well-known artists — including Rupert Bunny, George Bell, Daryl Lindsay and Charles Wheeler — refused to join the academy but, surprisingly, Grace Cossington-Smith and Roland Wakelin decided to accept the invitation.

A few months before the formation of the academy, Menzies, opening an art exhibition in Melbourne, had annoyed the more adventurous painters by saying: 'Great art speaks a language which a very intelligent person can understand. The people who call themselves modernists today speak a different language.' His observation sparked off a lively newspaper controversy. 'What does a layman know of craftsmanship or draughtsmanship ...?' asked George Bell, a Melbourne artist and teacher. 'Just as it would be ludicrous for an artist to argue a knotty point of law, so it is ludicrous for Mr. Menzies to lay down what is good drawing and good art ... Every great artist has been a "rebel" as an experimenter is always called.'

Menzies accused Bell of forgetting his good manners, and the debate continued for weeks, with artists of the old guard, including Max Meldrum and Harold Herbert supporting Menzies, and *avant-garde* artists, including Sali Herman and Adrian Lawlor, opposing him. The lay leader of the opponents was Mr Justice Evatt, later to become Menzies' bitterest political opponent. When Evatt declared that Australian galleries 'should be induced to buy or borrow modern pictures', J. S. MacDonald, director of Melbourne's National Gallery, replied: 'I don't think we should have modern art in the gallery at all. It is not liked by the galleries of Australia.'

Contemporary art

In 1938 the painter George Bell formed the Contemporary Art Society in Melbourne. Its first exhibition, opened by Mr Justice Evatt in June 1939, showed work by Sidney Nolan, Russell Drysdale, James Gleeson, Sali Herman, Albert Tucker, Noel Counihan, David Strahan, and many less known artists. The exhibition's success led to the establishment of similar societies in other states.

And later in 1939, on the eve of World War II, a comprehensive collection of more than 400 modern paintings was brought to Australia by the Melbourne *Herald*. It included works by Bonnard, Braque, Cézanne, Gauguin, Derain, Toulouse-Lautrec, Modigliani, de Chirico, Seurat and Rouault, most of them unknown to Australians, except in reproductions in expensive art books.

Art on trial

The rebels become respectable after a court case

Unlike many Australian artists, William Dobell did his finest work in portraiture, proving to be the successor of Tom Roberts and George Lambert, though his approach was very different. His unique psychological insight into his sitters, often misunderstood, led to a historic court case.

Yet Dobell said himself: '. . . I'm not looking for the "inner man". I paint just what I see. I'm not always aware of some idiosyncrasy in an individual even when I've put it down on canvas. I once painted a man, and later someone said to me, "I see you got his squint!" I took another look at the portrait, and, sure enough, one eye had a squint.'

But Dobell's prominence came in 1943 with the award of the Archibald Prize, which was then worth £500 ($12,000, although in 1985 the award itself was only $10,000). It was for a vigorous portrait of his friend and fellow-artist, Joshua Smith. Smith was a thin, bony man and Dobell exaggerated these characteristics. Two entrants in the competition asked the New South Wales Supreme Court to disallow Dobell's award on the grounds that his painting was a distorted caricature, not a true portrait.

The portrait was described by various witnesses for the plaintiff as a 'fantasy', a 'biological absurdity', and the representation of a long dead man who had 'dried up'. For the defence, witness argued that there were many types of portraits, that one of Cézanne's greatest paintings, *The Red Vest*, had more distortion than Dobell's and that a likeness alone did not constitute portraiture.

Dobell won the case and Mr Justice Roper's judgment vindicating him was, in effect, the Magna Carta of the modern art movement in Australia.

For Dobell the whole affair was a searing experience. By nature a rather shy man, he was seriously affected by the glaring publicity and he withdrew for some years from the society of his fellow-artists.

Sir William Dobell concentrated on portraits for many years. Margaret Olley sat for him in 1948

Tom Roberts painted *Bailed Up* in 1895, combining his love of landscape and people

Popular painters of the Australian scene

Travel broadens the mind but Australia has usually called its artists back, even if a great deal of the continent is a 'sunburnt country', more harsh than endearing. When John Longstaff returned in 1911, he replied to a speech of welcome in these words: 'Am I glad to be home again? I cannot tell you how glad. The Australian landscape has always seemed to me the most beautiful in the world as well as the most mysterious. When I first saw the brown, hot earth from the ship's decks at Fremantle I cannot tell you the emotion it gave me—after all that confounded sappy English green!'

Tom Roberts also spent years in Europe but he was quite happy to set himself up again in the heart of Melbourne, using a small studio in a diminutive two-storey building on a site in Bourke Street where the Myer Emporium stands today. He had a wonderful view up and down the busy street, with the Post Office nearby. Hansom cabs waited for fares, there were characters galore, and his keen eye did not miss any detail.

The Heidelberg school

In the late 1880s, Charles Conder shared Roberts' studio and they would go off at weekends to Eaglemont and Heidelberg, still surrounded by bush, to capture the light and effects in the landscape they loved.

Arthur Streeton was another of their 'Heidelberg school' but he found it difficult to draw the human figure. Nonetheless, in one of his best-known paintings, he dramatised the actions of a group of miners leaving a tunnel where they had just set explosives. Writing to Fred McCubbin, Streeton described the setting for this painting, *Fire's On*. 'There is a cutting through the vast hill of bright sandstone; the walls of the rock run high up, and behind is the deep blue azure heaven, where a crow sails along like a dot with its melancholy hopeless cry—long drawn, like the breath of a dying sheep. Right below me the men work, some with shovels, others drilling for a blast. I work on the w.colour drying too quickly and the ganger cries, *"Fire, Fire's on"*; all the men drop their tools and scatter and I nimbly skip off my perch and hide behind a big safe rock. A deep hush is everywhere—then, "Holy Smoke", what a boom of thunder shakes the rock and me . . . the rock is a perfect blazing glory of white, orange, cream and blue streaks here and there where the blast has worked its force.'

Australia has produced other painters, too, who have loved to record the country and its characters on canvas.

Donald Friend, for many years an expatriate painter living in Bali, described some of these subjects for pictures in his *Painter's Journal*, published in 1946. 'Today there are a lot of people in from the farms—lanky gnarled farmers with their amply shaped wives in sulkies and gigs—with their pink scrubbed bulky young sons (what enormous hands they have) yarning in the pubs about their crops, the shortage of oranges, of horse-breaking, the price of cattle, or rainfalls. The pink sons in uncomfortable best suits and hard hats that stick straight on their heads listen, uncomfortably self-conscious, silent, to the drawn-out yarns of their seniors. They look like Van Gogh characters, fresh-faced, strong, dumb, virginal.'

In 1958, Russell Drysdale travelled through the north-west with the author, Jock Marshal. His book, *Journey Among Men*, was illustrated by Drysdale, and, as Geoffrey Dutton points out, 'not only reflects Drysdale's fondness for pubs, but his countrymen's pleasure in standing around and yarning, and the pub provides him as an artist with incomparable opportunities for observing the relaxed human figure. Since he draws by memory, the informality is not disturbed ...'

And it was not only the acute observers of the rural scene who were becoming successful after World War II. As Ross Luck points out in the catalogue of a collection which was sent on exhibition tour to the United States in 1966: '... a new generation of artists has arrived. To these the struggles of the breakaway years are unknown. There are no restrictions to stifle their creative ideas, and there is a sympathetic audience for even their most experimental concepts ... They can draw on the whole world's traditions as well as their own. They live and work in cities that are almost as sophisticated as London, Paris, New York. Travel is easy and they travel, but they return. There are no significant reasons for staying away except further study. Their devotees are at home, waiting'.

A boom in art buying

In the early 1960s, too, a great art boom in Australian art began, prices soared and there was an astonishing proliferation of art galleries, often just a humble terrace-house transformed with a coat of paint, a fancy name, a few spotlights and a stock of cheap red and white wine for openings. The boom was largely promoted by the dealers, and supported by buyers who saw pictures as an investment, a status symbol, or both.

There were stories, too, of unscrupulous painters and dealers, perfectly content to produce pictures in tones to match somebody's decor or curtains, while even the famous, with no need for such tricks, were astonished to find plagiarists turning out fakes of their works. And sometimes rejected works even found their way into sales, with signatures neatly forged.

The number of galleries has risen remarkably too. In 1958, J. D. Pringle, then editor of *The Sydney Morning Herald*, wrote that he was impressed by the fact that Sydney had one large and three small galleries; but by 1985, over 240 galleries were flourishing, and there were 70 art dealers listed. As for the boom, whatever its origins, it greatly benefited artists, many of whom for the first time were able to earn a living by their work.

Prices of Australian paintings have reached extraordinary heights in more recent years. In 1949 the Art Gallery of New South Wales bought Sidney Nolan's *Pretty Polly Mine* for 45 guineas [$785] and his *Carron Plains* for 64 guineas [$1170]. Today he commands very high prices, his *Dog and Duck Hotel* being sold in 1972 for $60,000. In 1945 the gallery bought a Russell Drysdale painting for £250 [$5925]. Up to 1968 you could still buy one of his major works for $15,000 to $17,000; in 1981, *Hometown*, a 1943 painting, sold for $120,000. Art prices have continued to rise, the record being the $1.1 million paid for Arthur Streeton's 1889 painting, *Golden Summer*. The 1970s and 1980s saw more discriminating buying but as eager a procession to galleries and auctions.

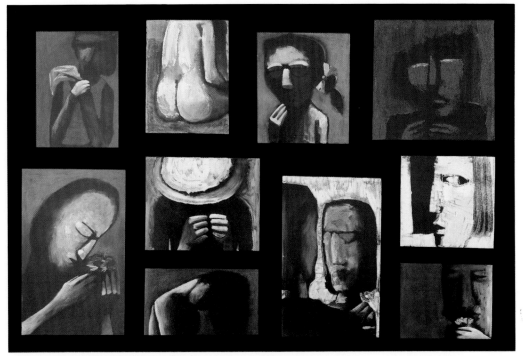

Suite V, a large panel in oils by Charles Blackman, was executed in 1960. His work is not only represented in all Australian state galleries but also in Paris, London and New York

A national gallery

In 1911, the Prime Minister, Andrew Fisher, mooted a national gallery made up of portraits of 'representative men'. Although the beginnings of a national collection date from that year, it was only in 1968 that the Australian National Gallery began to buy for itself. More that 80,000 objects have been purchased, in many cases with the aim of reflecting the location of the gallery in the Pacific and the Southern Hemisphere. At the core of the collection are Australian works—paintings, drawings and prints, as well as architectural, industrial and interior designs, sculptures, photographs and craft objects. Outbidding some of the world's most famous museums, the gallery has also acquired major works by such painters as Rubens, Tiepolo, Monet, Cezanne, Picasso and Miro, as well as important examples of North American, Asian, Pacific, African and pre-Colombian art.

In its massive, angular building on the shores of Lake Burley Griffin, the gallery received over 1.5 million visitors in the two-and-a-half years after it opened in October 1982. Seldom empty is the bench in front of *Blue Poles*, the huge abstract painting by Jackson Pollock, which caused a furore when it was purchased for $1.3 million in 1973.

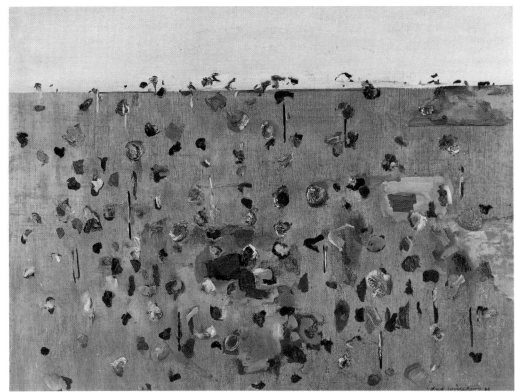

Fred Williams was one of Australia's most original and distinguished landscape painters. *Trees on Hillside II*, typical of his style, was painted in 1964

The performing arts

Great days of the theatre

The first performing artist to be officially recognised by the New Commonwealth was Nellie Stewart, Woolloomooloo-born star of musical comedy. She sang the ode *Australia* at the grand ball after the opening of the first Federal Parliament in Melbourne on 9 May 1901.

The precedent was followed when the new Parliament House in Canberra was opened 26 years later; a great Australian opera singer, Dame Nellie Melba, sang the National Anthem. Australians loved their singers. Nellie Stewart, Nellie Melba, Gladys Moncrieff and Peter Dawson, especially, enjoyed enormous popularity on stage and concert platform.

The object of a visit to the theatre was often a musical comedy. Opera too had a large following, and opera companies from Europe often made tours. Australian opera audiences regularly heard some of the greatest singers of the day, including Toti dal Monte in 1924 and 1928.

Many other world-famous artists toured Australia in the first half of the 20th century, including the Russian bass Feodor Chaliapin, the ballerina Anna Pavlova and her company, the pianist Jan Paderewski and the actor John Barrymore—who announced in Melbourne in 1906 that the Victorian capital was the only place on earth where being happy was made a crime.

But perhaps the most popular form of theatrical entertainment was one which has largely disappeared—vaudeville. It withstood the challenge of the cinema, but was killed by television. Australian vaudeville produced many stars in its long history, and the most famous of all was Mo, who could convulse his audience by 'just standing there and giving a slow leer'.

Yet if Mo was inimitable, Australia has continued to produce actors and actresses in the vaudeville tradition. Probably the most notable of these is Barry Humphries whose suburban creation, Edna Everage, has satirised the land of 'her' birth, with particular venom, since 1958.

And the live theatre has shown a new vitality since the 1970s, even if J. C. Williamson—the Firm—has gone out of business; and the Old Tote and the Pram Factory have come to an end. Sydney's Nimrod Theatre, and Melbourne's Universal Theatre to name only two, have continued to sustain exciting theatre, while every capital city has either a new theatre or a centre for the performing arts.

The role of the Australia Council too—and its Music and Theatre Boards—cannot be underestimated in proving a generous if exacting patron, and a stimulus to others to sponsor the arts.

The imperious Nellie Melba organised tours of Australia by the finest opera companies the country had seen. This portrait of her was painted by Rupert Bunny about 1902, the year she made a triumphal concert tour of Australia

Stars of the stage

Entertaining the new Commonwealth

The first citizens of the Commonwealth were offered a wide range of theatrical entertainment. There were seven live shows to choose from in Sydney theatres: *Monte Cristo*, with Alfred Dampier in the lead, at the Criterion; *A Message from Mars* at the Palace; *The New Barmaid* at the Lyceum; *Cast Adrift* at the Royal Standard; Harry Rickard's pantomime *Puss in Boots* at the Tivoli; and J. C. Williamson's 'Grand Original Spectacular Musical Pantomime Extravaganza, *Australia*,

or *The City of Zero*—a spectacle of a hundred years hence', at Her Majesty's. One of the great scenes in the latter depicted 'Semi-Circular Quay' in 2001 with an illumination of the Harbour Bridge—32 years before it was built. Melbourne theatregoers in 1901 could choose between three celebrated performers. Lottie Collins, the creator of *Ta-Ra-Ra-Boom-De-Ay*, was high-kicking at the Bijou Theatre under the management of Harry Rickard. At the Princess, Nellie Stewart was the hand-

some principal boy in George Musgrove's 'Gorgeous Operatic Pantomime—*Cinderella*'; and the dainty Viennese, Grace Palotta, had all Melbourne singing or whistling *Tell Me, Pretty Maiden*, from *Floradora*, J. C. Williamson's attraction at Her Majesty's. Bland Holt's *With Flying Colours* was at the Theatre Royal, and Mr Williamson was also presenting 'The Wonderful Anglo-American Bio-Tableau' at the Athenaeum Hall, which included films and tableaux.

George Musgrove's production of the 'Gorgeous Operatic Pantomime—*Cinderella*' displayed the pantomime in all its glory to the citizens of Melbourne in 1901. 'The hackneyed statement that the stage is decaying receives a salutary check from Melbourne,' wrote a columnist in the *Sydney Mail* on 5 January 1901. 'At the pantomime of "Cinderella", the boy's dress of Miss Nellie Stewart cost £350 [$17,650], while a cloak worn by Miss Darto for three seconds represents 80 guineas [$4235] or £28 [$1410] a second.' The columnist also noted that Cinderella's crystal coach had cost £500 [$25,215]

and commented: 'Shakespeare, Beaumont and Fletcher and "Rare Ben", with their wretched accessories and ricketty signboards, and ragged curtains, never dreamt of the heights that play-acting would be carried to by their successors.' Patrons of the Princess Theatre could see all this glory for admission prices ranging from 1s [$2.50] for the amphitheatre ('the gods') to 5s [$12.60] for the dress circle and reserved stalls. Musgrove also presented an opera season in 1901. He and Nellie Stewart were in San Francisco in 1906 and lost heavily in the earthquake

Joseph Bland Holt's blood-and-thunder productions thrilled audiences around the turn of the century. A skilful actor as well as a producer, Holt was known as Australia's Monarch of Melodrama

Actor-managers and pioneering 'little' theatres

The 19th century had been the age of the actor-managers—men like George Rignold and Bland Holt, who had great pride in their profession and vied with one another in the realism and lavishness of their productions.

Rignold's most popular piece, *Lights o' London*, boasted a 'River Of Real Water Into Which Seth Preene Will Be Thrown By Clifford Armaytage To Be Rescued By Harold'. Bland Holt, who made his stage debut at the age of six, was for 30 years—until his retirement in comfort in 1909—Australia's greatest actor-manager. In one of his plays he put horses, hounds and a stag on the stage; in another a realistic chariot race with real horses. His spectacular melodrama, *Riding to Win* (1901), included a bicycle race in which famous Australian cyclists took part, and a concealed tank of water on which a boat was rowed, and from which a dog rescued a drowning woman. A critic noted, 'the dog was the lion of the evening'.

When Bland Holt died in 1942, the actor-managers had long vanished, replaced by big

firms such as J. C. Williamson. However, 'little' theatres, where enthusiastic amateurs presented serious contemporary plays by overseas and Australian writers, had also sprung up in all the states.

Plays by Australian authors

The earliest was the Australian Theatre Society, founded in Melbourne in 1904 by Leon Brodsky; it survived until 1908. Then in 1909 Gregan McMahon, an actor-producer, started the Melbourne Repertory, with the backing of J. C. Williamson. Over the next seven years this company produced 57 plays, 13 by Australian authors, including Louis Esson, Arthur Adams, Blamire Young and Edward Dyson. After World War I, and backed by the entrepreneurs J. and N. Tait, McMahon moved to Sydney. In 1918 he founded the Sydney Repertory Theatre Society, which produced five or six plays a year with mixed professional and amateur casts. He introduced the work of Shaw, Galsworthy, Chekov and Pirandello to Australian audiences.

Duncan and Pakie Macdougall's Playbox Theatre, established in Sydney in 1920, was literally a little theatre. It occupied the living room of the Macdougalls' flat in Rowe Street, and its stage was only 1.2 m wide.

Meanwhile, the playwright and journalist Louis Esson joined the author Vance Palmer and others in establishing the Pioneer Players in Melbourne. On a visit to Ireland, Esson had talked with Yeats, Synge and Lady Gregory; and the Pioneer Players, founded in 1922, was a brave attempt to import the traditions of Dublin's famous Abbey Theatre.

In 1929, Gregan McMahon revived his Melbourne Repertory Theatre, and continued to produce good plays until his death in 1951. One of his stars in the 1930s was Coral Browne, who went on to be successful on the London stage and in films.

McMahon's successor in Sydney was his former pupil Doris Fitton, who, after many years of effort, was able to form a permanent repertory company with its own theatre—the Independent, in North Sydney.

138

Bert Bailey's bush dramas

When Nellie Stewart returned to Australia in 1901, after a long absence overseas, she said: 'I am really afraid the Australian taste has degenerated. It has been ruined by modern burlesque.'

Imported musical comedies remained the principal fare in the commercial theatre for many decades, with the Australian playwright represented mainly by simple 'hayseed' comedies, of which Albert Edward Bailey, known to the profession and public as Bert Bailey, was the most successful exponent. He was born in New Zealand in 1872, and came to Australia as a child. At 17, he joined a touring theatrical company, and within a few years became Australia's most popular character actor.

Bewhiskered as Dad Rudd

In 1912, with Julius Grant, he formed the Bert Bailey Dramatic Company, which produced a dramatised version of Steele Rudd's *On Our Selection*, with Bailey, wonderfully bewhiskered, in the part of Dad. It was a great success, not only in Australia, where it played for many years, but in England. This was followed by a number of Australian plays, including a dramatisation of C. J. Dennis' *The Sentimental Bloke*, in which Bailey was Ginger Mick. In collaboration with Edmund Duggan, Bailey also wrote two successful melodramas, *The Man From Outback*, and *The Squatter's Daughter*, later made into a talkie.

When in 1913 he produced *The Golden Shanty*, a comedy based on Edward Dyson's well-known short story, *The Lone Hand* congratulated his company 'upon the practical assistance they have given to the creation of Australian drama'. The contribution to drama can be assessed, not only by the 'Dad and Dave' sagas, but by *The Golden Shanty*. 'The plot,' said *The Lone Hand*, 'depends upon a backblock's public-house built of sun-dried bricks in which some Chinamen find gold. They are stealing it, brick by brick, until a lovely larrikin from Melbourne drops into the almost deserted diggings and is appointed by Mrs Public-house to the agreeable position of "chucker-out". Chiller Green, as this gentleman is named, pays his attentions to a girl who can "talk straight" and has a fine sense of what is appropriate in love making. These two provide the main interest of the play, and nearly all its humour.'

Authentic or false?

Bailey later played Dad in a number of talkies. Critics differ widely in the evaluation of his 'Selection' plays and films. He has been praised for presenting our nearest approach to an authentic Australian folk drama, and denounced for perpetuating a crude, false and sentimental picture of Australian outback life.

'It would be surprising if no writer in Australia could construct a tolerable play,' wrote the Australian poet and pioneer dramatist, Louis Esson, in 1928. 'Many people have the delusion that an Australian play must be something like *The Sentimental Bloke* or *On Our Selection* which are not plays at all.'

The firm of J. C. Williamson dominated Australian theatre for more than half a century. James Cassius Williamson himself died in 1913, but in 1920 The Firm came under the leadership of the entrepreneurial Tait brothers. During the 1920s, when this magazine came out weekly, The Firm's productions included comedies and melodramas, musicals such as *Rose Marie* and *The Student Prince*, two tours by ballet companies led by Anna Pavlova and tours by international opera companies

The Australian play establishes itself

After World War II, there was a significant change in the indigenous Australian theatre, with a greater emphasis on realism and social criticism. The first 'break-through' play was Sumner Locke-Elliot's *Rusty Bugles*, produced by Doris Fitton at the Independent Theatre, Sydney, in October 1948. This play about boredom and inactivity in a Northern Territory army camp was greeted with enthusiasm by audience and critics alike, despite its explicit language and the treatment of the soldier as an anti-hero. Two days after its opening, the Chief Secretary of New South Wales banned it because of its 'indecent and blasphemous words'. The resulting furore in the press was excellent publicity, and a week later *Rusty Bugles* was permitted to continue. It went on to draw packed houses and even made a successful tour of New Zealand.

An even greater success was Ray Lawler's comedy-drama *The Summer of the Seventeenth Doll*, which challenged the sacred traditions of toughness and mateship. Originally produced at Melbourne University's Union Theatre in 1955, it was taken up by the newly-formed Elizabethan Theatre Trust. *The Doll*, a play about cane-cutters and their relationships with women during the 'lay-off' periods, had an enthusiastic reception in Australia.

Richard Beynon's *The Shifting Heart*, which attacked Australian xenophobia, followed in 1957; then came Alan Seymour's *The One Day of the Year* (1961), which questioned the traditional veneration of Anzac Day.

In the later 1960s and early 1970s, the 'little theatres' continued to be the cradles of Australian plays that were later taken up by commercial organisations. The Australian Performing Group in Melbourne gave initial performances of works by Jack Hibberd, David Williamson and Alexander Buzo; while in Sydney, the National Institute of Dramatic Art inaugurated the very successful, vaudeville-style *Legend of King O'Malley* and the Nimrod and Old Tote theatres presented plays by Ron Blair and Peter Kenna, which examined the Australian experience with a sharply critical eye.

Vaudeville and musical comedy

Modernism runs wild in Australia's first revue

Australians had a feast of entertainment in 1914. Visiting overseas artists included Harry Lauder and W. C. Fields (touring as a juggler before he became a film star), the Cherniavsky Trio of child musical prodigies, actresses Ada Reeve, Grace Palotta and Carrie Moore, and American actor-director Fred Niblo. And Gladys Moncrieff made her Sydney debut as Josephine in *HMS Pinafore*.

That year, too, Australians saw what was billed as 'Australia's first revue'. Called *Come Over Here*, it ran for 13 weeks in Sydney and three months in Melbourne. The firm of J. C. Williamson, who presented it, explained in the programme that 'the revue has as its sole aim the amusement of audiences. It has no lesson to teach, and no other purpose than creating a spirit of gaiety. For people who don't want to laugh and are too superior to enjoy a frivol it is not recommended ... The music isn't Wagnerian nor has it the ache of the modern French School. For the most part it is ragtime, and not ashamed to own it.'

One of the stars of *Come Over Here* was the English comedienne Daisy Jerome, who sang *Do They All Go To See The Sea* and *Pulpit and Petticoat*. Another was the Australian dancer, Ivy Schilling, described as 'the terpsichorean with the most beautiful legs in the world'. These were most attractively displayed in her spectacular 'Spider and Fly' dance, which she performed with Fred Leslie on a gigantic reproduction of a spider's web that dramatically filled the whole stage.

Come Over Here was the first show that Sir Robert Helpmann remembers seeing. He was five years old. Fifteen years later, he and Frances Ogilvy danced the 'Spider and Fly' on the same web, in the pantomime *Sinbad the Sailor* at Melbourne's Theatre Royal.

'People ask the exact meaning of the dramatic "revue",' said the Melbourne *Punch* before *Come Over Here* arrived in Melbourne. 'A revue is a kaleidoscopic nightmare ... The ordinary conditions of time and space are set at naught and the revue laughs sequence and consistency to scorn.'

A later article elaborated: 'As futurist landscapes in the realms of art, and suffragettes in the arena of politics, so in the theatrical world is the "revue" the latest expression of modernism run wild.'

The legs of Australian dancer Ivy Schilling were star attractions in Australia's first revue. Another Australian dancer in the show was Madge Elliot

'Strike me lucky!'—a great clown

One day in June, 1920, when Melbourne was preparing a glittering reception for Edward, Prince of Wales (the future Edward VIII), staid citizens were astonished to find a banner stretched across Bourke Street in the middle of the city, proclaiming in scarlet letters: STIFFY AND MO WELCOME HIS ROYAL HIGHNESS!

'Stiffy and Mo' were a vaudeville team who for many years delighted Australian audiences with their rollicking and often bawdy humour. 'Stiffy' was Nat Phillips and 'Mo' was Roy Rene. They had joined forces in 1914 to become the most popular entertainers on the Australian stage, with Stiffy as the straight 'feed' and Mo as the slapstick comic. In this role, Roy Rene emerged as one of the world's great clowns, even compared by critics with Grock and Chaplin.

Roy Rene, whose real name was Henry van der Sluice, was the son of a Jewish cigar manufacturer who migrated to Australia from Holland in the 1880s. Henry was born in Adelaide in 1892, and began his stage career as a boy soprano, singing *Ave Maria* in front of a stained glass window. By the time of his death in 1954, Mo had become part of Australian folklore, and many of his sayings had passed into the Australian 'slanguage'.

Young Australians of the 1950s who sprinkled their conversation with expressions such as 'strike me lucky!', 'one of my mob', 'you little trimmer', 'very tasty, very succulent', 'cheeky possum' and 'suck it and see', had learned this idiomatic speech from listening to Mo on the radio—an educational process not always approved of by parents.

Like most great clowns, Mo was always on the side of the underdog, in constant battle with authority—whether represented by a policeman, a major-general or a mother-in-law. He cocked a snook at respectability, he punctured pretence and pomposity, he was unashamedly vulgar—and audiences loved it. He could rouse an audience to enthusiasm simply by standing on the stage with his chalk-white, unshaven face, and giving a long, slow leer. 'I've seen him stand there for minutes on end with the audience holding their sides, almost begging him to stop,' said the actress Neva Carr-Glynn.

Mo's only rival was George Wallace, a comedian of the old red-nosed, knockabout school. But while Wallace was the rough, tough Australian of the bush, in the tradition of Dad and Dave, Mo's humour was urban.

Edna Everage, Australian housewife from Moonee Ponds, was created by actor-writer Barry Humphries in 1958. Through Edna he satirises suburban life and values, and she and her sayings have become part of Australian folklore. Here Humphries as Edna relaxes before going on stage

Mo was a legend in his lifetime. There was a time when almost everyone in Australia—even those who disapproved of the bawdy humour he and his 'straight' partner, Stiffy (left), dispensed—would have recognised Mo. His act was developed for stage, but was also very successful on the radio

Viennese-born Grace Palotta, one of the 'postcard beauties' of her day, first came to Australia with the London Gaiety Company when it made a six-month tour in 1895-96. She became famous for her role as Lady Holyrood in the musical *Floradora*, which opened at Her Majesty's Theatre in Melbourne on 16 December 1900. *Floradora* ran for 200 performances—the longest run of any show in Australia before *Rose Marie*

Born in Woolloomooloo in 1858, Nellie Stewart was for years Australia's favourite 'pin-up' and singer. Her public career lasted 67 years, and she was always able to appear miraculously young on stage. When this photograph was taken, she was in her forties and playing Prince Charming in an Australian production of the pantomime *Cinderella*. In 1901, she sang the ode *Australia* at the opening of the first Federal Parliament

Gladys Moncrieff ('Our Glad') in one of her earliest stage appearances—as Marco in *The Gondoliers* at the West End State School, Townsville, about 1904. Her first professional role was also in a Gilbert and Sullivan opera, but she made her name when she played Teresa in *The Maid of the Mountains* in 1921. On the first night in Sydney she received 18 curtain calls. She went on to perform the role more than 3000 times and even late in life

Forty years as a star of musical comedy

Nellie Stewart, who had made her stage debut in Melbourne in 1863 at the age of five, was Australia's unchallenged light and comic opera favourite for at least half a century. She was nearly 70 when she revived her most successful part, Nell Gwynne in *Sweet Nell of Old Drury*, which she first played in 1902.

Nellie Stewart's successor was a dark-eyed, gypsy-like girl from Bundaberg, Queensland, named Gladys Moncrieff, who first appeared in public when she sang the *Merriest Girl That's Out* at a school concert in Maryborough. Her first professional appearance was in 1914 when, as understudy to soprano Pearl Ladd, she took over the role of Elsie Maynard for the opening night of the Brisbane season of *The Yeomen of the Guard*. She was paid £6 [$240] a week, and expenses.

Two years before, Melba had been impressed with the sweet, pure quality of Gladys Moncrieff's soprano voice and had recommended her as a pupil to Grace Millar, a concert singer, teacher and wife of J. C. Williamson's managing director, Hugh J. Ward. Miss Moncrieff's voice, wrote a discerning Sydney critic in January 1915, was 'absolutely free from what our critics snort at as "the Australian twang"'

Pigeons for peace

On the night of 11 November, 1918, Gladys Moncrieff was playing in the Sydney production of *Katinka*, and had made a triumphant entrance singing the popular song *Rackety Coo*, when the performance was interrupted with the announcement that World War I had ended. At the finale of the first act, white pigeons were released from the stage.

In 1921, Gladys Moncrieff played Teresa in J. C. Williamson's Melbourne production of *The Maid of the Mountains*—the musical with which her name was ever after associated.

The Maid of the Mountains ran for 27 weeks in Melbourne, and the Australian season lasted more than two years. During the season, Miss Moncrieff's salary was raised from £22.10s to £50 [$590 to $1315] a week—a considerable sum at a time when chorus girls were paid £3.10s [$90] a week and fined if late for rehearsals. When she last appeared as Teresa, in Perth in 1952, she had played the role more than 3000 times.

Her most devoted fans were the 'gallery girls', who would wait up all night and through the next day, equipped with vacuum flasks, sandwiches and rugs, to rush the cheap seats high up in the gods (the gallery) when the theatre doors were opened.

Advice from Melba

After the enormous Australian success of *The Maid of the Mountains*, Miss Moncrieff starred at the Gaiety and Daly's in London, then returned to Australia to play in *Rio Rita* and *Sybil*. More successes followed—in New Zealand, England, South Africa and the United States, where she added to her repertoire *The Girl in the Taxi*, *The Arcadians* and *The Merry Widow*. During a Melbourne rehearsal of *The Merry Widow*, when she was singing *I Love You So*, Melba, who was watching from the wings, confronted her as the song finished. 'Don't say "lov", dear,' said Melba. 'Always say "luv".' Years later, Miss Moncrieff said she had never forgotten this advice.

Her last appearance on the stage was at Hamilton, New Zealand, in 1961 when, in her 69th year, she appeared in a variety show, *Many Happy Returns*. Her salary was £375 [$3525] a week. For many years before her retirement she had been 'Our Glad' to thousands of affectionate Australian theatregoers. In 1966, a 'Gladys Moncrieff Club' was founded in Sydney.

On her 80th birthday, in April 1972, Miss Moncrieff was asked what she remembered most vividly of her days as a star. 'All the wonderful first nights and last nights,' she declared. 'The dressing and glamour. The usherettes walking down the aisles with the flowers and handing them over the footlights. Today they just walk in from the side. The queues outside the theatre and the marvellous sound you could hear in the dressing room of the feet going up the stairs to the gallery. When they started booking tickets for the gallery, a lot of the fun went out.

'They were wonderful days . . .'

Oscar Asche, actor and author of the famous 1920s 'oriental' musical *Chu Chin Chow*, was born in Geelong in 1891. Asche made his name in England acting in and producing Shakespeare, and toured Australia with his own company. He also brought *Chu Chin Chow* to Australia in 1921

Opera takes root on the Australian stage

Overseas companies give way to local organisations

On 1 January 1901, *The Sydney Morning Herald* in a review of most aspects of Australian life, noted that productions of opera had become less frequent during the later years of the 19th century. 'Just at the end of the century, however, Mr George Musgrove brought out to Melbourne a thoroughly cosmopolitan company, who sang seven or eight famous works there and in Sydney, Brisbane and Adelaide, including *Lohengrin* and *Tannhäuser* in English. Herr Slapoffski directed a fine orchestra, the staging was magnificent and the whole proved eminently successful. Mr Musgrove intends to arrange a yearly season. Moreover, Mr J. C. Williamson is just despatching Signor Hazon to Italy to form a company there for Italian opera early in 1901. So that the revival of operatic music should take firm root once more upon our stage.'

The *Herald's* confidence has been justified. Opera has become so firmly rooted in the Australian theatre that there is now a national company, the Australian Opera, playing all the year round. But for many years Australia relied on overseas companies for its diet of opera. Sometimes these companies brought with them Australian singers who had become famous overseas, and sometimes they allowed promising local singers to gain invaluable experience of professional opera.

The Musgrove company that played in Sydney and Melbourne in 1901 included an Australian, the bass Lempriere Pringle. He and another star of Covent Garden and the New York Metropolitan Opera, the soprano Ella Russell, were the most notable members of the company, which performed 13 works.

Later in 1901, Roberto Hazon returned from Italy with a company that performed six Italian operas, including Puccini's *La Bohème*, then only five years old. The stars included the tenor Carlo Dani and the famous mezzo-soprano Giulia Ravogli.

Musgrove failed to provide a yearly season, but in 1907 his Royal Grand Opera Company presented *Lohengrin, Der Fliegende Holländer, Die Walküre*, Gounod's *Roméo et Juliette* and Humperdinck's *Hänsel und Gretel*. The singers were German and Gustav Slapoffski was again the conductor.

Three years later J. C. Williamson presented *Carmen, Madama Butterfly* and *La Bohème*. The company included the Australian soprano Amy Castles, and the chorus was Australian. In 1911, Williamson and Melba brought to Sydney and Melbourne the finest opera company Australia had seen. Melba herself sang three times a week instead of her usual three times a fortnight. Other stars included the great tenor John McCormack, the soprano Janina Wayda and the mezzo-soprano Eleonora de Cisneros. The chorus was again Australian.

An even bigger venture was the visit of the Quinlan Opera Company from London in 1912. It brought out 200 people—including an orchestra of 60 and a chorus of 50—300 tonnes of scenery, 3 tonnes of music and 3500 costumes. Singing in English, the company performed a standard repertoire whose main novelty was a new Puccini opera, *The Girl of*

the *Golden West*, first performed only two years before. There was one Australian star, the soprano Lalla Miranda, from the Paris Opera. Another Quinlan company came in 1913, but audiences were smaller because of a small-pox scare.

The Gonsalez Opera Company—Italian singers of no great renown—performed 15

Melbourne-born soprano Amy Castles sang in J. C. Williamson's 1911 opera company. In Europe she was a star of the Vienna Imperial Opera

standard works in Sydney and Melbourne in 1916. Some of the singers stayed in Australia and sang again with the Rigo Opera Company in Melbourne in 1919. This company was taken over by J. C. Williamson's later in the year. Altogether 14 operas were performed. Several Australians sang with these companies, including Amy Castles, the soprano Gertrude Johnson, the tenor Browning Mummery and the baritone Frederick Collier. The singers sang in their native tongues.

Melba and J. C. Williamson's collaborated again in 1924 to present 18 operas performed by an Italian company that included three of the finest singers of the day—the soprano Toti dal Monte, the tenor Dino Borgioli and the baritone Apollo Granforte. The chorus was imported from Italy.

Granforte's powerful, sonorous tones were heard again in 1928, on the profitable tour of the Fuller-Gonsalez Opera Company, which staged 14 works. The principals were Italian, the chorus and orchestra mixed.

The same year saw another Williamson-Melba company. It included such great singers as the sopranos Toti dal Monte, Hina Spani and Giannina Arangi-Lombardi, the tenor Francesco Merli and the indispensable Granforte. Browning Mummery and the Australian baritone John Brownlee sang leading roles. The repertoire mixed standard classics with novelties such as Montemezzi's *L'Amore dei Tre Re,* Puccini's *Gianni Schicchi, Il Tabarro* and *Turandot*, Mascagni's *Lodoletta*, and *Deirdre in Exile*, a one-act opera by Fritz Hart, director of the Albert Street Conservatorium, Melbourne.

Every Sydney performance was sold out and large audiences attended in Melbourne, but Williamson's announced that they had lost thousands of pounds on the tour. The undertaking was on too large a scale for Australia; there was a demand for opera but not at the prices needed to make it pay.

The tenor Browning Mummery (left) and the baritone John Brownlee (right) sang leading roles with several visiting opera companies. Here they are seen with Melba, who chose them both to sing with her at her Covent Garden farewell. She also recorded duets with Brownlee, whom she discovered

But, undaunted, Williamson's tried again in 1932 with 17 French and Italian operas in Sydney, Melbourne and Adelaide. Only 15 principals were imported, including the soprano Lina Pagliughi, the mezzo-soprano Bruna Castagna, Granforte and Brownlee. The orchestra and chorus were entirely Australian and Joseph Post was given his first chance to conduct professional opera. Joan Hammond sang in the chorus.

The last opera company to visit Australia before World War II was Fuller's Royal Grand Opera, which toured all the state capitals in 1934-35 with a repertoire of 15 Italian, French and German works sung in English by Australian and British singers. The Australians included the soprano Florence Austral, Browning Mummery, Frederick Collier and the bass Horace Stevens. Joan Hammond sang one of the Valkyries in *Die Walküre* and, with only three days' preparation, Venus in *Tannhäuser*.

In 1939 the National Theatre Movement of Victoria, founded by Gertrude Johnson, produced *The Flying Dutchman* and *The Marriage of Figaro* in Melbourne with all-Australian casts. The conductor was Gustav Slapoffski, conductor of Musgrove's 1900-01 season.

After the war, in 1948-49, J. C. Williamson's brought out an Italian company which performed 13 Italian operas and Gounod's *Faust*. Williamson's aimed to present well-balanced performances rather than a few sensational stars, but there was criticism of both acting and singing. *The Sydney Morning Herald* observed severely that the lascivious Scarpia 'ought not to bite Tosca's neck before an Australian audience. This might excite appropriate feelings in a Latin audience, to Australians it is comic.'

In 1951 the National Opera of New South Wales was founded in Sydney. The next year it combined with the National Theatre Movement for a tour of Melbourne, Sydney and Brisbane, each company contributing its own productions and casts. Marie Collier

and John Brownlee were among the singers.

J. C. Williamson's next venture was its International Grand Opera Company in 1955. The principal singers were mostly Italians, but there were also several Australians, including the tenor Kenneth Neate.

The National Theatre Movement and the National Opera, which had continued to operate separately, were replaced in 1956 by the Elizabethan Trust Opera Company. The company toured Australia every year, except 1959 and 1961, until 1969 when the Australian Opera was formed. With its permanent home at the Sydney Opera House, it had its first season there in September 1973. In 1985, financial problems forced it to become a part-time company from 1987, abandoning the summer season in Sydney and performances outside Sydney and Melbourne. By then, most states had their own opera companies, and like the Australian Opera, they were becoming increasingly adventurous in their choice of repertoire.

A riotous wedding for Toti dal Monte

Toti dal Monte was a sensation of the 1924 Williamson-Melba Opera Company. She was a great singer and a pretty, if rotund, young woman with a sparkling personality. Australian audiences loved her. She sang 98 performances during that tour, returning for a concert tour two years later and again with the 1928 Melba-Williamson company. In 1928 she was idolised as much as ever. *The Sydney Morning Herald* said 'the men of Sydney were reduced to a hopeless state of adoration for Toti and were symbolically prostrate at her feet'. When it was announced that Toti was to be married to the handsome young tenor Enzo de Muro Lomanto, Sydneysiders were so enthusiastic that 25,000 uninvited guests turned up at St Mary's Cathedral for the marriage ceremony.

They began arriving at daybreak, 'secreting themselves in corners of the Cathedral under the pretence of hearing early Mass', said the *Herald*. At 8 o'clock, hundreds were there and the policemen were worried; at 11.30 thousands crowded the streets and Hyde Park. It was 'into a tempestuous, nightmare world of top hats, tears, tattered toilettes, red faces, mutilated millinery, collapsing people, and vast, shrieking crowds' that the bride, 'looking very small, and very white, and very nervous, and a million times more charming than ever, stepped from her car and searched for the steps of the Cathedral', wrote the *Herald's* reporter.

'For one instant she glimpsed 25,000 heads, hats and handkerchiefs fluttering and swirling down upon her; then she fled up the narrow carpet. In an ecstasy of abandon, a man threw his bowler hat after her . . .

'Everyone was very emotional, especially the little stout man with the top hat from which the bottom had been knocked. He was the most emotional of all, particularly when the policeman refused to admit him to the Cathedral, and an old lady, exasperated by the extensive area of his back, hit him several times over the head with a shoe she had removed for the purpose.'

The bridegroom, looking 'as though . . . he had just been asked to sing an opera in Chinese', stood nervously as the crowds inside the cathedral 'fought for seats, trampling lustily over the attendants, their ties adrift, their collars twisted back to front, footmarks in the middle of their backs, and signs of struggle in their coiffure.'

Outside, said the *Herald*, women fainted on top of one, stood up and fainted again. Men sat on the spikes of the fence and felt relieved that at last they discovered a comfortable retreat from the ordeal of fighting in that volatile crowd.

After the ceremony, the couple managed to reach the street and their car. But Toti had not yet shaken off her admirers. 'They charged upon her in a colossal, screaming flood which whirled the policemen along like moths in a monsoon . . .' said the *Herald*. 'In an instant they had torn down all the beautiful flowers that trailed around the car, the ribbons and the decorations . . . The chauffeur hastily reversed into a mounted traffic policeman, who hastily reversed into the cavaliers, who hastily reversed into the crowd . . . It was just short of a riot.'

Sydney had never known a wedding reception to surpass that held later at Romano's Cafe, said the *Herald*. 'There was an utter abandonment to the joy of the moment, such as only the Latin races can enjoy. There was no unseemly hilarity, but excitement was at its zenith. Men kissed each other on the cheeks, there were many handshakes, much clapping, and cries of "Bravo, Bravo".'

Stars of the 1928 Williamson-Melba Opera Company caricatured by the Italian bass Fernando Autori. The tiny Rosina is Toti dal Monte, darling of Australian audiences. Don Basilio, in the monstrous hat, is Autori himself and razor-wielding Figaro is Apollo Granforte, who sang in Australia with four visiting companies

Melba

Queen of Covent Garden

A reporter of the Richmond *Advertiser* who attended a concert in the Richmond (Melbourne) Town Hall on 11 December, 1869, wrote: 'Little Miss Mitchell, a young lady of the precocious age of 10 years, who did not content herself with singing in first-rate style *Can You Dance the Polka?* but also accompanied herself on the piano was, we think, the gem of the evening and rightly deserved the spontaneous encore she received, and responded to by singing *Comin' Thro' the Rye*.

'It took the audience by surprise to hear such sweet notes coming from comparatively a mere child . . . She is indeed a musical prodigy, and she will make crowded houses when she is announced again.'

Little Miss Mitchell, whose real age was eight, was Helen Porter Mitchell, the daughter of a well-known Melbourne builder, David Mitchell. She was born in Richmond, where she had first appeared in public at the age of six, singing *Shells of the Ocean*.

Married life in Queensland

In 1882, she married the handsome manager of a Queensland sugar plantation, Charles Armstrong, son of an Irish baronet, and went to live near Mackay. The marriage was not successful and two years later she was back in Melbourne, where she made her debut at a concert. 'The concert,' said the critic of the *Australasian*, 'if it were to be remembered in no other way, will never be forgotten on account of the delightful surprise offered by Mrs Nellie Armstrong's singing.' In 1886, Nellie Armstrong sailed for Europe, where she studied singing in Paris with Mathilde Marchesi, a teacher of great renown.

When she returned to Australia 16 years later, under her professional name of Nellie Melba, she had a world-wide reputation. She had been acclaimed in England, on the continent and in the United States. Gounod had coached her in the role of Juliette in his *Roméo et Juliette*. Puccini had chosen her as the ideal Mimi for his *La Bohème*.

Unrivalled in Britain

Her fame remained undiminished until her farewell appearance at Covent Garden in 1926—38 years after she made her debut there in *Lucia di Lammermoor*. For most of her career she reigned over Covent Garden, and after 1902 she appeared practically nowhere else. To British audiences she was the supreme soprano of her time. Other countries had other favourites, but Melba ensured that they did not appear at Covent Garden.

Her voice was acclaimed everywhere for its purity and silvery brilliance of tone and its perfect matching of one note to the next, like pearls on a string. An Italian critic has described her as a lyric soprano gifted with all the resources of a *soprano d'agilità*. But if the splendour of her voice was universally admired, there was also criticism of her interpretations. She was often accused of coldness, mannerism and lack of theatrical ability. 'Uninterestingly perfect and perfectly uninteresting' was how another great soprano described Melba's singing.

Melba's commanding personality shines from both these portraits, the upper one dating from 1902. Her single-minded pursuit of her career made successful marriage an impossibility, but she had a celebrated affair with the Duke of Orleans, Bourbon pretender to the French throne. This affair displeased both Queen Victoria and Melba's husband, who divorced her in 1900

Triumphant homecoming of a patriot

Melba's return to Melbourne in 1902 was like a royal progress. No homecoming Australian had ever received such a welcome. The city was decked with bunting, and tens of thousands of people thronged the streets as Melba drove by in her open carriage. When she visited the little town of Lilydale, 23 miles from Melbourne, where her father had limestone quarries, the local paper, the *Lilydale Express*, was printed in gold on blue paper. Her concert tour was an unprecedented success. The nine recitals she gave in Melbourne and Sydney earned her the huge sum of £20,000 [$948,000]. For one concert in Sydney she received £2350 [$111,390], reputedly the highest fee any singer had been paid for a concert.

After the tour, Melba returned to London, where she lived regally in her rococo mansion in Great Cumberland Place, which she had had remodelled at enormous expense in the style of the Palace of Versailles. But she periodically returned to Australia, and to Coombe Cottage, the quiet retreat she made for herself in the hills near Lilydale, where she collected friends and Australian paintings.

In 1909, she started singing classes at Melbourne's Conservatorium of Music and in 1911, in conjunction with J. C. Williamsons, she brought out the finest opera company that Australia had ever known. One of the company was the great Irish tenor John McCormack. More Melba-Williamson opera companies were brought to Australia in 1924 and 1928. Apart from three professional visits to the United States and Canada, Melba spent most of the war years, 1914-1918, in Australia, where she organised concerts for wartime charities often singing to informal

audiences in small country halls. She said she raised £100,000 [almost $3 million].

She also gave free singing lessons in Melbourne to many young girls, among them Marie Bremner, later to star in Australian musical comedy. Her other successful *protégées* included the sopranos Gertrude Johnson and Stella Power. In 1918 Melba was created Dame Commander of the British Empire, an appropriate honour for one who was a dedicated imperialist. In an article, headed 'Happy Australia', in the London *Daily Mail* in 1912 she declared Australia to be 'British to the backbone' and determined 'to assist Great Britain to retain the supremacy of the seas at any sacrifice'. She also wrote: 'The chicken in the pot policy is not a dream in Australia. It is a *fait accompli*. The general average of wealth and well-being is not excelled anywhere.'

'Sing 'em muck'

Less charitable views on Australia were ascribed to Melba in 1928, when a biography of Dame Clara Butt, the English contralto, was published. The author, Winifred Ponder, quoted Dame Nellie as telling Dame Clara, who was about to leave England on a tour of Australia: 'So you're going to Australia? Well, I made £20,000 on my tour there, but of course *that* will never be done again. Still, it's a wonderful country and you'll have a good time. What are you going to sing? All I can say is sing 'em muck! It's all they can understand.' The story made headlines in every English-speaking country. Melba denied it, and 1850 copies of the book had the offending passage excised. But the phrase 'Sing 'em muck' survives.

Melba made her first records in March 1904. She insisted that they should have this special lilac label and should sell for one guinea each—a shilling more than the discs of any other singer. Between 1904 and 1926 she made 150 recordings. Critics agree that Melba's records show the ease, purity and precision of her singing—and her marked Australian accent in Italian and French—but present only a pale reflection of the power and splendour of her voice. The acoustic process also imparted a hardness to her silvery tone

Farewells to stage and platform in Australia

'Goodbye is of all words the saddest, the most difficult to say,' Melba told the audience at her final appearance at Covent Garden in 1926. But she managed to say goodbye to many more audiences. In 1927, she made a farewell concert tour of Australia, during which she sang the National Anthem at the opening of Parliament House in Canberra.

The next year she said farewell three times, officially at a glittering charity matinee at Her Majesty's Theatre, Melbourne, on September 27. At this she sang in the third and fourth acts of *La Bohème* and the prayer scene from *Otello*. The theatre was packed, with seats costing up to £50 [$1330] each. 'The final scene was all that the most enthusiastic admirer of the great singer could have wished,' wrote a reporter. 'She stood, in the dress poor Mimi had worn as she sang her last song, against a screen, which was the entire width of the stage, composed of roses of all colours, set in a conventional design with a farewell inscription in rose-tinted electric lights. As she stood there, looking a little wan, and labouring under intense emotion, Dame Nellie was showered with thousands of posies of beautiful flowers, which came from all parts of the house, and they were followed by innumerable coloured streamers, which helped to break the inevitable sadness into

smiles.' Daryl Lindsay was commissioned by the Melbourne *Herald* to draw the scene and years later his wife, Joan, who accompanied him, recalled it vividly: 'An audience tense with the pent-up emotion of years of Melba-worship released at the final curtain an orgy of foot stamping, tears, bravos, cooees, kisses, streamers and the jungle drumming of moist kid-gloved hands.'

A month later, on October 27, Melba sang at a charity concert in Healesville, near Lilydale, and next day she sang Desdemona's *Ave Maria* in Geelong as a compliment to her American *protégée*, Elena Danieli (Helen Daniel), who was well-known in the city. This was Melba's swan song in Australia.

She left Australia for London with Elena Danieli on Melbourne Cup Day, 1928, and on October 5, 1929, sang at a charity concert at the Brighton Hippodrome. In November 1930 she arrived back in Melbourne, a sick woman, and was taken from the ship in an ambulance. She died in St. Vincent's Hospital, Sydney, on 23 February, 1931, and was buried at Lilydale. Inscribed on a stone above her grave are Mimi's words: '*Addio, senza rancore*'—'Farewell, without bitterness'.

The *New York Times* wrote another epitaph: 'Fortunate the generation that heard her, for we shall never hear her like again.'

Melba, looking tired and sad, stands amid a sea of flowers and streamers after her last operatic performance—in Melbourne in 1928. A reporter wrote that 'roses and lilies were everywhere. They bordered the edge of the stage, they adorned the ledges of the boxes, and they hung in baskets between the dress circles and stalls. The front of the balconies was inset with plaques, each of which showed a painting of an Australian song bird, surmounted with golden wattle and each was surrounded with golden electric lights'

Diversions and the Dance

The enthusiasms and eccentricities of Percy Grainger

One of the most curious museums in Australia is at Melbourne University. It houses a collection made by the Australian pianist and composer Percy Grainger. The exhibits include his suits made of towelling, his old boots, zithers and glockenspiels, eccentric letters, model ships, occult books and railway timetables—all enthusiasms of this extraordinary musician. Grainger was born in Melbourne. His mother, who gave piano lessons for a living, was his first teacher. He was a child prodigy. In a velvet jacket, with golden curls reaching to the collar, he gave concerts throughout Australia, and earned enough to enable him, at the age of 11, to continue his studies in Germany.

When the Graingers went to London in 1899, Percy was the breadwinner. With his shock of yellow hair, his bright blue eyes and his irreverent approach to the piano, he delighted London audiences. He would stop in the middle of a recital to talk to the audience, and laugh uninhibitedly as he played. And he played magnificently.

He toured Scandinavia with the Danish cellist Hermann Sandby, and Great Britain with the great soprano Adelina Patti. One of his admirers was the Norwegian composer Edvard Grieg. They became close friends and years later Grieg, who was born in 1843, wrote of Grainger: 'I had to reach the age of 64 to hear Norwegian music played with so much understanding and genius.'

Grainger became interested in folk songs—'because the singer is free', he said—and tramped the British Isles recording them on cylinders. (His priceless collection was bought by the United States Library of Congress.) He arranged many of these traditional songs, including the famous Londonderry Air, for concert performers.

To this period also belong *Shepherd's Hey*,

Molly on the Shore, Country Gardens, Mock Morris and *Handel in the Strand*, lively tunes which became enormously popular.

All his life Grainger rebelled against convention. His trousers were creased down the sides, not front and back. In the middle of a conversation, he was likely to do a standing jump. On tour, he liked to travel from town to town dressed like a tramp, with hunks of bread and cheese in his knapsack. On an Australian tour in 1924, he was hiking, swag on back, from Adelaide to Mount Gambier when a publican mistook him for a vagrant and threatened to call the police. Grainger sat down at the pub piano and proved his identity with a dazzling performance.

At orchestra rehearsals, he would often catnap under the piano until he got his cue. He was the eternal child, but a prodigious worker, and wrote more than 400 compositions in many musical forms.

Despite his unpredictability, he was in

Percy Grainger believed that unwashable worsted suits were unhygienic, so at home he often wore suits made from towelling—washable, warm and reminiscent of European folk costume. Other Grainger Museum items seen here include part of one of his 'free music' machines (which produced gliding tones), Swiss bells, a metallophone and a two-necked guitar, with extra bass strings

1932 appointed head of the music department of the New York University College of Fine Arts. His enthusiasm then was for bells, glockenspiels, dulcitones and marimbas. He evolved a theory that all music began with percussion and that it had originated in China. Though Grainger settled in the United States and became a US citizen, he retained his love for Australia. He returned several times. In 1933, he judged the senior piano section of the City of Sydney Eisteddfod, and in 1938 he went to Melbourne to establish and endow the Grainger Museum. He visited Australia again in 1950 to inspect his museum. He died in New York in 1961.

Grainger wrote this inscription for the entrance to his museum: 'Believing that great achievements in musical composition are seldom the result of a purely individualistic effort on the part of the composer, but are often the outcome of a coming together of several propitious circumstances of fructifying personalities, I have tried, in this museum, to trace as best I can the aesthetic indebtedness of composers to each other; the borrowing of musical themes or novel compositional techniques and the culturising influences of parents, relatives, wives, husbands and friends.'

Alfred Hill was probably Australia's busiest composer for much of his long life—he lived from 1870 to 1960. His output included operas, symphonies, concerti, string quartets and an almost endless list of smaller works, including this song. His Maori opera *Tapu*, performed in 1908, included perhaps the first ballet music written in Australia

Steps to professional ballet

Edouard Borovansky (above, at left in dinner jacket) looks justifiably proud as Dame Margot Fonteyn takes a curtain call after dancing with his ballet company. Czech-born Borovansky came to Australia as a dancer with Anna Pavlova (right) in 1926. He returned in her 1929 company and in Colonel de Basil's Ballet in 1938. This time he stayed, founded a ballet school and formed the Borovansky Ballet, which gave its first season in Melbourne in 1940. Over the next 20 years the company, though disbanded and re-formed many times, toured Australia and New Zealand and introduced ballet to thousands. Borovansky died in 1959 and the company disbanded in February 1961, but out of its ashes grew the Australian Ballet. Before 1940, the only Australian ballet groups were amateurs such as the Mosman Musical Society Ballet of 1916 (far right)

The well-trodden road to Gundagai

No place in Australia has been more acclaimed in song and verse than the New South Wales township of Gundagai, on the Murrumbidgee River, 480 km south-west of Sydney. In the 19th century, it was a popular meeting—and drinking—place for shearers and teamsters, as the old bush song, *The Road to Gundagai*, records:

Oh, we started down from Roto
*   when the sheds had all cut out,*
We'd ships and whips of rhino
*   as we meant to push about,*
So we humped our blues serenely,
*   and made for Sydney Town,*
With a three-spot cheque between us,
*   as we wanted knocking down.*
CHORUS:
But we camped at Lazy Harry's,
*   on the road to Gundagai,*
The road to Gundagai!
*   Not five miles from Gundagai,*
Yes, we camped at Lazy Harry's,
*   on the road to Gundagai.*

Well, we struck the Murrumbidgee,
*   near the Yanko in a week,*
And we passed through old Narrandera
*   and crossed the Burnet creek,*
And we never stopped at Wagga,
*   for we'd Sydney in our eye;*
But we camped at Lazy Harry's,
*   on the road to Gundagai.*

In the 1890s, Jack Moses, a travelling wine salesman and bush bard, wrote a song *Nine Miles from Gundagai*, about a teamster and his dog. It was based on an old bush song of the

1850s, *Bill the Bullocky*, which described what happened when Bill's team was bogged:

Bill lashed and swore and cried,
*   "If Nobby don't get me out of this*
I'll tan his bloody hide."

But Nobby strained and broke the yoke
*   And poked the leader's eye*
Then the dog sat on the tucker box
*   Five miles from Gundagai.*

'Sat' was a euphemism for what the dog really did.
Moses' song begins:

I've done my share of shearing sheep,
*   Of droving and all that,*
And bogged a bullock-team as well,
*   On a Murrumbidgee flat.*
I've seen the bullock stretch and strain,
*   And blink his bleary eye,*
And the dog sit on the tucker box,
*   Nine miles from Gundagai.*
I've been jilted, jarred and crossed in love,
*   And sand-bagged in the dark,*
Till if a mountain fell on me
*   I'd treat it as a lark.*
It's when you've got your bullocks bogged
*   That's the time you flog and cry,*
And the dog sits on the tucker box,
*   Nine miles from Gundagai.*

In 1922, Jack O'Hagan, a prolific Melbourne songwriter, wrote *Along the Road to Gundagai* which was first sung by Mona Magnet, the principal boy in the pantomime, *Ali Baba and the Forty Thieves*. The song was an instant hit.

Within two years, 97,000 copies of the sheet music were sold, as well as a great number of pianola rolls. Next year, Peter Dawson recorded it. It has since been recorded 29 times, the last version in 1972 by the comedians Barry Humphries and Dick Bentley. On the 50th anniversary of the song, Jack O'Hagan told an interviewer that it was originally going to be *Along the Road to Bundaberg*.

For many years in the 1930s, *Along the Road to Gundagai* was the theme-song in the popular radio serial *Dad and Dave*, presented four times a week on 58 stations, and O'Hagan wrote another song for the characters Dave and Mabel:

My Mabel waits for me,
*   underneath the bright blue sky,*
Where the dog sits on the tucker box,
*   five miles from Gundagai.*

O'Hagan's third Gundagai song was written in 1942 during the American 'invasion' of Australia. The title was *When a Boy from Alabama Meets a Girl from Gundagai*.

O'Hagen, who began his career as a songwriter for the silent movies in 1920, has had more than 200 songs published. Many commemorate Australian heroes of the day: *Hustling Hinkler, Amy Johnson, Kingsford Smith—Aussie's Proud of You, Our Don Bradman*, and *Our Marjorie Jackson*.

In 1932, Prime Minister Joseph Lyons unveiled a statue of the dog on the tucker-box, beside the Hume Highway at Five Mile Creek, a camping ground in the old days of the teamsters.

SUNFLOWER DISC CULTIVATOR

OWEN & FISCHER

HUGH V. McKAY
Manufacturer
SUNSHINE HARVESTER
SUNSHINE
VIC.

Showrooms
MELBOURNE
SYDNEY & ADELAIDE
Agencies **PERTH W.A.**
TOOWOOMBA Q
And all Agricultural centres

The printed page

Artists and writers who won popular favour

Before television arrived in Australia in 1956 the printed page was the chief medium of communicating ideas. Newspapers and magazines flourished, providing jobs for many talented writers and artists such as Henry Lawson, C.J. Dennis, Norman Lindsay, Stan Cross and George Finey. Some politicians became involved in journalism—Alfred Deakin, even during his terms as Prime Minister of Australia, was a correspondent for a London paper, and Billy Hughes, also while Prime Minister, negotiated contracts for the newspaper *Smith's Weekly*.

Many Australian artists and writers also owe a great debt to advertising. The perpetually hard-up Henry Lawson wrote poems extolling the virtues of various products from whisky to cough mixture, Ernest O'Farrell and Lionel Lindsay co-operated on a series of boot polish advertisements. And Troedel and Cooper, a Melbourne commercial printing firm, was a nursery for many Australian artists, including Blamire Young, Percy Leason and Arthur Streeton.

Many Australian writers captured the imaginations of their fellow countrymen during the first 80 years of this century—men like Lennie Lower, claimed by many to be Australia's greatest humorist, and C.J. Dennis, whose best selling first book *The Sentimental Bloke* was made into a silent film, a play and later a talkie and a stage musical. More recent is Patrick White, whose international stature as a novelist was acknowledged by the honour of a Nobel Prize for literature in 1973.

But the most colourful character in Australian literature and art during the 20th century was Norman Lindsay, a man of extraordinary talent who could turn his hand, with almost equal success, to cartooning, painting and writing. His bawdy paintings often attracted the wrath of wowsers, whom Lindsay delighted in satirising in savage cartoons. His novels were also successful although, *Redheap,* probably the best, was banned as obscene in Australia until 1956.

This elegant advertisement, with touches of *art nouveau* style, appeared in *The Lone Hand* in 1908

Newspapers and magazines

The life and death of *Smith's Weekly*

In its youth, *The Bulletin*, first published in 1880, was a hard-hitting, cheeky, republican, radical, nationalist, anti-clerical, xenophobic and very influential weekly, with a team of brilliant writers and cartoonists. After Federation, it dropped its republicanism and much of its radicalism. As its arteries hardened, it became more and more conservative and less and less influential.

Its function as a vigorous critical voice, and as a nursery for writers and black-and-white artists, was taken over in 1919 by a no less remarkable publication, *Smith's Weekly*. This was the brain-child of Claude McKay, a Victorian-born journalist and publicity expert, who, in 1918, had assisted Sydney's Lord Mayor, James (later Sir Joynton) Smith, to publicise a war loan.

Pawnbroker's apprentice

Joynton Smith, christened James John Smith, was the son of a London gas-fitter. At the age of 16, after an apprenticeship to a London pawnbroker who paid him 2s 6d [$6.50] a week, he sailed to New Zealand as a ship's steward. This job brought him 1s [$2.60] a month clear. When he was 23, Smith was a chief steward and had saved enough to take over the Prince of Wales Hotel in Wellington. By the age of 28, he was a wealthy man.

He returned to London, lost most of his savings of £10,000 [$520,000] by gambling and arrived in Sydney in 1890 with £54 [$2808]. He managed the Grand Central Coffee Palace for six years, and then acquired the Arcadia Hotel, in Pitt Street. This flourished, and Smith bought hotels and cinemas in the Blue Mountains, established the first electric lighting plant on the mountains, and transformed a lake near Sydney into the Victoria Park racecourse. In 1915, he was elected to the Sydney Municipal Council and in 1918 became Lord Mayor.

Claude McKay persuaded Smith to start a crusading weekly paper, and invited a journalist friend, Robert Clyde Packer (father of the newspaper owner Sir Frank Packer), to join them. Packer, a native of Hobart, had been a powder-monkey in a Sydney quarry and a labourer in a Sydney flour warehouse before becoming a successful newspaperman. With Smith providing the money, McKay the ideas and Packer the organisation, *Smith's Weekly* was born.

The first issue, a poorly printed, poorly displayed broadsheet of 24 pages, appeared on 1 March 1919. The front page had some abominable puns about the raging influenza epidemic—'At last N.S.W. Health Minister is happy. His position lately has been most influenzial'—and a demagogic criticism of

the authorities for the restrictive measures imposed on the public. There were a few joke drawings by Cecil Hartt, Mick Paul and Alex Sass but they gave no hint of the brilliant black-and-white work that was to become most characteristic and most popular feature of *Smith's Weekly*.

The editorial, published under what was to be the standing heading of 'Why I Publish *Smith's Weekly*', was signed by Smith, though it was, of course, written by Claude McKay. It declared: 'No country calls more clamantly today than ours for men of initiative and action. In every field we have it, save in politics. Governments by weakness and ineptitude succeed in one thing only—the creation of unrest. Who will find a way out? Not the party politician with eyes on the ballot box.

'Already the returned soldier, the cavalier, the cream of our country's manhood, has become the sport of the politician. Our soldiers fought for freedom in the broad sense of world

affairs. Now it falls for them, again in patriotism, to fight for real majority rule, the essence of democracy . . . Woodrow Wilson has pledged to make the world safe for democracy. It is for us to make democracy safe for Australia.'

Smith's Weekly, in effect, was to be 'The Digger's Paper', the clamant mouthpiece of Australian soldiers returning from World War I. In the first issue a page conducted by W. B. Dalley, who had served three years with the AIF, was devoted to their problems. This became a regular feature.

Smith's editors announced that they had cabled Prime Minister Billy Hughes, then in London, to offer Rudyard Kipling £500 [$13,000] for a 2000-word article on the 'glorious story' of the Villiers-Bretonneux victory, 'whereby the Australians saved Amiens.'

Hughes replied: 'Will approach Kipling if you wish, but as he declined our invitation to visit Australian battlefields, he can hardly

Australia's funniest joke and its sequel

'For gorsake stop laughing–this is serious'

Stan Cross's famous cartoon (above) appeared in Smith's Weekly in 1933. It convulsed Australia, sent a guffaw round the world, and briefly boosted the paper's circulation. Tens of thousands of reprints were run off on glossy paper and clerks were employed full time to post them to all parts of the earth. Requests for copies came from such curious places as the Khyber Pass (from British troops stationed there), Tristan da Cunha and Mombasa. The cartoon is still known to many as Australia's funniest joke, but few remember the sequel (right) published two months later

'Cripes, that was a narrow squeak!'
'Yairs—we were lucky to get out of it'

PRICE 4d
Smith's Weekly

FOUNDED BY JOYNTON SMITH   *The Public Guardian*

write effectively. Conan Doyle knows all about it. Shall I approach him?' *Smith's* cabled back: 'Exhaust Kipling Doyle unwanted.' Apparently, Kipling was exhausted. Hughes replied tersely: 'Kipling declines.'

This publicised offer of £500 for a short piece by a famous writer was typical of *Smith's* flamboyant, self-advertising editorial policy. Two years later, when Hughes was still Prime Minister, *Smith's* publicly offered him the enormous sum of £10,000 [$272,420] a year to become its editor for five years.

Smith's also derived publicity from the innumerable libel actions in which it was involved. In its first seven years, *Smith's* received libel writs totalling £400,000 [$10.5 million] and spent nearly £50,000 [$1.3 million] in legal fees—many of them paid to Bert Evatt, then a promising young barrister.

Drugs and white slaves

'In the 32 years of its life, it punched more noses and raised more belly-laughs than the rest of the papers in Australia combined,' says the paper's historian, George Blaikie. 'There was no limit to what *Smith's* could and did do. It smuggled opium into the country and peddled cocaine to prove there was a big drug-racket going on. It sold white girls by auction to Chinese merchants to spotlight a lively white slave-market in Australia. It fought for the right of a dog to attend golf matches at the exclusive Kooyonga Golf Club, Adelaide. It forced a Federal Government to give the inventor of the Owen gun a reasonable reward.'

Kenneth Slessor, who worked on *Smith's* for 13 years—four of them as editor—wrote: 'In its jaunty, irreverent and brilliant way, it created both history and legends.'

At its peak, *Smith's* had the biggest and most highly-paid staff of black-and-white artists in the world. They included Stan Cross, Cecil Hartt, Joe Jonsson, Vergil Reilly, Lance Driffield, 'Petrov' Turton, George Finey, Charles Hallett, Lance Mattinson, Syd Miller, Frank Dunne and George Donaldson. Most of them were paid on the

scale of pop singers and TV stars of today, according to Slessor. *Smith's* in its early days was an unprecedented success. The first issue sold 35,000 copies at 2d. By the end of 1921, the circulation had reached 150,000, and by 1927 it was more than 200,000. But during the Depression, sales began to drop and the decline continued till September 1939, when the circulation had sunk to an uneconomic 80,000.

World War II brought a temporary respite. Once more *Smith's* became 'The Diggers' Paper', beating a noisy war drum. Circulation rose to 250,000 in September 1944, and reached 300,000 before sliding again.

In October 1950, major shareholders decided to close the paper down. Like *The Bulletin* in middle-age, *Smith's* had lost its vitality, its brilliance and its purpose. Out of touch with post-war Australia, it desperately tried to whip up sales with front page stories with headings such as: 'Nude Dancing in the Slums', 'Black Men and White Women, Half-caste Harvest' and 'King's Cross—City of Sin'. The last issue was a poor production of 24 tabloid pages—exactly half the size of the first broad-sheet issue. The price was 6d [42c].

Claude McKay, 72 years old, emerged from retirement to write a valediction: 'The task of journalism did not beat *Smith's*,' he said charitably. 'Mounting costs did. It's goodbye to a loyal and devoted staff. Artists with grand reputations and talents. Journalists who relished the freedom to speak their minds. The death of a newspaper is a melancholy event. But we lived well and it was a good life while it lasted.'

A national daily

Australia's only national daily newspaper, *The Australian*, has not repeated the remarkable success of *Smith's Weekly*. Founded in 1964 by Rupert Murdoch, who later gained wider fame as the owner of a stable of major newspapers throughout Britain and the United States, *The Australian*, based in Sydney, was selling only 54,000 copies after two years. In 1985, its circulation was just over 119,000.

Vanished magazines

J. F. Archibald, the founder of *The Bulletin*, also started another successful magazine, a monthly called *The Lone Hand*; it had 116 pages of editorial and sold for 1s [$1.50]. *The Triad*, a smaller magazine, lasted until 1927 and sold for 6d [85c], while Australia's first journals of luxury in production and subject, Sydney Ure Smith's *Art in Australia* (1916-42) and *The Home* (1920-42) originally cost 12s 6d and 2s 6d [$20.85 and $2.90] respectively. World War II brought an end to both these magazines and several others, including the Melbourne publication *Adam and Eve*, which had enjoyed popularity through its coverage of social and women's affairs.

The Triad, a literary monthly, arrived from New Zealand in 1915. Its circulation reached 23,000

The Lone Hand appeared monthly from 1907 to 1921, and covered literary and general subjects

What the classifieds offered when 1901 began

The classified advertisements in the morning papers on the first day of January 1901, were, as always, interesting. An optimistic Sydney real estate agent offered land north of the harbour with this inducement: 'North shore bridge—the coming national work—Sydney and North Sydney to be connected—Foundation stone of the bridge to be laid within twelve months.'

In the section headed 'Horses and Vehicles', Mr Robbo, at the Square and Compass Hotel, Haymarket, advertised a hooded sulky and a blue-roan horse, complete with harness, for £13 15s [$695]. Mr Robbo also announced that he wanted to buy 'horses and cows, dead from 5s to 10s [$12.60 to $25.20] worn-out horses, 10s to £2' [$25.20 to $100.85].

An announcement in the 'Personal' column read: 'MARRIAGE legally celebrated by clergyman. All denominations, no notice, WIT-

NESSES FREE, fee 20s [$50.45], hours 9am to 10pm. WELDON'S 57 Phillip Street, next Metropole'. In the same column, more than a dozen clairvoyants and palmists advertised their services. One said: 'I'm the only gipsy palmist in Australia, 30 years a roving gipsy.'

In Melbourne papers, domestics offering their services often mentioned the fact that they were Protestants. A 'superior housemaid, Protestant' was available for 10s [$25] a week, a 'young Protestant general' for 8s [$20.15], East Melbourne preferred. Waitresses and pianists earned the same high wage, 21s [$52.95] a week.

A labour agency offered the services of a baker—'competent tradesman, bread, smalls, own yeast'—for 25s [$63] a week.

A 'splendid modern mansion 22 large rooms, in extensive grounds' on East Melbourne Hill was for sale for £7,000 [$352,980].

The Australian sense of humour

Laughing at drunks and misfortunes

Australia has produced many remarkable black-and-white artists. Magazines such as *The Bulletin* and *Melbourne Punch* and newspapers such as *Smith's Weekly* fostered local comic draughtsmen, and there was a recognisable Australian style. But today the market for joke drawings has shrunk, so talented artists draw political cartoons or go abroad.

OWNER (merrily): 'You had the whip going all the way down the straight, I noticed.'
BILLY (who rode a successful losing race): 'My word, I did! But once or twice I nearly 'it the 'orse, instead of my boot.'
Alf Vincent, 1900

'A typical Australian party! I wish I could think of a way of luring them from the keg and taking an interest in their womenfolk!'   **Stewart McCrae, 1961**

'In some respects the dead man doesn't resemble your husband.'
'Is he near enough to get the insurance?'
Joe Jonsson, 1935

THE MATE: 'Now then, lads, don't idle about. Find something to do.'   **Joe Jonsson,1935**

SPORTING MATRON (telling a story of how she didn't back the outsider): 'And so the end was I had absolutely nothing at all on, and the brute came home—actually walked home—at 20 to 1.'
FIRST WOWSER: 'Can you hear what she is saying, brother?'
SECOND WOWSER: 'She appears to be talking about the late hours her husband keeps.'   **Norman Lindsay, 1912**

'Any rags or bones today?'
'No, wife's away.'
'Any bottles?'   **Hal Gye, 1925**

'This is what comes from gettin' used to pouring
demi-johns!'   **George Donaldson, 1935**

'Do you approve of clubs for women, uncle?'
'Ye-e-es but only after every way of quietening them
has failed!'   **D. H. Souter, 1930**

'I've notished it time an' agen on these fishin' excursions, theresh always one damn fool wants to fish!'   **Stan Cross, 1935**

Laughing at the hayseeds

Cartoonists have fun with rural stereotypes

Country people have always been favourite targets for city cartoonists. Two themes occur repeatedly—the outback farmer on his yearly visit to The Show baffled by the strange ways of city folk, and the confrontation between the farmer and the swaggie looking for a free meal. The way of life that gave birth to the characters in these cartoons has now disappeared, and country jokes nowadays often rely on laconic understatement.

THE SWAGGIE: 'You might have stretched a point, and give a starving man a job!'
THE COCKIE: 'What! a starving man—and be eaten out of house and home.' **Ambrose Dyson, 1909**

HOTEL ATTENDANT (nervously): 'Shall I get you a cuspidor, sir?'
DAD WAYBACK: 'Thanks, young feller! Just a small one, and 'ave one yourself.' **Stan Cross, 1921**

'This war's livened things up, all right. That's the second time the 'phone's rung this week.'
Ted Scorfield, 1943

SARAH (at city hotel): 'Are you going to leave anything for the waiter?'
DAD: 'No hope! Ten to one 'e wouldn't eat it if I did!'
Joe Lynch, c. 1930

SWAGGIE: 'Any chance of a bit of meat, boss?'
COCKY: 'Well, I can't spare any meat, but I'm going to kill a pumpkin tonight, an' you can have the innards!'
Norman Lindsay, 1907

BUNG: 'Hey, Dave! Ye've left your whip behind.'
DAVE (too lazy to walk back): 'That's all right, Bill. I'll call f'r't comin' back. I got me langwidge.'
Norman Lindsay, 1907

'That's why I don't need to buy one of them milkin' machines.'
Unk White, 1939

FARMER: 'Tucker? Yes, there's plenty of tucker up at the 'ouse.'
WEARY WANDERER: 'I'll toss yer ter see 'oo goes fer it.'
Cecil Hartt, 1908

'Wot do yer mean, 'e needs a 'oliday, Doc? I give 'im a day orf last month ter go ter th' local show so's he could compete in th' woodchop, sheaf tossin' and th' boxin' events.
Ken Maynard, 1965

The long nose of the censor

Writers and publishers in the dock

The Commonwealth of Australia was only seven months old when the newly-formed Customs Department first exercised its power to censor books. It pounced on a consignment of French novels and launched a prosecution against the importers, in this case the highly respectable Melbourne firm of George Robertson.

The books were a translation of Balzac's *Droll Stories*—a minor classic—and Paul de Kock's *Monsieur Dupont*. Both were described by the prosecution as literary garbage of the worst kind. One of the crown prosecutors, Edward Ellis Morris, the Professor of English, French and German Literature and Languages at Melbourne University, said: 'I felt I defiled my mind by reading them. I needed a bath after it.' Other witnesses, including Edward Armstrong, librarian of the Melbourne Public Library, agreed. Robertson's were convicted and fined £25 [$1260.65]; the books were of course confiscated.

In 1971, another respectable firm, Angus and Robertson, was charged in Sydney with selling an edition of Phillip Roth's comic and sexually explicit *Portnoy's Complaint*, the importation of which had been prohibited. The juries in two trials disagreed; the charge was finally dropped.

Between these two prosecutions, 70 years apart, Australian censorship had passed through many stages, some of them absurd, culminating in a period during the Depression when Australia shared with the Irish Free State the distinction of being the most repressive English-speaking country.

Hansard in demand

Until 1973, when it was taken over by the Attorney-General's Department, book censorship in Australia was in the hands of the Customs Department. The department could prohibit the import of any book that it considered to be 'blasphemous, indecent or obscene'. This authority extended only to books published overseas. Independently, each state still has its own mechanism for banning books, whether imported—and passed by the Commonwealth authorities—or printed in Australia.

This has often led to the situation in which a book is banned in, say, Victoria, while it is on sale in other states. The result is usually a brisk sale of the book by Sydney booksellers to eager readers south of the Murray.

In 1964, copies of Mary McCarthy's novel *The Group*, which had been passed by the Commonwealth customs, were seized by the police vice squad in Melbourne. 'If I had a teenage son or daughter, I would not like to see them reading it,' said Victoria's Chief Secretary, Arthur Rylah.

A few days later Mr Rylah read the seduction scene from *The Group* aloud to Parliament. His speech was, of course, printed in Hansard, which was immediately in great demand. For a trifling fourpence [$1.55] studious Victorian readers who could not buy a copy of the book could read its most 'frightening' passage so obligingly quoted by the indignant Chief Secretary.

Norman Lindsay's writings and paintings were often in trouble with the censors: 'It would be impossible for me to write a textbook on arithmetic without having the censor ban it,' he complained. In this 1931 cartoon for *The Bulletin*, he depicted the shackled state of the arts in Australia

'A barrier of illiterate policemen and officials stands between the tender Australian mind and what they imagine to be subversive literature,' said the English writer H. G. Wells when he visited Australia in 1939. At that time, there were about 5000 books on Australia's prohibited list.

The main epidemic of book banning in Australia began in the early thirties, under a United Australia Party government. The 1920s had seen a new freedom for English novelists: books such as Margaret Kennedy's *The Constant Nymph*, in which a teenage music lover elopes with a married composer, were bestsellers and sold freely in Australia.

In the next decade, however, the Minister for Customs, Colonel T. W. White, was to proclaim that 'fine writing by prominent writers will not save them if their work is tinged with obscenity. My idea is that authors like Aldington and Huxley should not escape the provisions of the law.'

Nor did they. Richard Aldington had the distinction of a triple ban—*The Colonel's Daughter*, *All Men are Enemies*, *A Dream in the Luxembourg*. Aldous Huxley's *Brave New World* was banned. So were George Orwell's *Down and out in Paris and London*, John Dos Passos' *1919*, Ernest Hemingway's *A Farewell to Arms*, John O'Hara's *Butterfield 8* and *Appointment in Samarra*, Erskine Caldwell's *God's Little Acre*—and even Daniel Defoe's 18th century classic *Moll Flanders*.

Australian writers did not escape either. Norman Lindsay's *Redheap*, a vivid picture of life in a small Victorian country town, was published in England in 1930 and immediately banned in Australia. Lindsay commented: 'The average Australian is a slug and a moral coward whenever the noisy minority starts making a fuss over any frank statement of life and love.' *Redheap* remained on the banned list until 1956.

James Joyce's masterpiece *Ulysses* is distinguished by having been twice banned. The first time was in 1929, five years after the unlimited edition was published in Paris. In 1937 the ban was lifted, and no-one seemed to suffer moral damage. But in 1941 a church organisation succeeded in having it banned again. The Minister for Customs, E. J. Harrison, announced that *Ulysses* had so shocked him that his hair stood on end. The Minister for External Affairs, Sir Frederick Stewart, concurred: *Ulysses*, he said was a 'collection of unadulterated filth'.

Alarmed by Lawrence

About the same time, a member of the New South Wales Legislative Assembly named Lawrence said he would change his name if D. H. Lawrence's *Lady Chatterley's Lover* were ever admitted to Australia.

A hilarious interlude enlivened the hearing of an obscenity case in Sydney Central Summons Court in 1946. *We Were the Rats*, Lawson

'To classify *We Were the Rats* as obscene literature is the height of absurdity,' said the RSL. But the censorship laws at the time were absurd

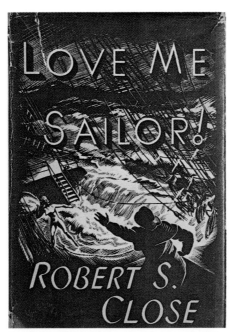

The first edition of Robert Close's *Love Me Sailor* landed its author in jail in 1948. These days the book would hardly raise an eyebrow

Angry Penguins

1944 Autumn Number
to Commemorate
the
Australian
Poet
Ern Malley

"I said to my love (who is living)
Dear we shall never be that verb
Perched on the sole Arabian Tree"

"(Here the peacock blinks the eyes
of his multipennate tail.)"

Painting by Sidney Nolan.

The special 'Ern Malley' edition of *Angry Penguins*, with cover by Sidney Nolan and comment by Max Harris, was found 'indecent' in 1944

Glassop's fine, realistic story of desert warfare and the siege of Tobruk, had been published in 1944. Seven months after the publication, a charge of obscenity was brought against the publisher, Angus and Robertson.

A vice squad sergeant, who said that part of his job was to seek out obscene literature, was cross-examined by Mr (later Justice) Dovey, and this dialogue took place:
Mr Dovey: Have you ever heard of Chaucer?
Sergeant: No.
Mr Dovey: You did not hear of him while in the vice squad?
Sergeant: No.
Mr Dovey: Have you ever heard of Byron?
Sergeant: No.
Mr Dovey: He was a Lord.
Sergeant: Yes, I've heard of him.
Mr Dovey: Do you know if he was on Lord Mountbatten's staff?
Sergeant: I don't know.
Mr Dovey: Do you know if he was a writer?
Sergeant: I don't know.
Mr Dovey: Do you know if he was a war correspondent?
Sergeant: I don't know.
Mr Dovey: Have you heard of Shelley?
Sergeant: I know a man named Shelley, but I take it you refer to an author or something. I have never heard of the name Shelley as a man who wrote anything.

However, the magistrate decided that *We Were the Rats* was obscene, and fined Angus and Robertson £10 [$232.35] with 8s [$9.30] costs. The book went under the counter and sold on the black market at £5 [$116] a copy. Although even the Returned Services League defended the book, it was 1965 before Australians were deemed sufficiently mature to read the original text of *We Were the Rats*.

In 1945, the Melbourne firm of Georgian House published a book called *Love Me Sailor*, by a Victorian, Robert S. Close, who had

spent six years at sea. It was a novel about the impact of a lone nymphomaniac on the crew of a windjammer.

Today the book would scarcely raise an eyebrow in a vicarage; but in 1948, three years after its publication, Close and his publishers were hauled before the Melbourne Criminal Court and convicted of publishing a book 'containing obscene matter'.

Georgian House was fined £500 [$10,130]; Close was fined £100 [$2025.60] and sentenced to three months imprisonment. Passing sentence, Mr Justice Martin thundered: 'The morals of a community, especially the youth of the community, are to be safeguarded. I regard your book as a gross assault on that morality.' Close was led from the court as a common criminal in handcuffs.

Many members of the community whose morals had been safeguarded were appalled at the severity of the sentence. 'Few will feel comfortable when they think of Australia being known abroad as a country where an author can be manacled and treated as a potentially dangerous criminal,' said the mass-circulation Melbourne newspaper, the tabloid *Sun News Pictorial*.

Later, the Court of Criminal Appeal annulled the gaol sentence, reduced the publishers' fine to £300 [$6076], and increased Close's fine to £150 [$3038]. Close 'tired of living in an atmosphere of parochial suburbanism', went abroad, and there was a happy end to the story. The book became a best seller in Germany and France, where it was sold with a note on the dust-jacket: 'The author of this book went to gaol.' In 1962 an unexpurgated paperback edition of *Love Me Sailor* was published in Sydney. It did not sell particularly well, despite the book's lurid history.

In 1944, two young Sydney poets, James McAuley and Harold Stewart, perpetrated a magnificent hoax on Max Harris and John

Reed, the co-editors of Adelaide's *avant garde* literary journal *Angry Penguins*.

McAuley and Stewart concocted a lot of meaningless verse, choosing words and phrases at random. These 'poems' were sent to *Angry Penguins* with a letter from a mythical 'Ethel Malley', saying she had found them among the papers of her brother 'Ern Malley', who had died in poverty at 25.

The two hoaxers said later that they wished to find out whether those who wrote and lavishly praised obscure poetry could tell the real thing from 'consciously and deliberately concocted nonsense'. They soon found out. Harris and Reed acclaimed the verse with enormous enthusiasm, and it was presented in a special edition of *Angry Penguins*.

Indecent nonsense

Even more amusing than the spoof, which was exposed in a Sydney newspaper, was the sequel: Harris, as the editor of the 'Ern Malley' poems, was convicted by an Adelaide court of publishing indecent matter.

One of the nonsense poems that Detective Vogelsang—the sole Crown witness—took exception to was called *Night Piece*. 'I think there is a suggestion of indecency about it,' he told the court. 'The whole thing is indecent. Apparently, someone is shining a torch in the dark . . . I have found that people who go into parks at night go there for immoral purposes . . .' Discussing another 'poem', the witness said: 'The word "incestuous" I regard as being indecent. I don't know what incestuous means. I think there is a suggestion of indecency about it.'

The comedy had an appropriate curtain when South Australia's Commissioner of Police commended Detective Vogelsang for 'zealousness and competency in securing evidence for the prosecution of an indecent publication'.

Advertising with style

Selling through poems and personalities

Rhymed advertisements in newspapers and magazines were the forerunners, in the days before radio and television, of singing commercials. They often exploited topical events shamelessly. Thus, during the Boer War, you were likely to find this in your paper:

The Boers keep up their useless war
To make the Transvaal free.
What they want to do it for
Isn't clear to see.
Far better they should settle down,
And make their homes secure,
To cure their colds and add renown
To WOOD'S GREAT PEPPERMINT CURE.

Some trade papers in the 1900s offered their readers a free 'Catchy Advertising Jingle' service. Here are a few specimens:

Two-thirds of your life is spent in your boots,
Whether at labour or leisure;
Two-thirds of your life is spent in your boots,
Why not spend it in pleasure?
Two-thirds of your life is spent in your boots,
Let us emphasise once more,
If you'd enjoy that much of life,
Buy your boots at (Blank's) Boot Store.

Fresh as the breath of a new-born day,
Pure as the morning dew,
Our butter is sent to us daily—
We'd like to send some to you.
'Tis the dimple of the dairy,
'Tis the pride of (Blank's) Big Store,
We stake our reputation that
A trial will mean buy more.

Our horses are swift but gentle
Our vehicles are light but strong,
Our harness is new and substantial,
In fact there's nothing wrong.
To serve you with the best of rigs,
You'll find we're always able,
Just write, or 'phone, or make a call
at (John Blank's) Livery Stable.

This advertisement for 'Australia's Elixir' had at least the virtue of brevity:

For coughs and chills and such like ills,
Why drench yourself with draughts and squills,
When Roberts' Whisky does the trick,
Makes young the old and cures the sick.

In 1918, the manufacturers of Heenzo, a quack remedy for asthma, bronchitis, colds, influenza, etc., commissioned the perpetually hard-up Henry Lawson to write doggerel such as this:

THE TRAGEDY—A DIRGE
by Henry Lawson

Oh, I never felt so wretched, and things never
look so blue,
Since the days I gulped the physic that my
Granny used to brew:
For a friend in whom I trusted, entering my
room last night,
Stole a bottleful of Heenzo from the desk
whereon I write!

I am certain sure he did it (though he never
would let on),
For he had a cold all last week, and today his
cough is gone;
Now I'm sick and sore and sorry, and I'm sad
for friendship's sake—
(It was better than the cough-cure that my
Granny used to make.)

Oh, he might have pinched my whisky, and he
might have pinched my beer;
Or all the fame or money that I make while
writing here—
Oh, he might have shook the blankets and I'd
not have made a row,
If he'd only left my Heenzo till the morning,
anyhow.

So I've lost my faith in mateship, which was all
I had to lose
Since I lost my faith in Russia, and myself and
got the blues;
And so trust turns to suspicion, and so
friendship turns to hate—
Even Kaiser Bill would never pinch his Heenzo
from a mate!

'I don't find much fun in writing rhymes for medicine advertisements, quack or otherwise,' Lawson wrote to his old friend, J. F. Archibald, then literary editor of *Smith's Weekly*, in May 1919. 'I think I'll get on with a tailoring, or a whisky firm; or a pork butcher — I like pork chops . . . Reminds me that when I was on the *Boomerang*, in Brisbane [in 1891] I wrote rhymes for J. P. D. Whisky advertisements for six months; but then I didn't drink. Think of the bottles I missed!' He mended the deficiency later.

The Senator's tribute

Lawson's acceptance of the Heenzo cheque is easy to understand. But his example was followed by many public figures who could not plead the excuse of poverty. For example, Senator Hattil Spencer Foll, later a Minister in four non-Labor governments, wrote during World War I: 'I must pay tribute to the makers of Heenzo. I had a fearful cold in the chest. It worked wonders with me . . . I am advertising it among my soldier friends, and will boost it for all I am worth.'

When Harry Lauder toured Australia in 1914, an advertisement depicted him in kilt, sporran and tam o'shanter, saying: 'I like your country, I like your people, and I like your Robur Tea. It's awfu' guid.'

The Minister's testimonial

In 1919, Clements Tonic, another patent medicine, proudly published this testimonial from a South Australian parliamentarian:

'During the early part of last year [1918] I went through a very strenuous campaign, addressing two or three meetings nightly, besides attending to my duties as Minister of Industries and Repatriation.

'The campaign lasted two or three months, at the end of which I felt completely fatigued and worked out.

'I had recourse to Clements Tonic, and derived great benefit from it in recuperating my energies.

Yours faithfully,
R. P. BLUNDELL.'

These preparations are now being used by nearly all the leading people in this country, and are daily being despatched to nearly every part of the world.

E. HOLLAND, Hair Specialist, 193 Collins St., Melbourne, Victoria.

This advertisement, for a preparation that apparently not only turned grey hair black but also made it grow, is an example of truly extravagant claims

The Governor's thanks

The device of persuading—and paying in cash or kind—well-known people to endorse commodities that they may never have heard of is, of course, probably as old as the practice of advertising itself.

Certainly in Australia it dates back at least to the regime of Sir Hercules Robinson, Governor of New South Wales from 1872 until 1879. When the Sydney firm of Washington Soul advertised its Australian Relish—'possessing the most delicious flavour for fish, game, wild fowl, curries, gravies, chops, steaks and roast meats'—it quoted this letter from the Governor's private secretary: 'I am directed by his Excellency the Governor and Lady Robinson to return you many thanks for your present of six bottles of the Australian Relish, and I am further directed to say that they consider it most excellent. They intend to use it regularly at Government House, and recommend it to others.'

Not a political imposter. The lithographers Troedel and Cooper produced these standard election posters so that a candidate could order one and have his own name and portrait inserted. These are samples, so the gentleman with the splendid moustache was probably neither Robinson nor Brown. The general-purpose illustrations in the background lent themselves to several interpretations. A candidate would not have had to stand on a platform of either retrenchment or federation.

Cobra was a widely advertised boot polish in the 1900s. In *The Bulletin* Cobra ran a series of full-page 'Chunder Loo' advertisements with drawings by Lionel Lindsay and verses by 'Kodak' (Ernest O'Farrell). Lindsay was paid £2 10s [$123.45] for each drawing and O'Farrell received 5s [$24.70] for the accompanying jingle. Lindsay was paid the same fee for each in a series of humorous advertisements for Schweppes, which for many years decorated pubs and railway stations in all parts of Australia. Two of his brothers also drew for advertising. Daryl Lindsay in the early days of his marriage not only drew realistic teapots for Robur Tea, but often posed in front of a mirror in tropical suit and sun helmet as the young Ceylon tea planter who advertised the tea from Melbourne's hoardings. The *Grocer of Australia* reported in 1904 that Percy Lindsay and another artist had just completed for Robur Tea 'a gallery of 600 paintings destined to adorn the festive tramcar'. Another painter who lived for a time by designing advertisements was John Longstaff. He turned to advertising in 1896, when he returned from England where he had exhibited at the Royal Academy, and found Australia in the depths of a depression. *The Bulletin* praised one of his whisky posters

"Cobra," The Boot Polish.

Chunder Loo,	That dread entrance—	He must pay	In he goes
Of Akim Foo,	Traitor's Gate—	In some degree	'Mid London's hoots!
Sees the grey	Where the Powers	For the world's,	"COBRA" will not
Ex-Kaiser through	Of Justice wait.	Long agony.	Clean *his* boots!

Advertisements of the past

Famous Australian posters

A Melbourne bill-poster, interviewed in 1934, said that of the 100,000 or so posters he had stuck up with flour paste over the previous 40 years, three remained indelibly in his memory. One was the famous English poster *Bubbles*, a reproduction of Sir John Millais' painting of his little grandson blowing soap bubbles from a clay pipe. This masterpiece of Victorian sentimentality was bought by Pears to advertise their transparent soap.

The other posters the bill-poster remembered were Australian, one advertising Carlton beer, the other Hutton's ham and bacon.

One day in the early 1900s, a Melbourne photographer, G. M. Sinclair, walked into a ramshackle bush pub at Walsh's Creek, north-eastern Victoria, and saw an old bearded fossicker raising a huge glass of beer to his lips with an air of beatific happiness. When the fossicker had drained the glass with a sigh of profound satisfaction, Sinclair remarked good-humouredly: 'You seem to be enjoying your beer, my friend?'

The old man replied with a sentence that was to become a catch-phrase in Victoria; 'I do indeed, sir, I allus has wan at eleven.'

Sinclair took a photograph of the old man, and a commercial artist adapted it as a poster for Carlton beer.

Other popular Australian posters were Pelaco's smiling Aborigine, clothed only in a shirt, saying: 'Mine tinkit they fit'; Kiwi's venerable cobbler with his slogan: 'They're well worn but they've worn well' (the model for the cobbler was a music teacher at Melbourne's Wesley College); and the monkey looking at himself in a well-polished frying pan to illustrate the slogan: 'Monkey Brand Soap—Won't Wash Clothes'.

Victorian classics of the billboards

The slogans on these posters, which both originated in the early 1900s, became part of Australian folklore. 'I allus has wan at eleven' was a popular catch-phrase in Victoria for many years. In Melbourne, football fans used to refer to a push in the face as a 'don't argue'. The bearded old-timer in the Carlton Brewery's posters was painted from a photograph taken in a Victorian pub in the early 1900s, but the vaudeville pair in the 'don't argue' poster originated in a drawing done by Mel B. Spurr, a well-known cartoonist. It was later registered as a trademark by J. C. Hutton Pty. Ltd. and became perhaps the most famous of all Australian posters. The full legend read: ' "Don't argue"—Pineapple hams and bacon "are" the best'.

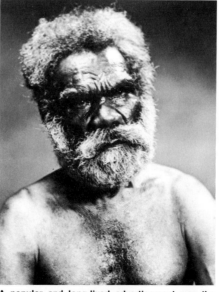

A popular and long-lived advertisement was the Pelaco shirt company's picture of a smiling Aborigine, clad only in a shirt, saying 'Mine tinkit they fit'. At left is the original painting for the poster, done in 1906 by A. T. Mockridge; above is the artist's model, a little later in life

Nursery for artists

For more than half a century, Troedel and Cooper, established in 1861, were Melbourne's leading commercial printers. The firm, which specialised in lithography, printed big 24-sheet posters as well as labels for biscuits, beers, soaps, teas and cigars. It was a nursery for many young artists, including Blamire Young, Charles Wheeler, Percy Leason and Arthur Streeton, all of whom worked on its lithographic stones.

Streeton was apprenticed to the firm at the age of 19. Fifty-one years later, when Walter Troedel, son of the founder, congratulated him on his knighthood, Sir Arthur replied: 'Thank you very much for your kind note of congratulation. The honour is for the art of Australia as well as for me. I have often thought of the original old firm of your Father's . . . and how kind he was to me. I did my first two or three good pictures during Saturday afternoons and Sundays when I was one of the apprentices.'

The novelist George Johnston also worked for Troedel and Cooper, before abandoning commercial art for writing.

Posters advertising seven different brands of Scotch whisky vie for attention with advertisements for cocoa and announcements of theatrical entertainments on this Sydney billboard about 1901. The billboard stood on the corners of Liverpool and Elizabeth Streets

A MESSAGE FROM MARS.
An Old Firm adopts a New Method of Publicity.

vid Jones' Anniversary Sale
To commemorate their 81st. Birthday.
Monday, June 2nd. —— Saturday, June 21st.

An exciting new stunt in 1919 was the aerial distribution of these pamphlets advertising a sale at David Jones' store in Sydney

The kangaroo with swag and billy and the bushman leaning against the tree are still to be seen on the Inglis's Billy Tea packets, but the original exotic trademark is no longer in use

Counter display from the mid 1930s

A billboard-size poster in a fashionable style of the early 1930s

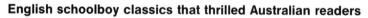

"BILL WATTLEBERRY V GINGER BLUEGUM
ONE TER WIN"

"SHAKE 'ANDS, LADS."

"SECONDS OUTER THE RING — BOX ON!"

GINGER GETS IN A STRAIGHT LEFT.

"BREAK AWAY, LADS!"

"CORNERS."

A KNOCK OUT.

NORMAN LINDSAY

"GINGER BLUEGUM THE WINNER."

Comics

Early Australian strips

The comic strip was known to English and American readers in the 1890s, but the Australian comic strip dates from 1907, when Norman Lindsay began contributing strips about animal characters to *The Lone Hand*.

The next year, a 16-page publication called *Vumps*, described as 'the first Australian comic paper', carried a full-page six-frame comic strip. This strip was drawn by Claude

The cover of the sole issue of *Vumps*, which carried the first Australian comic strip to relate the adventures of human characters. It shows Joe Vumps, an Australian urchin who looks oddly like the cretinous Alfred E. Newman, who many years later began to adorn the covers of the American magazine *Mad*. Vumps sports the Stars and Stripes in his cap out of enthusiasm for the United States fleet, which was visiting Australian ports at the time, August 1908. The first true comic strips in Australia had appeared the previous year in *The Lone Hand* magazine. These were drawn by Norman Lindsay and showed animal characters in human situations. The koalas in 'The Fight', at left, are an example, though they appeared in 1908

English schoolboy classics that thrilled Australian readers

English magazines enthralled many Australian boys. A thick bound volume of *Chums* was a treasure that endured for years

Marquet, who was better known as a leftwing political cartoonist. It presented two Sydney domain-dossers, Maryduke Miffles and Snoofter McSnickle—Australian counterparts of the English comic-strip tramps Weary Willie and Tired Tim. The strip showed how they tricked two 'somewhat shikkered' sailors from the visiting U.S. fleet.

The misadventures of Miffles and McSnickle were short-lived. Only one issue of the paper was published. It sold for a penny.

Vumps was edited by Hector Lamond, who later became editor of *The Worker*. Lamond wrote in his editorial: 'So interesting a personality as the Australian boy should not be allowed to live his life in obscurity, therefore this paper will chronicle his doings . . . He is a mischievous person . . . but he's as decent a lad as you ever met with a catapult in his pocket . . . Vumps' friends are as decent as he is, and there will be no indecency in his paper —we do not want your immoral support.'

The sole issue of *Vumps* had some notable contributors, including Henry Lawson, the ballad poet E. J. Brady, Norman Lilley (later editor of *The Lone Hand*) and Tom Mutch, a journalist and Labor member of Parliament.

The cautionary tale of Peter Wayback at the Melbourne Cup

This forerunner of the comic strip in Australia fits neatly into the urban tradition of making fun of unsophisticated people from the country. Titled 'Peter Wayback Visits the Melbourne Cup', it was published in Melbourne in 1904 by Charles Nuttall, a prolific black-and-white artist, etcher and journalist. It is not a true continuous strip but a sequence of thirteen comic drawings, originally printed one to a page. The sequence, which is not reproduced in its entirety here, begins with a frame showing a disgruntled looking Peter Wayback hard at work ploughing a paddock. The caption beneath it reads: 'For many years Peter has toiled, without ever a holiday, and the desire to see real life for once overwhelms him. The Cup season has come again, and so,--'. In the next frame . . .

He tells his wife and family that his mind is made up; he packs a bag, and after an affecting leave-taking, boards the express for Melbourne.

Arrived at Spencer Street, he is fortunate in meeting two agreeable young men, who warn him of the city's dangers, and volunteer to pilot him around.

They find lodgings for him, and arrange to meet the following day. Peter is tired, but will have a smoke before he turns in. Failing to light his pipe at the incandescent lamp, he retires in disgust.

Peter discovers that the siren of the bar has wonderful eyes, coupled with a frank disposition. Encouraged by her friendly manner, he boldly proposes a visit to the theatre.

It being her night off, she arranges to meet him. Peter spends a glorious night, topping off with champagne and oysters. When he rises to go home, he realises that the wine has affected his legs, as well as his head.

The lady kindly assists him a part of the way, until he falls unconscious, and is found by a policeman, who provides him with a lodging in a stone cell. Somebody — perhaps his lady friend — has taken charge of his watch and money.

. . . Cup Day at last! Acting on friendly advice, he hires a dog-cart, and goes to Flemington in style.

At the course his friends don strange clothes, and cry the odds. Peter backs the favourite.

The favourite wins. A cry of 'Welsher' is raised against his friends, who artfully turn the popular feeling against our hero. He runs in the direction of the Saltwater River.

After much ill-usage, he is thrown into the river, and swims across. From the opposite bank he addresses the crowd; most of his expressions begin with a capital D.

Once more in the bosom of his family. Peter has many regrets, but has still the satisfaction of having known what it is to see life.

Two perennial heroes

Long-running comic strips—and short-lived boys' papers

The first Australian comic strip to survive for a long time was *The Potts*, which Stan Cross began to draw for *Smith's Weekly* in 1919, under the title 'You and Me'. For many years it was based on the marital squabbles of Mr and Mrs Potts, who were still squabbling when the strip was taken over by Jim Russell, another *Smith's Weekly* artist, in 1939.

'The Potts' were subsequently syndicated in 35 American newspapers, and in Canada, New Zealand and Ceylon.

When *Smith's Weekly* closed down in 1950, 'The Potts' moved into the Melbourne *Sun-Pictorial*, cleaned up a bit for family-paper readers. The Potts were no longer constantly bickering, nor did Mr Potts give his wife an occasional slap on the behind.

Australia's best-known comic-strip character is perhaps Jim Bancks's Ginger Meggs, a tough, wily red-headed youngster with a great gift for getting into scrapes. Ginger Meggs made his debut in a strip called 'Us Fellers' in a colour supplement of Sydney's *Sunday Sun* in 1921. When Bancks died in 1953, the strip was taken over by other artists.

Although Ginge has a rich vocabulary of Australian slang, he has been syndicated in England and the United States and—in translation—in French-speaking regions of Canada and Spanish-speaking Argentina.

The cartoonist Vane Lindsay has pointed out that the major theme of the Ginger Meggs saga is 'You can't win!' The misdirected tomato splashes on the headmaster's face. The

innocently kicked football breaks an irate neighbour's window . . . Adversity dogs Ginger but he comes up smiling.

Second only to Ginger Meggs in longevity and popularity is Syd Nicholls' character Fatty Finn. Despite editorial vicissitudes, during which he disappeared from newspapers and survived in an eight-page comic paper, *Fatty Finn's Weekly*, this hardy Australian continued in the comic supplement of the Sydney *Sun-Herald* until June 1977. And, after more than half a century, he was still drawn by his creator. Syd Nicholls began the strip when asked for one to compete against 'Ginger Meggs' in the *Sunday Sun* and D. H. Souter's 'Sharkbait Sam' in the *Sunday Times*.

Daryl Lindsay drew this cover and many other illustrations for *Pals* during the 1920s

The Silver Jacket ran for 15 issues—from October 1953 to December 1954

Harold Herbert, a well-known landscape painter, drew this illustration for *Pals* in the 1920s, when it was hard for artists to make a living. The magazine survived for six years

THE GLAD SMILE OF GLADSOME GLADYS MAKES EVERYBODY CHEERFUL

Ginger Meggs made his first appearance in this episode of 'Us Fellers'. He is the bowler. He looks quite unlike his later self, but the mature style of the strip is foreshadowed in the little dog and the hatted fielder who urges: 'Now then Ginger work in a googley and they're done.' Fatty Finn was presented in his early days as a Billy Bunterish figure of fun, quite different from the popular and durable hero of his more tumultuous later years

165

Australian best-sellers/1

City man who extolled life in the bush

Perhaps the first Australian book to qualify for the title of best-seller would be 'Banjo' Paterson's *The Man from Snowy River*, which sold more than 100,000 copies. It was published in 1895. Ten thousand copies were sold within a year, and 20,000 before the end of the 19th century, when the population of Australia was fewer than 4 million.

It had enjoyed 'the biggest success ever made by any book in Australia', said *The Bulletin* in May 1900. Reviewing it, the English *Literary Year Book* said: 'The immediate success of this book . . . was without parallel in Colonial literary annals, nor could any living English or American poet boast so wide a public, always excepting Mr Rudyard Kipling.' High praise indeed!

Paterson, the son of a grazier, was born near Molong, NSW, in 1864. He was educated in Sydney and became a solicitor, a war correspondent and editor of the Sydney *Evening News*, the *Town and Country Journal* and the *Sportsman*. But although he lived and worked

in the city he had a practical knowledge of the bush, and a great affinity with bushmen, from whom he gathered material for many of his ballads.

In an age when recitations were a popular form of entertainment, his swinging verses had an immense appeal. They were recited in suburban drawing rooms as well as in shearing sheds and drovers' camps.

They perpetuated the myth of the devil-may-care, resourceful bushman. *The Man from Snowy River*, a dashing young horseman who outrides all others when he rounds up wild horses on the slopes of Mount Kosciusko, has passed into Australian folklore. A line in the last verse of the ballad still holds good: *The Man from Snowy River is a household word today*.

'Banjo' Paterson also wrote the words of Australia's unofficial national anthem, *Waltzing Matilda*. He was created Commander of the Order of the British Empire in 1939 and died two years later, leaving his wife all he possessed–£215 [$5725].

'Banjo' Paterson, a Sydney solicitor and newspaper editor, wrote bush ballads that won immense popularity in city and country alike

Comic misadventures on a Queensland selection

A contemporary of Paterson, Steele Rudd had an even greater success with his humorous novels of life on a small Queensland selection. Rudd, whose real name was Arthur Hoey Davis, was the son of a blacksmith who had taken up a selection at Emu Creek, near Toowoomba. As a boy he began to keep himself by picking-up in shearing sheds and stock-riding. He went to Brisbane in 1886 and worked in the Sheriff's office.

The first Steele Rudd book, *On Our Selection*, was published in 1899—after its first chapter had appeared as a sketch in *The Bulletin*—and was immediately successful. More than 20,000 copies were sold within four years. By 1940, sales had reached 250,000.

In 1903 it was followed by *Our New Selection*, and Davis left the public service. For the rest of his life, except for a few years farming on the Darling Downs, he was a full-time writer, producing more popular volumes in the Rudd saga, including *Sandy's Selection* (1904), *Back at Our Selection* (1906), *Dad in Politics* (1908), *From Selection to City* (1909), *The Book of Dan* (1911), *Grandpa's Selection* (1916) and *The Rudd Family* (1926).

The Rudd household consists of Dad, the bewhiskered patriarch; patient and uncomplaining Mother (Steele Rudd was angered when she was referred to as Mum); and many children, including gangling Dave, slow of speech but shrewd; his younger brother, barefoot, wild-haired Joe, forever doing the wrong thing; and their wholesome sister Sarah. There is also the dairymaid Fanny, for whom Dave has an amorous eye. Dad is the typical cocky-farmer of his day, always railing at the weather, the farm animals, unreliable fences and inept sons. But behind his comic anger lies the quiet courage of the pioneer, carving a strenuous living out of the bush, often down but never out. Drought, fire and flood cannot defeat him. He is a battler, a devoted family man in spite of his irascible outbursts, and a good neighbour.

'Some trouble with a steer' is the caption to this drawing from *On Our Selection*. Steele Rudd's tales of Dad's misadventures are in the sardonic Australian tradition of joking at misfortune

Australians as seen by a non-existent Italian

The most astonishing Australian best-seller in recent years was *They're a Weird Mob*, published in 1957 under the pseudonym of 'Nino Culotta'. It was written by John O'Grady, a Sydney man who had been a pharmacist and, later, a bricklayer's labourer. He had been a part-time writer of short stories, articles and verse for about 30 years when he drew on his bricklaying experiences to write *They're a Weird Mob*. The manuscript was rejected by Angus and Robertson, but published by a small firm, Ure Smith. Almost overnight it became a runaway best seller. By 1964, more than 500,000 copies had been sold, 350,000 of them in hard covers. The plot is simple.

An Italian writer, Nino Culotta, sent to Australia to gather material for an article, gets a job as a builder's labourer so he can mix with typical Australians. They either laugh at him for being a 'dago' or pity him. He is supposed to see life through the eyes of a new Australian, puzzled by Australian attitudes and Australian slang.

O'Grady paints a sentimental picture of the dinky-di Aussie, a man with a heart of gold despite his tough exterior, and probably this idealised image of the ordinary Australian was one of the reasons why the book became a best-seller. It had little success outside Australia, even though it was made into a film.

He sang songs of a sentimental larrikin

The best-selling Australian book during World War I was *The Songs of a Sentimental Bloke* by C. J. Dennis, a series of verse stories told in slang. Clarence Michael James Dennis, 'the laureate of the larrikin', was born in 1876 at Auburn, S.A. After working at a variety of jobs, including solicitor's clerk, barman and carpenter, he became a journalist. In 1906 he founded a short-lived satirical weekly, *The Gadfly*. His first book of verse, *Backblock Ballads*, appeared in 1913 under the pseudonym 'Den'.

In 1915, when Australia was mourning its dead on Gallipoli, Dennis published *The Songs of a Sentimental Bloke*. It had been rejected by a Melbourne publisher, but accepted by George Robertson of the Sydney publishing house of Angus and Robertson.

In July 1916, only nine months from the first appearance of *The Sentimental Bloke*, Robertson wrote to Dennis that the book was already in its fifty-first thousand. In less than 18 months—between 16 October 1915 and 31 March 1917—66,148 copies were sold in Australia and New Zealand. This figure did not include editions published in Britain, Canada and the United States.

In January 1918, Dennis sold the film rights of *The Sentimental Bloke* for £1,000 [$29,625]. It was produced as a silent film, a stage play and a sound film.

Critics in Australia and overseas acclaimed *The Sentimental Bloke* enthusiastically. E. V. Lucas, the English essayist, wrote: 'By virtue of truth, simplicity, and very genuine feeling, the story, though written in a difficult argot, which usually is anything but lovely, is convincing, and often too moving to be comfortable.' Lucas, H. G. Wells and W. J. Locke, the English novelist, sent congratulatory letters to the publishers.

A lone dissenting voice was the poet Kenneth Slessor, then only 19, who started a lively controversy in *The Bulletin* when he wrote: 'Fifty percent of modern Australian verse is written in the alleged dialect of the Outback—or of Surry Hills [a Sydney suburb] . . . Take the glaring example of *The Sentimental Bloke*. Mr Dennis makes his characters speak in a slang of Five Dock [another Sydney suburb]. Why not go the whole hog and have them speak in the prose of their everyday conversation? It would be no more improbable for them to speak in cultured English than to speak in verse . . .' Though Slessor attributed Dennis's slang to Five Dock, other critics have pointed out that it is a hybrid of Cockney and Australian. In any case, Dennis based the Bloke on a Melbourne larrikin, not a Sydneysider. *The Sentimental Bloke* was followed in 1916 by *The Moods of Ginger Mick*. Mick had first appeared in *The Sentimental Bloke* as 'a rorty boy, a naughty boy, wiv rude ixpressions thick'. In 1916, Dennis had him enlist and sent off 'to flamin' war to stoush the foe'. In less than six months, *Ginger Mick* sold 42,439 copies. Both the *Sentimental Bloke* and *Ginger Mick* appeared in a 'pocket edition for the trenches', the first Australian books specially produced for servicemen. They were immensely popular with the troops, Dennis produced more books, including *Doreen* (1917), *Digger Smith* (1918) and *Rose of Spadger's* (1924)—all in the same vein as *The Sentimental Bloke*—but he never had another best-seller. In later years he contributed topical verses to the Melbourne *Herald* under his old pseudonym 'Den'. When he died in 1938, the Prime Minister, J. A. Lyons, called him 'the Robert Burns of Australia'. He added: 'He created characters which have become immortal and captured the true Australian-spirit. Already his work has become world-famous, and future generations will treasure it.' As the Bloke would have said: 'I dips me lid!'

David Low drew his friend C. J. Dennis as a larrikin bard. The banjo, however, was not fanciful. Dennis who could play most musical instruments, had a banjo which he made himself

Hal Gye, a *Bulletin* artist for many years, illustrated *The Sentimental Bloke*, depicting its characters as curious roughneck cherubs

C. J. Dennis, seen here in his Melbourne home in 1922, was the only Australian writer of his time who had popular success with work set in the cities. He wrote about the larrikins of the Melbourne lanes, depicting them as soft of heart even though rough of speech and ready with their fists

Australian best-sellers/2

Alfred Rowlandson, the paperback pioneer

In 1883, an 18-year-old Victorian named Alfred Cecil Rowlandson sat in a tiny shop—only 76 cm wide—in King Street, Sydney, selling tram tickets for the New South Wales Bookstall Company, which owned all the bookstalls on Sydney's railway stations.

By 1897, Rowlandson, who had already worked his way up to manager, was able to buy the company. A few years later, he conceived the idea of selling shilling paperback editions of Australian novels on the company's book-stalls. This was 32 years before Allen Lane in England launched his Penguin series of sixpenny reprints.

Rowlandson wrote to Steele Rudd, asking him to write another book in the vein of *On Our Selection* and *Our New Selection*. Rudd tells how he called on Rowlandson—'a fair-haired, soft-skinned, well-built, well-groomed man with a fashionable moustache waxed and pointed'—in his dingy office. Rowlandson offered Rudd the large sum of £500 [$25,760] cash, plus 10 per cent on every copy sold outside Australia, and Rudd accepted.

First of the 'Bookstall' series

Rudd's first book for Rowlandson was called *Sandy's Selection*. Despite the fact that Rowlandson had to sell 10,000 copies of a book—or 20,000 in the case of *Sandy's Selection*—before its production costs were recovered, his book publishing business grew and thrived. And this was when Australia had a population of fewer than four million.

Sandy's Selection, the first of the 'Bookstall' series, appeared in 1904. When Rowlandson died in 1922, he had published about 200 Australian novels and sold nearly five million copies. Among his 70 or so writers were Louis Becke, Edward Dyson, Norman Lindsay and E. J. Brady: Arthur Wright was represented by 18 titles and Steele Rudd by 16. About 30 well-known artists—including Norman, Lionel, Percy and Ruby Lindsay, David Low and Will Dyson—drew the covers and illustrations. During World War I, the price of the books was raised to 1s 3d [$2.05], but was afterwards reduced to 1s [$1.50] again.

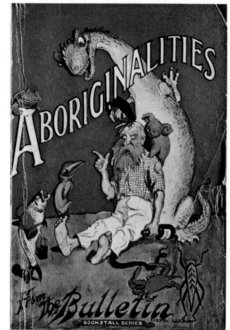
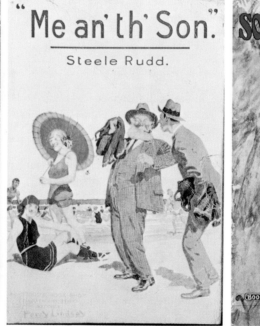
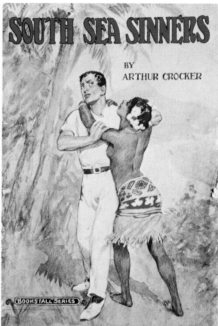
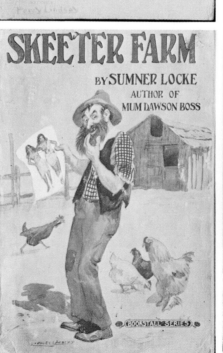
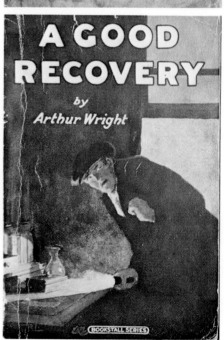

'Bookstall' series paperbacks like these once entertained many thousands of Australians. These tattered volumes are now collector's items

Lennie Lower, Sydney's laureate of laughter

Australia's greatest humorist, many claim, was Lennie Lower, whose novel *Here's Luck* was an immediate best-seller in 1930.

Leonard Waldemar Lower was born in Dubbo, New South Wales, in 1903, and was educated in a state school in Sydney. Soon after leaving school, he served briefly in the Royal Australian Navy. According to an obituarist in *Smith's Weekly*, his naval career ended when, impatient with naval methods, Lower gave the exact range to a gun crew, who caused severe damage to a valuable target.

Lower had begun writing when he was in the Navy, but his first funny piece was not published until he was 23. It appeared in *Beckett's Budget*, a Sydney scandal sheet of the late 1920s period.

For a time during the Depression, Lower joined the ranks of the unemployed, carrying his swag and 'jumping the rattler', doing a bit of road-mending, sleeping in the Sydney Domain. He then got a job on the *Labour Daily*, the voice of the Lang Labor Party, and wrote a daily column of humour, verse and comment under the name of T. I. Red.

Lower's social column

In the darkest days of the Depression, when Sydney's Sunday papers were devoting columns to so-called 'social news', reporting at length the languid inanities of the rich, Lower decided to publish his own social column. Here is a sample: 'The charming home of Mr. and Mrs. John Bowyang, tucked away in Pelican Street, Surry Hills, is a revelation in piquancy. From the backyard one has a view of every other backyard in the street, and the tall chimneystack of Tooth's Brewery looms majestically in the distance.

'Mrs. Bowyang has an artistic taste and an eye for effect. Two lines have been stretched between long poles at either end of the yard, and when these lines are full of clothes, the sight is bewitching in the extreme . . .

'The motif throughout the whole house is one of antiquity. The wallpaper is mellow with age, and the ceilings have not been kalsomined for forty-seven years . . .

'The bedroom furnishings are symbolic of that affectionate family life which seems to be fading into oblivion in these modern times. There are two double beds and a stretcher in the room, cleverly arranged so that one may walk from one bed to the other without climbing over.

'Mr. and Mrs. Bowyang and little Jacky sleep in one double bed, the three youngest girls in the other, and Mrs. Bowyang's brother-in-law, who is out of work, sleeps in the stretcher . . .'

Here's Luck gave Australia a much-needed tonic, and remains today a comic masterpiece, as ageless as the adventures of Mr Pickwick or Bertie Wooster. Reprinted year after year, it was still selling briskly more than 40 years after its first publication. 'Written as a mad, highly individualist extravaganza,' said a critic, 'it was soon seen to be much closer to the life and language of people . . . in Sydney and suburbs than many much more seriously conceived works. A book with a scene in it that recalls the glories of Falstaff, a book which showed Sydney people to themselves as they had never seen themselves before . . .'

Lower never wrote another novel, but he maintained a prodigious output as a newspaper and magazine humorist. At one period in the 1940s, he was turning out eight funny pieces, two of considerable length and all of considerable merit, every week. Lower became part of the Sydney scene, aptly described as 'a man of infinite legend, a man of infinite laughs, a much-loved man . . . Sydney's laureate of laughter' He was, in short, the Mo of the printed page.

He died in 1947, a funny writer almost to the day of his death.

Lennie Lower, prolific newspaper columnist of the 1930-40s, was one of Australia's great humorists

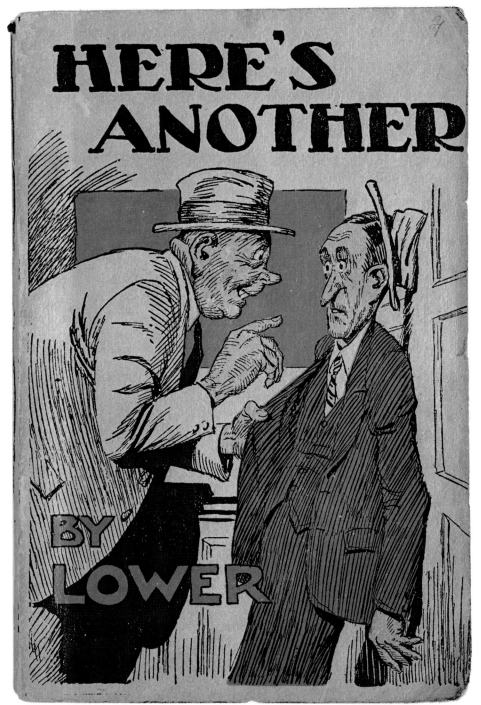

Lower's collection of humorous sketches, *Here's Another*, published in 1932, followed the novel that made him famous, *Here's Luck* (1930). His other two publications were also collections—*Life and Things* (1936) and *The Bachelor's Guide to the Care of the Young and other stories* (1941)

The Lindsays

At war with wowsers

When Norman Lindsay, on the eve of his 90th birthday, published a volume of pen drawings, some done only a few months before, a Sydney critic wrote: 'They speak with the voice of an exuberant young man in the springtime; a man who has had an unfading love-affair with life.' And Lindsay was in love with life—working, reading and talking till the day of his death a few months later.

For more than 60 years, he had maintained an astonishing output of black-and-white drawings, etchings, woodcuts and paintings in watercolour and oils. He had also published many books, contributed to periodicals, made exquisite model ships, decorated the grounds of his old stone house in the Blue Mountains with statues, fountains and pools, and written thousands of letters.

Norman Alfred Williams Lindsay was born in the Victorian gold-rush mining town of Creswick in 1879. His father was a cheerful Irish horse-and-buggy doctor, his mother the daughter of a tolerant Wesleyan missionary. The couple had ten children, in this order: Percival, Robert, Lionel, Mary, Norman, Pearl, Ruby, Reginald, Daryl and Elizabeth. All had a talent for drawing. Five of them—Percival, Lionel, Norman, Ruby and Daryl—became well-known artists.

At 16 Norman left Creswick for Melbourne to join Lionel in drawing 'news' pictures of prize-fights, fires, brothel raids, murder victims, chorus-girls and other lively subjects for a cheap scandal-sheet, *The Hawklet*, whose editor lived in a brothel. Norman began on 10s [$40] a week. 'It was an era,' he recalled, 'of the larrikin groups, of the street garrottings, of Little Bourke Street's Chinatown, of pubs open at all hours, and at night, Bourke Street a promenade of whores, openly soliciting custom.' A change for a country boy.

When *The Hawklet* folded, Norman and Lionel worked for a printer, turning out pickle and jam labels and illustrations for pamphlets and advertisements. Theirs was the world of poverty-stricken bohemians, dingy attics, sleazy wine-bars and amiable models. In seven years, they occupied no less than 37 different rooms.

Bulletin days

In 1901, J. F. Archibald, editor of *The Bulletin*, who had seen some of Norman Lindsay's better drawings, offered him a permanent job as illustrator and cartoonist. During this time he turned out more than 10,000 drawings for *The Bulletin* and its companion monthly, *The Lone Hand*. Much of this work reflected *The Bulletin*'s xenophobic and racist policies. As Lindsay's friend and admirer, Godfrey Blunden, wrote: 'His archetypal Australian is a muscle-bound simpleton; his Chinese are . . . sinister figures . . . aboriginals are comic; Jews tend to be pawnbrokers . . . The saving drawings of this period are the comic strips, cats and dogs, koalas and kookaburras, anthropomorphised with infinite tenderness and humour.' Lindsay also made countless joke-drawings about beer and boozers and declared war on the Australian wowser, lampooning him with enthusiasm.

The young Lindsays loved to play-act what they hoped would look like classical orgies. Here, about 1901, the bacchanals posing for the camera are from left: Reginald Lindsay, who was killed on the Somme; Will Dyson; Ruby, Pearl, Norman (foreground), Mary and Percy Lindsay. The Lindsays' mother, a daughter of a Wesleyan minister, watched these events with bemused astonishment

His first personal encounter with wowserism occurred in 1907 when his pen-drawing *Pollice Verso*, which showed naked Roman warriors and their women gesturing thumbs-down at the crucified Christ, was (to Lindsay's surprise) bought by the Melbourne Art Gallery for £150 [$7405]. When it was put on view, there was such an outcry from the public and press that the trustees relegated it to the gallery cellars. Another of Lindsay's pen drawings, *The Crucified Venus*, provoked even greater public fury when it was exhibited in Sydney; but Julian Ashton, who was in charge of the exhibition, refused to remove it, and a compromise was reached by turning its offending face to the wall.

Lindsay sailed for Europe in 1910, where his illustrations to Petronius' *Satyricon* were snapped up by a London publisher. But he was not happy in London or Paris, and returned after 16 months to accept a new offer from *The Bulletin*. While convalescing after a serious lung illness, he took up making model ships and writing. His first book, *A Curate in Bohemia*, based on his early Melbourne experiences, was published in 1913.

In 1918, Lindsay wrote his delightful children's book *The Magic Pudding*, which he said resulted from a discussion with a Sydney editor on child psychology, the editor maintaining that this was based on 'fairy fantasy' and Lindsay 'on its belly'.

Between 1913 and 1968, Lindsay published 13 works of fiction, four philosophical or critical works and one of reminiscences. His autobiography *My Mask*, written in 1957, was published in 1970 after his death.

Lindsay was careful to distinguish between bawdy, which he enjoyed, and pornography, which he disliked. 'Bawdy in art is extreme from pornography,' he wrote. 'Pornography is . . . dull, boring and humourless and to any mind sensitized to the intonation of wit and humour.' And: 'The richest, the rarest approach to life and art is by humour, and most of all, humour is the key of light-hearted bawdiness.' A doctrine not all accepted.

During World War I, Lindsay did a weekly full-page propaganda cartoon for *The Bulletin*, then infected with the prevalent war-fever. He also drew horrific enlistment posters for the Government. After the war, he became increasingly reactionary, vehemently condemning what he considered to be decadent art, as represented in painting by Cezanne, van Gogh and Gauguin, and in literature by James Joyce, T. S. Eliot and Ezra Pound. But his phenomenal creativity was undiminished.

He withdrew to Springwood, on the fringe of the Blue Mountains. In the most prolific period of his life, he worked furiously at drawings, etchings, watercolours, oils, sculpture, writing, landscape gardening, and, in his spare time, reading and talking.

Melba, one of his devoted admirers, made a pilgrimage to Springwood in 1924 with her secretary Beverley Nichols. In his autobiographical *Twenty-Five*, Nichols recalled the meeting with Lindsay: 'He did not walk towards us—he fluttered to us, like a bird . . . He was so thin, so fluttering, his eyes were so bright, his nose so like a beak, perched on top of his tiny neck. As for his talk—that too,

Norman Lindsay's gifts were many and varied. He delighted in conversation, writing, making model ships, and the whole gamut of art. Music alone seems to have eluded him

Censors plagued Norman Lindsay. He had to redraw the cover of his first novel (spot the difference). *Redheap*, a story of life in a small Australian country town at the turn of the century, was first published in England in 1930 with a cover by another artist. It was banned in Australia until 1956

was birdlike—the words pouring out one after the other, making one think of when the swallows homeward fly . . .'

That same year, the South Australian Society of Arts refused to show three out of 11 Norman Lindsay etchings because of the subject matter—nude men and women. One picture, said the Adelaide *Advertiser*, 'represented a wild licentious riot of the worst pagan times'. Among those who defended Lindsay were Melba and the composer Percy Grainger, but Lindsay angrily withdrew all his pictures from the exhibition and arranged for them to be shown in another gallery. Crowds thronged this rival show, concentrating their attention, of course, on the three banned etchings. Visiting Sydney one day in 1931, Lindsay saw a newspaper poster that read 'Will Norman Lindsay be Arrested?'. A police-court prosecution (later quashed) had been launched against a special issue of *Art in Australia* devoted to his work.

In August, 'to escape the splenetic furies of the national ego, in this case located in the carcass of Sydney's Commissioner of Police', as he put it, Lindsay spent a year in America. 'I am sick and tired of this most wowseristic country,' he declared.

When he returned, he flung himself again with demonic energy into creative work. A year before Lindsay's death in 1969, Godfrey Blunden wrote: 'A generation has arrived which happily seeks out Norman Lindsay . . . because in our drab and dangerous march to nowhere he is that rare, wonderfully reassuring and luminous event, a genius: perhaps the only authentic genius Australia has ever had.'

Norman Lindsay was a small bird-like figure, quite unlike the huge muscular voluptuaries he painted—as David Low noted in this drawing entitled 'Norman Lindsay takes his models for a walk'. Beverley Nichols wrote that Lindsay talked of wine like a devotee of Bacchus yet 'sipped only a mouthful . . . with pursed lips, as an old lady takes tea'. Lindsay's wife, Rose, said *he* was a wowser

THE OTHER LINDSAYS
Ruby Lindsay (right) also drew brilliantly. She contributed comic sketches to *The Bulletin* and *The Gadfly* under the name of Ruby Lind (left) until she married Will Dyson and went to England in 1910. Percy Lindsay also contributed to *The Bulletin*, but was best known for his small landscapes. Lionel and Daryl were both knighted for services to art. Lionel became famous for his woodcuts, etchings and watercolours, and was also a critic. Like Norman, he was opposed to modern art. Daryl, a war artist during World War I, was director of the National Gallery of Victoria from 1942 to 1955

171

Sporting Life

A land of champions and spectators

'The full force of fashionable patronage and interest is devoted to racing and cricket,' wrote the eccentric English poet, Richard Henry 'Orion' Horne, in his *Australian Facts and Prospects*, published in 1859. And he continued: 'The mania for bats and balls in the broiling sun during the last summer exceeded all rational excitement.' More than a century later—in 1971— another English observer, Jonathan Aitken, wrote in his *Land of Fortune:* 'Sport is the religion of Australia, and Saturday is the day of worship. Gallup Polls indicate that two-fifths of the population play some sport regularly, and that three-quarters of the population watch it.'

It is perhaps as a sporting nation that Australia is best known. A generally mild climate, cheap and abundant facilities, and, some say, a high-protein diet, have bred in Australia some of the world's greatest champions. To select just a few names: the cricketers Don Bradman, Richie Benaud and Dennis Lillee; the golfers Peter Thomson, Kel Nagle, Bruce Devlin and Jan Stephenson; the tennis stars Margaret Court, Evonne Cawley, Rod Laver and Ken Rosewall; the swimmers Dawn Fraser, Shane Gould, John Konrads, and Neale Brookes; the runners Robert de Castella, Herb Elliot, Ron Clarke and John Landy; the boxers Dave Sands, Lionel Rose and Jimmy Carruthers; the cyclist Hubert Opperman and the champion racing drivers Jack Brabham and Alan Jones.

Searching for a ball lost in the rough at the Kosciusko Chalet golf course in 1914

A nation of sports

New sports and new enthusiasms

A greater variety of sports is played in Australia than anywhere else in the world, including some that are indigenous: Australian Rules football, boomerang-throwing, sheep-shearing, speedway-racing, sphairee, skiing and—if you like to call it a sport—the gambling game, two-up.

The Australian Boomerang Association certifies that the world record for a boomerang throw stands at 114 metres, recorded at Parkes, NSW in 1967. The thrower was a white man, Frank Donnellan.

Speedway or dirt-track racing, originated at the Maitland (NSW) Agricultural Show in 1925, and was taken to England in 1928. The first race between Australia and England took place at Wimbledon in 1930.

Sphairee (pronounced 'Sf-i-ree') was invented by a Sydney student of Greek, Fred Beck, in 1961. It is a fast game played with a table-tennis bat and a perforated plastic ball on an indoor or backyard court, measuring 6 m by 2.5 m.

The South Melbourne Cricket Club's Ladies' Bowling Club, formed in 1899 under the name of the Albert Park Ladies' Bowling Club, is the oldest women's bowling association in the world. Bowls, once regarded as a game for old men only, is now attracting increasing numbers of young men and young women. Between 1952 and 1961, the number of women bowlers in New South Wales jumped from 4000 to 24,000.

Newer sports have been growing in popularity: boardsailing—the fastest growing sport in Australia—skin-diving, spearfishing, water-skiing, power boating, softball, skateboarding, orienteering and hanggliding. Squash, invented in 1890, was not much played until after World War II, but now about 1.25 million Australians play the game every week.

The rise and fall of tennis

The popularity of tennis, at its peak in the 1950s, declined in the 1960s, tennis equipment sales falling by over 40 per cent; but the 70s saw renewed interest and the estimated number of players in 1978 was about half a million. Surfboard riding continued to be a popular pastime. As much a way of life as a sport, Jonathan Aitken writes, 'Surfies are the hippies of the ocean.

'They sleep by the surf, live in the surf, and are psychologically and emotionally hooked on the surf . . .'

For the more mature and less vigorous, Australia's national sport is undoubtedly golf —a relaxing and relatively inexpensive game. You can take in 18 holes on a public course for four to six dollars. Australia's golfing population has been estimated at at least 286,000 men and 126,000 women.

Sport in Australia is truly democratic. It has no class barriers. Dawn Fraser grew up in the Sydney industrial suburb of Balmain, left school at the age of 14, and for a time had two jobs, dress-making in the day, serving in a milk-bar at night. John and Ilsa Konrads trained in public baths. Australia's 1960 Olympic swimming team included a carpenter, a plumber, a television compère, an apprentice mechanic, a bank clerk, a medical student, a ballet teacher and a travelling salesman. In the track and field teams, there were a doctor, a commercial artist, an accountant and a fitter and turner.

Hubert Opperman—from champion cyclist to government minister

In 1928, more than a million and a half readers voted in a poll, conducted by the French sporting magazine L'Auto, to discover the most popular sportsman in Europe. Hubert Opperman, the Australian cycling champion, won—he actually beat a Frenchman into second place.

That year had been Opperman's first in Europe, although he had been Australian road-racing champion since 1924. His first race in Europe was the marathon Tour de France, in which he finished a creditable (he had no team-mates to spell him) 17th. Then came the Bol d'Or, a 24-hour continuous slog around the Montrouge Velodrome.

In the first hour of the race, the chains on both of Opperman's racing bikes snapped—it was suggested that they had been sawn partway through by rivals. His manager, Bruce Small, could only borrow an old, heavy roadster for Opperman to continue, and by then he was 10 laps behind. Riding the heavy bike, he lost more time, and when he got his own cycle back he was 17 laps behind.

But by the 11th hour of the race Opperman had caught up to the field, and after 12 hours he was well in front. By the time he had covered 547 kilometres he had broken the race record at that stage by 10.5 kilometres, and the crowd went mad with excitement as he continued to break record after record. At the end of 24 hours he had covered a record-breaking 910 kilometres, and had broken seven intermediate course records.

The race was officially over, but Opperman's manager was not satisfied, and nor were the crowd. They wanted Opperman to break the world record for 1000 km. So the exhausted cyclist again took up circling the track until, 79 minutes later, he had broken that record as well.

L'Auto said that Opperman was so popular because of 'his courage, his perfect loyalty and his eternal smile'. It was suggested in Australia that the eternal smile was because he had no idea what the French were saying.

In 1931 he reached the climax of his cycling career when he raced in the 1170 kilometres Paris-Brest-Paris race—the world's longest and toughest non-stop road race. He kept awake by drinking black coffee, singing songs and smacking his forehead. Just 4.8 km from the finish four other riders overtook him and led the way into the crowded arena. But then, when everyone thought that Opperman could not possibly win, he swooped down from the top of the banked track and won the race by less than one length—after over 1126 kilometres.

Opperman's cycling fame helped him to become a Liberal member of the Federal Parliament in 1949. He was appointed Minister of Shipping and Transport in 1960 and Minister for Immigration in 1963. Some of his world records still stand, including that set at the Bol d'Or in 1928 (910 kilometres in 24 hours), and his time of 28 hours 55 minutes for 1610 kilometres (motor paced).

Hubert Opperman pedals along the main road between Fremantle and Kalgoorlie in 1937, on his way to setting a record of 13 days, 10 hours, 11 minutes for a ride from Fremantle to Sydney. Opperman was such a perfectionist that when he finished at night at the rear of his caravan he would insist on starting from there again in the morning—he would not start from the front

Toowoomba citizens gathered at the local race course in March 1912 for the publicans' races. Race meetings were major social events in country towns, especially where there was only one a year

A bookmaker's poster from about 1910. Australia was the first country in the world to set up a bookmaker's trust fund—to pay the debts of bookies who welched on punters who had laid wagers with them

Racing fever

Since Australia's first race meeting in Sydney in April 1810, horse racing has been a favourite pastime. In days when working hours were longer, leisure activities fewer, and travel more difficult, the local race meeting was a major social event.

Today, Australia has more racecourses and race meetings than any country in the world. Race clubs operate in every major city. Picnic races, long popular in country areas, now draw city people, too. The casual betting between neighbours at the early picnic races has grown into a profitable industry. In 1978-79 Australians bet more than $4300 million on horse racing, trotting and greyhound racing.

The year's richest—and greatest—race is the Melbourne Cup. In 1985 the prize money had risen to $1 million, the trophy is a $23,000 gold cup. On Cup Day, the first Tuesday in November, some 100,000 people flock to Flemington racecourse. The nation's business comes to a standstill as millions wait to hear the results of the big race. The Melbourne Cup is the only race day in the world to be declared a public holiday by a Parliament. During the last years of the Depression one Melbourne Cup-winner became a national idol that shone brightly through the gloom. It was Phar Lap, a wonder-horse that became a symbol of Australian achievement, even though he was born in New Zealand. When he died of accidental poisoning after winning his first big race in America, the Agua Caliente, in 1932, he had won 37 races from 52 starts, for total stake-money of £66,738 [$2,137,485]. His death was reported on the front pages of Australian newspapers, and people talked of it solemnly as a national tragedy. All the records he set, for races between 7 furlongs and 2¼ miles (.5km and 3.5km), have since been broken but the legend remains.

Jockey for a dog

In the 1930s a curious sport made a brief appearance on Sydney dog tracks—greyhounds ridden by monkeys. These animals raced at the Mascot track in 1938

Phar Lap, ridden by Jim Pike, wins the Melbourne Cup in 1930. No human being has been so triply honoured in death as this horse has. His 6.3 kg heart (twice the size of a normal horse's heart) is treasured in Canberra's Institute of Anatomy, his glossy skin is stuffed and preserved in the National Museum in Melbourne and his skeleton is in the national museum of his native New Zealand

Don Bradman

Australia's greatest batsman

When he went to England with the Australian touring team in 1930, the young batsman Don Bradman was already the idol of Australian schoolboys. In 1927, at the age of 19, he had scored a century in his first Sheffield Shield match, and in 1929 he had made 443 not out for New South Wales.

But the tour transformed him into a national hero as he ran up huge scores on English wickets. At Leeds he set a new world record test score of 334 runs, scoring 105 before lunch and 309 in the first day of his innings. At the end of the tour he had scored a total of 2960 runs in 36 innings.

Australians prepared to welcome their hero home. With true cricketing patience, more than 10,000 people stood at Melbourne's Essendon Airport waiting for Bradman's plane, which was two hours overdue.

In Sydney, three days later, there was a reception at the Town Hall and General Motors presented Bradman with a sports car. Until he moved to live in Adelaide a couple of years later, Sydneysiders could boast that they were 'three hours ahead of Melbourne—Our Harbour, Our Bridge and Our Bradman'.

When the South Africans played in Australia in 1931-32, Bradman made a century in every test he batted in, scoring 806 runs at an average of 201.35. His best score was 299 not out. The London *News Chronicle* made an interesting suggestion: 'As long as Australia has Bradman she will apparently be invincible ... In order to keep alive the competitive spirit, the Authorities might take a hint from billiards. It is almost time to request a legal limit on the number of runs Bradman should be permitted to make.'

For more than a decade Bradman was unquestionably the greatest living Australian. 'The boy from the bush'—he came from Bowral, NSW—took his honoured place in Madame Tussaud's waxworks in London

Bradman late in his cricket career, drawn by the great Australian slow bowler Arthur Mailey, who was also a journalist and caricaturist

Bradman in the 1930s. Between 1927 and 1948 he scored 117 centuries, including 37 scores of 200 or more, in first-class cricket

among kings, queens, archbishops and famous murderers. On the eve of World War II, in the selective pages of *Who's Who*, he rated 21 lines, 17 more than Josef Stalin.

The 1948 tour of England was a final triumph for Bradman, who lead Australia to win four of five tests. When he returned he made his last century at a testimonial match at the Melbourne Cricket Ground. He received a cheque for £9342 [$189,230], and on 1 January 1949, became Sir Donald Bradman.

Bradman cuts a ball through the slips. At the height of his career he was almost invincible. One admirer described him as 'the Phar Lap of cricket'. Seasoned sporting writers waxed lyrical about him, popular songs were written about him, and he was knighted for services to cricket

Batting against India at the Sydney Cricket Ground in 1947, Bradman plays the shot that completed his 100th century in first-class cricket

Test series that strained diplomatic relations

Since the first test match between Australia and England was played in 1877, after-dinner orators had acclaimed the noble game of cricket as a link of understanding between the two countries. But in 1932-33, when D. R. Jardine's MCC team toured Australia, the English 'bodyline' tactics started a crisis that seriously threatened English-Australian relations and nearly stopped the tour.

The term 'bodyline' was invented by an Australian cricketer turned writer, John Worrall. The English preferred the less provocative term 'fast leg-theory'. England's fast bowler, Harold Larwood wrote that the term 'bodyline' was 'maliciously coined by a cute Australian journalist for the express purpose of obscuring the issue, which it did with great success. This mere use of the word "body" was meant to damn me and damn me it did with great success ... The term being brief was very suitable for a sort of war-cry...'

Bodyline bowling consisted of directing fast, short-pitched balls at the leg stump with five or six fieldsmen grouped on the leg side close to the batsman. The ball rose sharply and flew around the batsman's head and shoulders, forcing him to defend his body as well as his wicket. This made him likely to pop a catch to one of the legside fielders.

These tactics were, of course, aimed at reducing Bradman's efficiency as a run-making machine. And an attack on Bradman in 1932 was an attack on the Australian nation.

Many Australian players received severe blows from England's fast bowlers. The Australian press echoed the indignation of the public. *Smith's Weekly*, custodian of Australia's honour on the cricket field as well as the battlefield, declared that England has 'sent a basher gang for the Ashes'. It accused Jardine of 'frightfulness'—a word associated with German atrocities in World War I—and published a blood-curdling Australian casualty list:

SYDNEY TEST: Fingleton—eight body blows; McCabe—four body blows; Ponsford—bruised arm, hand and thigh; Kippax—knocked on ribs, shoulder, leg and arm; Richardson—hurt hand. Bruises hip and thigh.

MELBOURNE TEST: Fingleton—three body bruises; Woodfull—blows to heart, hip, thigh, and chest.

ADELAIDE TEST: Woodfull—blows over heart; Ponsford—seven bruises; Oldfield—concussion; Richardson—thigh bruises.

Cyril Ritchard, appearing in *Our Miss Gibbs* at Her Majesty's Theatre, Sydney, brought the house down when he added an extra verse:

Now this new kind of cricket
Takes courage to stick it,
There's bruises and fractures galore.
After kissing their wives
And insuring their lives
Batsmen fearfully walk out to score.
With a prayer and a curse
They prepare for a hearse,
Undertakers look on with broad grins.
Oh, they'd be a lot calmer
In Ned Kelly's armour,
When Larwood the wrecker begins.

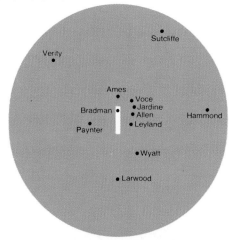

When the English fast bowler Larwood bowled to Bradman, this was his field. Five men clustered around the batsman, waiting for him to give a catch as he warded off a sharply rising ball

Australia's rage boiled over during the third test, at Adelaide, when W. A. Oldfield and the Australian captain, W. M. Woodfull, were both hurt. Woodfull was hit over the heart, and made his much-publicised remark to the Englishmen: 'There are two teams out there. One of them is playing cricket, the other is not.' During the match, the Australian Board of Control cabled the Marylebone Cricket Club: 'Bodyline bowling has assumed such proportions as to menace the best interest of the game, making protection of the body by the batsmen the main consideration. This is causing intensely bitter feeling between the players, as well as injury. In our opinion it is unsportsmanlike. Unless stopped at once it is likely to upset the friendly relations existing between Australia and England.'

The MCC replied chidingly that it deplored the cable, deprecated the suggestion of unsportsmanlike play, had every confidence in its captain, team and managers, and

D. R. Jardine, the English captain, speaks at a welcome to the MCC team in Sydney. Many Australians disliked his patrician manner off the field as well as his tactics on it

while it regretted the accidents to Woodfull and Oldfield, understood that the bowler was not to blame. However, if the Australian board considered the remainder of the programme should be cancelled, it would consent 'but with great reluctance'.

English newspapers offered varied comments. One said: 'Some things are not cricket. One of them is this undignified snivelling by a section of Australians because bowling tactics have defeated their Test batsmen.'

Diplomatic relations were strained up to the eve of the fourth test at Brisbane, but fortunately the trouble was smoothed out and the matches went on. England won the series by four matches to one. Bradman played in only four of the five tests and his scores were: 0 and 103 not out; 8 and 66; 76 and 24; 48 and 71. Larwood took 33 wickets in the series. After the series, a law was passed giving the umpire power to stop fast leg-theory bowling after he had once warned the bowler.

The NSW Northern Districts batsman Ray Robinson was injured when batting against the MCC at Newcastle in 1933. He dislodged a bail, but was given not out and carried off the field. The English players are, from left: Jack Hobbs, Wyatt, Voce, Chipperfield, Bowes and (obscured) Verity

Football fever

Aerial ping-pong and open-air wrestling

Australia is divided into seven states—and into four football codes, which are more divisive in the loyalties they inspire than are the boundaries between the states or the differences between their beers.

In New South Wales and Queensland the important game is rugby league, played on a semi-professional basis, with payment of top-grade players. Rugby league in New South Wales split away from the non-professional rugby union in 1907, and when top player 'Dally the Boot' Messenger defected to league he did so for the commercial lure of £150 [$7405] for three games. These days, a New South Wales league star is officially paid $100 to $150 for a losing game and about $200 to $500 for a win. A top player can expect to be signed on for about $40,000 with a guarantee of generous retirement benefits. Advertising and newspaper contracts, too, mean substantial rewards and a star can get as much as $50,000 a season. Rugby union, the original brand of rugby, which is entirely amateur, still comes a close second to league in New South Wales and Queensland. Then comes association football, or soccer, which has a big following on the New South Wales coalfields. It has been steadily increasing in popularity with the post-war influx of migrants from the United Kingdom and Europe.

'Up there, Cazaly!' was the cry of the followers of South Melbourne's rules team in the 1920s—and here is Roy Cazaly himself, showing how to mark one-handed. Cazaly, seen here in a match against Essendon in 1926, so popularised the game with his spectacular leaps that the yell of 'Up there, Cazaly!' is still heard today when a player is 'pulling one down'—that is, marking the ball. Marking is probably the most exciting feature of the Australian rules game

The makers of Capstan cigarettes enticed Australian rules fans in the 1900s with cards showing flags and guernseys of Victorian clubs. Australian rules developed from a game devised in Melbourne in 1858 to keep cricketers fit. The first interstate carnival was played in 1908; Victoria won

Australian rules—more a cult than a sport?

In Victoria, South Australia, Western Australia and Tasmania, the predominant game is Australian rules, which its impassioned followers call national football, or the Australian game. In Victoria particularly, Australian rules is more like a cult than a sport.

It seems likely that Australian rules first developed as a means for keeping cricketers fit. The first recorded game was played in August 1858, between Scotch College and Melbourne Grammar School. There were 40 boys to a side, the goalposts were half a mile apart, and the game lasted from noon until six in the evening. The match was to have lasted until one team scored two goals, but neither did. A round ball was used and the rules were apparently a combination of rugby, Gaelic football, soccer and anything else that came to mind.

As the game developed, it took many rules from Gaelic football, which is also a rough-and-tumble contact game. Some sociologists attribute the popularity of Australian rules to the considerable Irish strain in Australia's population. It has developed into a game of quick movement, long and accurate kicking and spectacular high-marking—that is leaping high into the air to catch the ball. Because of this, its critics (from other states) sometimes compare it sneeringly to ballet dancing, or dismiss it as 'aerial ping-pong'.

In the same way, rugby of either code is 'open-air wrestling' to Australian rules followers. But there is no question that Australian rules is a splendid, fast-scoring spectator sport, full of action.

The famous English international cricketer and soccer player, C. B. Fry, paid this tribute to it: 'The Australian game is easily the finest form of football ever invented—the most athletic to play and the most exciting to watch.'

Some of the teams have popular nicknames which testify to their toughness. Melbourne, once known as 'The Fuchsias', now has the more appropriate name of 'The Demons'; Richmond, whose home ground was once known as the Jungle, has become 'The Tigers', with a resonant battle-cry of 'Eat' em alive!'

Pilgrimages to Mecca

In 1912, when the population of Melbourne was less than 600,000, a record crowd of 54,463 saw Essendon defeat South Melbourne in the grand final, and *The Australian*, in a brilliant flash of journalese, described the Melbourne Cricket Ground as 'the Mecca of all League football pilgrims'. It has remained the Mecca of ever-growing pilgrimages. In 1956, a crowd of 115,902 paid to see Melbourne defeat Collingwood in the grand final and, according to officials, at least 2000 broke in without paying, while 25,000 frustrated fans were locked out. Melbourne's population was then just over 1,500,000.

From the opening of the season, Australian rules is front-page news in Melbourne. Football writers and TV commentators are influential and revered men. 'At the very heart of Melbourne's popular culture, sport means Australian rules football,' writes the Victorian poet Chris Wallace-Crabbe in his

Portrait of Melbourne. 'Footy, is, after the weather, the universal subject for small talk and every little girl or boy that's born . . . becomes a supporter of one of the twelve league clubs. About 150,000 fans pour to the six matches every Saturday with coloured rosettes, ribbons and scarves, miniature team sweaters for the kids, binoculars and campstools, bottles and thermoses . . . the barracking is wittily colloquial and dislike of the umpire is universal . . . In various spirits, the spectators trail home and Melbourne prepares to endure another Sunday and then to bustle through another week before next Saturday's matches. And so life goes on.'

Every cult requires a folk-hero, and Australian rules adopted the South Melbourne high-marker, Roy Cazaly, whose prodigious leaps were greeted by an equally prodigious roar of 'Up there, Cazaly!' The exhortation has passed into the language; Australian infantrymen of World War II yelled it as they made bayonet charges.

Australian rules fever even infected a white cockatoo, which barracked vociferously for Carlton during the 1930 season. Standing on its owner's shoulders behind the goalposts, the bird acclaimed every Carlton goal with flapping wings and uncouth squawks.

Flying high: Australian rules players for the VFL club of Footscray. This team's nickname, 'The Bulldogs', is typically aggressive. The game can be very tough; a former boxing champion, Ambrose Palmer, once said that no fight ever left him as sore as did a hard game of Australian rules

Roman gladiators cast in bronze? No, these heroes are Sydney rugby league stars Norm Provan (left) and Arthur Summons after a big mud-match in 1963

How Wallabies turned into Kangaroos

In 1907, Alec Burdon broke his arm playing rugby union for the Sydney club. He got no compensation from the club for time lost at work, or for medical expenses. Consequently, a group of footballers voted to quit the union and start a professional game.

The first season of Australian rugby league football was played in 1908, and at the end of the season a league team called the Kangaroos went to England. The Australian rugby union players, the Wallabies, happened to be touring England at the same time.

After their return to Australia, the Kangaroos and Wallabies met for three matches played under league rules. The Wallabies won, but union triumph was short-lived—most of the team switched to league. The defecting players were followed by their fans and attendance at union matches shrank. In 1910 the Rugby Union tried unsuccessfully to regain support by staging an international tournament involving a New Zealand Maori team, a combined team from two American universities and local sides. League made further gains in players and public support when the Rugby Union suspended competition matches during World War I.

Flying low: Tom Radonikus of Sydney's Western Suburbs rugby league team. Rugby league is the most popular football game in New South Wales and Queensland; but the biggest crowd for a league grand final in Sydney is 78,000, while an Australian rules grand final in Melbourne has drawn 122,000

Boxing

The big fight of 1908

A blow for women's lib was struck, more than half a century before the movement was born, when Charmain London took her seat beside her husband, the famous American writer Jack London, in the front row of the Sydney Stadium on Boxing Day 1908. She was there to see a white Canadian, Tommy Burns, and a black American, Jack Johnson, fight to the finish for the heavyweight boxing championship of the world.

'No lady has ever been admitted to an important fight in Australia before,' reported the Melbourne *Argus*, 'but when it was known that Mrs London was going, half-a-dozen other ladies were present in different parts of the stadium. One wore a boxer hat, probably to appear as much like a man as possible in the cinematograph pictures.'

Jack London was at the fight because the *Argus* had commissioned him to write a special article about it. He had interrupted a Pacific cruise in his 45-foot yacht *Snark* to spend six months in Australia, suffering from an obscure skin malady.

Pieman turned entrepreneur

The fight was promoted by Hugh D. McIntosh, a soldier of fortune who had conducted a boxing academy in North Sydney, and claimed to be middleweight champion of New South Wales. Before this he had had a variety of occupations from miner to chorus boy, from bread carter to pieman.

In 1908, he bought a Chinese vegetable garden at Rushcutters Bay in Sydney and built one of the world's biggest open-air boxing arenas. There, in August 1908, Burns successfully defended his title for the third time against the New South Wales heavyweight, Bill Squires. Johnson then challenged Burns, who at first refused to fight a black man. But McIntosh, with an enormous offer of £6000 [$278,820]—win, lose or draw—overcame his racial objections. Johnson was to get the lesser reward of £1500 [$69,705].

The fight was publicised on an unprecedented scale and aroused unprecedented interest, not only in Sydney, but throughout Australia and the world. 'People in Sydney set out before six in the morning by the hundreds,' reported the *Argus*. 'Long before the fight it was difficult to reach the Stadium. Cabs were at a premium. Trams were overflowing. The old omnibuses were out, with three, and four horses, charging exorbitant fares.' Among those in the more expensive seats were the Federal Attorney-General, Billy Hughes, and a former Labor Prime Minister, J. C. Watson.

Tommy Burns was 15 centimetres shorter than Johnson, and weighed just over 76 kilograms, to Johnson's 87 kilograms. He had no chance against the heavier opponent, and took terrible punishment before the fight was stopped in the 14th round, not by the referee—McIntosh—but by the police.

The *Argus*, like *The Sydney Morning Herald*, devoted a whole broadsheet page to its own correspondents' reports, as well as two columns to Jack London's special story. 'When Johnson smiled, a dazzling flash of

Twenty thousand people packed the huge open air stadium at Rushcutters Bay in Sydney to see Canadian boxer Tommy Burns mercilessly beaten by the black American, Jack Johnson. Thousands, unable to get in, gathered outside, some climbing telegraph poles or standing on the roofs of omnibuses or trams

gold teeth filled the wide aperture between his lips, and he smiled all the time,' wrote London. 'The fight? The word is a misnomer. There was no fight. No Armenian massacre would compare with the hopeless slaughter that took place . . . Burns never landed a blow . . . A golden smile tells the story, and the golden smile was Johnson's.

'The fight, if fight it can be called, was like unto that between a colossus and a toy automaton, and had all the seeming of a playful Ethiopian at loggerheads with a small

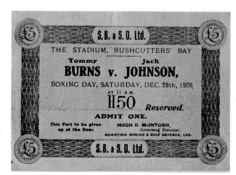

Tickets for the fight were at a premium. Hundreds of people who had bought £1 and 10s unreserved tickets were unable to obtain admission

and futile white man, of a grown man cuffing a naughty child, of a monologue by one Johnson who made a noise with his fists like a lullaby, tucking one Burns into his little crib in sleepy hollow, of a funeral with Burns for the late deceased and Johnson for the undertaker, grave-digger and sexton. There was never so one-sided a world championship fight in the history of the ring.'

The prevailing attitudes of the time were reflected in London's report, despite the fact that he was a fellow countryman of the challenger. 'Personally, I was with Burns all the way,' he wrote. 'He is a white man, and so am I. Naturally, I wanted to see a white man win.'

Norman and Lionel Lindsay, who had known McIntosh in Melbourne, were both given free tickets for the fight. A few days before it took place, Norman Lindsay called on McIntosh and noticed on his desk a piece of music rolled round a length of lead pipe. There had been a dispute between McIntosh and Johnson over the choice of a referee, and McIntosh explained the purpose of the pipe. 'It's for that big black bastard if he ever comes any funny business with me,' he said. The title of the music was *Sing Me to Sleep, Mother*.

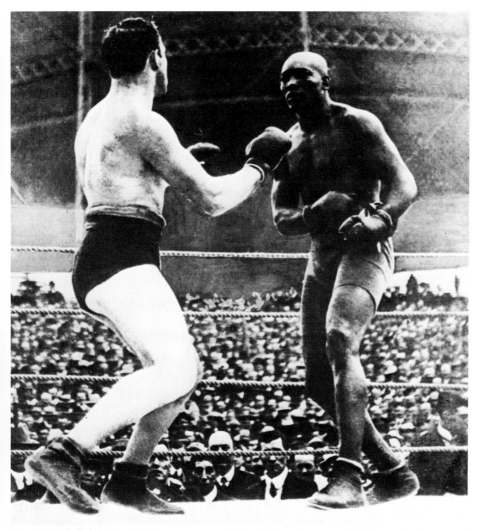

It was immediately obvious that Burns was no match for his heavier opponent. Johnson played a cat and mouse game, offering such pleasantries as 'Come on now, Tommy. Jewel won't know you when she gets you back from this fight.' Burns replied less good humouredly with 'You cur!' or 'You big dog!'

Burns took a terrible beating before police had to eventually stop the fight. The referee and organiser of the contest was Hugh D. McIntosh, widely known for his amazing schemes as 'Huge Deal' McIntosh. McIntosh 'borrowed' the timber to build the stadium with the promise that he would return it afterwards

Les Darcy at the height of his career, in 1916, when he was regarded as probably the greatest middleweight boxer in the world. He never gained the official title of world champion

Australia's greatest boxer?

James Leslie Darcy, perhaps the world's greatest middleweight, was born in East Maitland, N.S.W., in 1895, the second of 11 children. His parents were poor, and Darcy went to work as a child. He spent his spare time boxing with local boys, and had his first professional bout at West Maitland in 1911. Darcy moved to Sydney and his first appearance at the Stadium, in July 1914, was the biggest event since the Burns-Johnson fight in 1908. He fought Fritz Holland, one of America's most skilled boxers, and lost on points after 20 rounds. The decision was angrily and loudly contested by Darcy's followers, who tried to burn the Stadium down.

In 1916, Darcy met many well-known Americans, and defeated them all. 'This boy Darcy is the real middleweight champion of the world,' wrote Snowy Baker, after Darcy had twice outpointed the American champion Jimmy Clabby. During 1916, Darcy lost only one out of 23 fights.

Darcy enlisted in the AIF during World War I, but his mother had him discharged because he was a minor. In 1917 he was invited to fight in the United States, and in defiance of the War Precautions Act, which forbade people from leaving the country without permission, he sailed to New York. Darcy never fought in America because of rumours that he was dodging war service. He joined the US Flying Corps, but his health broke down and on 24 May 1917, at the age of 21, he died from septicaemia and pneumonia.

Darcy's body was brought back to Sydney, where a sinister legend arose that he had been poisoned by wicked Americans. But it was an American, the undefeated heavyweight champion Gene Tunney, who paid Darcy the most eloquent tribute: 'Les met and defeated all the best middleweights at a time when the greatest galaxy of middleweights the world has ever known was in existence,' he said. 'Les was the greatest boxer that ever fought.'

Competing on water

Yachtsmen of the inland and the coast

Australia is not only a motorised country. It is also a nation of sailors. One person in three is estimated to participate regularly in some sort of boating, from the tycoon's luxury ocean cruiser to the schoolboy's 2.5 metre dinghy. In 1983, Australians were spending some $600 million on boating and a vigorous industry had developed to meet this rapidly growing demand.

The explanation of the popularity of boating is simple. Every Australian capital city is either on a navigable river, a harbour or a bay. Nearly 90 per cent of all Australians live in coastal cities. Few are more than 50 kilometres from a boatshed or marina. And the climate makes it possible for sailing to be enjoyed for most of the year.

But sailing is not confined to those who live near the coast. Irrigation canals and huge dams have produced a breed of inland sailors. Rice farmers on the Ord River in the far north-west of Western Australia disport in shallow-draught ski-boats and graziers in western New South Wales drive for hundreds of miles to compete in 16-foot (4.8 metre) sailing dinghy races on the giant Burrendong Dam, which is bigger than Sydney Harbour.

The nursery (or kindergarten) for thousands of young Australian sailors was the VJ (Vaucluse Junior), a small unsinkable plywood sailing boat designed by Charles Sparrow, a Sydney naval architect, in 1932. It was 3.5 m long, and 33 cm deep, with a 1.3 m steel keel. The first VJ cost about £13 [$415]. By 1952, more than 6000 had been built, many by young amateurs.

The start of the interstate sailing championships on Sydney Harbour in January 1910. The ferries carried punters and bookmakers

It is often asserted that Australians will bet on anything. That claim is lent support by the crowds of eager punters who pack Sydney ferries every weekend to bet illegally on the racing 18-foot yachts.

The first 18-footers (5.5 metres) were seen on Sydney Harbour in the 1890s. They were vastly different from the modern 18-footer—a light, 1.8 m beam boat carrying about 150 m² of sail and crewed by three men. Running before the wind, they can average about 26 km/h. The first 18-footers were much heavier and slower—they probably averaged about 12 km/h—in spite of the fact that they carried nearly twice as much sail. They carried 16-man crews—earning them the scornful nickname of 'troop ships'—to counterbalance the power of the sails.

This 18-footer, *Vera*, seen here running down Sydney Harbour before a stiff breeze in 1907, carried a 12-man crew and a good deal of sail

Somewhere beneath this vast area of sail—probably about 280 m² of it—is a 22 ft (6.5 m) boat. The weight of heavy japara sails, large crews, solid wooden spars, hundreds of metres of natural fibre rope and steel centreboard so slowed the yachts that they could only travel at about 11 km/h—less than half the speed of their modern counterparts. Yachts that capsized during a race, a not uncommon occurrence, were disqualified

Australians are sculling champions of the world

On 30 July 1904 a crowd of about 90,000 people, nearly 20 per cent of Sydney's population, lined the banks of the Paramatta River to watch two Australians—John Towns and Richard Tressider—battle for the title of sculling champion of the world.

This was only the second time that the championships had been held on the Parramatta River. Edward Trickett raced on the Thames in England in 1876, when he became the first Australian to win the title. Sculling was then a popular sport so that when Trickett returned from the race a crowd of 25,000 people packed Circular Quay in Sydney to give him a hero's welcome. His fans even took up a public subscription and gave him £850 [$48,000] to buy his own hotel. Trickett lost the title four years later to a Canadian who was so superior that he stopped several times to wave to watching friends.

The 1904 contest was almost as uneven a match. George Towns, the reigning champion, won the race and £1000 [$51,520] by a margin of 20 lengths over the 5 kilometre course. The *Sydney Mail* reported that Tressider had 'proved quite a disappointment for his friends and . . . was quite outclassed'. The *Mail* then went on to consider the profits to be made by wily entrepreneurs: 'The steamers which followed the race were very full, particularly the *Cobar*, that being the 5s [$13] boat. The *Kirribilli* was well filled at 10s [$26] a ticket and there were about 200 people on the *Bronzewing*, tickets for which were £1 [$52]. The amount of money taken was about £560 [$28,850] and the total expenses are about £50 [$2575].' The rowing world celebrated the contest for days. Twelve days later, when the Sydney Rowing Club held its first annual ball in Baumann's New Rooms, the ballroom, according to the *Sydney Morning Herald*, 'was artistically decorated with a profusion of flags, a charming effect being produced by skilful arrangement of oars'.

Part of the 90,000-strong crowd that lined the banks of the Parramatta River from Putney to Henley to watch two Australians compete for the world sculling championship in July 1904. Some spectators paid £1 [$52] to watch the race from the deck of one of the ferries

Members of a Tasmanian rowing club, eccentrically costumed by modern standards, pose outside their ramshackle clubhouse before World War I. The Derwent River at Hobart was the scene of the first regatta ever held in Australia—in January 1827

Australian champions

Australia and New Zealand join forces to win the Davis Cup

The Davis Cup was first contested in 1900, but it was not until 1907 that Australia took part in the competition, and then it was in partnership with New Zealand.

The Australasian team consisted of only two men—Norman Brookes, a Victorian, and Anthony Wilding, a New Zealander. Both men had to pay their own fares to England for the contest, but they must have thought their money well spent for not only did they win the Davis Cup, but Brookes won the Wimbledon singles, doubles and mixed doubles as well.

On their return the *Australasian Star* re-ported with satisfaction that: 'America held the cup for some years, and it is to be expected that Australasia will hold it for many years to come. Our riflemen are to bring back the King's [Cup], and Towns [George Towns] still sits on the world's rowing champion-ships. Soon there will be nothing left for the sports of the old land.'

The next year, the winners were hosts and two Americans—Fred Alexander and Beals Wright—came to Melbourne to play Brookes and Wilding in a challenge round that left Australian tennis fans breathless.

Wilding, in his book *On the Court and Off*, recalls the last of three days of desperately hard tennis, fought in temperatures over 37.8 °C, with characteristic calm: 'I was called upon to play the deciding match against Alexander, but he appeared to be more overawed by the importance of the oc-casion than I was. Thus Australia won the most exciting Davis Cup contest ever held, or I should think ever likely to be held for many a long day.'

Australia won by three matches to two. Both Brookes and Wilding lost to Wright and won against Alexander. Australia won the doubles three sets to two.

Norman Brookes—poker-faced as always when on the court—looks on while A. W. Dunlop returns the ball during the 1912 Davis Cup final in Melbourne.

Australasia lost the cup to Britain that year. Brookes always played in a grey tweed cap and con-tinued to use a flat-topped racket long after the

newer styles became available. His unusual style of play and uncanny anticipation earned him the nick-name of 'The Wizard'

Percy Cerutty—trainer of champions

In 1939, a doctor told 44-year-old Percy Cerutty that his health was so bad that he would never work again. Cerutty refused to accept his doctor's verdict and embarked on a plan of intensive mental and physical train-ing of his own invention. Seven years later he was fit enough to set a Victorian record for the 26 miles (42 kilometres) of the mara-thon. When he was 55 he became the third Australian ever to run 100 miles (161 kilo-metres) in less than 24 hours—he ran 101 miles (162.5 kilometres), the extra one for good measure, in 23 hours 45 minutes.

In 1947 Cerutty set up a training camp for athletes at Portsea near Melbourne. His fol-lowers ran for miles on heavy sand, in knee-deep surf and up 'Cerutty's hell dune', a sandhill 24 metres high with a grade of 3 in 1, Cerutty himself leading the way. All of the inmates of the camp were on a vegetarian diet, were not allowed to eat salt, smoke or drink alcohol. Many of his followers were in-spired and goaded to spectacular success. In

one year John Landy reduced his time for a mile (1.6 kilometres) from 4 min. 14.6 sec. to 4 min. 2.1 sec. It seemed that Landy would be the first man to run a mile in 4 minutes, but he was beaten to it by Roger Bannister in 1954. Landy himself ran the 4-minute mile 46 days after Bannister.

Herb Elliott, a Western Australian who had come to Cerutty in 1957 at the age of 19 as a self-confessed 'lazy', won the 1500 metres at the 1960 Rome Olympic Games by the widest margin in the history of the race, and within a period of two years ran the mile in less than 4 minutes 17 times. Dave Stephens and Dave Power became two of the world's best six-milers. Eleven world records were set by ath-letes that Cerutty trained. At the 1958 Em-pire Games in Cardiff runners whom he had trained or influenced won every event from the 880 yards (805 metres) to the marathon.

Sixty-nine year old Percy Cerutty chases Herb Elliott up 'Cerutty's hell dune'—a 24 m sand dune at the Portsea Training Camp

A champion who ran out of opponents

The top of one of the graves in the Melbourne Cemetery is a marble billiard table, complete with pockets, and on it are a bronze billiard cue and three billiard balls of bronze. This unique memorial is that of Walter Lindrum, unbeaten world champion billiards player for 26 years, and holder on his retirement in 1950 of 57 world records.

Walter Lindrum, who came from a family of brilliant billiards players, was so good that the billiards authorities changed the rules of the game to try to even up the chances of his opponents. This was after his devastating win over the reigning world champion, Joe Davis, in England in 1932. On that occasion Lindrum broke his own world record with a score of 4137. Davis' best break was only 1247.

The Melbourne *Herald's* London correspondent reported that when Lindrum played his record-breaking shot a 'great roar of applause' broke out, and 'cooees and shouts of "Good old Walter", such as might have been heard in a crowded stadium . . .'

Lindrum's score included 15 sequences of nursery cannons. Very few players in the history of billiards have perfected this difficult shot. The authorities decided to limit the use of nursery cannons, in order to curb Lindrum. The attempt was unsuccessful. In his first game under the new rules, the champion made a score of 3905.

From the mid-1930s a Lindrum match became virtually a Lindrum exhibition—he had run out of opponents. In a game of 1000 in 1940, for example, he made an unfinished break of 1002 at his first turn at the table; his opponent did not even score.

Later in his life, however, Lindrum spent much of his time playing matches in aid of charities, and he is said to have raised some millions of dollars at these exhibitions.

This marble billiard table marks the grave of Walter Lindrum, whose skill at billiards was so great that it ruined his career—the public grew tired of watching him win overwhelmingly. Below, Lindrum plays a shot in an Australian competition in 1929—the year before he took England by storm

The versatile Snowy Baker

All-round sportsman who became a film star

Australia has produced no more versatile athlete than Reginald Leslie ('Snowy') Baker, who distinguished himself in 26 different sports, from swimming to tent-pegging, from boxing to polo. He also became a successful actor in Australian and American films.

Baker was born in Darlinghurst, Sydney, in 1884, and attended the Crown Street Public School, where he won school running championships as well as 18 prizes for other sports. At Sydney University, where he studied engineering, he was awarded blues for cricket, football, rowing and athletics. In 1904, he played rugby union for New South Wales against England. In 1905, he became amateur middleweight boxing champion of Australasia, and the following year, in one night, defeated the middleweight champion of New South Wales and the heavyweight champion of Victoria.

A draughtsman with the Colonial Sugar Company in private life, Baker also found time to row with championship crews, to play international polo, and to do a bit of rifle shooting. 'He is a fairly good rifle shot,' said a writer in *The Lone Hand* 'and altogether a handy man in the event of a foe descending on our peaceful shores.'

Hero on horseback

Baker was always a keen horseman, and served with the New South Wales Lancers for seven years. In military tournaments he won 20 first and five second prizes for wrestling on horseback, tent-pegging, rescue races and tourneys with sword and bayonet.

In 1908, representing Australia at the London Olympic Games, he lost the middleweight championship on points in a controversial fight with J.W.H.T. ('Johnny Won't Hit Today') Douglas, the famous English cricketer. The judges gave a vote each to Baker and Douglas, but the referee, who was Douglas' father, gave the title to his son. Baker accepted the decision sportingly.

A few days later, when he and Douglas were dining at the National Sporting Club, they were persuaded to remove their dinner jackets and have a return bout. Fighting bare knuckle, Baker knocked Douglas out.

Baker gave demonstrations of diving, water-polo, boxing and military athletics in many parts of the United Kingdom, and was equally active on the Continent, setting swimming records in Denmark, winning water-polo matches in Finland and Holland, and giving exhibitions of diving, boxing and wrestling in Sweden and Germany.

Return to Australia

When he returned to Australia, he opened a physical culture school in Sydney. He published a physical culture monthly, *Snowy Baker's Magazine*, and a book on fitness.

In 1912, he bought the Sydney Stadium from Hugh D. McIntosh, and next year called a conference of fighters, trainers, managers and rubbers, to establish championship conditions and rules to govern Australian boxing, including the standardization for all divisions, from flyweight (51 kg) to heavy-

Snowy Baker flexes his muscles to demonstrate the benefits to be gained by attending his recently opened physical culture school in Sydney. In 1912, when this photograph was taken, Baker was a national hero as a result of his prowess at boxing, wrestling, swimming, athletics, football and many other sports

weight (unlimited). This, the first conference of its kind ever held in Australia, brought the Commonwealth into line with Great Britain. The new weights were later adopted in America and are now universally accepted.

Then in 1918 the rugged, blond idol of the sporting public made his debut as a film star in *The Enemy Within* produced by E. J. Carroll. Baker played the role of Jack Airlie, Australian special agent, who foils the stratagems of the Kaiser's spies in Australia. 'He performs stunts which other actors can only fake,' said the publicity. 'See his terrific fight against four men, his 24 metre dive into the harbour, his leap from the flying cars.'

The film, described as 'The Mighty Australian Superfeature', was directed by Raymond Longford, and the leading lady was an

American, Lily Molloy. It did not lack action. In the opening sequence, Baker discovers Miss Molloy, drugged and tied to a wave-lashed rock by the German villains. As he clambers down the cliff on a rope to rescue her, they open fire on him. One shot cuts the rope, and he falls to a ledge 24 m above the water, from which he dives to her aid.

In his second film, *The Lure of the Bush*, made the same year, Baker knocks out the bully of the shearing sheds, rides a wild buck-jumper and wins the beautiful heroine, Rita Tress, herself 'a dashing horsewoman, and as pretty as a picture'.

Baker then decided to go into film production. He engaged an American director and actor, Wilfred Lucas, who had made a very successful thriller, *Tarzan of the Apes*, and

E. J. Carroll
Presents
"The JACKEROO of COOLABONG"
"The Jackeroo arrives... eyeglass and all"

In his fifth Australian movie, *The Jackeroo of Coolabong* (1920), Baker played the part of a posh monocled Englishman who had come to learn the ropes on an outback station. Baker, second from left, looks so tough that it is hard to believe one of the Australians called the Englishman 'dear'. At right is Charles Chauvel, then about 19, who later became a successful film director. The cast also included Arthur Tauchert, star of *The Sentimental Bloke*. E. J. Carroll, who made the film in partnership with Baker, was a pioneer film exhibitor

Astride a galloping horse, Snowy Baker drags a couple of villains from their horses in *The Man from Kangaroo*. Here he lifts the evil pair clear of the ground, one gripped by each mighty hand, as his horse thunders along. *The Man from Kangaroo* was the first of three movies Baker made in 1920 in partnership with E. J. Carroll. All were directed by Wilfred Lucas, an American who specialised in action pictures. He provided plenty of opportunities for Baker to show off his talents as horseman, swimmer, diver, wrestler, boxer and all-round athlete, ready to try anything

in partnership with E. J. Carroll, took over a 28-roomed house, *Palmerstone*, in Waverley, Sydney, as a studio. The house was set in two hectares of grounds, with gardens and lakes.

Parson and bushranger
The Carroll-Baker company made three films in 1920. In the first, *The Man from Kangaroo*, Baker played the part of a fighting parson. The film, some of which was shot on location in the Kangaroo Valley and Gunnedah, NSW, was a great success. It was followed by *The Shadow of Lightning Ridge*, in which Baker as a mysterious bushranger terrorises the countryside on his big grey steed, Boomerang. There is a spectacular scene in which Baker jumps from Boomerang's back to a moving train. 'See the terrific all-in fight with 15

powerful men,' said the advertisements. 'And the leap on horseback through the roof of a hut to 40 feet [12 metres] below.' The third film, the last he made in Australia, was *The Jackeroo of Coolabong*, in which Baker was a Piccadilly swell, complete with monocle, who arrives at a rough outback station. According to the publicity, 'the fun started when someone called him "dear".'

In August 1920, Baker left for Hollywood, where he soon starred in he-man films. His first American picture was *His Last Ride*, in which a horse called Boomerang appeared.

He was followed to America by Charles Chauvel, who as a young man had attended Baker's physical culture school and had worked for him as a stable hand. To publicise one of his Hollywood films, Baker gave a dis-

play of whipcracking on a Californian variety circuit, and Chauvel had the job of standing to attention while Baker flicked a lighted cigarette from his lips with a stockwhip.

From film-acting, Baker in 1923 moved to the management of the Riviera Polo Club in Santa Monica, California, where he instructed wealthy Americans in horsemanship, polo and boomerang-throwing. He taught Rudolf Valentino horse-riding tricks for *The Sheik*, and Douglas Fairbanks how to crack whips in *Son of Zorro*. One of his closest friends was the comedian Harold Lloyd. He was still playing polo at the age of 59, when he led a Californian team.

He lived in America until his death in 1953, visiting Australia only once, in 1952. But he never became an American citizen.

The lure of speed

Motor sports were early favourites

Australians were quick to see that the motor car offered opportunities for competition. Hill-climbs, rallies, reliability trials and inter-city record-breaking all soon attracted large followings, but it was racing that provided the thrills and drew the big crowds. Probably the first motor race in Australia was held at the Maribyrnong gymkhana in Victoria in 1903.

Racing tracks were built at Phillip Island, Victoria, and Penrith, NSW, in the early 1920s but these had cinder or dirt surfaces that limited speeds to about 96 km/h. Then in the mid-1920s two high-speed concrete tracks were opened—one at Olympia Park in Melbourne in 1924 and the other at Maroubra in Sydney in 1925—and for the first time Australians could drive their powerful imported racing cars to the limit.

Rallies like this one at Aspendale, Victoria, in 1904 were often organised so that proud owners could show off their latest acquisitions. There was no race—the cars drove around the track and went home—but cars were still something of a novelty so a small crowd gathered to watch

A short life for Sydney's killer race track

The track at Maroubra was a smooth concrete dish 1.5km in circumference, with high banking which enabled the cars to take corners at top speed—often up to 160 km/h. Many of the famous racing cars of the day such as Bugattis, Alvises, Sunbeams, Jewetts and Italas were raced at the track by equally famous—but now forgotten—drivers including Charlie East, Phil Garlick, Fred Barlow, Hope Bartlett and Don Harkness.

Opening of Maroubra

The first meeting at Maroubra was held on 5 December 1925 and drew an enormous crowd of 72,000 spectators. On the following Monday morning a reporter in *The Sydney Morning Herald* described the scene: 'A low, beautiful, slim machine screams down the track, shedding a mist of petrol smoke.

'Banking steeply you see it, like a toy motor, far across the course, then its exhaust grows to a thunderous staccato, and you realise that it is bearing down towards you.

'For a moment you see a muffled driver crouched over his wheel and a mechanic leaning out far to balance the turn.

'Your exclamation is obliterated by the roar of the engine, the whirr of beaded tyres on the concrete track, and that terrible clatter of the cut out (a device for by-passing the silencer), and before you realise it has entered the straight the machine is whirling up the steep bank on the far side as tiny as a toy again.'

Despite this stirring spectacle, the crowd at the opening meeting remained strangely silent, and the *Herald's* writer speculated on the reason: 'When a horse or a man races and one goes to the front the audience always watches in tense fearful expectation for the moment when he shall begin to tire, to fail, but these superlatively powerful cars never tire, never fail. After three or four laps one can tell just exactly how, barring accidents, the race will end.'

High-speed death

But accidents happened frequently at Maroubra, and it rapidly acquired the reputation of being a killer track. Within a week of the opening a Jewett racing car flew over the top of the banking at 128 km/h, with its driver and mechanic inside. Both men were killed. In the next two years many men were killed, including the well-known drivers Phil Garlick and Fred Barlow.

After the death of Garlick in January 1927 *The Sydney Morning Herald* seemed to have lost much of its enthusiasm for motor racing. An editorial denounced this 'reckless waste of human life' and declared: 'The fatal accident which occurred at the Maroubra Speedway on Saturday night last must shock the community into insisting upon some restrictions upon a sport whose short annals in Sydney are already too deeply blackened with tragedy for its continuance under present conditions to be regarded with equanimity.'

But in the end restrictions were not necessary. Attendance at the track fell off because of its bad reputation, and many drivers refused to take part in races there. By the end of 1927 the track was closed—less than two years after its triumphant opening. Today nothing remains of the Olympia Speedway; the area is now occupied by Housing Commission homes.

Phil Garlick in an Alvis (left) and Hope Bartlett in a Bugatti battle for the lead in this under-1500 cc race held at Maroubra in 1926. Cars like these used to lap the track at 145 to 160 km/h

This race at Aspendale in 1923 was organised by the importers of Itala cars to demonstrate their performance. The contest was declared a draw

A rousing cheer for Bill Conoulty after he won the 350 cc championship at Penrith, NSW, in 1925 on his Douglas motor-cycle. Motor-cycle racing—especially speedway, which was invented in Australia—was as popular as car racing in the 1920s and 1930s. The opening of the Speedway Royale in Sydney was one of the reasons why spectators deserted the Maroubra speedway. They found skilful racing on a small dirt track more entertaining than the spectacle of sheer speed

A German NSU racing car at high speed. The mechanic is crouched low in his seat to reduce wind resistance. Part of his job during a race was to keep the engine oil pressure up by laboriously working a hand pump in the cockpit. He also had to lean out to balance the car on corners

Chasing records

Racing against the clock

On 1 December 1929 a sleek, gold-painted car flashed along the sands of Seven Mile Beach on the New South Wales south coast. At the wheel, setting a new Australasian land speed record, was Norman 'Wizard' Smith. He was an extraordinary driver who took part in hundreds of hill-climbs, inter-city record attempts and reliability trials during the 1920s and 1930s, and won most of them. Smith's car for the 1929 record attempt, the *Anzac*, was powered by a 20-litre, 268 kW aeroplane engine and had a top speed estimated at 273 km/h. Smith hoped to break the Australasian mile (1.6 km) record of 175 km/h and the world ten-mile (16 km) record of 209 km/h. The world land speed record was held at that time by Henry Seagrave with 371 km/h.

Curiously enough, Smith's record attempt —in an Australian built car—attracted little attention. A paragraph in *The Sydney Morning Herald* recorded that: 'Mr Norman Smith . . . stated that according to the engine revolution counter he had done a speed for a brief period of 130 mph [209 km/h] without extending the engine. In the course of his fastest run however he struck one of the sand ridges caused by a storm the day before and the car leapt and bounced in a thrilling way, indicating what might be expected with a serious attempt at record breaking . . . Yesterday the opportunity of improved conditions on the beach was seized to make an attempt which proved so successful that the Australasian record was lowered by more than 19 mph [30 km/h] the speed averaged for the mile being 128.5714 mph [206.9156 km/h].'

Despite the new record—which was to stand for 27 years—Smith decided that the car was capable of even higher speeds, and in January 1930 he took the car to Ninety-Mile Beach in New Zealand in search of a better track. Then, despite a shower of rain during the critical high-speed run, Smith raised the world ten-mile (16 kilometres) record to 239.208 km/h. His top speed during these attempts was 258 km/h.

In 1964 Donald Campbell became the first man to establish both land and water speed records in the same year—both in Australia. On 17 July 1964 he sped across the dry bed of Lake Eyre in South Australia (below) to establish a land speed record of 648 km/h. Five months later, with only hours before the year ended, he broke the water speed record on Lake Dumbleyung in Western Australia with an average speed of 444.71 km/h

The *Anzac*, with 'Wizard' Smith at the wheel, speeds down Ninety-Mile Beach in New Zealand in January 1930 to establish a new Australasian ten-mile (16 kilometre) record of 239 km/h. Sharp toheroa shells cut the car's tyres to pieces, and it was feared that they would cause punctures during the high-speed run

Around Australia the hard way

Between 1953 and 1955 the Redex Company organised three round-Australia car trials that attracted enormous interest throughout Australia and around the world. The cars had to average a specified speed between towns, and they lost points for late or early arrival. Points were also lost if parts were missing from the cars. The last of these trials, in 1955, covered 16,900 kilometres over some of the worst roads in Australia. Of the 176 cars that started, only 63 crossed the finishing line 21 days later—many almost wrecked by the terrible roads in the outback.

'Gelignite' Jack Murray—nicknamed for his habit of carrying the explosive for clearing obstructions—took part in all the trials, and won the 1954 event. Twenty years later he recalled the weeks of preparation for these trials, and some of the unexpected hazards of outback motoring:

'When you had carried out all the mechanical modifications you would say that the car was ready. Then you would sit down in front of it, until you thought of something else and then you would pull it to bits and start again ... This would go on and on until you could just touch the car and it would start.'

'You didn't know what was going to happen to you, so you couldn't carry too many spares. The Darwin highway is 900 miles [1448 kilometres] long, and you don't go through anywhere on it. In order to save weight my navigator cut the handle off his toothbrush and cut the bristles down so that there were only four tufts left at the end ... It's marvellous what you can cut out when you have to.'

'The Cloncurry to Mt Isa road was the worst road that I have ever driven on in the world. The first 20 miles [32 kilometres] from Cloncurry was a good gravel road, but then

suddenly the road dips down and rises up again steeply. If you are going over 40 mph [64 km/h] your bumper bar digs straight into the other side. There are three of these dips, and all the warning you got was a shadow in your headlights, and then it was too late.

'You rely a lot on following the car in front, but if he goes wrong, so do you. We got on to a clay pan one night—it was about 15 miles [24 kilometres] round and hard and smooth like glass. There were cars everywhere, and nobody knew where anybody was going. We spent an hour there driving round and round until we found the right track.

'At one stage we were in one of the remotest parts of Australia when we came to a creek crossing and saw a car parked by the side of the road with three ladies having a picnic. We stopped and asked them what they were doing and they said they had driven 350 miles [563 kilometres] from a nearby station to watch the trials cars go by. But generally when you saw a crowd of locals you would know that they had gathered at a spot where they thought you might crash. So when you saw a crowd you would slow down, put your hand out and wave a finger. "I'm awake," you'd say, and they would all cheer and laugh.

'Australians—especially if they have been up in the bush—compromise and use imagination to keep the car going. For example, what do you do when you get water into your petrol? Water and petrol won't mix, and water won't burn. So you pour methylated spirits into your tank—meths and water will mix and still burn, and meths and petrol will also mix. If your radiator leaks, a mixture of mustard and fresh egg will block up the hole.'

Bad roads like this were the downfall of nearly two-thirds of the cars that entered the 17,000 kilometre Redex round-Australia trial in 1955

World champion who builds his own cars

In 1949 a writer in *Australian Motor Sport*, previewing a forthcoming speedway race, summed up by saying: 'It is generally considered that young Jack Brabham, who has drawn number one position, will be a hard man to beat.' It was a prophetic statement that might well have applied to the rest of Brabham's motor racing career.

Brabham started racing in midget speedway cars when he was 21, and in 1949 he had won the Australian, New South Wales and South Australian championships. In 1951 he left speedway for 'proper' racing cars and soon established himself as an outstanding driver. He was placed sixth in the New Zealand International Grand Prix in 1954 and by 1959 he was world champion.

Much of Brabham's success in motor racing can be attributed to his meticulous planning. In order to reduce the weight of his car to the minimum he even calculated the exact amount of fuel necessary to win the race. This trick nearly cost him the 1959 world championship when he ran out of fuel on the last lap of the final race. He pushed the car about 182 m over the line. Brabham later won the world championship twice more.

In this home-made car Jack Brabham became Australian speedway champion in 1948. Seventeen years later, also in a car he made himself, he won his third world Grand Prix championship

Record-breaking swimmers

The Cavills—royal family of swimming

The history of swimming in Australia is in part the history of the remarkable Cavill family. The dynasty begins with 'Professor' Fred Cavill, born in London in 1839, who took up swimming after serving in the Royal Navy. A London newspaper, reporting in 1876 that Cavill had won three Royal Humane Society medals for saving life at sea, described him as 'one of Sir Charles Napier's sea-dogs who . . . bears the stamp of a noble specimen of British sailor'. It is uncertain when he left the navy, but in 1862, he won the swimming championship of England over 500 yards (457 m). In the early 1870s, he opened baths in London and taught many distinguished people to swim, including Princess Mary of Teck, the future Queen Mary.

In 1877, in a second attempt, he swam the Channel from Dover to Calais in a little over 12 hours. Two years later, he migrated to Australia with his large family, and took over baths at Lavender Bay, Sydney. These were resumed when the North Shore railway was being built, and Cavill made a brief return visit to England.

Defying the sharks

On the return voyage he leaped into the sea off Cape Town to rescue a woman passenger who had tried to drown herself. A contemporary account of the exploit said that Mr Cavill, who was on deck, stripped to the trousers and 'telling the female passengers to turn their heads away, the noble fellow threw off his remaining garment and shot overboard on his fearfully dangerous mission'. The danger included a school of sharks which had followed the ship for days. This noble and decorous act earned Cavill his fourth Royal Humane Society award. The Professor also had the honour of posing for a statue of the future King Edward VII, Cavill's body being combined with the Prince of Wales' head.

Professor Cavill's natatorium

Back in Sydney, Cavill opened an elegant 'natatorium' in Farm Cove, Sydney, by the Botanic Gardens. The natatorium, which became one of the sights of the town, was an open-slatted baths supported by iron buoyancy tanks. The dressing cubicles were equipped with mirrors, brushes and combs. The Professor advertised his natatorium in verse:

Come everyone, each mother's son and
*   every bonnie daughter*
And learn to swim with sturdy limb and
*   sport amid the water.*
For should you wish to swim like fish,
*   you have not far to travel,*
To Farm Cove go and soon you'll know the
*   famous teacher Cavill.*
His bath secure, the water pure, no fear
*   of monsters finny,*
For Cavill's there—his charge is fair
*   He'll teach you for a guinea.*

In 1909, a gale swept away the natatorium and deposited it on a beach across the Harbour, some miles away, but the Professor lived on till 1927, watching his sons distinguish themselves as swimmers.

The eldest, Ernest, at the age of 15 won the New South Wales championship. The second son, Charles, went to the United States and was the first man to swim the Golden Gate, San Francisco. He was killed by poisonous gas in baths in Stockton, California, in 1897, while demonstrating underwater endurance.

Champion swimmer's disappearance

The third son, Percy, won the 440 yards (402 m) and five miles (8 kilometres) championships of the world in 1897. He went to the United States in 1900 as a swimming coach, and disappeared from the headlines until 1930, when the Australian flier Mrs Keith Miller was forced down on the island of Andros, in the Bahamas. 'I thought I was on a cannibal island,' she said. The only white residents were the Commissioner, his wife, a priest and 'a fellow Australian, Percy Cavill, who at one time had been the champion swimmer of the world.' Before his death in 1940 at the age of 65, Cavill was still swimming up to five miles (8 kilometres) from one part of the island to another.

The fourth son, Arthur Roland Cavill (nicknamed 'Tums', because as a child he chewed his thumbs), was born on the night of his father's second attempt on the Channel. At 18, he won the 500 and 1000 yards (457 and 914 m) amateur championships of New South Wales; at 20 was awarded a Royal Humane Society medal for saving a man's life in Sydney Harbour; and at 21 was the professional 220 yards (200 metres) champion of Australia. 'Tums' went to the United States in 1901, and like his brother Charles, swam the Golden Gate. He coached many great swimmers, and introduced the Australian crawl to Americans. He died in 1914, frozen to death, after swimming across Seattle Harbour in cold weather.

'Tums' Cavill is credited with the invention of the crawl. According to family records, this arose from a challenge match in Sydney when he agreed to swim with his feet loosely tied, allowing them slight freedom, and using arm and body movements.

Development of the crawl

That was in 1898. Next year, his 15-year-old brother Richard Theophilus (Dick), the Professor's sixth son, experimenting with the new style, developed an independent leg thrash. (The universal stroke of the period was the trudgeon, or double over-arm with scissor kick.) Using this leg movement, Dick in 1899 won the 100 yards (91 metres) New South Wales championship. The word 'crawl' was first used by a competitor who, finishing behind him, said: 'I won't have Cavill crawling over me.'

Dick Cavill was certainly the greatest swimmer of his time, perhaps of all time. He was virtually unbeatable. Using the crawl stroke, he was the first man in the world to swim 100 yards (91 metres) in less than a minute. His time was 58.6 seconds. He won every championship from 100 yards to one mile, both in New South Wales and national events. After swimming in England and coaching in New Zealand and the United

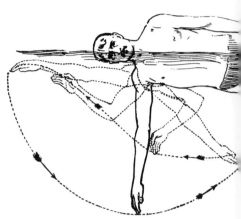

Sidestroke was one of the laborious strokes in general use before the crawl was invented. The invention is generally credited to 'Tums' Cavill

States, he returned to Australia in 1913, and joined Wirth's Circus.

The fifth son, Sydney St Leonards Cavill was the amateur 220 yards (200 metres) champion of Australia at the age of 16. He too went to the United States as a swimming teacher. In California, he invented the butterfly, or double over-arm stroke, which enabled breaststroke swimmers to cut times almost as greatly as the crawl had cut times for over-arm swimmers.

Madeleine, one of Cavill's several daughters, was also a notable swimmer, and, true to the family tradition, received a Royal Humane Society medal for bravery.

Frank Beaurepaire toured Europe in 1910 and raced against swimmers from many countries over distances from 100 yards (91 metres) to a mile (1.6 km). He won all 48 races. He had won three events in the Australian Championships at Perth in 1908, when he was 17. He reached Perth from Melbourne, despite low funds, by donning short pants and a schoolboy's cap and travelling at half-fare on the steamship. Beaurepaire represented Australia at the Olympic Games in 1908, 1920 and 1924

She ate a banana under water

The Melbourne Aquarium, in an annexe of the Exhibition Building, was a curious 19th century pleasure-palace, offering a variety of unusual diversions. The most popular was the aquarium itself, with its hundreds of live marine creatures, from long-tailed Chinese carp to stately sea-horses. There were also acrobatic seals that leapt high in the air for their fish lunch; a maze in which you could easily lose yourself; a musty dimly-lit chamber of Egyptian mummies and mummy-cases; a gallery of moralistic Victorian paintings; plaster casts of naked Greek goddesses; a cool fernery; haughty peacocks; an aviary; ingenious slot-machines; and a museum.

To these delights was added, in 1903, the exciting spectacle of a lissome young lady in a bathing-suit 'fearlessly gambolling', as Melbourne *Punch* put it, in a tank 'among various types of fishes and eels'. *Punch* predicted she would become the rage of the town. And she did, especially when she added to her gambols the remarkable feat of peeling and eating a banana under water. This accomplished performer was a girl named Annette Kellerman, who was born in Sydney in 1887 and took up swimming therapeutically at 'Professor' Cavill's natatorium after her legs had been weakened by poliomyelitis.

From the age of 15, she set a number of sprint and distance records in New South Wales and Victoria. And in 1905, when she swam 4 miles (6 km) in the Upper Yarra in 1 hour 48 minutes, she was described as 'The Champion Lady Swimmer in Australia'.

The next year her father took her to Europe and she won a 23-mile (37 km) race in the Danube in 13 hours 11 minutes, and set several endurance records in other rivers. In the third of three unsuccessful attempts to swim the Channel the hard way—from Dover to Calais—Annette Kellerman was in the water for 10½ hours.

In the summer of 1905, a London *Daily Mail* photographer followed her round the English south coast resorts, but she was photographed either fully clothed, or with only her head visible. The reason, apparently, was that she wore a one-piece bathing suit at a time when women took to the water only when swathed in a concealing multiplicity of garments. More than any other woman, she was responsible for the introduction of the one-piece bathing suit.

'Women of advanced thought who have the well-being of the rising generation of girls at heart have done much, very much, in encouraging girls in bathing and swimming by establishing societies and clubs for the instruction of these arts,' reported *Weigall's Journal of Fashion* in December 1905. 'Miss Annette Kellerman, the clever young girl swimmer and diver, has assisted by her example. Thus at the present time there are almost as many girls as boys who cultivate these arts now in our state [Victoria].'

Annette Kellerman went to America in 1909 to give swimming and diving displays. Within a few years she had become a film star and a physical culture expert. In 1912, when she was running a fashionable physical culture school in New York, she contributed quite a number of articles on health and fitness to *Snowy Baker's Magazine*.

Advanced views on diet

Her views were well ahead of her time. For example, slender women who wanted to put on weight were advised to eat scientifically, and not to stuff themselves like 'a silly goose'. 'Vegetables are especially good for everyone ...' she wrote. 'The spring vegetables have a real medicinal effect, and salads are splendid for you, lettuce, tomatoes, watercress, celery, onions, etc., with a dressing of lemon juice and olive oil. When you can have things like that, who in the world wants to eat foods with hot and highly seasoned dressings and heavy greasy pastries?'

'I avoid the use of white bread and substitute whole wheat bread, brown bread and corn bread. I use all the olive oil I can on my salads and green vegetables. I like meat broths, oyster soup, broiled fresh fish, poultry or game, oatmeal, hominy, boiled onions, brussels sprouts, cauliflower, potatoes, asparagus, peas, string beans, stewed prunes, figs, baked apples with cream, all kinds of fruit, the desserts I have mentioned, cocoa, new cider, orange juice, unfermented grape juice. All alcoholic liquors are tabooed.' Billed as 'the perfect woman', in 1917 she starred in a spectacular million-dollar film.

In this costume Annette Kellerman performed sensational high dives in Melbourne in 1903 in a spectacle entitled 'The Breaking of the Drought'. She was one of the first women to wear a one-piece bathing costume and she inspired others to follow her example. In later years she appeared in a silent movie wearing no costume at all. She starred in two silent films and was the subject of *Million-Dollar Mermaid*. Made in 1952, this film starred Esther Williams as Annette Kellerman

Ilsa and John Konrads astonished the Australian public in the 1950s with a succession of world records. Both set their first world records when they were only 15—John in 1956 and his sister in 1958. Born in Latvia, they came to Australia in 1949 and learned to swim at a migrant camp at Uranquinty, NSW. They were pioneers in training by lifting weights and swimming for hours on end

Andrew (Boy) Charlton broke world records and won Olympic medals for Australia but he never swam in the Australian championships. At 17, he won the 1500 metres freestyle, breaking the world record, at the 1924 Olympic Games in Paris. In Amsterdam in 1928 he won silver medals in the 400 and 1500 metres. He represented Australia again at the 1932 games but was unplaced. His modest willingness to do surf patrols when at the height of his fame brought him national popularity

The battle of the beaches

Gocher bounds in for a daytime bathe

'Prior to 1900 one "bathed in the open sea",' says the 1963 *Australian Encyclopaedia*. 'In 1901, one "bathed in the surf" or "went surfing".

'By 1905, the verb, "to surf" was in common use. Half a century later, it could reasonably be claimed that after a summer weekend, a million people might say, "I surfed".'

The emancipation of the surfer was a slow process. Way back in 1833, the New South Wales Government passed an act prohibiting bathing in Sydney Cove or Darling Harbour between 6 a.m. and 8 p.m. Five years later, a more repressive act banned bathing 'near or within view of any public wharf, quay, bridge, street, road or other public resort within the limits of any of the towns . . . between the hours of six o'clock in the morning and eight in the evening'. In Melbourne, where the Yarra River had become a favoured place for bathing, a similar act passed in 1841 forbade bathing close to the town between 6 a.m. and 8 p.m.

By the turn of the century, bathers on Sydney beaches were frequently defying the law, which had changed little since the 1830s. At Manly, where the time-limit had been extended to 7.30 a.m., a man armed with a big dinner-bell gave the signal for all to leave the water.

Local authorities were not pleased by this outbreak of sea-bathing, which, as C. Bede Maxwell puts it in her history of surfing, they regarded 'much as they would have regarded an outbreak of scarlet fever or smallpox'. Manly imposed a £2 [$101] fine for bathing during prohibited periods, and you could be fined up to £10 [$505] if your costume did not enshroud you neck to knee. But it was at Manly, in 1902, that a historic blow was struck for the freedom of the beaches. The hero of this battle against bumbledom was Mr William Gocher, the 43-year-old proprietor and editor of the local paper, *Manly and North Sydney News*.

On 1 October 1902, Gocher boldly announced in his paper that at midday next day—Sunday—he would challenge the law by 'bounding in for a bathe', and gave the police every opportunity to arrest him. He bounded in but nothing happened.

'No posse of police came flying down with drawn batons to the water's edge to yell out to me to come out and be arrested,' said Gocher. 'There was no mighty concourse of citizens to cheer me as I came shooting in on No. 4 breaker, breathing salt spray and defiance. Outside my few bosom pals . . . the passing pedestrians took but a tired interest in my plunge for public liberty . . .'

On the following Tuesday, the Manly Council met. When the Mayor declared firmly that he would not tolerate all-day bathing, only one alderman dissented. Undeterred, Mr Gocher twice repeated his defiant plunge, and even reported his public law-breaking to the New South Wales Inspector-General of Police, Edmund Fosberry. But the police took no action, and almost a year later, on 2 November 1903, the Manly Council quietly rescinded its forgotten by-law. All-day bathing was now legal, provided everyone over the age of eight years wore a neck-to-knee costume.

William Gocher, a newspaper owner described by a contemporary as 'a little shrivelled-up sort of a cove', was Australia's first surfing hero

Gocher was made a vice-president of the Manly Lifesaving Club, and later given a watch inscribed: *Presented with a purse of fifty sovereigns [$2470] to W.H. Gocher Esq., Pioneer of all-day surf bathing, by his Manly friends, February 11th 1907. Entered the water 2nd October, 1902.*

Gocher died on 18 August 1925. No monument has yet been erected in Manly to commemorate his epochal victory.

These exuberant surfers at Manly in 1906 owed their freedom to bathe by day to the heroic William Gocher. He defied a by-law against daytime bathing and in 1903 the Manly Council rescinded it. But attention was soon excited by the brief V-trunks worn by some day-time bathers, and in 1907, the **Mayors of Manly, Randwick and Waverley joined forces to rule that all costumes must extend from neck to knee and have a skirt**

Nakedness at Bondi shocks the mayor

With all-day bathing permitted, crowds flocked to Manly's beaches. 'The immense popularity which surf-bathing has assumed at Sydney's chief watering-place has caused during the past two years a "Manly boom",' reported the *Sydney Mail* in February 1905. The latest development was evening bathing, and each morning the council erected a temporary canvas enclosure for ladies to dress in, and removed it discreetly after the morning rush slackened.

But the battle of the bathing costume had yet to be won. In 1907, Mr R. G. Watkins, Mayor of Waverley, an eastern Sydney suburb, received complaints about the costumes worn, or not worn, on the beach at Bondi, in his municipality. Alderman Houston, for example, said he could no longer take his daughters for a walk by the sea. 'The recumbent nakedness is too indecent,' said the alderman. And morality apart, it reduced the value of property. Accompanied by his town clerk, Mr Watkins boldly inspected the recumbent nakedness and was appropriately shocked. 'What we saw was . . . disgusting!' he told the *Sydney Daily Telegraph*. And he elaborated: 'Some of these surf-bathers are nothing but exhibitionists, putting on V trunks and exposing themselves, twisted into all shapes on the sand. Their garments after contact with the water show up the figure too prominently. Women are often worse than the men, putting on light gauzy material that clings when wet too much to be decent. But they won't continue it at Bondi Beach, not so long as I am Mayor Watkins!'

'A costume that seems graceful to one generation seems disgraceful or outrageous to the next, as witness the crinoline,' commented the *Daily Telegraph*. 'And the sufficiency or otherwise of a dress designed to be worn in public is not likely to be decided for all time either now or at any later period.' It expressed the hope that 'no Draconian ordinances on the subject of voluminous attire would be promulgated . . .'

Skirting the problem

The paper's hopes were not realised. Mayor Watkins conferred with the Mayor of Manly, Mr J. Learmonth, and the Mayor of Randwick, Mr J. C. McDougall, and the three custodians of seaside decency issued a stern combined directive. Henceforth, all bathers, male and female alike, were to wear skirts! The required costume was to be 'a combination of a guernsey with sleeves reaching to the elbow, and trouser legs reaching to the bend of the knees together with a skirt covering the figure below the hips'. 'A suitable decoration would be red tape along the seams,' suggested the *Sydney Mail*.

Bathers were further warned that 'no persons shall continue bathing in public swimming baths for a greater period than half-an-hour', nor should '"sun-bathing", *i.e.* loitering on the beach' be indulged in 'except within a special enclosure (if any) set apart by the council for such purpose'.

And: 'No person shall while in bathing costume, mix with the general public who are not bathing, unless such person wears over the bathing costume, an overcoat, macintosh, or other sufficient wrapper or clothes.'

A fine of up to £10 [$494] could be imposed for any breach of these edicts. A correspondent signing himself 'Another Injustice to Ireland' wrote to the *Daily Telegraph*: 'As a self-respecting Irishman my feelings were outraged by the edict that I must wear skirts when I go into the surf. What will I be at all—a Highlander in kilts, or a serio-comic Aphrodite in the foam? Neither is to my taste.'

Another wrote: 'To compel sensible men to dress in a pantomime dress, half-skirt, half-petticoat, is an insult to twentieth century civilization'; and another asked: 'If a member of the Life Saving Brigade took off his skirt to go and rescue someone, would he be liable to a fine of £10?'

'Skirts are as much out of place in the water as tights would be at church, or bell-toppers amongst the players of a football-match,' commented the *Daily Telegraph*.

Surfers in petticoats

'In all civilized countries the sexes dress differently,' said Mr A. W. Relph, honorary secretary of the Manly Surf Club. 'If custom is to be revolutionised and a man forced to wear women's wear merely because he is bathing, our beaches will become a laughing stock. Men who cannot afford such an expensive costume as is planned will bathe in their sister's petticoats, regardless of colour or type . . . To be logical, these mayors should also introduce an ordinance enforcing skirts to be worn in the streets by men, and abolishing evening dress among women.'

Mr Relph suggested as an alternative the new Canadian costume, consisting of a pair of knickers reaching half-way to the knees, and a sleeveless guernsey, reaching halfway down the thighs outside the knickers.

While Sydney newspapers carried columns of protesting letters, surfers on two beaches organised a picturesque demonstration. At Bondi, they marched in madcap procession, some wearing their sisters' flounced and embroidered petticoats, others in grandmotherly red flannels, or frothy ballet skirts or sarongs made from kitchen curtains. Some of the skirted marchers had train-bearers. The procession was led by a man holding a dead sea-gull on a flagpole, the symbolism of which was not clear. A similar charade was enacted at Manly, where surfers paraded in a variety of grotesque garbs: poke-bonnet and shawl, a doormat tied round the waist, a diaphanous trailing red skirt. A band accompanied them as they sang *Hang Mayor Learmonth on a Sour Apple Tree*.

Routing Mrs Grundy

Sydney newspapers reported these fashion parades sympathetically. Under the heading 'The Fiasco in Skirts', the *Sydney Mail* denounced 'the absurdities of official prudes'.

'Mrs Grundy has been ignominiously routed, and we may be quite sure we will hear no more of skirts . . . The neck-to-knee costume meets all requirements, even when its

What the mayors wanted

Public derision swept away the 1907 decree that men must wear long-skirted bathing costumes, but the man on the left was wearing one as late as 1914, when he was photographed at Avoca, NSW

occupants are lying down on the sand . . . Health and happiness for many thousands are considerations too important to be played with by stodgy individuals who have got beyond the age of enjoyment,' it said.

The reaction of the three 'official prudes', Messrs Watkins, Learmonth and McDougall, was not recorded, but their repressive edicts were swept away in a great gale of popular laughter. The Canadian costume became standard wear on Australian beaches.

These surfers, resting on the steps of a bathing machine, are wearing the Canadian costume which was standard for men and women for many years

The beach cult grows

Sunbathing, the 'new form of idleness'

While the inhabitants of Sydney to the north were learning to body-surf and gaining freedom to bathe during the day, things were different in Melbourne. In January 1908, when Melbourne was limp under a heatwave with temperatures up to 44°C, the suffering citizens could find relief only in paddling.

'Prudery flies to the winds with advent of the hot spell,' wrote 'Clio', a woman columnist in Melbourne's *Punch*. 'Down at South Melbourne on the hot nights I saw dozens of the "very nicest people" sensibly paddling about in the water with skirts and frillies

In 1906, *The Bulletin* showed readers in other states the perils and pleasures of mixed bathing; in Victoria at the time, it was still forbidden

kilted up to well above the knee, and their shoes and stockings under their arm or "planted" on shore. Paddling is an adorable pastime.' 'Clio' deplored the fact that 'mixed bathing' was impossible in Melbourne; she blamed the 'moral atmosphere', and the absence of surf. 'But,' she asked, 'why should there not be plenty of mixed paddling?'

Queer things at Black Rock

'Clio' reported on a curious happening at Black Rock, a seaside suburb on Port Phillip: 'Queer things arrive by the sad sea waves on hot nights,' she wrote. 'Down at the Red Bluff, a man and a girl made for the water's edge, the girl puffing a cigarette vigorously. After a moment's hesitation, she slipped off her shoes and stockings, tucked up her petticoats, etc., and waded into the sea, much to the admiration of the mere men in the vicinity, who shouted out, "Ain't they bonzer", and "What boshter legs" . . . I too became interested while she moved up and down, while the man carried dainty shoes and stockings. "How would she dry herself" was the thing that puzzled me. Out she came, and sitting on the sand, she lifted a dainty leg. The man drew out a silk handkerchief and flicked it delicately, as one does old china. The divinity opened her lips, and we all listened for a caressing, beautiful voice. What we heard (in strident tones) was "Ain't yer got a Cambrich 'andkerchief? Silk don't take the sand off".'

Not safe for girls

'Why, oh why, are we still so morbidly, prudishly modest that mixed surf bathing is virtually unknown?' asked another writer in *Punch* in December 1908. 'Surf bathing—breaker shooting as it is called in Sydney—is not safe for girls by themselves. It is essentially a mixed sport, unless a girl happens to be very

'Paddling,' said Melbourne's *Punch* in 1908, 'is an adorable pastime.' The camera caught these Launceston ladies wading as early as 1901, when showing the calf was still considered shocking and bathing was not permitted during the day

adept . . . It is time Victorians threw off this yoke of foolish sedateness they have worn so long . . . In Sydney, it is not fashionable to have a pink and white complexion. The admired skin is the brown, healthy surf-bather's skin, and the browner it is the better.'

In 1910, *The Lone Hand*, a Sydney monthly magazine, published an article on 'Australia's Amphibians' by Egbert T. Russell, who wrote: 'The surf-shooter, born in Sydney, has spread round the whole map of Australia: and in New South Wales, Queensland and Western Australia has become an institution as important to Australia as standing armies, established churches, music halls and sturdy beggars are in older civilisations.' He noted that 'one of the strangest features of Sydney surf-bathing to the stranger who hails from Presbyterian Victoria . . . is the casualness of the sexes on the beaches. They are partially naked but so unashamed as not to notice the fact.'

Shooting the breakers with body and board

Before the art of body surfing came to be understood in Australia, so-called 'surfers' merely swam about or bobbed up and down in the waves. The sport of shooting the breakers was introduced to Australia in the 1880s by a South Sea Islands boy called Tommy Tanna, a gardener in the township of Manly. Tommy was from one of many islands in the New Hebrides from which, between 1863 and 1904, thousands of Kanakas were bribed—or kidnapped—to work long hours on Queensland plantations.

Tommy Tanna astonished the bathers at Manly with his skill in swimming out through the breakers and then allowing the waves to propel him shorewards, while he whooped with delight. One 17-year-old Manly boy, Freddie Williams, was particularly fascinated. Tanna taught Williams how to throw himself, shoulders hunched and head lowered, along the path of a wave, and ride it to the beach.

Freddie Williams passed on what he had learnt to other local boys. Slowly he and his companions learned which waves to choose and when to start swimming before the wave so as to be carried along in its rush like a human torpedo, rather than be 'dumped' in its trough and half drowned in the turbulent water.

Soon the surf at Manly was full of enthusiastic youngsters, and surfing began to spread up

and down the coast. The first surf life-saving club began at Bondi in 1906, though Manly and nearby Freshwater remained the main centres, and it was at Freshwater that the photograph at right was taken in 1915. It shows Freddie Williams (left with moustache), who was still a champion surf-shooter, with Duke Kahanamoku, the Hawaiian who introduced surf-board riding and its excitements to Australia.

A world-champion swimmer, Duke Kahanamoku was invited to come to Australia in 1915 to swim in Australian competitions. When he arrived, he was surprised to find no boardriders at the beaches, for surfboard riding was already popular in California, where it had been introduced from Hawaii seven years earlier. The Duke therefore bought himself a length of sugar pine, carved out his own board, and gave a dazzling display on it, astonishing the crowd which soon gathered on Freshwater beach.

When the Duke left Australia he presented his board to 15-year-old Claude West from Manly. West soon became the country's leading board rider, holding the championship for 10 years. The Duke's board still stands as a memorial in the Freshwater Surf Club today.

Surfboard riding has grown enormously in popularity in recent years. It now has more participants than any other sport in Australia

'Presbyterian Victoria' for the most part remained obdurate. On some of its beaches, bathing was banned altogether; on others, it was permitted only if the sexes were strictly segregated, men on one side of a division, women and children on the other. Mixed bathing was allowed on part of the beach at Port Campbell, perhaps because it was 258 kilometres from Melbourne, but in January 1911, Councillor Scudds reported an alarming situation at the bayside suburb of Moorabbin. In defiance of a stern by-law, men and women were bathing together. The matter was so serious and of such concern to decent people, declared the Councillor, that he would be pleased to use the horsewhip.

The horror of mixed bathing

Councillor Scudd's horror at the thought of men and women plunging into the water together was echoed by the Reverend T. Adamson at the Methodist conference in Melbourne in 1912. 'No modest man can be associated with mixed bathing and no man who respects the opposite sex could take part in it,' he declared. But that year, South Melbourne allowed mixed bathing on their beaches any day except Sunday. Next, 'sun bathing' came under attack in Melbourne.

The *Argus*, which had campaigned for mixed bathing, described this new practice of lolling on the sand, imported from wicked Sydney of course, as a new form of idleness ('almost fanaticism') which should be strictly forbidden. Some councils obligingly passed by-laws forbidding it, and did not repeal them for 30 years.

Getting the necessary tint

On Sydney beaches, 'sunbathing' had become an accepted corollary of surf-bathing. 'There is only one thing that jars the harmony of the beaches,' wrote Egbert T. Russell. 'That is the advent of a newcomer whose horrible white arms and legs seem to indicate that he is first brother to the gruesome insects found when you turn up a stone. The average healthy man or woman looks horribly unhealthy and degenerate when their white limbs appear side by side with those which have acquired the rich brown tint of the sun.' Though the shooter represented the aristocracy of the beaches, the ordinary bather could 'rise to full rights of citizenship by lying in the sun until he acquires the necessary brown tint'.

On 26 December 1917, only about five years after mixed bathing was first officially permitted on Victoria's beaches, Melbourne *Punch* carried this photograph of women lifesavers. It was taken at Half Moon Bay, near Black Rock, an outer bayside

The first life-savers

In 1906, three Bondi surfers, Lyster Ormsby, Percy Flynn and Sid Fullwood, formed the Bondi Surf Bathers Life-Saving Club, and conceived the plan of having a rescue line on a portable reel which could be moved quickly to any part of the beach in an emergency. Ormsby worked out this idea with a cotton reel, a couple of hair pins, and a rough plan on the back of a cigarette pack.

The reel which resulted, and came to be copied all over the world, was first demonstrated on Bondi Beach on 23 December 1906. Eleven days later it was used to rescue two small boys. One, when he recovered his speech, gave his name as Charles Smith, of Yates Street, North Sydney. He grew up to be one of the world's greatest fliers, Sir Charles Kingsford Smith; many years after he had been saved from the sea in Sydney, he disappeared into the sea while on a flight from England in 1935.

suburb of Melbourne—which is not a surf beach. There are women lifesavers at many still-water beaches around Australia, but women have seldom qualified as surf life-savers because they are not considered to be strong enough swimmers

Although very few women ever qualified as surf life-savers, they often took part in surf carnivals—the first were seen at Bondi in 1910. This trio paraded in Western Australia in the 1930s

In 1909, when the Bondi Surf Life-Saving Club team was photographed in this march-past in a carnival at Manly, surf clubs were attracting young men to all the main beaches around Sydney. Then, as now, the life-savers were all volunteers; their surf-rescue methods are copied world-wide

Players in petticoats

Women rid themselves of cumbersome costumes

By the early 1900s, women had abandoned the languors of croquet for the greater excitement of lawn tennis, cycling and cricket, and were moving into other sports previously regarded as exclusively male preserves—swimming, netball (or basketball), rowing and athletics. But they were slow to distinguish themselves in any of these fields except swimming. One reason was the limitations imposed on them by cumbersome 'lady-like' costumes. It was many years before women achieved emancipation in sportswear, even for swimming. When Australia's Fanny Durack won the 100-metres freestyle at the 1912 Stockholm Olympic Games in the world record time of 1 minute 10.8 seconds, she had to wear a long towelling robe to the starting block; she did not remove it until a signal seconds before the start, when she was revealed in black woollen bathers,

high at the neck and reaching to her knees.

When women tennis players in the first decade of the Commonwealth were hobbling across the courts in dark blue serge skirts, flannel shirts and sailor hats, they were advised to have 'the cleanest and prettiest of white underskirts, as these show when running for a stroke far more than one can imagine'.

Duck-footed tennis players

There were gradual changes, but in 1908 'Clio', a woman columnist on Melbourne's *Punch*, complained that clothes then worn by women tennis players were uncomfortable and unattractive. 'It is a pity that someone cannot think of a picturesque dressing for women who play tennis,' she wrote. 'The short washing skirt looks so ungraceful while the duck-footed appearance of the tennis shoe adds to

the awkward appearance of the skirt. The ordinary blouse, too, is quite unsuited for a strenuous game of tennis. It wriggles out of the belt, and wrinkles and gathers up under the arms.' The 'flop hat' tied down over the ears and under the chin was hot and inelegant, 'Clio' added. She hoped that with the increased popularity of tennis there would come new and more attractive methods of dressing.

Her hopes were realised. From the days of shapeless dresses, women's tennis outfits have grown progressively briefer, with a gay interlude when frilly pants became the rage.

When women's rowing started in Melbourne in 1901, the approved costume was a sailor-style jacket over a long-sleeved blouse, long black bloomers, black stockings, lace-up boots and hats tied on with scarves. Now women rowers wear very short stretch shorts.

In the late 1890s, the pneumatic-tyred, chain-driven safety bicycle came on the market, and women took to cycling. A few bold pioneers, like the girl in black in the centre here, appeared in 'rational dress'— breeches and a shorter or divided skirt. The majority of women cyclists, however, stuck to their conventional long skirts, like the rest of this decorously behatted group of South Australians with their one male escort

Costumes like these must have been a handicap, but golf was an established sport for women by the turn of the century. The first Australian women's championship was held in 1894. These golfers were photographed at Gundagai, apparently playing on a makeshift course

Hitting the ball was only one of the skills required by a woman tennis player in 1905; she also had to be able to control her petticoats and hat

When Australian all-rounder Betty Wilson scored a century and took seven wickets for seven runs in the test against England in Melbourne in 1958, her outfit included cream gaberdine culottes and a broad-brimmed white hat. Except that skirts are now much shorter, the style has not changed much

Beautiful batswomen

Women cricketers at the turn of the century wore ankle-length skirts with black boots peeping from under layers of petticoats, ruffled blouses with puffed sleeves, straw hats and men's ties. They had no pads, relying on the barrier of petticoats to protect their shins. (This practice, however, was condemned by one cricket writer as bad form.)

By the 1930s, skirts had crept up to the calf. The first women's cricket tests between Australia and England were played at Brisbane in December 1934 and Sydney and Melbourne in January 1935. A crowd of 300 gathered to watch the first day's play in Brisbane. Under a heading of 'No Powder-Puffs at Play', the Brisbane *Courier-Mail* commented poetically: 'The two umpires seemed quite lonely among so many bright young ladies who tripped like sylphs across the brilliant green oval . . . If the girls lacked the strength of men players, the spectators found compensation in their graceful bearing and willowy movements. Figures flying across the green after the ball, as if swept by a stiff breeze, denoted great resilience, and the upright poses of the fair ones knocked out all the unpleasant arguments associated with "bodyline" . . .' The English girls, it was also noted, 'resembled Grecian statues'.

In a more down-to-earth tone, the reporter continued: 'But why worry about clothes and slim figures? The girls were intent only on playing the game. Sceptical fellows who went out expecting to see a better display of powder puffs and legs than batting found no such silliness in evidence, and some of them growled because the girls had left high heels, mirrors, lipsticks "and all that" in the dressing room.'

A cricket team from Launceston, Tasmania, in 1906. A newspaper commented that these women had attained 'more than ordinary feminine pro-ficiency in batting and bowling', but it is a wonder, considering the restrictive clothing they wore. Even in 1934, when the first women's test was held in Brisbane, the *Courier-Mail* noted how the Australian players' more conservative skirts fettered their 'fast career of leg'

Discovering the snowfields

Australians were pioneers of skiing as a sport

Australia has imported most of its sports, but in skiing it was a pioneer. Skiing in Australia has a longer history than Switzerland. As far back as the 1830s, fur-trappers in Tasmania were using a ski made of local timber and shaped like a snowshoe, and in 1855, when alluvial gold was found in the Australian Alps at snowbound Kiandra, NSW, 1310 m above sea level, Scandinavian miners got around by strapping fence-palings to their boots. These primitive skis were known as butter-pats. Later the miners made skis of more orthodox patterns from the local mountain ash.

Skiing began in Switzerland—whose total area is smaller than the area of the seasonal snowfields of Victoria—in the mid-1890s, but it was already an established sport at Kiandra by 1862. The ski club at Kiandra, formed in 1878 as the Kiandra Snow Shoe Club, is one of the oldest in the world. Among its early members were 'Banjo' Paterson and the Sydney photographer Charles Kerry, who took some of the pictures on these pages. Kerry, an early champion of snow sports, took part in the first winter ascent of Mount Kosciusko in 1897.

Hotels and chalets

Around the start of the 20th century, a few adventurous sportsmen became interested in skiing in the Australian Alps. In 1909 a hotel was built at Kosciusko and in 1910 a chalet was built at Mount Buffalo, Victoria.

Skiing did not increase much in popularity until the late 1920s, when Australians who had skied overseas brought back their enthusiasm for the sport. In 1927 a party of skiers made the first major cross-country run—from Kiandra to Kosciusko. They were led by Herbert Schlink, director of the Royal Prince Alfred Hospital, Sydney. He was

'The ladies toboggan race'—a photograph taken in the Australian Alps early in the 20th century by Charles Kerry, a Sydney photographer who was an early champion of snow sports

made a Fellow of the Royal Geographical Society for the feat, and Schlink Pass, the highest in Australia, was named after him.

In the mid-1930s, some Austrian ski instructors came to Australia to work during the European summer, and just before World War II ski tows were built at Charlotte Pass, Mount Kosciusko, and at Mount Buffalo. After the war, there was a great development of skiing—clubs were formed, ski lodges and

huts were built and roads were opened to the snowlands of Victoria and New South Wales.

Australian skiers now compete not only in Australian and New Zealand contests, but also in Europe, Canada, the United States and South America. A unique contest is the Summit Trophy, awarded to the skier who records the fastest time of the year from the Hotel Kosciusko to the summit of Mount Kosciusko and back, a distance of 55 kilometres.

Cold wind rustled the skirts of these young skiers as they posed resignedly for Kerry. Their skis are secured only by straps over the instep

The well-dressed woman skier of 1926 (above) was more appropriately clad than her counterparts of 1909 (right), or 1914 (below). The early skiers used a single long pole for braking

Just a passing craze

When table tennis bats went ping and pong

Organised table tennis began in Australia about 1902, the year of this tournament in Tasmania. The game was played in those days with hollow vellum-covered bats, long-handled like tennis rackets

The up-to-date young Australian who whistled 'Tell Me Pretty Maiden' from *Floradora* as he walked to work in 1901, probably looked forward to a game of ping-pong when he got home. Ping-pong, though invented in England about 1890, had not become popular there until the end of the century, when it was played under a variety of names, including 'Gossima'. The boom reached Australia a little later and gained many enthusiasts.

At first the game was played with vellum bats, similar to those used in the children's game of battledore and shuttlecock. The sound of the ball on these bats suggested the onomatopoeic name 'ping-pong'. When the vellum bats were replaced by wooden ones, the game was given the more impressive name of 'table tennis'. In its early days, the ball was patted gently back and forth.

The New South Wales Table Tennis Association was formed in 1902. 'It would be difficult to find a pastime in which skill, control of temper and moderate exercise are so well combined,' said the official handbook of the Association, published in 1903.

The popularity of ping-pong was briefly challenged by 'puff billiards'. This, said *Table Talk* in January 1902, 'calls for rather more skill and good judgment than ping-pong . . .'

Diabolo mania

'Puff billiards'—like the hula hoop of the 1950s—was soon forgotten. Ping-pong met a more serious rival when diabolo came to Australia in 1908. 'Now we leave ping-pong to children,' a writer in Melbourne *Life* announced rather patronisingly in November 1907. 'The latest craze is diabolo.'

In England, where it had taken a firm hold on every class, diabolo was the chief topic of conversation in trains, in the streets and at meals. Newspapers devoted whole columns to it. A great tournament was being organised at the Crystal Palace. There were fashionable 'diabolo teas', and 'correct' diabolo costumes. And on the Continent it had ousted every other game. Continental beaches were crowded with 'solitary diabolists, families of diabolists, battalions of diabolists'.

The diabolo itself was made of celluloid or rubber and looked like a narrow-waisted hour-glass. By manipulating with a see-saw motion a long cord attached to two short sticks, the diabolo was made to rotate at a very high speed, up to an estimated 2000 revolutions a minute, which gave it a gyroscopic steadiness. When the sticks were sharply drawn apart, the diabolo flew into the air, to as high as 15 metres. As it came down, the player caught it and repeated the action, hurling it into the air and catching it for as many as a thousand times in succession.

In competitive play, the diabolo was thrown from player to player; they stood about 22 metres apart, separated by a net. Or it could be played by sides, with a field set out like a football field.

While the chauffeur changes a tyre, these elegant creatures pass the time at diabolo—the fashionable game in 1908 in Australia

This looks like an eccentric kind of surfboard riding but the artist was probably trying to depict aqua-planing, a voguish sport of the years after World War I. In reality, the board was towed by a yacht, the rider gripping the reins for stability. Aqua-planing was followed by water-skiing, which became very popular

Cyclorama to glaciarium

Roller-skating, or 'Rinkomania' enjoyed a boom in England in the 1870s, but never became popular in Australia. 'Timber floors and roller skates were tried some years ago, but though it caught on for a time this poor substitute soon failed to attract,' said *Australasian Hardware and Machinery* in 1905.

It reported that an Adelaide building, formerly used as a cyclorama, had been refitted as a glaciarium, under the name of the Ice Palace Skating Rink. There was room for 500 skaters on the oval floor, which measured 35 by 22.5 m and was lit at night by six 2000 candlepower electric lamps. Sydney followed Adelaide's lead in 1907, when an old cyclorama in George Street was converted into a glaciarium, with a rink 55 by 28 m accommodating 800 skaters. Ice-skating became a fashionable amusement.

Forerunner of water-skiing

Table Talk in March 1916 reported that 'aqua-planing' was Sydney's new sport. It had caught on strongly for it supplied 'the thrill and spice of danger that seems to be desired by modern athletes.' Many Sydneysiders had become so expert that they rode 'triumphantly' with a companion seated astride their shoulders.

The new sport came to Melbourne in the summer of 1918 when *Punch* reported: 'The latest thrill of the seaside summer girl this season is a sport she calls "sea-planing". The so-called sea-plane is a broad wooden plank attached to a yacht by two reins of rope. The planist stands on the plank and steadies herself by the reins while the plane rushes madly through the water after the yacht . . . To the onlooker it appears a frightfully exciting, if not absolutely dangerous game, and none but expert swimmers are allowed to take part in it.' Aqua-planing remained popular until the 1940s, when the faster water-skiing took over.

Depression diversion

A curious phenomenon of the Depression years was the fantastic proliferation of 'miniature golf' courses. The craze swept America in 1929, and reached Australia towards the end of 1930. A miniature golf course was like a tiny Disneyland, crammed with all sorts of strange obstacles and cunningly contrived devices, such as a mysterious castle which returned your ball if you putted into the wrong entrance.

Courses erupted everywhere—on vacant land behind city buildings, in shops, halls, and suburban backyards, on beach-fronts. 'Links are springing up like mushrooms all over the city and suburbs, proving that folks have money to spend, even in hard times, if their fancy be captured sufficiently,' said Melbourne *Fashion and Society* in December 1930.

But *Table Talk* recalled that diabolo had once been all the rage, and then died a sudden death. 'These crazes come and go,' it reflected philosophically. 'And perhaps midget golf will travel the same road, who can say?' It was an accurate prediction.

The miniature golf craze prompted *Table Talk* magazine in 1930 to suggest a further improvement—miniature miniature golf

Going places

The passing of a more leisurely era of travel

The development of fast road, rail, sea and air transport has brought enormous benefits to Australia, a vast land separated by 20,000 kilometres of ocean from the origins of most of its people. At the turn of the century, before the first heavier-than-air machine had left the ground, even travelling from one state capital to another meant a major journey.

Roads in the outback were little better than dusty tracks over which interstate travellers bumped in horse-drawn coaches; camels were still the principal carriers in many parts of the outback. Travellers wealthy and daring enough to attempt a long trip by automobile fared little better. In 1900, when Herbert Thomson and Edward Holmes attempted the first long-distance drive in Australia—the 793 kilometres between Bathurst and Melbourne—the trip took them ten days at an average speed of only 14 km/h.

Australia was very well off for railways; by 1921 it had a greater length of track in proportion to population than any other country. However, it was not until 1917 that the Commonwealth finished the transcontinental railway to provide the first land link between Perth and the eastern states, and changes in rail gauge meant that the six-day rail trip from Brisbane to Perth involved changing trains six times.

In the first decade of the century it was still possible to travel to England by sailing ship. Although by that time the steamers out-numbered the sailing ships, they still came to Australia in ballast in the hope of finding cargoes and passengers. River steamers still plied for vast distances along the Murray and Darling, carrying passengers up and down stream, bringing stores to remote settlements and taking wool, wheat and timber to the coast.

A New South Wales Railways C38 locomotive labours up Cowan Bank, north of Sydney, in 1956

Days of camels and coaches

Carrying goods and passengers in the outback

Plodding through the outback, a string of pack camels, such as this one photographed in 1910, would cover about 32 kilometres a day. A pack string usually consisted of two to three dozen animals, each carrying two 90 to 130 kg packs, one slung on each side of the hump

Railways were predominant among the many forms of public transport functioning when the Commonwealth was born, their total length of track having increased from 391 kilometres in 1861 to 20,651 kilometres in 1901. But many Australians living in 1901 had never seen a train. Settlements on the coast and in the interior were often hundreds of kilometres from the nearest railway line. Horses, bullock teams, mules, donkeys and camels were their only means of transport.

The first camel

As early as September 1839 *The Sydney Herald*, forerunner of *The Sydney Morning Herald*, had advocated the introduction of camels to Australia as animals 'admirably adapted to the climate and soil of New South Wales'. In October 1840, a dromedary was landed in South Australia, where it was worked on a sheep station near Clare for several years. In December 1840 two more camels, a male and a female, were landed at Melbourne and exhibited to the public. They were then overlanded to Sydney and, with an offspring, bought by the New South Wales Government for £225 [about $13,500] and exhibited to the public.

In 1860, the Victorian Government imported 24 camels from India for use by the explorers Burke and Wills. Soon after, Thomas Elder, a South Australian pastoralist, imported 120 Indian baggage and riding camels for use in the interior. In 1886 two 'Afghans' brought 259 camels from India to South Australia which were later used for carrying supplies to the Western Australian goldfields.

Thereafter camels played an indispensable part in developing the interior, carrying goods and produce as well as mails and missionaries. At the time of Federation, there were about 6000 camels in use in Australia and they were the principal carriers in more than half the continent.

Camels lived off the country and, unlike bullocks and horses, could travel for days without water. In the survey of the route of the trans-Australian railway in 1908, camels transported water for distances up to 500 kilometres into the desert.

At many railheads in New South Wales, South Australia, Victoria, Queensland and Western Australia, trains were met by strings of hobbled pack camels. These were driven by Muslims whom Australians, for some mysterious reason, called 'Afghans' or 'Ghans'—though nearly all of them came from the Indian regions of Rajasthan and Baluchistan.

A pack camel normally carried weights of 180 to 270 kg and could carry two bales of wool. Harnessed to a wagon, however, a camel could move twice as heavy a load. On the Western Australian goldfields, teams of up to 18 camels were harnessed to loaded wagons and they pulled them 32 or more kilometres a day. An additional advantage of using camels to draw wagons was that, unlike pack camels, they did not have to be unloaded each night and loaded again in the morning.

Camels were also ridden and hitched to light buggies, and in some places they even pulled earth scoops and ploughs. Their replacement by motor vehicles was only gradual and as late as the 1950s outback police and dingo fence patrols were sometimes made by camel riders. In 1939, Dr C. T. Madigan carried out the last of the great explorations of Australia—the first crossing of the Simpson Desert—with the help of camels. Nineteen camels carried supplies for his team of nine men, who included two 'Afghans'.

Official records are incomplete but they indicate that the working camel population of Australia reached a peak about 1922, when about 20,000 of the animals were in use. Nowadays there are probably no more than a few dozen working camels in Australia, but about 25,000 are running wild in the outback that their ancestors helped to develop.

The decline of coaching

Coaches still served vast areas of the outback at the beginning of the 20th century. In 1904, Cobb and Co., the biggest coaching company, was still operating 42 mail services covering a total distance of 6,500 kilometres, and it owned 1114 horses, valued at £8008 [$216,000].

Cobb and Co. was founded in 1853 by Freeman Cobb and three other Americans who provided a much-needed coaching service between Melbourne and the goldfields. The company later under different owners moved its headquarters to Bathurst, NSW, but by the 20th century, Queensland was where the business was most strongly developed. In 1911, Cobb and Co. coaches carried passengers and mails in most parts of the state, from Cunnamulla in the south to the head of Cape York in the north.

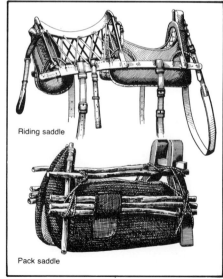

Riding saddle

Pack saddle

On the Indian riding saddle favoured in Australia, the rider sat behind the hump, with his baggage loaded in front of him

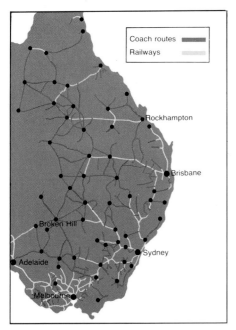

Cobb and Co. coach routes about 1900 linked many country towns with the railways

One of the last Cobb and Co. coaches to run. This was a concord type coach pulled by a team of two to seven horses, depending on the terrain. Six passengers sat inside with two beside the driver

A Cobb and Co. timetable about 1917 for the service between Cunnamulla and Thargomindah, to the west, gives some idea how arduous coach travel must have been. Jolting over rough roads, the coach—either a 14 passenger vehicle drawn by seven horses or an eight-passenger coach with a team of five—took 35 or 36 hours to make the 56 kilometre trip. This included an overnight stop, but the timetable does not say whether the cost of the night's lodging was included in the price of £3 10s [$110]. Nowadays, the trip takes 12 hours by mail car.

Cobb and Co.'s last service was in southwestern Queensland, where a 14-passenger coach ran between Surat and Yuleba until 1924. The coach was bought by the Federal Government for £100 [$2695] and is now in the Power House Museum in Sydney.

Mail coaches await departure time in Franklin Street, Adelaide, about 1908. Though the front coach looks almost overloaded, there is still room for more passengers alongside the driver

The discomfort of coach travel is evoked by this 1910 photograph of a mail coach jolting along behind its galloping team on a rough dirt road between

Broken Hill and Tibooburra on the western plains of New South Wales. Until the 1920s, coaches like this were the only means of public transport in some

parts of Queensland. It was in the southwest of Queensland in 1924 that Cobb and Co. ran its last service in horse-drawn transport

The tyranny of the horse

When there was one horse to every two Australians

In 1901 the motor age was still a long way off and horses were everywhere. They pulled omnibuses, horse-trams, lorries, ploughs, harvesters, hansom cabs, huge drags capable of seating 150 people and a great variety of private vehicles—buggies, sulkies, dog-carts, landaus, broughams and wagonettes. There were 1,662,000 horses in Australia—about one horse for every two inhabitants, men, women and children.

The clip-clop of horse-shoes on the wooden blocks of city streets, the jingle of harnesses, the grinding of brakes, a gleaming fire-engine drawn by galloping horses, huge Clydesdales gaily decorated for an Eight-Hour Day procession were all familiar sounds and sights to Australians everywhere.

Familiar also was the all-pervading smell of the horse manure that lay in heaps in streets and gutters—from where it was eagerly gathered to fertilise kitchen gardens—the resulting swarms of flies proving as much a threat to public health as the exhaust fumes of modern motor-cars. The vast army of horses ruled the lives of an equal army of city-dwellers who were forced to rise at the crack of dawn to feed, harness and prepare them for the day's work.

Advice to grocers

Horses required more than the superficial attention that most motor-cars receive. *The Grocer of Australia* offered readers the following advice on caring for a horse:

'The delivery horse should be watered and fed long enough before the driver has himself breakfasted to allow it time to rest after feeding before beginning the day's work. Four quarts of oats is an average feed. While the driver is eating, the horse may be left with a little hay with which to finish off. Just before starting off in the morning the horse should be curried (combed).

'At noon the horse should have a full hour's rest. He should be watered and fed another four quarts of oats. This will do him until evening, when he should be fed again, watered and curried. Don't put your horse to bed without cleaning him.

'A delivery horse should be well shod once a month at least, and his hoofs regularly examined. During working hours care should be taken to blanket the horse whenever he is sweating and compelled to stand in an unsheltered place.'

Horse breeding was an important industry, and horse-traffic provided employment for more than stable-hands. *Sands' Sydney Directory* for 1901 lists 122 retail saddlers and harness-makers, 211 coach, carriage and buggy proprietors, 114 coach-builders, 51 livery-stables and 69 horse-trainers. Following Queen Victoria's lead, many genteel women favoured phaetons, elegant vehicles that swept down in the middle, so low that passengers could enter or alight with little

effort—or exposure. Phaetons were useless in the bush, where the tough, all-purpose buckboard, the utility vehicle of the horse-drawn era, was widely used. To board it, you had to climb first to the step and then on to the seat. The only disadvantage was that ladies had to raise their skirts, thus revealing a brief glimpse of black-stockinged ankle to the vulgar gaze. The most popular vehicle of the day was the Sydney sulky.

The introduction of the first motor-cars into this horse-dominated society failed to impress many people. A magazine, *The Australasian Coachbuilder and Wheelwright*, told its readers in February 1906 that the motor-car was just a passing craze, and said: 'In our opinion the automobile is simply, speaking broadly, an added luxury to our twentieth century civilisation. We believe time will

A Brisbane baker on his rounds in 1937. The tradesman with his horse-drawn cart was a common sight until the late 1940s

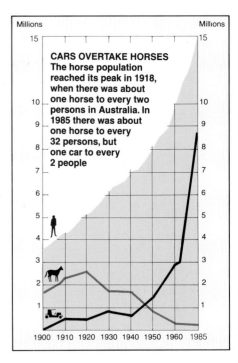

CARS OVERTAKE HORSES
The horse population reached its peak in 1918, when there was about one horse to every two persons in Australia. In 1985 there was about one horse to every 32 persons, but one car to every 2 people

The sight, sound and smell of horses dominated the cities and dictated the pace of life at the turn of the century. When this photograph was taken in George Street, Sydney, there was about one horse to every two persons in Australia. Nearly all transport throughout the country was horse-drawn. Large firms kept their own stables, and in 1911, MacRobertsons, the confectioners, boasted a stable of 108 horses

In the heyday of horses, the cab ranks of the cities were lined with hansoms and four-wheelers, their horses patiently munching in nosebags, while the drivers waited for fares. By 1920, when this Sydney cab was photographed, horses were beginning to disappear from city streets

show that people will own and maintain both horses and carriages as well as autos. Just as many families who formerly got along without any telephone now have one and even two in their homes and have their homes equipped for both gas and electric light.'

But the article warned carriage-dealers that the automobile had really come to stay, and advised them to 'get into the game' and handle both commodities.

This view was not, however, shared by Thomas Alva Edison, when he announced in October 1907 that he had perfected a compact electric storage battery for use with the motor-car. The American inventor confidently predicted that horses were destined to disappear from the streets.

Edison was right. Despite growing mechanisation of transport and farming, the number of horses in Australia increased until it reached a peak of 2,527,149 in 1918. The population was then about 5 million. By 1978, the number of horses had fallen to 444,523 against 14 million people.

Horse troughs, hitching posts and municipal dung collectors were once common sights in city streets before the introduction of the car

Rosa buggy

Two-seat station waggon

Queensland buckboard waggon

Hansom cab (Melbourne style)

Victoria

The carriage-builder's art

Some of the dozens of types of carriages available in 1902. Many designs had been developed by Australian coachbuilders to cope with the bad roads that they had to travel over. When Lord Hopetoun, Australia's first Governor-General, arrived from England in 1900 he brought with him three landaus, a brougham, a dog-cart and a victoria. The *Australian Coachbuilder and Saddler* magazine was not impressed, and declared that they would prove too heavy for Australian conditions. Whether they proved to be is not recorded

Single brougham

Open drag

The arrival of the horseless carriage

The first imported automobiles scare Australian horses

At Federation, on 1 January 1901, the motorcar was still a novelty to the Australian public. Karl Benz had built his first petrol-driven car in Germany in 1885, and the first car seen in Australia had been imported in 1897, twelve years later. Already some bold Australians had predicted that the car would soon replace the horse as the main means of transport, but the majority doubted it.

On 2 January 1901, Mr J. W. C. Elliot wrote in the Sydney *Daily Telegraph* that after carefully examining all other makes in Paris and London, he had imported a De Dion Voiturette—one of Sydney's first cars. The De Dion, which looked like a small buggy on bicycle wheels, was a two kilowatt, water-cooled car. It had two facing seats and was capable, on a fair road, of a top speed of 40 km/h with three passengers. Mr Elliot had recently made the trip from Melbourne to Sydney in 38 hours.

Beware of the hay motors

Not long after Mr Elliot's adventurous journey, the Sydney retailers Mark Foy's announced proudly that their first steam-driven parcel delivery car had gone into service. It had four brakes and could travel at 80 km/h. However, Mark Foy's drivers were instructed not to exceed nine kilometres an hour so as to avoid accidents with frightened horses, or 'hay motors' as they were then termed.

The fourth car to chug through the streets of Sydney was a 10-12 kW Coventry Humber which Mr Alfred Lee, a champion cyclist, imported in 1901 at a cost of £650 [$32,777]. The Coventry Humber had no hood or windscreen, but with it came a motor-head-dress for Mrs Lee and a supply of dustcoats and goggles for Mr Lee. The white silk headdress, which enclosed the whole of the head, had a talc window in the front and a drawstring to fasten it tightly round the neck.

'My father had a great deal of trouble with the Coventry Humber car,' his daughter recalled. 'He kept it for six months, during which he spent £750 [$37,820] on maintenance and repairs, and he felt he had suffered enough. He had the car packed up in the same case it had come out in and sent it back to the Humber company with his compliments. As he had always ridden Humber bicycles when making his records in Sydney, they immediately sent out to him a Becston Humber 16-18 hp [12-13.5 kW] with their compliments.'

In 1901 a Melbourne citizen bought a car for £700 [$35,300] from an Indian prince who had got tired of towing it home behind an elephant. The Melbourne *Argus* later described it as the summit of the car-builder's art. It had a short, snub-nosed bonnet, no hood and, of course, no windscreen. The body was entered from the back, but there was no leg-room anywhere. The back wheels—huge wooden artillery wheels with absurd little tyres perched on their rims—were as high as those of a spring-cart. The engine was a two-cylinder model. Gear-changing was a job for a craftsman, and when the driver did get in his gear, the scream could be heard half a kilometre away. It was chain-driven, while the ignition was from tubes heated by burning petrol—a method which cost many a driver his moustaches and eyebrows. There was no silencer, and the noise made by the car with its rattling chain-drive and screaming gears was terrific.

In 1911, there were 3896 cars in New South Wales, and you could buy a booklet listing their registration numbers and their owners. Many motorists owned more than one car. The market was international: you could buy an American Ford, an English Crossley, an Italian Bianchi or a Belgian Metallurgique.

In the early days of motoring, most car owners employed chauffeurs to drive and service their temperamental machines. Chauffeuring became a skilled profession, and chauffeurs in Melbourne and Sydney formed their own clubs. By 1908, the Chauffeurs' Club of Victoria had 60 members, and a waiting list of 18. A report of a club smoke night held in 1908 says that after an enjoyable evening enlivened with song and refreshments, the meeting broke up in time for the chauffeurs to pick up their masters at the city theatres.

Doing the grand

'The taxicab seems to add much to the motorish appearance of Melbourne streets,' said a woman writer in *The Australian Motorist* in March 1909. 'I notice that many working girls, and boys also, are gaining their first taste of the delights of motoring by their means. They save up and club together, and hire a taxi for as long as their money will suffice, and do the grand on their weekly half-holiday or, at times, in the evenings.' But 'doing the grand' was a costly amusement.

Cars had to be started by cranking until self-starters were introduced in 1911. Cranking could be slow, with up to four levers to set

The fare from the city to St Kilda and back via Albert Park, a distance of about 10 kilometres with two five-minute halts, worked out at £1 [$46.45].

When the Sydney-based Australasian Motor Cab Company issued its prospectus in 1910, there were only 14 'motor cabs' in Sydney, compared with 822 licensed horsedrawn vehicles—four-wheelers and hansom cabs. Sydney's population was 577,180. Melbourne, with a population of 538,000, had 42 motor cabs and 832 licensed horsedrawn vehicles; Adelaide, population 178,000, had 27 motor cabs and 123 licensed horse-drawn vehicles.

The company proposed to operate 270 four-cylinder Napier cabs in Sydney, and estimated each would travel 77 kilometres a day at a tariff of one shilling [$2.30] per 1.6 kilometres.

One of Australia's first motor cycles, built in South Australia. This state was the home of many of the country's motoring pioneers, including David Shearer, the builder of Australia's first car

Bodies built to order

Phaeton

Landaulet

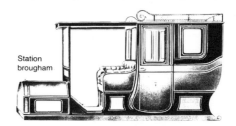
Station brougham

Until the introduction of mass-produced cars, most buyers had their car bodies built to order. Chassis were imported, and the buyer would specify the type of body he wanted, as well as any special features he required. Bodies were made up with a framework of wood, usually ash, to which were fitted the hand-beaten, shaped steel panels. Three examples of basic body types available in 1906 are shown above

The basic coach shape for cars persisted for many years. This 1901 American car even seems to have provision for a footman

Queensland's first petrol-powered car, this two-cylinder De Dion Bouton, was imported in 1900 by James Trackson, a Brisbane electrical engineer

Visiting magistrates in South Australia. Many early car owners employed chauffeurs to drive and service their temperamental machines

When is a car a traction engine?

W. J. Proctor, general manager of the Dunlop Rubber Company, claimed to have been the only motorist in Victoria to be convicted under the Steam Roller and Traction Engine Act. This Act, passed in 1865, limited the speed of a self-propelled vehicle to five kilometres an hour and said it must be preceded on a public highway by a man carrying a red flag. In November 1901, unaccompanied by a flag-carrier, Proctor was driving a $2^1/_2$ kW one-cylinder De Dion on the Flemington road, Melbourne, when he was charged by a frightened race-horse which broke a leg on the step. In a subsequent court case, the Chief Justice ruled that a motor-car was a traction engine and found against Proctor.

Melbourne motorists complained of being harassed by the police. One of them was Dr

Renard, a medical practitioner, who drove his small Rochet car past a cable-tram at about 19 km/h. A police inspector travelling on the 'dummy' of the tram leaped off, hailed a horse gig and gave chase, overtook the doctor and fined him 10s [$25].

In 1909, New South Wales introduced Australia's first Motor Traffic Act. Before then, cars were not registered and drivers not licensed. In its first year 16 convictions were recorded for exceeding 9 km/h across intersections and 6 km/h around corners.

In December 1924, when it was proposed to introduce compulsory driving tests in South Australia, the Automobile Association objected strongly. It pointed out that no tests were required to drive a horse or ride a bicycle. The horse driver found drunk while driving had no licence to lose, it argued.

Nosegays for sweet motoring

'The custom of carrying a vase containing a small posy of flowers suspended in the motor-car is spreading,' said *The Australian Motorist*, which ran a regular women's section, in 1909. 'It is a dainty and pretty conceit, but, judging from the fact that the flowers chosen are almost always highly scented roses, violets or daphne, I fancy that the idea is rather to disguise even the faintest suggestion of the odour of petrol than for any other reason.'

In the same article, the writer recommended a new silk waterproofed hood with attached cape as a protection for women motorists. 'It entirely envelopes the head, hat and all, and protects hat, hair, face and neck from all dust. It has a clear mica mask let into the net, which, when in position, is nearly invisible.'

Dressed for a spin

A New South Wales Government Tourist Bureau vehicle in Sydney in 1909. This was the year when taxis were first introduced to Sydney. It was to be many years, however, before they entirely replaced the hansom cabs and four-wheelers. Even in 1934 there were still 80 four-wheelers on the road in Melbourne.

In the early years, motoring could be uncomfortable for drivers and passengers who were not well wrapped up. Most clothes shops before World War I stocked a great variety of motoring clothes and accessories such as goggles, masks, rugs and veils for both men and women. This lady's lined leather coat was priced at 16 guineas [$781] in 1909. The man's double-breasted coat, Scottish tweed with leather lining, cost 10 guineas [$488]

Sydney to Melbourne in five days

Gruelling trial proves the reliability of the motor car

Cover of the official Dunlop
guide to the motor trial

In February 1905, eight years after the first motor-car had been seen in Australia, the Dunlop Tyre Company sponsored a five-day reliability trial for cars and motorcycles from Sydney to Melbourne.

Much of the course lay over rugged bush tracks that played havoc with the thin treadless tyres of the cars; one competitor repaired 13 punctures on the first day's run. The sole woman entrant, Mrs Ben Thompson of Adelaide, excited admiration and wonder by finishing the arduous 920 kilometre course in her single-cylinder 4.5 kW Wolseley.

Cars ranged in size and price from a single-cylinder 5 kW Oldsmobile at £200 [$9875] to a 4-cylinder 26 kW Talbot at £1500 [$76,065]. Fastest time was made by a young American, H.L. Stevens, in a 10.5 kW two-cylinder Darracq, which averaged about 38 km/h. A booklet issued before the contest warned the public not to run out on the road for the purpose of watching passing cars, as there was a danger of other cars being close behind hidden by dust. But it was reassuring to be told by the organisers that it was impossible for a petrol car to blow up.

'All the competitors complain of the V-shaped open culverts frequently met with,' said the Sydney *Daily Telegraph*. 'In several instances bent axles were thereby caused, the whole car being bodily thrown into the air and falling again with a crash, occasionally being flung clear from the crown to the side of the road.'

Each car had to carry a passenger as well as a driver. One passenger was 'Banjo' Paterson, then editor of the Sydney *Evening News*,

Daring American driver H. L. Stevens in his Darracq fords Paddy's River, 43 kilometres north-east of Goulburn. Stevens completed the run from Sydney to Melbourne in a record 23 hrs 42 min. at an average speed of over 39.5 km/h—a virtuoso performance that not all the other competitors approved of. Stevens claimed that he used low gear only once—on the Razorback near Picton. He took all the other hills in medium gear who sent back daily reports of the trial. 'Ruts and loose metal, sidings and sand-drifts, washed-out creeks and heart-breaking hills—these are the items on the bill of fare,' he wrote. And he described the contestants who by common consent wore 'breeches and gaiters, a high-peaked cap, a white macintosh, a pair of awful goggles, and possibly a mask with a false leather nose'.

Paterson thought the chauffeur was more important than the driver: 'To compare it to horse-racing, the driver is the jockey, while the chauffeur is the trainer. The driver must take the risk of sending her along, must save every bit of the road, and let her out on the level, and a lot depends on his skill, nerve, and judgment. But the chauffeur has to know by the slightest sound if anything is wrong, and he must know what is wrong. Anyone with a little skill in steering, a fair share of pluck, and a quick decision, can drive and perhaps drive well, but it takes years of training to make a man a really first-class chauffeur.'

The contest finished in Melbourne on February 26, with no clear winner, because nine contestants had completed the course without losing any points at all. A run-off was organised from Melbourne to Ballarat and back on March 6, and this was won by Colonel Tarrant in his Argyll.

If nothing else, the motor contest proved the value of the motor-car as a reliable means of transport. On the day that the contest started, a sceptical leader writer in *The Sydney Morning Herald* had observed that it was very interesting and thrilling to cover hundreds of kilometres at a speed of more than 80 kilometres an hour, but did anyone suppose that motors would ever be allowed to career at that hurricane rate along the public roads? By the time the contest had finished, another

The route and the winner

Start	●	**Sydney**
First day	●	Liverpool
▲▲▲▲▲	●	Picton
▲▲▲▲▲	●	Berrima
▲▲▲▲▲	●	Marulan
	●	**Goulburn**
Second day		
▲▲▲▲▲		Yass
▲▲▲▲▲	●	Jugiong
	●	**Gundagai**
Third day		
▲▲▲▲▲	●	Upper Tarcutta
	●	Kyamba
	●	**Albury**
Fourth day		
	●	Wangaratta
	●	Benalla
	●	Violet Town
	●	**Euroa**
Fifth day		
▲▲▲▲▲	●	Seymour
Finish	●	**Melbourne**

Good road	▭
Bad road	▨
Hill country	▲▲▲▲▲▲▲▲▲▲

Colonel Tarrant, in his Argyll, was the eventual winner of the contest. He completed the course without losing any points. Tarrant entered the second Dunlop trial held later in 1905, this time in a car that he built himself, and was one of the five contestants who tied for first place

leader was extolling the virtues of the motor-car, and even suggested that they might mean the end of the railways. The paper now seemed less concerned with the dangers of speeding cars, but more with the fact that poor roads prevented one from driving high-powered cars at 96 km/h.

The success of the first trial prompted Dunlop to hold a second trial from Melbourne to Sydney in November 1905. Six competitors arrived in Sydney without loss of points. A run from Sydney to Medlow Bath in the Blue Mountains failed to break the tie, so the remaining competitors were sent back to Melbourne. Five completed the run without the loss of a single point, even though they had covered 2054 kilometres over some of the worst roads in the country.

Mrs Thompson at the finishing line in Melbourne. As the only woman competitor she attracted a lot of support from the crowd

Taking a corner at speed. Fallen trees and open culverts added to the hazards of driving fast over poor gravel roads. One commentator felt that the danger of having the car reduced to a heap of scrap-iron at a moment's notice merely added to the excitement of the contest

213

Automobiles conquer the outback

Pioneer motorist tells of the drive to Darwin

In November 1907, Harry Dutton and Murray Aunger left Adelaide in a 15 kW Talbot in an attempt to drive across nearly 3500 kilometres of roadless country to Darwin. After they had travelled 2219 kilometres, torrential rains and mechanical breakdown forced them to abandon the car between Barrett's Creek and Tennant Creek. In June the following year, they set out in another Talbot, picked up the abandoned car, and took both vehicles through to Darwin, completing the first car journey across the continent. In an interview, Murray Aunger described some of the obstacles they had encountered:

'At Stewart's Creek and the Finnis, we had difficulties in crossing, particularly on the former, where the banks are 60 feet [18 metres] high. Presently we came across a succession of sandhills. We pushed the car and endeavoured to take the rises at speed; but in one day we were not able to do more than 10 miles [16 kilometres]. Crossing the Warrender, we had to make a corduroy track of branches and saplings, for in the bottom of the creek was a treacherous quicksand. We pressed on to Oodnadatta, 675 miles [1086 kilometres] from Adelaide. The country was riddled with washouts. At Neil's River we had to dismount and break a causeway through the high banks. We used the earth broken from the banks to fill up a passage across the water course, wide enough to let the car cross. Half a mile from Oodnadatta, we struck Alburga Creek, half a mile wide, the bottom rumpled into lumps of uneven sand.

'This region led us on to a labyrinth of boulders and sharp-edged stones, over hundreds of acres of which we rattled frightfully. From Charlotte Waters, the country is sand all the way to Alice Springs, and there are 49 sandhills to be crossed in 45 miles [72 kilometres]. The majority of the hills are about 60 feet high [18 metres], and the grades as much as one in three. The McDonnell Range is very rough and sandy. At one part we had to get out of the car and roll away many boulders. On Burke's plain we crunched for 80 miles [96 kilometres] through the thick, harsh grasses of the desert—which had sprung

Heading for Oodnadatta, Aunger and Dutton's Talbot rattles along beside the railway line. This was the second attempt to cross Australia from south to north by car. The first was by Francis Birtles early in 1907; it had ended when his car caught fire and was burned out 320 kilometres north of Alice Springs

up everywhere after the rains. 'The growth clogged our wheels and tangled in the engines and gear, but worse were the thousands of anthills hidden in the grass ...

'The sandy spinifex desert extends for about 500 miles [800 kilometres]. Sometimes our pace was beaten down by natural obstructions to 10 miles [16 kilometres] a day and at one place, we took three hours to do five miles [8 kilometres]. We blundered into a mass of thick scrub where it was impossible to see fifty yards [45 metres] ahead.

'Crossing the Catherine and Lucy rivers, we simply raced the car into the water, and

the momentum carried her through before the engine got properly wet. At Pine Creek, the southern terminus of the Northern Territory railway, we were told it was simply impossible to go any further, but we pushed on to Bridge Creek. Here the tropical jungle fairly swallowed us up. As the branches swished down above us, myriads of abominable insects dropped upon us like rain. The jungle extended for 40 miles [64 kilometres]. Then, on 20 August, we broke out, hot and happy, upon the main road to Darwin.'

Their only mishaps were two broken springs and three punctures.

Sand was a constant problem—on one 72-kilometre section between Charlotte Waters and Alice Springs there were 49 sandhills to cross. Although the wheels could be widened by the addition of extra rims to give more grip, the car still became bogged. Here the Talbot is being towed by a donkey team

The Talbot ploughs through high grass near the Adelaide river, about 110 kilometres south of Darwin. Grass seeds frequently clogged the radiator

Across the Nullarbor with a bicycle for spares

Setting records for driving between state capitals became a popular sport in the first three decades of the Commonwealth.

The first car to cross Australia from west to east was the Brush, a 7.5 kW American machine with a very slender wooden chassis. In 1912, Francis Birtles, who worked for a Sydney bicycle firm, and S. R. Ferguson, whose employers had imported the first Brush cars that year, shipped the car from Sydney to Fremantle. Birtles insisted on taking a new bicycle with him on the trip.

They left Fremantle on a fine March day with four waterbags, a fortnight's supply of tinned food, and the bike strapped on behind. Birtles carried a pocket compass, but they had no spare wheel. Petrol, oil and tyres had been deposited along the route.

When they were well out of Perth, they lifted the car on to the Coolgardie railway line and drove steadily eastward. Though repeatedly bogged, they finally struck the overland telegraph line and followed it, at times

extricating themselves from deep sand by tying a rope to the car and hauling it forward from telegraph post to telegraph post.

About halfway across the continent, they repaired a fractured big end by cutting up Birtles' new bike for parts. Another improvised repair was carried out some days later near Broken Hill, when an axle broke. Near the Darling River, one side of the chassis broke in half. The men walked back to a settler's hut and had a new piece of wood shaped to replace it. Night driving was abandoned after one attempt when the car dropped into a hole 'as big as a house'.

The intrepid pair reached Sydney in 28 days 4 hours, and were escorted to the General Post Office from the outskirts of the city by a honking fleet of new Brush cars. Top speed on the journey was 32 km/h. If they drove faster, the radiator boiled.

In 1909, B. Barr Smith and Murray Aunger drove a Napier from Adelaide to Melbourne in 22 hours 24 minutes, averaging 42.6 km/h.

This record was broken in 1910 by G. H. White in a 26 kW Talbot, with a time of 20 hours 6 minutes.

In 1915, Fraser and Armstrong drove from Fremantle to Sydney in 8 days, 23 hours and 35 minutes. In 1917, in an 18.5 kW Prince Henry Vauxhall, Boyd Edkins made a Brisbane-Sydney record, covering 1025 kilometres in 26 hours 3 minutes. He also held the Melbourne-Sydney record: 909 kilometres in 16 hours 55 minutes. In 1918, Burton and Smith drove in a Hupmobile from Fremantle to Sydney via Broken Hill, a distance of 4308 kilometres, in 7 days 2 hours.

In 1924, Don Harkness became the first man in Australia to exceed 160 km/h when he drove his Hispano-Suiza engined Minerva on Gerringong beach, south of Sydney, at 174 km/h. But the motoring hero of the 1920s was Norman 'Wizard' Smith who ran up an amazing score of reliability trial victories and interstate records.

In November 1922, he drove his famous Essex racer from Adelaide to Melbourne in 13 hours 21 minutes despite an encounter with a flock of sheep at Salt Creek beyond Menindee. One landed on top of the bonnet, tearing off the radiator cap and smashing the windscreen. The following year, he drove from Sydney to Melbourne in the record time of 13 hours, averaging 73 km/h.

In 1926, he drove a Chrysler 1038 kilometres from Brisbane to Sydney in 16 hours 5 minutes, an average of 64 km/h over roads which were often only cart tracks. In 1929, he achieved 238 km/h on Gerringong beach in a car built by Don Harkness and powered by a 12-cylinder Rolls Royce engine. In 1932, he took another Harkness-designed car, powered by a 12-cylinder Napier engine, to New Zealand's 90-Mile Beach in an attempt to break Malcolm Campbell's world record of 397 km/h. He reached 367 km/h before rising tides forced him to stop.

In 1934, he reduced his Brisbane-Sydney record to 11 hours 38 minutes. The following year, the New South Wales police banned interstate record-breaking. It is now banned in all states.

Francis Birtles was the most prolific long-distance record breaker in the world. Apart from his numerous trips across Australia by car and bicycle, he also made two attempts at driving from London to Canberra in 1927. The first ended in Delhi, and the second was defeated in Burma by the monsoons

Norman 'Wizard' Smith in his famous Essex 4 racer on his way to establishing a record for the drive from Melbourne to Sydney in the late 1920s. Inter-city record breaking was banned in 1935 because of the danger to life

The *Enterprise*, designed by Don Harkness, speeds along 90-Mile Beach in New Zealand at 367 km/h with Smith at the wheel. The car failed to beat Malcolm Campbell's world record of 398 km/h because of bad conditions

Henry Ford's Tin Lizzie

The mass-produced car reaches Australia

For the first eight years of the Commonwealth, motor cars remained a luxury for those who could afford £1000 [$46,470] to buy them and £6 [$295] a week to maintain them. The arrival in 1909 of the first model-T Fords ushered in a new era not only in Australian transport but in Australian life.

The first Ford car to appear in Australia was the model-S roadster which was imported in 1907 by Harley Tarrant. The model-S had a four-cylinder, 11 kW engine, two gears and extraordinary hill-climbing ability. Shortly after testing one of these cars Tarrant decided to give up manufacturing his own cars and took up the agency for Ford in Australia. Tarrant was alone in seeing the potential of the cheap Ford car, as its arrival in Australia was greeted with little enthusiasm. The model-S cost £250 [$11,618], and became quite popular, but its popularity was nothing to that of the model-T. The 'Tin Lizzie' was a tough, reliable, simply operated, two-speed four-cylinder machine, and the touring model cost only £275 [$12,780]. A 'country' model with a removable back seat was £15 [$680] less.

The men who sold these cars also had the sometimes difficult job of teaching customers to drive them. Farmers were particularly difficult pupils; having spent their entire lives with horses, they expected cars to have enough road sense not to run off the road or bump into trees.

Other drivers too had difficulties with Fords, particularly after electric lighting replaced acetylene gas in 1917. As a catalogue of accessories published by the Auto Import Company, Sydney, pointed out: 'The lighting system of the Ford is notoriously bad. Electric light taken from the magneto is a constantly changing light, and at low speed over rough and dangerous roads, it is dim and useless. It changes with every change in the speed of the engine and goes out when the engine stops.'

Ford owners were advised to replace this system with a battery-operated lighting unit supplied by the Auto Import Company.

One year after the model-T made its debut, Australians owned just under 5000 cars—about one to every 900 persons. The number grew rapidly until imports were curtailed by World War I, but increased even more rapidly after the war. The popularity of the model-T more than kept pace and at one stage it had captured almost a third of the Australian market. Ford's were able to bring the price of the standard model down from £275 to £199.10s [$12,780 to $9295].

The 1920s saw an astonishing boom in Australian motoring, a boom that did not collapse until the Depression arrived. In Victoria, for example, car registrations increased from 21,722 in 1920 to 144,596 in 1930. By 1930, with a population of about six million, Australia had nearly 600,000 motor-cars and trucks, more than most European countries of much greater population.

In the 1960s, cars were multiplying three

The model-T Ford caused a revolution in motoring in Australia. Its low price brought cars within the reach of the middle-classes. At one stage, one-third of all cars sold were model-Ts

'Any colour you like—so long as it is black'

The model-T Ford is probably the most famous car ever made. Between 1908 and 1927 over 15 million model-Ts were made. It was not until 1972 that Volkswagen passed Ford's record for the greatest number of cars made of a particular model.

It was in 1909 that Henry Ford made his famous announcement: 'In future we are going to build one model, and that model will be the model-T. Any customer can have the car painted any colour he wants, so long as it is black.'

The car was an immediate success. Annual sales rose from 12,000 in 1908 to 2 million in the peak year of 1923—figures only made possible by the perfection of the first assembly line. These huge sales brought the price of the car down from $US950 in 1909 to $US290 in 1925. In the lifetime of the model, Ford manufactured half of all American passenger cars. He concentrated on selling to what he called 'the other 95% of the market'—working men and farmers who could not afford the more expensive cars. By 1927, when Ford ceased production of the model-T, mass-production techniques had started a world-wide revolution in industry

Petrol was pumped from an underground tank into the graduated glass cylinder at the top of the bowser. From there it was allowed to run down the hose into the tank of the car

times as fast as people. In 1966, motor vehicles registered in Australia numbered 4,018,000; in 1970, 4,600,000; and in 1984 the figure was 8,832,800. Of this latter number, 5,462,200 were cars and station wagons, meaning about one car to every 2.3 people.

Petrol by the jar

In the early days of motoring, a regular supply of petrol was something of a problem. It was fairly readily available in the cities, where four-gallon (18 litre) cans of Pratt's motor spirit sold for 10d to 1s a gallon [$1.95 to $2.30 per 4.5 litres], but it could be scarce in country areas. Even when it was available, it was often at more than twice the city price. This shortage often had the effect of limiting excursions to the maximum distance that could be reached on half a tank of fuel. Pharmacists also sold petrol, or gasoline as it was then called, in large stone jars.

By the mid-1920s, garages were installing roadside bowsers in which petrol was hand-pumped from underground tanks into a graduated glass cylinder from which it flowed into the tank of the car.

No parking space at Bondi Beach—a result, in 1929, of the motoring revolution started by the model-T

The forgotten cars

An Australian car buyer in 1920 had a selection of over 90 imported and locally made cars to choose from. Competition between the small manufacturers was fierce, and most of these makes have now disappeared. Here are some of the vanished makes and their badges. How many of them do you remember?

Alvis, Amilcar, Anderson, Ansaldo, Arrol-Johnson, Auburn, Aurel, Barley, Bean, Benz, Berliet, Bianchi, Buchet, Cass, Ceirano, Chalmers, Chandler, Chenard-Walcker Cleveland, Columbia, Cottin, Crossley, De Dion, Desgouttes, Diana, Diatto, Dort, Elcar, Erskine, Essex, Federal Six, Flint, Gardiner, G.N., Graham, Gray, Haynes, Hotchkiss, Hudson, Hupmobile, Hurtu, Itala, Jewett, Lanchester, La Salle, Lexington, Locomobile, Lorraine-Dietrich, Marmon, Maxwell, Mercer, Milburn Electric, Minerva, Moon, Mors, Nash, Oakland, O.M., Page, Pierce-Arrow, Phoenix, Renown, Reo, Rickenbacker, Rochet-Schneider, Rollin, Rugby, Scat, Sizaire-Berwick, Stanley Steamer, Star, Stephens, Stoewer, Stutz, Summit, Talbot, Templar, Turcat-Mery, Velie, Vermorel, Vulcan, Willys-Knight, Wilton, Zedel.

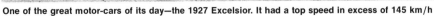

One of the great motor-cars of its day—the 1927 Excelsior. It had a top speed in excess of 145 km/h

A 1926 Bean fitted with a touring body

Making cars in Australia

Early mass-production attempts that failed

The only Tarrant car still in existence. Harley Tarrant started his car manufacturing business in 1900, and sold his first car in 1901—the first petrol-driven car built in Australia. He designed and made cars until 1907, when the company took the agency for Ford cars

Designers had toyed with plans for a mass-produced all-Australian car since the Thomson steam buggy chugged through the streets of Melbourne in 1897, but it was not till World War II, when Australia was forced to make its own tanks, Bren-gun carriers and military lorries, that the idea became feasible.

The first all-Australian petrol-driven car was built by two Melbourne enthusiasts, Colonel Harley Tarrant and Howard Lewis, in 1899. It had a two-cylinder engine in the rear of a buggy-type body, and chain-driven back wheels. It was not a success, but the performance of an improved machine, made in 1901, encouraged the makers to build another

two-cylinder and two four-cylinder cars in 1905. Several more were made before World War I. One was still running in 1954.

In 1907, Felix Caldwell, a young Adelaide engineer, invented a device by which power was transmitted equally to all four wheels of a car. After four years of experiment, he built the first Australian-made motor-lorry, and fitted it with his four-wheel drive. His firm, the Caldwell-Vale Company of Auburn, NSW, made 50 of these lorries which were sold to the Government and to private firms for £1250 [$61,270] each.

Before the depression hit the car market in the 1930s, many attempts to mass-produce

an Australian car were made, but nearly all had the major components from the United States. A notable exception was the Wege.

In 1920, William Wege, a 29-year-old mechanic of Peterborough, South Australia, invented a valveless petrol engine, operating on what he described as the two-cycle principle. It had no operating rods, timing wheels, cams or camshafts. Charges compressed in the lower portion of each cylinder were trans-

The Thomson motor-phaeton, a 3.5 kW steam car designed in 1900 by Herbert Thomson

The Summit—described in contemporary advertisements as the car wonder of 1923. It boasted electric stop lights and a cigar lighter, and one car was fitted with an experimental radio

ferred to the upper part of the next cylinder, where they were fired.

Wege designed a three-cylinder and a six-cylinder engine. The six-cylinder was shown at South Australia's first Automotive Show in 1920. Wege Motors Ltd was formed to exploit the invention, and Wege took it to England, where he had a chassis and body built for it. He planned to mass-produce Wege cars in Adelaide, but nothing came of the project.

The Australian Six, launched in 1920, was a conventional six-cylinder car designed by the American engineer, Louis Chevrolet. A Sydney car dealer, F. H. Gordon, assembled the cars at a factory in Ashfield, NSW, using 75 per cent Australian-made components. Some of these cars were exported to New Zealand before the Australian Six went out of production in 1924. It was the most successful of many short-lived Australian cars, none of which could compete with much cheaper American models.

Two other successful but short-lived partly Australian cars of the period were the Eco and the Summit. The Eco was designed by a Melbourne engineer, G. Hamilton Grapes. He had a prototype built to his specifications in Detroit, USA, and planned to build the car in Melbourne from American parts, and export it to India, China and the Dutch East Indies.

A car radio in 1924

The Summit was designed by W. T. Kelly, of Kelly's Motors, Alexandria, NSW. It, too, was assembled in Australia from American components. It boasted such refinements as an electric stop light and a cigar lighter. In 1924, a Summit was fitted with a wireless set, powered by the car battery, with the aerial attached to the waterproof hood. Passengers listened on headphones.

In 1932, the Marks Motor Construction Company of Sydney planned to mass-produce a 10.5 kW plywood chassis-less car. One of the company's directors was Sir Charles Kingsford Smith, whose wife christened the car 'Southern Cross' at Mascot airport under the wing of the famous plane of the same name. It was to be marketed at £240 [$7690], but only one car was made.

The utility model of the first Holden released in 1951. The car was named after the firm of Holden Motor Bodies Ltd., a firm originally established in 1856 to supply the needs of the carriage trade. The company merged with General Motors in 1931 to form General Motors-Holden's

During the twenties, American car manufacturers saw the advantage of assembling their products in Australia. The first was the Ford Motor Company of Canada, which in 1923 bought land at Geelong in Victoria and two years later turned out its first Australian-assembled car from a woolshed on the farm site it had acquired. In 1925-26, Ford set up plants in New South Wales, Queensland, and Western Australia.

The General Motors Corporation of America followed in 1926 with assembly plants in all Australian States. In 1939, Richards Industries of South Australia arranged with the Chrysler Corporation of America to establish a plant for assembling Chrysler and Dodge cars in Adelaide. This began production in 1940. In 1948, the British Motor Corporation began assembling its Austin and Morris cars in West Melbourne and in 1950 opened a plant in Sydney.

Debut of the Holden

Towards the middle of 1948, five nameless cars drove each day around a 132-kilometre test course at Lang Lang, near Melbourne. By July, one had covered more than 80,000 kilometres and another, 65,000 kilometres. They were the prototypes of a new Australian-made car, designed by American engineers, which

General Motors-Holden's expected to sell at from £400 to £600 [$8100 to $12,155]. Four years of planning had gone into its production.

The car was launched and named 'Holden' by Prime Minister Chifley at the GMH plant at Fishermens Bend in Victoria on 29 November 1948.

The price of the first model was £733 10s. [$14,860]. At first only ten cars a day were produced and only 163 were built by the end of 1948. When the millionth Holden came off the assembly line in 1962, the output had reached 600 a day. The peak was 760 a day in 1973, but the day of the wholly Australian car has passed as components now come from many countries. GMH itself exports over $1 million worth of parts every day.

The spread of the motor-car and the motor-bus changed the development of Australian cities by making people willing to build houses away from railways and tramways, and changed the habits of city dwellers. Before World War I, it was rare for an Australian to travel beyond his own state for a holiday. Today, the Sydneysider on holiday thinks nothing of driving to Adelaide by way of Canberra, and the Melburnian will pursue the sun in national holiday centres—such as Surfers Paradise, Queensland—which the motor-car has created.

The people's car that never was

In May 1950, when the cheapest car in Australia was the Ford Anglia tourer at £483 [$8175], Lawrence Hartnett announced that he hoped to sell a 'people's car' for £416 [$7040].

Hartnett, an English-born engineer, came to Australia in 1934 to take charge of General Motors-Holden's. He was largely responsible for the creation of the Holden car, but he left GMH in 1947 after a disagreement with his American principals. One of the main reasons was his insistence that the Holden be Australian in character and design.

The four-seater Hartnett was designed by the famous French car designer J. A. Gregoire. Four test cars were built and sent to Australia where they were thoroughly tested over the toughest roads. The cars had an aluminium-alloy chassis, a two-cylinder, 4.5 kW engine and a top speed of 115 km/h. The Hartnett never went into production, although 2000 cars were ordered. The collapse of the project had two causes—the Victorian government withdrew important concessions it had promised, and the Commonwealth Engineering Company broke its contract to supply panels

The railway that took five years to build

Forging the land link from east to west

Until 1917 neither road nor rail crossed the 1600 kilometres of waterless desert that separate Port Augusta from Kalgoorlie. Travellers between Western Australia and the eastern states had to go by sea—an eight day voyage.

In 1908 surveyors from east and west began to plan a transcontinental railway. It was a strenuous job. The Western Australian party of four men took three months to reach the South Australian border from Kalgoorlie, a distance of about 720 kilometres. There was no sign of the South Australians, so they built a cairn of limestone rocks to mark their final peg—at latitude 30° 45', longitude 129°, near where the town of Deakin stands today. The Western Australian party was led by R. J. Anketell, a red-headed Irish-Australian who some years before had built 1600 kilometres of rabbit-proof fence.

The four surveyors engaged on the Western Australian section lived for six months on tinned meat and a gallon of water a day.

'There was no motor transport at that time,' one of them, Geoffrey Drake-Brockman, recalled. 'Our drinking water was carted up to 150 miles [240 kilometres] in small tanks on the backs of camels. We struck and pitched our tents on a new site every day for seven days a week, month after month. We saw no one, not even a native, outside our own party, throughout the whole distance. When we reached the South Australian border, we ran a line south for sixty-five miles (105 kilometres) to Eucla, a tiny telegraph repeating station on the Great Australian Bight, in order to check our longitude. Here we camped for a few days before turning back with our camels along our pegged route to Kalgoorlie. Riding a camel is rather like being on a small boat on a rough sea, but you either got your camel legs or you walked 30 miles [48 kilometres] a day.'

At Port Augusta, South Australia, on 14 December 1912, the Governor-General, Lord Denman, turned the first sod, and heroically pushed it in a barrow for 14 metres along a plank, and back to the starting point. Speaking later at a luncheon, he prophesied that the transcontinental line would create a widespread spirit of nationalism.

A contemporary account describes the celebrations that followed:

'Three loud reports were heard and three large rockets were seen in the sky. As they burst successively, small parachutes emerged from them and carried across the heavens a Union Jack, an Australian flag, and a Stars and Stripes.'

The American flag was in honour of the Federal Home Affairs Minister, King O'Malley, who, though Canadian-born, was widely believed to be an American.

Four kilometres a day

Construction of the line went on from both ends. Transport of supplies, particularly water, across great stretches of uninhabited country was the greatest problem.

Earth was moved mainly by horse-drawn scoops and navvies with shovels. But the track was laid by machines—at rates up to 4 kilometres of sleepers and rails a day—for the first time in Australia.

'The great continental line is being finished in spite of exasperating difficulties, while this young nation is feeding blood and treasure into the Allied Cause on the other side of the world,' said a writer in *Land and Transport* in May 1917. And he described the life of the people working on the line:

'The march of the approaching railheads from the east and west is a unique progression. At each end a working village is always to be found. There are all the services of community life in these moving townships. There is a boarding-house to accommodate four or five hundred men, a bakery, a butcher's shop, a general store, a smithy, and a travelling parson. Children are born at the railhead towns and duly baptised, and when death takes its toll of the worker in the desert, the minister there performs the last offices of the Church.'

A village on wheels

'Sunday mornings the men devote to their laundry-work. For the rest of the week-days it is a case of steady labour on the long track. At the rail-head village there is a hospital car with a dispenser and medical attendant, a house on wheels and working office for the staff, and every other day the train comes up from civilisation bearing vital supplies of water. Out beyond the railhead, water is supplied to the gangs of navvies by means of movable pipe tracks.

'Day in, day out, the little community labours, and at night sleeps under the most brilliant of starry skies. Every three weeks a change is made. The whole village bestirs itself. The boarding-houses and temporary storehouses are pulled down in sections, loaded on to rail-road wagons, and the whole population moves on into the desert.'

The east and west lines were linked at Ooldea, 1000 kilometres east of Kalgoorlie, on 17

In the middle of the Nullarbor Plain, over 600 kilometres from the nearest settlement, the chief surveyor for the transcontinental railway stands at the border between South and Western Australia

Camels and horses were widely used on the transcontinental line. At one time there were more than 750 animals in use. These camels are carrying well timbers from the railhead to the workmen

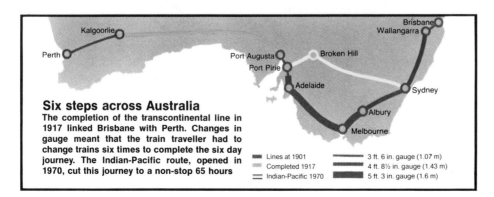

Six steps across Australia
The completion of the transcontinental line in 1917 linked Brisbane with Perth. Changes in gauge meant that the train traveller had to change trains six times to complete the six day journey. The Indian-Pacific route, opened in 1970, cut this journey to a non-stop 65 hours

Kalgoorlie · Perth · Port Augusta · Port Pirie · Adelaide · Broken Hill · Brisbane · Wallangarra · Sydney · Albury · Melbourne

Lines at 1901
Completed 1917
Indian-Pacific 1970

3 ft. 6 in. gauge (1.07 m)
4 ft. 8½ in. gauge (1.43 m)
5 ft. 3 in. gauge (1.6 m)

October 1917, and five days later, the first transcontinental train left Port Augusta, cheered by 1500 people. The first-class single fare between Kalgoorlie and Port Augusta was £5 10s [$174], with 10s [$15.80] extra for a sleeper. A second-class single ticket was £5 [$158], with 5s [$8] extra for a sleeper. Running time was 31 hours 20 minutes, but with stops, the trip took 42 hours 48 minutes.

'The carriages are fitted with electric fans and a refrigerating plant conveying food and drink for the travellers, and the bunks are sufficiently wide for a mother with two infants to sleep in any one of them,' said *Land and Transport* in December 1917.

But despite electric fans, cool drinks and wide bunks, travel across the Nullarbor Plain —where one stretch of track runs for 478 kilometres without a curve—was not pleasant. 'A lady who has just arrived per the medium of the new and awfully up-to-date transcontinental line tells us how Society travels when

the sun is shining on the saltbush,' wrote 'Clio' in Melbourne *Punch* in January 1918. 'Convention is discarded as easily as a dust-coat, and swarthy, perspiring Adoni step forth in the glory of muscles, singlets, and, of course, trousers.'

The great gauge muddle

Brisbane was now linked by rail with Perth. But the traveller who made the 5,611 kilometre journey was bedevilled by frequent breaks of gauges, legacies of inter-colonial jealousy and intransigence. From Brisbane he travelled 376 kilometres to the New South Wales border via Toowoomba, on a gauge of 3 ft 6 in. (1.07 m). From here to the Victorian border at Albury, there were 1426 kilometres of standard 4 ft 8½ in. (1.43 m) gauge. From Albury through Melbourne to Adelaide and 225 kilometres northward to Terowie, the gauge was 5 ft 3 in. (1.6 m). From Terowie, his train crawled on a 3 ft 6 in. (1.07 m) gauge

to Port Augusta at the head of Spencer's Gulf, where he joined the standard-gauge transcontinental line for the 1691 kilometre journey to Kalgoorlie. The last lap of 505 kilometres to Perth was again on a 3 ft 6 in. (1.07 m) gauge. This meant he had been in six different trains. 'It is now possible to travel from Perth to Brisbane, roughly speaking, in six days,' said *Land and Transport* in July 1918. By then the transcontinental train had become so popular that the service was increased from two to three trains a week.

By 1962, a uniform gauge of 4 ft 8½ in (1.43 m) connected Brisbane, Sydney and Melbourne and by 1982 it linked the five mainland states as well as running north to Alice Springs. One can now go from Brisbane to Perth in three-and-a-half days. The 'Indian-Pacific' makes the 3960 kilometre run from Sydney to Perth via Broken Hill in under three days. The 'Alice' a two-day service between Sydney and Alice Springs began in 1983.

The Roberts tracklayer was used for the first time in Australia for the construction of the transcontinental railway. Despite the fact that the ground had to be laboriously prepared by navvies and horse-drawn scoops, the builders were still able to lay a record 4 kilometres of track a day. Under ideal conditions modern equipment can lay about 7 kilometres of track a day

The four-day journey from Sydney to Perth in 1938 has now been whittled down to 65 hours

The 'Tea and Sugar' train makes a weekly trip along the transcontinental railway to supply maintenance workers who look after the track

The first train on the Indian-Pacific route leaves Sydney on 23 February 1970. East and west were now linked by a standard-gauge line

The Indian-Pacific bound for Perth. Before the completion of this line travellers from Brisbane to Perth had to change trains six times

221

The great days of steam

The austere reality of a romanticised era

For almost a century after Australia's first steam train—a puffing, grunting rattle-trap plying between Melbourne and its port—started its services in 1854, the railway offered little comfort to its passengers.

The carriages of a generation ago, in which many passengers had to sit up all night, were antiquated and filthy. On cold days, one shivered, and when it was hot, one had to choose between opening the windows and being half blinded by dust, soot and cinders, or closing them and being stifled. Even on the longest journey, the only food available was an unappetising snack in dingy refreshment rooms.

Travellers of the 1930s will have vivid, if not very pleasant, memories of the early morning horrors as trains pulled in for a breakfast stop. Dishevelled, bleary-eyed passengers staggered on to the mournful grey asphalt in various stages of undress, and the cold meat pies, drenched in tomato sauce and served by yawning waitresses in grimy white uniforms, did little to lift their morale. Often, just as the famished traveller received his scalding hot tea in a grubby, thick cup, the bell would ring, forcing him to scurry back to the departing train.

But gradually this primitive era of railway transport came to an end. The man responsible for many of the changes was Harold Clapp, the Melbourne-born son of Francis Boardman Clapp, an American who had settled in Australia in the 1850s.

After 19 years as a railway engineer in the United States, Harold Clapp returned to Australia in 1920 and was commissioned by the Victorian Government to take over the reorganisation of Victoria's railways. As a result, a carriage proudly publicised as the 'first air-conditioned passenger carriage in the British Empire' was introduced on the Victorian section of the Melbourne-Sydney 'express' as early as 1935.

Clapp went on to revolutionise Melbourne's electric suburban railways—and in 1937, produced Australia's first all-steel, fully air-conditioned train, the famous *Spirit of Progress*, which set an unforeseen standard of luxury in rail travel. Among its attractions were a high-class dining car and Australia's first train hostess.

World War II brought a sudden halt to the new ventures, but after 1945, all states resumed their efforts to bring the quality of their passenger services up to par with the rapidly developing times. In 1952, the year of Sir Harold Clapp's death, Victoria's first diesel-electric locomotive went into operation. It was named *Harold W. Clapp*, and Sir Harold rode in the cabin and acted as assistant engineer. The Sydney-Melbourne 'Daylight Express' followed in 1956, when passengers could, for the first time, see the landscape between the two cities from their carriage windows in the clear light of day.

Eventually, the high-speed XPT is expected to reduce the Sydney to Melbourne journey time to about 10 hours. Luxury trains with sleeping, dining, lounge and club cars now run on several long-distance routes.

Passengers stretch their legs at Gundagai railway station in the early 1900s. Carriages had no connecting corridors, so stops were a welcome relief on long journeys

A C36 locomotive pulls out of Casino station. These engines were the main workhorses on New South Wales railways, usually used for pulling local passenger or mail trains

Despite the primitive facilities, early rail travel had its charm. The timber station at Hill Top with its plank platform and overhanging trees conjures up memories of a less hectic age

An early morning scene on the Mullet Creek causeway, which forms part of the Sydney-Newcastle line. The locomotive is a C38, the principal express engine used in New South Wales to haul passenger trains in the 1950s, when steam was unchallenged as a source of motive power

Streamlined giants that pulled the crack expresses

A romantic aura surrounded the engines that pulled the expresses during the great days of steam. These machines, often weighing over 200 tonnes, were capable of speeds of more than 160 km/h.

The Victorian S class ran from 1928 to 1933 and was the fastest steam engine to run in Australia. It had a top speed of over 192 km/h, and was best known as the engine that pulled Australia's first prestige express, the *Spirit of Progress*.

The New South Wales C38s hauled all the crack expresses out of Sydney—the 'Melbourne Limited' to Albury, the 'Riverina Express' to Junee and the 'Newcastle Flyer' to Newcastle.

The South Australian 520 class looked, at first sight, more like a submarine on wheels than a steam engine. It hauled the 'Overland' from Adelaide to Melbourne and was still in active service in the 1960s.

Victorian railways S-class locomotive—fastest steam engine in Australia

The C38 was the most famous locomotive to run in New South Wales

The record-breaking, 200-tonne, South Australian railways 520-class engine

Railway posters of the 1930s extolled the pleasures of train travel

Riding to work on the dummy

When tramways ruled the city streets

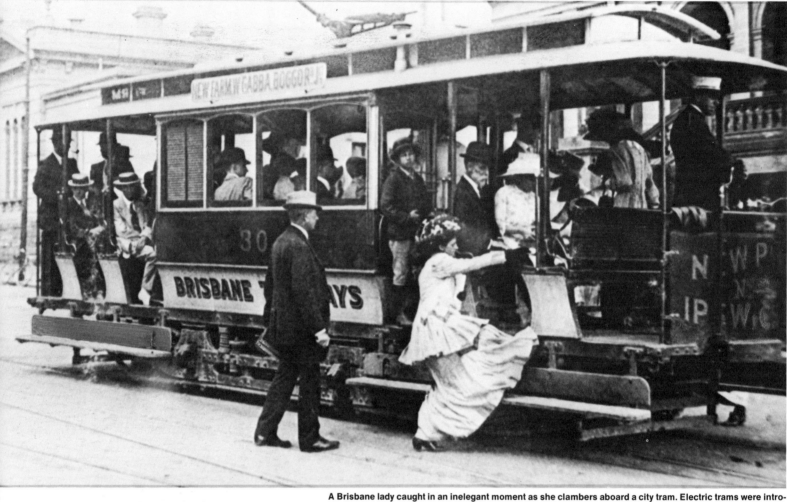

A Brisbane lady caught in an inelegant moment as she clambers aboard a city tram. Electric trams were introduced in Brisbane in 1897, and stopped in March 1969. At that time there were over 192 kilometres of track

In 1901, citizens of Sydney could travel to work by steam-train, steam-tram, cable-tram, electric tram or horse-drawn omnibus. The omnibuses, painted brilliant yellow, were drawn by four or five horses. Some were double-deckers. The outside passengers, men only, sat back to back with their feet braced against a rail. When a passenger wanted to alight, he pulled a strap that ran through to the front of the bus where it was conveniently attached to the driver's arm.

Melbourne in 1901 boasted one of the biggest and most efficient tramway systems in the world. Its cable-trams trundled along at a comfortable 20 kilometres an hour, hauled by a heavy steel cable beneath the road. The trams consisted of a closed car hauled by an open 'dummy', where the gripman, or driver, stood, manipulating his heavy levers. This car was intended for ladies, children, old people and non-smokers. On fine days, there was always a rush for seats on the 'dummy'.

In 1913, Melbourne had 73.5 kilometres of cable tramways, 24.3 kilometres of electric tramways, and 21 kilometres of horse tramways. On 31 January 1916, when Hawthorn's horse tram service ended after operating since 1890, *Table Talk* commented: 'The horses are well-nourished beasts and reflect the care which the company has bestowed on its properties. The old horse tramway has had its

day, but it departs amid general regrets.'

On 6 April 1916, electric trams began a service from Hawthorn to Princes Bridge—the first electric trams to serve the city.

Melbourne had a great affection for its cable-trams, the last of which disappeared in 1940. An English visitor, Thomas Wood, who was in Australia in 1930-31, wrote:

'Most trams are hateful. They are noisy, imperious and hide-bound despots but the cable-tram is a docile friend. If the cable-tram were done away with, people in Melbourne would be robbed of that hope of relief from

Mick Phelan, tram signal-man at Sydney's busiest intersection in 1929. At peak periods about one tram every eight seconds passed this point

Straw boaters were evidently standard dress for ticket collectors in 1909, when this group of Adelaide horse tramway employees were photographed

Commuters at Mundoora, SA, in 1907 after the 80-minute, 16-kilometre trip from Port Broughton

Steam trams near Central railway in Sydney. The last government-owned steam tram ran in 1937

A cable and an electric tram meet in a Sydney suburb. Cable-trams stopped running in 1905

An electric tram in Hobart during World War II. Some Hobart trams had a net catcher at the front

the humdrum which every true traveller sets out with.' When double-decker buses were introduced in Melbourne in 1902, *Table Talk* reported:

'The new omnibuses are at present a great Melbourne attraction, and draw numbers

into the city from distant suburbs, solely for the purpose of going for a journey on the roof. It needs an effort to mount to the roof at first, but the feeling soon wears away, and the experience is quite thrilling. Soon these roof rides will be the correct thing.'

In December 1905 the Victorian Railway Department inaugurated a steam omnibus service between Malvern and Prahran, competing with the horse buses of the tramway company, but it was discontinued after six months. Sydney motor buses that had been running for five months on the Potts Point service were also discontinued about the same time. 'Horse buses have driven the motors off,' *The Australasian Coach Builder* reported with satisfaction.

Adelaide in 1897 boldly experimented with an electric tram powered by storage batteries, but went back to its horse trams until 1909, when they were replaced by more orthodox electric trams.

Brisbane introduced electric trams in 1897, and Perth in 1889. Perth trams were equipped with a rope mesh 'cow-catcher' at each end, lowered according to the direction the car was travelling. This was supposed to scoop up not cows but careless citizens.

The conductor on Sydney's 'toast rack' trams often collected fares while balanced precariously on a 30 centimetre-wide plank running along the tram

Electric trolley buses were introduced in Sydney experimentally in 1934. They replaced the steam trams on one route where they ran until 1959

When a cable-tram reached a corner, the gripman had to disconnect the cable and coast. If the tram lacked sufficient momentum, passengers and conductor would leap off and push the tram around the curve. Melbourne, where this photograph was taken, is the only Australian city to have kept its trams

225

When boats had sails and paddle-wheels

River boats that brought prosperity to the inland

The fast and cheap transport provided by the river boats brought prosperity to many inland stations. Instead of carting wool over hundreds of kilometres of bad roads, bullock teams only had to cart it as far as the nearest river loading point. Freight costs from Wilcannia to Echuca were as low as £1 [$35] a ton. Barges and boats could carry enormous quantities of wool. One barge, the *Vega*, was 33 m long and could carry 1700 bales of wool

The *Decoy* was one of the best known boats on the Murray. She was built on the Clyde in 1898 and sailed out to Australia. In 1905, after seven years towing barges on the Murray, she carried miners from Adelaide to the goldfields in Western Australia. She was sold in Fremantle and used on the Swan River as a pleasure boat before returning to the Murray, where she remained in active service until 1932

The *Marion* was built in 1897 and in the 1920s she was used as a passenger boat between Mildura and Murray Bridge. The fare for the seven-day return trip from Murray Bridge to Renmark was £4 10s [$118]

By the start of the 20th century, the great days of the river boats had passed. In their heyday, the 1870s and 80s, the boats and their barges, piled high with wool from the inland stations, had been a common sight chugging down the Murray, Darling and Murrumbidgee river systems to the rail heads at Bourke and Echuca.

At that time the boats were the only reliable means of taking wool to the coast. But as the network of railways grew so did competition for the wool trade, and by the early years of the 20th century the river traffic was virtually defunct. In 1900 only 76 boats called at Echuca wharf with wool to be transported by rail to Melbourne and the waiting British wool clippers, whereas in the peak year of 1872 the figure had been over 240.

The major disadvantage of river travel was its unreliability. The boats depended on winter rains and melting snow in the spring to make the rivers navigable between July and January. In a bad year the river might dry up altogether and traffic would be impossible. On the other hand, a severe flood would swell the river so that it spread over many kilometres, and boats that lost their way or tried to take short-cuts might eventually find themselves stranded kilometres from the main channel of the river.

Many people on the river thought that the boats would be saved once locks were built to make the river navigable all year round. Work on the Murray locks started in 1917, but it was too late to recapture the dwindling trade. At Echuca and Morgan in the 1920s scores of old steamers and their barges slowly rotted away. At that time it was possible to buy a good boat for only £50 [$1350].

But although the wool trade was finished forever, timber boats still used the river. In the 1900s nearly 500 men worked in the Barmah forests near Echuca and the river boats, often towing two or three barges, would cart the logs downstream to the sawmills. But once again progress overtook the boats, and motor transport had ousted them from the timber trade by the mid-1950s.

Passenger boats were another feature of the rivers, playing an important part in transporting people and goods to the river towns. As the wool traffic declined, many cargo boats were converted to passenger use.

The last steamer to come up the Darling to Bourke was the *J. G. Arnold* in 1931, and by then the river was silted up and the piles of the wharf were rotting.

Sailing ships fight a losing battle with steam

At the turn of the century, 'clipper packets' of several lines were still carrying passengers, and cargo, from Melbourne to London and Hull. The Loch Line, with a fleet of over five ships, advertised:

Saloon passengers will be supplied with bed, bedding, towels and table-linen; second-class passengers will be supplied with all table requirements.

Just as the steamships plying around the Australian coast fought a losing battle with trains and aeroplanes, so the overseas sailing ships which had long dominated the sea lanes to Australia fought a losing battle with steamships. In the late 1890s the tonnage of steamships leaving Australia passed that of sailing ships, and by 1910 there were three times as many steamships as there were sailing ships. Many of these sailing ships, despite the fact that they often had to wait in port for months at a time, still came to Australia in ballast, confident of getting a cargo. Norwegian, Finnish, American, German and Italian sailing ships were common in Australian waters and harbours in the first years of the century.

Sailing ships carried coal from Newcastle to Chile until World War I, when much of the world's shrinking fleet of sail was lost to enemy action. The disappearance of sail was also hastened by the opening of the Panama Canal in 1914, and by the widespread substitution of oil fuel for coal.

While sailing ships were tied up in Australian ports awaiting cargoes, the sailors had to fend for themselves ashore, and hordes of unscrupulous boarding-house keepers found them easy prey. Boarding-house keepers solicited custom by handing out their business cards, such as this one from a Newcastle establishment in 1905:

J. O'SULLIVAN & BRIDGES, Boarding-master. Gentlemen sailors attended to Aucher Frères pianos, pills and salts for use of boarders.

The coastal steamers

At the outbreak of World War I, before the trans-Australian railway had linked Perth with the eastern states and the Sunshine Route had linked Brisbane with Cairns, no fewer than 164 steamships, with accommodation for 16,000 passengers, plied between Australian ports.

The names of the ships which served ports from Cairns to Fremantle, and the Tasmanian ports of Hobart, Launceston and Burnie were familiar to most Australians. They included the *Dimboola*, the *Karoola*, the *Zealandia*, the *Canberra* and the *Katoomba*.

The voyage from Fremantle to Melbourne took seven or eight days, and the Melbourne to Sydney two days and one night.

After World War I new ships, most of them motor-ships, were added to the passenger fleet. But by 1938, the available passenger accommodation on coastal ships was only 40 per cent of what it had been in 1914. The coastal fleet gradually faded away, losing business to the railways and airlines.

The paddle steamer *Hygeia* was the fastest and one of the finest ships of her type in Australia. Built in 1890 for the excursion trade on Port Phillip Bay, she ran for 40 years until she was scrapped in 1932. She was officially credited with a top speed of 36.7 km/h in trials, but it was claimed that she later reached 40 km/h. The *Hygeia* weighed 987 tonnes, and could carry over 2000 passengers

Coal ships at anchor in Newcastle harbour in 1906. Many sailing ships of all nationalities carried coal from Newcastle across the Pacific to Chile until the outbreak of World War I

The grain races

At the turn of the century, hundreds of four-masted steel barques were carrying wheat to Europe from South Australian ports. The ships would arrive in Australia in ballast, load their cargoes of up to 5000 tonnes of grain, and race back to Europe. The first ships to arrive got the best prices for their cargoes. These grain races took place every year until 1939. In 1921 68 vessels still took part, but in 1939, only 13 remained.

Grain was the only cargo that the sailing ships could load and carry more economically than the steamers. The crews of the sailing ships were poorly paid, so it was not important that the ships might sit at anchor for several months waiting for a cargo.

A fast journey from South Australia to Europe was 90 days, although some ships took over 150 days. The race in 1939 was won by the *Moshulu*, a 5385-tonne barque which completed the trip to Europe in 91 days.

The race to be airborne

Who was the first Australian to make a powered flight?

When the Commonwealth was born, in 1901, no man anywhere had ever left the ground in a heavier-than-air, powered machine. Many flights in balloons and airships had been made since the first ascent by Jean-François Pilâtre de Rozier in France in 1783, but these depended on the lighter-than-air principle. There had also been a good deal of experimenting with kites and gliders in the late 19th century, but the real race was to be the first to fly a steerable, powered, heavier-than-air machine.

The story of aviation began on 17 December 1903, when the Wright brothers, Orville and Wilbur, made man's first controlled flight in a heavier-than-air machine at Kitty Hawk, North Carolina, USA.

In Australia, as in America and Europe, the answers to the problems of human flight were eagerly sought by a few enthusiasts. Among them was Lawrence Hargrave, a scientist and inventor whose experiments with kites and powered models influenced many early British and European designers, though his discoveries were not utilised by the Wrights. Hargrave never achieved true flight, but he was lifted to a height of 4.8 metres by four box kites at Stanwell Park near Sydney in 1894.

Collaborating with Hargrave in experiments with box kites in the 1890s was George A. Taylor, a man of extraordinary versatility: an artist, editor, journalist, inventor, astronomer, town-planner and radio engineer, with a messianic belief in the future of radio and aviation. Taylor came far closer to manned, controlled flight than Hargrave had done, when on 5 December 1909 he was lifted from the ground in a glider at Narrabeen Heads, near Sydney. His glider had a wingspan of 5.4 m and weighed 58 kg, and in the course of 29 flights made that day—not only by Taylor, but also by his wife Florence, Edward Hallstrom, the inventor, Charles Schultz and Mrs Schultz—Taylor achieved the maximum distance in a flight of 100 metres.

When Taylor was persuaded by his wife to abandon such tests, he turned his attention to other fields of experiment. In 1911, he fired a field gun by radio, and succeeded in exchanging wireless messages between speed-

Lawrence Hargrave suspended beneath one of his box kites to test its lifting power during experiments at Stanwell Park, NSW, in 1894. Hargrave never achieved free flight, although on one occasion a train of four box kites lifted him 4.8 metres into the air in a 33 km/h wind

ing trains. 'The world may see wireless dirigibles go forth with camera, photograph a position, drop bombs, and mechanically return to their base,' he prophesied.

On 28 April 1909, the inaugural meeting of the Aerial League of Australia was held in Sydney's Hotel Australia. Lawrence Hargrave, who took the chair, was appointed a vice-president, and George Taylor honorary secretary. The objects of the league were:

To watch the latest achievements in aerial engineering.

To secure the best recognition for Australian efforts in that direction.

To awaken public attention to the grave danger in allowing foreign nations to excel in aerial navigation.

To join forces with the Aerial League of the British Empire in advocating that the Empire should secure the same supremacy in aerial navigation as it has enjoyed in the command of the Sea.

On 11 September 1909, the Australian Defence Department announced in the *Commonwealth Gazette* a competition with a prize of £5000 [$232,350] for the best and most suitable aeroplane for military purposes. Only native-born Australians or naturalised British subjects were eligible and the machine had, as far as possible, to be constructed in

Hargrave spent many years experimenting with aeroplane engines. He invented the rotary engine, although he never developed it. This partially built sea-plane was powered by a small steam engine

George Taylor soars over the sand dunes near Narrabeen Heads, NSW, on 5 December 1909. This was the first heavier-than-air flight in Australia. Of the 29 flights made that day, the best covered 100 metres

Harry Houdini in his Voisin biplane during his Australian tour in 1910. The Voisin was a development of the box kite pioneered by Hargrave

Colin Defries in his Adamson's Wright biplane at Victoria Park racecourse in Sydney. Defries made his first flight on 9 December 1909, four days after Taylor's flights at Narrabeen. As there is no proof that he could steer the machine he is not given credit for the first controlled flight

Australia by Australians. It also had to be capable of remaining over a given area long enough for military observations to be made, of attaining a speed of at least 32 km/h, and of staying in the air for five hours.

The Government's offer was discussed at a crowded meeting held in the vestibule of the Sydney Town Hall on October 7. Many members of the Aerial League were present, and several of their model flying machines were exhibited on the platform. Two were 'flown' round the chamber.

The £5000 offer was subsequently withdrawn because, perhaps not surprisingly, there were no entrants.

The first powered flight

Who had the distinction of making the first *powered* flight in Australia is a much disputed question. There are three contenders: two obscure Australians, Colin Defries and Fred Custance, and the famous American escapologist Harry Houdini.

On 4 December 1909, the day before Taylor's historic ascent at Narrabeen, Colin Defries made three attempts to fly a Wright biplane at Victoria Park racecourse, Sydney. This plane and a Bleriot monoplane had been imported by L. A. Adamson, headmaster of Wesley College, Melbourne, who had sent Defries to England and France to buy them.

The Great Mechanical Bird

Thousands of people paid 2s 6d [$5.80] each to see Defries fly. His biplane, *Stella*, was adver-

tised as 'The Winged Wonder of the World', and 'The Great Mechanical Bird', but it did not live up to these flattering labels. At first towed by a car, and later in two unassisted attempts, it failed to take off. Five days later, Defries was more successful. Again watched by a big crowd, his machine left the ground and covered a distance of 105 metres in 5½ seconds, at heights of half to four and a half metres. The crowd cheered enthusiastically. 'As he left the ground there was an involuntary cry from about 150 spectators, "He's up" and he was up,' reported the *Sydney Morning Herald*.

On 18 December, in the early hours of the morning, Defries flew 400 metres in a straight line, again at a height of 0.5 to 4.5 m, and crashed. He lost control of the machine when his cap was bumped off and he grabbed for it. He was unhurt.

'Never in the history of human ingenuity had invention moved with such swiftness as in the improvement of the aeroplane,' Defries said, when interviewed while playing billiards in a leading Melbourne club. And in another interview he said:

'I have felt the thrill of rushing in a motor car over curving roads at 90 mph [145 km/h]; I have experienced the sudden surprise of the earth dropping away from me as I sat in the basket of a balloon; but there is no thrill, and there is no sudden surprise when flying. It is, after the feeling of security is fixed in the mind, simply a state of ecstasy.'

Many aviation historians deny that Defries flew, in the strict sense. He was airborne, but

he did not show that he could turn or otherwise control the machine.

Some give the credit for the first controlled flight to Fred Custance, a young Adelaide mechanic. On 17 March 1910, at Bolivar near Adelaide, Custance flew a Bleriot monoplane for 5 minutes 25 seconds, making three circuits of a paddock, a distance of about four kilometres. The machine had been imported by F. H. Jones, an Adelaide businessman, at a cost of £1000 [$45,560], and Custance, who had helped to assemble it, had taught himself to fly simply by reading the handbook which came with the aeroplane.

Houdini takes the trophy

The day after Custance's flight, Houdini made three flights in a Voisin biplane at Diggers Rest, near Melbourne. The flights ranged from one minute to 3½ minutes, and nine witnesses certified that Houdini had attained a height of 30 m and covered more than three kilometres on a circular course. On 21 March, he made another certified flight of seven minutes 37 seconds, covering about nine kilometres. 'The rope is unleashed and the machine starts off with me in it downfield like a bounding greyhound set at liberty . . . The sensation is indescribable . . .' he said. Houdini, whose real name was Erich Weiss, was on a theatrical tour of Australia, and had been invited by the Aerial League to bring his French-built biplane with him. The League awarded him its trophy in the belief that he had made the first flight in Australia.

Aeroplanes to defend Australia

Three models exhibited at the Aerial League's meeting on 7 October 1900 in response to a Defence Department offer of £5000 [$232,350] for an Australian-built military aeroplane. Despite the fact that flights in America and Europe had demonstrated the form that an aeroplane must take, many Australians were still experimenting with alternative designs. The offer had to be dropped because there were no candidates

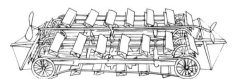

Ewing's aerocar

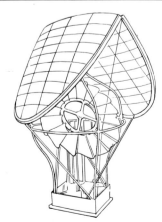

Green's floating aeroplane

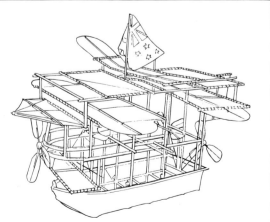

Garty's flying ship

John Duigan—Mia Mia's flying farmer

First successful Australian plane was built in a farm shed

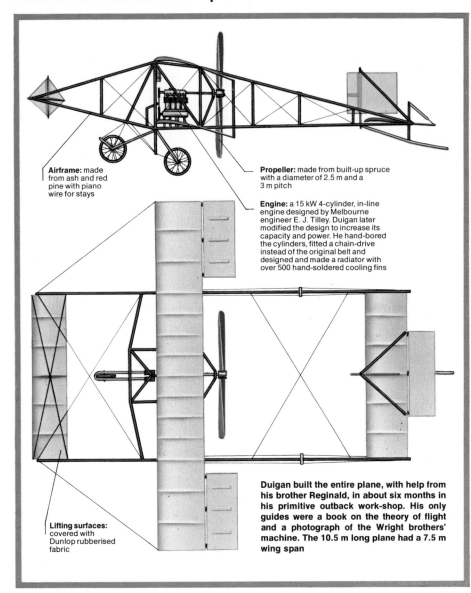

Airframe: made from ash and red pine with piano wire for stays

Propeller: made from built-up spruce with a diameter of 2.5 m and a 3 m pitch

Engine: a 15 kW 4-cylinder, in-line engine designed by Melbourne engineer E. J. Tilley. Duigan later modified the design to increase its capacity and power. He hand-bored the cylinders, fitted a chain-drive instead of the original belt and designed and made a radiator with over 500 hand-soldered cooling fins

Lifting surfaces: covered with Dunlop rubberised fabric

Duigan built the entire plane, with help from his brother Reginald, in about six months in his primitive outback work-shop. His only guides were a book on the theory of flight and a photograph of the Wright brothers' machine. The 10.5 m long plane had a 7.5 m wing span

The first Australian-built aeroplane to fly was made and flown at an isolated Victorian farm by a 28-year-old farmer and engineer who had never seen a plane.

John Robertson Duigan decided to build an aeroplane early in 1910 after seeing a photograph of the plane in which Orville and Wilbur Wright made man's first flight in a heavier-than-air machine at Kitty Hawk, North Carolina, in 1903.

Wings but no theory

Duigan began his flying career in 1907, with a pair of large home-made wings. Attempts to fly with the wings ended in a heavy fall, and they were discarded. In 1909, spurred on by the news of the Wright brothers' demonstrations in France, he built a half-scale model of their aeroplane, without a motor. This plane, tethered by 109 metres of fencing wire, carried him to a height of one to one and a half metres.

Duigan's early experiments with gliders convinced him that his main problem was that he knew nothing of the theory of flight. In June 1909, however, he borrowed a copy of Sir Hiram Maxim's book *Natural and Artificial Flight*, and at last found accurate calculations on which he could base the design of a powered aircraft.

Duigan decided to build a biplane based loosely on the French Farman. Working in a makeshift corrugated iron lean-to on his property at Mia Mia, with Melbourne 96 kilometres away over difficult roads, Duigan had to improvise most of the components and many of the tools.

The airframe was made from ash and red pine with piano wire for stays. Sheet-metal fittings were made from old steel bands off wool bales, and the entire frame was bolted together for strength. No glue, nail or screw was used in the entire construction. Duigan also included several devices of his own

Duigan at the controls of one of the three gliders that he built. His first, unsuccessful, attempt at flight was with a large pair of wings. This glider was a half-scale model of the Wright brothers' first aeroplane, without the motor. The machine was tethered with fencing wire and was lifted into the air by a strong wind. The limited experience gained on gliders was all that Duigan had to guide him when he made his first flight on 16 July 1910

With the engine roaring at full throttle Duigan climbs rapidly into the air at the start of one of his early flights at Mia Mia.The flights at Mia Mia were made more difficult by the size of the flying ground, which was only 800 metres long, 400 metres wide and surrounded by trees

design, such as air-springs for the running wheels instead of the conventional rubber shock-absorbers then in use.

The only part of the aircraft that Duigan did not make was the engine. This he had specially designed by Melbourne engineer E. J. Tilley, but even here Duigan later made extensive modifications himself.

Airborne for seven metres

Duigan's flying ground was a smooth paddock near the homestead, surrounded by ploughed fields and trees. In order to get the machine there, three men had to manhandle it down a 1-in-4 hill, across two fences and over a neighbouring creek.

On his first trial Duigan tried several practice runs along the ground at half-throttle. The machine handled well, despite a strong cross-wind, and Duigan was soon able to steer it using the rudder and ailerons. Then on 16 July 1910, with the engine roaring at full throttle, Duigan ran the machine fast downhill, raised the elevating plane, took off and was airborne for about seven metres. At last he could actually fly.

Not satisfied with the performance of the engine, he improved it by enlarging the cylinders and increasing the compression ratio. He also substituted a chain drive for the belt that drove the propeller. Duigan continued his trials during July and then, on October 7, in the presence of six awed spectators, he flew 180 metres at a confident height of about three and a half metres.

After this Duigan made many public demonstration flights, but within 18 months he decided he did not know how to fly and he left for England and the Avro flying school. He gained his Royal Aero Club pilot's certificate on 30 April 1912.

Duigan sits at the controls of his plane, perched precariously on the lower wing, with his head only a metre away from the engine and propeller. There was no protection in the event of a crash. Take-off speed was 19 to 24 km/h and top speed during flight was about 40 km/h

Forgotten names in Australian aviation

The aerial acrobat who flew Australia's first air mail

Maurice Guillaux in the clouds over Victoria Park in 1914. About 60,000 people watched as he 'looped the loop', a daring acrobatic manoeuvre

Australia was becoming increasingly aircon-scious, spurred on by a sense of distance and isolation from the rest of the world, when Maurice Guillaux, a dashing and accomplished French aviator, arrived in Melbourne in April 1914 with his Bleriot-type monoplane. He was an expert in aerial acrobatics, particularly in 'looping the loop', a spectacular manoeuvre in which the plane flies upside down in a circular dive.

More than 60,000 people turned up when he gave a demonstration at Victoria Park Racecourse, Sydney, in the presence of the Governor of New South Wales. He looped the loop ten times and, said the *Sydney Mail*, 'concluded his wonderful exhibition by flying round the course not more than three feet [nearly a metre] above the ground, to the accompaniment of salvos of applause'.

Lebbeus Hordern had imported a Maurice Farman 'hydro-aeroplane' which remained unpacked because no-one could fly it. Guillaux offered his services. He broke a bottle of champagne over the machine, named it *Olga* after Mr Hordern's wife, and made a number of flights. On one, his passenger was a Miss Bessie Mulligan, an Albury girl working in Sydney. As the *Olga* was circling Double Bay, Guillaux said, 'Put your arms around me and kiss me.' Someone who had field glasses intently focused on the pair exclaimed, 'My word! That was a bonzer kiss he gave her!'

Guillaux became the first pilot in Australia to use aircraft for commercial purposes. An American aviator, Arthur ('Wizard') Stone had been engaged to fly Australia's first air

mail from Melbourne to Sydney. A few days before the fixed date, his plane crashed and he was injured severely. Guillaux took over the arrangements and left the showgrounds at Flemington at 9.12 a.m. on 16 July 1914 with 1785 specially printed postcards and parcels of tea, cordial and lemon squash. One shilling [$1.95] was paid by each person for the privilege of sending a card to Sydney by air. Hundreds paid double on the black market, realising the value of these cards.

On the first day, Guillaux landed in paddocks at Wangaratta, Albury, Wagga Wagga and Harden. He had to return to Harden three times because of impossible weather, but on July 18 he made a successful flight to Goulburn through cloud and driving rain. After lunch with the Mayor he pushed on and arrived at Moore Park, Sydney, at 2.50 p.m. His total flying time was 9 hours 33 minutes at an average speed of 103 km/h.

'It was an epoch-making performance,' said the *Sydney Mail*. 'It gives us proof of the practical value of the aeroplane more convincingly than anything we could get from books. We realise the extraordinary pace at which the machine can travel as well as its stability in the roughest weather.'

During the war, Guillaux became a captain in the French Air Force, and later trained Australian airmen at Shrewsbury in England. There are countless anecdotes of his daring escapades—once, to win a bet, he took off in a Farman trainer with four men on the wings and two in the cockpit. He was killed in 1917 when his plane crashed at Villa Coublay near Paris.

Bert Hinkler—'Australia's lone eagle'

It was early morning on 7 February 1928 when a tiny Avro Avian biplane took off from Croydon aerodrome near London and set its course for Australia. At the controls was Herbert John Louis (Bert) Hinkler, who had sworn to beat the record of 28 days for the journey still held by Ross and Keith Smith.

Bert Hinkler had always been crazy about flying. As an 18-year-old youth in Bundaberg, he had built a glider called *Aviette*, which he based on his study of the flight of ibises. In 1912, he became mechanic to 'Wizard' Stone; the following year, he worked his passage to England, eventually to join the Royal Flying Corps. By the time he set off for Australia he was an experienced pilot having made a record flight of 1900 kilometres from London to Riga, Latvia, and a non-stop flight to Turin in 1920. The latter won him the Britannia Trophy for the most meritorious flight by a British aviator that year.

Nonetheless, few believed he would make it to Australia. The Avro Avian was a flimsy single-seater with fabricked folding wings, and experts doubted that such a frail machine could survive the perils of the route. But Hinkler pushed on, and reached Darwin in the record time of 16 days on February 22. It was the longest solo flight ever made, and it was to Australians what Charles Lindbergh's Atlantic flight had been to Amer-

icans. Hinkler was given a hero's welcome. More than 80,000 people greeted him at Sydney, where Sir Keith Smith gave him the title 'Australia's Lone Eagle'. The Commonwealth Parliament interrupted a debate to acclaim his feat and adjourned to allow its members to attend a function at which he was presented with a prize of £2000 [$53,260].

The Queensland Government gave him £500 [$13,315]. He received the Air Force Cross and was made an honorary squadron leader of the Royal Australian Air Force.

Hinkler went on to further triumphs. In 1931 he flew a Puss Moth across the South Atlantic from Brazil to West Africa. Bad weather plagued him throughout the 3,200 kilometre journey, yet after 22 hours of blind flying, he landed only 160 kilometres from his destination. The news flashed across the world that Hinkler had made the first west-east crossing of the South Atlantic and the first trans-Atlantic flight in a light aeroplane.

On 7 January 1933, Hinkler left London in an attempt to beat C. W. A. Scott's record of 8 days 20 hours from England to Australia. He passed over France and was not heard of again. Four months later, the wreckage of a plane was found in the Italian Apennines. Beside it was Hinkler's body. He was buried in Florence with military honours at the insistence of Benito Mussolini.

Hinkler created a craze in Australia. Anything that moved fast was said to 'hinkle', and a popular Hinkler hat was modelled on his flying helmet

Bert Hinkler and his Avro Avian after the record-breaking flight in 1928. His mother was among the first to welcome Australia's new hero

The flying dentist

The holder of Australia's first pilot's licence was W. E. Hart, a Parramatta dentist, who bought a Bristol biplane in 1911 and taught himself to fly it well enough to qualify for the Royal Aero Club's Aviator's Certificate in November that year.

On 29 June 1912, Hart won Australia's first air race. He challenged the visiting American flier, 'Wizard' Stone, to a 32 kilometre race from Sydney to Parramatta for a stake of £250 [$10,045]. It was a cold, windy and rainy day and Stone lost his way, landing at Lakemba. Hart, though a much less experienced pilot, finished the flight in 23 minutes.

Flying in those days had hazards on the ground as well as in the air. Hart once crash-landed in a Chinese market garden and had to compensate the infuriated owners. On a flight to Penrith, a storm forced him to land on the railway tracks near Mt Druitt, and he barely escaped being overrun by the Blue Mountains Express.

In 1912, he was hauled to the Sydney District Court by a Waterloo dairyman and charged with 'propelling ... an aeroplane over, upon and against the plaintiff's land and making great noise and disturbance therewith and frightened, disturbed and stampeded a herd of dairy cows, whereby two of the cows were killed and others injured'. Hart offered to settle for £10 [$400], but the Judge gave a ruling for the full claim of £20 [$805].

In 1916, Hart went to the Middle East as a trainer with the No. 1 Squadron of the Australian Flying Corps. After the war, he returned to dentistry. He died in 1943, a forgotten pioneer.

W. E. Hart prepares to land his Bristol biplane in Parramatta Park after beating 'Wizard' Stone in Australia's first air race in 1912. In spite of rain, he completed the 32 kilometre course from Botany, Sydney, in 23 minutes. Stone followed the wrong river and landed at Lakemba

Hart at the controls of a two-seater monoplane which he built on the lines of the French Nieuport in 1912. When making his third trial flight, he crashed from 60 m at Richmond, NSW. The plane was wrecked and Hart suffered multiple injuries which took him to hospital for two months

First attempt at Atlantic crossing

Harry George Hawker was the most famous Australian airman of his time and the first Australian flier to achieve a world reputation. He was one of a number of young Australians who saved their fares to go to London to learn the new art of flying.

After taking poorly-paid jobs with motor companies, Hawker joined the Sopwith Aviation Company in 1911 and became their top flying instructor. He made a series of speed and altitude records, and in 1913, competed for the £5000 [$200,850] *Daily Mail* prize for the first person to circumnavigate the British Isles within an elapsed time of 72 hours. He had covered 1678 kilometres in 55½ hours, when he crashed in the sea near Dublin. The *Daily Mail* awarded him a consolation prize of £1000 [$41,200], as his nearest contender covered only 320 kilometres.

Hawker returned to Australia in 1914 to demonstrate the new Sopwith biplane he had designed. To keep an appointment with the Governor-General, he landed on the lawns of Melbourne's Government House.

'The great lesson which has been taught by Harry Hawker,' said Melbourne *Punch*, 'is that in a properly constructed aeroplane of modern design, flight is as safe and simple as any other means of locomotion.'

Hawker's was also the first attempt to cross the Atlantic Ocean. Accompanied by Lieu-tenant-Commander K. Mackenzie Grieve, he took off from Newfoundland in a specially built Sopwith biplane on 8 May 1919. Soon after, gales blew them 240 kilometres off course, and when they were about 1600 kilometres out to sea, the engine failed and they were forced to ditch their machine close to a Danish tramp steamer, which picked them up. The ship had no wireless, and the fliers had been given up for lost when they were landed in Scotland on May 25. They were invested with the Air Force Cross by King George V, and awarded £5000 [$130,220] by the *Daily Mail*.

On 12 July 1921, when Hawker was practising at Hendon for an Aerial Derby, his machine caught fire and he was killed while trying to parachute from it.

Harry Hawker toured Australia in 1914 with a Sopwith Tabloid biplane. He gave demonstrations and carried joyriders at £20 [$780] a trip

Hawker landing on Caulfield Racecourse in Melbourne on 12 July 1914. 'Hawker the aviator is the hero of the moment,' said the Melbourne *Punch*

Heroes of the turbulent air

Nightmare flight that opened the London-Sydney air route

Ross Smith climbs into the cockpit of the Vickers-Vimy biplane in which he and his brother Keith pioneered the London-Sydney air route in 1919. The flight took 27 days 20 hours—a total actual flying time of 135 hours 50 minutes for the 18,500 kilometre journey

In 1919 aviation in Australia needed popular acceptance. The public still regarded the aeroplane as either a suicide machine or some sort of freak show. However, the Prime Minister, W. M. Hughes, had learned to appreciate the mobility offered by the plane on his frequent trips between Paris and London during the Versailles peace discussions. He offered a prize of £10,000 [$160,000] for the first Australian crew to fly between London and Australia in less than 720 hours before 31 December 1919 in a British-built machine.

The prize was won by the brothers Ross and Keith Macpherson Smith, with J. M. Bennett and W. H. Shiers as their mechanics, after a testing flight from England which made them public heroes in Australia.

Ross Smith, the Adelaide-born son of a station manager, was working in an Adelaide hardware store when World War I was declared on 4 August 1914. He enlisted seven days later, served at Gallipoli as a sergeant with the 3rd Light Horse, was promoted to lieutenant on the field of battle and then invalided to England.

After returning to his unit in Egypt in 1916,

he joined the Australian Flying Corps and received his wings in July 1917. During 1918 he was T. E. Lawrence's pilot in the Middle East and, a few weeks after the war ended, piloted a Handley Page bomber on the first flight from Cairo to Calcutta.

Keith Smith, two years older than his brother, was also a salesman in an Adelaide shop when war broke out. After being rejected by the AIF for health reasons, he went to England and was commissioned in the Royal Flying Corps. He did not, however, take part in any war action. The other two members of the team, Sergeants Bennett and Shiers, had been Ross Smith's mechanics on the Cairo-Calcutta flight.

Several other groups of intrepid fliers, attracted by both the challenge and the £10,000 prizemoney, also entered the race. Several dropped out because they could not meet the requirements of the Royal Aero Club and others failed to complete the journey. Two entrants, Howell and Frazer, flying a Martynside A1 with a single Rolls-Royce Falcon engine, died when their plane crashed into the sea off Corfu.

Ross and Keith Smith took off from the snow-covered Hounslow field, near London, at 9.12 a.m. on 12 November 1919 in a Vickers-Vimy biplane powered by two Rolls-Royce 268 kW Eagle VIII engines.

The plane carried 4386 litres of petrol, which gave it a cruising range of 3800 kilometres. The registration number was G-EAOU, interpreted by the fliers as 'God 'Elp All Of Us'. The motto began to seem apt soon after take-off, as the four men froze in the open cockpit and ice coated their goggles.

The early part of the flight was a nightmare because of terrible storms that swept across Europe. Conversation was impossible because of the roar of the engines, the fliers had no radio or navigational aids and only sketchy maps of many of the countries they passed over. Bennett and Shiers suffered almost more than the pilots. They were unable to sleep in the plane during the day because of the noise, cold, and vibration, and they had to spend most of each night servicing and repairing the plane. Every drop of the 90,920 litres of petrol used on the flight had to be laboriously pumped into the tanks from 18 litre tins.

The flight almost ended in Iraq when a severe gale sprang up while the Vimy was on the ground at Ramadie, near Baghdad. The plane was saved only because 50 soldiers spent the entire night physically holding it down.

At Calcutta there was another near miss when two hawks flew into and severely damaged one of the propellers as Ross Smith was taking off. He managed to regain control, but almost crashed into trees surrounding the airport.

On the last leg of the flight, the fliers struck monsoon weather, but the Vimy lumbered on at its steady pace of 128 km/h. The last accident occurred at Surabaya in Java, where the plane sank through the crust of an airfield improvised on a rice-paddy. It was only able to take off after villagers laid 400 metres of

The cheque presented to Ross and Keith Smith at the end of their flight by Prime Minister W. M. Hughes and the Governor-General, Sir Munro Ferguson

Queensland Railways save the day

how that our Rolls Royce engine has been tested I would like to say how pleased I am with the results of the test, and also how very much I appreciate the great assistance which we have been given by the Ipswich Works. The work carried out here has been done quietly and skilfully and reflects the greatest credit on all concerned. I am now quite confident that the engine will carry us on safely to the end of our flight. The new propeller which has been made is an excellent piece of workmanship and I am sure it will carry us along successfully.

Ross Smith.

The Vimy was held up for 11 days at Charleville in Queensland while workmen at the railway workshops repaired the engine and made a new propeller. Ross Smith records his satisfaction with the work in this letter to *Land, Sea and Air* magazine

bamboo matting stripped from their homes.

At 3.05 p.m. on December 10, the fliers landed at Darwin. They had flown approximately 18,500 kilometres in 27 days 20 hours—668 hours altogether. Actual flying time was 135 hours 50 minutes.

But their troubles were not over. They left Darwin on 13 December 1919, and the flight across Australia—the first from Darwin to Sydney—was punctuated with mishaps.

The hawk-damaged propeller was temporarily repaired with fencing wire and angle iron at Anthony's Lagoon in the Northern Territory. At Charleville, Queensland, they were held up for 11 days while workmen at the Queensland Railway Workshops at Ipswich repaired one of the engines. The railwaymen also made a replacement propeller of Queensland maple capped with brass.

The well-known photographer, Captain Frank Hurley, joined the plane at Charleville and accompanied the crew to Melbourne.

.After spending three days in Sydney, the fliers went on to Melbourne where they landed on Flemington racecourse on February 25. They were welcomed by the Governor-General, Sir Ronald Munro Ferguson, Prime Minister Hughes and a large crowd. Huges handed over the cheque for £10,000 to be divided equally among the crew members. Both the Smiths were knighted and Sergeants Bennett and Shiers were awarded Air Force medals and given the honorary rank of lieutenant in the Reserve of Officers as an added honour.

Ross Smith, who was 27 at the time of the flight, lectured on his experience in Australia and England. Early in 1922, he made

plans for a flight around the world. In England in April he took off for a trial flight with Lieutenant Bennett in a Vickers-Vimy amphibian. The machine went into a spin and crashed, and both men were killed.

Sir Keith Smith joined the staff of Vickers Limited in 1923 and became their Australian representative as well as a director of several Australian companies. He died in Sydney in 1955.

After the flight the Smith brothers toured Australia giving lectures and showing Frank Hurley's film of the final stages of the flight

Huge crowds turned out all over Australia wherever the battered but triumphant Vickers-Vimy landed. At Mascot, in Sydney, spectators clambered over the plane for three days before it left on the final leg of the flight to Melbourne, where the fliers were given an official state reception

The first trans-Pacific flight

Kingsford Smith's extraordinary career ends in tragedy

Kingsford Smith (right) and his co-pilot Charles Ulm in front of the *Southern Cross* in May 1928, before their historic flight across the Pacific

After World War I ended, the race to develop the potential of aviation began. One of the world's greatest pioneer airmen, Charles Edward Kingsford Smith, put Australia among the leading contenders.

Kingsford Smith had served with the Australian Imperial Force as a motor cycle despatch rider in Egypt, Gallipoli and France at the age of 18. In 1916 the Imperial Government called for 200 volunteers from the AIF to train as pilots in the Royal Flying Corps. Kingsford Smith, then 19, was among those selected, receiving his commission in March 1917. After three months' service in France, during which he shot down two planes, he was wounded, invalided back to London and awarded the Military Cross.

A medal from the King

'I went to Buckingham Palace and got my medal from the King,' he wrote to his family. 'He was awfully nice and spoke to me for about five minutes about my scrap.'

On his demobilisation after the war, Kingsford Smith joined forces with two other Australians who had been pilots in the Royal Flying Corps, Cyril Maddocks and Val Rendle, to earn a precarious living giving joy-rides in two DH-6 planes they had bought.

In March 1919, the Australian Government announced a prize of £10,000 [$160,440] 'for the first successful flight to Australia from Great Britain, of a machine manned by Australians'. The three young men decided to enter, proposing to fly a two-engined Blackburn biplane, the *Kangaroo*, powered with the latest Rolls-Royce 126 kW engine. However, their entry was disallowed by the Prime Minister, Billy Hughes, on the grounds that they lacked experience in navigation.

First set-back

Opportunities for aspiring pilots were few and Kingsford Smith lingered in England until winter, nursing his disappointment. Then, in November 1920, his partnership with Maddocks and Rendle broken up, he went to the United States. It was there that Kingsford Smith had the idea of flying across the Pacific, but he failed to get the necessary backing.

He spent about a year in the USA 'flying for a crust', as he put it, with the Moffett-Starkey Aero Circus, until having been swindled by Moffett, he abandoned this to paint signs for a petrol company. In January 1921, he returned to Australia.

In Australia, too, commercial aviation was still more saleable as a novelty than a utility, and Kingsford Smith went to work for another joy-riding firm, the Diggers' Aviation Company. During this time he distinguished himself when, on a joy-ride at Dubbo with three passengers, he made a safe landing with a collapsed wing—a remarkable demonstration of skill. But later he wrecked his plane and broke two ribs in a champagne-assisted take-off, an escapade which lost him his job. However, he found a new job in 1921 with the inauguration of the first Australian airline service. Western Australian Airways Ltd., under contract from the Commonwealth Government

and with a subsidy of 4s [$5.30] a mile, flew the 1600 kilometres between Geraldton and Derby, and Kingsford Smith was among the five pilots hired by the company. He worked for them until 1924. Then, with a pilot friend, Keith Anderson, he started a transport business, the Gascoyne Trucking Company, which so flourished that by the end of 1926 the partners were able to sell the business for £2300 [$60,570]. With money in their pockets they returned to Sydney. Here Kingsford Smith met Charles Thomas Ulm.

Like Kingsford Smith, Ulm had served in Gallipoli and France—under the name of Charles Jackson, for he was just under age at the time. However, it was not until after the war that he qualified as a pilot.

His meeting with Ulm revived Kingsford Smith's determination to make the flight across the Pacific, and the two men decided to attempt the trip together. But they had first to arouse public interest and attract funds. Accordingly, they set out in June 1927 from Sydney in a seven-year-old Bristol machine, to break the round-Australia record. They accomplished the trip in 10 days, less than half the time of the previous record held by Jones, Buchanan and Brinsmead.

Assembling the plane

As a result, Jack Lang, Labor Premier of New South Wales, guaranteed £3500 [$93,205], a sum subsequently increased by private donations to £9000 [$239,700], towards the cost of the proposed Pacific flight. Eventually, the fliers were able to buy the airframe of a badly damaged Fokker triplane that had been used by Sir Hubert Wilkins in his Arctic explorations. Using some parts of another of Sir Hubert's planes, this became the *Southern Cross*.

On 31 May 1928, with Ulm as co-pilot, and two Americans, Harry H. Lyon and Jim Warner, as navigators, Kingsford Smith took off from Oakland, California.

The farthest distance flown westward till then was 3862 kilometres to Honolulu—only one third the distance from America to Australia. The Southern Cross trip was to be made in three stages with landings at Honolulu, Fiji and Brisbane, and the lap from Honolulu to Fiji involved the longest non-stop flight ever attempted—the *Southern Cross* was in the air for nearly 35 hours before it touched down on the tiny Suva airfield. On 9 June 1928 they arrived in Brisbane; their total flying time had been 83 hours, 38 minutes. Kingsford Smith nd Ulm were jointly awarded £10,000 [$226,300] by the Commonwealth.

Coffee Royal Affair

After the Pacific flight, the aviators continued to notch up records. In August of that year, in the *Southern Cross,* Kingsford Smith and Ulm made the first non-stop flight from Melbourne to Perth—3363 kilometres. In September they made the first east-bound flight across the Tasman—from Richmond, NSW, to Christchurch in 14 hours 25 minutes. The return trip to Richmond, NSW, the first westbound crossing, took 22 hours 51 minutes.

Then, for a time, there fell the shadow of

what came to be known as the Coffee Royal Affair. On 31 March 1929, Kingsford Smith, Ulm, H. A. Litchfield (navigator) and T. H. McWilliams (radio operator) set off from Richmond on the first lap of a westward flight to England to buy airliners for a projected Australian service, expecting to make their first landing at Wyndham, in northern Western Australia. But after crossing the Overland Telegraph line in Central Australia, the *Southern Cross* ran into a storm, the fliers were disoriented, and with fuel almost exhausted made a forced landing on a mosquito-infested mud flat of the Glenelg River estuary at Coffee Royal.

Nothing was heard of them for 12 days. An intensive air search was made. Among the searchers were two of Kingsford Smith's friends Keith Anderson and Bobby Hitchcock. They too became lost in the air and made a forced landing at Wave Hill in Central Australia. They died of thirst, having drunk the alcohol in their broken compass.

The *Southern Cross* was eventually found, provisions and fuel were dropped, and a small plane landed to pick up Litchfield and McWilliams. With the lighter load, Kingsford Smith was able to take off. The reception he and Ulm faced on their return was a good deal different from what they might have expected. A rumour, arising from a *Smith's Weekly* report, that the landing on the mud flat had been a premeditated publicity stunt had been widely believed. An official inquiry completely exonerated them, but Kingsford Smith was understandably bitter.

Complete circumnavigation

In June 1929, he took off from Sydney and reached London in the record time of 12 days 18 hours. A year later, he completed his circumnavigation of the world by flying from Portmarnock, Ireland, to New York by way of Newfoundland, and then to San Francisco. It was the first westward crossing of the Atlantic against the prevailing winds.

In October 1930, he set a light aircraft solo record from England to Australia, flying an Avro Avian Sport, the *Southern Cross Junior*, to Darwin in 9 days 22 hours 15 minutes elapsed time. He was made honorary Air Commodore of the Royal Australian Air Force in 1930 and knighted in 1932.

In October 1933, in a Percival Major Gull, *Miss Southern Cross*, he set a new record of 7 days, 4 hours and 44 minutes for a solo flight

Australia issued this stamp in 1931 to celebrate Kingsford Smith's record breaking world flights

The *Southern Cross* on a demonstration flight over New Zealand. Shortly after this photo was taken, in September 1928, Kingsford Smith and Ulm set another aviation record—the first trans-Tasman crossing

Half of Christchurch, NZ, turned out to greet the aviators when the *Southern Cross* landed there. Despite his popularity, Kingsford Smith had a constant struggle to get backing for his flights

from England to Australia, and in August-September 1934, flying a Lockheed Altair, *Lady Southern Cross*, he set the following Australian inter-city records: Sydney to Perth, 10 hours; Melbourne to Sydney, 2 hours 11 minutes; Adelaide to Sydney, 3$\frac{1}{2}$ hours. In October-November the same year, with Gordon Taylor as navigator and relief pilot, he made the first flight from Australia to America in a single-engined plane.

Kingsford Smith came close to disaster in May 1935. He and Taylor were flying the King George V Jubilee air mail from Sydney to New Zealand, when the *Southern Cross* developed engine trouble about 965 kilometres from the Australian coast. At enormous risk, Taylor climbed out under the wing five times to transfer oil from one engine to another, an amazing feat of courage for which he was awarded the Empire Gallantry Medal.

This was the last time Kingsford Smith flew the 'Old Bus', as he called his historic machine. Soon after, he offered to sell it to the Australian Government to be preserved. After haggling, the Government bought it for £3000 [$96,000] (the initial offer had been £1500 [$48,000]!)

If the Government's parsimonious reluc-

tance to part with a reasonable sum for the *Southern Cross* gave Kingsford Smith cause for bitterness, so did its continued failure to give him any kind of real financial backing. Public adulation was no substitute for a secure living. For some time he had sought Government support of his scheme for the establishment of a regular trans-Tasman service. Some promise of help was forthcoming from New Zealand, but Australia was still evasive.

His funds were low. The Australian Government was holding up the payment for the *Southern Cross*. Kingsford Smith decided that his best course was to try for yet another record, hoping the publicity would help raise the necessary funds for his trans-Tasman venture. Ill, and dispirited by continued rebuffs, he left London on 6 November 1935 with copilot Tommy Pethybridge, to fly the *Lady Southern Cross* back to Australia. Two days later they took off from Allahabad for Singapore. They were never seen again.

Sir Charles Kingsford Smith left an estate totalling £12,875 [$412,360]. Three years after his Atlantic flight in 1927, Charles Lindbergh, whose achievements were immeasurably less than Kingsford Smith's had a personal fortune estimated at over $40 million.

237

Record-breakers and daredevils

On 7 January 1920, too·late for the 1919 London-Sydney air race but not for the pages of history, Lieutenants Raymond Parer and John McIntosh left Hounslow, near London, in a battered DH9 biplane, which had been condemned as not airworthy upon examination by the British Air Ministry.

They arrived at Darwin on 2 August, after an incredibly hazardous flight of 206 days which included two crashes—in Burma and Java. They flew on from Darwin on 10 August and reached Sydney 11 days later. On the last lap, their machine was wrecked in a nose dive at Culcairn, 374 kilometres from Melbourne, but the fliers escaped unhurt.

A Sydney aviation writer described them as 'two lame ducks in a comic opera bus'. He itemised some of the troubles they had encountered: '. . . carburation troubles galore—floats leaking, jets loosening and needles jamming. Propeller bolts, bearer bolts and cylinder bolts all worked loose periodically. Their magnetos frequently required resetting. They had bad trouble, too, with their oil filters and petrol connections . . . of their instruments, practically every one failed at some stage of the flight . . .'

The fliers used up five propellers, three undercarriages and three radiators between England and Australia. One of the substitute radiators consisted of two motor car radiators bolted together in makeshift fashion.

In 1924, two RAAF fliers performed a feat that did much to convince the public that flying was safe—they flew round Australia.

Wing-Commander Stanley Goble and Lieutenant Iver McIntyre left Point Cook on 6 April 1924 in a Fairey 3D seaplane to survey the coastline for the RAAF. They completed the 13,680 kilometre journey 44 days—some 90 flying hours—later.

The plane had a very short range, and the fliers were forced to make dozens of landings. They did all their own maintenance, refuelling from 37 depots laid down by an oil company. On most nights, each took it in turn to have two hours' sleep while the other watched the plane. Often, after a hard day's flying, they had to struggle to keep the plane from drifting on to rocks or reefs.

Solo flights from England

Francis Chichester, who later became world-famous as a yachtsman for his single-handed circumnavigation of the world, was another flier of the 1920s who made a solo flight to Australia. He flew a DH Puss Moth, arriving on 29 December 1929, at the very end of a great decade of flying.

In the 1930s two women made flying news. Amy Johnson was the first woman to make the England-Australia flight. She left England on 5 May 1930, flying solo in a DH Moth, and reached Darwin in 19 days. Later,

she married James Mollison, who in July-August 1931, also flying a DH Moth, made a record flight from Wyndham to England in eight days, 19 hours and 25 minutes.

Jean Batten, a New Zealander, flew her DH Moth from England to Darwin in May 1934 and, the next year, flew it back from Darwin to England. In 1935 she made the first flight from England to New Zealand via Australia, and in 1937, flew from Australia to England in five days, 18 hours and 15 minutes—14 hours better than the record.

Melbourne Centenary Air Race

On 22 March 1933, when Melbourne was preparing to celebrate its centenary with elaborate junketings, her Lord Mayor, Harold Gengoult Smith, wrote to the confectionery millionaire Sir Macpherson Robertson: 'Dear Sir Macpherson—will you give £10,000 [$333,800] for the greatest air race the world has ever seen—for our Centenary?' Sir Macpherson replied in nine workds: 'Re yours of even date my reply is yes.'

Twenty planes carrying entrants of many nationalities left England on 20 October 1934 to compete for the prize. Eight crashed or withdrew between England and India. Two days and 23 hours later 50,000 excited spectators saw a scarlet DH Comet—forerunner of the famous Mosquito—flown by C. W. A. Scott and T. Campbell-Black flash over the finishing line at the Flemington race course, Melbourne.

'In an age of extraordinary mechanical progress one takes many things for granted, but flight half-way across the world seems too remarkable for analysis . . .' said the Melbourne *Argus*. 'If the present conquest of speed be maintained at its present rate, an air journey to England in these days will become a commonplace and Australia, that vast land over the edge of the beyond, will become part of a great world.'

An American, Roscoe Turner, came second, in three days 21 hours and five minutes.

The most spectacular performance was that of two Dutch airmen, K. D. Parmentier and J. J. Moll, who won the handicap section of the race in a Dutch-built Douglas DC2 of the Royal Dutch Air Lines. It was the first modern airliner seen in Australia. Towards midnight on 23 October, flying from Charleville to Melbourne, they lost their bearings in severe thunderstorms near the Victorian border. Their radio call for help was picked up by station 2CO at Corowa, which broadcast appeals to motorists to assemble at the Albury Racecourse and light the field with their headlights. Meanwhile, the Mayor of Albury, Alderman Alf Waugh, had the street lights switched on and off to signal the name of the town in morse code.

The airmen, told by radio where to land, dropped parachute flares and made a perfect landing through blinding torrential rain. The machine was bogged, but was pulled out next morning by about 300 enthusiastic citizens. Leaving their mail and passengers behind, Parmentier and Moll flew on to win the handicap section in three days, 18 hours and

Stanley Goble and Iver McIntyre flew round Australia in this Fairey 3D seaplane in 1924. The two fliers completed the hazardous 13,680 kilometre survey of the coast for the RAAF in a series of short hops over 44 days. Their flight greatly encouraged public acceptance of aviation

Handsome 21-year-old Jimmy Melrose was mobbed by women when he reached Melbourne after the 1934 air race. Melrose, the youngest entrant, came second in the handicap section. This beam wireless picturegram, one of the earliest received from England, shows him preparing his kit for the race

There was no airfield nearby and Arthur Butler's little Comper-Swift needed refuelling, so he landed in the main street of Tooraweenah, northern NSW, and filled it up. Butler's flight, in October 1931, clipped two hours off C. W. A. Scott's two-day, 23-hour England-Australia record. The plane was the lighest ever flown on the route, and Butler only had sufficient room in the cockpit for one suit of clothes and very little food

18 minutes. The Dutch airmen, who claimed they were not really racing, but simply proving that commercial aircraft could make long, fast flights, waived second place in the overall section to take the handicap prize.

Queen Wilhelmina of the Netherlands conferred the Order of Oranje-Nassau on Alderman Waugh and made personal gifts to those who had helped the fliers, and the Dutch people subscribed for a plaque which was placed in Albury's council chamber.

Second in the handicap section of the race was Jimmy Melrose, who reached Melbourne in his Puss Moth after a leisurely flight of ten days, 16 hours and 23 minutes. But he was not the last entrant to arrive. That distinction belonged to Messrs Davies and Hill, flying a Fairey 3F—time, 36 days.

Greasy overalls gave warmth

Early in 1916, a 22-year-old Queenslander, Sidney Cotton, arrived in England to join the Royal Naval Air Service. A few weeks later he sat in a cockpit of a plane for the first time and flew solo. Three weeks later he passed his final test, which included flying, navigation, plotting and morse code. He was soon flying on bombing raids over Germany.

Pilots in those days suffered severely from cold in their open cockpits. One day in the very cold winter of 1916, Cotton was tuning his engine when there was a sudden alert, and he took off still wearing his dirty blue overalls. When he returned to base, his fellow pilots, who had worn their flying kits, seemed to be frozen stiff, while he was quite warm. Cotton thought a lot about this, and decided that his

overalls, thick with oil and grease, had acted as an airtight bag, retaining his body heat. He went up to London and had a flying suit made on the basis of this theory. It had 'a warm lining of thin fur, then a layer of light Burberry material, the whole being made in one piece just like a set of overalls'.

Thus was born the famous 'Sidcot' flying suit which, after searching tests, was adopted by the RNAS and the Royal Flying Corps. The Germans paid Cotton the compliment of copying it. The famous German ace, Baron von Richthofen, was wearing a similar suit when he was shot down, and Alcock and Brown each wore one when they made the first direct flight across the Atlantic in 1919. But Cotton refused to patent his suit or to make any claim for inventing it.

In the 1920s, Cotton pioneered air mail services in Newfoundland. In 1931, he conducted an air search for Augustine Courtald, who was stranded on an ice-cap off Greenland. In 1939 he attempted to stop World War II with a plan to fly Goering to England.

In May 1930, the 28-year-old Amy Johnson piloted this little DH Moth from England to Australia, and became the first woman to fly the route solo

The rise of the airlines

When passengers played quoits on the promenade deck

Organised commercial flying in Australia began on 5 December 1921, when Major Norman Brearley began a weekly mail and passenger service between Geraldton and Derby in Western Australia. The route took in Carnarvon, Onslow, Roebourne, Port Hedland and Broome, and covered 1948 kilometres of rugged, sparsely populated country. The service was necessarily subsidised by the Commonwealth Government.

War-surplus aeroplanes

After war service with the Royal Flying Corps, Brearley had returned to Perth in 1919 with two war surplus Avro 504 biplanes. The Avros, which he assembled on the Belmont Park racecourse, had a wing span of 11 metres and a maximum speed of 128 km/h. In them Brearley gave flying exhibitions in Perth and country towns. He took passengers on ten-minute joyrides for which he charged £3 15s—the equivalent of about $98 today.

When he was awarded the mail contract, Brearley imported Bristol three-seater biplanes with a speed of 168 km/h. The Bristols were gradually replaced by DH50s, and within a few years Brearley's company, Western Australian Airways Ltd, grew to be the biggest airline in Australia.

. In 1924, it extended its services to Perth, and in 1929, operating DH Hercules 14-seat biplanes with a cruising speed of 160 km/h to Adelaide. This gave the company a 4828 kilometre network extending from Wyndham to Adelaide. The fare between Perth and Adelaide was £18—about $470 now.

Foundation of ANA

In 1943, Western Australian Airways lost its north-west contract to MacRobertson Miller Airlines. Two years later, faced with problems of reorganisation, it sold the Perth-Adelaide service to a new company that was to be known as Australian National Airways—which for a decade dominated Australian commercial aviation.

In 1919, the same year that Brearley returned to Western Australia with his Avros,

This T-model Ford, being helped across a dry Queensland river bed, carried pilots Hudson Fysh and P. J. McGinness when they surveyed an air route to Darwin in 1919. They later founded Qantas

A group of graziers who realised the need for air services in Queensland backed Fysh and McGinness when they started Qantas in 1920. This was the company's first office, in Longreach

a young man called Reginald Lloyd registered a company called Aerial Services Ltd in Sydney. His aim was to bring Australia within 150 hours of London.

At first the Postmaster-General had refused to grant registration to Lloyd's company. With classic lack of foresight, he said that 'the whole question of aerial mails is absolutely impractical as far as this country is concerned.' However, registration was finally granted, and on 31 January 1919 Lloyd led a convoy of seven motorcycles to survey an air route across Australia from Sydney to

Cape York. It took them more than four months to reach Darwin.

Later that year, the Federal Government commissioned two ex-RFC lieutenants, 23-year-old Hudson Fysh and 22-year-old P. J. McGinness, to survey a route from Longreach to Darwin for use by contestants in the £10,000 [$160,440] England-Australia air race. On August 18 they set out from Longreach in a T-model Ford utility, finally reaching Katherine on October 8.

In their report Fysh and McGinness condemned the route they had taken in favour

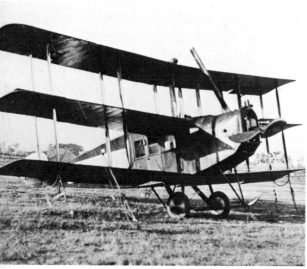
This Avro triplane, a post-war design, was introduced by Qantas in 1921 but was not a success

The bearded man here was the holder of Qantas ticket No. 1—Alexander Kennedy, born in 1837

On-the-spot repairs—not a sight to bolster the confidence of nervous fliers

of the one surveyed by Lloyd, and landing grounds were eventually prepared along Lloyd's route. His company's plans, however, came to nothing.

It was from Fysh and McGinness' expedition into remote Queensland that the international airline of Qantas was born. Backed by Fergus McMaster, a Queensland grazier, and a number of his friends, the two men founded Queensland and Northern Territory Aerial Services Ltd (QANTAS), registered as a company on 16 November 1920. It began operations with one plane, an Avro 504K, which cruised at about 105 km/h and provided joyrides at £3 3s [$72] for ten minutes and charter flights at 2s [$2.30] per mile.

First Qantas passenger

In February 1922, Qantas was awarded the contract for a weekly subsidised mail and passenger air service between Charleville and Cloncurry, a distance of 928 kilometres. The service was inaugurated on November 2 with two Armstrong Whitworth FK8 biplanes carrying two passengers and cruising at 136 km/h. The first passenger was 85-year-old Alexander Kennedy, a Western Queensland pioneer who, 53 years before, had taken eight months to drive his cattle from Longreach to Cloncurry. The plane journey took him four hours and 35 minutes.

In 1924, Qantas flew its first cabin plane. Thereafter passengers no longer had to suffer the full force of icy winds or the equally uncomfortable heat of high summer.

A Qantas handbook published in the 1920s offered this comforting advice to passengers: 'Flying caps or goggles are unnecessary. Sit at ease in the machine; your movements cannot possibly affect its balance ... The fact that many invalids have used our facilities, including people with weak hearts, women just out of hospital and infants three weeks old, demonstrates the ease of air travel.'

Commercial flying within Australia was now established; it remained only to provide an air link with the rest of the world.

The Journey from Sydney to Southhampton by flying-boats like *Cooee* (above) took nine and a half days. The service was very popular. The 15 passengers were provided with reclining chairs, a smoking cabin and a promenade deck, and a cabin crew of three. Mail was carried for 1s 6d [$2.15] per 14 g

In 1931 a single experimental airmail service was run between London and Darwin by Imperial Airways of Britain, with Qantas carrying the mail on to the southern Australian cities. However, it was not until 1934, when Qantas joined with Imperial Airways to form Qantas Empire Airways, that the first regular air mail service between England and Australia began in earnest.

Thirteen days to London

Soon after, Qantas put four-engined, ten-passenger DH86s into service, and Australians could fly the 7018 kilometres from Brisbane to Singapore in three and a half days. Imperial Airways took over from Qan-

tas at Singapore. The complete journey to London took 13 days, and the passengers slept in a different country almost every night.

By 1938, a new route suitable for flying-boats was surveyed, and the first west-bound flying-boat departed from Sydney on July 5. The Short Empire flying-boats took off from Rose Bay and reached Singapore four days later; but though they were slow, they were comfortable and introduced a new luxury to long-distance travel. You could move around them freely, and if you happened to be a ballet dancer, there was space on the promenade deck for you to do your daily exercise *à la barre*—as Serge Lifar did when he flew from England to Australia in 1939.

The *Brisbane* was one of Qantas' original fleet of ten-passenger DH86s which flew to Singapore

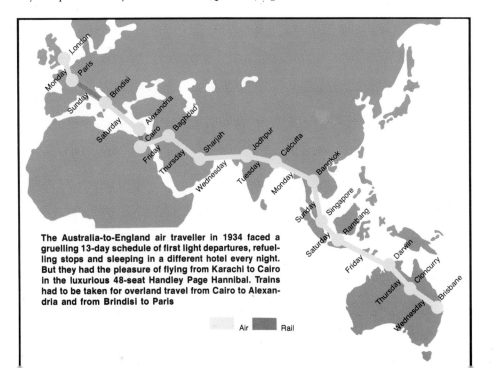

The Australia-to-England air traveller in 1934 faced a gruelling 13-day schedule of first light departures, refuelling stops and sleeping in a different hotel every night. But they had the pleasure of flying from Karachi to Cairo in the luxurious 48-seat Handley Page Hannibal. Trains had to be taken for overland travel from Cairo to Alexandria and from Brindisi to Paris

Air   Rail

Fashion Parade

Learning to dress for the Australian climate

The clothes that Australian men and women, living between the southern latitudes of 42° (Hobart) and 27° (Brisbane) wore in 1901 would not have been out of place between the northern latitudes of 56° (Edinburgh) and 51° (London). They did not adapt their dress to the demands of the Australian climate but copied exactly the clothes that the British middle classes found appropriate for their much cooler weather.

Australian women sweated through scorching summers in tight-laced corsets, voluminous underclothes and long dresses in heavy fabrics. Men wore three-piece suits of serge or tweed and did not discard the waistcoat in even the hottest weather. Everyone wore a hat.

Children suffered too. Boys wore serge Norfolk suits with trousers tucked into knee-length woollen socks, and girls were dressed in miniature versions of their mothers' elaborate dresses, complete with lace and embroidery. Boys and girls alike wore ankle-length boots. Infants, the risk of heat-stroke notwithstanding, were enveloped in matinee jackets, pelisses and gowns.

But these Edwardian fashions vanished in World War I. The war left women with a new, freer role in society, and this new freedom was reflected in their clothes. Yet during the next six decades, the path of Australian fashion passed through some obscure byways, with the not infrequent imitation of past styles, even some fads of the Edwardian era making their reappearance. The mini-skirt came and went, to be overtaken by the maxi-skirt. Easier travel overseas also had an influence, with kaftans all the rage, and the looser and more colourful garments of Asia bringing innovation to Australian dress. It all spelt more freedom and Australians now feel free to dress as they please—and as a rule they do.

The Melbourne Cup has always been used by women as an excuse to show off the latest fashions. These women, obviously in the grip of Cup fever, display the modes of 1909

Farewell to Edwardian fashions

Women start to buy their clothes ready-made

In 1901 materials were rich and lustrous, and costumes were elegant. The vogue was for laces, beads, pleats, flounces, frills and feathers. Silk blouses, intricately adorned with masses of tucking and lace insertions, were worn with navy or royal blue skirts. 'Castor-oil blue'—the colour of the slim bottles in which castor-oil was sold—was fashionable. A stylish gown of floral organdy muslin, trimmed with guipure lace and baby ribbon, made to order, cost £2 12s 6d [$132.35]. Capes of velour, trimmed with fur, feathers, or jet, cost from 69s 6d to 5½ guineas [$175.25 to $291.20].

Hats were wide, decorated with artificial flowers and fruit, with sweeping ospreys—the milliner's name for egret plume—or curling ostrich feathers. Many older women still wore bonnets. Hatpins, which came in a variety of designs, became a hazard to pedestrians. Often people in crowds were injured by them. The menace was overcome by the introduction of a device, sometimes resembling an acorn, which covered the point.

Women as well as men carried sovereign cases, women in their muff-chains, men on their watch-chains. You opened them by putting the thumb-nail between the two halves. When the top coin was pressed down, the spring was depressed and the coin easily slid out. If you were short of gold coins, you could put shillings in the sovereign slots, and sixpences in the half-sovereign slots.

In the early years of this century most women had their clothes made to order. The idea of ready-made clothes had only been introduced in the late 1890s, and it was some years before it became the popular way to shop. Women who lived in the country ordered their clothes from mail order catalogues—lavishly illustrated books put out twice a year by the large department stores. The catalogues included a complex order form which called for 18 body measurements plus the buyer's height and weight. The form also noted that 'any peculiarity of figure, if desired, will be carefully attended to'.

The summer 1914 catalogue from Buckley and Nunn, the Melbourne department store, was nearly 130 pages long and contained over 1500 illustrations. Most of the clothes by then were 'ready made only' in three sizes—SW, W and OS. The limited range of sizes was compensated for by the offer to alter to special measurements for only 3s6d [$6.80] extra.

These women at the Victoria Racing Club's autumn meeting in 1918 wore egret plumes despite a Commonwealth edict forbidding their sale or possession from 1 January 1918

These two dresses—the pride of Buckley and Nunn's summer collection in 1914—adorned the cover of their mail order catalogue. On the right is a 'charming frock of satin or chiffon taffeta, in cornflower blue or preferred tones, trimmed with pretty lace and Medici collar, made to order, £8 10s' [$330]. And on the left an 'elegant visiting gown of new pink radium taffeta, lined Japanese silk, lace lined ninon, giving a very soft effect, and conveniently made to order, £10 5s' [$400]

The Countess of Dudley, wife of Australia's fourth Governor-General, in her study in 1910

The Melbourne Cup has always been an occasion to display fashions. The clothes worn here by Lord and Lady Fuller and the Government House party in 1912 were in the best taste and latest fashion

Garden party gown, 1903

1909

1914

Evening coat, 1914

Bodice and skirt, 1914

1918

The years before World War I saw the end of the S-shape and the tiny waist, and a return to high waists and a straight line. For a brief period the orient exerted an influence—seen here in the evening coat from 1914. Then came World War I and social upheaval that completely changed fashion. Women felt they were emancipated and this was reflected in the simple, free clothes that they began to wear more and more

A quiet, informal afternoon on the river in 1909 demanded rather formal dress for men and women alike. Sports clothes for casual wear had not then been introduced

Wholesome scents

Perfumes used by women in 1914 had floral, rather than sexy names. Popular lines were Atkinson's English perfumes: wild lilac, wild rose, wild honeysuckle, wild opponax, all 1s 9d [$1.45] a bottle, and Californian poppy, 2s 6d [$4.85]. Rimmel's lavender water and smelling salts—a survival from the days when Victorian women suffered the 'vapours'—were also popular. Colgate's Violet Talc Powder cost 1s 3d [$2.40], and Buttermilk Soap for the complexion was 3d [46c] a tablet. Piver's French perfumes had more exotic names—'Safranor', 'Azurea', 'Flormaye', 'Pompeia' and 'Incarnat'—and cost a good deal more at 4s 6d [$8.75] a bottle

THE GIRL: 'I was weighed yesterday—ten stone and half-a-pound'

THE GALOOT: 'Ah! And the half pound—that I suppose represents the clothes?'

This girl's dress in 1914 would have seemed brief to anyone used to 19th century fashions

Fashionable discomfort

How women achieved the ideal figure

Women suffered heroically from the dictates of fashion in the early 1900s—if they could afford to be fashionable. As Rose Lindsay puts it: 'A woman walked in beauty in those days, and in pain.' She wore 'a choking, boned neck-band, padded hair, padded hips, squeezing high-heel shoes, hour-glass corsets that cupped the breasts and viced one in their steel, and garters—wide elastic ribbon-frilled—which burnt into one's legs'.

Beneath her dress, the woman of fashion wore layers of underthings—petticoat, chemise and drawers. The long formidable corset, stiff with steel or whalebone, compressed her waist to a fashionable, and unhealthy, 55 centimetres. The ideal figure, achieved by tight-lacing, was S-shaped, the bosom pressed forward to balance an equally protuberant behind. In the great days of corsetry, whaling was Australia's most important industry, and countless whales were sacrificed to the ideal of a tiny waist.

The Sydney firm of Grace Brothers announced in their 1908 catalogue: 'Should a pair of Model Corsets rust in ordinary wear, we will replace them free of charge.'

Uplifting influences

Flesh-coloured 'bust improvers' had been on sale in Australia early in the 1900s, but the bra as we know it was invented—or at least first patented—by an American heiress, Caresse Crosby, in 1914. She was a granddaughter of Robert Fulton, an inventive engineer who launched a steamboat on the Hudson River in 1807. 'I can't say that the brassiere will ever take as great a place in history as the steamboat, but I did invent it,' she wrote modestly. She explained how one night when she was dressing for a dance, she rebelled against wearing a corset and devised the prototype of the bra from two handkerchiefs and some pink ribbon. Her patent was bought by a corset company, and, within a few years, uplift had swept round the world.

In Sydney, Farmer's *Autumn and Winter Catalogue* for 1917 advertised 'Gossard bust improvers for slim figures in silk-finished batiste filled with lambswool and mohair', for 3s 6d [$5.50], and Gossard back pads, 'filled with lambswool and mohair, to be sewn lightly in the back of the corset for figures sinking at the back below the waist', for 2s [$3.15]. There was no mention of brassieres.

But when Mrs Percival Shaw wrote an article titled 'Mainly about brassieres' in the October 1918 issue of *The Lone Hand*, she said: 'The advantages of the brassiere are becoming so widely recognised, it has passed from the exclusive use of stout women for whom it was originally intended.' Mrs Shaw went on to catalogue some of the varieties:

'There are many developments of the brassiere: the bandeau, which without producing undue warmth, takes excellent care of the figure; the hock-front brassiere, an extremely comfortable type; the cross-over back, giving a bracing effect to the shoulders and rounding the bust; the elastic back, and the laced back brassiere, particularly valuable for reduction.' Brassieres were then made in pink and white batiste, hemstitched or trimmed with cluny. Some were fashioned entirely of cluny, torchon, or filet lined with net. For evening wear, there were brassieres of silk jersey and crêpe-de-chine, and 'delicate arrangements of black with fine gold lace'.

In 1925, David Jones, Sydney, offered troubled women 'hip confiners', rubber brassieres, and brassieres of 'pink rubberised tricot' that assured 'perfect control and reduction of the bust', as well as brassieres of madapolam, calico, pink net, and broche batiste. 'By present modes,' said the catalogue, 'a brassiere is as essential as a corset.'

But the corset still had its devotees. 'It is said that society women everywhere are regretting ever having discarded the corset, and are now endeavouring to recover their lost figures through careful corseting,' reported *Madame Weigel's Journal* in February 1924. 'Most women recognize that they require at least three pairs of corsets in use, one for general wear, one for sports, and one for evening wear. And there should always be one fresh from the laundry and one on its way there.'

This combined 'bust form' and brassiere—advertised in 1914—was designed for the slender figure. It incorporated horse hair pads inside front pockets to give 'natural roundness to the bust'. In 1918 a writer in *The Lone Hand* lamented that there were still many Australian women who did not use a brassiere. She explained that its true purpose was to keep the back of the corset tight to the figure, 'increasing its gracefulness, and giving a rounded and supporting effect to the bust'

And six years later, a writer in the Sydney magazine *Fashion and Society* said: 'The corset, as I predicted, has come again much into use and we are treated to visions in black, green and heliotrope, as well as the more usual shades of pink, generally a salmon, in these useful garments.'

CORSETS C.P. A LA SIRÈNE Fabrication française PARIS SAN-SEBASTIAN

Mail order catalogues early this century always devoted several pages to their large range of corsets. It was assumed that every woman needed one, and there was even a range for young girls

246

Ostrich feathers were very much in demand for hats, boas and fans in the early years of this century, and ostrich farming became a lucrative business. Birds like these on a farm in Port Augusta yielded about £3 [$135] worth of feathers annually in 1911, compared with about 7s [$15.65] for wool from one sheep

Fine feathers for fine ladies in the 1900s

When George Ernest Morrison, the future London *Times* correspondent in Peking, voyaged down the Murray River in 1880, as a youth of 18, he visited Mr Officer's ostrich farm at Murray Downs, near Swan Hill. 'For the first time in my life, I saw these magnificent birds,' he noted. The farm, which was probably the first in Australia, had been established in 1875.

Ostrich feathers were very fashionable at the turn of the century, and farms were established in South Australia, Victoria, and New South Wales. South Australia had 1345 birds in 1912, 843 near Port Augusta and 495 near Miningie. By 1936 only a few remained.

For many years the show ostrich-farm in Australia was Mr J. Barracluff's, which occupied 4.5 hectares near South Head, Sydney, overlooking the Pacific, on sandy rises now thickly-infested with flats and houses. The farm was subdivided in 1925, when feathers were no longer fashionable. In 1902, it had a flock of about 100 birds. There was a keen demand for the feathers, which were 'plucked'—that is, cut—while the customer waited. Mr Barracluff also sold boas and 'other beautiful and graceful things'. When the Princess of Wales was in Sydney in 1901, she was presented with an ostrich-feather fan, mounted in gold. The feathers came from a noble bird called 'The Duke', the pride of Mr Barracluff's flock, some of whose feathers were 68 centimetres long and 38 centimetres wide.

'Mating the good birds is often a troublesome business,' warned a romantic writer in the *Royal Agricultural Society Annual*. 'The ostrich is as amorous as Narcissus and it selects its mate by falling deeply in love with one fair lady on the spot. One glance of the big, seemingly impressionless eye and the great bird falls a victim to Cupid's dart, and he is as constant as the sea. Man has not yet devised means to cure or subdue the flame of his passion and any attempt to separate him from the lady of his choice will provoke him to fury.'

But a consolation for the farmer was the remarkable longevity of his birds. The ostrich was said to live as long as the swan, often attaining an age of 100 years, and ostriches were much more profitable than sheep, especially after South Africa banned the export of ostriches and their eggs. In 1905, 14 birds at the Hawkesbury Agricultural College produced feathers said to be worth from £70 to £80 [$3455 to $3950] annually.

In the days when weddings were big news

Social papers in the 1900s reported weddings in extraordinary detail. Not only were the dresses of the bride and bridesmaids described down to the last sequin, but the glittering array of gifts was also meticulously catalogued. For example, when Hugh Trumble, the eminent Victorian cricketer (he took two hat-tricks in test matches) married Florence Christian at St George's, Malvern, in Melbourne in March 1902, *Table Talk* said of the 'petite and pretty bride':

'The bridal robe of rich ivory white satin had a fluted skirt, plain of design, to suit her graceful figure, and a long flowing train, with a vandyked basque trimming of satin rolls in a small latticed design, each square set with a pearl; the same trimming was on the lower part of the Russian vest, with a waist finish of pearl applique; the long Venetian sleeves and yoke were of very finely hand-tucked chiffon; the bodice was finished with a drapery of beautiful duchesse lace, rosette of white chenille and bebe ribbon, with long ends of chenille reaching to the hem of the robe. A long veil of bridal net delicately embroidered with true lovers knots was worn, and a spray of orange blossom in the hair. One of Paton's shower bouquets was carried, of white roses, gardenias, water lilies and fine ferns, tied with a wide white satin sash.'

The list of presents occupies a column of small type. From it you learn that the Trumbles set up house with an enormous collection of silver cake basquets, candle-sticks, salvers, entree dishes, coffee-pots, tea trays, tea-pots, tea-kettles, hot-water jugs, card trays, asparagus-dishes, cheese and butter stands, vases, cream and sugar stands, jardinieres, toast-racks, fish-knives and forks, fruit-knives and forks, cake-forks, photo frames, crumb scoops, preserve dishes, afternoon teaspoons, nut-dishes and crackers, sugar-basins and tongs, scentbottles, flower stands and saltcellars, as well as carved tables, travelling-clocks, marble clocks, bronze and terracotta statuettes, house and table-linen, lampstands, a diamond and sapphire brooch, silver-backed hairbrushes and mirrors, and assorted cheques.

The intricate detailing in the dresses worn by these bridesmaids at a Brisbane wedding in 1904 involved the dressmaker in hours of painstaking hand stitching

The roaring twenties

Women suddenly want to look like men

Beige was the dominant colour of the 1920s, not only in women's clothes, but in interior decoration. 'The cynical theory is that the manufacturers had so much khaki dye on their hands that it took them ten years to use it up,' writes the great authority on fashion, James Laver. 'But such rationalistic explanations are never the whole story,' he adds. 'Fashion has its roots on the deepest level of the collective psyche.'

By 1924, the 'tubular' look, derived from men's fashions, was supreme, in Australia as overseas. Breasts disappeared and waists were anywhere from below the hips to a very low waistline. Dresses had as much shape as a flour-bag, with magyar sleeves and plain round necks. Never had dressmaking been so simple and straightforward a matter.

To the American social historian Frederick Allen, these fashions were signs that 'consciously or unconsciously, the women of this decade worshipped not merely youth, but unripened youth. They wanted to be—or thought men wanted them to be—men's casual and light-hearted companions, not broad-hipped mothers of the race, but irresponsible play-mates'.

In the early 1920s, bobbed and then shingled hair became popular and hairdressers flourished in Australia as never before. During the war, bobbed hair was introduced in England as a practical measure for girls doing war work.

Cloche hats became fashionable with the introduction of bobbed hair in the 1920s. This 1924 model in green silk cost £1 19s 6d [$53.20]

Short hair produced the *cloche* hat, which dominated hat fashions for the next five years. It was a hat with a very narrow brim and a crown that fitted the head like a helmet. The hat was pulled right down over the eyebrows. Early in 1927, the shingle was succeeded by the Eton crop, a short, boyish style of haircut.

Perhaps the most typical women's garment of the 1920s was the jumper, loose and sloppy, worn over a blouse, and covering the hips. Girls knitted jumpers in trains, trams and buses, on the way to work, and at spare moments during the day.

In the mid-1920s skirts became shorter and shorter, until not only flappers but middle-aged women wore knee-length skirts. Legs were news. In July 1928, a versifier in Sydney's *New Triad* wrote *A Seasonable Rhyme:*

Half an inch, half an inch, half an inch shorter, the skirts are the same for mother and daughter, when the wind blows each one of them shows, half an inch, half an inch, more than she oughter.

Clergymen in many countries were loud in their condemnation of this new evil. When there was an earthquake at Amalfi, south of Naples, the Archbishop of Naples declared that it was caused by God's anger at the shortness of women's skirts.

A girl's complete equipment often consisted only of a one-piece undergarment, a short one-piece overgarment, a slender stocking-suspender belt, shoes and stockings. 'A woman can be fully dressed this summer and have only 20 ounces [566 grams] of clothing,' an English fashion magazine calculated in 1926. This included an allowance of 454 grams for shoes.

In 1928, the indestructible 'Madame Weigel' counselled girls in her *Journal of Fashion* on the appropriate 'undies' for sports wear: 'Sports clothes need undies all their own, and different sports call for different lingerie. For golf, nothing is more suitable

In 1921 the Sydney store David Jones advertised their high-necked, sleeveless evening gowns—the 'most moderately priced reproductions and adaptations of Paris fashions'

Hot but hard-wearing

In the summer of 1923-24 Mark Foy's store in Sydney advertised these clothes for young children. The boy's Cotswold suit was available in fawn or grey tweed or English worsted—materials specially selected for their hard-wearing characteristics, but hardly for their comfort in hot weather. The girl's pleated skirt was available in navy blue serge. Although both children here are wearing shoes, 'sensible' ankle-length boots were more usual for everyday wear

In the early 1920s dresses became narrow tubes in which both waists and breasts disappeared. Women no longer possessed a 'figure'. But then in the mid-1920s came the sensational discovery that women possessed legs, and hemlines rose suddenly from ankles to knees

than the fashionable cami-bloomers, as the petticoat is not necessary under the substantial materials used for golf-skirts. The best fabric to choose for these undies is artificial milanese. It is not so expensive as it sounds, for it stands an enormous amount of wear. They should be kept extremely plain, and not on any account trimmed with lace; it looks so very idiotic and out of place on the golf course if one's skirt happens to blow up, or if it is necessary to leap into a bunker after a ball.

'Then tennis requires its own particular undies. Very few girls bother about having any special lingerie for tennis; but, as a matter of fact, they should be just as thoughtful of them as they are of their frocks. To begin with, every woman, however slim she is, should wear a bust bodice when playing any game, tennis especially, as there is so much running to be done. A slim woman need wear only a brassiere of net or lace, but a stouter person needs one of some stronger material.

'Like golf undies, anything worn under a tennis dress should be very plain, and they should also be made of silk. If the dress is a Fuji silk or crêpe-de-chine, a petticoat will be necessary, in which case, as a minimum amount of underwear is always aimed at, the popular petti-bockers are the correct thing to choose. These do away with any bulkiness around the waist and bodice.'

Dressing-up fashionable legs in lisle and silk

As skirts got shorter, stockings became more important. Until 1924 they were usually made of cotton, cashmere or lisle, and black, tan, or white were the popular colours. Then stockings were of silk, or artificial silk, and followed the current vogue for shades of beige. Silk leg hose with lisle feet and tops cost in Sydney from 8s 11d to 12s 6d [$6 to [$16.85]. Some of the tints were flesh-coloured, and if the stockings were seamless, it was not always easy to tell whether a woman was wearing stockings or not. This raised the ire of the wowsers, who, for some inexplicable reason, considered bare legs more wicked than stockinged legs. Moralists were also dismayed by the fact that young women when they crossed their legs sometimes showed bare thighs and suspenders above the stocking tops. Below the knees, they wore elaborate floral garters whose function was purely decorative. This advertisement appeared in *The Triad* in 1922

Dancing was all the rage in 1924, when this fashionably-dressed couple took to the floor

By 1926, when this Hobart store was photographed, ready-to-wear clothes were widely sold, but many women made clothes at home. They could have them machine-stitched at shops like Capron's

A decade of disorder

Paris is still the fashion capital of the world

The boyish look of the 1920s vanished with the French collections of 1930. Femininity was back in fashion. Skirts became longer, and the new silhouette was narrow and elongated with an indented waistline, a rounded bosom and moulded torso. Halter necklines and deep *décolletages* at the back exposed necks, shoulders and backs. 'Sometimes the whole outfit looked as if it had been designed to be seen from the back,' wrote the fashion historian James Laver.

Berlei, the underwear manufacturers, saw the possibility of increased sales and greeted the new fashions with rapturous metaphors: 'The change from straight flat-chested slimness to rounded slenderness, and from rounded slenderness to a decided waist, and

gently accentuated bust, is a connected sequence—three jewels upon the thread of feminine beauty—three milestones upon the pleasant high-road of fashion.'

Paris speaks

Australian women also applauded the new fashions, but resisted the longer skirts. A writer in *The Berlei Review* in April 1930 reported that: 'The modern Australienne quite vigorously disputes the authority of any one who wishes to rob her of the clean-limbed freedom of the knee length skirt . . .' However, the writer revealed that cables received at Berlei House from Paris reported that Jacques Worth had issued a statement designed to settle the matter once and for all:

'Proportions of Frock-length for average sizes should be 14 in. [36 cm] from shoulder to belt, 28 in. [71 cm] from belt to bottom of skirt and 14 in. [36 cm] from hemline to floor.' Paris had spoken.

Milliners added to the confusion by offering a bewildering variety of hats—the brim, the toque, the beret and the turban—in fabrics to match dresses. One thing, however, was generally agreed—a well-dressed woman wore gloves. There were long gloves of striped and spotted materials for day, and gloves of contrasting colours and matching materials for night. Long white gloves were invariably worn with the popular white satin evening gown.

In the mid-1930s the padded look, which emphasised wide, square shoulders and

The latest in chic nightwear is the centrepiece of this Buckley and Nunn shop window display in Melbourne in 1939. The purpose of the curious chair is a mystery

Stockings from wood-pulp

The history of rayon, or artificial silk made from wood-pulp, goes back to 1889, when a French scientist, Comte Hilaire de Chardonnet, exhibited samples he had made at the Paris Exposition. The English firm of Courtaulds, which had begun making rayon commercially in 1905, registered the trade-mark 'Celanese' in 1921. In its early days, rayon was used mainly in knitted fabrics for underclothing, and in stockings which were shiny, coarse and ill-fitting. Not till the 1930s was rayon so improved that it was almost indistinguishable from real silk. It then became important in the world of fashion. Rayon brought the possibility of 'silk legs' within every woman's reach, though the cheapness was largely illusory, because rayon stockings had a much shorter life than silk stockings. 'Australia is following a world fashion by adopting the new Celanese fabric made of wood-pulp,' said a writer in *Madame Weigel's Journal* in 1930

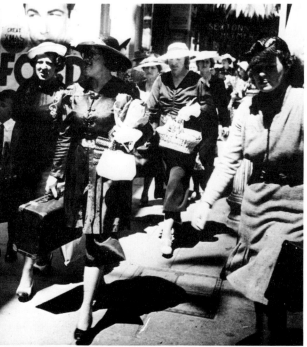

How Paris styles were interpreted for the mass market. An Adelaide street in December 1938

Dressing for formal occasions

Silks and satins were in vogue in 1938 when this debutante (left) and bride and bridesmaid were photographed in Adelaide. Pastel shades of green, pink and yellow were popular colours

minimised waists, became popular. Tailored clothes in tweeds and other woollens were fashionable for day wear and there was a glamorous black cocktail dress with hat, veil and suede gloves for the evenings. Fox fur was much used for trimming—there were fur cuffs, collars and hemlines, in red, silver, black and white. Complete fox skins were also popular, and the glass eyes of these unfortunate animals stared from many a fashionable shoulder.

In the 1930s, for the first time, women could buy coloured leather shoes, open-toed sandals and rayon stockings. Rayon, an artificial silk made from wood-pulp, had now become so cheap that all women could afford silk-type stockings. A few women in Melbourne tried to start a vogue for bare legs, but 'the side glances and comment outpoured have not been the kindest', *Fashion and Society* reported. 'Extremists get a bad time, for we are nothing if not sensible.'

Frantic search for style

The fashion scene in the late 1930s was disordered. Directoire, Edwardian, Oriental and geisha-girl were all styles hailed as fashionable. 'It was as if designers were absolutely frantic to explore every possibility and express every idea before it was too late,' wrote Madge Garner, a former editor of *Vogue*.

With the outbreak of World War II, a new woman emerged. Her concern was survival, not fashion. Already these words of Mademoiselle Madeleine, a style pacesetter of the 1930s, seemed frivolous: 'Woman has no joy to surpass that of dressing attractively. This is her great privilege. Whether she votes or not is of no consequence, for everything beautiful that has ever been created being hers to wear about with the glory of an almost heavenly creature.'

Evening dress 1932

1933

1934

1939

Fashions varied widely during the 1930s. Hemlines plunged from the knee-length of the 1920s to below the calf, but they gradually crept up again as the decade wore on. The padded look, with square shoulders and slender waists, was popular just before the outbreak of World War II

Fashionable racegoers at Brisbane in 1937, complete with fox furs and ample hats

Melbourne Cup day 1931. The dress worn by the girl on the right was exceptional. The others, especially the partly obscured girl in the white dress at left, show the accepted silhouette at that time

The rebirth of fashion

A new look emerges from wartime austerity

World War II put an end to the frantic experimentation with styles that had characterised the 1930s. For six years it was Canberra—not Paris, Rome, New York or London—that dictated Australian fashions.

Frills and personal extravagances were out. Austerity was in. Women had to conform to regulations issued by the National Council of Clothing Styles. On 27 July 1942 the council issued tables that told women exactly how long their skirts could be. The council did, however, relax the regulations for tall women—those standing over 172 centimetres in bare feet.

Petticoats, aprons, evening wear and accessories other than belts were banned. Clothing manufacturers, and eventually home dressmakers, were given detailed instructions which reduced the range of styles.

However, the council's 'Fashions for Victory' showed more imagination than some women had expected. A Sydney woman echoed the generally favourable reaction when she told a *Daily Telegraph* reporter: 'Fancy the government thinking up styles for women that are not just a lot of boiler suits.'

The new look

Two years after the end of the war, Christian Dior, the French designer, ended austerity with his 'new look'. Skirts were wider and fuller and had nipped-in waists. The hemline dropped from just below the knee to 17 cm. above the ground. Small hats, high shoes with ankle straps and long elegant umbrellas usually completed the look.

Not all women welcomed the rebirth of high fashion. In October 1947 a woman wrote to *The Sydney Morning Herald* and asked: 'Have these "modern" dress designers no originality that they must lead women back to the era before World War I for fashion . . . We agree that grandma looked sweet, according to the fashion of her day, but the modern lass does not want to filch her bonnet and long, hampering hemline. She looks to fashion to clothe her as befits her life in a modern world.'

From teddy boys to hippies

The writer need not have worried. Fashion moved on, and in the 1950s and 1960s it moved faster than ever. Almost every year saw the introduction of a new style—some of which still influence clothing today. In the early 1950s there were the teddy boys with long jackets and thick, crepe-soled shoes. There was the Mary Quant look in the mid-1950s—mad clothes that broke every rule in the couturier's book—followed by Dior's A-line in 1955 and the Cardin bubble look in 1957. The 1960s saw the beatnik image—scruffy hair, beards and duffle coats. In Paris in 1964 both Courrèges and Rabanne unveiled their futuristic looks—Courrèges with clean-cut lines, long white boots and PVC helmets and Rabanne with clothes of metal, plastic and wood based on armour and chain mail. The late 1960s saw the hippies wearing exotic clothes using eastern fabrics and designs, and in the early 1970s jeans became the uniform of the young.

These Adelaide women in 1948 disregarded Dior's 'new look', but the pleats and bows on the dress of the woman in the foreground were a departure from wartime austerity

Clothes that celebrated the end of a war

Two versions of Dior's new look that was first seen in 1947—winter (left) and summer (right). Women were no longer limited by regulations on the amount of material they could use in a dress, and they celebrated their freedom by making dresses with hems up to 18 metres around

These models at a Sydney fashion show in the 1950s are all made-up in the glamorous Hollywood film star image. Marilyn Monroe—at the height of her career then—epitomised the look

Long dresses with many layers of stiff petticoats underneath were very popular in 1957

Shocking scenes at Flemington racecourse

On Melbourne Cup day 1965 the English fashion model Jean Shrimpton scandalised Australia's arbiters of good taste by wearing a simple white dress that stopped 10 cm. above her knee, no stockings, no hat and no gloves. 'This Shrimpton is a child and showed very bad taste,' commented Lady Nathan, former Lady Mayoress of Melbourne.

The following Thursday the author Douglas Lockwood wrote humorously in the *Melbourne Herald*: 'Listen, Jean Shrimpton, I'll have you know that women wear hats and gloves and mink and diamonds even at bush race meetings in the Northern Territory. That's the way we have it in Australia ... There are no lawns. There is no members' enclosure. The dust is sometimes two or three inches deep, and whipped up by trade winds blowing across a flat that is several hundred miles wide. But you must understand that the women out there wear hats, they wear gloves, and the shoes, that you perhaps cannot see for dust, may be crocodile hide with a matching bag ... As for bare heads and skirts four inches above the knee ... unthinkable. My dear Miss Shrimpton, don't you see there is a race meeting on?'

The English model Jean Shrimpton shocked women racegoers at the 1965 Melbourne Cup with this dress; they thought it too short

How not to board a bus in the new mini-skirt—*The Sydney Morning Herald* staged the picture at left as a warning to girls in 1966. Later that year, however, tights were introduced and girls could display their legs, like the Sydney girls above in 1971, without showing their stocking tops

253

Clinging to British tradition

Edwardian men's clothes took no account of the climate

Men, as well as women, endured great discomfort at the turn of the century—and for many decades later.

Professor A. R. Chisholm, recalling his undergraduate days at Sydney University from 1908 to 1911, wrote:

'Men always wore stiff collars, either double (like the modern soft collar) or with two peaks (like a dress collar). One felt rather shabby without starched cuffs, held in place by means of small metal clasps inside their coatsleeves. Trousers were tight, and trouser cuffs came in only about 1909.

'Towards the end of my course, coats became rather long, with a slit in the back that made them look like ghosts of the old tailcoat. Shorter coats forthwith became rather ridiculous, and were known as bum-freezers. Lapels came down almost to the top of one's trousers.'

A waistcoat was always worn by conformists, even in the heat of a Sydney summer. 'In particularly hot weather', wrote Professor Chisholm, 'a cummerbund was often substi-

tuted, a sort of wide cloth belt with pockets'.

The most popular hat with sober citizens was the round-crowned hard hat which Englishmen called a bowler and Americans a derby. In Australia, it was variously called a boxer, a bocker, a hard-hitter, a pee-wee or, derisively, an egg-boiler, hop-harry or pea-dodger. Young men preferred the hard straw hat, the straw-decker (known in England as a boater) with its ribbon of silk round the crown. The disrespectful called it a nan-nan. As the straw-decker was likely to become airborne in a wind, it was usually moored to the coat lapel by a black cord.

With the more adventurous, the soft felt hat was slowly coming into favour, but it was to be many years before it completely replaced the boxer.

Australian men clung determinedly to their traditional sombre and uncomfortable clothes, though from time to time there were bold attempts at innovation. 'I am grateful to the merchants and tailors who are endeavouring to combat the dreary drabness of civil-

isation that oppresses our sex, and still more so to those men who, taking their courage in both hands, flaunt themselves abroad in coloured garments,' wrote a Sydney fashion writer in 1908. 'I saw a man in brilliant purple the other day—hat, tie, suit and boots. I did not like it, but he fairly livened up the whole street with his splash of colour.

'Another man I met on Sydney Station had a rich brown velvet knickerbocker suit—hat, tie, shirt, stockings, and boots, all in accord—and he was a pleasure to see. A perfect tone poem in clothes, with everything in harmony. But it would not do for the average man in Australia.'

A devotee of spats

The same writer deplored the disappearance of spats. Spats were small gaiters worn over the instep, and usually fastened under the boot or shoe. 'The only persons wearing them have been smart military men of middle age, and then only white ones,' he wrote. But white spats had a loyal devotee in Stanley

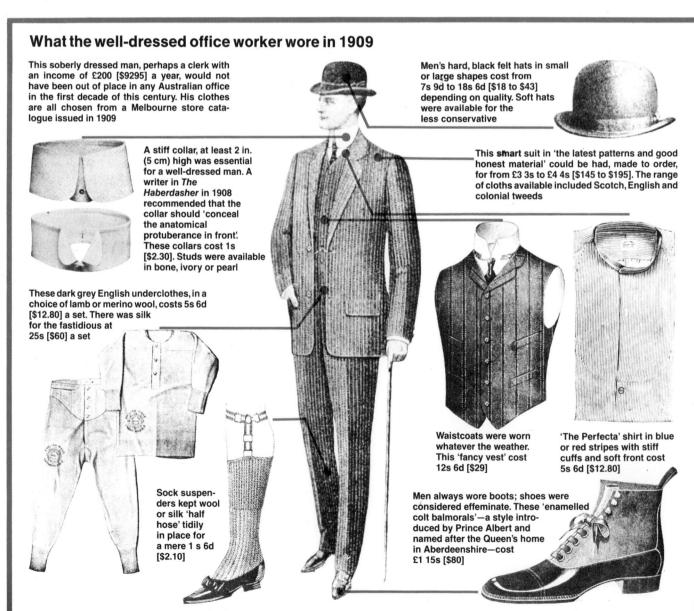

What the well-dressed office worker wore in 1909

This soberly dressed man, perhaps a clerk with an income of £200 [$9295] a year, would not have been out of place in any Australian office in the first decade of this century. His clothes are all chosen from a Melbourne store catalogue issued in 1909

Men's hard, black felt hats in small or large shapes cost from 7s 9d to 18s 6d [$18 to $43] depending on quality. Soft hats were available for the less conservative

A stiff collar, at least 2 in. (5 cm) high was essential for a well-dressed man. A writer in *The Haberdasher* in 1908 recommended that the collar should 'conceal the anatomical protuberance in front'. These collars cost 1s [$2.30]. Studs were available in bone, ivory or pearl

This smart suit in 'the latest patterns and good honest material' could be had, made to order, for from £3 3s to £4 4s [$145 to $195]. The range of cloths available included Scotch, English and colonial tweeds

These dark grey English underclothes, in a choice of lamb or merino wool, costs 5s 6d [$12.80] a set. There was silk for the fastidious at 25s [$60] a set

Sock suspenders kept wool or silk 'half hose' tidily in place for a mere 1s 6d [$2.10]

Waistcoats were worn whatever the weather. This 'fancy vest' cost 12s 6d [$29]

'The Perfecta' shirt in blue or red stripes with stiff cuffs and soft front cost 5s 6d [$12.80]

Men always wore boots; shoes were considered effeminate. These 'enamelled colt balmorals'—a style introduced by Prince Albert and named after the Queen's home in Aberdeenshire—cost £1 15s [$80]

Melbourne Bruce, who, to the delight of cartoonists, was still wearing them when he became Prime Minister in 1923.

By 1908, the soft-fronted shirt was gradually replacing the shirt with a stiff, starched front. Many soft-fronted shirts had double cuffs that could be folded over when one side became soiled and unsightly.

In 1907, the corpulent King Edward VII appeared at Homburg in a double-breasted jacket, a mode which helped to disguise his considerable girth. This led to a revival in England of the double-breaster, which inevitably spread to Australia. More than half a century later, another Australian Prime Minister, Robert Menzies was consistently wearing double-breasted jackets, but they never became generally accepted.

Melbourne had a reputation for being even more conservative than Sydney. 'The men of Melbourne live in starched shirts and expensive broadcloth,' wrote Alfred Buchanan, an English visitor, in 1907. 'They cling tenaciously to that fading relic of an earlier civilization—the bell-topper hat. Social life in the city would be impossible without one.'

Revolt in Melbourne

But even in Melbourne, there was an occasional sartorial revolt. Under the heading 'A Revival of the Dandies', *Melbourne Punch* in February 1908 devoted an editorial to the exciting colour that was creeping into men's wear; 'It is extremely hard for a man to be distinctive in an ordinary tweed suit and a commonplace "bowler" or "boater". But times are changing . . . Go down Collins Street or Bourke this afternoon and mark the shop windows that flare with colours. Are they the windows of the milliners or the ladies' drapers?

'Not they; it is the mercer's window which is richest in crimson, gold, purple, blue, orange, plaids, checks and tartans. The mere socks of the Johnnies of our time transform a prosaic window into a kaleidoscope. Add the ties, the vests, the hatbands, the hats and the handkerchiefs now popular with the young man who wishes to be just "it" and you get a feast of colour. Already a brave dresser may parade Collins Street garbed from head to foot in purple, warmed up with lemon-coloured gloves. Suits may be purple, green, puce, or blue, or a little of each, and the colour is becoming more pronounced.

'Your up-to-date Johnnie in addition to his purple or lavender suit wears a boater hat, into the rim of which is woven strands of coloured straw, the band about it is deep, as bright as the dyer dares, and tied with . . . a big bold flaring bow with fluffed out edges . . . His socks are gaudy tartan and his trouser legs . . . actually built with cuffs on the bottom, in order that a startled public may not miss those delectable socks.'

The young 'Johnnie' also wore 'assertive shoes of tan, tied with broad silk laces in big, conspicuous bows' and his shirt was 'as bright as the rest of the peep-show, while his vest is simply deafening'.

Staff of the Queensland Lands Department in 1904 clutch the three styles of hat popular at that time—the traditional bowler, the soft felt hat and the straw hat for young men

There were few of these young men as yet, *Punch* admitted, but others would follow their example. They were mostly bank clerks and the 'curled darlings' of the Civil Service.

The revolt of the bank clerks and 'curled darlings' had little lasting effect. 'We build, dress and eat according to British ideas; we try to make British social habits conform with the tropical and sub-tropical climate,' said Mr H. A. Hunt, Director of Melbourne's Weather Bureau, in March 1914. 'Our clothing is unseasonable. We should wear sandals in the summer, not footwear of stiff leather, and black boxer hats should be replaced by soft felts, or straw hats with brims as broad as those worn by Chinese market gardeners.'

The Australian male remained doggedly conservative in dress, even up to World War II. When Robert Helpmann was touring Australia with Pavlova in 1926, he had the temerity to walk along the Bondi beachfront in fawn 'Oxford bags'. These trousers had recently enjoyed a brief vogue among Oxford under-graduates. They were cut so wide at the cuffs—up to 56 cm—that they flopped around like skirts as you walked, sometimes with only the tips of the shoes visible. And they came in unusual colours, fawn and mauve, as well as grey.

Helpmann was soon followed by a curious crowd. Then a number of young men picked him up and, without comment, pitched him into the surf, Oxford bags and all. Recalling the incident in an interview with John Hetherington in 1964, Helpmann said he was convinced that such an incident would no longer take place in Australia. 'My God', he added, 'in 1930 you wouldn't have dared to wear a pair of suede shoes in public unless you wanted a fight on your hands!'

Visitors continued to express amazement at the Australian male's inappropriate garb. Writing in 1946, the American historian C. Hartley Grattan said: 'The great surprise with regard to clothing is the almost complete absence of lightweight and light-coloured suits for men, even in summer time. White is confined almost entirely to sports wear.

'The Australian men favour greys and grey-blues in suits, and black shoes. A few blossom out in symphonies in brown. To American notions, they wear ridiculous underwear, even sticking to the old-fashioned, long-sleeved, long-legged heavy shirts and drawers for cold weather. This is because Australian houses and business establishments are usually imperfectly heated in the colder months.'

Traditional hats made from palm trees

Cabbage-tree hats, which had been made as far back as 1799, were still being worn at the beginning of the 20th century by bush workers and farmers in parts of New South Wales and Queensland. The hats woven from narrow strips of the cabbage-tree palm, were light, and stood

up to hard wear. They cost up to £3 [$151] according to quality. Many country women were expert hat-makers. The long narrow leaves of the palm were soaked in hot water for a few minutes, and partly dried. Each leaf was then shredded with a hand shredder, the teeth of which were set about 32 mm apart for fine grade hats, and 48 mm for coarser hats. The strands were plaited by hand into suitable lengths for working, and rolled up on an oval spool until required. Four of the broader strands were used for the cheaper hat, and six of the finer strands for the better hat. The flat plaited strips of cabbage leaf were worked round and round and stitched through by hand with stitches about 63 mm apart. Sometimes a basin was used to shape the crown. The finished hat was lined throughout with a strong red or green material

The vanishing swimsuit

Australian girls in search of a sun-tan

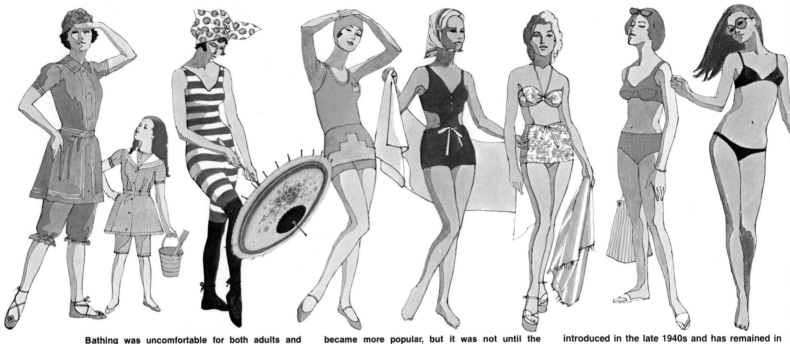

Bathing was uncomfortable for both adults and children before World War I. Modesty demanded that as much as possible of the body was well covered. Women often wore stockings as well as the all-enveloping costume. Most women adopted the one-piece woollen costume as swimming became more popular, but it was not until the 1920s that costumes started to become smaller and more sensible. The 1930s and 40s saw the first moves towards separating the top and bottom halves of the costume, and these eventually culminated in the two-piece swimsuit. The bikini was introduced in the late 1940s and has remained in fashion. Each year has seen even briefer costumes. Despite the ensuing barrage of outraged letters to newspapers, topless bathing is now tolerated on many Australian beaches and a number of metropolitan nudist beaches exist

It was sunbathing rather than swimming that brought about the revolution in bathing costumes after World War I.

Mixed bathing became legal on many Australian beaches in 1903, and by 1910 most women had adopted the Canadian costume. This costume was usually made from wool and consisted of knickerbockers and a tunic. *The Lone Hand* magazine approved of it. 'This costume seems specially designed by providence to meet the requirements of feminine bathers,' it said. 'The average girl, when she commences surf-bathing shrinks from notice, and chooses a costume of amplitude. After a few weeks, she no longer shrinks, but the costume does and gradually assumes proportions at once useful and picturesque.'

For many years costumes remained largely unchanged. When Fanny Durack won the women's 100 metres freestyle for Australia at the 1912 Olympic Games, she wore a long towelling robe to the starting blocks, and disrobed coyly to reveal black woollen bathers, high at neck and back, and reaching to her knees. It was not until World War I ushered in a more emancipated era that costumes started to become briefer.

The backless swimsuit made its appearance in the 1930s, and soon became popular despite the denunciation of clergymen and shire councillors. The costumes were no more backless than the evening gowns of the period, but one Melbourne minister described them as the hottest things ever seen on the beaches. Much hotter things were to come in the following years.

The Canadian costume, worn here at Bondi beach in 1919, was adopted by most women bathers when surf bathing became legal in 1903

Bathing costumes had become much briefer by 1936, when this group strolled along a Melbourne beach, but they still had a long way to shrink. Even in 1960, regulations in Sydney demanded that everyone over four years old—male or female—wore a costume with an eight centimetre leg and a chest covering

In July 1946 the United States began its atomic bomb tests at Bikini atoll in the Pacific, and in that month Louis Reard, a Parisian fashion designer, made world news by introducing the first bikini swimsuit. The impact of the bikini was almost comparable to that of the bomb and Micheline Bernadini, the dancer who modelled it, received more than 50,000 fan letters when photographs of her in the bikini were published.

It was, however, to be some years before the bikini became accepted in Australia. The summer season of 1949-50 saw the introduction of the strapless swimsuit on Australian beaches. The new lastex, self-supporting swimsuits had cunningly placed stiffeners of bone and metal to prevent them from slipping off in even the heaviest surf.

Guarding public decency

The bikini gradually gained acceptance during the early 1950s, although most local councils attempted to enforce strict regulations governing their dimensions. The last recorded skirmish on a Sydney beach took place in 1961, when Miss Joan Barry was ordered from the sands at Bondi and later fined £3 [$28.20] for offensive behaviour. The offence was wearing a small gold bikini. 'I've never seen anyone wearing less than you are, and I've seen many put off the beach,' said the prosecuting detective-sergeant. 'I never thought for a moment my bikini would be objected to,' replied Miss Barry. Nor would it actually be today.

In July 1964, Tuija Pakerinen, a 20-year-old Finnish model, plunged boldly into the surf at Mona Vale near Sydney in a topless swimsuit. But she was ahead of her time. A Sydney swimsuit manufacturer revealed that although his firm had already produced topless swimsuits, it was holding them in cold storage. Sales would still be few.

Seaside councils have long guarded public decency. This girl had to satisfy beach inspectors at Bondi in 1961 that there was at least eight centimetres of material at the side of her bikini. At Clovelly in 1900 the young bathers below were defying a law that forbade bathing between 6 a.m and 8 p.m. Unlawful bathers in those days often wore pyjamas or—as here—underclothes. The decently dressed women in the background are presumably acting as look-outs

A Sydney fashion writer suggested these swimsuits in blue and green beribboned taffeta as alternatives to the unflattering Canadian costume

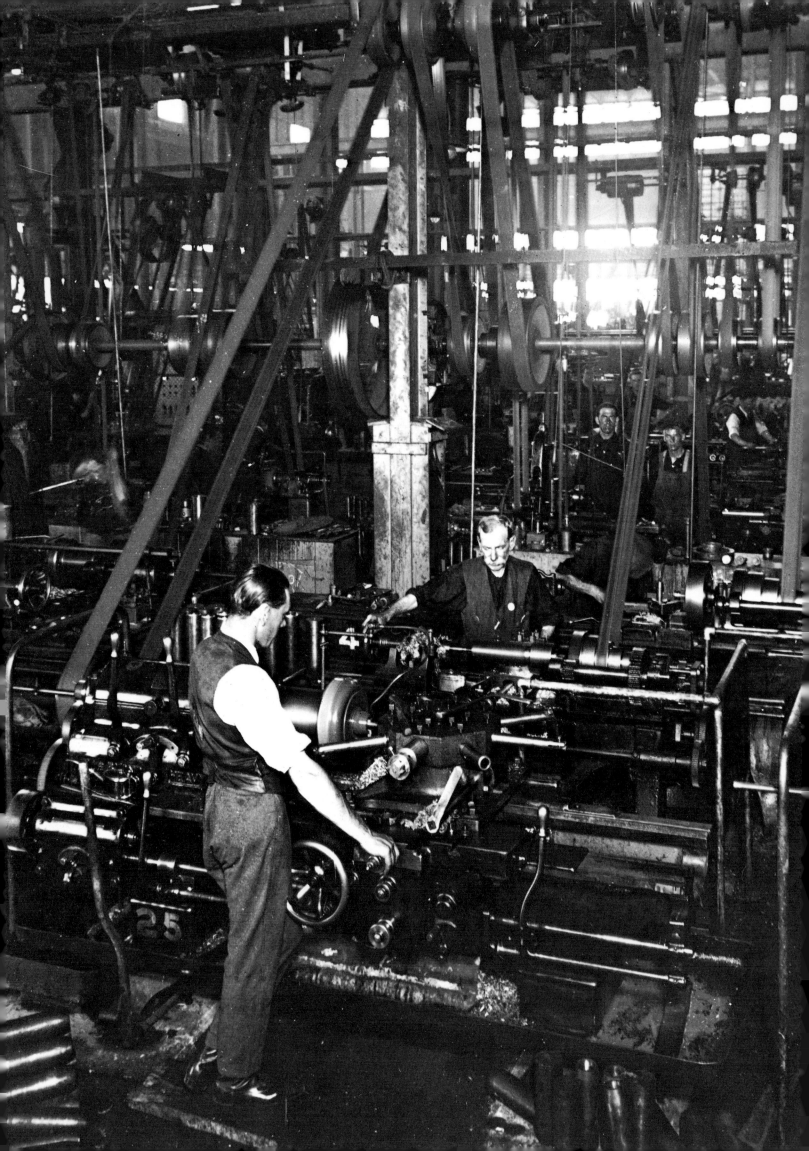

Earning and spending

Poverty and sweated labour amid increasing prosperity

On the first day of the 20th century, the Sydney *Daily Telegraph* looked back with satisfaction on man's recent achievements:

'Inventors have found ways of communicating at lightning speed over thousands of miles, over the ocean's bed, even, by the grace of Marconi, across mere waves of air. The telephone, the phonograph, even the cinematograph that reproduces events in life-like forms and occurrences, are all instruments in aid of commerce and association . . . The mass of men are far better off than ever before . . . Labour-saving devices have not debarred the labour from employment. On the contrary they have made what were luxuries necessities virtually within the reach of all.'

Exactly a year later a Melbourne trade journal, *Australian Hardware and Machinery*, was less optimistic. 'Whether our present day race for wealth and our high pressure living, with the comforts and luxuries we enjoy, is real improvement on the life of a century ago, is a question to which different answers may be given,' it observed.

And it discussed the 'almost continuous warfare between capital and labour': 'While the one has the tendency to sweat the employee, the other is apt to intimidate capital. It will require the harmonious combination of the two in patient, honest effort to ensure the commercial prosperity of this great continent.'

The mass of men may have been far better off than ever before, as the *Daily Telegraph* leader-writer confidently claimed, but there was still widespread poverty throughout Australia. And many employees were certainly sweated.

Unguarded belts and closely placed machines endangered workers in this Sydney munitions factory in 1916. Lathe operators were paid a minimum of £3 16s—about $127 in 1984—for a 44-hour week

The right to a fair and reasonable wage

(Equivalent amounts in today's *purchasing power* are given in brackets.)

The Commonwealth was born in an age of great economic differences. The 'take-home' salary of the first Governor-General, the Earl of Hopetoun, was £10,000 a year (say $504,260 today), equal then to the wages of 100 skilled workers. And he was a man of great personal wealth—he owned about 17,240 hectares in Linlithgowshire, Scotland, and had a private income of about £40,000 [$2,017,040] a year. Yet, though he received an additional £10,000 to pay for expenses incurred during the visit of the Duke ad Duchess of York, he complained that his pay was inadequate, and resigned after being in office for the short period of only 17 months.

The Bulletin bade Lord Hopetoun farewell with a typical comment: 'He spent £22,000 [$1,109,370] a year on the guzzlers and gorgers who invested his halls, giving them frozen fish and pheasant from 'Ome . . .'

In 1901, the maximum wage in New South Wales for a skilled worker was 60s [$151.30 a week. The aristocrats of the work-force who could earn this maximum were the boiler-makers, platers, moulders, plumbers, felt hat body-makers and finishers, asphalters, slaughtermen and blacksmiths. Lower down

the wage scale watchmakers earned 30-40s [$75.65-$100.85], manufacturing jewellers 20-40s [$50.45-$100.85], cigar-makers 20-30s [$50.45-$75.65], portmanteau-makers 16-35s [$40.35-$88.25], whipmakers 18-30s [$45.40-$75.65]. Women's wages were much lower. A female folder and sewer earned 5s to 12s 6d [$12.60-$31.50] a week; a female boot-maker's machinist, from 5s to 10s [$12.60-$25.20]; a tailoress, from 10s to 12s 6d [$25.20-$31.50]. Nursemaids and general servants who lived in were paid from 6-8s [$15.15-$20.20]. Even in Victoria, where wages were generally higher, women were often miserably paid.

In December 1900, a woman wrote to *Women's Sphere*, a Melbourne feminist magazine, urging that it should be illegal to pay skilled women workers, such as dressmakers, *less* than 3d [60c] an hour. 'Starting as an apprentice at 2s 6d [$6.30] a week,' she wrote, 'it takes a young girl about four years before she can earn the extravagant sum of 10s [$25.22] a week. Is that a living wage?'

A 48-hour week was standard in most Australian industries in 1901, but an eight-hour day was not. In order to enjoy 'the boon of a Saturday half-holiday', most had to work eight and three-quarters hours on weekdays.

Food prices in 1901

	Melb.		Syd.	
	s	d	s	d
Best bacon, per lb		8		8
Butter, per lb	1	0		10
Cheese, per lb		5		5
Cocoa, per packet		5		4
Coffee, per lb	1	0	1	0
Eggs, per dozen	1	0	1	4
Flour, per 25 lb	1	9	—	—
Ham, per lb		8		8
Herrings, per tin		6½		5½
Jam, per tin		3½		4
Kerosene, per case	10	8	10	0
Lollies, per lb		2½		4
Marmalade, per lb tin		5½		7
Matches, per doz. boxes		3½		3
Oatmeal, per 7 lb bag	1	2	1	3
Rabbits, per pair		6		7
Rice, per lb		2		2½
Sago, per lb		2		2½
Salt, per lb		½		1
Soap, per cwt	11	0	12	6
Starch, per lb		4		3½
Sugar, per lb		2½		2
Tapioca, per 12 lb	2	0	2	0

In 1901, 10s bought about the same as $25.21 in 1984 and ½d, ten cents

Sweated labour in a Melbourne starch factory

Mr Robert Harper was one of Melbourne's most respected and godly citizens, a member of the Federal Parliament, a pillar of the Cairns Memorial Church, and a regular subscriber to many well-advertised charities.

Myoora, his magnificent white stone mansion in the heart of Toorak, set in spacious grounds, was often the scene of picturesque garden parties and elegant balls, attended by the cream of Melbourne society.

Mr Harper's wealth derived from Silver Star starch, and other popular commodities. Unfortunately, the benevolence exhibited in his publicised charities was not extended to his hundreds of employees. In evidence to the Industrial Appeal Court in 1907, David Simmons, employed at Robert Harper and Co's no.1 factory, said:'I have been with the firm for four years, and am in receipt of 30s [$74.06] per week of 54 hours. I do general starch work and repairing. I started when I

was 21 years of age, at 25s [$61.70]. I am a married man, with one child. It takes more than 30s [$74.05] per week to live, but I occasionally make some overtime and occasionally I get £2 [$98.75] in a week. I pay weekly 7s [$17.30] for rent, 6s [$14.80] for groceries, 2s [$4.95] for baby's food, 1s 3d [$3.05] lodge fees, 2s 6d [$6.15] for firewood, 1s 3d [$3.05] for milk, 1s 6d [$3.70] for bread, 2s 6d [$6.15] on time-payment sewing-machine, and 4s to 5s [$10 to $12.35] for meat.

'For clothes we generally have to go on the time-payment system at 2s 6d [$6.15] a week, or 1s [$2.50]. I get a pair of boots when I can. If I wear a good pair of boots to work they are gone in four weeks. We are paid time and a quarter for overtime. As a rule, I make 32s [$76.55] per week by going to work for three hours on Sunday morning.'

Robert Burns, a starch-worker employed at the same factory, told the court that he had worked there for five years. His wages were 32s 6d [$80.25] per week. He worked alternate fortnights on day and night duty. Day work was 54 hours a week, and night work 63 hours a week. He had received 25s [$61.70] a week to start and used to get 8s [$19.75] a day on the sewers. He was a married man, and his weekly expenses were: rent 6s [$14.80], bread 2s 9d [$6.75], meat 5s 3d [$12.95], milk 2s [$4.95] groceries 10s [$25.20], wood 1s 10d [$4.55], lodge fees 2s ½d [$5.45]— newspaper 6d [$1.25], vegetables 1s [$2.45]—a weekly total of £1 11s 4½d [$77.40], without clothes.

Mr Harper's employees rarely got sick pay, and were forced to take three or more weeks' unpaid holiday each year, at times when work was slack.

In July 1907, *The Lone Hand* visited two homes of Mr Harper's starch-workers. One was 'a two-roomed hovel, in a dingy court, reached by a sewer-alley'. It consisted of a living-room and one bedroom, with a lean-to shed outside for the washing boiler. There were three children in the family.

A bed was kept on the little verandah during the day and put up every night in the small living room, which was about 3 m square. Two small girls slept in this bed, one at the top, the other at the bottom.

The other home was 'one of a row of small hutch houses, in a grey, squalid-looking street'. The plain deal furniture and the family clothing had all been bought on time-payment. In the living room there was a penny-in-the-slot gas meter which, when the family could afford it, provided four continuous hours of good light.

Working when ill

The father had had two bad spells of illness. Pleurisy once, and then lumbago. There had been no chance of rest during sickness. Someone else would have taken his place; so he had worked on, ill, in spite of doctor's orders, and had taken some months to get over an illness that could have been cured, with proper care, in a week or two.

Though he showed little interest in the housing conditions of his employees, Mr Harper took a pious interest in their spiritual life. He questioned them frequently about their religious activities. How often did they attend church? Did their children go to Sunday School? And sometimes he offered them a little sermon of his own composition, or he ponderously recited a prayer.

The wealth that enabled Robert Harper to build this palatial home in Melbourne was founded on the sweated labour of his employees

One way to find a job in Sydney in 1918 was to do what the man at right has done—consult the NSW Central Labour Exchange. The 55-year-old clerk who interviewed him, when he was not posing for the camera, was paid £230 [$6815] a year. The 26-year-old shorthand writer and typist with her back to the camera earned £150 [$4444] a year and the 20-year-old typist at right £130 [$3850]. At the top of the salary tree was the director of the exchange on £500 [$14,815] a year

These children who posed outside their corrugated iron shack on the outskirts of Sydney in 1913 were victims in a society that allowed great social inequality. Yet the Commonwealth Year Book for that year claimed: 'the distribution of wealth in the Australian Commonwealth . . . operates to prevent the development of a permanent pauper class . . .'

Victorian workers march through the streets of Melbourne on Labour Day 1939. Labour Day marks the struggle to achieve an eight-hour working day

Living on the basic wage

The Commonwealth Arbitration Court was established in 1904 for the settlement of industrial disputes. In 1907 the Court gave an award to shop-assistants in Sydney and Liverpool, New South Wales. Boys under 15 started at 5s [$12.35] and their wage rose to 7s 6d [$18.50] at 15, to 10s [$24.70] at 16 and then rose at 5s a year until it reached £2 5s [$111] at the age of 23. Girls under 15 started at 5s [$12.35] and their wage rose at 2s 6d [$6.20] a year until it reached £1 5s [$61.70]

A month later, the Court was asked to decide what was 'a fair and reasonable' wage for the Australian worker. Mr Justice Higgins decided that the minimum wage should be based on 'the normal needs of the average employee regarded as a human being in a civilized community'. After examining current living costs, he fixed the 'basic' wage for an unskilled worker at £2 2s [$103.70] a week.

An ironworker earning 11s [$27.15] a day told the Court: 'We look at it this way. We build cities, railways and palaces. We prepare the best of food and clothing, and we get very little of these things. We think we have a right to enjoy a little of them. If we build palaces, it is not right that we should have to live in hovels'.

When a counsel for employers said: 'I don't think you live in a hovel,' the ironworker said: 'But I'm not a labourer, I'm not getting 6s [$14.80] a day. It's him I'm thinking of.'

No money for savings

Another witness, an iron-pipe moulder earning 10s 6d [$25.90] a day, presented a typical domestic balance sheet. He was married with two children. His weekly household expenses were £2 5s 9d [$112.90], made up of: rent 12s 6d [$30.85], groceries 10s [$24.70], lodge 1s 3d [$3.05], newspapers 6d [$1.25], firewood 2s 6d [$6.15], vegetables 3s [$7.40], milk 3s 6d [$8.65], bread 5s [$12.35], meat 5s [$12.35], butter 2s 6d [$6.10]. There was no provision for clothes, gas, fares or tobacco, and he had been unable to save money.

Many alterations to the method of determining this minimum wage have taken place since 1907, but the concept of a 'basic wage' remains a fundamental part of Australian life.

Scraping by on the minimum

The shrinking pound

'Ever since the advent of Federation, the burden of taxation upon the people of Australia has steadily increased,' said *The Advisor*, the organ of New South Wales store-keepers, in 1910. And it pointed out that the 'once treasured sovereign' was now worth only 14s or 15s [$31.90 or $34.20]. (Thirty-nine years later, Robert Menzies, in the 1949 elections, promised 'to put value back into the pound.')

Since 1901, taxation per head had increased 45 per cent, from £2 14s 1d to £3 18s 3d [$123.25 to $178.30], compared with about £2 16s [$127.60] in Britain. *The Advisor* blamed 'a multiplicity of parliaments and an overwhelming number of representatives, who are paid exhorbitant salaries'.

In 1914, before the outbreak of war, Mr Justice Heydon said that the living wage in Sydney for a family of two parents and two dependent children was not less than £2 8s [$93.25] a week. He suggested a minimum wage of 8s 6d [$16.50] a day for light work, 8s 9d [$16.98] a day for ordinary work and 9s [$17.50] a day for heavy work.

At the end of World War I, the cost of living in Sydney had gone up by one-third, and the basic wage had risen to £3 [$88.88]. By 1920, commodities that had cost £1 in 1911 cost £1 17s 10d.

By 1973 the New South Wales basic wage had risen to $44.50 and the Commonwealth minimum wage to $60.80 (in Sydney), yet later that year Professor Ronald Henderson of the Commonwealth Commission of Enquiry into Poverty declared the poverty level to be $63 a week.

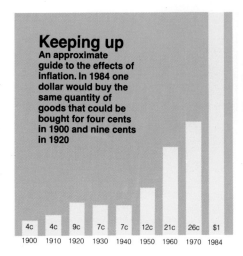

Keeping up

An approximate guide to the effects of inflation. In 1984 one dollar would buy the same quantity of goods that could be bought for four cents in 1900 and nine cents in 1920

4c	4c	9c	7c	7c	12c	21c	26c	$1
1900	1910	1920	1930	1940	1950	1960	1970	1984

The high price of eating out

In December 1913, popular Sydney restaurants made a move to increase the charge for a three-course meal—soup, meat and dessert—from 6d to 9d [$1 to $1.49]. The Sydney *Sun* reported that the lot of restaurant keepers had not improved since a similar attempt was made unsuccessfully a year before. Food was a little cheaper, but rents higher.

The *Sun* quoted figures that showed that meat had fallen since Easter from 3-3½d a lb. to 2½d [48-56c to 40c per 454g] in December, and potatoes from £7-10 [$280-400] to £4-5 [$160-$200] a ton. Groceries were unchanged. Meanwhile, wages had risen from £2-3 [$80-$120] a week to £2 4s-£3 2s 6d [$88.40-$125.55] for cooks, from 17s 6d-£1 [$35.15-$40.20] to £1 [$40.20] for dinner waitresses, from 15s to 17s 6d [$30.15 to $35.15] for tea waitresses, and from 15s-17s 6d to 18s [$36.15] for kitchen hands.

The newspapers said the wages were even higher than they appeared on paper. Before, a waitress might have worked any number of hours and had only one day off a week. Now she must work not more than 56 hours, and have a day and a half off; that meant employing extra hands. All employees received three meals a day.

The reason why restaurant proprietors had difficulty in obtaining a higher price for meals was the wide difference between 6d and 9d, the *Sun* said. A rise to 7d or 8d [$1.15 or $1.35] would, it was considered, cause dissatisfaction, whereas a 50 per cent rise to 9d [$1.50] would be unjust. It quoted one restauranteur who had experienced unpopularity through charging more than 6d [$1].

'When eggs were 2s [$4] a dozen and bacon 1s [$2] a pound, I charged 7d for a plate of two eggs and bacon', he said. 'When the price was 6d about every second man took eggs and bacon for breakfast, but when they had to pay a penny more, we did not sell a tenth of the quantity. The people went right off them.'

Some proprietors tried to solve the problem by providing a meal of soup and meat for 6d and charging an extra 3d [50c] for dessert. This, they claimed, turned a loss into a profit.

Kenneth Slessor recalled the restaurants of William Street, Sydney, in days when the price of a three-course meal had risen to 1s: 'On a cold evening, the smell of those lowly eating houses was as provoking to the nose as the fragrance from a Cunard kitchen.'

What was a living wage?

In 1919 the 'living wage' for men in New South Wales was £3 a week and the average wage was £3 14s 11d for men and £1 17s 1d for women. In industry the highest paid men were in mining, with an average weekly income of £4 8s 4d, and the lowest paid were those in domestic and hotel work, with an average wage of £3 8s 7d. That year *Smiths Weekly* compared various weekly earnings:

Governor-General	£192 6s 2d
New South Wales Governor	£96 3s 1d
Victorian Governor	£96 3s 1d
SA Governor	£76 18s 3d
WA Governor	£76 18s 3d
Chief Justice of Australia	£67 6s 1d
Tasmanian Governor	£52 17s 8d
Prime Minister	£40 7s 8d
Shearers (seasonal)	£12 0s 0d
Plumbers	£4 16s 0d
Boilermakers	£4 4s 0d
Painters	£3 12s 6d
Ironworkers	£3 12s 0d
Hairdressers	£3 8s 0d
Tailors	£3 7s 6d
Wharf labourers	£3 1s 6d
Labourers	£3 0s 0d
Teachers	£3 0s 0d
Tailoress	£1 18s 0d

Melbourne shops were boarded up against looters when the police went on strike in 1923. On the second day of the strike part of the city was at the mercy of hooligans who smashed shop windows and stole goods

A car load of specials—businessmen and their employees—patrol Melbourne streets during the police strike. The specials, with the help of police pensioners, kept peace in the city for several weeks

The girls who operated these looms in a Sydney spinning mill in 1922 earned about £1 17s [$50.40] for a 48-hour week—about half the men's pay rate.

In that year in New South Wales about one in three factory employees was a woman, whereas in 1903 it had been one in four. In 1982 the proportion was

one to two and three-quarters. Over 20,000 children under 16 worked in factories in 1922. They represented about 5 per cent of the work force

The men who built these beautifully finished car bodies in Melbourne in 1919 were craftsmen, but they were not highly paid. Firms that built bodies on imported chassis to the customer's order eventually disappeared in the face of competition from mass-produced cars

Living on a pension in 1905

Victoria in 1905 was the only state to provide old-age pensions. Payment of Commonwealth pensions, age and invalid, did not begin until 1909 and 1910 respectively. The Victorian old-age pensioner in 1905 received a meagre 7s [$17.30] a week.

The art historian William Moore, in his *City Sketches* (1905) discussed 'The Science of Cheap Living' in Melbourne. A single man, he explained, could manage with comparative ease on 10s [$24.70] a week; '. . . a decent bed for half a crown [$6.20] a week, and three fourpenny meals a day. The fourpenny [84c] meal is pretty filling at the price—oxtail or gravy soup, *à la mode*, an entree composed of either beef, steak, or sausages; sweets, bread and butter and tea.'

The half-crown for lodgings included free soap and blacking, the use of a smoke-room and a kitchen where the lodger could cook.

How did the old-age pensioner fare? One questioned by Moore said his living expenses were 6s 7d [$16.25] a week—'a late breakfast, threepence; tea, fourpence and a bed for the week, half a crown.'

Running the household

What it cost in working time—are we better off now?

Because both prices and wages rise together, it is difficult to judge whether people are better off now than they were earlier this century. One way to judge is to compare the time worked in order to buy a particular item.

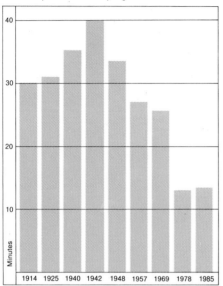

The length of time that a Sydney man earning the average minimum wage had to work to buy a bottle of beer. There was little difference in other cities

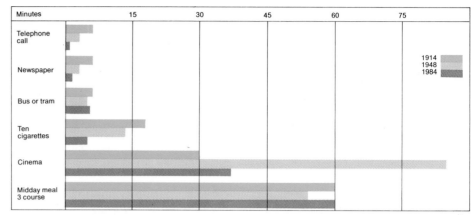

These graphs show the amount of time that a man earning the average wage in 1914, 1948 and 1984 had to work to buy various goods. In 1914 the average wage was £2 8s [$93.25] for a 48-hour week, in 1948 it was £5 16s [$111.40] for a 40-hour week, in 1984 it was $397.80 for a man working 39 hours

The decimal currency equivalents given here, of course, only show the comparative purchasing power of wages. As a result, in 1901 Sydney was the most expensive capital in which to live, as it remains today. A 1914 survey showed that it was followed by Perth, Adelaide, Hobart and Melbourne

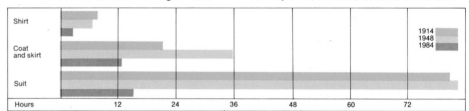

Complete household drapery for £12

In 1904 the Sydney department store of David Jones offered this collection of household drapery for £12. In 1985, the same goods cost well over $1000. The 1904 prices are given in dollars, in terms of today's purchasing power.

	1904
2 pairs strong cotton sheets for double bed	27.69
1 pair embroidered frill pillow cases	6.00
1 pair plain pillow cases	2.25
1 pair blankets	29.85
1 underblanket	5.65
1 white quilt	19.85
1 duchess table over and mats	8.35
2 pairs strong cotton sheets for double bed	23.45
1 pair hemstitched pillow cases	5.65
1 pair blankets	19.20
1 underblanket	5.65
1 white quilt	16.35
1 duchess table cover	2.65
2 pairs cotton sheets for maid's bed	15.65
1 pair pillow cases	2.10
1 pair blankets	14.95
1 underblanket	4.95

	1904
1 coloured quilt	6.95
1 toilet cover	1.40
2 double damask table cloths 1.8x2.3 metres	35.50
1 double damask table cloth 1.8x2.7 metres	21.30
6 damask napkins	8.35
2 kitchen table cloths	7.00
6 huckaback towels	8.95
3 Turkish towels	5.90
3 large bath towels	10.55
3 maid's coloured Turkish towels	4.25
6 glass towels	4.10
6 tea towels	5.05
6 kitchen rubbers	6.10
2 round towels	3.80
6 dusters	2.70
6 dish cloths	1.20
	343.34

Women enter business and professions

'Women are now a recognised force in many classes of business, and they have come to stay,' said an editorial in *The Model Trader*, a monthly magazine published by the Sydney firm of Grace Brothers, in October 1908.

'It is not many years since women had little or no choice in a vocation,' the editorial said. 'They could be a dressmaker, a milliner, and governess, a nurse or a domestic servant ... But now, after years of repression and heaps of abuse, they have won their way into nearly every branch of business and most of the professions. Even those most conservative professions, law and medicine, have had to open their portals, although unwillingly, to the modern woman ...'

First woman doctor

Women had succeeded in entering the medical profession before the turn of the century, and a woman graduated from the faculty of law at the University of Sydney in 1902, but it was not until 1918 that a woman in New South Wales was allowed to practise law.

But the editorial pointed out that though the woman in business was recognised as a factor in the great machinery of commerce, particularly as a confidential clerk, she worked only until 'Mr Right' came along. The loving wife and mother would always be with us. 'We must admit that there are dangers to the body politic from the excessive employment of female labour; the emancipation of women has caused a certain amount of aversion among educated women against the duties of a wife and mother, but this is only the natural swing of the pendulum after years of subservient submission to the whims and caprices of men,' the editorial said.

Careful housekeeping in 1938

In June, 1938, the Melbourne *Herald* published an article headed 'She feeds five on 25s a week'. It examined the budget of a 'Mrs Brown', whose husband earned the basic wage of £3 17s a week. They had three children, aged 12, ten and five.

'Every week Mrs Brown has 25s and anything she can get from the bone and bottle man, to buy food,' said the article. 'With great care and forethought she manages to keep within this amount.'

This is how she did it: 'Mrs Brown is very careful with little economies—for instance, she never buys dripping, but suet, and renders it. She keeps a stock-pot and never sells the bones until the marrow and last scraps of nourishment have been wrung from them. And, of course, she never sells any fat.

'Twice a week she goes to the market for meat, eggs, fruit and vegetables and keeps them in a drip-safe . . . She is quite content to pass by fruit and vegetables which are out of season—not for her either those handy but expensive tins of pork and beans, those fascinating little snacks, which are not really necessary for the family diet. Instead her meals draw their inspiration from the stock-pot, with its vegetable waters, bacon rinds, cheese parings and whisper of garlic, and an appreciative feeling for salt and cayenne pepper. So she has plenty of liquid rich in mineral salts for soups and gravies and extra money is not needed for tonics or patent medicines or pick-me-ups.'

In their pocket-handkerchief back garden, the Browns grew mint, parsley, marjoram, sage and thyme in boxes and they grew in tubs silver beet, spring onions, lettuces and other vegetables that do not have deep roots.

Each week Mrs Brown divided her food money into five amounts of 5s and allotted them for bread and other cereals, milk and cheese, meat and eggs, fruit and vegetables, fats and sugar and sundries.

Mrs Brown had a neighbour with a lemon tree with whom she exchanged pots of home-made jam for lemons so there was always fresh lemonade for the children.

The Browns used 680 g of oatmeal a week and porridge was made twice a week and well swollen. Mrs Brown rarely fried anything and had roasts only on special occasions because they were apt to be wasteful. She never used custard powder.

The article quoted typical meals:

A week day
Breakfast: porridge, milk and honey. One slice each of bread and butter—after that bread and dripping. Cocoa and tea.

Lunch: scrambled egg sandwiches, jam sandwiches, fruit, tea and sugar for Mr Brown. Boiled egg, bread, butter and fruit for the smallest child. Mrs Brown has cheese, bread, jam, fruit, tea.

Dinner: tripe, delicately seasoned with nutmeg, garlic, onions, and mashed potatoes; stewed prunes with plenty of juice (prunes are rich in iron and balance the easily-digested but nearly iron-less tripe).

Sunday
Breakfast: same.
Dinner: lamb's fry soufflé (half pint of white panada, 2 eggs, minced liver and heart, herbs), potatoes, boiled cucumber and white sauce—baked unpolished rice custard with sultanas.

Tea: grated cheese omelette, bread, butter, dripping, jam, and the last of the cocoa.

What Mrs Brown got in her five-shilling shopping baskets in 1938

In 1938 this food fed a Melbourne family of five for one week. Each group of food cost 5s, making a total of £1 5s a week out of the husband's income of £3 17s a week—one third of his wage. In 1985, this food cost $66.08, just under a quarter of the average minimum wage paid to a man

2.25 kg of apples, 12 bananas, 1 kg of pears, 7.75 kg of potatoes, 2.75 kg of onions, 1.35 kg of tomatoes, one cucumber, 1 kg of swedes, 1 kg of carrots, 1 kg of peas. Cost in April 1985—$19.04

8 litres of milk and 1 kg of cheese. Cost in April 1985—$9.21

1 kg of suet, 1 kg of butter, 450 g of sugar, 250 g of cocoa, 450 g of honey. Cost in April 1985—$7.12

One fish, 18 eggs, 450 g of liver, 1 kg of steak, 1 kg of black pudding and 450 g of tripe. Cost in April 1985—$20.64

1 kg of oatmeal, 1.85 kg of flour, seven loaves of bread and 450 g of unpolished rice. Cost in April 1985—$10.07

The great depression

Terrible years that followed the Wall Street crash

In the first half of 1929, America's stock-market boomed with a crazy rise in prices, and the nation plunged into a wild orgy of speculation. But on 'Black Thursday', 24 October 1929, the market suddenly collapsed. Share prices dropped sensationally. Thousands of investors were ruined. Some committed suicide. Businessmen went bankrupt, industrial production declined, unemployment rose to staggering heights, and international lending dried up.

The Depression spread to the rest of the world. Australia suffered very severely because her economy relied on overseas loans, and on the sale of primary products. The value of her exports fell by nearly half. Wool, previously selling for up to 16s 6d [$22] a kilogram fell to about 1s 8d [$3.10], and wheat dropped from £6 17 6d [$183.10] to less than £2 15s [$91.80] per m³.

Share prices slumped, as they had in America. Dunlop shares, for example, selling at 28s 2d [$62.70] in March 1929, were down to 7s 4d [$11.15] in September 1931, and Mt Lyell had dropped from 42s 9d to 17s 1d [$55.65 to $25.95] in the same period.

As spending power declined, shops closed, farms were abandoned, rents were unpaid, debts mounted, and unemployment rose

tragically. For a time, more than 30 per cent of the Australian workforce was unemployed. Moratorium acts were introduced in New South Wales, Western Australia and Tasmania to protect people who could not find work. The Labor Government in New South Wales, under Premier Jack Lang, was the first to introduce such measures. In his book *The Great Bust*, Lang recalls the situation: 'We had promised a moratorium. Within a fortnight of taking office we had a Moratorium Bill drafted and presented to Parliament . . . 10 December 1930. For a period of two years it restricted the foreclosure and power of sale under mortgage, bills of sale and hire purchase agreements. Before a lender could sell up the security he had to get the permission of the court. In short, the onus was on him to prove that the person who had borrowed the money was in a position to repay and was seeking to evade his obligations. The only exception was when interest payments were more than 12 months in arrears.'

Those lucky enough to keep their jobs often had to take a cut in wages. The federal basic wage fell from £4 14 6d [$123.05] at the end of 1929 to £4 8s [$119.85] by the end of 1930. In February 1931 the Commonwealth Arbitration Court reduced the basic real wage for

unskilled labour by 10 per cent. Peter Fallon of the Clothing Trades Union is quoted by Lang as saying: 'This [the basic wage reduction will mean that my members will lose 18s 6d [$28.10] a week when the basic wage reduction is taken into account. I do not know how they are going to live. They are already working part time. The people will have less money to buy clothes. This is the kind of thing that makes communists.'

Barefoot to school

No Australian who lived through the Depression, either as adult or child, could ever forget the traumatic experience of those terrible years. The Sydney poet Nancy Keesing, writing 30 years later, remembered the many children in the Sydney suburb of Darlinghurst who went barefoot to school; the 'greasy cabbage-sulphurous smell' from cafes next to prawn-shops in William street which advertised: *3 Course Meals for 9d. [$1.17] Dole tickets accepted;* and the women with little children who often knocked at her parents' back door, asking for food—'sometimes our half-worn clothes leave with them when their meal in the kitchen is finished'.

The novelist George Johnston, in *My Brother Jack*, recalls how the Victorian auth-

When the Depression was at its worst more than 30 per cent of Australia's workers were unemployed, white-collar and blue-collar workers alike. Men became desperate for work and were prepared to try anything to find a job. This Sydney man stood in city streets wearing a placard proclaiming: 'A challenge! For 16 months all efforts to obain a job have proven useless! I am in excellent health. First class civil and military record. Wide experience. References available. I require employment!' It is not recorded whether his vigorous appeal won him a job

Many unemployed men left the cities to search for work in the country. But work was scarce there too, and many tramped for hundreds of kilometres and managed to find only enough work to earn their keep. The fierce competition for rural jobs meant the end of the old-time Australian swagman

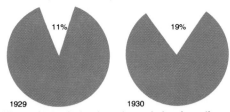

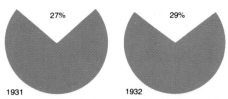

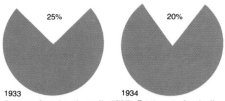

11%	19%	27%	29%	25%	20%
1929	1930	1931	1932	1933	1934

The wedges missing from these circles dramatise the statistics of unemployment among members of Australian trade unions. In the first quarter of 1929 the unemployment rate was just over 11 per cent. In the depths of the Depression, in mid-1932, it was over 29 per cent. Unemployment did not fall to pre-Depression level until 1937. Post-war Australia knew almost full employment until the mid-70s; in 1983, the unemployment rate was 10.3 per cent

orities 'unlocked the Defence Department warehouses, and out of the mothballs they took the old surplus great-coats and tunics and they dyed them a dull black—all that brave khaki of 1914-18—and against the contingency of a Melbourne winter issued them out as a charity to keep the workless warm. So that as the unemployed grew in number the black army coats became a kind of badge of adversity, a stigma of suffering. As the situation grew worse desperate attempts were made towards alleviation, and the "black coats" moved then in the more regimental bands of the "sustenance-workers" and you would see them with their brooms and picks and shovels and council tip-drays working in slovenly unison on pointless municipal projects.'

Another Victorian writer, Alan Marshall, who worked during the Depression in a shoe factory in the inner Melbourne suburb of Collingwood, recalls how each evening 'ragged children with bare feet and dirty faces' took home waste pieces of leather in their billy carts. 'Their meals were cooked over these scraps of leather, their thinly-clad bodies were warmed by it, the air above their homes was tainted by the smell of its burning.' It was called 'Collingwood coke'.

And Marshall tells how men queued in an alley beside a hotel in Elizabeth Street, Melbourne. Each in turn spread a sheet of newspaper on the cobblestones. A man carrying a rubbish-bin tightly packed with refuse upended it, and divided the hotel's waste among the waiting men.

'The heaps, speckled with sodden tea leaves, contained chop bones, the fatty selvedges of steaks, pie-crusts, saturated bread, the stringy sections of roasts, corned beef fat, scrappings of potatoes stained with gravy, blobs of rice custard, cabbage, pieces of carrot and nibbled portions of cheese. Permeating them all was the black sand of coffee grounds. They wolfed the goo like dogs,' he writes.

In Fitzroy, another inner-Melbourne sub-urb, a number of cafes served a three-course meal for 7d [92c]: 'In the early morning a spring-cart drawn by a bony horse pulled up in front of these cafes. It was laden with hessian bags stuffed with vegetables and fruit swept from the stalls of the Victoria Market or gathered from the gutters . . . Apples bearing brown patches of decay, sprouting onions, shrunken potatoes, sat amid sodden horse dung that had spread along the gutters . . . These bags of vegetable refuse were bought by the cheap cafes and tossed into stock-pots for soup or used with servings of meat . . .'

'These are the things in Australia I have hated,' wrote the Western Australian novelist, Katherine Susannah Prichard. 'To see relief workers with their wives living under shacks of bagging and boughs. To know that hundreds of Australians, young and old, have lived on the brink of despair because they could not find work or wages to feed and clothe themselves, in this rich and lovely country of ours.'

The hardships of the Depression forced many of the unemployed to live in parks or on any piece of vacant land they could find. Groups of unemployed men, like these in Perth, were a familiar sight to anyone who lived through the Depression. Ramshackle camps of flimsy hessian shacks sprang up in every city. They housed families that had been thrown out of homes they could no longer pay for

267

Living with unemployment

The search for work and somewhere to live

'Jumping the rattler'—travelling free on goods trains—was a favourite method of moving about the country during the Depression. Those who travelled in this way risked sudden death under the wheels if they missed their grip while jumping aboard, and risked imprisonment if they were caught

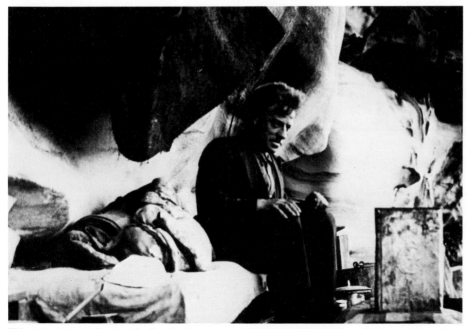

This man was one of many who lived in the meagre shelter of sandstone outcrops in Sydney's Domain, a park in the centre of the city. The men who lived there were usually single—married men had to stay with their families or they could not collect unemployment relief

At the height of the Depression, in 1932, nearly one Australian worker in three was un-employed. When one Sydney firm advertised for a night watchman, more than 500 men applied for the job.

But newspapers frequently cheered up the homeless and workless in reassuring prose: 'Apart from expensive cigars, cars, more clothes and more food, what does the poor devil of a rich man obtain that is not just as easily obtained by the poor man?' asked the Sydney *Sun* in September 1930. 'Sunsets are just as beautiful, spring morning just as fair, love as tender, music just as consoling for Lazarus as for Dives. The things which really matter are not purchased with money.'

Swelling ranks of beggars

In the same month, *The Sydney Morning Herald* said: 'During recent months the growth of begging in Sydney's streets has been a feature of the city's life. Many of those who have swelled the ranks are obviously victims of the financial crisis.' It was an offence to solicit alms, or sell on the street without a licence, but the newcomers, said the *Herald*, were 'fur-tive, quick people, darting and dotted in the jostling crowds.

'Lurking in an alley-way, a man pushes his stunted child forward to offer onion pickles, home-made toffee. "Has the gentleman a coin? . . . sick mother . . . please sir!" Thin faces dart from doorways—ties, handker-chiefs, face cream, shoe laces, posies, fish that waggle fins; unshaved chins, unwashed necks, collarless, shirtless, sockless, tense faces: "Buy, buy, buy, give, give, give"; fierce whispers, the failure, the dart back to cover, the next prospect; "'ere y'are, sir, very cheap, sir"; eager thrusting, tenacious, imploring.

'Some offer nothing, some sing, make pre-tence at playing violins, clarinets, anything. Some just stand and look with hunger in their eyes. When the sun dips, the still low orders rake the garbage tins—hooking, stirring; "nothin' 'ere, Jack", banging of lids, the prowl beyond the lights. By the time the theatre crowds are home, they have all gone—somewhere.'

But where did they go? To hessian shacks in parks and race-courses, flimsy camps on sand-dunes, rough shelters in the caves of the Sydney Domain.

Door-knockers

As numerous as the street beggars and pedlars were the droves of 'door-knockers', men, women and even children who trudged sub-urban streets imploring housewives to buy camphor, mothballs, darning wool, pins, writing-tablets, pens, collar studs, soap, stockings, plants, artificial flowers, gumtips, holy pictures, rabbits, fruit or clothes-props.

Some men, working on commission, tried to sell insurance policies, Fuller brushes, sewing-machines or vacuum-cleaners.

In November 1930, Nettie Palmer, living in Melbourne, noted in her diary 'the sense of wheels running down: the shabby hawkers drifting from door to door: the line of de-feated men sitting on the Post Office steps'.

The Melbourne *Herald* reported a typical police-court case. William Burke, 41, pleaded guilty to begging on a street-corner in Prahran. He told the Court: 'I went to two or three cars. I admit that I did ask one for money. I have had no work for 10 months. I am willing to work. I walked 1100 miles [1770 kilometres] to the last job I had.' The case was adjorned for three months 'to give Burke a chance'.

Men tramped bush roads prepared to do any work for their bare keep. They lined their shoes with cardboard, huddled in shanty towns, ate boiled wheat, and sang:

I'm spending my days in the doss house,
I'm spending my days on the street,
I'm searching for work but can find none.
I wish I had something to eat.

Jumping the rattler

Thousands 'jumped the rattler', a dangerous practice, as one of them, the humorist Lennie Lower, recalled:

'The temptation to "jump the rattler", is great: twenty miles [32 kilometres] that would take a day to walk can be covered in less than an hour on a goods train. And the man who walks all day must have food. The gain is worth the risk of imprisonment or sudden death, from one point of view. But death is always within call, the policeman is never far away. I saw one poor old man who missed his grip on a flying truck and clung to the buffer for half a mile, clawing like a feeble monkey to retain his hold—and wouldn't let go his swag! The look in his eyes when at last I managed to get his hands on to the edge of the truck, I shall never forget. I have ridden smothered in coal on an engine tender, astride a buffer in the dead of night, in an empty truck which had contained lime, and still contained sufficient to blind and choke a man as the motion of the truck stirred it, while the train shunted about a clamorous depot—and I lay on my stomach breathing lime. I have clung to the side of a high wheat truck, afraid to move, and sweated under tarpaulins; but for sheer hell commend me to the under-the-seat method. The space is so narrow that chest and backbone seem as one, and breathing is both staccato and pianissimo.'

A typical day

Writing in *The Sydney Morning Herald* in January 1931, an unemployed man in Sydney described his typical day: 'Out of bed; but what to do? The drab routine of clearing the bread tin and making a cup of tea for "her", lying in a troubled slumber; the effort to convince the kiddies that dripping is better for them than butter; the equally heroic effort to shave with a hopeless blade, and the jumping out of one's skin when the baker, not this time the landlord's agent, raps at the door for payment of his account.

'The routine continues, in dread and anxiety, and tears. For there is yet the landlord's man—most fearsome of all—and one or two collectors whom it is becoming impossible to placate. Then there is the gas account, which the wife weeps over, and the impending electric light bill. To stay at home seems effortless; to walk the streets without definite purpose is futile.'

Evictions of tenants unable to pay their rent were frequent, and not always peaceful. *The Sydney Morning Herald* in June 1931, under the heading 'Desperate Fighting: Communists and Police', reported: 'The most sensational eviction battle Sydney has ever known was fought between 40 policemen and 18 Communists at 143 Union street, Newtown, yesterday morning. All the defenders were injured, some seriously, and at least 15 of the police were treated by ambulance officials. Only one man was hit by bullets fired at the walls of the house by the police, and it is not known how the injury was inflicted. Probably the wounded man was struck by a bullet which had been deflected in its path.'

Hostility to the police

'Entrenched behind barbed wire and sandbags, the defenders rained stones weighing several pounds from the top floor of the building on to the heads of the attacking police, who were attempting to execute an eviction order. After a desperate battle, in which iron bars, piping, rude bludgeons and chairs were used by the defenders, and batons by the police, the defenders were dragged, almost insensible, to the waiting patrol waggons. A crowd hostile to the police, numbering many thousands, gathered in Union street. They filled the street for a quarter of a mile [440 metres] on each side of the building until squads of police drove them back about 200 yards [180 metres], and police cordons were thrown across the roadway.

'At times the huge crowd threatened to become out of hand. It was definitely antagonistic to the police. When constables emerged from the back of the building with their faces covered in blood, the crowd hooted and shouted insulting remarks. When one patrol waggon containing prisoners was being driven away, people standing well back in the crowd hurled stones at the police driver.' The *Herald* did not explain how it identified the 'defenders' in the eviction from the Newtown house as communists.

Life in 'Happy Valley'

In July 1931, about 350 homeless men, women and children lived in a straggling collection of tents and huts at La Perouse, on Botany Bay, Sydney, 'waiting till the sun shines through the murk of depression', as *The Sydney Morning Herald* poetically phrased it. When the settlement, known as 'Happy Valley', was visited by the Governor of New South Wales, Sir Philip Game, his wife said she had seen one little home in which she would not mind living herself.

The *Worker's Weekly* described the settlement in February 1934. There were then 400 men, women and children living in bag humpies in the 'flea-infested stretch of scrubby sandhills' at La Perouse.

'This camp is one and three-quarter miles [2.8 kilometres] long, and scattered at random, sheltering in the lee of hillocks of sand and bushes from the southerly busters that swept across Botany Bay are 129 shacks,' it said. 'Have a look inside the shacks that look so dilapidated from the road. Bags, these walls, flour bags, bummed from the baker, cut open and resewn into squares to fit the white-anted, second-hand timber that forms the jerry-built walls; painted with a mixture of lime and fat boiled up in salt water to make them weatherproof. The roofs are mostly made of scrap sheets of tin rescued from the garbage tip . . . the floors are wet sand, smoothed out and covered with more bags.

'Fleas? Millions of 'em.'

The scrubby sandhills of Sydney's seaside fringes erupted into a rash of shacks and tents that housed unemployed workers and their families who had been evicted. Shacks were built in any materials that came to hand, including old rotten timber and sacks waterproofed with lime and fat

On the susso

Meagre handouts but generous advice for the unemployed

Each state had its own system of relief for the unemployed, usually in the form of either wages for relief work or a weekly dole, more politely called 'sustenance', and more popularly, 'susso'.

Children of the Depression used to chant:

We're on the susso now,
We can't afford a cow,
We live in a tent,
We pay no rent,
We're on the susso now.

'Work, sustenance or dole. What's in a name?' asked the Melbourne society weekly, *Table Talk*, in July 1930. 'In Britain they call it boldly and callously the "Dole"; here we prefer the more genteel term "Sustenance", but fortunately a move is afoot to wash out both Sustenance and Dole, and to substitute Work—even if it be work for two days a week only. The danger lies in giving something for nothing. The better course is to demand work in return for the cash, and if the Government hold boldly to that course, it will be doing the right thing.'

Administering relief

F. A. Bland, writing in the *Economic Record* of May 1932, explained how unemployment relief was administered in New South Wales: 'To obtain food relief, an applicant must be registered at the State Labour Exchange for at least seven days, and he must make a declaration that he has been unemployed for at least fourteen days, and is without resources which he might use for his support.

'If he possesses any property (with the exception of a house) which he might realise, he cannot obtain relief until all his resources are exhausted. An applicant relieved through

the Labour Exchange attends at assigned depots at a regular day and hour, and, having made a declaration regarding his continued unemployment and his destitution, he received coupons relative to his scale of relief for the ensuing fortnight. Separate coupons are issued for milk, bread, meat and groceries, and are made negotiable only with traders nominated by the applicant.'

Drawing numbers for food

In August 1930, there were 4000 unemployed in the Melbourne suburb of Brunswick. 'As there is not sufficient food to go round for relief distribution to the Brunswick unemployed today, 622 tickets bearing numbers and 200 blanks will be drawn from a hat,' reported the Melbourne *Sun-Pictorial* on August 23. What the unlucky drawers of blanks ate that day was not recorded.

About the same time, Dr Hilda Kincaid, of the Melbourne City Council, drew up a chart showing how a man, woman and two children could live on 13s 4d [$18.20] a week. And a Tasmanian MLA named Ockerby told an unemployment demonstration that he personally could bach on 10s [$13.60] a week. (His parliamentary pay was £10 [$272.40] a week.)

'It's an ill wind that blows no good and the present hard times are teaching valuable lessons in domestic economy,' said *Table Talk* in a paragraph headed 'The Advantages of a Light Diet'. 'For instance, Dr Arthur, New South Wales Minister for Health, advised the local Food Relief Kitchen that skimmed milk in soup enhances its food value 300 per cent, and that dripping, plus pepper and salt on bread, is more nutritious and cheaper than treacle or jam. He also became lyrical on the subject of bread fried in dripping, which he describes as a kingly dish.'

Applying for relief in 1933. The officials who distributed relief had wide discretionary power to grant or refuse applications. This was because there were so many applicants—as many as 22,000 a fortnight at one city depot. Some got neither food nor relief work and were sent on their way

Table Talk followed this report with a cautionary tale headed 'A Case in Point'. 'Apropos of dieticians, an unemployed Parramatta house-painter, living on rations provided under the dole system, died the other day quite unexpectedly, and it was at first thought that malnutrition was a contribution cause. However, the medical man who examined him after death found that cerebral haemorrhage was responsible for his sudden end, and he said that if the man had eaten more meat, or more food of any kind, he would have died much sooner,' it said.

In September 1931, Dr Harris, the unofficial leader of Victoria's Legislative Council, complained that the diet provided to the unemployed was 'too luxurious'. There was no starvation, he said, when people could eat 'such luxuries as cocoa, tripe and kidneys'. (Tripe cost 6d a pound [76c per 450g]; cocoa the same; and kidneys 1½d [18c] each. Tea was 1s 6d [$2.30] a pound; cheese 1s 6d; barracouta 1s 3d [$1.88]; eggs 1s 6d a dozen; and butter 1s 10½d [$2.85] a pound.)

The sustenance allowance in Victoria for a single man was then 5s [$7.60] a week if he lived away from home, but only 1s 6d [$2.28] if he lived at home or with a relative. A married man with a wife and child received 8s 6d [$12.90] a week, plus 1s 6d for each additional child. The amount allotted for food represented 2d [24c] a meal. The Victorian Government sent about 10,000 men to fossick for gold on abandoned fields. In eight months, they dug out 312,000 g, equivalent to 31 g a person or about £4 15s [$144.30] worth each.

'Although I realise that men and women aged from 30 to 40 years who are now unemployed are becoming absolutely demoralised and completely beyond hope, I must maintain that there is no more serious phase of unemployment than the idleness of adolescent children,' said the organising secretary of Melbourne's Unemployed Girl's Relief Fund, Miss Muriel Heagney, in July 1932. 'Some of the unemployed girls are solving their problem by saving themselves physically, and sacrificing certain other standards. Another section are breaking down physically. Girls aged 14 to 16 years are showing definite signs of malnutrition, which will be difficult to cure.'

A year later, there were about 4400 girls out of work in Melbourne, among them nurses, stenographers, cashiers and dress designers. If they lived with relatives, they had to work one day a week, and received 7s 6d [$12.50] unemployment allowance, or sustenance. If they boarded, they had to work two days a week, and received 12s 6d [$20.85]. (Board cost at least 7s or 8s [$11.70 or $13.35] a week, leaving 5s 6d [$9.20] a week for clothing, travelling and other necessities.)

To qualify for sustenance in Victoria was a lengthy process, taking up to a month. It involved interviews at several scattered labour and welfare offices. After the girl got her registration card, an official inspected her place of residence to question her about her circumstances and qualifications. Then after about a fortnight, she received a notice telling her to attend one of the work centres.

A special correspondent of the Melbourne *Herald* who spent two weeks among unemployed girls reported that they talked mostly about 'boy friends' and 'sex questions'. 'A very rare type is the girl who thinks about deeper things,' he wrote.

Secession moves in the west

In Western Australia, with a population of about 440,000, 70,000 men, women and children lived by earnings from relief work, or on sustenance. The sustenance allowance was 7s [$11.70] a head per week for men, women and children. Only foods named on an official list could be bought with sustenance money.

Unemployed single men were sent to a canvas camp in a jarrah forest in the Darling Ranges, and had to earn sustenance by cutting firewood for a day and a half a week. The wood was given to unemployed families in Perth.

One result of the Depression in Western Australia was the revival of the secession movement. At a referendum held April 1933, the people by an overwhelming majority voted to secede from the Commonwealth, and to return to their former status as citizens of a self-governing independent state. But no action was taken and the movement faded when prosperity returned.

The Australian economy began to recover in 1934, but memories of the Depression remained and it became the objective of governments to maintain full employment. This ideal was fulfilled in post-war years until, with renewed fears of depression, unemployment figures rose in the 70s, and remain a problem.

At one stage of the Depression, Sydney men in search of food relief had to report to this wharf at Circular Quay and queue for dole tickets. Then they had to go to the other end of the city, near Central Railway, to collect the goods. Many could not afford fares and walked from the suburbs and through the city

Relief was available for many only in return for work, and thousands of men were employed in public works. This gang is forming a road in what is now a populous Sydney suburb. In other states men were sent to work at timber cutting, on irrigation schemes and on the goldfields

Shopping in more leisurely days

The baker cooked the Sunday roast for forty cents

In the days before supermarkets, housekeeping had a pleasant leisurely and personal flavour. The Sunday joint was delivered by the butcher, who usually had time for a chat at the back door—he used the tradesmen's entrance, of course.

The Chinese market gardener went from house to house, carrying his vegetables and fruit in two baskets suspended from a yoke over his shoulders. At Christmas he gave his customers presents such as preserved ginger in blue-and-white jars, embroidered silk handkerchiefs or peacock-feather fans.

The 'rabbito' or 'rabbio' cried 'Rabeet' up and down the street, his rabbits strung in rows in his horse-drawn cart. When he sold one he skinned it on the spot. Down Melbourne lanes echoed the resonant cry of 'TumAHtoes, tumAHtoes, r-r-ripe Bendigo tumAHtoes!'

At the beginning of the century housewives—and not only those who were poor—made most of their own preserves.

Delicatessens, then known as ham and beef shops, were few. The poet and essayist Frederic Macartney, who was a boy in Melbourne at the start of the century, has written of one where 'we bought beef dripping, striated with gravy, for fourpence [85c] a pound. Butter at from two to three times that price was too dear for us for general use'.

Macartney remembers too how sometimes on a Sunday, 'to save firewood and the bother of cooking, we were sent with a joint in a dish to a nearby baker, who put it in his oven to be collected later nicely cooked for threepence'.

Another Melbourne writer, John Hetherington, has described the grocer's shop his father kept at Sandringham, on Port Phillip Bay. The period was about 1914. Packaging was almost unknown. There were tins of biscuits, deep tins filled with sultanas, dates and dried apricots, and wooden drawers with walnuts, almonds and brazil nuts.

'The grocer and his men had to weigh and

wrap all the regular items in which they traded,' Hetherington writes. 'Even butter came in fifty-six pound boxes [25 kilogram] and had to be cut into one-pound and half-pound portions which were patted into cubes or oblongs, then wrapped in greaseproof paper and stored in the ice-chest . . .'

Chemist shops, which today sell everything from pantyhose to cameras, were much more austere in the 1900s. The chemists usually displayed in their windows, as curious symbols of their craft, two tall, bulbous bottles, one filled with red liquid, the other with green. The shelves of the shop displayed an impressive array of jars, labelled with the names of the medical drugs and chemicals listed in the British Pharmacopoeia; thus common salt bore the thoroughly enigmatic label *sod. chlor*.

The chemist was a dispenser of medicines then, not a mere distributor of ready-made pills, cosmetics and fancy goods as, for the most part, he is today.

This row of shops in Port Pirie, South Australia, is typical of those built along the main streets of prosperous country towns around the start of the century. Decorative verandahs shade the shop windows from the sun, while on the elaborately moulded facade built-in letters proudly announce the proprietor's name. In this case he was a chemist and druggist; the 'etcetera' of the sign refers to the Boot Palace next door

Smallgoods were made in this butchery at the turn of the century in conditions that were far from hygienic by today's standards. But then, as now, there were complaints about the contents of sausages. Bran, flour and water were some of the substances that swelled out the meat

Chinese market gardeners were a familiar sight around the suburbs up to World War II. Some hawked their vegetables from a cart, usually a black, covered one; others carried their wares from door to door by the traditional Chinese device of two large baskets suspended from a pole

The grocer's burden

'Can anyone be a Grocer?' asked *The Grocer of Australasia* ('The only Purely Grocers' Paper in Australasia') in February 1901. And it answered itself:

'A clerk or joiner may buy a business and wear an apron behind the counter, but that does not qualify him a grocer . . . There are no trades in existence requiring more care and practical intelligence than that of a grocer. The multiplicity of articles which he stocks—all more or less of a perishable nature—demand the closest attention . . . In order to be successful, he must in very truth have a special training for the work.'

From time to time, the paper advised its readers on the subtleties of selling groceries. For instance, the shop should always have a characteristic 'lovely odour'. And this was very easy to achieve: 'All that is necessary is to make a shovel hot and sprinkle an ounce of coffee on it every morning and that odour will stay with the store nearly all day . . .'

Another useful device was to pick out 'a few nice pieces of candy suitable to the standing of the customers', and hand them to the customer's eldest child. 'There is nothing that warms the cockles of a parent's heart to the storekeeper as to witness this little act on his part.' And the grocer should remember to send a little bag of sweets home to the children with his monthly bill.

Despite these sugary blandishments, customers did not always pay up, and a poet in 1907 addressed the reluctant 'bad eggs' thus:

Take up the Grocer's burden
Go pay him for your feed;
He stood your friend in trouble,
Served you in time of need;
And now to wait forever,
On unpaid bills high piled,
Of never-pay-up people
Will starve his wife and child.

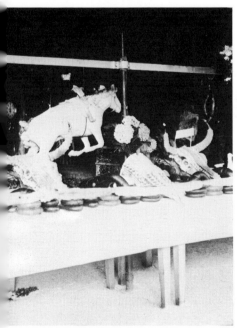

Before World War I, butchers' shops were windowless, open to the street. This one's counter is enlivened with decorated carcasses and flowers

Behind the counter the carcasses hung in rows. This photograph was taken in the early days of Silvester's butchery in Redfern, Sydney, a big business which installed its own refrigeration plant in 1904. Smaller butchers kept their meat in rooms rather like large ice-chests

The cash-and-carry revolution

'Nothing Over 1s' was the motto

On 11 April 1914, hundreds of eager housewives stormed a small shop in Smith Street, Collingwood, an inner Melbourne working-class suburb. Their curiosity—and cupidity—had been aroused by a widely distributed dodger announcing the opening of a 'Nothing Over 1s' [$1.95] variety store.

On opening day, the principal attractions were 66 cm imported enamel mixing bowls which had previously cost 1s 8d [$3.60] and which were there priced at 1s [$1.95]. The stock of 20 dozen was quickly snapped up, and the brothers George and Jim Coles closed their first day's tradings with more than £100

[$3,885] in the till. This was the beginning of a business that was to revolutionise retail trading in Australia.

The Coles brothers were sons of a Victorian country storekeeper. George, who had run a successful store at St James in northern Victoria, sold it in 1913 and made a trip around the world. In the United States, he studied the five and ten cent chain stores, and in England the '3d, 6d and 1s' stores. When he returned to Australia in 1914, he and his brother Jim, who had managed one of their father's country stores, decided to open a '3d, 6d and 1s' store in Melbourne.

The first Coles store was in Smith Street, in the Melbourne suburb of Collingwood, and it opened in April 1914. When the two Coles brothers floated the business as a public company in 1927, its annual turnover was already £1 million [$26.6 million]. In 1984, Coles had 893 stores and a turnover of $5442 million

Before supermarkets, most housewives shopped at their local grocer and had the goods delivered. However, shops like the Owl Store in Gosford, NSW, offered cheaper goods and did a thriving 'cash-and-carry' business during the 1930s. A number of the smaller stores were consequently put out of business

All merchandise was to be openly displayed, customers were not to be pressured to buy, and money would be cheerfully refunded on request. These principles, on which the huge Coles empire was to be built, were novel in the Australia of 1914. After three months' trading, the store showed a trading loss of £120 [$4,660], but by spring it was making a perfectly respectable profit.

During World War I, George and Jim Coles and their two brothers Arthur and Dave all served in the AIF. Jim and Dave were both killed in France. After the war, George and Arthur opened another store in Smith Street, with the slogan 'Nothing over 2s 6d' [$3.25] (this remained their policy until 1938). The new store was an immediate success, and by 1927, when the business was turned into a public company with a paid up capital of £272,660 [$7.26 million], nine Coles stores were operating in Melbourne, with a turnover approaching £1 million [over $26 million] a year.

In 1928, Coles moved into Sydney, taking over a six-storey building in Pitt Street—near King Street (opposite the present store). It was taken on a 21-year lease at £20,000 [$532,600] a year—an unprecedented Sydney rental. When the doors opened on June 1, police were called in to control the crowds struggling to buy enamel buckets for 1s [$1.33], sleeping dolls for 2s 6d [$3.33], winceyette bloomers for 1s and striped towels for 6d [66c].

'The Coles brothers began their brilliant and meteoric career ... with £1000 cash and a small shop,' said *Table Talk* in 1930. 'Last year they cleared a profit of £90,000 [$2,344,000]. If they have done nothing else, they have set the younger generation an example of how two young men without influence and precious little capital, can achieve the apparently impossible.'

Australia's own Woolworths

In 1933, Coles had moved into every State and were operating 29 stores. By 1933 also, the rival Australian firm of Woolworths was operating 31 branches (including eight in New Zealand), and had opened its first store in Coles-dominated Melbourne.

The first Woolworths—advertised as 'Woolworths Stupendous Bargain Basement'—had opened in Sydney in 1924, in the basement of the Imperial Arcade. The company was founded by five Australians; it had no connection with F. W. Woolworth of the United States and Great Britain, whose name had become synonymous with the cash-and-carry, open-display method of selling that the Australian company adopted along with the celebrated name.

Woolworths and Coles proliferated at such a rate that in 1933 there was an attempt to control the growth of chain stores. Retail traders held several meetings in Melbourne to protest against the spread of chain stores in Victoria. At one, a speaker said that chain stores had been abolished in Denmark, and drastic action was being taken against them in the United States and Germany. Another meeting was told that 142 hardware stores had closed in Melbourne during 1931, and 162 mixed stores in country towns, because of chain store competition. It was suggested that chain stores be subjected to a special tax. Some big department stores of today have grown from businesses established more than 100 years ago. In Sydney, David Jones was founded in 1838 and Farmers (later Myers and then Grace Brothers) in 1840, and Buckley and Nunn began in Melbourne in 1851.

Early in the century, when a woman visited one of these exclusive emporiums, a uniformed flunkey opened the door and a shopwalker in striped trousers and frock coat bowed her graciously to a chair. Her purchases were of course delivered.

Most of the department stores also did a thriving business by mail order. Some posted out catalogues which were almost magazines, containing recipes, anecdotes, snippets of news and a children's corner.

Grace Brothers' New Year catalogue for 1918, for example, ran to 45 pages of advertisements for goods ranging from bathing costumes (men's all-wool two-piece, 9s 11d [$14.65]) to gas stoves (the 'Kookaburra', £6 11s [$194]; crating 7s 6d [$11.10]). Between the wars, Farmer's sent out 75,000 catalogues five times a year; these went all over Australia and throughout the Pacific Islands.

Paying by instalments

During the Depression, retail stores introduced the lay-by system, which enabled customers to reserve expensive items until they were paid for by weekly instalments.

However, many shoppers still preferred the established system of hire-purchase or time-payment, by which the purchaser gets immediate use of the goods in return for regular interest-bearing payments. If the purchaser defaults, the company which has advanced the money can repossess the goods.

In a cautionary article headed 'Time Payment and Its Pound of Flesh', *The Lone Hand* in 1909 said that time-payment was general throughout Australia, and it listed as articles bought in this way 'furniture, home utensils, pianos, phonographs, sewing-machines, bicycles, picture books, jewellery and a thousand things more.'

'Women are . . . especially prone to enter into hire-purchase agreements,' said *The Lone Hand*. 'The itinerant vendor of jewellery comes to the door with an alluring show of alleged gold and gems . . . a watch, a ring, a bangle, or a bracelet is dangled before her eyes, and the fluent and loquacious traveller adds his persuasions to the natural attraction of the gew-gaw. The price is only £4 [$185], or whatever the sum may be; this may be paid at the rate of 2s 6d [$5.80] a week, a sum the good lady will "never feel"; and in a few months the ornament will be wholly paid for . . . The lady signs an agreement, by which she becomes merely the hirer of the gew-gaw until thirty-two half-crowns have been paid.' And in doing so, she was charged from 50 to 150 per cent more than the cash price. But hire-purchase had come to stay.

Woolworths Stupendous Bargain Basement in 1924—the year it opened in the basement of the Imperial Arcade in Sydney. On opening day staff had to turn their lunchroom into a casualty station to cope with people injured in the excited rush to buy such remarkable bargains

Australia changed from pounds, shillings and pence to dollars and cents on 14 February 1966, the day known as C-Day (C for Changeover). The transition was quite smooth, probably because of an intensive and carefully planned programme of education on decimal currency. At one stage there were xenophobic fears of loss of national identity and alternatives to 'dollar' were suggested. Among the suggestions were 'koala', 'Menzies' and 'royal', the last being put forward by Sir Robert Menzies himself. During the transaction period goods were priced in both currencies—as on these supermarket signs, which have been converted with notable accuracy

Country life

Tales of rural hardships

In the early years of the 20th century, farming life was still a dawn-to-dusk round of work, interrupted by large meals cooked by the farmer's wife or the station cook. Only on Sundays would there be a break, perhaps for church-going, or for gatherings of relatives and friends. Even in the remote huts of the boundary-riders, the men reckoned out which day was Sunday, and 'spelled out'.

By 1900 the days of the isolated shepherds, the mad 'hatters', were over. Fences stretched across the land, and on the big sheep runs the shepherds were replaced by boundary-riders, who often lived at the homestead or came back to it once a week, or worked with a mate. On the outback runs, however, the boundary-rider's life could still be lonely. The historian C. E. W. Bean, who travelled around outback New South Wales in 1909 to write a series of articles (later collected into a book) for *The Sydney Morning Herald,* visited a lone boundary-rider at his tiny log hut, and wrote that to look into its interior was like prying into the privacy of a man's mind.

'Some solitary man had lived there for months together,' Bean wrote, ' . . . and the hut was simply the shell of him. There were solid log walls, the fireplace an old ship's tank, two beds of flat tin, a sack of flour, several bottles of sauce, and a tin of "cocky's joy" . . . golden syrup in 2 lb. [908 g] tins, then costing

A welcome visitor to lonely homesteads was the itinerant hawker. He filled his van in the city and took it from station to station, selling clothing, dress materials and books as well as small practical items. Some hawkers told fortunes too; others peddled liquor illegally

7d [$1.35], four times as cheap as jam and six times as portable'.

Mutton, damper and 'cocky's joy'

The golden syrup brought sweetness into a diet consisting mainly of damper, mutton and tea. The menu was likely to be monotonous at the smaller homesteads too, although it might be supplemented by eggs and milk and even fresh vegetables from a precious garden tended by the farmer's wife.

On many of the big inland runs there was a station store, which often carried a much larger stock than the store in the nearest town. The station store at *Dunlop,* a large sheep-run on the Darling River in New South Wales, in 1909 listed among its stock such exotic foodstuffs as bottled olives and ginger, vermicelli and coconuts. These were in addition to the usual station supplies—which included three tonnes of sugar, three tonnes of flour and 508 kg of salt, guns and cartridges, every-

A wealthy squatter built this mansion as his homestead at the turn of the century

A caption written on the mount of this 1902 photograph of a bark hut tells this dismal story: 'Young squatter with young wife, 1500 sheep, orchard and run seven miles (18 km²) square. Five children and 25,000 sheep at 35 years of age. Then drought, foreclosure, death of wife and children, and at 71 years of age pension and hut.'

The country children below rode their pony to school in town each day, but many other children lived far from school. Some of the larger stations had their own school, or a resident governess. Wealthy graziers sent their children, especially boys, to boarding schools run on English lines

Harvesting grain used to be a lengthy process. First a reaper and binder cut the stalks and tied them into sheaves. These were stood in stooks for a few days, then pitchforked on to drays and carted to the threshing machine, which separated and bagged the grain. It was driven by a wood-burning traction engine—the drive-belt between the two machines has not yet been fitted when this 1905 photograph was taken

thing for the horse, every type of tool and '40 team collars'.

Dunlop was a property of 405,000 hectares which in 1894 had shorn 276,000 sheep; ten years later, drought had reduced its carrying capacity to 100,000. But it was still a big run, and its centre was almost a village. Besides the store, there were the main house where the manager and his wife lived with their children and a couple of jackaroos; the overseer's cottage and a hut for the station hands; a carpenter's shop and wagon factory, a smithy, an engine-room, a sawmill and a saddler's workshop, and a school.

The bushman's day

Whether he worked for a 'squatter' on a large run, or was himself a 'free selector' on a small farm of his own, the bushman had to be versatile. In the course of a day's work he might milk a cow, yard and dip some sheep, do some blacksmithing—repairing horse or bullock wagons, making iron hinges for gates—and a bit of saddlery work. On Sundays, he might turn soap-boxes into furniture, golden syrup tins into quart pots, kerosene tins into anything that seemed useful.

'According to his work, the bushman carried sheathed dagging shears to attend to fly-blown sheep, an axe in a short saddle-scabbard or wire strainers—or the three,' says Harry Hodge in *The Hill End Story*. 'He never went far without his multi-bladed pocket-knife for cutting up plug tobacco, shaping wood, marking (castrating) lambs and a dozen other uses . . . Strapped to the pommel of the saddle he carried a nosebag of feed for his horse. It was usually a sugarbag folded partly back with a leather or rope loop to hold it on the horse's head.'

Many Australian bushmen were itinerant workers—drovers, shearers or harvest hands. But by 1912 farmers—in the Wimmera district of Victoria, for example—were complaining that it was difficult to get seasonal workers in time of harvest, for the old nomadic bush workers were beginning to disappear. It was hard to tempt farm workers into the more isolated districts for a wage of 30–40s [$60.25-$80.35] a week, although food and board was also provided.

The harshness of life on a small selection is powerfully evoked by this photograph of pioneers and their home early in the century. Their clothes suggest they were prosperous enough, but the skeleton trees all round them tell a story of back-breaking toil to clear the land

Up to the 1920s, Australian farmers were still dependent on the horse. These teams are pulling (from left to right) a seed drill, a roller, a spike-tooth drag harrow, another roller and a fertiliser box. Tractors began to take over in the 1920s, and nowadays the draughthorse is a rarity

277

Health and education

Enlightened attitudes swept away the miseries of the past

One of every 13 children born in Australia in 1901 died before it could reach its first birthday. Parents then had cause to fear for their children's lives when they became ill—diseases such as diphtheria, typhoid and whooping cough were all killers. Adults feared for their own lives when major epidemics struck. The influenza epidemic of 1918-19 killed more than 10,000 Australians—in Sydney alone 37 per cent of the population were infected. These diseases were defeated this century—many doctors today have never encountered a case of diphtheria—but they have been replaced by new killers. Heart disease killed fewer than one person per thousand in 1910, but in 1983, heart-related diseases accounted for nearly four deaths per thousand persons or almost half of all deaths. Despite these new killers, however, Australians can hope to live longer, and there are even signs that deaths from heart disease are falling in number. Life expectancy for Australian men has risen from 55 years in 1907, to over 71 years in 1982; and women may expect to live on till 78 years.

Among people ignorant of the causes of disease, quackery flourished. Unscrupulous men adopted bogus titles to peddle a range of cure-alls more likely to hasten the patient's death than to cure any disease. The horrifying details of the ways in which gullible people could be exploited were revealed in 1907 when Octavius Beale released the results of his one-man Royal Commission into quackery.

Dentistry was also a favourite activity of quacks. No qualifications were necessary to pull or fill teeth, and for many years after the turn of the century all that a would-be dentist needed were some forceps and a lot of self-confidence. At 1s [$2.52] an extraction, it was a profitable business when you consider that the average weekly earnings of a worker were about 30s [$75.64] at the turn of the century.

Education in the new Commonwealth consisted mainly of teaching children to recite stereotyped information, rather than to understand it. Those unfortunate enough to fall behind were thrashed. Some attempts were made to introduce enlightened methods—in 1912, for example, the New South Wales Education Department sent a primary schoolteacher to study a new informal method of teaching developed by Maria Montessori in Rome. But for the most part the rigid, unyielding discipline of the Victorian education system was not relaxed until late this century.

Milk at morning break for children at Blackfriars Infants School, Sydney, in 1923

Winning the war against disease

Conquering the old killers—and discovering the new

On 2 January 1901, a Sydney doctor, A. Jarvie Hood, M.B., Mast. Surg. (Edin.), wrote an article for the *Daily Telegraph* which complacently summed up the 'enormous strides in the science of medicine in the last hundred years'. There had been great developments in practical pathology and bacteriology, he wrote: 'The means of clinical investigation have also been added to and now we have clinical thermometers, electricity, blood tests, Röntgen Rays, etc., to assist in arriving at a correct diagnosis ...' Preventive medicine had also made great strides; not only in hygiene and public health departments, but also in the inoculation against certain 'dire diseases'—typhoid fever, smallpox and plague, for example.

Other great innovations had taken place: 'The serum treatment, the use of organic substances made from the glands of the lower animals, the hypodermic application of certain strong drugs such as morphia and strychnine, the use of electricity, and the application of X-rays in certain forms of skin diseases. Tropical medicine, so long neglected, has now a special school ... and one result of its investigations show what part the mosquito plays in the incidence and causation of malarial fever.'

What they did not know

But despite Dr Hood's reassuring summing up, medicine at the turn of the century was by today's standards primitive. None of Dr Hood's contemporaries knew of vitamins or hormones. They did not know that rickets was a diet-deficiency disease, or that raw liver was specific for pernicious anaemia. They had never heard of intravenous anaesthesia; the anaesthetist of 1901 dropped ether or chloroform on a bit of gauze held over the patient's face. The anaesthetist of today operates a complex and delicate apparatus, controlling several anaesthetics and administering oxygen or carbon dioxide if necessary.

In 1901 many such epochal discoveries still lay in the future. Some of the most important of them were to be salvarsan, the first of the specific drugs, which selectively attacks the micro-organism causing syphilis; penicillin, which saved thousands of servicemen's lives during World War II; sulphonamide, the first of the modern 'miracle drugs'; streptomycin, the forerunner of a big family of antibiotics; and the Salk and Sabin vaccines which have eliminated the scourge of poliomyelitis.

The scourge of TB

Another important discovery was BCG, the vaccine which conquered tuberculosis. In 1901, when the population of Australia was less than four million, there were 3557 deaths from tuberculosis—representing 93.8 per 100,000 of population. TB was then Aus-

Baby clinics such as this helped to reduce the infant mortality rate. In 1901 babies under one year of age died at the rate of 103.6 to every 1000 born. By 1916, when this clinic was photographed, the rate was down to 70.33 per 1000; but even that meant 5186 deaths in the year

tralia's biggest killer. Figures for later years show how this one-time scourge has been conquered. In 1931, deaths were 49 per 100,000; in 1950, 21 per 100,000; in 1970, 2.0 per 100,000; and in 1983, 0.49 per 100,000.

The mortality figures for typhoid and diphtheria tell a similar story. In 1905, when Australia's population was just over four million, there were 630 recorded deaths from typhoid, and 314 from diphtheria. In 1983, there were no deaths from typhoid or diphtheria recorded among a population of 15.4 million. Diphtheria has become so rare that many Australian doctors have never encountered a case of the disease.

Before the discovery of insulin in 1922, diabetes was nearly always fatal. Insulin treatment was introduced to Australia the following year. In March 1923, a diabetic returned soldier, J. F. Loveday, was admitted to the Melbourne Hospital; to all appear-

ances he was a haggard and tottering old man of 60, though he was only 43. He was treated with insulin and by December was cured.

In 1941, the Sydney ophthalmic surgeon, Norman Gregg, discovered that rubella (German measles) contracted by a woman during pregnancy can cause many defects, including blindness and deafness, in new-born babies. This observation led to the use of an effective anti-rubella serum, and, more recently, of a prophylactic vaccine.

The debit side of progress

But the medical balance sheet has a debit side. While there has been a dramatic decline in the incidence of communicable diseases, noncommunicable diseases, such as heart disease and lung cancer, have increased alarmingly. Australia today has one of the highest death rates in the world from heart disease, which has become the main cause of death.

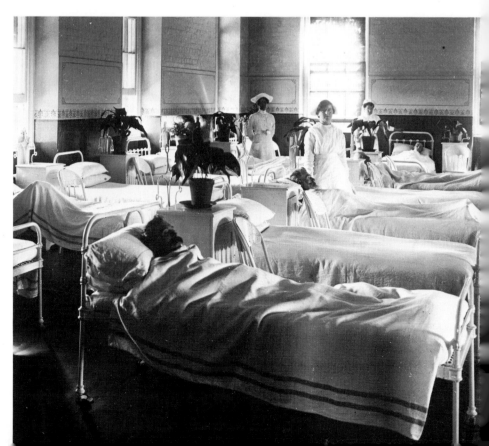

Liverpool Hospital, near Sydney, in 1918, had an air of austere elegance with its potted palms and polished linoleum gleaming in the light from many windows. But in those days hospital was not a place that one entered with a light heart. Sufferers from tuberculosis and cancer, in particular, had little or no hope of a cure. Tuberculosis was second to old age as the main cause of death

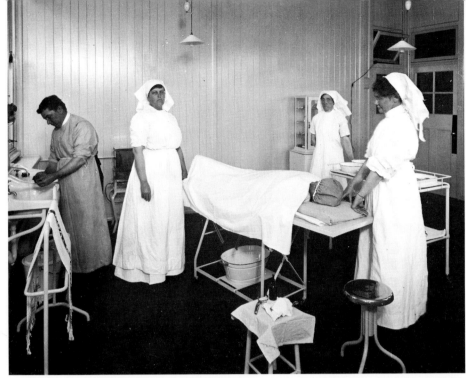

A doctor scrubs up before an operation at a Sydney hospital in 1918. He has hot water, provided by an electric heater, and ordinary electric lights to work by. On the table in the foreground are a chloroform bottle and mask, and an instrument for holding the patient's mouth open

The longevity of the Australian male decreased slightly in the late 1960s, reversing for the first time the improvement which had been continuous since the birth of the Commonwealth; and in May 1973, Professor John Bloomfield, head of the Physical Education Department of the University of Western Australia, reported to the Federal Government that Australians were dangerously unfit by world standards. He attributed this to the physical inactivity of people living in a predominantly urban and motorised society.

The tranquillised society

Another result of the concentration of people in big cities has been a great increase in the consumption of tranquilliser drugs. In the year ended 30 June 1984, Australian doctors wrote National Health prescriptions for: 4,059,000 tranquillisers; 3,598,000 anti-depressants; and 2,785,000 sedatives and

hypnotics; a total of 10,422,000 prescriptions. The professor of pharmacology at Melbourne University, Professor M. J. Rand, said that tranquiliser consumption showed the degree of pressure caused by modern life.

'The fact is people, a lot of people, are living miserable bloody lives,' he said. 'They are in the depths of misery and the drugs are a help. There is always a risk factor but it is insignificant compared with the help they give.'

Australians, too, consume an enormous quantity of often worthless vitamin preparations and of potentially dangerous headache powders and tablets. They are still the victims of unscrupulous patent medicine manufacturers. These are now prevented by law from claiming that their products 'cure'; they have been forced to substitute the more cautious word 'relieve'. But aided by the persuasiveness of television advertising, they still sell their products on an enormous scale.

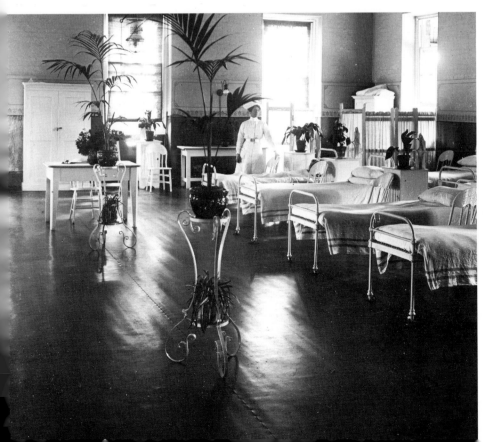

Patterns of life and death

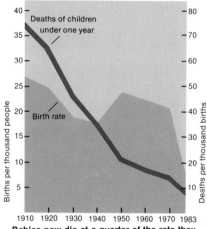

The death rate has declined during the 20th century. So have deaths from pneumonia and tuberculosis, but cancer and heart disease deaths have risen. Heart disease is responsible for half of all deaths

Babies now die at a quarter of the rate they did early in the century. The birth rate is lower too, but it has climbed back after plummeting during the Depression

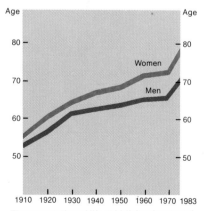

The expectation of life at birth has increased dramatically during this century, through improvements in medicine, hygiene and diet

Living in fear of disease

Drastic government action halts the spread of 'black death'

One hot Friday morning in January 1900, 33-year-old Arthur Payne was driving his horse-drawn truck from Darling Harbour wharves in Sydney to a city warehouse when he was overcome by an attack of nausea and giddiness. He reached the warehouse, but was forced to lie down for a while before he could unload the truck and return to the docks. Payne worked on through the afternoon, although he still felt ill, and at about four o'clock he was alarmed to find that he had developed a lump in his groin. At six o'clock in the evening he stopped work and walked the few blocks to his house in the Rocks district and went straight to bed. The next morning a doctor summoned by Payne's wife diagnosed bubonic plague.

Private alarm

The appearance of the disease alarmed the health authorities but the public did not learn of the outbreak until five days later, when a constable was stationed outside the Paynes' house. News of the unusual event spread rapidly and a large crowd gathered to see a horse-drawn ambulance arrive to take Payne to North Head quarantine station.

Arthur Payne was the first case in a serious outbreak of plague which later spread to all states except Tasmania. Between January and August 1900, 303 cases were reported and 103 people died.

Billy Hughes, then member for West Sydney in the New South Wales Legislative Assembly, claimed that the plague came to Sydney from Mauritius in a sailing ship which berthed in Darling Harbour near the foot of Erskine Street, in the heart of his constituency. But as steamers regularly arrived at Sydney from Hong Kong, Bombay and Noumea, in all of which plague was endemic, it was not possible to say where the epidemic had actually originated.

On March 24 the area around Darling Harbour wharves was quarantined. The people who lived there were given the option of moving to North Head quarantine station

for observation, or of staying in the quarantined area until there was no further risk of infection. Tradesmen were allowed to remove account books, but all other goods had to be left behind. Every *bona fide* resident who was quarantined was paid 6s [$15.15] a day during the period of enforced detention. In the more affluent parts of Sydney, thousands fled to the health-giving Blue Mountains, or even to the distant far west.

On March 28 gangs of men moved into the quarantined area and started cleaning it out. Wooden outhouses were pulled down, floors were torn up and bedding and furniture were taken from the houses and burned to kill the vermin that infested it. Refuse that could not be burnt was removed—more than 1000 tonnes of rubbish were carted away from one block alone. All that remained was thoroughly drenched in disinfectant and whitewash. Many of the people whose homes were thus purified complained that they were no longer homes fit to live in.

'My constituents suffered fearful indignities, their privacy was invaded; their pianos and sewing machines ruined with whitewash and strong disinfectant,' wrote Billy Hughes on his house-to-house tour of the quarantined area. He was appalled at the crowded and unsanitary conditions in which many families had to live. 'The slums of London before the Great Fire could not have been any worse,' he wrote.

Wholesale demolition

The City Council took the opportunity to demolish as much slum housing as possible. If a building was thought to be sub-standard then it could be closed, and if the necessary repairs were not done within a certain period, the building would be pulled down. This was hard on the residents, as most of them were poor and unable to carry out repairs. Many people could not afford to replace boundary fences and lavatories that had been demolished. Houses were often demolished without notice to the occupiers.

The wharves were cleaned out in the same way. All the dangerous buildings were pulled down and tons of refuse were removed. Dead sheep, pigs and fowls were found in the mud below the wharves, and nests of up to 30 rats, some killed by the plague, were uncovered.

The role of the black rat in spreading the disease was still disputed at that time. An inter-colonial Plague Conference rejected the theory of a Frenchman, P. L. G. Simond, that the infection was carried only by fleas to which the black rat is host; but the New South Wales Medical Officer, in charge of Sydney's anti-plague measures, was able to establish this as an irrefutable fact.

The last case in the 1900 epidemic was reported on August 9, by which time the disease had spread to all states except Tasmania. Victoria had one fatal case, and Queensland 16. There were fresh outbreaks until 1907, and of the 1121 people that were infected, very nearly half died.

'Flu strikes Australia

But plague was not the only epidemic disease to be seen in Australia in the early part of this century. The world-wide influenza epidemic of 1918-19 killed more than 10,000 Australians. In Sydney alone 390,000 or 37 per cent of the population were infected.

The virus, popularly known as 'Spanish 'flu' may have been brought to Australia by returning servicemen. The first outbreak was in Melbourne late in January 1919, and reached its peak in the second week in February. A second wave, of even greater virulence, began in the last week of March, and reached its peak a month later.

When, on 28 January 1919, *The Sydney Morning Herald* announced that 'Pneumonic influenza has appeared in Sydney' the health authorities were at least prepared. Over 30,000 people had already been inoculated, all theatres, schools and places of public entertainment were closed, and many of them turned into emergency hospitals.

Day after day, men and women of all

Many of those forced out of work by the plague turned to rat-catching to earn a living. The government paid a bounty of 2d [40c] a head for rats, and this was later increased to 6d [$1.20]. The amateur rat-catchers were instructed to dip the dead rats into boiling water to kill the fleas before taking them for burning

During the plague, old outhouses containing lavatories and 'bathrooms' were torn down. Often residents could not afford to replace them

The SOS cars of the Influenza Administration Committee were a common sight in Sydney during the epidemic. The committee was made up largely of voluntary helpers and they visited the poorer areas of Sydney to keep in touch with infected people, and provide food, clothing and sometimes money.

Houses where flu victims had lived were quarantined for four days, during which time none of the occupants was allowed to leave

classes queued up at Melbourne Town Hall to be inoculated. Others managed to combine immunisation with entertainment. 'Inoculation parties are all the rage,' reported Melbourne *Punch* early in February. 'The idea is that one should collect a nice gathering of young men, preferably with a sprinkling of those still in khaki, and about an equal number of girls with good arms. When the doctor comes along with his little bag and gets to work, the operation, which proves trying to some of us, becomes an excellent joke.'

It was compulsory to wear gauze masks in public, and these appeared in great variety, from a plain contrivance that looked like a small wire meat-cover, favoured by most men and many women, to elaborately coloured models, worn by more fashion-conscious women. 'Black ninon [silk voile] yasmaks over rose-coloured masks are popular about William and George Streets,' it was reported, not uncritically, in *The Bulletin*.

Schools, churches, racecourses, billiard saloons, theatres, picture-shows and libraries were closed throughout New South Wales, and meetings of all kinds were prohibited. Hospitals were erected on racecourses and in parks. Later, when the regulations were relaxed, hotels were allowed to open, but customers were forbidden to remain in them longer than five minutes.

Advertisers exploited the epidemic en-

thusiastically, and many patent medicine manufacturers enjoyed a record year in 1919. Advertisements in newspapers and periodicals advised citizens: 'Keep clean inside and out and minimise the risk of influenza—take Dr Morse's Indian Root Pills freely,' and 'In these serious epidemics, get Clement's Tonic for your blood.'

By the end of 1919 the epidemic had run its course. 'The striking feature of the epidemic in 1919 was the very heavy death rate among persons at the most vigorous period of life,' said the *Victorian Year Book* for 1919-20. Approximately 72 per cent of the 3561 people afflicted who died in Victoria were between 20 and 50 years old.

Policemen guard the barricades around the quarantined area near Darling Harbour. Thousands of tonnes of refuse were removed from this area

Influenza quarantine camps, similar to this one at Jubilee Oval in Adelaide, were set up in most Australian cities. Camps were also established along the New South Wales-Victoria border, and interstate visitors were forced to spend seven days waiting for any symptoms of the disease to appear

The home of quackery

When mountebanks and cure-alls flourished

'Australia, like America, is the home of quackery,' wrote Queensland's first Commissioner of Public Health, Dr Burnett Ham, in a memorandum to the Home Secretary in October 1906. 'A large army of imposters, so-called "Professors", "Herrs", "Nurses", "Herbalists" and "Specialists", who, with little if any professional training . . . are allowed at the present time to exist, and find a flourishing means of livelihood among our community,' he said. 'Such imposters, and in many cases palpable humbugs, pursue their nefarious calling under no legal restraint or control.'

Dr Ham had been striving since 1900—he was appointed when the menace of plague spurred Queensland to action—to improve the environment in which the quacks flourished. His health inspectors reported on the appallingly primitive sanitation over widespread areas of the state. Many houses had no privies, and polluted water supplies were common. Few towns had protected drinking water, garbage removal systems or sanitary services. Rats and other vermin were to be found everywhere.

Dr Ham pointed out that meat was sold locally without supervision and was often unfit for human consumption, whereas all export meat was strictly supervised. Fruits, vegetables and other foodstuffs were exposed on footpaths, open to contamination by dust and dirt, horses and stray dogs.

Adulteration of food and drink was gross. Samples of Schnapps from a Brisbane hotel were found to contain 18 grams of sulphuric acid to every 4.5 litres. At the same hotel were found 680 litres of rum diluted with 15 per cent of water. The flavour of the watered rum had been strengthened, however, by the addition of tobacco.

Queensland was then 'medically speaking, an outpost State', with no medical school, and inadequate medical services, according to Sir Raphael Cilento, the state's first Director-General of Health and Medical Services. He quotes the endemic and epidemic disease statistics for 1902-3, a typical year, to show how prevalent were many diseases that today have disappeared or are very rare: plague, 108 cases; diphtheria, 239; erysipelas, 72; scarlet fever, 219; and typhoid 2362. In the second half-year typhoid affected 2.7 per cent of the whole population. Deaths from tuberculosis totalled 413, and about the same time a 'new and rare disease' called infantile paralysis or poliomyelitis made its appearance with 108 reported cases.

Eye-testing quacks

'The surest money-getting occupation by which to fleece the public in the shortest possible time is that of quack optician,' said *The Lone Hand* magazine in March 1908. 'All that is necessary is a face of brass, a glib tongue, a total contempt for the truth, and absolute indifference as to whether the poor unfortunate you supply with glasses has his or her eyes positively and hopelessly ruined by your treatment.'

Quack opticians operated in cities and in the outback. The city quack usually had a shop with a big pair of gilded wooden spectacles hanging outside and a notice in the window such as: 'HEADACHES are frequently due to eye-strain. CONSULT US, IT COSTS NOTHING.'

Or: 'IF YOUR CHILD SQUINTS don't imagine he will grow out of it, SPECTACLES WILL CURE SQUINT if used constantly.'

The quack's equipment consisted of a few gross of common spectacles costing about 3½d [65c] a pair—he charged 5s to 10s [$11.60 to $23.25] a pair—a few sight-testing cards such as legitimate oculists use, and perhaps some sulphate of zinc solution.

Headache powder habit

'What the "drink habit" is among men in Australia, the "headache powder" is among women' said, *The Lone Hand* in 1907. 'Just as the unwell city man, when he got a touch of "tired feeling" or is a little worried by business cares, sallies out for a "nip", women, especially the "fashionable woman" . . . takes from her satchel a headache powder when she feels a bit "off".

'The headache may be due to the fact that she has had no breakfast, a hurried lunch of two buns and a chocolate cake, and four lots of afternoon tea; or it may arise from the fact that her waist is made unnaturally waspy, so that she may appear well in the eyes of desirable acquaintances, it may be tight boots or a cold in the head, or defective eyesight, or a spotted veil, or the fact that another woman has a new dress. The remedy is always the same—a "headache powder" from her favourite chemist.'

Popular powders analysed

The Lone Hand had eight popular headache powders analysed. All contained acetanilide, mixed with caffeine and phenacetin, or with caffeine and carbonate of soda. (Acetanilide is a deadly drug, toxic when taken in repeated doses.) It pointed out that the 'promiscuous

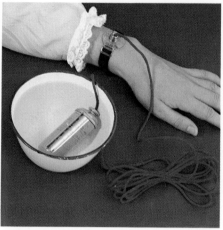

An extravagant claim from 1919

Dr Hercules Sanche's Oxydonor, one of the great quack devices, was claimed to cure all forms of disease. The metal tube, containing carbon, was placed in water and the disc was strapped to the wrist or ankle. Then, claimed Dr Sanche, the body absorbed blood-purifying oxygen

consumption' of these powders affected the heart and the alimentary canal, as well as stopping women from finding out what caused their headaches. 'Will the pharmaceutical societies co-operate in stopping a dangerous trade?' it asked. The pharmaceutical societies did not respond.

In 1921, Aspros (a proprietary name for aspirin) were advertised under the slogan '20 ASPROS A DAY KEEP A MAN'S PAIN AWAY', and were strongly recommended for the relief of 'Headaches, Neuralgia, Malaria and Sciatica'.

Headache powders and tablets are still consumed in enormous quantities by Australians. They no longer contain acetanilide,

Strong men made from weaklings by the power of electricity

Quacks enthusiastically exploited electricity as a cure-all in the 1900s. Dr Kelly of Phillip Street, Sydney, sold an electric girdle, guaranteed to cure any case of 'nervous debility', for £1 1s [$52.95] At £10 10s [$529.50], Dr McLaughlin's Electric Belt—whose benefits are dramatically illustrated at left—performed a similar service for more affluent citizens. The Dr McLaughlin Co. claimed that the belt made strong men from weaklings and promised that it would cure 'varicocele, atrophy of the organs, bladder or kidney disease, blood poison or lumbago . . . Men who *were* weak and puny now declare their strength is enormous; that their functional organs work perfectly . . .'

In 1903 the American Electrical Novelty and Manufacturing Co., of Sydney, introduced the Ever-ready electrical medical coil, powered by a dry-cell battery. It was described as specially suited for every form of electrical massage.

At the same time hospitals were being equipped with electrical devices, many of them worthless. 'The medical coil and battery has long been in constant use, and more recently Roentgen rays (X-rays), electric light baths, and medical exploring lamps are being largely employed,' said *Australasian Hardware and Machinery* in 1901. 'The Melbourne Hospitals are adding a quantity of electrical apparatus to their equipment . . . a cedar table 3 ft x 2 ft [91 cm x 61 cm] is to be fitted with an induction coil, a regulating rheostat of 10,000 ohms resistance and . . . electrodes of pewter, for applying the current to various parts of the body.'

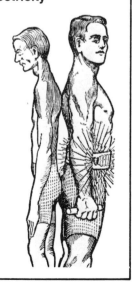

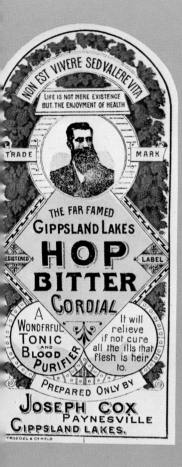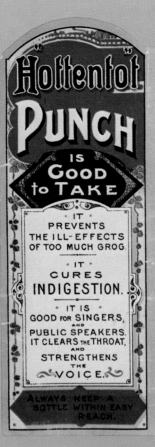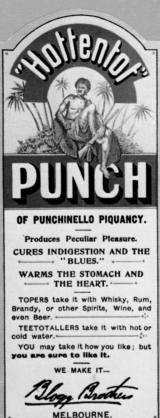

The labels of patent preparations in the 1900s were often as flamboyant in design as in their claims to curative properties

but the principal ingredient, aspirin (acetyl salicylic acid), can cause serious stomach trouble if it is taken regularly, and another common ingredient, phenacetin, can lead to kidney damage.

Mail-order medicine

From his elegant headquarters in Collins Street, Melbourne, Dr L. L. Smith advertised consultations by letter for £1 [$50.45], or at home, £1 1s [$52.95], 'including medicine'. Dr Smith, who was one of the best known citizens of Melbourne, claimed to spend more than £3000 [$151,278] a year on advertising and to have patients in such distant places as Japan, China and India. His income was said to be about £40,000 [$2,017,000] a year.

He specialised in the treatment of 'acquired diseases', a genteel term for venereal diseases. A typical advertisement, headed 'To Persons About to Marry', read in part: 'No one within either visiting or writing distance should marry without communicating with DR L. L. SMITH, who has made the Incapabilities and Diseases of Married Life his especial study... If they do not desire to do so personally, they can avail themselves of his admirable and now perfect system of Consultations by Letter. By this means they have but to retire to their room, and in privacy pen a letter or ask any question, and enclose a fee of £1, and by return posts, with equal secrecy, they can have their queries answered.'

Or you could consult many other Melbourne mail-order 'specialists', such as Mr T. W. Bull, who modestly described himself as a medical clairvoyant, or Dr Langston's Institute, 129 Collins Street, which offered to cure effectively by post drunkenness, diseases of men, and rupture.

Social disabilities

Blushing and red noses seem to have been common social disabilities in the early 1900s, judging by advertisements. Here are extracts from two typical advertisements:

'RED NOSES. There is no doubt that it is one of the worst infirmities to suffer from. It is a disfigurement and attracts unpleasant attention. Hundreds of testimonials attest to the real efficacy of my treatment. Average time of cure, seven days...'

'BLUSHING. Men and women who suffer from involuntary blushing need no longer despair. Their self-consciousness can be so thoroughly removed that they themselves will wonder if they ever really had this embarrassing complaint... Men and women previously nervous and shy, now take their places in Society with pleasure and ease, and get greater profit from their business.'

Other advertisers offered a patent nose machine ('scientific yet simple') to 'improve ugly noses of all kinds', and 'patent rubber ear caps to remedy ugly outstanding ears'.

Or you could have your height increased by as much as 12 centimetres in a few weeks, by a system of 'stretching the cartilage'.

Folk medicine lingers on

Despite the competition of quack doctors and quack medicines, traditional folk medicine was still practised in many Australian households at the start of the century. In 1905, for example, a Sydney magazine called *The Wardrobe* gave its readers this medical advice: 'A raw onion, sliced fine, placed in a muslin bag and applied to the throat, has curative powers.'

Onions were often recommended for curing colds, worms, croup and rheumatism. Other

widely-held beliefs that lingered on well into the 20th century included:

- A bag of camphor hanging on the chest prevented influenza.
- A mustard plaster on the chest cured bronchitis.
- A bib of red flannel worn next to the chest was good for 'weak chests'.
- Rheumatism could be cured by ant-bites, by carrying a potato in the pocket, or by winding copper wire around the wrist.
- Parsley tea was good for kidney trouble.
- A paste of mashed garlic and lard applied to the soles of the feet was good for treating whooping cough.
- Children who suffered from a curious malaise known as growing pains should have their limbs massaged with eucalyptus oil.
- Children who studied too assiduously were likely to 'overtax their brains'. In any case, they should eat plenty of fish because fish was 'brain food'.
- Bad toothache could be relieved by applying neat whisky to the affected part.
- Condy's crystals (permanganate of potash) was a good gargle for sore throats (as well as a good stain for floorboards).

Epsom salts, liquorice powder and castor oil (sold in the thin blue bottles that are now eagerly collected) were administered freely to move the children's bowels, and mothers warned their children against putting coins in their mouths because Chinamen were said to keep coins in their ears.

People still thought that appendicitis was contagious, though the operation to remove the appendix became fashionable after it was performed on King Edward VII in 1902.

285

Exposing the quacks

'Soothing' medicines that hastened the patient's demise

Irish-born Octavius Beale in 1893 established Australia's first piano factory in Sydney. He became wealthy, and interested himself in social problems. In 1905, he served on a New South Wales Royal Commission inquiring into the decline of the birthrate and into child mortality. The commission examined the trade 'in secret nostrums, in proprietary child-foods, and in secret preparations for the prevention of conception, and for the destruction of the human embryo'.

One-man Royal Commission

Beale was so horrified by some of the evidence that two years later he persuaded the Commonwealth Government to let him act, at his own expense, as a one-man Royal Commission inquiring into 'patent or proprietary medicine . . . drugs, alleged curative agents, toilet articles, foods and drinks, the composition of which is not disclosed, and which are alleged to have medicinal or remedial properties'.

The huge two-volume report that Beale presented in August 1907 was a horrifying record of the criminal unscrupulousness of manufacturers and advertisers and of the limitless gullibility of the public.

'The whole present practice of self-dosing, induced by universal and uncontrolled lying and deception, exposes the people, poor and rich, clever and simple, to ill-health, discomfort, misery, suffering and untimely death,' Beale wrote.

Of the hundreds of quack remedies sold to the gullible Australian public in the 1900s, perhaps the most widely advertised were Beecham's Pills, Dr Williams' Pink Pills for Pale People, Hearne's Bronchitis Cure, Bonnington's Irish Moss, Dr Collis Browne's Chlorodyne, and Doans' Backache Pills. Most of these had little or no therapeutic value, and some contained dangerous ingredients.

Beecham's Pills—'worth a guinea a box', according to the manufacturer, who generally sold 56 pills for only 1s 1½d [$2.80]—were advertised to cure 'Constipation, Headache, Dizziness or Swimming in the Head, Wind, Pain and Spasms at the Stomach, Pains in the Back, Restlessness, Insomnia, Indigestion, Want of Appetite, Fullness after Meals, Vomitings, Sickness of the Stomach, Bilious or Liver Complaints, Sick Headaches, Cold Chills, Flushings of Heat, Lowness of Spirits, and all Nervous Affections, Scurvy and Scorbutic Affections, Pimples and Blotches on the Skin, Bad Legs, Ulcers, Wounds, Maladies of Indiscretion, Kidney and Urinary Disorders, and Menstrual Derangements'.

'These renowned pills are composed entirely of Medicinal Herbs,' the manufacturer claimed. The renowned pills in fact consisted entirely of aloes, ginger and soap. The ingredients of 56 pills cost about half a farthing [1c].

Dr Williams' Pink Pills, which were said to cure almost every disease from rheumatism to St Vitus' dance, consisted of sulphate of iron, potassium carbonate, magnesia, liquorice and sugar. A box of 30 pills cost 2s 9d [$6.75]; the ingredients cost one-tenth of a penny [just over one cent].

'Every picture tells a story'

Advertisements for Doan's Backache Pills always included a harrowing drawing of a man or woman agonised by backache, with the slogan 'Every Picture Tells a Story'. The pills, guaranteed to cure rheumatism and diabetes as well as kidney and bladder complaints, were said to be purely vegetable. They consisted mainly of potassium nitrate (saltpetre), hemlock pitch, powdered fenugreek seeds, flour and starch. The estimated cost of 40 pills (price 2s 9d) was ½d [10c].

Most patent medicines were worthless, but others, though freely advertised and sold, were also dangerous. 'Soothing powders' and 'syrups' for infants cutting teeth often contained morphine or opium and could cause death. So could a number of abortifacient pills, sold under such innocent names as Mrs Harle's Pansy Packet, Steel and Pennyroyal Pills, and Towle's Pills ('Invaluable to Ladies—Will quickly Cure all Irregularities').

There was no restriction on the sale of 'catarrh snuffs', which contained cocaine, while morphine and cocaine tablets with apparatus for hypodermic injections, were easily obtainable. Savar's Coca Wine boasted that it contained 32 milligrams of pure cocaine to every 28 millilitres while the same manufacturer's Cubeb Cigarettes ('to be smoked through the nose for hay fever') contained *Cannabis indica* (marijuana) and stramonium, a drug like belladonna. The ingredients of a Melbourne firm's 'cough cartridge' included heroin, described as one of the 'most effective agencies in the world for curing coughs and colds'.

Dr George Rennie, a Sydney physician who edited the *Australian Medical Gazette,* was asked by Beale in January 1907 whether to his knowledge many people, without medical prescriptions, were accustomed to taking sulphonal, acetanilide, cocaine, morphine and other drugs. Dr Rennie replied, 'Yes.' The four medical members of the Queensland Board of Health gave the same reply to the questions.

Drugged sweets

In most Australian 'lolly' shops, as well as in chemists, children could buy octagonal linseed, liquorice and chlorodyne cough lozenges. Chlorodyne was a mixture of morphine, chloroform, *Cannabis indica*, prussic acid, peppermint and treacle. A doctor told Beale that children bought them 'for the sake of prompt intoxication, and having once acquired the taste, will use no other sweet'.

In its first issue, in June 1907, *The Lone Hand* exposed fraudulent claims of a popular patent medicine called Peruna. This contained 25 per cent absolute alcohol, plus flavouring, colouring and water. It cost about 4d [84c] a bottle to make and sold for 5s [$12.35]. It was supposed to cure, among other disorders, consumption, pneumonia, dyspepsia, enteri-

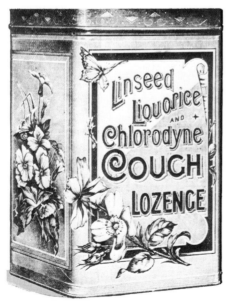

Gaily decorated tins of these addictive lozenges, containing morphine, chloroform and cannabis, stood on sweet shop counters for many years

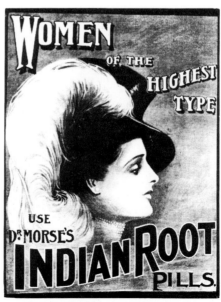

Dr Morse's pills were advertised as a cure for biliousness, constipation, indigestion, sallow complexion, piles and female ailments

Beecham's Pills were still on sale in 1972, with the same ingredients as in 1909, but they were no longer offered as a cure-all

tis, heart disease, measles, colic, mumps, appendicitis and 'women's complaints'.

In subsequent articles under the same heading, 'For The Public Good', *The Lone Hand* denounced other popular nationally advertised nostrums, including Tuberculozyne and Liquozone. Tuberculozyne, which was *guaranteed* to cure consumption, consisted of little more than flavoured and coloured water. It was said to have been invented by an eminent American physician, Dr Derk P. Yonkerman, 'after 20 years of ceaseless research and experiment'. A month's supply cost £2 [$98.75]. *The Bulletin* echoed *The Lone Hand's* denunciation, describing the stuff as 'bottled slush' and commenting that 'only an utterly heartless wretch could delude miserable and often impoverished consumptives into spending pounds on it.'

Liquozone claimed to be a certain cure for eczema, goitre, hay-fever, malaria, rheumatism, throat, kidney and liver troubles 'and half a dozen other diseases too unpleasant to mention.' On analysis, it proved to be merely an impure diluted solution of sulphurous acid, made for about ½d [10c] per four litres and sold for 6s [$14.80] a bottle.

Despite its anti-quack campaigning in early issues, *The Lone Hand* continued to accept advertisements for a variety of frauds. In 1913, the Falliere Flesh-Food Company was guaranteeing in its pages to increase the bust measurement of 'thin, flat-bosomed scraggly women' by some 20 to 25 centimetres in no less than a week.

Sugar for diabetics

Senior's Dugong Oil and Lard were proclaimed 'the most marvellous remedies in the world for consumption, coughs and colds, asthma, general debility and physical weakness'. And the manufacturers of Hollaway's Ointment were repeating their bold claim that 'the Ointment quickly cures Bad Legs, Wounds, Piles, Sores, Eczema, and all skin affections'. It consisted of olive oil, lard, resin, white wax, yellow wax, turpentine and spermaceti, none of which has curative properties.

Octavius Beale continued his crusade, but with little result. He told a convention of advertising men in Sydney in September 1920: 'A cure for diabetes still advertised consists of large pills like marbles, of plain sugar with no medication that analysis can discover. A much puffed hair restorer contains a few grains of boric acid in water, and nothing else.'

The blood-makers

Quackery lingered on in all the states. In 1926, H. T. Gould was advertising in the *Illustrated Tasmanian Mail:* 'Gould's Mutton Bird Oil—for wasting diseases, coughs, symptoms of consumption, 2s 6d, 4s 6d [$3.30, $5.95]. Gould's Nerve Food makes new, rich blood — useful for both men and women. 2s 6d a bottle.'

And the mythical Dr Williams was still in business. His advertisements read: 'To make rich, red blood, you have only to take Dr Williams' Pink Pills: You will soon feel the new blood tingling in your veins; your backache will go, your appetite will improve . . .'

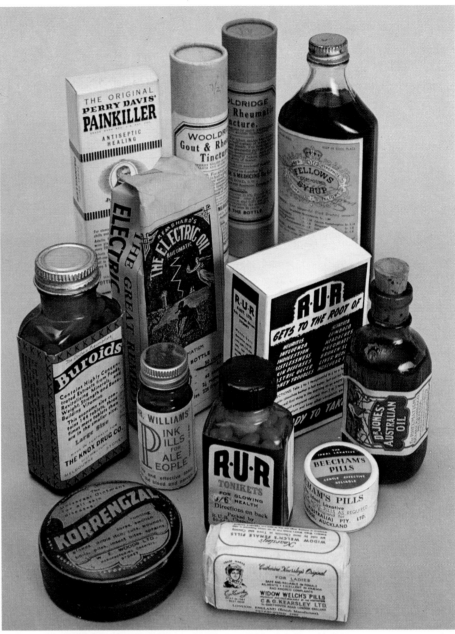

All these old-established patent medicines remained available until the mid-1960s, for people who wished to treat themselves rather than go to a doctor. Patent medicine manufacturers now claim that their preparations relieve symptoms rather than cure diseases

The fictitious Mr Forde and his Bile Beans

Most of the villainous patent medicines peddled in Australia originated in England or the United States. But at least one, Charles Forde's Bile Beans for Biliousness, was an indigenous Australian invention. It had an instructive history. English-born Ernest Gilbert was a young man of 21 working in Sydney in a stationery and printing business when he met a Canadian, Charles Fulford, who had been a shopman in a chemist's shop in Canada. Fulford had also been employed by Dr Williams Medicine Company, manufacturers of Pink Pills for Pale People. Neither had any knowledge of chemistry or medicine, but realising there was money in pills, and in alliteration, they invented their Bile Beans and a fictitious scientist named Charles Forde, to whom they attributed the formula.

In many thousands of booklets distributed from house to house, they explained how the non-existent Forde had made his discovery:

'More important than the whereabouts of hidden gold was the secret of the ancient natives of Australia. For untold ages they have handed down to them the great secret

of how certain native herbs cured the diseases to which they were subject . . . When Captain Cook made his great Australian discoveries the amazing health of the natives was one of the chief things which impressed him. Writing on this very subject, he afterwards said: "I did not observe (among the natives) any appearance of disease or bodily complaint, or eruption of skin . . . and the most severe wounds healed most rapidly." '

The booklet went on to describe how the 'eminent scientist' Charles Forde, after years of scientific research, had discovered the secret Australian herbs that were the main ingredients of his wonder-working Bile Beans, 'the most perfect medicine of modern times'. The beans were in fact compounded of cascara, rhubarb, liquorice, and peppermint, and were made to order in the United States.

In 1905, when Gilbert and Fulford took legal action in Edinburgh against another quack manufacturer who used the words 'bile beans', the court, dismissing the case, said their business was 'founded entirely upon fraud, impudence, and advertisements'.

Outlawing the amateur dentists

'There isn't a tooth in the world that I am afraid of'

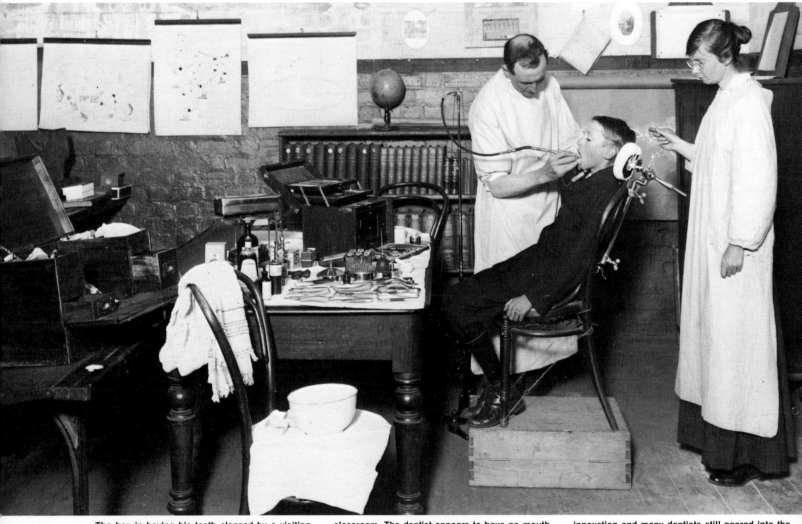

The boy is having his teeth cleaned by a visiting dentist who has made a surgery in the corner of a classroom. The dentist appears to have no mouth mirror. At the time, 1916, the mirror was a recent innovation and many dentists still peered into the patient's mouth as they worked

Australia's first university dental school was established in Sydney in 1901, but for years afterwards dentistry represented a goldmine for quacks. Despite legislation in some states, anyone with sufficient cheek and muscle could set himself up to pull and fill teeth and make false teeth, provided he did not call himself a dentist. Chemists often made a sideline of extractions, and dental apprentices, who were unpaid, invariably made money with their forceps.

But bigger profits came from dentures than from extractions. In Sydney, for example, one Macquarie Street dentist charged 10s 6d [$24.40] for an extraction, but £16 16s [$780] for a full set of false teeth in 1909. This was not regarded as expensive, even though false teeth were generally made by a dental mechanic working full time at a dentist's surgery for a wage of only about £4 [$185.90] a week.

Country patients sometimes received their sets of teeth through the mail. One Sydney dentist recalls being handed a biscuit tin full of impressions of gums and being asked to make teeth to match. But being one of those who were earnestly attempting to upgrade the profession, he declined.

Qualified and unqualified men alike advertised freely in the press:

'No pain! This is my Watchword. No soreness. No swelling. No after-effects. Nothing but pleasure.' 'A gold filling for 10s 6d [$24.40]. Other fillings 5s [$11.60]. None but specialists employed. Extractions 1s [$2.30] each. The only safe and painless method.' 'Teeth one guinea [$48.80] a set. Perfect suction! Teeth two guineas [$97.60] a set. Mastication guaranteed!'

The advertised guinea and two-guinea sets were merely a means of enticing a patient in. He would invariably be told, 'I'm afraid these would not come up to your requirements,' and be persuaded to spend a great deal more.

The dentists who advertised were held in considerable disrepute by the more ethical men, but even among these there were some

Many dental surgeries used to carry eye-catching displays such as this one in Newcastle. A Sydney dentist once displayed a devil with a placard reading 'extractions one shilling' [$2.30]. Evening newspapers also carried many dental advertisements, in which 'painless' was a favourite word

Bygone equipment

A filling from this treadle drill might have meant an hour in the chair. Some who could afford it had the dentist visit them at home. For a home extraction, the patient would lie on a bed or kitchen table, within the reach of a sink which ran an aspirator sucking the blood from his mouth

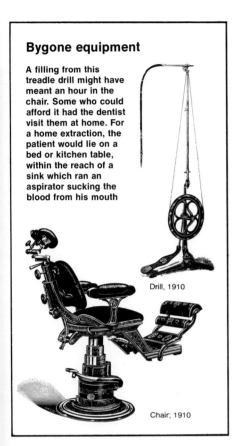

Drill, 1910

Chair, 1910

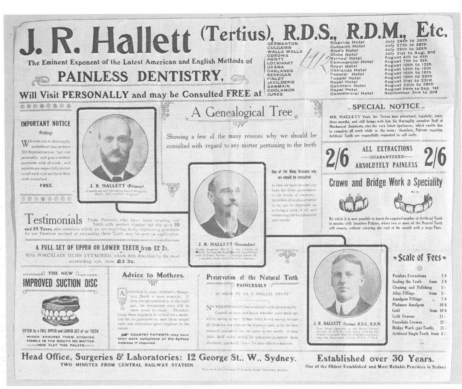

This handbill, probably displayed in a hotel window in advance of Mr Hallett's visit, carried on its reverse 38 enthusiastic testimonials to his painless method of extracting teeth. One patient in Lockhart, NSW, had all 32 badly decayed teeth or roots extracted by Mr Hallett in one sitting. Dentistry remained largely an itinerant profession in Australia until well into the 20th century

distasteful practices. One woman was examined by a dentist in 1919 who put his hand in the pocket of his big black alpaca coat, produced a forceps and removed her tooth—charge 1s. As late as 1920, instruments were kept in a jug of sterilising fluid and merely wiped on a towel. The mouth mirror sometimes went from mouth to mouth without cleaning, let alone sterilisation.

Laughing gas (nitrous oxide) was used as a general anaesthetic. The hilarity it caused in the patient was not shared by the dentist, on whom the strains of working with inefficient pain-killers and unco-operative patients were enormous. Laughing gas also made some of the patients become rigid or involuntarily struggle.

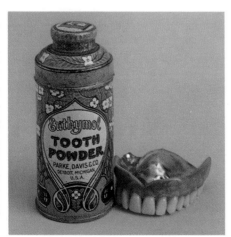

Tooth cleaner (early 1900s) and dentures (1930s). Artist Cedric Flower says his grandmother kept spare dentures in case guests mislaid their own

X-rays—also called radiographs and radiograms—were being used by 1910. The early operators, ignorant of radiation dangers, held the film in the patient's mouth. One dentist lost most of his fingers and eventually died from radiation poisoning.

The photographic chemicals gave many dentists dermatitis, as did the copper sulphate used to treat trench mouth, a gum disorder which was widespread during World War I. Another gum complaint, pyorrhoea, was treated with a teaspoonful of powdered charcoal in the mouth at bedtime. The patient bandaged his head to protect his pillow.

Country people had to rely on a travelling dentist, qualified or not, who toured the district, setting up practice in a hotel room, hall or schoolroom. He might have no white coat, no special chair, no running water. There would be a basin to spit in, a foot-operated drill, many forceps and a supply of ether or chloroform. This was poured on a cloth which was placed over the patient's nose.

After a rough journey of perhaps 30 or 40 kilometres with toothache, it was no wonder the sufferer allowed an extraction. It was preferable in any case to the tooth being filled without full excavation of the cavity—something that was done for the sake of speed.

The introduction of anaesthesia to dentistry in the 1880s, and improvements in the appearance and fit of false teeth, led to four decades of almost reckless tooth-drawing, with and without the benefit of anaesthesia.

In 1901, the Australian representative of a London dental instrument manufacturer advertised in *The Chemist and Druggist of Australasia* that his firm kept in stock 120

patterns of tooth forceps, 'but *Twelve Pairs* as a rule will do the work and are quite sufficient for beginners'.

The advertisement carried a testimonial headed 'How I Paid my rent—a fact'. It read: 'I commenced Business eight years ago last June, and whilst giving my opening order to Mr——— you know him, one of Ayrton & Saunders Travellers, he said "You will want some Tooth Forceps," "Tooth Forceps," I replied—"never pulled a Tooth in my life."

"Well," Mr——— said, "you are not an old man yet and why shouldn't you learn, there is more profit in Teeth Extraction than in selling Patent Medicine, and, when once the Forceps are paid for, all that comes in, is so much for the good."

'I thought the matter well out and as Thursday afternoon is early closing day, I arranged with a friend, a Dentist, in a neighbouring town, to run over for a lesson every week, and he very soon initiated me into the mysteries of Tooth Drawing, and now, there isn't a Tooth in the world that I am afraid of, and . . . have done well indeed, have more than PAID MY RENT.'

In the second decade dentistry veered toward saving rather than extracting teeth, but for some years afterwards there were still dozens of unethical practitioners who would pull out all a victim's teeth when perhaps only three were affected.

Slowly the loopholes were closed. By 1917 the last state (South Australia) had made it illegal for anyone but a qualified dentist to practise, and by 1934 advertising was banned. Dentistry had raised its status, and outlawed the dental bandits.

Flynn of the inland

Providing the only medical care in two-thirds of Australia

In 1912, fewer than 50,000 white people in the Australian inland occupied an area the size of Western Europe. Life was hard, lonely and hazardous. Letters took weeks, or even months, to arrive. Over every remote station hung the fear of accident or sickness.

There were doctors in Darwin, Oodnadatta, Cloncurry, Burketown, and in some Western Australian ports, but it was impossible for them to meet an emergency hundreds of kilometres away. If a boundary rider fell from his horse on the perimeter of a run of 25,000 square kilometres, or a station man-

ager's wife had an acute attack of appendicitis, no medical help was possible.

Ernestine Hill tells a typical story of 'Old Jack Cameron who fell from his horse on Burnside country... and dragged himself for two days in agony to try to reach the railway line in time for the passing of the little weekly train. When it did pass he was no more than 300 metres away. With superhuman effort, on a crippled spine, he raised himself and waved and shouted—somebody waved back and the little train went... on. They thought it was merely a greeting. They found Jack

Cameron in time, his water-bag bone dry, his tucker-bag full of ants—a year in the hospital set him right.'

Such incidents, many with more tragic endings, were common in the outback. But in 1912, the Presbyterian Church of Australia founded the Australian Inland Mission and John Flynn, a 31-year-old minister, was appointed superintendent.

The mission built a number of nursing hostels in the outback—the first in Oodnadatta and the second in Port Hedland—dedicated 'to suffering humanity without preference for

John Flynn (right) and George Towns, a radio expert, leave Adelaide in 1925 to make the experimental broadcasts from the outback which confirmed the feasibility of long-distance radio communication

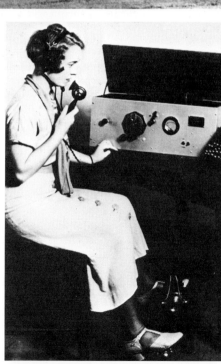

The pedal-operated radio transceiver was conceived by Flynn and developed by Alfred Traeger (left), a young engineer. The morse key was soon replaced by the microphone. Outback homesteads without electricity were now no longer isolated

nationality or creed,' and staffed by trained nurses. But Flynn realised that two great problems had to be overcome—transportation and communication.

In 1917 a young Victorian medical student, Clifford Peel, suggested that aerial ambulances would solve the problem of transport, but the problem of communication remained. It was solved in 1928 when an Adelaide electrical engineer, Alfred Traeger, at Flynn's suggestion designed a pedal-operated radio 'transceiver' with a range of about 480 kilometres. No technical knowledge or skill was required to operate it. Later, battery-operated sets replaced the pedal transmitters, and microphones replaced morse.

Radio station in a church

The first flying doctor base was established at Cloncurry. A transmitter was installed in the vestry of a church, and the service began in May 1928 with a Qantas DH50 plane carrying Dr K. H. Vincent Welch and a pilot. During his first year's operations, Dr Welch flew 32,000 kilometres and attended 255 patients.

In 1931, another flying doctor, Allan Vickers, flew 2092 kilometres from Normanton to Brisbane in a vain attempt to save the life of a hotel-keeper injured by the explosion of a kerosene refrigerator. On the return journey to Cloncurry, Dr Vickers took back a tube of poliomyelitis serum that saved a 12-year-old boy from crippling paralysis.

As well as treating patients personally, flying doctors often prescribe by radio—in Ernestine Hill's words, 'for babies with gastritis, toddlers with measles and whooping cough, children with trachoma or sprained ankles, a lad badly burnt, a woman bitten by a red-backed spider, an old bushman in his billabong camp crippled with sciatica—anything in the seven ages of man'.

An expensive service

The Royal Flying Doctor Service—the prefix was granted in 1955—grew rapidly, with bases in New South Wales, South Australia and Western Australia. Nowadays it is the only form of medical help available to two-thirds of the continent, and the cost of running it is high. In 1984 total expenditure was $14.1 million, of which the Federal and State Governments contributed two-thirds, the remaining one third being raised from private donations from within the Service. Patients contribute something towards the cost of treatment, which is provided without regard to colour, creed, race or ability to pay. Some graziers, however, pay a contribution based on the number of animals they own.

Flynn died in 1951, and was buried near Alice Springs. Two years later a commemorative cairn was erected 27 kilometres north of Tennant Creek. On it are these words:

His vision encompassed the continent.
He established the Australian Inland Mission
And founded the Flying Doctor Service
He brought to lonely places a spiritual ministry
And spread a mantle of safety over them
By medicine, aviation and radio.

In 1927 this hired Qantas De Havilland DH50 mail plane flew the 1802 kilometres from Cloncurry to Mt Isa to pick up a miner with a broken pelvis and returned him to Cloncurry. This was the first flight to demonstrate the practicability of a flying doctor service. Pilot Norman Evans is on the right, with Dr George Simpson—one of Flynn's chief medical advisers—in the centre, and Jack Lisson, a member of the Queensland Ambulance Transport Brigade, is in uniform on the left

Morning in the bush—Flynn strops his razor while his wife attends to the breakfast. Flynn, as superintendent of the Inland Mission, spent his entire working life driving around the outback, visiting homesteads and welfare centres. His aim was to provide both physical healing and spiritual help for the people of the outback; it was achieved through the establishment of the Flying Doctor Service and a team of patrol padres. Flynn was an able administrator as well as a visionary

The time of their lives

Learning by rote to the swish of a cane

For most young Australians of the new Commonwealth, schooling was, in words Thomas Hobbes used in another context, 'nasty, brutish and short'. It was nasty, because school buildings were primitive and overcrowded. It was short, because few children went beyond third class at primary school.

In most states, there were no high schools or junior technical schools. Teachers' salaries were low, facilities for teacher-training limited, and teaching methods mechanical and uninspiring. It was more important to tame children than to teach them. Curiosity and individuality were discouraged, high spirits and disobedience sternly repressed.

The headmaster was a dictator, godlike in his authority and remoteness. Pupils sat at desks and worked out their problems on squeaky slates, which were supposed to be cleaned with a small wet sponge. More often, they were wiped with spit on the hand.

Conditions varied from state to state, but the overall picture was the same; Norman Lindsay remembered his State School in Creswick, Victoria, in the 1890s: 'The fusty odour of crowded classrooms ... the discomfort of hard seats' and the sadistic headmaster who believed that 'the intellectual faculties are stimulated by raising blue welts on the epidermis.'

When Professor A. R. Chisholm attended the Milson's Point (Sydney) Public School in the early 1900s, teachers stalked the classroom in frock coats, always with cane in hand. The punishment for playing the wag

Punishment Book.						
Name of pupil.	Age.	Nature of offence.	Amount of punishment.	Instrument of punishment.	Date of punishment.	By whom inflicted.
Eory Williams	7.10	Disorderly conduct,	3 strokes one hand	Cane	26 April	J.W. Teacher
Bert McMurray	13.10	in Class.	3 hand	do	26 April	" "
Corporal punishment should not be inflicted for unpunctuality.					5/7/10	S.W.
Harold Wood	11½	Deliberate	3 strokes on hand	Cane	23rd June	Jw. Reader
John Wood	9¾	Falsehood	2 " "	"	23rd June	

A teacher who caned a pupil had to record the details in a book for the inspectors. Here an inspector has noted, of an earlier entry, that 'corporal punishment should not be inflicted for unpunctuality'. Small comfort, though, for a victim such as the one Norman Lindsay depicted above

(truancy) was, he recalls, 18 strokes of the cane, 'six on each hand ... and six more on a fleshier part ...'

The writer John Hetherington describes the curriculum at the Sandringham (Victoria) State School, which he attended in 1914: 'Multiplication tables from Once One to Twelve Times Twelve were chanted by the whole class ... I could chant many other things also including the principal imports and exports of the British Isles, the names of the major rivers of Europe in their order of importance, the names of Kings of England from William the Conqueror down to George V. Geography as taught proved the existence of Europe, notably and above all of Great Britain, and, rather less clearly, the existence of America. The existence of Australia was also conceded if somewhat unwillingly, but, for us, Asia, hardly existed at all ...'

Pupils marched to their class-rooms singing *Three Cheers for the Red, White and Blue*, to a piano accompaniment thumped out by a junior teacher. Senior boys had the duty of hoisting the Union Jack on the school flag-pole every morning, and lowering it in the

These children, solemnly posing for the photographer, were pupils of a New South Wales State School in 1909

School used to be an austere place. Even in a winter as mild as that of Sydney, these pupils of the Petersham Continuation School evidently found their bare classroom extremely cold, for several of them are wearing two coats. The boy fourth from left in the front row appears to be cheating

afternoon. Swearing was punished by washing the foul mouth out with soapy water.

Discipline was tougher at Hetherington's next school, All Saints' Grammar, Melbourne. The headmaster, he says, 'flogged not only those boys who wilfully misbehaved but also those of sluggish mind who were slow to learn . . . He would single out any troublesome or slow-learning boys and thrash them on the spot to encourage the others.'

Another writer, Hal Porter, recalling his education at the Bairnsdale (Victoria) State School, says all he had to do was to sit back, hands clasped behind his back, in classrooms smelling of chloride of lime, chalk dust and cedar pencil-shavings, and 'decorously and unquestioningly' accept the teacher's assurance that seven eights were 56, Berlin was on the Spree, Henry VIII had six wives and William Wordsworth was an English poet.

The psychiatrist Reg Ellery was a pupil at the East Adelaide State School in the early 1900s. 'The schoolhouse stood at the street corner in the midst of an asphalt yard, which was accurately bisected for girls and boys . . .', he said. 'Here the youngsters marched into classrooms to the sound of drum and fife, forty or fifty in a class, the girls on one side, the boys on another . . . the portrait of a bearded Edward VII reminded them of their allegiance to the distant throne . . .' The pupils 'strengthened their down strokes, polished their pothooks . . . learned to read and write and to honour the King.'

Flax and hemp are exports of Russia.
Flax and hemp are exports of Russia.
Flax and hemp are exports of Russia.
Flax and hemp are exports of Russia.
Flax and hemp are exports of Russia.
Flax and hemp are exports of Russia.
Flamborough Head, East of Yorkshire.
Flamborough Head, East of Yorkshire.
Flamborough Head, East of Yorkshire.
Flamborough Head, East of Yorkshire.
Flamborough Head, East of Yorkshire.
Flamborough Head, East of Yorkshire.

Geneva, a Swiss lake.
Geneva, a Swiss lake.
Geneva, a Swiss lake.
Geneva, a Swiss lake.
Hague, town in Holland.
Hague, town in Holland.
Hague, town in Holland.
Hague, town in Holland.
Hague, town in Holland.

In the early years of the century, a child learning to write practised in a copy book, copying the printed examples over and over again to get the letters perfect. In 1924, this little girl was posed to demonstrate what was considered to be the correct posture for writing with a steel-nibbed pen

Critics and pioneers

Attacks on stereotyped teaching in NSW schools

The shortcomings of New South Wales education were discussed at a lively conference of government-employed teachers held in Sydney in 1901. The main complaints were that teaching was too mechanical and stereotyped, that teachers were inadequately trained or paid, that the examination system was oppressive, and opportunities for higher education were limited. These objections remained valid for many years.

The New South Wales Attorney-General, Bernhard Ringrose Wise, summed up the situation perceptively. The very word 'education', he said, meant not only the acquisition of facts but the exercise of faculties. However, a young country, for reasons he could never comprehend, was generally sup-posed to be too occupied with material cares to take an interest in art. There was so little appreciation of the very best in Australia that the country might be called 'the paradise of mediocrity and the grave of genius'. The educational system was too exclusively concerned with testing knowledge and fell short in developing the imagination.

At the same conference Francis Anderson, Professor of Philosophy at Sydney University, said it was disgraceful that pupil teachers should have to teach classes of 60 to 80 children in any subject whatever, and that there was little or no systematic training of teachers in New South Wales. 'Our methods are grievously defective,' he said. Schools were under-staffed, classes too large, and teaching methods were dull and mechanical.

The conference was concerned only with government schools. For those who could afford the fees, the so-called Great Public Schools—that is, the private or church schools—provided, like their English models, an education based on a complacent conservatism, with sport taking precedence over scholarship. They inherited the 19th century English belief that team games produced men of character and resource. The Australian public schoolboy was trained, in Kipling's words, to keep 'his pores open and his mouth shut'. And as in England, the Old School Tie became a status symbol.

The Montessori system

In 1911 and 1912 the American *McClure's Magazine* ran a series of articles about revolutionary teaching methods employed in Rome since 1907 by an Italian physician, Maria Montessori. She had set up a little school where children from three to six years were led by apparatus offered to them to teach themselves to read and write and to grasp fine differences of size, shape, number, colour and so on.

The articles were read enthusiastically in Sydney by the New South Wales Minister for Public Instruction, A. C. Carmichael, and Miss M. M. Simpson, infant mistress at Blackfriars Demonstration School. Miss Simpson later read the English translation of Montessori's book *Pedagogia Scientifica*, and in July 1912 she wrote a report to Carmichael, suggesting that an experienced, unprejudiced person be sent to Rome to study the doctor's methods. Carmichael decided that Miss Simpson herself should be the one to go.

Before she left Miss Simpson had the Montessori apparatus copied and began using a modified version of the system.

Democratic teaching

Miss Simpson's report, published in March 1914, recommended that the Montessori method be generally adopted. '. . . based as it is on liberty, the Montessori system is particularly well suited to the educational needs of a free, democratic country like Australia, where self-reliance, individuality, resource and freshness of thought are qualities much to be desired in future citizens', she wrote.

The Montessori system did not become general in primary schools, but its influence did spread throughout the state. By 1930, when Miss Simpson retired, the Montessori system no longer aroused much interest among teachers, but its salient features had been adopted into pre-school education throughout Australia.

These children at the Blackfriars Demonstration School, Sydney, were photographed in 1913 to show the merit of a new system of education. The school's infant mistress returned to Sydney in that year after studying with Maria Montessori in Rome. The upper picture shows a traditional class, the children sitting stiffly erect, arms folded behind backs, as the teacher lectures. In the Montessori class, below, the teacher is a guide, offering help when she judges the individual child is ready for it. The children sit naturally, learning from special books and apparatus

---

More pupils per school

In 1902, 781,000 pupils attended 9600 government and private schools in Australia. In 1982, however, there were 9868 schools, but they shared 2,994,650 pupils and 188,860 teachers. The number of schools rose until the 1930s, and then gradually declined

Horse-and-buggy teachers

Despite the many defects of Australia's educational systems, attempts were made early in the century to bring schooling to children of the outback. In 1901, Queensland, with a population spread over 1,727,528 square kilometres, appointed its first travelling teacher. He was supplied with a specially-designed buggy, a complete ambulance outfit, camping equipment, and a boy assistant who looked after the horses, helped pitch the tent, lit the camp-fire, lowered slip-rails and opened the boundary gates.

By 1915, there were 17 travelling teachers in Queensland. All still used buggies. 'The motor-car and motor-cycle are also being tried as a quick means of locomotion,' said a departmental report. 'But so far, owing to the nature of much of the country to be crossed—sandy tracts, heavy black soil plains, hilly districts, treacherous billabongs, etc.— the motor-car has not been an unqualified success . . . The Department is anxiously waiting the perfection of aeroplanes.'

The teacher was expected to visit each family in his district at least four times a year. 'We do not pretend to produce University graduates under this system,' said the report. 'But we are teaching these children to read, to write, and to count. And what a tower of strength the lads will be in the defence of their country! They can ride well, can shoot straight, are skilled in bush-lore, can find their way in strange country as unerringly as a homing pigeon . . .'

The travelling teacher had to be a handyman as well as a pedagogue. 'He must be a man of infinite resource,' said the report. 'He must be able to splice a broken pole, mend a wheel, doctor a sick horse, and, if threatened by fire or flood, be able to extricate himself and his boy and save His Majesty's property.'

In 1913, Queensland travelling teachers visited 846 families and instructed 1893 children at a cost per pupil of £3 11s 4d [$143.30]. The teachers covered a total distance of more than 96,000 kilometres.

The travelling school

In 1908 the New South Wales Department of Public Instruction became worried about the education of isolated families in the north of the state, so the department decided to appoint a special travelling teacher.

Much thought was given to selecting a suitable teacher, and it was considered that he should be a self-reliant single man, used to the bush and to managing a horse. Such a teacher was found in 23-year-old Albert Biddle, who had taught in several bush schools.

He was appointed to the Eton-Harrow Travelling School in August 1908, with instructions to teach a week at a time at each place on his circuit. The department kept in touch by sending his mail to a central township with the curious name of Come-by-chance.

From 1908 to 1923 six young teachers successively travelled and taught in northern New South Wales in this little van. Half-time schools at Namoi View and Evandale replaced the Travelling School

The teacher was equipped with a specially-built covered van 2 m long and 1 m wide with a waterproof canopy 1.5 m high. There was a bunk so that he could sleep in the van, and there were lockers and shelves for his school equipment and personal belongings. The construction was kept light so that the van could carry a load of 305 kilograms weight, yet not be too heavy for one horse. The equipment included a 3.6 x 4 m tent which was used as a schoolroom when no other suitable room was available.

Charges of regimentation and snobbery

In 1935, John Francis Cramer, superintendent of schools in Oregon, USA, made a study of Australian educational methods. After visiting many city and country schools, he came to the conclusion that they were much more regimented than American schools.

School uniforms stressed conformity rather than individuality. 'Neither American pupils nor their parents would tolerate any prescribed uniform,' he wrote. Other evidences of regimentation were 'marching in and out of school buildings...standing to answer questions, rising when the head or an inspector comes into the room, addressing teachers as "Sir" . . .'

And as for the expensive private schools: 'The Englishman likes to point to the Great Public Schools as the flowering achievement of English education. The type of education obtained in these schools . . . was designed to accomplish efficiently a certain end. This purpose was to develop, in a rigidly stratified society, a professional and governing class. They touched only a small percentage of the people, but they conferred a social distinction that no other type of school could claim. Such schools are excellently adapted to preserve a society of caste and class, but become . . . an anachronism in a democratic community.

'Australia's government is democratic, and Australians are loyal to democratic ideals, but they have built up in every State small copies of the Great Public Schools, and these are increasing their influence.'

Cramer conceded that these private schools had been responsible for some interesting developments in education, but said they were more interested in examination passes and university matriculation even than the State Schools, if that were possible. And they were very important socially. The social side of these schools was noted many years later by Malcolm Muggeridge. When he came to Australia in the 1950s he found one of Victoria's famous private schools, Geelong Grammar, to be more snobbish than Eton.

In 1952, Mr H. C. Dent, editor of *The Times Educational Supplement*, said much of what he had seen in Australian schools perturbed and depressed him. 'With rare exceptions the school conceives its task in the narrow light of preparing children for examinations instead of future citizenship,' he said. He found Australian education authoritarian, hierarchical and stereotyped. And David Holbrook, a well-known English educationist, found most teachers in Australia worked in an atmosphere of repression which reflected 'a traditional assumption in Australian society that people are not to be trusted'.

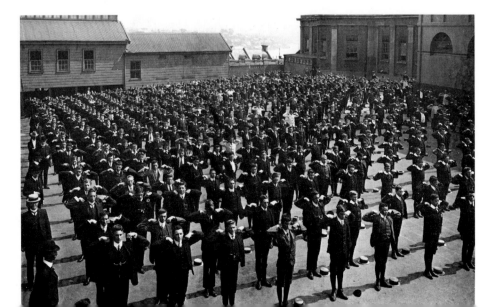

Morning exercises were performed with parade-ground precision at Fort Street Boys' High School, Sydney, in 1910

Wartime life

Australia finds nationhood in defeat

When the Australian States federated in 1901, they were already at war; separately, they had committed themselves to supporting Britain in South Africa against the Boers. The Commonwealth Horse was raised to fight in South Africa, and Australians soon became proud of their bushmen soldiers.

When war broke out in Europe in 1914, Australia did not hesitate to back Britain again. Political leaders from both conservative and socialist camps loudly offered the country's last man and last shilling, and enthusiastic patriotism engulfed the people. On the day that the news came through of the Gallipoli landing, the Melbourne *Argus* was able to announce that Australia had 'in one moment stepped into the world of great manhood'. The Anzacs were the martyrs who had to die to make the birth of the Australian nation real.

During World War I, two referendums were held on conscription, and twice the majority of Australians voted against it. However, the people were united again in their jubilation when the armistice was signed, and all over the country there were scenes of wild celebration.

Because of the war, Australia now had a national day—Anzac Day. Naturally, in a country which commemorated its nationhood by celebrating a military defeat, the question 'Will there be another war?' often recurred, and when Britain declared war on Germany in September 1939, Australia declared war too—though with less enthusiasm than in 1914.

The war with Japan, however, brought enemy bombs to Australian soil for the first time, and soon the war seemed very close and very real. At home there were rationing, censorship and the American invasion.

During World War I, lurid posters like this frightened patriotic Australians into joining the army to fight the Germans

The Commonwealth fights its first war

Labor leaders stand alone in opposition to war in South Africa

When war broke out between Britain and the two South African Republics of the Transvaal and Orange Free State in October 1899, the Australian States immediately offered their support. At first each state sent its own units, but after the formation of the Commonwealth, these were combined as the Australian Commonwealth Horse. There was a great deal of pride in this contribution, and in the well-tested skills of the Australian bushman turned cavalryman.

But although the public in general welcomed the opportunity to display its loyalty to Crown and Empire, support for the war was by no means universal in Australia. Some members of the Labor Party had their reservations, and in New South Wales, its two most brilliant leaders, William Holman and Billy Hughes, both British-born, vehemently opposed the war. Holman declared in the House Assembly: 'While I am loyal to the Empire, I see with emotions of shame and indignation which I can hardly express, the name and reputation of that Empire being dragged in the dust . . . ' When, towards the end of an eloquent anti-war speech, he was asked by Edmund Barton whether he wanted the Boers or the British to win, he replied: 'Whilst my country is fighting in a just cause I hope I shall be as ready to support its claims as any other member. But as I believe from the bottom of my heart that this is the most iniquitous war ever waged with any race, I hope that England may be defeated.'

Arnold Wood, Challis Professor of History at the University of Sydney, became president of an Anti-War League which advocated immediate termination of the war and self-government for the Boers. In Victoria, the league was supported by the eminent lawyer Henry Bourne Higgins who denounced the war as 'unnecessary and unjust', and opposed the despatch of Australian contingents 'on the simple old-fashioned ground of justice'.

But Australians, on the whole, enjoyed an unprecedented orgy of jingoism. They decorated their shops, houses and lapels with pictures of their heroes—the British commanders Lord Roberts ('Bobs') and Kitchener of Khartoum ('K. of K.').

The popular poets were kept busy churning out patriotic verses, such as this one by Will Ogilvie that told of the Bushmen's Contingent, men from the outback who were trained and equipped by public subscription:

You have taken down the sliprails, set the mustered
cattle free,
You have put the snaffle-bridles on your best.
You have kissed a sobbing sweet-heart by the
moonlit wilga tree,
You are riding from the North and from the
West.
You are bushmen of the bushmen and your steeds
are bridle-wise
And if your leaders learn to lead you right
You will show the Transvaal rebels when the
Mauser bullet flies
That the back-block boys are not afraid to
fight.

Patriotic fervour reached a hysterical climax in May 1900, when Mafeking, an unimportant little South African township which had been besieged for 218 days, was relieved by a force under Lord Roberts. For two days, all Australia celebrated madly, with bands, processions, fireworks, bonfires, bell-ringing, flags, songs, and great torrents of oratory.

But war fever had subsided by March 1902, when Melbourne *Table Talk* reported: 'Very little interest is being taken in Adelaide in the South Australian quota of the Second Federal Contingent for South Africa. The men are drilling daily, but scarcely anyone has enough interest in them to watch them.'

When the peace treaty was signed on 31 May 1902, the news was received quietly. 'There was no horse-play and no riot of rejoicing in the city,' said Melbourne *Punch,* and 'none of the ribaldry that marked the Mafeking demonstrations. There were no anti-Boer demonstrations; even the street songs that were favourites at previous demonstrations were out of favour, and although strains of *Up With the Dear Old Union Jack and Down With Kruger and the Boers* were heard here and there, they were not popular.'

Australia, it seemed, had grown tired of the war. But its real significance, said *Punch,* was that 'it had put the young Australian on his trial, and enabled him to demonstrate to Australia's complete satisfaction, that here in the new hot southerly land the descendants of fathers bred in the cold northern world have not degenerated and can be trusted to face the enemy with the pluck and determination that have made the British islands the firmest stronghold on earth.'

The New South Wales Bushmen's Contingent marches along William Street in Sydney on its way **to embarkation for South Africa. These troops took part in the relief of Mafeking on 18 May 1900, an** **event that was greeted with scenes of patriotic hysteria throughout Australia**

LORD KITCHENER.

This silver-framed portrait of Lord Kitchener, a national hero, was sold for 4s 6d ($6.40) in 1900

A farewell luncheon held in the Exhibition Building in Adelaide for South Australian troops about to leave for South Africa. Each state sent its own troops until Federation on 1 January 1901

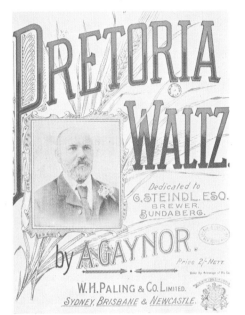

Cover of one of the many music sheets recording popular feeling about the Boer War in song

Part of the second New South Wales contingent preparing its horses for loading on to the *Southern Cross* bound for Cape Town in 1900. Australia sent 16,175 men and 16,314 horses to war

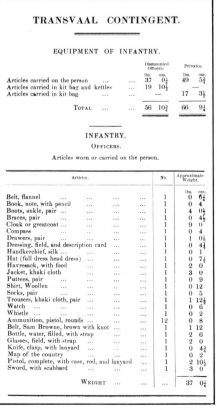

TRANSVAAL CONTINGENT.

EQUIPMENT OF INFANTRY.

	Dismounted Officers.		Privates.	
	lbs.	ozs.	lbs.	ozs.
Articles carried on the person	37	0¼	49	5¾
Articles carried in kit bag and kettles	19	10½	—	—
Articles carried in kit bag	—	—	17	3½
Total	56	10¾	66	9¼

INFANTRY.
OFFICERS.

Articles worn or carried on the person.

Articles.	No.	Approximate Weight.	
		lbs.	ozs.
Belt, flannel	1	0	6¼
Book, note, with pencil	1	0	4
Boots, ankle, pair	1	4	0½
Braces, pair	1	0	4½
Cloak or greatcoat	1	9	0
Compass	1	0	4
Drawers, pair	1	1	0½
Dressing, field, and description card	1	0	4¼
Handkerchief, silk	1	0	1
Hat (full dress head dress)	1	0	7½
Havresack, with food	1	2	0
Jacket, khaki cloth	1	3	0
Puttees, pair	1	0	9
Shirt, Woollen	1	0	12
Socks, pair	1	0	5
Trousers, khaki cloth, pair	1	1	12½
Watch	1	0	6
Whistle	1	0	2
Ammunition, pistol, rounds	12	0	8
Belt, Sam Browne, brown with knot	1	1	12
Bottle, water, filled, with strap	1	2	6
Glasses, field, with strap	1	2	0
Knife, clasp, with lanyard	1	0	4¾
Map of the country	1	0	2
Pistol, complete, with case, rod, and lanyard	1	2	10½
Sword, with scabbard	1	3	0
Weight		37	0¼

A private carried equipment weighing 30 kg, an infantry officer 16.8 kg. Drawers were optional for privates

A few army nurses accompanied the troops to South Africa; this group came from South Australia. Australian troops only suffered 1400 casualties during the Boer War; 518 of these died

Australia prepares for the worst

9000 men to defend 8 million square kilometres

The last British soldier left Australia in 1870. After that it was up to the colonies to organise their own defences. The next year, New South Wales raised a permanent battery of artillery and two permanent companies of infantry; the other colonies soon followed suit.

In March 1877, Major-General Sir William Jervois and Lieutenant-Colonel Peter Scratchley of the Royal Engineers came to Australia to advise on a co-ordinated sys-

tem of seaport defence. Their report—presented a leisurely six years later—said that as Britain commanded the seas, all the Australian colonies needed was defence against raids by armed vessels, shore batteries and 'torpedo' mines. The report finally set in motion a military reorganisation which remained the basis of Australia's defence planning until Federation in 1901.

After the reorganisation of the colonial

troops, the armed forces of the Australian colonies totalled 9423 men, but numbers rose during the Boer War, so that the new Commonwealth Government inherited about 29,000 soldiers—all volunteers. The country had just over 3.5 million people at the time.

Two years after Federation, the Australian Parliament passed a Defence Act authorising compulsory military training, but nothing was put into force.

'Shamefully unprepared!' said the Defence League

Many Australians in the early 1900s felt isolated and threatened. They saw most of their countrymen as sports-mad fools oblivious to the threats that menaced them. This cartoon cover from *The Call*—magazine of the Australian National Defence League—illustrates a few of their fears

Norman Lindsay—an ardent supporter of the Defence League—illustrated what he saw as the beneficial effects of military discipline on the idle youth of the day

'A coming test match'—the title of this 1909 cartoon from *The Call* which depicts a woefully ill-equipped Australia facing the 'Yellow Peril'

In 1905, the Australian National Defence League was formed to advocate effective national defence and compulsory military training for all. Supporters of the League included politicians of various parties, university professors, barristers, businessmen, clergymen and Tooths, the Sydney brewers. Those who supported the League proclaimed that the Australian lad was a bad lot, entirely out of hand, a lawless larrikin who could only be brought to reasonable behaviour and moral improvement by military discipline.

For many years, the League published an

expensively-produced magazine, *The Call,* whose recurring theme was that Australians were so obsessed with sport that they were shamefully unprepared to meet the foe. It was not clear whether the main foe was a belligerent Germany or the mysterious 'Yellow Peril'; but it was obvious that *The Call* considered drink, gambling, strikes, immigrants from Asia and even professional sport foes of equal importance.

In its exhortations to militarism, *The Call* did not overlook women, whom it urged to take up rifle shooting. 'It has no sordid or

doubtful surroundings,' said *The Call*. 'There is nothing in it unbecoming to a lady.'

The article continued: 'Some say rifle-shooting for ladies is not safe. The same has been said of matches, mail coaches, steam railways, electric trams . . . our ladies should practise rifle-shooting, for indirectly it would benefit all. By their enthusiasm they attract the attention of men and boys to the subject. Thus a spirit of patriotism is nurtured, and patriotism is one of the highest, if not, indeed, the highest sentiment that can animate any human being.'

Lord Kitchener and the Defence Act

In 1909-10 the British army commander, Field Marshal Lord Kitchener, visited Australia at the request of the Government to advise on defence. During two hot summer months, he inspected nearly all the military establishments in the country. He also attended numerous receptions in his honour, and was generally lionised by the Australians, to whom he was famous as the hero of Khartoum.

The newspapers, however, were less taken with the hero, for he was a man of few words. After Kitchener visited the Liverpool army camp—a festive occasion on which about 7000 people went to the camp, many of them on special trains from Sydney—the *Sydney Mail* observed:

'In the field at Liverpool he uttered many an expressive "Ah" and to a very important field officer he observed, "Do you not think your orders are rather—er, rather—er, rather?" There was no doubt they were. In his report Lord Kitchener may be relied upon to tell us in no uncertain manner how to escape being "er, rather, er, rather, er, rather". The Commonwealth has every faith in Kitchener.'

However, Kitchener did prove reliable. In his report, issued early in 1910 before he had even left Australia, he left the government in no doubt that he thought Australia's defences were inadequate.

He recommended that the country should have a trained military force of not less than 80,000 men, one half to defend the big cities, the other half to be a mobile striking force. Boys between the ages of 12 and 14 were to drill as 'junior cadets' for a total of 120 hours a year; boys between 14 and 17 would train as 'senior cadets' for four whole days and 12 half days and attend 24 night drills. Young men from 18 to 25 years would serve in the citizen forces, with 16 whole-day drills, eight in camp, and a year in the reserves.

As a result of Kitchener's report, a new Defence Act was proclaimed on 1 January 1911, and Australia became the first English-

Lord Kitchener (centre, in white uniform) visited Australia in the summer of 1909-10 to survey the country's defences and advise on their future. Here, at Liverpool, NSW, he inspects the Metropolitan Cadets—some of the Australians Kitchener considered to be 'excellent fighting material'

speaking country to introduce conscription in peacetime. However, the system was workable only in the more populous areas, so country boys—about a quarter of those eligible for military training—were automatically exempt. This may have been one reason why the Act was bitterly resented by many people, while being hailed as progressive by many others. Another reason was perhaps the traditional Australian dislike of regimentation.

Compulsory cadet drill began in July 1911, but thousands of boys failed to enrol, often with the approval of their parents. Only 17,000 of the 40,000 boys eligible registered in the second year of the scheme. Between 1 January 1912 and 30 June 1914, there were

no less than 27,749 prosecutions for evasion of the Act—an average of 250 per week for two years; 5732 boys and youths were imprisoned, in military or civil gaols. Even more evaders were fined.

Sympathy was often with the defaulters. For example, miners at Broken Hill gave a medal to a boy who was imprisoned for two weeks on bread and water.

One celebrated case was that of 19-year-old John Size and his 18-year-old brother William, both sentenced in South Australia to 20 days' detention for refusing to drill. They were put on a diet of bread and water, but remained obdurate. Yet, when World War I broke out, both youths volunteered for the Australian Imperial Force.

'Unspeakably mean!' said the Freedom League

In 1912, a non-party Australian Freedom League was formed to oppose the implementation of the Defence Act. Its manifesto read in part: 'The Australian Freedom League . . . denounces as unspeakably mean a system which places the brunt of the training upon lads between 14 and 18 years old, who are liable to detention in a military fortress if they "fail to render the personal service required of them . . ." New Zealand and Australia alone among the civilised countries of the world have allowed a cowardly set of politicians to impose the burden of national service on the boy who has no vote . . .

'But the League's chief and most fundamental objection to the present Defence Act is that it, in times of peace, places the military power above the civil power. Any offence against the Act itself or the Military Board's regulations is defined as a "military offence" . . . appeal to the civil court . . . is forbidden.'

One curious objection to compulsory mili-

tary service was that it would expose well-brought-up boys to moral contamination. A founder of the Australian Freedom League, Mr F. J. Hills, wrote of the degradation of 'the finer and more delicately nurtured young minds' that would result from 'enforced companionship with the worst elements of society . . . A decent lad during the training must stand and listen to the blasphemies and obscenities, not merely of the loose lads of the district, but of the larrikin and criminally inclined ones.'

A contributor to *The Lone Hand* pointed out in October 1912 that under the Defence Act 'an Australian youth who has been allotted to the Navy may be called to go to China or to the North Sea, and to try to kill the King's enemies, even if they are opposing injustice . . . In 1841, the British Government used its ships of war to compel China to admit Indian opium . . . If the British Navy were in the future to be called on to act for any other purpose of oppression, the Aus-

tralian lad may be compelled to aid in the oppression . . .'

In fact, what most Australians wanted in 1912 was a Navy of Australia's own; unlike Canada and New Zealand, Australia was not content to rely solely on Britain for naval defence. The movement towards forming an independent navy culminated in the passing of the Naval Defence Act in 1910, and in that year the Royal Australian Navy came into existence with the arrival of the destroyers *HMAS Parramatta* and *HMAS Yarra*. A third destroyer, *HMAS Warrego*, shipped out in parts and assembled in Sydney, was commissioned in 1912.

When the battle cruiser *HMAS Australia* and the light cruisers *HMAS Melbourne* and *Sydney* sailed into Sydney Harbour in 1913, the dream of an Australian navy seemed to have come true—although Admiral Henderson's ambitious 1911 proposals for an Australian fleet of 53 ships, to be run by 15,000 men, were never to become reality.

Jubilation greets declaration of war

Patriotic fervour ends with Gallipoli casualty figures

Army recruiting teams toured Australia during the war urging all fit young men to join their mates in the trenches of Europe

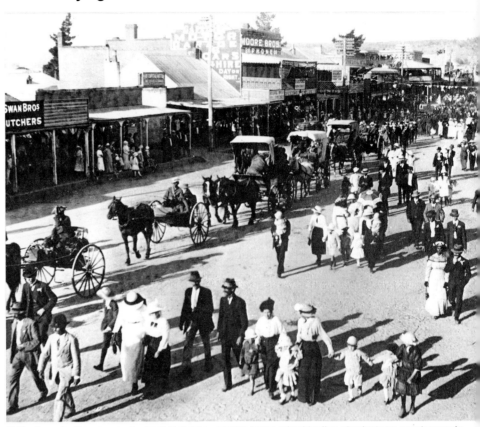

Enthusiasm for the war was so great that many country towns raised bodies of volunteers spontaneously. The men would be given a banner with their own self-styled name, such as this group in Queanbeyan called 'The Men from Snowy River', and they would march to the capital gathering recruits on the way

On the night of 31 July 1914, when events in Europe were moving swiftly to a crisis, Andrew Fisher, leader of the Labor Opposition, and soon to be Prime Minister, declared: 'Should the worst happen, after everything has been done that honour will permit, Australians will stand beside the Mother Country to help and defend her to our last man and last shilling.' The next night, the Prime Minister, Joseph Cook, gave a similar promise: 'If there is to be a war, you and I shall be in it,' he said. 'We must be in it. If the Old Country is at war, so are we.'

On August 4, Britain declared war on Germany. 'The lamps are going out all over Europe,' said the British Foreign Secretary, Sir Edward Grey. 'We shall not see them lit again in our lifetime.' The news was received in Australia with wild enthusiasm. Dense and excited crowds gathered outside newspaper offices. The Melbourne *Age* reported the scene in Collins Street:

'It needed only a single voice to give the opening bars of a patriotic song and thousands of throats took it up, hats and coats were waved, and those who were lucky enough to possess even the smallest of Union Jacks were the heroes of the moment and were raised shoulder high as the crowd surged hither and thither. *Rule Britannia, Soldiers of the King* and *Sons of the Sea* were sung again and again. The National Anthem had a sobering effect from time to time, and woe betide anyone who failed to remove his hat without hesitation.

'Suddenly, a Frenchman got up on the steps and commenced singing the *Marseillaise*. The crowd grew frantic with enthusiasm. He was lifted bodily in the air shouting, "Vive l'Australie! Vive la France!"

'About 11.20 p.m., in response to the persistent cry of "We want more news" a notice was put up stating that there would be no more news till morning. "We won't go home till morning", shouted someone and every voice took up the chorus. Suddenly two bluejackets arrived on the scene. They were pounced upon. A procession formed and they were carried up and down the street to the tune of *Rule Britannia, Boys of the Bull-dog Breed* and *Sons of the Sea*. Finally the procession or part of it marched up the steps of the office, deposited the jovial tars on the counter and asked, "Is there more news?" The notice already posted was confirmed and the crowd gradually dwindled away.'

The *Annual Register* recorded Australian reaction to the declaration of war rather patronisingly: 'The declaration of war against Germany was not taken quite so calmly by the Australian people as by the people of the United Kingdom. The Australians, as a youthful community naturally exercise less restraint in time of Imperial stress than the experienced veterans of the Mother Country.'

Recalling the early days of the war, Dr Herbert Moran, who was practising in the Sydney suburb of Glebe at the time, wrote: 'There was much rhetoric from politicians and aldermen, flag-flying and flag-flapping. Kipling's poems were in great demand as recitation pieces. Old men were exhorting young men to go to the war—"If only I were your age." A mass hysteria was being whipped up by the tom-toms of the newspapers and sing-song politicians ... White feathers were constantly sent by mail.'

Within a few months, Melbourne warehouses were offering 'a fine assortment of patriotic goods', imported from England—Commonwealth flags, Union Jacks, coloured flag brooches, tricolour ribbon, bunting and patriotic neckwear, fancy bows, etc., in the English, French and Belgian colours. The new autumn millinery included the Tipperary cap, the Russian turban, the Glengarry and other military styles, while men could buy black cashmere half-hose with red, white and blue designs.

The day before Britain declared war Australia offered to place the brand-new vessels of the Royal Australian Navy under the control of the British Admiralty, and to despatch an expeditionary force of 20,000 men to be at the complete disposal of the British Government. This was gratefully accepted on August 6. New South Wales and Victoria were to supply four battalions each, and the other states another four between them. Pay for the private was fixed at 6s [$6.65] a day when he was overseas. Both the Governor-General, Sir Ronald Munro Ferguson, and King George V thought this excessive, though the basic wage in New South Wales was 8s 6d [$9.45] a day.

Labor was elected to power in September 1914 and the new government, headed by

Sydney volunteers, with their sweethearts, on their way to embarkation for Europe. Australian privates were paid 6s [$6.65] a day, while their British equivalents only received 1s [$1.10]. This earned the Australians nicknames such as 'six-bob-a-day tourists', although all were expected to be front-line fighting troops

The Diggers' uniform, criticised as dull and drab when first issued, proved to be far more suited to trench warfare than the conspicuously colourful French and German outfits

Andrew Fisher with Billy Hughes as Attorney General, immediately passed the Federal War Precautions Act, based on Britain's Defence of the Realm Act. The act gave the government wide-ranging powers, including those of censorship.

On September 1914, the First Victorian Regiment paraded through the streets of Melbourne. The crowds that watched showed little enthusiasm at first but as the men passed Parliament House, where the Governor-General took the salute, cheers rang out, drowning the bands, and flags and handkerchiefs waved in wild profusion.

The units of the first contingent were ready to sail by September 21, and by late October, troopships from every part of Australia were assembling in King George Sound, on the south-western coast. Early on the morning of November 1, the fleet of 36 troopships and three escorting cruisers moved out to sea.

'The scenes of enthusiasm which attended the departure of the first contingents from Australia found no parallel in the United Kingdom,' said the *Annual Register*. 'And the people of Australia were at the same time far more anxious and "jumpy".'

The anxiety and jumpiness increased in May 1915, when the heavy casualty lists from Gallipoli first appeared, black-edged, in the papers. 'The tone of the press . . . grew more sober,' wrote Dr Moran. 'The strident braggart voices were not so loud.'

Entirely by voluntary effort, Australia, with a population of less than 5,000,000

raised 416,809 men for the war, and sent 330,000 overseas. Total casualties were 226,073 of whom 59,258 were killed, died or missing. About 40 per cent of all Australian men between the ages of 18 and 45 enlisted and more Australians than Americans died in battle. The war, with its tragic losses, and its bitter divisions over conscription, left an enduring scar on Australian life.

The first Victorian troops prepare to leave from Melbourne on 19 October 1914. The convoy assembled in King George Sound, Western Australia, and steamed to Egypt; the troops disembarked in November

'Business as usual' on the home front

Stockwhips and boomerangs suggested as weapons of war

Sacrifices for the war effort were made enthusiastically on the home front. In Melbourne, for example, the ballroom at Government House was turned over to the Red Cross (above). In Melbourne, too, a woman sought permission from the Defence Department to name her daughter 'Queen of the Allies'

Just after the war began, the Melbourne store of Buckley and Nunn prefaced its spring and summer catalogue with this special note

After the first excitement over the war died down, the prevailing mood of the Australian public at home was 'business as usual'. Sydney people interviewed in the street thought it would all be over within a month.

On December 10, four months after fighting began, the Sydney magazine *The Australian Bystander* made two comments on the war: 'Since the war started ... the swarms of people disporting in the surf at the weekend are larger than ever ... not a game of cricket the less has been played; not a picture-show, not a vaudeville has closed because of the war; not a pub has closed; not a race-club has held fewer meetings; there is not a motorcar less in the streets; concerts, entertainments and side-shows have increased in numbers; judging casually by evi-

De Mole's caterpillar fort

This tank was designed by an Australian engineer, Lancelot de Mole. While engaged on survey work in south-west Western Australia, he was working out methods for hauling heavy loads over rough country and evolved an idea for a chain-track vehicle. He then realised the value of the idea in relation to defence, and in 1912 submitted his design to the War Office in Britain, accompanied by a working model. The design was never accepted, although it was later realised that de Mole's model for a 'caterpillar fort' with a double climbing face was in advance of its time—the tanks that went into action during World War I were far inferior to de Mole's. The photograph above is of his final model, which he presented to the Australian War Museum, Canberra; for many years, information about it was classified as secret

dence met in the streets, the beer and whisky trade is very brisk; the trams, the streets and the harbour ferry-boats are crowded, Parliament is talking as much as before and doing as little ...'

The Australian Bystander's other comment concerned the business world. 'From the very start,' it noted, 'Sydney looked forward in expectation of blessings to come out of the war. Of course, they were to be of a trade nature, monetary benefits, and that optimistic feeling is sustaining the commercial community yet.

'When Germany has been rubbed out, there will not be occasion to fasten Sydney second-hand pianos with new German nameplates; the food product made at Surry Hills will sell as Sydney sausage, and need not be labelled "German". And Sydney will make miles of other things and none of them will be labelled "Made in Germany".'

The Australian Storekeeper and Trader's Journal reported with satisfaction on February 29, 1916 that 'one result of the British victory in Mesopotamia was the liberation of last season's date crops'. The satisfaction was premature—in April, General Townshend's forces, besieged in Kut-el-Amara, surrendered to the Turks. In the same issue, the *Journal* told its readers of a recent 'abnormal' advance in the prices of spirits, especially whisky. The reason for this was the demand for spirits for the manufacture of high explosives—England's Ministry of Munitions had taken over all the distilleries.

There was brighter news for Scotch whisky drinkers in the *Journal's* issue of April 29. It revealed that there were 590,000 litres of the stuff in bond in the United Kingdom, a quantity sufficient for three or four years' normal consumption of the liquor.

However, the wholesale price of Scotch whisky in Australia was still only 25s to 29s

[$41.75 to $48.40] per 4.5 litres, including 17s [$37] excise. Even after 18 months of war, Australian drinkers were still offered a very wide range of Scotch whisky, Irish whiskey, French brandies, champagne and still wines, and imported beers—including German beer.

Winning the war at home

One significant contribution to the war effort on the alcohol front was made by the staff of the University of Melbourne. Inspired by the example of King George V, who had undertaken to abstain from alcohol for the duration, the academics made a similiar sacrifice.

Also in Victoria, an 'Australian League of Honour' launched a thrift campaign for economical cooking, and distributed two free books of cheap recipes. In the foreword to one of these, Lady Helen Munro-Ferguson wrote: 'The avoidance of waste is in this crisis no longer a matter of personal concern, but one of extreme national importance.'

To avoid waste ('For the Empire'), housewives were advised to cook such dishes as:

JAM FRITTERS. *Ingredients:* 1 egg, $1/2$ teacup of milk, 1 pennyworth stale bread. *Method:* Beat up the egg with the milk, cut the bread into squares or fingers, dip each piece in the egg and fry in hot fat. Serve with a little jam on each. (Four Persons.)

In 1916, a Necessary Commodities Commission was given authority to determine the prices of 'foodstuffs, necessary commodities and services', and the *Commonwealth Gazette* was enlivened with frequent proclamations such as 'The following shall be a foodstuff for the purposes of the War Precautions (Prices) Regulation, namely, Lemon Peel.'

Inspired patriots all over Australia were

keen to make their contributions to the war effort. A composer wrote a piece of music called *The Dead March for the Federal Troops*; it was rejected by the military bandmaster, who thought the traditional dead marches were good enough. Melbourne's Prahran and Malvern Tramways Trust sent an illuminated electric tramcar each night through busy shopping streets; it carried a brass band and a tableau in which Britannia was supported by her sea and land forces (portrayed by senior cadets). In a Sydney theatre, Mr Marshall Crosby aroused great patriotic fervour by singing *Australia's Bonny Boys in Blue;* the 'bonny boys' who accompanied him were six buxom, flag-waving girls dressed as sailors.

Other patriots volunteered suggestions for war weapons, ranging from stockwhips to boomerang-shaped bayonets. Many inventions were submitted to the Government; they included one for finding the exact position of an aircraft by means of a balloon and electric wires, and another for an aerial torpedo. 'And countless people sought financial assistance in order to complete prototypes of inventions whose full powers of destruction would be revealed when the money was forthcoming,' writes the historian L. L. Robson.

One invention of which the Government might have taken good advantage, but did not, was a 'tank' (as it afterwards came to be called) designed in 1912 by a South Australian, Lancelot de Mole. By 1919, it was recognised that de Mole's tank was far better designed than the ones which did go into action in 1916. But its inventor could not get it accepted by either the Australian or British Government during the war.

In 1911, when the last census before the outbreak of the war was taken, Australia had 32,990 German-born citizens, and 2774 born in Austria-Hungary. During the war, 6739 men (most of whom were eligible to be called

up by the German army), 67 women and 84 children were interned.

However, wild stories proliferated about the traitorous acts of those Germans who remained free. For example, it was rumoured that in the Barossa district of South Australia the teacher in a German school used to haul down the Union Jack, wipe his feet on it, spit on it and then raise the German flag. The story was no doubt apocryphal, but in November 1917 South Australia prohibited the teaching of German in primary schools, and closed 49 Lutheran schools.

Spy hysteria

No German spies were discovered in Australia during the war, but there were frequent outbreaks of spy hysteria. Many thousands of letters about suspicious happenings bedevilled the authorities. A cricket club could not put down a concrete pitch without being accused of preparing gun emplacements. Flights of birds at night were reported as enemy planes, whales disporting off a seaside resort as enemy submarines. One Melbourne patriot reported sinister flashing lights in the Dandenongs; when investigated, they proved to come from a rabbit trapper inspecting his traps by hurricane lamp.

Feeling against Germans was most bitter in South Australia, where many towns had been given German names in the early years of settlement. In 1918 British names were substituted for all of these except Adelaide (named after Queen Adelaide, wife of William IV and daughter of the Duke of Saxe-Meiningen). German names were also changed in other states. For example, in New South Wales Germanton became Holbrook and German Creek, Empire Vale; in Victoria, Hochkirch became Tarrinton; in Queensland, Bergen became Murra Murra; Western Australia's Mueller Park became Kitchener Park, and in Tasmania Bismark was renamed Collins Vale.

War Chest Day in Sydney in 1917 raised £170,000 [\$5.4 million] to buy tinned food, boxing gloves, gramophones and cigarettes for the troops

German nationals relax at the bar in the internment camp at Berrima. The camp was set up in 1914 to hold enemy aliens

Relics of the Battle of Broken Hill

Great Britain declared war on Turkey on 5 November 1914. On New Year's Day 1915, a train of ore trucks set out from Broken Hill, crowded with members of the Manchester Unity Order of Oddfellows off on their annual picnic. A few kilometres out of town, two men with rifles, flying the Turkish flag from an icecream cart, opened fire on the train. Four people were killed, and many other picnickers, including children, were wounded, some badly.

Police, soldiers and rifle club members were summoned, but the two 'Turks' took to the hills and were able to hold hundreds of armed men at bay for over an hour. Finally one of the men was killed and the other fatally wounded.

It was discovered that the two gunmen were both well-known in Broken Hill. They were Gool Mohammed, an icecream vendor from north-west India, and Mullah Abdullah, an Afghan butcher. They had decided—apparently under the influence of narcotics—to die fighting for Turkey and their religious faith, Islam

Conscription divides the nation

Violence and intimidation mar two referenda

Prime Minister Billy Hughes, known for his fiery oratory, appealed passionately for conscription to large crowds like this one in Martin Place, Sydney. His campaign was unsuccessful

The Crime of those who Vote "NO!"

Supporters of the 'no' vote were subjected to considerable harassment. Pro-conscriptionists leaned heavily on the line that a 'no' vote meant death to the volunteers in the trenches

Anti-conscriptionists felt that a 'yes' vote would mean the death of thousands more young Australians. This lurid poster dramatised their arguments in verse

The conscription issue of World War I had a devastating effect. It split the country and the Labor Party and left scars that remained throughout World War II and beyond.

In August 1916, while the disastrous battle of the Somme was still raging, the British Army Council urgently demanded reinforcements from Australia. In the first seven weeks of the offensive the Australian Imperial Force had 27,000 casualties. British losses on July 1, the first day of the infantry assault, were 60,000 dead, and when the last futile attack took place on November 13 they had lost no less than 420,000 men.

Prime Minister Billy Hughes had powers under the War Precautions Act to introduce conscription, but decided, because of bitter opposition from unions and his own Labor Party, to avoid a direct fight and take the issue to the Australian people by popular referendum. 'I am going into this referendum campaign as if it were the only thing for which I lived,' he declared. Others, including the Irish-born Roman Catholic Coadjutor Archbishop of Melbourne, Dr Daniel Mannix, threw themselves just as uncompromisingly into the fight against conscription.

Bitter personal duel

The campaign was a bitter one, punctuated by personal abuse of opponents, street fights, and physical violence against leading anti-conscriptionists. Some were tarred and feathered. It also became a duel between the gnome-like Hughes and the tall, ascetic Mannix. Both were gifted speakers. Mannix believed Britain was engaged in a 'sordid trade war'. Her failure to resolve the Irish question had also helped to precipitate hostilities.

But the Anglican Synod in Melbourne announced that God was on the side of the Allies and conscription was morally necessary. The New South Wales Premier, William Holman, told the story of a man who had removed the wooden seat from his new toilet pan so as to frame Mannix's portrait in it. The Roman Catholic Archbishops of Sydney, Perth and Hobart supported conscription.

'Muddy-mettled wastrels'

Almost the entire Australian press urged a 'yes' vote and the advocates of 'no' were subjected to severe and often grossly unfair censorship restrictions. The Melbourne *Age* denounced those who had not enlisted as 'muddy-mettled wastrels who disgrace the country in which they skulk'. One of the few papers to speak out for the other side was the Sydney *Worker*, which declared that the war was 'a brutal conflict between decadent military castes'. Also among the anti-conscription campaigners was Monty Miller, an 83-year-old survivor of Eureka Stockade.

A. W. Foster, later a judge, was one of those subjected to harassment for his stand against conscription. His criticism of the Prime Minister in a speech that he made resulted in prosecution and a long trial. He escaped conviction, but later wrote: 'Few public men on the anti-conscription side escaped prosecution or conviction, though they, as it turned out,

Women's Auxiliary Army Corps volunteers, carrying the sign 'All for Empire', march through Melbourne during the early stages of the war. Australians readily and patriotically supported the war when it first began, and over 400,000 people out of a population of 5 million volunteered for service overseas. Of those who went, one in five was killed and almost half were wounded

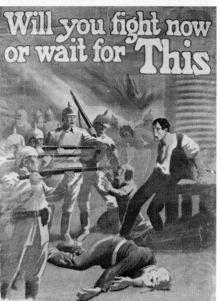

represented the majority of citizens and soldiers ... Military squads were continuously posted in printing offices where anti-conscription literature was being printed ...'

To assist its propaganda campaign the Commonwealth accepted 25,000 blood-curdling cartoons from the Dutch artist Raemaekers and distributed them throughout Australia to libraries, Government departments and, despite their often disgusting, even obscene nature, to schools.

Thousands of people attended impassioned meetings on Sydney's Domain, Melbourne's Yarra Bank and Perth's Esplanade. Men and women screamed abuse at their opponents, made bonfires of campaign leaflets and attempted to set fire to rival speakers' platforms. A Melbourne Women's Army fighting against conscription had its own flag of purple, white and green—purple for international justice, white for international life, green for international peace. Waving the flag at anti-conscription meetings, the Melbourne contralto Cecilia John would sing plaintively:

I didn't raise my son to be a soldier
I brought him up to be my pride and joy
Who dares to put musket to his shoulder,
To kill some other mother's darling boy?

On the other side, Dame Nellie Melba appealed to Australian women to vote "yes". If Germany won the war, the first thing the Kaiser would demand would be Australia, she said. The *Argus*, in an adulatory leading article, pointed out that Melba had a knowledge of the world, particularly Germany.

When the vote was held on 28 October 1916: the result was 1,160,033 votes against conscription and 1,087,557 for. Soldiers, including those on active service, voted 72,399 for conscription and 58,894 against.

The immediate result of the referendum was a split in the Labor Party. Hughes walked out of a Labor parliamentary meeting, exclaiming: 'Let all who support me follow me!' Twenty-three of the 65 members of the party went with him.

The strong 'no' vote apparently did not indicate that the majority of Australians were anti-war; rather that they felt that the war should be fought in the Australian manner—one of the principal 'no' slogans had been 'Fight for Freedom's cause in Freedom's way'. The new federal Nationalist Party formed by Hughes as a coalition of his followers and the Liberals seemed now to be the more warlike of the parties, and accordingly this coalition was voted into power shortly after the referendum, in an election held on 5 May 1917.

But enlistments in Australia continued to fall and the war situation to deteriorate. Undeterred by his previous experience, Hughes decided to hold another conscription referendum. The second campaign was even more virulent than the first, with a greater abuse of the Government's powers of censorship. Opposition to the war was increasing among trade unionists, but once again the chief antagonists were Hughes and Mannix.

'Fortunately the Roman Catholics and Irish in this country are not all blind and foolish sheep to be led to dishonour by a blatant prelate,' *The Lone Hand* said on 1 December 1917, a few weeks before the referendum. 'Remember that every No vote is a vote to dishonour Australia, to tarnish the glory that has been won by the Anzacs.'

But despite this almost constant press hostility, the people of Australia again voted against conscription, even more decisively than they had in the first referendum. This time the figures were: 'no', 1,181,747; 'yes', 1,015,159. The soldiers' vote was: 'no', 93,910; and 'yes', 103,789.

In an effort to scare Australians into joining the AIF, the Commonwealth Government commissioned thousands of lurid posters by many well-known artists and sent them to libraries, schools and householders. Most of them leaned heavily on themes of rape, mutilation and murder for inspiration. The 'Hun' was always portrayed as a bestial creature who, if he were not shooting soldiers, was murdering grandmothers and babies. Stirred by this propaganda, a 'shrieking sisterhood' of women dedicated to forcing men to join the army would persecute physically fit-looking men in the streets. Often the men they persecuted were in reserved occupations and unable to leave the country. However, the results of an intensified recruiting campaign were not encouraging. Australians were becoming thoroughly war-weary

Cheers and tears as armistice is signed

Returned soldiers quickly forgotten as life returns to normal

Crowds jammed into Martin Place, Sydney, to celebrate the signing of the armistice on 11 November, 1918. In all Australian cities there were wild celebrations that carried on late into the night

In March 1918, while the slaughter on the Western Front continued, 'Clio' reported in *Punch* that Melbourne was crowded for the Victoria Racing Club Autumn meeting and that Sydney visitors could be identified by their very low-cut bodices and extremely abbreviated skirts.

'The pleasure-as-usual brigade is having a gorgeous race carnival in more sense than one. Oysters and champagne, peaches Melba and cocktails figure largely on their menus. The contemplation of these gorged pleasure seekers gives thinking people a positive nausea,' 'Clio' said. 'Dinner parties with roulette to follow, are the order of the evening; men discuss betting prices while women rail at dress prices; but it is not considered good manners to make anyone feel uncomfortable by mentioning the Big Offensive.'

Recruiting was in the doldrums, despite new measures taken to stimulate it. Streets were placarded with a revolting poster which depicted the 'German Monster' as a horrifying gorilla dripping blood everywhere. In Adelaide, members of six ladies' choirs sang persuasively at open-air lunch-hour appeals, and on the steps of Melbourne's old GPO, 'Skipper Francis', who had been rejected

because of a deformed foot, sang his own stirring compositions, *Australia will be there* and *Keep Smiling Mother*.

On November 11 Gladys Moncrieff was playing the lead in a Sydney production of *Katinka*, when the performance was interrupted with an anouncement that the Armistice had been signed. Bells, whistles and sirens proclaimed the news and the city's streets were jammed with shouting, cheering and singing crowds.

In Melbourne, Wirths' Circus was staging a performance when Mr Phillip Wirth stepped into the ring shortly after 8 p.m. and anounced the news of the Armistice. The crowd immediately leapt to its feet and sang the National Anthem and sang it once more when Mr Tex Bailey with his 'posing horses and dogs' put on an impromptu patriotic tableau entitled 'Victory'.

Patriotic hooliganism

In the city, crowds surged into Swanston Street and started to attack tramcars in their enthusiasm. They succeeded in derailing a Carlton tramcar and crashing another through the front window of the Australian

Electric Company's office. Hundreds of people then surged into the Chinese quarter in Little Bourke Street, attacked the barricaded stores and stole firecrackers. The next day the Melbourne *Age* published an appeal by the Defence Department which urged people not to explode bungers, 'in the interests of invalided soldiers and particularly those suffering from shell shock'.

Dame Nellie Melba, who had fervently supported the war, sang at a service in Melbourne Town Hall. After a stirring rendition of the National Anthem, she sang *Home Sweet Home* as an encore, 'evidently under the stress of deep emotion', reported the Melbourne *Age*.

Similar scenes were repeated in cities and towns all over Australia. The Victorian town of Geelong was typical when, after the flag waving had ended, the Mayor moved a resolution, which was unanimously acclaimed, 'thanking God for the great victory' and congratulating the Allied nations on the success of efforts to bring about a 'triumph of righteousness over barbarism'. Everywhere people believed that the world's long agony had finally ended and a sigh of relief went up.

The climax of four years of uncertainty—relatives and friends of returned soldiers await their arrival at a reception in Sydney. But the relatives of the 60,000 dead had no one to wait for

The forgotten soldiers

Discharged soldiers found that life was not easy at the end of the war. Lloyd George, the British Prime Minister, had voiced the hope that Britain after the war should be 'a fit country for heroes to live in'. It wasn't, and neither was Australia.

In September 1919, *The Bulletin*, which had been a strong supporter of the war, attacked the growing number of street bands in cities. With typical xenophobia, it commented: 'The business in its present form was originated by the Hun, who borrowed and improved on the method of the Dago organ-grinder of half a century ago. The war freed Australia of these invaders, but it promises to give the country more and worse music.'

There were three types of 'noise makers', *The Bulletin* said. The first were bands of soldiers, 'some disabled, some fit'. Then there were civilians hoping to be mistaken for 'damaged soldiers' and finally bands of blind soldiers. The magazine commented that no man who had lost his sight in the service of his country should be forced to depend for his living on street collections.

'Can you spare a deaner (1s) Mister, for a Digger down on his luck?' became a familiar cry from men in shabby uniforms, often with the letter A, denoting Anzac, over the flash of their battalion colours. Four years after the end of the war limbless and maimed returned soldiers were eking out a bare existence. As their association pointed out: 'Able-bodied men find it hard to secure employment . . . in the labour market, with more applicants than vacancies, the war-battered are left behind.'

Two pounds a limb

Urging the Federal Government to increase pensions for disabled soldiers, the association quoted some details of compensation then paid. A man who had two arms amputated received 80s [$104.20] a week at a time when the average weekly wage was 74s 11d [$97.55]. For one arm and both legs amputated above the knee, the pension was also 80s. But if the solider had one leg amputated above the knee and the second leg amputated below the knee, he received only 42s [$54.70]. One arm and one eye; two legs and an eye; one leg, one arm and one eye; and one leg and an eye were worth 42s. But a single leg amputated below the knee was only worth 31s 6d [$41].

A happy moment for the family of a wounded Digger as they are reunited. Wounds had disabled over 90,000 soldiers by the end of the war

Australia follows Britain into war

Little excitement, but plenty of volunteers

The *Queen Elizabeth* (left) leaves Sydney Harbour as the *Queen Mary* enters, in April 1941. For the duration of the war, both these great ships, painted battleship grey, carried troops around the world. On short journeys they were packed with as many as 8000 troops, whereas in peace time they carried only some 2000 passengers. Both ships ended service with the Cunard Line in 1968

When the famous English writer H. G. Wells came to Australia in January 1939 to attend a science congress, he described Hitler as a 'certifiable lunatic' and Mussolini as a 'fantastic renegade' from socialism. He compared both to the 'criminal Caesars'.

For this, he was severely rebuked by the Australian Prime Minister, Joseph Lyons, who said his Government did not endorse Mr Wells' 'disparaging remarks', which were to be deplored.

Wells' realistic comments were little appreciated in the complacent Australia of 1939, even though Italy, Germany and Japan were obviously on the march—Italy had conquered Abyssinia in 1936, Japan invaded China in 1937, and Germany annexed Austria in 1938. The Australian coalition Government under Lyons, like the British coalition Government under Chamberlain, still believed that the aggressors could be appeased.

Wells, however, continued his 'deplorable' utterances, and warned Australia of her isolation in the Pacific. 'No longer is the British fleet your fleet,' he said. 'The so-called Japanese menace to Australia is no bogey.' Less than three months later, on 14 March 1939, Hitler's tanks rolled into Czechoslovakia, and on April 7, Italy invaded Albania. Lyons died of a heart attack on the same day, to be succeeded for 20 days by Sir Earle Page, leader of the Country Party. The United Party leader, Robert Gordon Menzies, became Prime Minister on April 26.

On the morning of September 1, Australians read in their newspapers that schoolchildren and expectant mothers were being evacuated from London, though this did not mean that war with the Germany was inevitable. That night Menzies was booked to hold a political meeting at Colac, Victoria, in the Victoria Hall—the hall where, on the eve of World War I, the Federal Labor leader, Andrew Fisher had made his historical pledge that Australia would defend the Mother Country to the 'last man and . . . last shilling'.

Menzies was dining before the meeting when he was told on the telephone that Hitler had invaded Poland. He went to the meeting and told the audience of the invasion, and returned to Melbourne at 11 p.m. to confer with some of his ministers.

Australia at war

At 9.15 on the night of September 3, he broadcast to the Australian people: 'It is my melancholy duty to inform you officially that, in consequence of a persistence by Germany in her invasion of Poland, Great Britain has declared war on her and that, as a result, Australia is now also at war. No harder task can fall to the lot of a democratic leader than to make such an announcement . . .'

'There can no be doubt that where Britain stands there stand the people of the entire British world,' he added.

Parliament was not consulted. It had been adjourned on June 16 and was not recalled until September 6.

Menzies' announcement that Australia was at war evoked no wild scenes of patriotic fervour. The mood of the nation was calm and purposeful, not excited and enthusiastic as it had been in August 1914.

Police rounded up enemy aliens for internment, amateur radio operations were prohibited, and compulsory military training was introduced for home defence. Service overseas was voluntary throughout World War II, which may account for the fact that few Australians—only 2791—applied for exemption from service because they were conscientious objectors.

First volunteers leave for Europe

Within a few months, about 20,000 men had volunteered for the Australian Imperial Force and in January 1940, the first contingent sailed for Europe from Sydney Harbour, some in giant liners such as the *Queen Mary*.

Australia's permanent army at the outbreak of war consisted of only 2800 officers and men. There was also a part-time voluntary militia of 80,000 with no obligation to serve outside Australia. By the end of the war in 1945, 993,000 persons had enlisted in the three services, more then twice as many as in World War I. Casualties—95,746, including 28,753 killed—were much fewer, however; this was because medical services were better, and there were no bloody years of trench fighting.

During the course of the war, about 550,000 men and women—one in 12 of the population of seven million—served outside Australia. At one stage, more than 52,000 women were in the women's services, and more than 160,000 men and women were engaged in munitions production.

Robert Menzies in April 1940. Menzies was Prime Minister from April 1939 until he resigned in August 1941, and was succeeded by Arthur Fadden

A window display in Melbourne urges women to join the Land Army. Women could enrol for full or part-time rural work; most were sent to help in the fruit and vegetable growing areas. Most of the recruits came from the cities, and by April 1945 there were 2364 full-time and 610 part-time volunteers

Posters urging Australians to join the forces in World War II had a businesslike almost matter-of-fact tone, quite the opposite of the hysterical posters used in World War I. By 1945 nearly one million men and women had enlisted in the three services—more than twice the number that enlisted in World War I. Casualties were, however, much lower in the second war

War comes to Australian soil

Japanese bombers strike and Darwin panics

A shell from a Japanese submarine hit this house in Rose Bay, Sydney, in June 1942. Three ships were torpedoed off the coast in the same month

Darwin was bombed many times during 1942. In the first and most severe of these raids, the office of the Administrator was destroyed, as well as many other buildings. The lack of warning of the raid and Darwin's general unpreparedness were the subject of an immediate Royal Commission

In February 1941, Arthur Fadden, the acting Prime Minister and leader of the Country Party, warned that Australia was in danger of hostile action 'near, if not upon our coast line'. But in London, Prime Minister Menzies told a London audience that we should not drift into 'a dubious and possibly dangerous atmosphere' about Japan.

The next month, the first Japanese Minister to Australia, Mr Tatsu Kawai, arrived in Canberra. He said that Australia and Japan must meet any difficulties with 'an untiring determination to reach a peaceful solution,' and rebuked John Beasley, a Labor member of the War Council (a non-party advisory board set up to formulate defence policy) for saying Australia should guard against a Japanese military move. 'In all the history of Japan, we have never launched upon a war of conquest,' he said reassuringly.

In August, Menzies, having lost the confidence of his party, resigned, and Fadden took over as Prime Minister. His government fell in October, and the leader of the Australian Labor Party, John Curtin, became the next Prime Minister.

Pearl Harbour attacked

At 5.30 am on 8 December 1941, Curtin was awakened by his secretary and told that Japan had attacked Pearl Harbour. Soon came the news that Thailand and Malaya, Guam and Wake islands had been invaded, while Manila, Shanghai, Singapore and Hong Kong had been attacked from the air. 'Australia is facing the gravest hour in her history,' Curtin said in a national broadcast.

Recognising the gravity of the hour, J. C. Williamson's cancelled a Sydney performance of *The Mikado*.

The danger of a Japanese invasion seemed very real. All civilians over 16 were issued with identity cards; the government thus had data on everyone so that they could deploy manpower to best advantage. Air-raid war-

dens were given steel helmets, and the National Emergency Services, manned by more than 300,000 male and female volunteers, were trained in first aid, fire-fighting and aircraft-spotting. Respirators were stored against possible gas attacks. Surface air-raid shelters were built in the cities, and buildings were protected from blast by sandbags or baffle walls. Householders dug slit trenches or built covered shelters, many of dubious value, in their backyards.

Air-raid drill was held in schools, offices and factories. A modified blackout, called a 'brownout', was imposed.

Confusing the Japanese

Signposts that might guide a Japanese invader were taken down—even the names of hotels were removed if they gave a clue to locations. Beaches were fortified with tank traps and barbed wire. Headlands and hills sprouted concrete pill-boxes, gun emplacements, searchlights and anti-aircraft batteries; anti-submarine booms were stretched across harbours.

Australian towns attacked by Japanese in World War II

Darwin
Drysdale
Derby
Broome
Port Hedland
Wyndham
Katherine
Millingimbi
Mossman
Townsville
Newcastle
Sydney

⬇ Bombing raid ◀ Shelling raid

The tower of Sydney's General Post Office was dismantled, and its numbered stones were put into storage—until well after the war was over and they could be presumed safe.

A top-secret 'denial squad' was trained to destroy important industrial plants and machinery in the event of a Japanese invasion. The squad stored supplies of explosives and inflammable material and learned how to light strategic fires; it cut the steel roof structures of some of Sydney's biggest factories at critical points, so that the buildings could be demolished easily.

While all these precautions were being taken in the south, it seems that Darwin, which was then an important naval, airforce and supply base, was quite unprepared for war. On the morning of 19 February 1942, a large force of Japanese bombers, dive-bombers, and fighters carried out two raids on Darwin. At least 238 persons were killed and between 300 and 400 wounded.

Five merchant ships and three warships, including the US destroyer *Peary*, were sunk; 13 other vessels were damaged or beached, including the hospital ship *Manunda*; 23 aircraft were destroyed in the air or on the ground. The RAAF station, the civil aerodrome and the port buildings were severely damaged. Scores of houses were destroyed.

Prime Minister Curtin announced the first of the raids from his bed in St Vincent's Hospital, Sydney, where he had been confined for a few days with gastritis. 'The Government has told you the truth,' he said. 'Face it as Australians.'

The Adelaide River Stakes

However, Australians were not told casualty figures, nor were they told of the looting by civilians and servicemen that followed the raids, nor of the panic flight from Darwin by most of the residents.

The looting, writes the journalist Douglas Lockwood, who was in Darwin at the time of

Midget submarines raid Sydney Harbour

Street lights were blacked out as precaution against attacks on Australian cities. Street signs were taken down to confuse invaders

On the night of 31 May 1942 three Japanese midget submarines attacked Sydney Harbour. That the attack was relatively unsuccessful was perhaps due more to the defenders' luck than to their organisation. *Midget 21*, sunk by depth-charges, was brought to the surface on the day after the raid

the bombing, was 'on such a scale that the soldiery openly consigned goods by ship to their home addresses in the south'. The goods included furniture, radios, refrigerators, cameras, stoves, pianos, clothes—even toys. The frenzied retreat to Adelaide River and the train south, 72 miles [116 kilometres] away, became known as 'the Adelaide River Stakes'.

People fled on bicycles, in pushcarts, trucks, a road grader, an icecream vendor's bicycle cart and even a sanitary cart (Darwin was without a sanitary service for five days). 'There had never been greater loss of life in a single day in Australia,' says Lockwood, 'nor, in some respects, a day of greater ignominy.'

Damning report

On March 3, less than a fortnight after the raids, Mr Justice Lowe was appointed Royal Commissioner to inquire into the circumstances surrounding the raids. His reports were not tabled in parliament until October 1945, and the transcript of the Commission was only released publicly in October 1972—with 118 of its 911 pages still censored.

The report tells a story of warnings of an impending raid received but, as at Pearl Harbour, inexplicably ignored or mis-interpreted; of woefully inadequate defences, lack of leadership and want of training to cope with an enemy attack; of breakdown in civil administration, and failure of military command to take control, leaving residents confused and leaderless; of a panic-stricken stampede for 'the bush' by airforce personnel and civilians; and of a rampage of drunkenness and looting, astonishingly led by members of the military police.

Darwin was bombed 58 more times between March 1942 and November 1943, when the last Japanese raid on the Australian mainland took place. Some raids were mere nuisances, others full-scale attacks. Nine other Australian towns were also bombed.

On 23 March 1942, a Japanese plane was

Nineteen naval ratings died when the former ferry *Kuttabul* was hit by a torpedo aimed by the submarine *Midget A*—which was never seen again—at the US cruiser *Chicago*. In the city nearby, many people slept through all the noise and gunfire of the raid, or thought it was the navy practising

launched from a big mother submarine off the New South Wales coast and reconnoitred Sydney Harbour in broad daylight undetected. The plane returned to the submarine and reported that battleships and cruisers were in the harbour.

At 2.30 a.m. on May 30, another reconnaissance flight was made from Japanese submarine *I21*, which had surfaced 56 kilometres north-east of the Heads. Its observer sketched the position of the boom across the harbour and the position of the two cruisers.

On the bright moonlight night of May 31, Sydneysiders heard the loud reports of heavy guns, the whistle of shells, the sharp crack of machine-gun fire, the muffled detonations of depth-charges. Searchlights swept the water, tracer bullets gleamed red, patrol vessels dashed here and there. Three Japanese midget submarines, launched from a convoy of five mother submarines, had entered the harbour. Each was 24 m long, and carried two 46 cm

torpedoes and a crew of two men, crouched in a space no bigger than a telephone box.

One submarine became entangled in the boom; its crew blew it up and themselves with it. The other two got through. One launched a torpedo which missed the US *Chicago* but hit an Australian naval depot ship, the converted ferry *Kuttabul*, killing 19 ratings. This submarine was not heard of again, but the third was destroyed by depth charges and later dredged up.

A week later, one of the mother submarines surfaced off Bondi and shelled Sydney's eastern suburbs between Rose Bay, Bondi and Bellevue Hill. Several houses and a block of flats were damaged. The only casualty was a refugee from Nazi Germany who, according to which newspaper one read, was either injured by flying masonry or broke his ankle leaping out of bed.

The same night another of the submarines shelled Newcastle, but caused no damage.

The Americans in Australia

A brisk trade in second-hand orchids

Fourteen days after Pearl Harbour, 4600 American troops, diverted from the Philippines, arrived in Brisbane. Five days later, Prime Minister Curtin made a historic declaration: 'Without any inhibitions of any kind I make it quite clear that Australia looks to America, free of any pangs as to our traditional links or kinship with the United Kingdom . . .

'We know . . . that Australia can go and Britain can still hold on. We are therefore determined that Australia shall not go, and we shall exert all our energies towards the shaping of a plan, with the United States as its keystone, which will give our country some confidence of being able to hold on until the tide of battle swings against the enemy.'

Australians generally acclaimed Curtin's policy as realistic, though Menzies accused him of making a great blunder in describing Australia's ties with Britain as 'merely traditional', and Billy Hughes predicted that Curtin's attitude would cause the break-up of the British Empire.

On 17 March 1942, General Douglas MacArthur, who had commanded the United States forces in the beleagured Philippines, landed at Batchelor Field, south of Darwin, after a hazardous journey through enemy lines. 'The President of the United States ordered me to break through Japanese lines and proceed from Corregidor to Australia, for the purpose, as I understand it, of organising the American offensive against Japan, a primary object of which is the relief of the Philippines,'

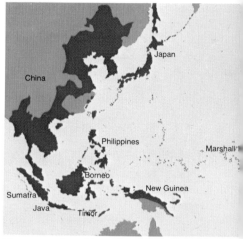

The areas coloured brown show the extent of Japanese conquest in the Pacific area during World War II. At the height of the war, the Japanese General Tojo mockingly referred to Australia as the 'orphan of the Pacific'

MacArthur told reporters in Darwin. 'I came through and I shall return.'

The casually spoken 'I shall return' became, in MacArthur's own modest words, 'the battle cry of a great underground swell that no Japanese bayonet can still'.

Simultaneously with MacArthur's arrival in Darwin, the American President sent a message to Curtin saying it would be very acceptable if the Australian government were to nominate General MacArthur as the Supreme Commander of all Allied forces in the South-West Pacific; he and his Cabinet agreed at once. Four days later, on March 21, MacArthur reached Melbourne by train from Alice Springs, and was welcomed by Australian service chiefs, a guard of honour and thousands of spectators. In his *Reminiscences*, written in 1964, MacArthur says: 'As the train puffed into Melbourne cheering thousands lined the streets in a tumultuous welcome. But heartening as the welcome was, it did not disguise the fact that a sense of dangerous defeatism had seized upon a large segment of the Australian people. The primary problem was to replace the pessimism of failure with the inspiration of success.'

A few days later MacArthur drove to Canberra to meet Curtin. 'He was the kind of man the Australians call "fair dinkum",' MacArthur wrote. 'As I rose to leave I put my arm about his strong shoulder. "Mr Prime Minister," I said, "we two, you and I, will see this through together. We can do it and we will do it. You take care of the rear and I will handle the front." '

No defeatism

Historians do not share MacArthur's view that there was a defeatist mood in Australia when he arrived. Sir Paul Hasluck, for example, has written: 'The Australian people in March 1942, as far as their opinion is revealed in the press, by their actions, and by their acceptance of the direction of their lives, were aroused by the danger as they had never been stirred before, and having been aroused, they had not turned away but were bracing themselves to grapple with their foes no matter how numerously they might come.'

Or, as the left-wing newspaper the *Australian Worker* put it: 'It is not in the Australian make-up to squib a fight, no matter how hard and bitter the conflict may be.'

Huge influx of troops

At the end of March 1942, when MacArthur became Supreme Commander, there were only 33,500 American troops in Australia. By June, however, the number of Americans in Australia had risen to 88,569, excluding sailors. At the end of September 1943, there were 120,000. By the end of the war, 862,737 Americans were serving in the South-West Pacific area, and hundreds of thousands of them had passed through Australia.

Inevitably, this great influx of American troops created tensions, which sometimes led to brawls between Americans and Australians. The American GI, with roughly twice the spending power of the Australian

digger, soon acquired the reputation of being a free-and-easy spender. Not only was he well paid, but he was also often ignorant of the value of Australian money, and would carelessly offer a handful of assorted Australian notes or coins in payment for goods or services, innocently trusting to the honesty of the recipient. The trust was not always justified. Petty crooks and black-marketeers were quick to pounce on the affluent Yank.

And Americans, because of their recklessness with money, generally got preferential treatment from shopkeepers, barmaids and taxi-drivers. Australian soldiers resented this favouritism. They also resented the success with Australian girls won by the smartly-dressed, gregarious Americans, armed with prized cartons of Camels and Lucky Strikes, local orchids, blackmarket liquor, perfume, even nylon stockings, and smooth talk.

General Douglas MacArthur was popular with Australians, who were able to buy souvenir portraits of him, such as this plaster bookend

General MacArthur, Supreme Commander of the South-West Pacific Area, with President Quezon of the Philippines in Melbourne; March, 1941

A widely-circulated story told of a GI who boasted that the Americans have pinched all the girls from the Australians, to which a digger replies laconically, 'You didn't pinch our girls. You just helped us sort them out.'

The Americans, with their pleasant habit of giving flowers to girlfriends, created a curious trade in orchids. Girls would accept these expensive blooms at night and next morning sell them back to florists at half price.

Racial tension

Some Australians disliked having black American troops in their vicinity, others disapproved of the white American's attitude towards his coloured comrades. Black troops based near Sydney were segregated in their own club, and newspaper editors were instructed by the New South Wales Publicity Censor—at the request of the US command—not to publish pictures or stories of black soldiers being entertained by white hostesses.

When American soldiers wrecked a Sydney dance hall because the manager refused their request to exclude blacks, newspapers were forbidden to mention the incident.

Office and hotel buildings all over Australia were taken over by the Americans to accommodate headquarters and administrative staffs, or servicemen on leave or in transit. A curious result of the American presence was an increase in sales of liquid carbon dioxide and dry ice, a response to the Americans' appetite for ice cream and soft drinks.

A satirist expressed a cynical view of the intentions of Americans in a verse entitled *The Passionate (US) General to His Love:*

Come live with me and be my bride,
And you'll have orchids five feet wide,
Unrationed robes from Saks to swathe in
And Chanel No. 5 to bathe in.
With sheer stockings by the mile on
You'll be my serpent of the Hylon . . .
We'll take a flat at Darlinghurst
Big enough for Randolph Hearst;
At breakfast, as we sip our Bourbon,
I'll tell you how I met Miss Durbin;
       ☆ ☆ ☆ ☆
And when I'm back in U.S.A.,
I'll send you a cable on Mother's Day!

But despite the poet's cynicism, it was estimated at the end of the war that more than 12,000 Australian girls would go to the United States with American servicemen.

'Wot'll you do, Cabby, when the Yanks go?'
'Wot'll YOU do, sister?'

From the first, American servicemen were eagerly welcomed by Australian girls. They had money and ready access to exotic goods such as Coca-Cola and Camels, which became status symbols

The first American troops to arrive on Australian soil disembarked at Brisbane on 22 December 1941 to an enthusiastic reception. Australia had declared war on Japan on December 9, and already it seemed that the USA might be a more valuable ally than Britain in the Pacific area

315

Business not quite as usual

Rationing and restrictions impose austerity

At the outbreak of war in 1939, Prime Minister Menzies advised businessmen to revive the World War I slogan 'business as usual'. But it became progressively harder to follow this homely advice as the government introduced price controls, commandeered factories for war production, restricted the sale of essential materials, and began to control imports, exports, foreign exchange transactions, even homing pigeons.

When petrol rationing was introduced in October 1940, private cars were allowed only enough petrol to travel about 25 kilometres a week. Hundreds of motorists turned to charcoal as a substitute fuel; when burned, it gave off a gas that powered the engine. Clumsy Heath-Robinsonish devices called gas producers were fitted to cars and trucks; some were hidden in the boot of the car, others were mounted behind, yet others waddled after on clumsy trailers. The average range with one filling of fuel was 160 kilometres.

Charcoal fuel was cheap—a Chevrolet sedan on a test run did 1178 kilometres at a cost of 18s 6d [$13.15]—but unpleasant. A young woman who left Adelaide as a platinum blonde arrived in Melbourne as a brunette.

Another but less popular substitute fuel

Rg. D.1

No. **V. B 114421**

COMMONWEALTH OF AUSTRALIA

RATION BOOK

JUNE, 1943, ISSUE

Name_____
(BLOCK LETTERS)

Address_____

Civilian Identity No.
Or Alien
Registration No.

Age at 13th June, 1943_____years_____months
(if not holding Civilian Identity Card or Alien Registration Certificate)

If this Book is found it must be returned at once to the
DEPUTY DIRECTOR OF RATIONING
for the State

	SUGAR	SUGAR	SUGAR	SUGAR	SUGAR	SUGAR
	D 43	D 38	D 27	D 22	D 11	D 6
	SUGAR	SUGAR	SUGAR	SUGAR	SUGAR	SUGAR
	D 44	D 37	D 28	D 21	D 12	D 5
	SUGAR	SUGAR	SUGAR	SUGAR	SUGAR	SUGAR
	D 52	D 45	D 36	D 29	D 20	D 13	D 4

The ration book and its coupons were closely guarded possessions during the war years. Friends who came to stay invariably brought a gift of coupons; soldiers on leave were issued with books so that their families could feed them

was household gas, carried on the roof of the vehicle in a balloon-like container.

Controls became more severe after Japan entered the war in 1941, and Australia moved to a total war economy. Rationing of clothing and footwear began in June 1942. When the manufacture of cloth was standardised to one thickness, angry citizens pointed out that suits worn in a sweltering Townsville summer would be of the same weight as those worn in a freezing Hobart winter.

One style of suit

More angry criticism followed the introduction in July 1942 of the 'victory suit', better known as the 'Dedman suit' after the efficient but unpopular Minister for War Organisation of Industry, Scottish-born John Johnstone Dedman. The 'Dedman suit' was restricted to one style: a single-breasted, two-button coat with no buttons on the sleeves, and cuffless trousers not more than 48 cm wide. It cost £7 7s [$104], required 38 ration coupons out of an annual allowance of 112, and was expected to last from nine to 12 months at least.

Waistcoats and double-breasted coats were banned. 'Fancy a man who has has worn a waistcoat all his life suddenly going without one,' wrote a typically indignant reader to *The Sydney Morning Herald*. Eventually, after many such protests, waistcoats were added to the 'victory suit' in December 1942.

Riding breeches, too, were banned, and patterns on socks were prohibited.

Women did not escape. They were advised to substitute leg paint for stockings. A National Council of Clothes Styling—which included the singer Gladys Moncrieff and Mrs F. M. Forde, wife of the Army Minister—fixed the maximum length for skirts and banned dolman, balloon and leg-of-mutton sleeves to save cloth. Belts could not be wider than a regulation 5 cm.

Because of the shortage of elastic, panties were to be substituted for bloomers, but *Madame Weigel's Journal* rose to the national emergency and published a pattern for bloomers that fastened just below the knee and required no elastic.

Dry cleaning of evening frocks, dinner suits, cream trousers and furnishings was prohibited. Permits to have evening frocks—which were no longer allowed to be made—and cream trousers drycleaned could be granted in 'specially urgent cases', but it was not clear what constituted special urgency.

Black market in drink

Attempts were made to reduce spending on drink. Hotel trading hours were shortened and the production of beer and other alcohol was reduced. However, black markets flourished openly, especially near military bases. At one base, a bottle of Scotch cost £9 [$240], the legal price being £1 1s 6d [$28.65].

Despite police vigilance, black market liquor flowed in seemingly inexhaustible supplies to nightclubs and cabarets, where transient servicemen were viciously exploited. Price did not matter to servicemen having

fun. The Sydney black market price for beer was 5s [$6.65] for a bottle worth 1s 7d [$2.10]; for Australian whisky or gin £3 or £4 [$79.90 or $106.50] for a bottle worth 12s 9d [$16.95] and for Scotch £5 to £6 [$133 to $160]. One American admitted spending £84 [$2237] in less than a week on liquor and girls.

Sir Paul Hasluck writes in his official history of Australia during World War II: 'Wartime experience makes it clear that beer and betting mean more than anything else in life to a considerable number of Australians.'

Substitutes for tea

Tea rationing was introduced in July 1942, the limit being 226 grams a person for five weeks. Newspapers suggested substitutes: tea-tree, as used by the early settlers, maidenhair fern, red clover blossom and lucerne. The American troops' demand for coffee led to a search for coffee substitutes. W. S. Scully, Minister for Commerce and Agriculture, proudly served at Parliament House, Canberra, a dubious beverage brewed from bran, oatmeal and treacle, which he hoped would become popular. It was never heard of again.

Tobacco was in short supply, and musk leaves, cured gum leaves and 'native' tobacco were recommended as substitutes. Sugar rationing began in August 1942. The manufacture of non-essentials was prohibited. These included bath-heaters, lawnmowers, lounge suites and some other furniture, toys, dishwashing machines, men's evening wear, garters, suspenders, horse-racing equipment, swimsuits and pyjamas. Even livestock felt the heavy hand of Dedman. Salt-licks were abolished and it was necessary to have a permit to buy salt for sheep.

Killing Father Christmas

The unfortunate Dedman became even more unpopular in November 1942 when he banned advertising that mentioned Christmas, New Year or Easter, and such expressions as 'Yuletide' and 'the festive season'. 'Austerity Amok!' said *The Sydney Morning Herald*.

Dedman explained that he was not trying to kill Father Christmas, only check 'undue commercialisation' of the bewhiskered old gentleman. Despite criticism and ridicule, he continued his austere rule. The pastrycooking trade was 'rationalised', releasing 300–400 men for other work. Pink icing on wedding-cakes was prohibited, but only in New South Wales; a pastrycook estimated that this would save about 100th part of a penny [0.09c] per cake. Christmas cakes were permitted as long as they did not look like Christmas cakes.

Confectionery, too, was rationalised; the 6479 varieties on the market were reduced to 70. Typewriters were controlled, cigars were rationed, and the export of pigeons was prohibited. Four thousand confiscated Chesterfield cigarettes auctioned by the Customs Department in Sydney realised an average of over 6d [61c] each.

Controls on servants

Another of Dedman's decrees which brought

A Melbourne maker of 'personality clothes' produced this suit made from sugar and rice bags, brands and all, to emphasise austerity fashions

Many motorists overcame petrol rationing by fitting their car with a gas producer like this. It burned charcoal, which gave off a gas that powered the engine. A gas producer was expensive to buy—from £42 to £72 [$986 to $1690]—but economical to use. One filling of charcoal fuel took a car about 160 kilometres

much angry debate was one concerning domestic servants. In December 1942 there were about 90,000 domestic servants in Australia. Dedman decreed that from 1 January, 1943, no person without a permit could employ a servant for more than 24 hours a week, unless the household included three or more children under ten years, or for a period starting six weeks before and ending six weeks after the birth of a child.

The Housewives' Association described the edict as a 'crowning act of madness to a mad career'. 'Calvinistic communism', thundered *The Sydney Morning Herald*.

But Prime Minister Curtin defended his colleague's measures: 'There is only one way to get rid of wartime restrictions,' he said. 'Get on with the war and win it.'

'Austerity dinners' for 5s

Austerity meals were announced, with maximum prices: breakfast, 3s [$3.50]; lunch, 4s [$4.70]; dinner, 5s [$5.90] Some hotels tackled the price problem by serving half portions of 3s 6d [$4.10] dishes for 2s [$2.35]. For 5s, you could have asparagus soup, roast chicken and bacon, and ice-cream Melba; or *consommé claire*, grilled sirloin steak, and *bisquit glacé*—or you could spend your entire 5s on a grilled spatchcock.

Despite all these restrictions, and the fact that taxi-hire was banned after 12.30 a.m., a squalid night-life spawned in Sydney. In November 1943, a *Sydney Morning Herald* reporter described what he had seen early one morning:

'Young girls sat on the kerbs of the city's

principal streets, with their stockingless legs posed so that their knees would support their drink-sodden heads. Some sang, others argued, all shouted to every passing car. There were couples in doorways on dustbins, and on grass plots off the pavement under the full glare of the street lights.'

On the 2 a.m. tram to Vaucluse, 'women stormed up and down the centre gangway shouting and insulting other passengers.'

Towards Christmas 1943, black-marketeers discovered the toy market, and peddled gimcrack toys, made illegally in backyard workshops. Thirty thousand Canadian

alarm-clocks arrived in Australia, but only essential workers could buy them.

However, much to the great relief of Robert Menzies and others who clung tenaciously to the style, the ban on double-breasted suits was lifted. On the other hand, it was still difficult for a man to be well dressed; umbrellas disappeared from the shops, and barbershop shaves became almost unobtainable. It was difficult, too, for women to achieve elegance, as the manufacture of many cosmetics was prohibited, as was the making of fur coats and all jewellery—except for wedding rings which were always available.

In a demonstration as part of the war loan appeal in Perth in 1942, these schoolgirls industriously converted felt hats into slippers, not even looking up to see the army band go by

The prelude to peace

Tighter rationing, strikes and censorship—then jubilation

Rationing became more severe in the latter stages of the war. Meat rationing was introduced in January 1944—680 g to 1.8 kg per week, according to the type of meat, for those over nine, and a half ration for children under nine. Poultry, rabbits, bacon, ham, sausages, tripe, liver, brains, pigs' heads, cowheels, hearts, sweetbreads and other items were not rationed at all.

Housewives would arrive at the butcher's as early as possible in the morning and simply ask: 'What can I have?' They took along their prams or pushers to carry their purchases, because home deliveries were no longer allowed.

A Sydney butcher put a notice in his window: 'Wanted—One Thousand Men to Build an Asylum for Mad Butchers!' The demand for unrationed sausages tempted some butchers to use horsemeat and it was alleged that hundreds of young horses were slaughtered in New South Wales, where the sale of horsemeat for human consumption was banned.

A confectionery manufacturer was ordered to change from making sugar pigs to 'a more useful type of confectionery'. It was explained that sugar pigs were not confectionery because they might be used as decoration. Manufacturers were also told to save labour by leaving the stripes off 'bulleyes'.

No beer for thirsty soldiers

The beer shortage worsened. Over Easter 1944, hundreds of Australian soldiers on leave from New Guinea vainly tramped the city streets in search of beer. Most hotels were closed or beerless, but there were still ample supplies on the black market.

Home-brewing, both for domestic use and for sale, became widespread, and the Customs Minister, Senator R. V. Keane, was urged to legalise it, but refused.

There was a brisk trade in adulterated or home-made liquor sold under authentic labels. Wine-drinkers were warned against poisonous 'bombo'—a 6 cm lizard had been found pickled in one bottle—and spirit-drinkers against the deadly products of backyard stills, indiscriminately labelled gin, whisky, brandy or rum. Many servicemen were rushed to hospital after drinking these concoctions.

Coal and censorship

To unite the country in the war effort, the Federal Government took over many of the powers of the states. Australian life had never before been so closely controlled. By mid-1942, the government had the power to say what every man and woman should do, whether they were in the armed services, in war industry or civilian industry.

The government made efforts to bring the trade unions fully into the war effort and to avert strikes. But stoppages continued and strikes were extensive on the New South Wales coalfields. In 1943 unauthorised stoppages of coal production were made an offence under the National Security Act. Moderate union leaders supported the government, and 400 extra men were employed on the coalfields, but disputes multiplied and production fell.

Curtin announced that there was not enough coal to meet an emergency, and imposed further restrictions on industrial and domestic use. The strikes continued and the government, despite its legislation, made elaborate efforts not to antagonise the miners. This conciliatory attitude resulted in a dispute over government censorship of newspaper reports of strikes and unrest on the New South Wales coalfields.

The government's attitude was that anything that might damage morale should be censored. The Newspaper Proprietors' Association objected to the application of this rule to military communiques and industrial disputes. By the end of 1943 the Sydney newspapers were pressing for a full investigation into censorship. *The Sydney Morning Herald* told its readers that censorship had developed 'an unblushing political character, a zest for suppression, and a fussy preoccupation with matters supposed to relate to public morale'.

Newspapers that criticised the Government's handling of the coal crisis were censored. An average of eight censorship orders a day were served on them. On 15 April 1944 the *Daily Telegraph* appeared with three blank columns—an obvious implication that the censor had cut an article. Under the censorship regulations no indication of cutting should have been made.

Seized by the police

The conflict between press and censor reached its climax on 17 April, when the *Sunday Telegraph* was seized by Commonwealth police for publishing a front page with a blank space replacing a leading article and a box reading: 'A free Press? The Great American democrat, Thomas Jefferson, said: "Where the press is free and every man able to read, all is safe".'

Next day, papers in Sydney, Melbourne and Adelaide were seized—one at gunpoint—for reproducing the banned front page of the *Sunday Telegraph*. Sydney University students led a march of about 2000 people through Sydney, protesting against political censorship and singing 'The freedom of the press lies a-mouldering in the grave'.

Newspaper proprietors appealed to the High Court, and finally after complex legal actions the censorship regulations were amended to cover only breaches of security. Strikes in the coal industry, however, continued throughout the remainder of the war.

Toasts to victory

On 8 June 1944, Australian newspapers carried the greatest story of the war—the Allies had invaded northern France. All over the country thousands listened to the BBC broadcast of the long-awaited announcement by General Eisenhower.

The European war ended on 7 May 1945, and on 8 May, VE (Victory in Europe) Day was celebrated, more or less exuberantly in Sydney, less so in other capitals. Rejoicings were damped by the knowledge that the Pacific war had still to be won. 'Wait until all the fellows are home and the men of the 8th division swing down Martin Place,' said a digger in Sydney. 'That will be the day!'

Worn out by the strain of the war years, Prime Minister Curtin died five weeks before the unconditional surrender of Japan on August 14. General MacArthur described him as 'one of the Great of the Earth'.

At 9 a.m. eastern standard time on August 15, the new Prime Minister, Joseph Chifley,

Burnt-out huts of the prisoner-of-war camp at Cowra, NSW, after 1000 Japanese attempted a mass breakout early in the morning of 5 August 1944. The prisoners, armed with baseball bats, mess knives and other improvised weapons, killed four guards and wounded three, and set fire to the barracks. In the riot, 234 Japanese died and 108 were wounded. Another 378 prisoners got through the barbed wire and scattered over the countryside. All were accounted for within nine days.

Newspaper proprietors held that wartime censorship regulations were too strict. The *Sunday Telegraph* caused an uproar with this 1944 front page

Servicemen and civilians celebrated Victory in the Pacific Day—15 August 1945—in Sydney streets. A two day holiday was declared and all over Australia, even in the tiniest settlements, people came together to celebrate the peace they hoped would never end

announced the Japanese surrender with the words, 'Fellow citizens, the war is over.' He then proclaimed a two-day holiday in celebration.

Australia enjoyed the holiday uninhibitedly. In Sydney, where an estimated million people celebrated, a naked female window-dummy was carried high above the crowd and an effigy of a Japanese soldier was burned in Martin Place. Girls traded kisses for autographs, and wore hats snatched from servicemen. The hokey-pokey was danced wildly through the city. Loudspeakers roared out *Roll out the Barrel*, competing with *Rule Britannia.*

Kerbside peddlers quickly sold out of flags, rattles and whistles. Torn-up telephone directories, income-tax, manpower and permit forms carpeted the streets. Soldiers, sailors, airmen, marines and nursing sisters formed conga lines. Equally exuberant scenes took place all over Australia. Rockets flared above Parliament House, Canberra, and in Gosford, New South Wales, crowds danced around a barbecued 270 kg bull. Pubs were shut, but tea drinkers were allowed an extra four ounces a person to help quench victory thirsts.

It was a long time before rationing ended. Sugar became unrationed in 1947, meat and clothing in 1948, butter and tea in 1950. Petrol rationing ceased in June 1949 but was reintroduced in November in all states except Tas-

mania. It was finally abolished in February 1950, after Menzies led the anti-Labor parties to a great electoral victory in December 1949.

Labor was not to regain power for 23 years. But it could look back on success in maintaining a fairly stable economy through the war years, despite the pressure of inflation—a house that cost £913 [$26,388] to build in 1939 cost £1267 [$30,027] in 1945.

The war stimulated industrial development enormously, but seriously affected primary industry. There had been an acute shortage of manpower in rural areas and supplies of phosphate from Nauru for fertiliser had been cut off. As a result of a disastrous drought in 1944-45, the harvest failed and the number of sheep in Australia fell by nearly one-third; it took 10 years for sheep figures to recover.

The end of the war did not bring an end to rationing and shortages. Butter, tea and petrol remained rationed until 1950. Hard-to-get goods were rushed when they appeared in the shops. These frantic shoppers besieged counters at Selfridges in Perth in 1949

Part two: The passing years 1901-85

Nine decades are charted year-by-year in this part of *Australia's Yesterdays*. Significant and interesting events of each year are grouped in five sequences. Four of them are concerned with Australian affairs—life in general, politics and government, the arts and entertainment and sport—and the fifth deals with events abroad.

Events at home and abroad have been included for their intrinsic interest and for the light they cast upon one another.

Some of these events have brought important social and political change, with Australia coming of age in a century of new nations and frequent conflict.

If Australia's role in international affairs has been limited, it can still claim to have established its national entity and to have contributed to the world community.

Pitt Street in Sydney was renamed the 'Avenue of Nations' for the Commonwealth celebrations in 1901. The gaily decorated French arch, with a gallic cock and an emu surmounting its twin towers, marked the northern end

The passing years 1901-10

	1901	**1902**	**1903**	**1904**

The Australian scene

1901: Commonwealth population is 3,773,801. An act restricting immigration officially introduces 'White Australia' policy. Victoria pays old age pensions. The Rocks area of Sydney cleared after outbreak of bubonic plague: first example of redevelopment in Australia. Black opals found at Lightning Ridge. 33,000 telephones in use

1902: Women given the vote. Western Australia passes the first Worker's Compensation Act. End of seven-year drought, worst in Australian history; half the nation's sheep have died. Explosion at Mt Kembla colliery kills 95 men—Australia's worst mining disaster. Cable communication begins between Australia and North America

1903: Empire Day (May 24) proclaimed as holiday. Coolgardie-Kalgoorlie water supply scheme completed. Automobile Club of Australia formed in Sydney by motorist who had been apprehended by police for leaving his stationary car unattended. Tasmanian scallop industry is beginning. Broome pearling fleet numbers 300 vessels

1904: NSW sets up Royal Commission on decline in fertility rate and effects of contraception, first such inquiry in world. Sydney gets electric street lighting. Kidnapping South Sea islanders for work in Queensland is finally halted. Cyclone destroys all Broome except stone houses. First aerial photograph in Australia taken from balloon 274 m above Sydney

Politics and government

1901: Lord Hopetoun proclaims Commonwealth. Edmund Barton forms first Federal Ministry. First Federal Parliament opened in Melbourne by Duke of York. Australian national flag flown for first time. Interstate free trade established. Australian mounted and medical units serving in Boer War. Protective tariffs introduced

1902: Lord Tennyson acts as Governor-General after Lord Hopetoun is recalled at own request. A committee reports in favour of adoption of decimal currency (plan shelved as Britain unwilling to change its system). Queensland relinquishes interest in British New Guinea. External Affairs Department attempts to curb emigration to South Africa

1903: Federal High Court constituted with Sir Samuel Griffith as Chief Justice and Sir Edmund Barton and Richard O'Connor as associate judges. Alfred Deakin becomes Prime Minister. Australia tries unsuccessfully to buy West New Guinea from Holland

1904: First Australian Labor Government formed by J. C. Watson; lasts three and a half months. Conciliation and Arbitration Act sets up means to deal with industrial disputes. Lord Northcote is Governor-General. Defence Act sets up volunteer army and gives power to conscript

Arts and entertainment

1901: J. C. Williamson and George Musgrove present opera seasons. Nellie Stewart sings *Australia* at opening of Federal Parliament. Tom Roberts commissioned to paint opening of Parliament. Norman Lindsay joins *The Bulletin*. Books: *My Brilliant Career* (Miles Franklin); *Joe Wilson's Mates* (Henry Lawson)

1902: Sydney University receives bequest to further music education (not used until 1948 when first professor of music appointed). *Art nouveau* style in decoration is the rage. House planning revolutionised: north exposure and exploitation of sun advocated. Concert tour by Melba. Book: *Bush Studies* (Barbara Baynton)

1903: Brisbane *Daily Mail* begins publication. Hans Heysen returns to Adelaide after study abroad and begins to paint the Australian landscape. Ada Crossley tours with Percy Grainger as accompanist. Books: *Such is Life* (Joseph Furphy); *Our New Selection* ('Steele Rudd'), sequel to the enormously popular *On Our Selection* (1899)

1904: Leon Brodsky forms repertory company, Australian Theatre Society, in Melbourne. Bequest of Alfred Felton enables National Gallery of Victoria to spend £100,000 [$3 million] on art works annually. Norman Lindsay's allegedly 'obscene' drawing *Pollice Verso* causes public outcry. Pianist Jan Paderewski tours Australia

Sport

1901: Australian bowlers rout English batsmen in test match in Melbourne; M. A. Noble takes 7 wickets for 17 runs, and Hugh Trumble takes a hat-trick. England all out for 61 runs. Australia wins by 229 runs

1902: W. H. Gocher forces authorities to permit surf-bathing in daylight by bathing at Manly and unsuccessfully demanding to be arrested. In test at Manchester, which Australia wins by 3 runs, Victor Trumper becomes first batsman to score 100 runs before lunch; he makes 2570 runs and 11 centuries this season

1903: Dick Cavill wins every men's freestyle event at Australian swimming championships. Hugh Trumble takes his second hat-trick in test against England in Melbourne. Automobile Club of Victoria formed and first car race in Australia held at Maribyrnong, Vic. Pioneer Motor Cycle Club (Australia's first) formed in NSW

1904: Only one Australian competitor in third modern Olympic Games held in St. Louis, USA. Acrasia wins Melbourne Cup at 14 to 1, equalling Carbine's 1890 record time of 3 min. 28¼ sec. First Australian open golf championship held at the Australian Golf Club, Botany, NSW; winner is the Hon. Michael Scott

The outside world

1901: Queen Victoria dies and is succeeded by Edward VII. President William McKinley assassinated in USA. Marconi signals letter S across Atlantic from Cornwall to Newfoundland. Trans-Siberian railway opened. First motor-cycle. Boxing legalised in England. Safety razor invented by American K. C. Gillette. Died: Verdi and Toulouse-Lautrec

1902: Boer War ends with signing of treaty at Pretoria. In Russia, peasants' revolt is suppressed and Armenian Church despoiled. Hormones are discovered. Book: *Just So Stories* (Rudyard Kipling). Drama: *Three Sisters* (Chekhov). Opera: *Pélléas et Mélisande* (Debussy). Caruso makes his first records. Died: Emile Zola; Samuel Butler

1903: First successful flight in heavier-than-air machine by Orville and Wilbur Wright at Kitty Hawk, North Carolina. Robert Scott makes first expedition into Antarctica. Lenin founds Bolshevik party in Russia. Drama: *Man and Superman* (Shaw). Died: Gauguin; Hugo Wolf; Pope Leo XIII

1904: War between Russia and Japan begins. Photoelectric cell devised. Ultra-violet lamp made. Rolls-Royce company founded. Drama: *Peter Pan* (J. M. Barrie); *The Cherry Orchard* (Chekhov); *Riders to the Sea* (Synge) Opera: *Madama Butterfly* (Puccini). Died: Dvorak; Chekhov

1905	1906	1907	1908	1909	1910
Population reaches four million. NSW reintroduces assisted immigration.'Yellow peril' propaganda spreads in Australia. Walter Rose delivers 4000 cattle 3460 kilometres in 17 months. Silver rush to field at Coppabella, NSW. Baby show in Hobart, a novelty, causes amusement. Annette Kellerman pioneers the one-piece bathing costume	Wireless telegraphy established between Victoria and Tasmania. The night shift is abolished in coal mines. Kiwi shoe polish company founded. Electric trams run in Melbourne suburbs. 'Patterson's Curse' plant first recorded in South Australia	First Industrial Workers of the World ('Wobblies') clubs established in Australia. First trunk telephone service between Sydney and Melbourne opens. Rabbit-proof fence, 1833 kilometres long, finished in Western Australia after five years. Octavius Beale publishes severe report on patent medicines. First electric stoves imported from USA	Douglas Mawson's party (on Shackleton's expedition to Antarctica) climbs Mt Erebus, 3962 m volcanic cone. Railway accident at Sunshine, Vic., kills 44, injures 431. Natural gas bore at Roma, Qld, blazes for six weeks. Wilsons Promontory, Vic, made a national park	First old age pensions paid by Commonwealth. Coal miners in NSW persist in strike despite 'Coercion Act' providing jail for strike initiators, but finally concede defeat. Ship *Waratah* vanishes on way to CapeTown with 211 passengers and crew. G. A. Taylor flies in glider; Colin Defries is airborne in powered machine	First Commonwealth bank notes issued. Railway accident at Richmond, Vic., kills nine, injures 400. Cyclone at Broome: 26 pearling vessels, 40 lives lost. John Duigan, Fred Custance, Harry Houdini, fly in aeroplanes. NSW is first state to require motor driving test. There are 14 motor cabs in Sydney; 42 in Melbourne. Mt Stromlo Observatory built
Deakin becomes Prime Minister for second time. Arbitration and Conciliation court constituted, revolutionary in its acknowledgement that trades unions are equal to employers in disputes. National Defence League begins to agitate for compulsory military training. Sugar growers seek deferment of deportation of 'kanakas'	British New Guinea renamed Papua and administration taken over by Australia. Bureau of Census and Statistics formed. Constitution is amended so that no state may independently borrow overseas money	Basic wage, 'fair and reasonable living wage', established by Mr Justice Higgins in 'Harvester' cases; amount for family of five—£2 2s [$62] MPs' salaries raised from £400 to £600 [$11,500 to $17,000] a year. After Imperial Defence Conference in London, Deakin announces Australia is to have its own fleet. Parliament allocates £20,000 [$600,000] for survey of trans-Australia railway	Canberra chosen as site of national capital. New protection policy almost doubles previous customs and excise duties and introduces imperial preference. Andrew Fisher (Labor) is Prime Minister. Lord Dudley is Governor-General. US fleet visits Australia. Federal Weather Bureau set up	Deakin is Prime Minister for third time at head of 'fusion' Government of non-Labor parties. New Defence Act provides for compulsory military training. First federal/state financial conference held in Hobart. Sir George Reid appointed first High Commissioner to London	Andrew Fisher is Labor Prime Minister. Lord Kitchener reports on Australian defence; advocates army of 80,000 and establishment of a military college. Admiral Sir Reginald Henderson arrives to advise on naval defence. *Yarra* and *Parramatta*, first vessels built for RAN, arrive. First attempt to extend federal powers by referendum defeated
Widespread use of concrete as structural building material begins in Australia. First French Impressionist painting bought by an Australian gallery (Melbourne). An 'Exhibition of Living Pictures' showing shearing, buckjumping, street and other scenes, screened at Government House, Hobart. Book: *The Little Black Princess* (Mrs Aeneas Gunn)	A. G. Stephens resigns as editor of *The Bulletin's* literary Red Page. Melbourne Symphony Orchestra formed: first permanent orchestra in Australia. C. J. Dennis and others in Adelaide publish satirical weekly magazine *The Gadfly*. Film: the world's first full-length feature, *The Story of the Kelly Gang*. Book: *Fact'ry 'Ands* (Edward Dyson)	Adelaide Amateur Repertory Company established. *The Bulletin* launches *The Lone Hand*, general and cultural magazine. Dame Clara Butt tours Australia; Melba gives series of concerts. Mitchell Library founded in Sydney (opens 1910). Arthur Streeton has large and successful show in Melbourne	Prime Minister Deakin founds Commonwealth Literary Fund to support aged and infirm authors and assist impoverished authors to continue writing. Books: *We of the Never Never* (Mrs Aeneas Gunn); *Maurice Guest* ('Henry Handel Richardson')	Japanese-designed prefabricated house displayed in Brisbane influences architects. C. J. Dennis' magazine *The Gadfly* folds. Melba gives series of concerts. Painter Charles Conder dies in London. The first science-fiction film: Franklyn Barrett's *A Message from Mars*. Book: *Satyrs and Sunlight: Silvarum Libri* (Hugh McCrae)	First fully steel-framed building in Australia, Nelson House, Sydney, constructed at cost of £12,758 [$283,000]. Australian painters begin to be influenced by Cubism and Cézanne. Film: *Heroes of the Cross* directed by J. H. Perry, sequel to *Soldiers of the Cross* made 1899. Sydney *Sun* begins. Book: *A Little Bush Maid* (Mary Grant Bruce)
R. W. Heath is Australia's first tennis champion. Australia and New Zealand first enter a team in the Davis Cup tennis competition. Annette Kellerman swims six kilometres in Yarra River in 1 hr 48 min	Poseidon, at 4 to 1, wins Melbourne Cup after winning AJC Derby, Caulfield Cup and VRC Derby, a record still unbroken. Bondi Surf Bathers' Life Saving Club is formed, the first of its kind. Champion rider Lance Skuthorpe brings to a standstill buck-jumper Bobs, which has tossed all 800 people who have tried to ride him before	Norman Brookes is first non-British player to win Wimbledon tennis championship, and partners Anthony Wilding of New Zealand to win the Davis Cup for Australasia. Rugby league begins in Australia; first players guaranteed 10s [$14] a day plus 7s 6d [$10.65] a day on tour. First women's rowing club formed in Sydney	Australia wins one gold medal at London Olympic Games—for rugby union. Canadian Tommy Burns fights American Jack Johnson for world heavyweight boxing championship in Sydney and loses when police stop fight. First Australian surf carnival held at Manly. Davis Cup final in Australia for first time; Australasia beats USA 3-2. Diabolo becomes fashionable game	Building of hotel at Kosciusko stimulates skiing. First reliability trial for power boats held—Sydney to Newcastle and back. Dan Cooper shears 316 sheep in one day with machine shears	Frank Beaurepaire tours Europe, competing in 48 races against the best swimmers in the world over distances from 100 yards to one mile (91 metres to 1.6 kilometres), and wins all of them. In Johannesburg, Australian professional runner Jack Donaldson runs 100 yards in 9⅗ sec; record stands until 1948
Treaty of Portsmouth ends Russo-Japanese war; Russia concedes territories to Japan. 'Bloody Sunday' massacre of workers in Russia and mutiny on battleship *Potemkin;* Tsar Nicholas II crushes revolution but allows creation of a parliament. Norway becomes independent of Sweden. Music: *The Merry Widow* (Lehar); *Salome* (Richard Strauss)	San Francisco devastated by earthquake and fire. First Labour MPs elected in England. Simplon rail tunnel between Switzerland and Italy (world's longest) opened. Zuider Zee drainage scheme begun. Vitamins discovered. Book: first volume of *The Forsyte Saga* (Galsworthy). Died: Ibsen; Cézanne; Pierre Curie	New Zealand becomes a dominion. USA restricts Immigration. Lenin exiled from Russia. Baden-Powell founds the Boy Scouts. Colour photography invented by Auguste Lumière. Bakelite invented. Cubist exhibition in Paris. Opera: *Elektra* (R. Strauss). Drama: *Major Barbara* (Shaw); *Playboy of the Western World* (Synge). Died: Edvard Grieg	Belgium annexes the Congo. The King and Crown Prince of Portugal murdered. 'Young Turks' revolution in Turkey. About 75,000 people die in earthquake in southern Italy. The Geiger counter is invented. Books: *The Old Wives' Tale* (Arnold Bennett); *The Wind in the Willows* (Kenneth Grahame). Died: Rimsky-Korsakov	Union of South Africa formed. Old-age pensions for people over 70 introduced in England. Admiral Robert Peary reaches North Pole at sixth attempt. Louis Blériot crosses English Channel in mono-plane. Henry Ford introduces his Model T car. Girl Guides founded. Diaghilev's Russian Ballet visits Paris. Music: *Symphony No. 9* (Mahler)	Edward VII is succeeded by George V. Braganza dynasty overthrown in Portugal, which becomes a republic. First roller bearings produced. Music: *The Firebird* ballet (Stravinsky). Books: *Clayhanger* (Bennett); *Howard's End* (E. M. Forster); *Mr Polly* (H. G. Wells). Died: Mark Twain, Tolstoy and Florence Nightingale

The passing years 1911-20

	1911	**1912**	**1913**	**1914**

The Australian scene

1911
First federal census shows population 4,455,005. Mawson leads expedition to Antarctica; he covers 160 kilometres alone on foot to reach base after losing two companions. First pilot's licence in Australia issued to Sydney dentist W. E. Hart. Opals found at Coober Pedy. University of Queensland opens in Brisbane. Hobble skirts in fashion

1912
First free university in British Empire opens in Western Australia. Francis Birtles and S. R. Ferguson make first motor car crossing of Australia; top speed of their 7 kW Brush was 32 km/h. Australian Inland Mission founded by Rev. John Flynn. Work on Murrumbidgee irrigation begins. First advertising agency formed. Perth gets electric street lights

1913
First Commonwealth postage stamps issued. Outbreak of smallpox in NSW. H. C. Hawker of Australia sets world air speed record of 148 km/h at Farnborough Air Show. King George V lays foundation stone of Australia House in London. First branches of Workers' Educational Association founded

1914
Severe nation-wide drought; wheat harvest much reduced. All exports to and from Germany cease; censorship imposed. Probate tax introduced. First Coles store opens, in Collingwood, Melbourne. Air mail service between Sydney and Melbourne begins. Correspondence schools originated in Victoria

Politics and government

1911
Commonwealth takes over control of Northern Territory from South Australia. Lord Denman is Governor-General. Commonwealth Bank set up despite strong opposition in Parliament. Duntroon Military College founded. First Commonwealth wireless station built. HMAS *Warrego* launched. Compulsory cadet drill begins; thousands of boys fail to enrol

1912
Maternity allowance of £5 [$110] per child first distributed. Restrictions on old-age pensions eased. Water Conservation and Irrigation Commission formed

1913
Capital is named Canberra; foundation stone laid by Lord Denman, Prime Minister Fisher and Home Affairs Minister King O'Malley. Norfolk Island becomes Australian territory. Second referendum on extension of federal powers fails narrowly. Joseph Cook becomes Prime Minister. HMAS *Australia* commissioned. Jack Lang enters NSW Parliament

1914
Double dissolution of Parliament. Fisher becomes Prime Minister. War declared on Germany. Australian navy transferred to British command. HMAS *Sydney* conquers German cruiser *Emden* off Cocos Islands. Australian Flying Corps formed. Australia seizes German southwest Pacific territories. ANZAC corps formed under Sir William Birdwood

Arts and entertainment

1911
Melbourne Repertory Company founded—to produce 57 plays in next seven years. 'Bungalow' houses built. Melba tours Australia with opera company including John McCormack. Raymond Longford produces his first feature film *A Fatal Wedding*, starring Lottie Lyall. Books: *Jonah* (Louis Stone); *Mateship* (Henry Lawson)

1912
Building of Taronga Zoo begins in Sydney. Walter Burley Griffin wins prize for design of new city Canberra. Australia's first 'skyscraper', Culwulla Chambers, 52 m high, is being erected. Australasian Film Studio built by Couzens Spencer in Sydney. Bert Bailey stars in play *On Our Selection*

1913
Russian Imperial Ballet tours Australia. Raymond Longford's film *Australia Calls* stars W. E. Hart, Australia's first licensed pilot. J. C. Williamson dies. Books: *Backblock Ballads* (Henry Lawson); *A Curate in Bohemia* (Norman Lindsay)

1914
Conservatorium of Music established in Sydney with Belgian Henri Verbrugghen as director. Australian tours by Harry Lauder and W. C. Fields (as a juggler). Stiffy (Nat Phillips) joins Mo (Roy Rene). C. J. Brennan publishes his *Poems*. Film: Raymond Longford's *The Silence of Dean Maitland*, with Lottie Lyall

Sport

1911
Second Kangaroos rugby league team tours England and wins 'Ashes' in test series, a feat not repeated until 1963. New South Wales Trotting Club buys Epping racecourse (later Harold Park) from Metropolitan Rugby Union. The Australasian Professional Golf Association is founded

1912
At Stockholm Olympic Games Fanny Durack wins 100 metres freestyle; men's swimming team wins Australia's other gold medal; electric timer first used. Australia's first air race won by W. E. Hart from 'Wizard' Stone, the only other competitor. T. J. Matthews takes two hat-tricks in one test (only time ever done) against South Africa

1913
For the second of three times—others were in 1912 and 1914—Bill Longworth wins all NSW and Australian swimming titles from 182 metres to 1.6 kilometres. 'Snowy' Baker, owner of Sydney Stadium, organises boxing to conform with British regulations. Middleweight Jerry Jerome first Aboriginal national boxing champion

1914
Norman Brookes wins Wimbledon men's singles, and doubles with Anthony Wilding of New Zealand. Kingsburgh sets new record of 3 min. 26 sec. in winning Melbourne Cup. Rugby league test at Sydney nicknamed 'Rorke's Drift' because of courage of the English team; they won 14-6 though at one stage they had only nine of 13 men playing

The outside world

1911
China's Manchu dynasty is overthrown; a republic is proclaimed; an edict abolishes men's pigtails. Amundsen reaches South Pole. British members of Parliament paid for first time. War between Italy and Turkey. Suffragette riots in London. Music: *Der Rosenkavalier* (Richard Strauss); *Alexander's Ragtime Band* (Irving Berlin). Died: Mahler; W. S. Gilbert

1912
Captain Robert Scott reaches South Pole; dies on return journey. SS *Titanic* strikes iceberg and sinks; 1513 drown. War in Balkan states. Italy and Turkey sign peace treaty. Woodrow Wilson becomes US President. Stainless steel and Cellophane are invented. Charles Pathé produces first news film. Music: *Petrushka* (Stravinsky). Died: Strindberg; Massenet

1913
Further war in Balkan states ended by Turkey conceding control of her European territories. First ship passes through Panama Canal. Henry Ford introduces the assembly line. More suffragette agitation in Britain. Books: *Sons and Lovers* (D. H. Lawrence). Music: *The Rite of Spring* (Stravinsky). The foxtrot becomes popular.

1914
World War I erupts. USA and Italy declare neutrality. Germany capitulates in New Guinea. Pope Benedict XV is elected. British protectorate over Egypt is declared. Panama Canal opens. Book: *Dubliners* (Joyce). Music: *London Symphony; The Lark Ascending* (Vaughan Williams)

1915	1916	1917	1918	1919	1920
Drought continues. BHP begins making steel at Newcastle. NSW introduces six o'clock hotel closing after referendum; Victoria, South Australia, Tasmania follow suit. Federal income tax introduced. NSW is first state to employ women police. NSW Government sets up an aviation school. Census of wealth and income and service-age males	Hughes Government establishes national merchant shipping line with 15 steamships bought in England. Aliens required to report weekly to police. Miners strike; Hughes intervenes and rules in favour of strikers. 'Wobblies' imprisoned for sedition. Tasmania has hydro-electric power and is first to have daylight saving	Railway from Port Pirie to Kalgoorlie completed. South Australia bans teaching of German; closes 49 Lutheran schools. Railway workers' strike leads to paralysis of ports and transport and general strike involving some 75,000 men. Wonnangatta murders in Victoria: station manager and cook, found nine months later, shot; mystery never solved	Labor Party protests to Prime Minister about wartime censorship. Population reaches 5 million. Victims of world influenza epidemic quarantined on arrival; Australia wards off the disease this year. Names of many towns changed from German to English. First wireless message received from London	Influenza epidemic sweeps Australia; 10,000 die. War Service Homes scheme begins, encouraging move to suburbs. Victorian bushfires kill 71. Huge rises in price of wool. First public demonstration of broadcasting in Australia by Ernest Fisk. Strikes by seamen and Broken Hill miners. Ross and Keith Smith win London to Darwin air race in 27 days 20 hours	Returned Services League formed. Wholesale prices now double 1914 levels. Harry ('Possum') Lasseter leads expedition to find 'lost reef' of gold and disappears. Ten 'Wobblies' convicted in 1916 released after three separate inquiries. Prickly pear infests 50 million acres. Qantas formed by Hudson Fysh and P. J. McGinness
Anzac force lands at Gallipoli. Only two casualties in retreat from peninsula but over 10,000 killed in campaign. Australians mobilised total 250,000. Department of Navy created. First war loan raises over £13 million [$288 million]. Billy Hughes becomes Prime Minister after Fisher resigns to become High Commissioner in London	First Australian flying unit leaves for Egypt, by ship. Australian troops train in Egypt for French campaign. Australian Light Horse in Syria and Palestine. After bitter debate, a referendum rejects conscription; Hughes expelled from Labor Party and 23 members follow him out; he retains office as National Labor Prime Minister	More harsh dissension over conscription, decisively rejected by a second referendum; Hughes resigns, is re-elected. Australian Flying Corps in Palestine and France. At Passchendaele and Ypres 38,000 Australians killed. Luxuries Board bans import of non-essential goods. Entertainment tax imposed, also heavy wartime profits tax	Earle Page founds Country Party. Labor Party adopts abolition of state parliaments as policy. Sir John Monash succeeds Sir William Birdwood in command of Australian forces in France. By end of war, 329,000 Australians have served overseas; 59,330 killed; 152,171 wounded; 66 receive Victoria Cross. Mobs in Darwin demonstrate against NT administration	Hughes negotiates aggressively for Australia at Versailles peace conference and gains mandate over former German south-west Pacific territories including New Guinea. Australia becomes founding member of League of Nations. Referendum to increase federal powers fails. King O'Malley defeated in election; retires from politics	Hugh Mahon first and only member expelled from Federal Parliament — for calling British Empire 'bloody and accursed'. Hughes defeats maritime strike; his popularity steadily decreases. Visit by Prince of Wales. MPs' salaries raised to £1000 [$13,000]. Australian Communist Party founded. Lord Forster is Governor-General. Edmund Barton dies
Triad, monthly literary periodical, first published. Melba starts a singing school in Melbourne. Post-Impressionist paintings exhibited in Sydney by Grace Cossington-Smith and Roland Wakelin judged 'daring'. Books: *The Pioneers* (Katherine Susannah Prichard); *The Songs of a Sentimental Bloke* (C. J. Dennis)	Sydney Zoo moves to Taronga Park with 406 animals, including 329 birds. Sydney Ure Smith's magazine *Art in Australia* first issued. Roland Wakelin's picture *Down the Hills to Berry's Bay* stirs interest. Books: *The Moods of Ginger Mick* (C. J. Dennis); *A Short History of Australia* (Ernest Scott)	First national conference of town planners. Frank Hurley is appointed official war film photographer. Max Meldrum founds 'tonal realism' art school in Melbourne. Books: *Australia Felix*, first volume of Henry Handel Richardson's trilogy *The Fortunes of Richard Mahoney*; *Saltbush Bill* ('Banjo' Paterson)	Melba created Dame Commander of the British Empire. *Smith's Weekly* begins. Post-Impressionist movement begins in Melbourne with work of William Frater and Arnold Shore. Books: *Snugglepot and Cuddlepie* by May Gibbs; *The Magic Pudding* by Norman Lindsay	J. F. Archibald, founder of *The Bulletin*, dies. By his bequest the Archibald Prize, for a portrait of a distinguished Australian, is instituted. Post-Impressionist painting attacked by influential teacher Julian Ashton. Film: Raymond Longford's *The Sentimental Bloke*. Films are shown in 750 cinemas and theatres in Australia	J. C. Williamson Theatres merges with Tait Brothers organisation. Royal Commission into planning of Canberra leads to resignation of Walter Burley Griffin as director of design and construction. *The Home* magazine started by Sydney Ure Smith. Books: *Ways and Means* ('Furnley Maurice'); *Colombine* (Hugh McCrae)
Duke Kahanamoku introduces surfboard riding to Australia at Freshwater beach, NSW. First state championship for surf lifesavers held at Bondi. R. Lewis on Patrobus wins Melbourne Cup: his second of four wins out of 38 mounts in this race. Sydney Rugby Union suspends competition because of war; rugby league continues	Les Darcy becomes Australian heavyweight boxing champion; he successfully defends this and his (unrecognised) world middleweight titles in nine fights this year. First gliding club is formed at Granville, NSW	Les Darcy dies from blood poisoning in US after failing to get a fight there. Automatic totalisator first used in Australia, at Randwick. Westcourt wins Melbourne Cup by short half-head, 4 to 1. Annette Kellerman, starring in film, *Daughter of the Gods*, dives 28 m from a cliff into Pacific—a world record dive by a woman	Alick Wickham dives into the Yarra River from 62.7 m, 5.9 m higher than Sydney Harbour Bridge. The cricket over is increased from six to eight balls. Nightwatch, at 12 to 1, breaks record by winning Melbourne Cup in 3 min. 25¾ sec	Australasia retains Davis Cup in first competition since 1914; Norman Brookes and Gerald Patterson win doubles 6-0, 6-0, 6-2, clearest win in Davis Cup history. Brookes beats Patterson in first all-Australian Wimbledon singles final. Australian Imperial Force rowing eight wins Royal Henley Peace Regatta blue ribbon event; their trophy becomes the King's Cup	No gold medals for Australia at Olympic Games in Antwerp. Arch Smith sets 160 km/h world speed record for motorcycles at Sellicks Beach, SA. Poitrel wins Melbourne Cup carrying 63.5 kg. R. Spears wins world professional sprint cycling championship. First national handball championship
Fighting all over Europe continues. Italy enters war on side of Allies. Sinking of *Lusitania*, with loss of 1198 lives, brings USA to brink of war with Germany. Poison gas first used, by Germany. Gallipoli campaign fails. Science: Einstein's general theory of relativity; theory of continental drift. Film: *Birth of a Nation*. Died: Keir Hardie; W. G. Grace	Battles of Verdun, Ypres, Isonzo, Somme and Jutland. British first use tanks. Portugal enters war on Allies' side. Lloyd George becomes British Prime Minister. Easter rebellion in Dublin. Treatment of war casualties leads to development of plastic surgery. Book: *Portrait of the Artist as a Young Man* (Joyce). Died: Henry James; Lord Kitchener	USA declares war on Germany, and so do Cuba and China. Battle of Passchendaele. Germany intensifies submarine attacks. Russian revolution begins at St Petersburg; Lenin returns from exile to lead Bolsheviks. By Balfour Declaration Britain favours Palestine as home for Jews. Died: Degas; Rodin; 'Buffalo Bill' Cody	Second battles of Somme and Marne. Germans shell Paris from 120 kilometres away. Armistice between Germany and Allies is signed. Royal family is executed in Russia. Influenza kills 20 million people. Traffic lights installed in New York. Music: *Il Trittico* (Puccini); Original Dixieland Jazz Band tours Europe. Died: Debussy	Peace conference in Paris adopts principle of League of Nations. Captured German fleet scuttled at Scapa Flow, Scotland. Austrian empire broken up. Alcock and Brown make first direct flight across Atlantic. Mussolini founds Fascist Party in Italy. Nazi movement is born in Germany. Died: Renoir; Adelina Patti	Prohibition and slump in USA. League of Nations comes into being with headquarters at Geneva; USA not represented. The Ottoman Empire of Turkey is broken up. Earthquake kills 180,000 in China. First public broadcasting stations open in USA and England. Women receive vote nationwide in USA. Mary Pickford marries Douglas Fairbanks

The passing years 1921-30

	1921	**1922**	**1923**	**1924**
The Australian scene 	Second census shows population 5,436,794. Mining disaster at Mt Mulligan, Qld; 76 killed. Airmail service begins between Geraldton and Derby—1948 kilometres. South Australian Motor Association succeeds in having speed limits raised to 32 km/h in city, 30 in country. Sugar-cane harvester patented. Bobbed hair—the Eton crop—begins to be smart	Queensland is first state to abolish death penalty. First lock on Murray River opened at Blanchetown, SA. Smith Family founded. World's first Legacy Club founded in Hobart. Country Women's Association formed—NSW branch is first	John Miles accidentally discovers silver-lead areas at Mt Isa. Serious riots and looting in Melbourne when police strike for five days; public is antagonised and Government pressure defeats strikers. Last horse-drawn trams run in Melbourne. Construction of Sydney Harbour Bridge begins. Waists on women's dresses descend to the hips	S. Goble and I. McIntyre fly round Australia in 44 days. First commercial production of rice in Australia, at Leeton, NSW. Last Cobb and Co. coach runs in Queensland. Order of the Star of the East builds amphitheatre at Balmoral, Sydney, to view second coming of Christ; seats cost £5-£100 [$65-$1325]. First Woolworths store opens in Australia
Politics and government 	Labor Party introduces creed of 'socialisation' of industry, production, distribution and exchange as major policy. Tariff Board is created to advise Government and prevent exploitation of consumers. First Australian woman MP, Mrs Edith Cowan, elected to lower house of Western Australia	Quarterly adjustments to basic wage in accordance with cost of living variations introduced. Northern Territory first represented in Federal Parliament. Queensland abolishes Legislative Council	Hughes resigns as Prime Minister. Stanley Bruce heads party led by coalition of Nationalists and Country Party. Work begins on Parliament House, Canberra. Federal Government guarantees price of cotton; acreage of cotton increases	HMAS *Australia* scrapped and five submarines broken up to conform with decision to limit naval armaments. First land leases sold in Canberra. British Government proposes loan of £34 million [$448 million] to increase opportunities for settlers from Britain. Wine export bounty greatly increases wine sales abroad
Arts and entertainment 	Leslie Wilkinson becomes Australia's first professor of architecture, at Sydney University. Gladys Moncrieff stars in *The Maid of the Mountains*. *The Lone Hand* ceases publication. Books: first two volumes of official Australian war history by C. E. W. Bean; *A Book for Kids* (C. J. Dennis); *Black Opal* (K. S. Prichard)	Henry Lawson receives state funeral. Louis Esson and Vance Palmer form Pioneer Players in Melbourne to foster Australian drama. Sculptor Bertram Mackennal is first Australian artist to become member of Royal Academy. 'American' or 'Californian' bungalow style in full vogue. *Sun News-Pictorial* begins in Melbourne	Regular broadcasting begins. Adelaide *News* starts publication. Exhibitions: Australian art at Royal Academy, London; European art in Sydney and Melbourne. First edition, by Jack Lindsay and Kenneth Slessor, of *Poetry in Australia*. D. H. Lawrence visits Australia and writes *Kangaroo*, hailed as 'true picture of Australia'	Singers Evelyn Scotney and Elsa Stralia make tours of Australia. Dame Nellie Melba presents opera company which stages 16 works; her 'farewell' appearance is first opera broadcast. Arthur Streeton returns to Australia after 16 years. Book: Nettie Palmer's *Modern Australian Literature*, one of the first collections of criticism
Sport 	Australian cricket team captained by Warwick Armstrong wins all five tests in series against England. Arthur Mailey takes 9 wickets for 121 runs in fourth test at Melbourne, and takes 36 wickets in the four tests for which he is chosen. First national diving championship held. Kangaroos rugby league team tours England; loses 'Ashes' but is first to make profit	Gerald Patterson wins men's singles at Wimbledon. Jack Chalmers and Frank Beaurepaire receive the first two Meritorious Awards in Silver for rescue of a swimmer attacked by a shark at Coogee	New Zealand and Australia now compete separately for Davis Cup. Bitalli wins Melbourne Cup in record-equalling time of 3 min. 24½ sec. Crowd of 47,000 watches China play Australian soccer team at Sydney Showground. South Australia forms first state table tennis association	'Boy' Charlton wins one of Australia's three gold medals at the Paris Olympic Games. He defeats world champion Arne Borg over 200, 400 and 800 metres at Sydney Domain baths in world record times. Speedway racing is invented at West Maitland, NSW. The Brownlow Medal for best and fairest Victorian Football League player is first awarded
The outside world 	French troops occupy German towns in Ruhr after Germany fails to make first war reparations payment. Economic crisis in Germany. USA, Britain, Italy, France and Japan sign treaty at Washington to limit naval armaments. Night clubs proliferate in Europe and USA. Film: *The Kid* (Chaplin). Died: Caruso; Saint-Saens	Heavy fighting in Ireland; British troops leave after treaty is signed creating Irish Free State. Turks defeat Greeks in war. Mussolini leads Fascist 'march on Rome' and forms government. Tutankhamen's tomb found. *The Reader's Digest* founded in New York. First Austin 7 produced. Literature: *The Waste Land* (Eliot); *Ulysses* (Joyce); *Babbitt* (Lewis)	USSR is formed by confederation of 14 states. Economic crisis deepens in Germany. Earthquake wrecks Tokyo and Yokohama; 143,000 die. Kemal Ataturk elected President of Turkey. First F. A. Cup final at Wembley. *Time* magazine first issued. London's Big Ben chimes first broadcast. Music: *Facade* (Walton). Died: Sarah Bernhardt	First British Labour Government, under Ramsay MacDonald, lasts nine months. France agrees to evacuate Ruhr. A talking picture system and the first insecticide are developed. Music: *Rhapsody in Blue* (Gershwin). Books: *A Passage to India* (E. M. Forster). Drama: *St. Joan* (Shaw). Died: Lenin; Puccini; Joseph Conrad

1925	1926	1927	1928	1929	1930
First exports of Australian sugar. Population reaches 6 million. 'Big Brother' immigration scheme for boys from Britain founded by Sir Richard Linton. Briquettes first produced. Prickly pear infests 26 million hectares. Brisbane and Sydney joined by uniform-gauge railway. Short skirts and exposed knees scandalise some	Auction sales of wool begin. Council for Scientific and Industrial Research set up. Sydney Mint closes. Sydney *Guardian* conducts first 'Miss Australia' quest. Fires in Victoria last six weeks; death toll 31. Western Australian goldfields murders: two detectives shot by gold stealers. Women begin to wear trousers for first time	Lang Government in NSW introduces Australia's first child endowment scheme. Australian Council of Trades Unions (ACTU) formed. Beam wireless transmission begins. Liner *Tahiti* rams Sydney harbour ferry; 40 die. 'Squizzy' Taylor and another gangster shoot each other dead in Melbourne	Flying Doctor Service begins. Charles Kingsford Smith and Charles Ulm cross Pacific by air in ten days. Bert Hinkler flies solo from London to Darwin in 129 hours. First traffic lights in Australia installed at Collins/Swanston Streets, Melbourne. Bottled milk first available in NSW	Depression begins. Police fire on striking miners at Rothbury, NSW; one dies, over 50 seriously hurt. First train runs from Adelaide to Alice Springs. Export of merinos banned. Dam bursts and 340 million litres of water flood Derby, Tasmania; 14 die. First Russian Orthodox church built, in Brisbane. Over 500,000 telephones now connected	Australia proportionately worse hit by unemployment than Germany: 125,000 out of work in Sydney. Radio-telephone links with Britain inaugurated and all mainland states linked by telephone trunk lines. World's first milk bar opened in Sydney by Clarence and Norman Burt. Amy Johnson is first woman to fly from England to Australia (19½ days)
Voting in federal elections becomes compulsory. Jack Lang becomes Premier of NSW. Bruce-Page Government returned, campaigning against communist militancy in unions. Lord Stonehaven is Governor-General. Rural credits section of Commonwealth Bank established to aid primary producers	Referendum to extend federal powers over arbitration and essential services fails. Lang Government fails to abolish NSW Legislative Council. Central Australia, separate territory of the Commonwealth, administered from Alice Springs (for next five years). At Imperial Conference in London dominion status is defined: all colonies to be equal	Dame Nellie Melba leads singing of the national anthem when Parliament House, Canberra, is opened by Duke of York. Seat of government transferred from Melbourne to Canberra. Voting becomes compulsory in Victorian state elections	Referendum to set up Loan Council approved: Commonwealth takes over states' debts. Visit by British economic mission to report on development of Australian resources. Attempt to reform arbitration and conciliation raises storms of protest. Sir John Salmond of the RAF invited to advise on Australia's air force	Australia's overseas debt alarmingly high. Export prices fall. Bruce-Page Nationalist-Country Party coalition Government defeated over amendments to conciliation and arbitration system; Bruce is first sitting Australian Prime Minister to lose own seat. J. H. Scullin's Labor Party returned to power. Compulsory military training abolished	Treasurer E. G. Theodore forced to resign by Royal Commission report on Mungana Mines scandal. Tariff embargoes and import rationing imposed. Export prices fall to half 1928 levels. Visit by Sir Otto Niemeyer of Bank of England, who advises severe deflationary measures
Bernard Heinze appointed to Melbourne University's chair of music. Poet C. J. Brennan dismissed from Sydney University for drunkenness and immorality. Spanish Mission style of architecture introduced. Amelita Galli-Curci and Fritz Kreisler tour Australia. Lottie Lyall dies at 34. Over 60 films produced this year; there are now 1200 cinemas in Australia	Anna Pavlova receives great adulation on tour; Robert Helpmann, aged 17, joins company as student. Dame Clara Butt, Toti dal Monte, Chaliapin tour. 'Contemporary Group' artists including Wakelin, De Maistre, Cossington-Smith, Lambert, formed in Sydney. *Canberra Times* begins publication. Charles Chauvel produces his first film, *Moth of Moonbi*	Tours by pianist Jan Paderewski, violinist Jascha Heifetz, soprano Frances Alda. Fourth film version of *For the Term of His Natural Life*. Books: *An Australasian Anthology*, historical collection of verse edited by P. Serle; *My Crowded Solitude* (Jack McLaren)	*The Bulletin* literary prize established. Dame Nellie Melba gives farewell performances in opera with J. C. Williamson touring opera company. Gonzales Opera Company also tours Australia. Painter John Longstaff knighted. Books: *Up the Country* by 'Brent of Bin Bin' (Miles Franklin); *The Montforts* (Martin Boyd); *Wanderings in Wild Australia* (W. B. Spencer)	Second tour by Pavlova. Visit of Arthur Benjamin, Australian composer and pianist. First radio broadcast of an orchestral concert. *Australian Quarterly* begins publication. Books: the first 'Boney' novel, *The Barrakee Mystery* (Arthur Upfield); *A House Is Built* (M. Barnard Eldershaw); *Coonardoo* (K. S. Prichard)	Doris Fitton launches Independent Theatre in Sydney. An entertainment tax means increased theatre seat prices and theatrical unemployment. Sydney *Daily Telegraph* begins. Australia's first talkie film, *The Cheaters*, produced. Books: *Here's Luck* (Lennie Lower); *Redheap* (Norman Lindsay)—published in England, banned in Australia
Windbag wins Melbourne Cup in record time of 3 min. 22¾ sec. The Australian Gold Cup for polo is instituted. Maroubra speedway, Sydney, opens	Record crowd of 118,877 see Spearfelt win Melbourne Cup. Victoria makes 1107 runs in one innings in Sheffield Shield match against NSW. Charlie Macartney scores a century before lunch on first day of test at Leeds; series ends with four draws and one match to England. Sydney Showground speedway is opened	The Ashes are presented to Marylebone Cricket Club by widow of Australian captain Ivo Bligh. First meeting of 'electric hare racing' conducted at Epping (later Harold Park) racecourse, Sydney. Waratahs rugby union team from NSW tours Britain and France; scores 400 points to 177 in 28 games	H. R. Pearce (single sculls) wins Australia's one gold medal at Amsterdam Olympics. Hubert Opperman wins French Bol d'Or 24-hour cycling event with 909 kilometres. First Australian Grand Prix car race held on Phillip Island. Don Bradman plays in his first test match	Don Bradman scores world record 452 not out for NSW in 415 minutes in match against Queensland. Phar Lap, even-money favourite, beaten into third place in Melbourne Cup behind Nightmarch, after winning AJC Derby in record time. In Sydney-Perth Trans-Continental Air Race, Hereward de Havilland makes fastest-time in a Gypsy Moth	Phar Lap wins Melbourne Cup at 11 to 8 on, the shortest-priced favourite for this race, and carrying 62 kg; jockey Jim Pike's first Cup win in 14 attempts. First British Empire Games (events for men only) held in Canada; Australia wins three gold medals. At Leeds Bradman scores highest individual score in test cricket with 334 (309 in one day)
Treaty of Locarno, guaranteeing European borders as in 1919, is signed. Chiang Kai-shek becomes leader of Chinese Nationalist Party, Kuo Min Tang. Christiania is renamed Oslo. Clarence Birdseye freezes cooked foods. Books: *The Great Gatsby* (Scott Fitzgerald); *The Trial* (Kafka). Film: *The Gold Rush* (Chaplin)	General strike in Britain lasts ten days. Hejaz renamed Saudi Arabia and Ibn Saud proclaimed King. Adoption legalised in Britain. J. L. Baird demonstrates television in London. Jack Hobbs scores 16 centuries in first-class cricket. Books: *Winnie the Pooh* (A. A. Milne). Opera: *Turandot* (Puccini) produced. Died: Monet; Rudolph Valentino	Charles Lindbergh flies from New York to Paris in 37 hours in *The Spirit of St. Louis*. Britain breaks off diplomatic relations with USSR after Soviet intrigues against Empire are revealed. Trotsky is expelled from Soviet Communist Party. Germany's economic system collapses on 'Black Friday'. Nylon is discovered. Film: *The Jazz Singer*	German airship *Graf Zeppelin* with 60 passengers crosses Atlantic. Women in Britain allowed to vote at 21 instead of 30. Penicillin discovered by Alexander Fleming. Herbert Hoover elected US President. Turkey adopts Latin alphabet. First 'Mickey Mouse' film in colour produced by Walt Disney. Music: *Bolero* (Ravel). Died: Thomas Hardy; Ellen Terry	Financial panic on Wall Street, New York, leads to the Great Depression. Fascist government in Italy after single-party 'elections'. Serbo-Croat-Slovene kingdom renamed Yugoslavia. Commander Richard Byrd flies over South Pole. Books: *A Farewell to Arms* (Hemingway); *The Good Companions* (Priestley). Theatre: *Bitter Sweet* (Coward). Died: Serge Diaghilev	Allied troops finally evacuate the Rhineland. Economic crisis spreads. British R101 airship crashes in first flight. Mahatma Gandhi opens civil disobedience campaign against British in India. Haile Selassie becomes Emperor of Ethiopia. Constantinople renamed Istanbul. Planet Pluto discovered. Perspex invented. Died: D. H. Lawrence

The passing years 1931-40

	1931	**1932**	**1933**	**1934**

The Australian scene

1931 Depression deepens. Basic wage cut by 10 per cent. First experimental airmail between England and Australia, takes 26 days and 45,288 letters. Aeroplane *Southern Cloud* disappears in Snowy Mountains with loss of eight lives; Kingsford Smith and Ulm's Australian National Airways collapses. Argentine ants enter Australia about this time

1932 Unemployment situation begins to improve. Taxation reduced and assistance given to wheat-growers. Restrictions on imports eased. Sydney Harbour Bridge opened unofficially by Captain W. de Groot of the New Guard, forestalling Premier Lang. Japanese fishermen killed by Aborigines in Gulf of Carpentaria

1933 Unemployment is quarter of work force but begins to ease. The 10 per cent wage cut is abandoned in some industries. Third census taken: population 6,629,982. Record wheat harvest. BHP takes over steelworks at Port Kembla. Gold rush to Tennant Creek; town of 600 springs up. Pedal wireless introduced by Inland Mission

1934 Egon Kisch, Czech anti-fascist writer, barred from Australia after failing dictation test in Gaelic. Race riots in Kalgoorlie; prejudice rages against Italians and Yugoslavs. 'Pyjama girl' case—a burnt body is found near Albury; it is identified and murderer found ten years later. Duke of Gloucester opens Victorian centenary celebrations

Politics and government

1931 Arthur Calwell becomes President of Victorian Labor Party. United Australia Party formed. Sir Isaac Isaacs is first Australian to be appointed Governor-General. Premiers' Plan, reducing expenditure of all kinds to counter Depression, adopted by Federal Government. In NSW, road transport tax is imposed to bolster railways

1932 Joseph Lyons heads Ministry of anti-Labor United Australia Party. Sir Philip Game, Governor of NSW, dismisses Premier Lang for 'breaches of the law'; Lang Labor party loses subsequent election. Premiers meet four times in year to discuss Depression

1933 Western Australia votes in referendum to secede from Commonwealth. Australian Antarctic Territory awarded to Australia. NSW Legislative Council reduced by referendum. Rearmament of Australia begins with accent on air force

1934 J. G. Latham leads Australian goodwill mission to East. Sir Langdon Bonython, owner of Adelaide *Advertiser*, gives £100,000 [$1,320,000] to complete South Australia's Parliament House

Arts and entertainment

1931 'Tivoli circuit' formed to present variety shows. Students of Mischa Burlakov form the first Australian Ballet. Cinesound is founded in Sydney, and Efftee in Melbourne. Book: *Man-Shy* (Frank Dalby Davison). Died: Tom Roberts; Melba

1932 Australian Broadcasting Commission set up. The Contemporary Group of painters founded in Melbourne includes George Bell, Arnold Shore, William Frater, Daryl Lindsay. Films: *His Royal Highness* starring George Wallace; *On Our Selection* with Bert Bailey. Books: *The Cautious Amorist* (Norman Lindsay); *Under the Wilgas* (Mary Gilmore); *Flesh in Armour* (Leonard Mann)

1933 Archibald Memorial Fountain built in Sydney's Hyde Park. Theatre Royal in Sydney and Her Majesty's in Melbourne close due to Depression. Films: Charles Chauvel's *In the Wake of the Bounty* starring Errol Flynn; Raymond Longford's *The Hayseeds*. Robert Helpmann joins Sadler's Wells Ballet

1934 Bust of Adam Lindsay Gordon placed in Westminster Abbey's Poets' Corner, the only Australian poet so honoured. Sulman Award for architecture established. Anzac memorial unveiled in Sydney; Shrine of Remembrance in Melbourne. 'Mo' makes film *Strike Me Lucky*. Books: *Seven Poor Men of Sydney* (Christina Stead); *Sea and Spinifex* (Vance Palmer)

Sport

1931 Shots fired at Phar Lap one week before the Melbourne Cup, for which he is 3 to 1 favourite, carrying 68 kg; he finishes eighth behind White Nose. Ivo Whitton is open golf champion for fifth time. First amateur and professional squash championships are held

1932 Phar Lap dies in USA; strong suspicion of poisoning. Swimmer Claire Dennis at 15 is youngest competitor in Los Angeles Olympics; she wins one of Australia's three gold medals. Walter Lindrum sets world record with billiards break of 4137 in 2 hr. 55 min. over three sessions. 'Bodyline' cricket test series begins

1933 England keeps Ashes after controversial 'bodyline' tour. Bill Hunt takes five hat-tricks in one year in top grade cricket, two in Sydney and three in Lancashire. Jack Crawford wins Wimbledon singles. Walla Walla wins a 2414 metres trotting race from a handicap of 165 metres

1934 In second win, Peter Pan carries 62 kg to take Melbourne Cup: his time of 3 min. 40½ sec. is slowest since 1880. Don Bradman (244) and W. H. Ponsford (266) make record second wicket score of 415 in test against England; in series Ponsford averages 94.83; Bradman 94.75. Charles Scott and Campbell Black win Melbourne Centenary Air Race (London-Melbourne)

The outside world

1931 Economy measures in Britain provoke riots in London and Glasgow and a naval mutiny. Japan besieges Mukden in Manchuria, using bomber seaplanes. The 102-storey Empire State Building is dedicated in New York. Russia bans Rachmaninov's music as 'decadent'. Films: *Frankenstein* with Boris Karloff; Chaplin's *City Lights*. Died: Edison; Pavlova; Arnold Bennett

1932 Japan creates puppet state Manchukuo out of Manchuria. Sixty nations at disarmament conference in Geneva. Hindenburg re-elected German President with 19 million votes against Hitler's 13 million; Nazis very active. Famine in USSR. Zuider Zee drainage system completed. Shirley Temple makes first film, at 3½. Book: *Brave New World* (Huxley)

1933 Hitler becomes Chancellor of Germany. His Nazi government suspends civil liberties after Reichstag fire (arranged by Nazis and denounced as Communist plot). Japan occupies China north of Great Wall. Japan and Germany resign from League of Nations. Roosevelt plans 'New Deal' for USA. Synthetic detergent first made. Opera: *Arabella* (Strauss)

1934 Hitler becomes both President and Chancellor of Germany as Fuehrer. 'Night of the Long Knives'—Nazi purge of powerful party factions. Austrian Nazis murder Chancellor Dollfuss. Dionne quintuplets born in Canada. *Queen Mary* is launched. Driving tests introduced in Britain. Cole Porter composes *Anything Goes*. Died: Delius; Elgar; Holst

1935	1936	1937	1938	1939	1940
P. C. Taylor, crossing Tasman with Kingsford Smith, saves plane by walking along wings over sea to transfer oil from engine to engine. Kingsford Smith killed in crash in Bay of Bengal. Reginald Ansett begins operating Ansett Airways. 'Shark arm' murder case begins when shark in Coogee Aquarium disgorges man's tattooed arm	Tasmania linked to mainland by submarine telephone cable. Second Australian National Airways formed. Centenary of South Australia. Hume reservoir completed, provides storage for Murray Valley schemes	Invalid pensions raised to £1 [$13.20]. Tasmania is first state to change from 6 p.m. to 10 p.m. closing. Authorities alter policy of protecting Aborigines to encouraging assimilation. Epidemic of infantile paralysis. Hurricane causes huge damage in Darwin. One million radio licences now issued. Refrigerators becoming widely used	Qantas starts Australia-to-Europe service in flying boats. NSW celebrates its 150th anniversary. Pleasure ferry capsizes in Sydney harbour, 19 drown. Hundreds of people swept out when surfing at Bondi; 70 rescued by lifesavers; five die despite hours of artificial respiration. Coca-Cola first made in Australia	Population reaches seven million. BHP leaves Broken Hill after 54 years' mining there. First pre-mixed concrete business in world starts in Sydney. Victorian bushfires kill 71. Steel workers refuse to load pig-iron for Japan. The last grain clipper race to England held	Volunteer Defence Corps set up by RSL: 50,000 join in six months. Age limit for AIF raised from 35 to 40. Bass Strait temporarily closed to shipping after British ship is mined there. General manager of BHP becomes Director-General of Munitions. Petrol is rationed
John Curtin becomes leader of Labor Party. Britain refuses Western Australia's petition to secede from Commonwealth. Royal Commission recommends that NSW be divided into three states. Excise on locally-produced tobacco is reduced. Australia imposes sanctions against Italy; sends HMAS Sydney to Gibraltar to serve in international force	Restrictions on Japanese and American imports lead to loss of export market in Japan and USA. Lord Gowrie becomes Governor-General. Commonwealth Aircraft Corporation set up to design military aircraft.	Referendum to increase federal control over aviation and sale of Australian products is defeated. Royal Commission on money and banking favours change to decimal currency	New defence program to spend £63 million [$830 million] over three years. Citizens' Military Force to be increased to 70,000 men. Two cruisers purchased from Britain: HMAS Hobart and HMAS Perth	Death of Prime Minister Lyons. Page and Country Party refuse to support Menzies, who becomes Prime Minister. War declared on Germany. Navy placed at Britain's disposal. Citizens' Military Force recruits 75,000 men. Compulsory training for home defence reintroduced. Advance party of Australian Army leaves for Middle East	Australian enlistments total 48,496. HMAS Sydney and destroyers in action. First legation or embassy established: R. G. Casey becomes Minister to USA. Three Cabinet Ministers killed in plane crash at Canberra. United Australia Party and United Country Party form coalition government under Menzies. Communist Party banned
ABC begins schools broadcasts. Manchester Unity building (copy of a Chicago building) erected in Melbourne. Percy Grainger begins lecture tour of Australia. Yehudi Menuhin tours. Charles Chauvel's second talkie Heritage wins £2500 [$33,000] in a Commonwealth film competition. Books: Tiburon (Kylie Tennant); Human Drift (Leonard Mann)	Mary Gilmore created Dame of the British Empire. ABC decides to form orchestras in each state and inaugurates subscription concerts. Tour by De Basil ballet company. Ezio Pinza tours. Expressionism and social realism begin with the paintings of Danila Vassilieff. Books: All That Swagger (Miles Franklin); The Inheritors (Brian Penton)	Australian Academy of Art founded with support of R. G. Menzies; many painters refuse to join. 'Constructivist' paintings by Frank Hinder shown in Sydney. Lottie Lehmann tours. Death of Walter Burley Griffin. Books: The Great Australian Loneliness (Ernestine Hill); The Young Desire It (Kenneth McKenzie)	'Waterfall front' houses popular. Contemporary Art Society formed in Melbourne to oppose Academy of Art which is considered reactionary. Sydney Mail ceases publication. C. J. Dennis dies. Visits by Ruth Draper, Kirsten Flagstad, Richard Tauber. Books: The Passing of the Aborigines (Daisy Bates); Capricornia (Xavier Herbert); Foveaux (Kylie Tennant)	Melbourne Herald exhibition of contemporary European art has deep effect on Australian art. First Contemporary Art Society show in Melbourne includes work of Nolan, Drysdale, Tucker and Sali Herman. Radio Australia first broadcasts. H. G. Wells visits Australia. Books: Patrick White's first novel Happy Valley; Five Bells (Kenneth Slessor)	First Australian classical ballet company formed by Edouard Borovansky in Melbourne. First issues: Meanjin edited by Clem Christesen; Angry Penguins edited by Max Harris. Contemporary Art Society starts in Sydney; first exhibition contains abstract and surrealist works. William Dobell, back from England, paints The Cypriot. Film: Forty Thousand Horsemen
Jack Crawford and Adrian Quist win Wimbledon men's doubles. Jim Ferrier is national amateur golf champion for first of four times. Joan Hammond is NSW women's golf champion for third time; she leaves Australia to study singing in Europe. Jack Metcalfe sets world triple jump record of 16 metres. J. Turner invents game of cricko	At Berlin Olympics, Jack Metcalfe is Australia's only medal winner, with a bronze for triple jump. Speed skater Ken Kennedy is Australia's first competitor in Winter Olympics. Don Bradman is appointed Australian cricket captain. Australian Lionel van Praag wins first world speedway title at Wembley, London. Water-skiing begins in Australia	Australia's first team of women cricketers tours England, losing only one game, the single test played. Polo team from Goulburn comprising four Ashton brothers, wins England's premier polo trophy, the Hurlingham Cup. Gymnastics is organised as a sport with formation of an association in Victoria	Australia wins 24 of the 70 gold medals at British Empire Games held in Sydney; Decima Norman wins five. Bradman's average on Australian tour of England is 115.66. Bathurst Mount Panorama racing circuit is completed: Peter Whitehead of England wins first Grand Prix held there	Australia wins Davis Cup for first time since competing alone. Rivette wins Caulfield and Melbourne Cups—first mare to achieve this double. Ajax, at 40-to-1 on the shortest-priced favourite to lose in Australia, comes second in minor race at Rosehill. Jim Ferrier is national open golf champion for second successive year	Olympic Games, to have been held in either Tokyo or Helsinki, cancelled. Horace Lindrum wins world snooker championship. His brother Walter makes an unfinished break of 1002 points on his first turn in a 1000-point billiard game; his opponent did not score. Jockey Billy Cook rides 126 winners, including three dead heats, in one season
Hitler deprives German Jews of citizenship. Italy invades Abyssinia; League of Nations imposes ineffective sanctions against Italy. Persia renamed Iran. Robert Watson-Watt devises radar. Polyethylene discovered. T. E. Lawrence ('of Arabia') dies. Opera: Porgy and Bess (Gershwin)	Army revolt against failing government in Spain starts the civil war. King Edward VIII accedes then abdicates to marry American Mrs Simpson; Duke of York becomes George VI. Abyssinian war ends. Penguin books start the paper-back revolution. BBC starts TV service. Film: Charlie Chaplin's Modern Times. Died: Kipling; Dame Clara Butt; Maxim Gorky; Houdini	Japanese take Peking, Shanghai and Nanking. Fascist rebels win victories in Spain. German airship Hindenburg burns in New Jersey USA; 36 die. Irish Free State is renamed Eire. Women are unveiled in Iran. Divorce for grounds other than adultery made possible in England. First jet engine; first nylon stockings. Died: Ravel; Marconi; Lord Rutherford; Gershwin	Austria is annexed by Germany. In first Czechoslovakia crisis Britain and France resist Hitler's demands. Germany mobilises; British navy mobilises. Britain and France agree to Hitler's ultimatum at Munich, so postponing war, but Germany is dominant power. Ball-point pen invented. Picture Post first issued. Died: Chaliapin; Stanislavsky; Kemal Ataturk	General Franco's Nationalist forces win Spanish civil war. Pius XI dies after 17 years as Pope; Pius XII elected. Conscription begins in Britain and evacuation of women and children from London. Germany invades Poland and war begins. In Battle of the River Plate, the Graf Spee is sunk. Polythene and DDT are invented. Film: Gone with the Wind. Died: Freud	Norway, Holland, Belgium and Luxembourg invaded by Germany. Churchill becomes British Prime Minister. France falls. Britain wins air Battle of Britain. London blitz begins. Latvia, Lithuania and Estonia annexed by USSR. BBC Radio Newsreel begins. Films: Walt Disney's Fantasia; Charlie Chaplin's The Great Dictator. Died: Trotsky

329

The passing years 1941-50

	1941	**1942**	**1943**	**1944**

The Australian scene

1941
Adelaide and Darwin linked by telephone. Royal Commission in NSW recommends compulsory retirement for miners at 60. Newsprint is rationed to 55 per cent of pre-war level. Federal child endowment of 5s [$3.55] per week for first child and 10s [$7.10] per week for others, begins. Owen sub-machine gun patented

1942
Daylight saving introduced. Commonwealth becomes sole tax-levying authority. Widows' pensions introduced. Darwin bombed; 243 people killed. Attacks on Broome and Wyndham. Volunteer Defence Corps members increase to 100,000. Sale of liquor limited. Mobs of cattle driven inland in case of invasion. Clothes and commodities rationed

1943
Speed limit for cars set at 64 km/h. Sales of cooking appliances restricted. Household drapery rationed. Scottsdale, Tasmania, introduces first free medical service in Australia. Airgraph service begins: letters received from UK on micro-film, magnified by GPO to 12 x 10 cm. Record £73½ million [$1043] for wool clip

1944
Meat rationing introduced. Pay-as-you-earn taxation begins. Hospital benefits scheme inaugurated. Large rice-growing area at Wakool, NSW, developed by Italian prisoners of war. First Aboriginal army officer commissioned. Death toll of 51 in season's bushfires in Victoria. Worst dust storms on record sweep south-east Australia

Politics and government

1941
Menzies resigns as Prime Minister; Fadden succeeds him. Coalition Government collapses; Curtin heads new Labor Government. War declared on Japan. HMAS *Sydney* sinks with all 645 crew off WA coast, fighting German ship. Australian troops besieged at Tobruk. RAAF squadrons fighting in Britain, Middle East, Singapore

1942
Three Japanese midget submarines destroyed in Sydney Harbour; barracks ship *Kuttabul* torpedoed; 19 die. General MacArthur sets up headquarters in Melbourne. Battle of Coral Sea: HMAS *Australia* and *Hobart* engaged. Australian troops in North Africa, Middle East, Malaya, Papua, Britain. First federal subsidy to dairy industry. Ban on Communist Party lifted

1943
Australians in fighting services number 790,000. Hospital ship *Centaur* torpedoed. Darwin suffers the last of 59 bombing raids. Industrial conscription introduced. By payment of subsidies Government brings down prices of tea, milk, coal, firewood. Jack Lang expelled from Labor Party. Dame Enid Lyons becomes first woman MHR (enters Cabinet 1949)

1944
First two Victory Loans, £150 million and £155 million [$2130 and $2201 million], oversubscribed. Referendum to increase federal powers in post-war period defeated. Liberal Party formed by Menzies from remnants of United Australia Party. Japanese prisoners of war attempt mass break-out from camp at Cowra, NSW; 234 killed

Arts and entertainment

1941
Douglas Stewart becomes editor of *The Bulletin's* Red Page. Sydney *Daily Mirror* begins publication. James Joyce's book *Ulysses*, banned 1929-1937, is banned again. 'Banjo' Paterson dies. Russell Drysdale depicts drought and country life and becomes well known. *Australian Poetry* (annual) first issued. Book: *The Timeless Land* (Eleanor Dark)

1942
ABC begins Kindergarten of the Air. *Art in Australia, Triad, The Home*, cease publication. Douglas Stewart wins two ABC play competitions with *Ned Kelly* and *The Golden Lover*. Exhibition of anti-fascist art in Melbourne and Adelaide by Contemporary Art Society includes work by Arthur Boyd and John Perceval. Dr A. E. Floyd begins his concert presentations on ABC

1943
Theatre staff in Melbourne and Sydney strike for three weeks. Arthur Streeton dies. Sidney Nolan exhibits his *Dimboola* landscapes. Books: *The Persimmon Tree* (Marjorie Barnard); *The Vegetative Eye* (Max Harris)

1944
Dobell wins Archibald Prize for portrait of Joshua Smith and is unsuccessfully sued by other artists. Eugene Ormandy comes to report on Australian music. Ern Malley hoax perpetrated by James McAuley and Hal Stewart on *Angry Penguins*. Lawson Glassop's book *We Were The Rats* prosecuted for indecent language

Sport

1941
Skipton wins the Melbourne Cup, last three-year-old to do so. Walter Lindrum scores 100 billiards points in only 46 sec. Arthur Dunstan wins a bicycle race riding backwards; he has achieved 42 km/h in this manner

1942
War-time restrictions are imposed on horse and greyhound racing: no racing mid-week or on first Saturday of the month. Colonus wins Melbourne Cup by seven lengths. Softball is introduced to Australia

1943
Dark Felt wins Melbourne Cup—run on second Saturday in November. Australia's heaviest boxer, Les McNabb is weighed at 141 kg on a railway weighbridge at Lithgow

1944
Greyhound Chief Havoc breaks five track records in one night at Harold Park, Sydney. Olympic Games, to have been held in London, are cancelled

The outside world

1941
President Roosevelt's Lend-Lease bill aids Britain against Axis powers. North Africa campaign against Rommel's Afrika Corps. Allies evacuate Greece. House of Commons destroyed in air raid. Japan bombs Pearl Harbour and USA enters war. Japan invades Malaya, Philippines, Hong Kong. Terylene invented. Died: James Joyce; Virginia Woolf; Paderewski

1942
Singapore falls and Seventh Division is captured but Major-Gen. Gordon Bennett and staff escape. Naval battles of Coral Sea and Midway. George Cross is awarded to Malta for courage under siege. Montgomery defeats Rommel at El Alamein. Worst mine disaster in history in Manchuria; 1549 die. Night club fire in USA kills 493. Magnetic tape invented

1943
Russians destroy German army near Stalingrad. German forces in North Africa surrender. Allies invade Italy. Mussolini overthrown; Italy surrenders and declares war on Germany. Churchill, Stalin and Roosevelt meet at Teheran. Massacre in Warsaw ghetto. Civil conscription of women in Germany. Theatre: *Oklahoma*

1944
Massive bombing raids on both England and Germany. D-Day landings of Allied forces in Normandy. First flying bombs hit London. Leningrad relieved after 876-day siege. Bomb plot on life of Hitler fails. New Guinea cleared of Japanese. At Dumbarton Oaks conference in Washington, Russia, USA, Britain and China propose formation of United Nations

1945	1946	1947	1948	1949	1950
Child endowment now 7s 6d [$5.30] a week; old age and invalid pensions 32s 6d [$23]. Captain Cook Dock in Sydney opened. Occupation survey of all male civilians aged 14 and over. Estimated 2 million sheep dead in two-year drought. Lancastrian air service begins between Sydney and England. Alcoholics Anonymous set up in Australia	Commonwealth sets up Trans-Australia Airlines (TAA). Immigration scheme plans mass emigration of Europeans to Australia. Woomera rocket range established. Australian National University established in Canberra. Fire danger begins to be broadcast daily. Eight-kilometre-wide lake in Queensland disappears after earth tremor	Calwell's great immigration drive begins. First displaced persons arrive in Australia. Antarctic research station set up at Heard Island. Sugar rationing ends. S. M. Bruce becomes first Australian in House of Lords. First successful rain-making experiment in Australia in NSW. Freighter *Mahia* burns in Melbourne dock; 10 men killed	Meat and clothes rationing ends. First mass-produced Australian car, the Holden, appears. Tuberculosis Act initiates campaign to eliminate the disease. State of emergency declared in Queensland over rail strike. Forty-hour week established throughout Australia. NSW University of Technology (later University of NSW) opens	Work begins on Snowy Mountains hydro-electric scheme. Rum Jungle uranium deposit discovered in Northern Territory. Cyclone destroys most of Cooktown, Qld. Asian migration under strict control; many Asians deported. Australia has 10 million telephones in use. The New Look in fashion: the hemline drops to near ankle	Petrol rationing ends. Modified free medicine scheme introduced. Huge stock losses in floods in NSW. ANA plane crashes near Perth; 29 die. School of the Air founded at Alice Springs. Jindivik pilotless jet aircraft invented. Myxomatosis introduced to control rabbits. Androman Khan returns to Karachi after many years as foremost Australian camel man
Curtin dies in office; J. B. Chifley becomes Prime Minister. Australia signs UN Charter at San Francisco. Duke of Gloucester becomes Governor-General. Third Victory Loan (£100 million) [$1420 million] over-subscribed. Fourth Victory Loan (£85 million) [$1207 million] filled. War ends; demobilisation of 500,000 men and women begins	Referendum approves increase in federal social security powers. United Nations grants trusteeship of New Guinea to Australia. Federal-state housing agreement to employ 130,000 men over ten years. Broadcasting of proceedings in Federal Parliament begins. Commonwealth Employment Service set up. Mission in USA raised to embassy status	All Australian troops demobilised. NSW pioneers introduction of 40-hour working week. Qantas fully nationalised. Laws to nationalise banks introduced. Australia joins World Health Organisation. Sir William McKell is second Australian-born Governor-General. H. V. Evatt is chairman of UN commission on Palestine	Membership of House of Representatives increased to 123; Senate to 60. High Court invalidates parts of bank nationalisation legislation. Referendum to increase federal powers over rents and prices fails. Australian citizenship created. ACT given parliamentary representation. H. V. Evatt becomes President of UN General Assembly	Chifley sends in troops to break seven-week miners' strike during which stringent power restrictions imposed. Chifley Government falls over nationalisation of banks; Menzies becomes Prime Minister. Administrations of New Guinea and Papua merged. Some Aborigines given federal vote. HMAS *Sydney*, Australia's first aircraft carrier, arrives	Australian troops join British Commonwealth brigade in war in Korea. Australian airmen aid British in campaign against Communist terrorists in Malaya. Compulsory military training introduced. Female basic wage increased from 54 per cent to 75 per cent of male rate. Sir Thomas Blamey becomes Australia's first field marshal
National Film Board and Commonwealth Film Unit set up. National Trust formed in NSW, first in Australia. Gracie Fields tours Australia. Sydney group of neo-romantic painters includes Jean Bellette, Francis Lymburner, Justin O'Brien, Donald Friend. Books: *The Cousin from Fiji* (Norman Lindsay)	Musica Viva society formed in Sydney to promote chamber music. Dorothy Helmrich establishes Arts Council of Australia to present the arts to the youth of Australia. Nolan begins his *Ned Kelly* paintings. Film: *The Overlanders*, with Chips Rafferty, a great success. Judith Wright publishes first book of poetry, *The Moving Image*	ABC inaugurates youth concerts. Shortage of building materials leads to pre-fab houses. First professor of fine arts appointed, at Melbourne University. *Angry Penguins* ceases publication. Contemporary Art Society collapses. Rupert Bunny dies. Film: *Bush Christmas*. Book: *The Fatal Days* (Henrietta Drake-Brockman)	Eugene Goossens becomes first permanent conductor of Sydney Symphony Orchestra and suggests building an opera house. Old Vic company with Vivien Leigh and Laurence Olivier tour Australia. Sumner Locke Elliott's play *Rusty Bugles* causes outcry then acclaim. Robert Close's book *Love Me Sailor* lands its author in jail	Cumberland County Council master plan for Sydney approved. Tyrone Guthrie reports on state of Australian theatre; his advice to set up a national theatre is rejected. Serial *Blue Hills* begins on ABC. Sydney Ure Smith dies. Sir Kenneth Clark visits Australia, admires Nolan and Drysdale	Première in Sydney of ballet *Corroboree*, music by John Antill, choreography by Rex Ree. Joan Sutherland wins Mobil Quest. Drysdale and Nolan hold their first London exhibition. Publication of *Power Without Glory* leads to unsuccessful libel suit against author Frank Hardy. Nevil Shute's *A Town Like Alice* is published
Nine yachts enter first Sydney-Hobart yacht race, which is won by Commander John Illingworth's *Rani*. A triple dead-heat is declared by judges of Wollongong Wheel, the first recorded for any cycling event. The new Australian Rough-riders' Association standardises championship saddles. T. F. Schwerdt tosses a sheaf 16.6 m	Russia wins Melbourne Cup by five lengths, in time equalling Wotan's 1936 record. Sydney Turf Club introduces photo-finish camera for its race meetings. Shannon, ridden by Darby Munro, loses Epsom Handicap in Sydney by only half a head, after being left 91 metres at the start. First national championship of marching girls teams	Ray Lindwall takes three wickets in four balls in test against England in Adelaide. Shannon equals world record times in winning two US horse races. Australian Jockey Club opens its own laboratories in Sydney for testing horse blood samples for drugs. Jim Ferrier is US professional golf champion	Australia wins two gold medals at London Olympics; Shirley Strickland is Australia's first female athletics medal winner with one silver and two bronze. Don Bradman retires from test cricket after scoring a duck in his last innings. His team scores a world record 721 in one day against Essex. 18-year-old Trevor Allan captains the Wallabies rugby union team	Don Bradman is knighted. Dave Sands wins Empire middle-weight boxing title from Dick Turpin of England. Sid Patterson is world amateur sprint cycling champion. Croquet achieves status with formation of Australian Croquet Council. Greyhound racing's largest crowd—18,600—gathers at Wentworth Park to watch Chief Havoc	At Empire Games in Auckland Australia wins every rowing event but one. Australian jockey Rae ('Togo') Johnstone wins all four English classic horse races in one season. Australia wins Davis Cup, first time for 11 years. Walter Lindrum retires from billiards, holding 57 world records. Jack Hoobin wins world amateur road cycling title
Heavy US air raids on Tokyo. US marines invade Iwo Jima. President Roosevelt dies; Harry Truman new President. Mussolini killed by Italian partisans. Hitler commits suicide. Germany capitulates. USA drops atomic bombs on Hiroshima and Nagasaki. Japan surrenders. Black markets in food, clothes and cigarettes all over Europe. Died: Bela Bartok	United Nations General Assembly meets for first time, in London; Trygve Lie of Norway elected Secretary-General. War crimes trials in Nuremberg and Japan. Vietnamese begin revolt against France. First bikini designed after US atom bomb tests at Bikini Atoll. Opera: *War and Peace* (Prokofiev). Film: *Great Expectations*. Died: H. G. Wells; Damon Runyon	Partition of India to create Pakistan; thousands die in Hindu-Moslem terror. Worst floods recorded in England. Princess Elizabeth marries Prince Philip Mountbatten. UN plans partition of Palestine into Jewish and Arab states. Thor Heyerdahl crosses Pacific on *Kon-Tiki* raft. First supersonic flight. Died: Henry Ford	Mahatma Gandhi assassinated by Hindu fanatic in Delhi. By Marshall Aid Act, USA grants US$5.3 million for European recovery. Berlin blockaded by Russians and air lift begins. Israel becomes a state. Declaration of Human Rights adopted by United Nations. Antibiotics are prepared. Long-playing records marketed. Transistor invented	NATO treaty signed by 12 nations in Washington. Berlin airlift ends after 277,264 flights. Apartheid begins in South Africa. Indonesia and Vietnam gain independence. Mao Tse-tung proclaims People's Republic of China. Siam renamed Thailand. Clothes rationing in Britain ends. Cortisone discovered. Film: *The Third Man*. Died: Richard Strauss	Korean War begins. UN troops under General MacArthur suffer reversals. Marshall Aid to Britain ceases. Chinese forces occupy Tibet. Klaus Fuchs found guilty in London of spying for Russians. Communist bogey in USA. Leopold III of Belgium abdicates; Baudouin is King. 'Bebop' dancing popular. Films: *Rashomon; La Ronde*. Died: Jan Smuts; George Bernard Shaw

The passing years 1951-60

	1951	**1952**	**1953**	**1954**

The Australian scene

1951 Wool reaches record £1 per lb [$9 per 453 g], and makes over half total rural earnings. Colombo Plan begins operation: free tertiary education for Asians. Federation jubilee celebrations. Immigration of displaced persons reaches 170,000. NSW is first state to set up long-service leave measures. Mechanical letter sorters used in Melbourne GPO

1952 Restrictions on imports and funds for overseas travel. Nuclear experiments begin at ANU. Santa Gertrudis cattle introduced. Large bushfires in Victoria and NSW. Heavy rain ends severe drought in northern NSW but sets off worst floods in history in south of state. James Stirling becomes first fully qualified Aboriginal teacher

1953 Wool prices drop after four-year boom. Oil discovered at Exmouth Gulf. Bauxite discovered at Weipa. Australian Atomic Energy Commission established. Commonwealth medical benefits scheme begins. *Women's Weekly* sells 960,000 copies of special Coronation issue

1954 Queen makes first tour of Australia by a reigning monarch. Antarctic research station set up at Mawson. Referendum in NSW favours ten o'clock hotel closing. Uranium discovered at Mary Kathleen, Qld. WA declares 1 million hectares wild life sanctuaries. Electric typewriters first used in Australia. Seamless stockings arrive. Hula hoop craze

Politics and government

1951 ANZUS pact between Australia, New Zealand and USA signed. Menzies fails in attempts to dissolve Communist Party, first in High Court then in referendum. Commonwealth takes over from States payment for free milk for primary school children. Government calls conference to discuss inflation

1952 Second battalion of Australian troops leaves for Korea. Ambassadors to Japan and West Germany appointed. Immigration programme reduced. RAAF group sent to Malta for Middle East peace-keeping operations. Billy Hughes dies

1953 More Australian troops sent to Korea. Automatic basic wage adjustments abolished. Premiers' conference fails to return income tax powers to States. Australia and Japan agree to refer fishing and pearling dispute to International Court. UN Trusteeship Council urges Australia to end use of pidgin in New Guinea. Sir William Slim becomes Governor-General

1954 Russian diplomat Vladimir Petrov and his wife Evdokia defect to Australia and are granted asylum; Russia and Australia withdraw ambassadors. Royal Commission into espionage set up. Troops withdrawn from Korea. South East Asian Treaty Organisation founded for collective defence against aggression

Arts and entertainment

1951 First Blake prize for religious painting won by Justin O'Brien. Open-air sculpture exhibition in Sydney shows some abstract work. Drysdale is influenced by Aboriginal art. Books: *Come In Spinner* (Dymphna Cusack and Florence James); *Adam in Ochre* (Colin Simpson); *Dead Men Rising* (Kenneth Mackenzie)

1952 Marie Collier makes star debut in Melbourne. Commonwealth buys one of only 14 authentic copies of Magna Carta. Dobell, Drysdale, Nolan and Friend exhibit in USA. Film *Kangaroo* made in Australia. Books: *The Cardboard Crown* (Martin Boyd); *The Naked Island* (Russell Braddon); *The Far Country* (Nevil Shute)

1953 Melbourne Union Theatre founded. Shakespeare Memorial Theatre company with Anthony Quayle and Diana Wynyard tours Australia. Exhibition of Australian paintings in London includes work of Dobell, Drysdale, Nolan, Friend, O'Brien, Boyd, Miller. Exhibition *French Painting Today* influences painters towards abstraction. 'Dad' Bert Bailey dies

1954 Australian Elizabethan Theatre Trust formed at instigation of H. C. Coombs. Walter Susskind becomes resident conductor of Victorian Symphony Orchestra. Ray Lawler's play *The Summer of the Seventeenth Doll* first produced. Books: *The Australian Tradition* (A. A. Phillips); *Fourteen Men* (Mary Gilmore). Died: 'Mo'

Sport

1951 Australia wins Davis Cup. Wimbledon men's doubles won by Frank Sedgman and Ken McGregor, who are the first pair to win the Australian, French, Wimbledon and US doubles. Frank Sedgman is first Australian to win US singles title. The world's quickest boxing match lasts seven seconds: Ian Gordon beats Frank Brooks at Brisbane

1952 At Helsinki Olympics, Marjorie Jackson wins gold medals for 100 and 200 metre sprints but a dropped baton costs Australia a certain win in relay race. Four other gold medals are won. Ken Rosewall and Lew Hoad, both aged 17, win Wimbledon doubles. Jimmy Carruthers is Australia's first world boxing champion, winning bantamweight title from Vic Toweel

1953 Ken Rosewall, aged 18, is youngest Australian singles tennis champion. He and Lew Hoad retain Davis Cup for Australia. Ian Craig, 17 years 8 months, is the youngest cricketer to play in tests for Australia. Amateur cyclist Russell Mockridge wins open Grand Prix of Paris; amateurs are banned from future races

1954 John Landy is defeated by Roger Bannister (UK) in mile race at Vancouver Commonwealth Games when he turns his head in last 90 metres. Peter Thomson and Kel Nagle win Canada Cup world professional golf event for Australia. Thomson wins British open (first of five times). Bantamweight world champion Jimmy Carruthers retires undefeated

The outside world

1951 President Truman dismisses General MacArthur in Korea. Armistice talks fail. British diplomats Guy Burgess and Donald Maclean flee to Russia. Festival of Britain. British Witchcraft Act of 1735 repealed. Musical: *South Pacific*. Opera: *The Rake's Progress* (Stravinsky); *Billy Budd* (Britten). Book: *The Catcher in the Rye* (Salinger).

1952 Elizabeth II proclaimed queen on death of George VI. US aircraft launch massive bombing in Korea. Britain explodes its first atomic bomb off Monte Bello Islands, north-west Australia. First H-bomb exploded by Americans in Pacific. Mau Mau terrorism in Kenya. John Cobb killed on Loch Ness, setting water speed record of 333 km/h. Died: Eva Peron

1953 Korean War ends. Edmund Hillary and Norgay Tensing climb Mount Everest. Beria, head of USSR secret police, shot as traitor. Dr Jonas Salk develops polio vaccine. 'Piltdown Man' skull, found in 1912, revealed as hoax. Laos gains independence. Ian Fleming writes first James Bond thriller *Casino Royale*. First Cinemascope and 3-D films. Died: Stalin

1954 Vietminh capture Dien Bien Phu from French. France evacuates North Vietnam, Communists withdraw from South Vietnam. Nasser becomes head of state in Egypt. Terrorism in Algeria. Roger Bannister runs mile in under four minutes. Books: *Lucky Jim* (Kingsley Amis); *The Lord of the Rings* (Tolkien). Drama: *Under Milk Wood* (Dylan Thomas). Died: Matisse

1955	1956	1957	1958	1959	1960
One millionth immigrant arrives. Kwinana (WA) oil refinery begins production. First power generated by Snowy Mountains scheme. Disastrous floods in NSW; 22 die and 10,000 homes destroyed. Pearlers gather 1300 tonnes of pearls. Newspaper competitions and crosswords proliferate; one prize reaches £62,000 [$558,000]	One millionth road casualty in Australia. Duke of Edinburgh opens Olympic Games in Melbourne. Television begins. Tobacco crops destroyed in Queensland floods. Darling and Murrumbidgee Rivers flood vast area of NSW and Victoria. Severe floods also in Tasmania. First parking meters installed in Sydney. First computer installed at Sydney University	Commonwealth public servants awarded long-service leave. Three air companies merge to form Ansett Airlines of Australia. Severe drought in eastern states. First Volkswagen assembled in Australia. Sydney Opera House lottery opens; tickets cost £5 [cheaper now at $6] each	Qantas becomes first airline to start round-the-world service. First nuclear reactor opened at Lucas Heights, Sydney. Mort's Dock, Sydney, closes after 104 years. Oil discovered in New Guinea. Last trams run in Perth and Adelaide (except Glenelg line)	Population reaches 10 million. Consumers' Association founded. NSW workers granted three weeks' holiday a year. Thirty thousand live sheep exported to USA. First Billy Graham crusade in Australia. Aboriginals, except nomads and primitives, become eligible for pensions and maternity allowances. Chemists begin to charge 5s for dispensing free medicine	Aborigines become Australian citizens and eligible for social service benefits. Warragamba and Keepit dams opened. Credit squeeze begins. Severe floods in Tasmania. Macfarlane Burnet awarded Nobel Prize for work in immunology. Country television stations approved
Labor Party splits over Petrov affair and Evatt's defence of alleged spies; Democratic Labor Party formed. Australia commits forces to a southeast Asia strategic reserve. Cocos Islands become Australian territory. Journalists R. E. Fitzpatrick and F. C. Browne found guilty of breach of parliamentary privilege and are sentenced to three months' imprisonment	Australia agrees to accept refugees from Hungarian revolution. Menzies appointed chairman of committee of Suez Canal users which leads to breaking off diplomatic relations with Egypt. Australian troops fight in Malaya against Communist terrorists	National service intake reduced by two-thirds. By treaty there is no more discrimination in trade with Japan. Japanese Prime Minister Kishi visits Australia. First non-Labor Government for 23 years comes to power in Queensland. National Capital Development Commission set up to co-ordinate development of Canberra	Visit by Harold Macmillan is first by incumbent British Prime Minister. NSW legislates for equal pay for men and women performing similar tasks. Dictation test for immigration abolished. All elected members of Northern Territory Legislative Council resign in protest against treatment of report on constitutional reform; all re-elected	Australia signs Antarctic Treaty in Washington. Commonwealth agrees to spend £720 million [$3600 million] on roads and bridges. Diplomatic relations with Egypt and USSR restored. Australian mission in South Vietnam raised to embassy status. Four government departments, involving over 1000 public servants, move to Canberra	Australia sends ambassador to European Common Market. Phone tapping prohibited except for national security. Reserve Bank established. Number of native members of Papua New Guinea Legislative Council increased. R. G. Casey is made a life peer. Viscount Dunrossil becomes Governor-General
Eugene Goossens knighted. American abstract art begins to influence Sydney painters, including John Olsen. Chauvel films Jedda in Northern Territory. Max Meldrum dies. Books: The Tree of Man (Patrick White); The Shiralee (D'Arcy Niland); I Can Jump Puddles (Alan Marshall); The Wandering Islands (first book of verse by A. D. Hope)	Joern Utzon wins prize for design of Sydney Opera House. ICI House is first building to break 40 m barrier in Melbourne. William Dargie's portrait of Albert Namatjira, Aboriginal painter, wins Archibald Prize. Direction I exhibition marks turning point in abstract painting in Sydney. Dorian Le Gallienne's Sinfonietta first performed. Royal Ballet tours Australia	Critics laud Nolan's exhibition in London. Margot Fonteyn dances in Australia. First performance of Richard Beynon's play The Shifting Heart. Books: Voss (Patrick White); They're A Weird Mob (John O'Grady—"Nino Culotta")	National Institute of Dramatic Art started by ABC, University of NSW, Elizabethan Theatre Trust. Fonteyn again dances in Australia. Museum of Modern Art of Australia founded in Melbourne under direction of John Reed. Barry Humphries creates 'Edna Everage'. Books: To The Islands (Randolph Stow); The Australian Legend (Russel Ward)	Construction of Sydney Opera House begins. Sidney Myer Music Bowl opens in Melbourne. 'Antipodean' group of artists formed in Melbourne includes Boyd, Perceval, Clifton Pugh; issues manifesto against Sydney abstraction. My Fair Lady opens in Melbourne (to play for four years). On The Beach is filmed in Australia	First Adelaide Festival of Arts. Bolshoi Ballet tours Australia. Charles Blackman wins Helena Rubinstein travelling scholarship. Maurice Chevalier visits Australia. Eric Worrell opens reptile park at Gosford, NSW. Book: The Australian Ugliness by Robin Boyd. Film: The Sundowners. Died: Alfred Hill
Australia wins Davis Cup 5-0 against US. Jockey 'Scobie' Breasley begins record of riding 100 winners each season (mostly in England). Sir Norman Brookes retires after 29 years as president of Lawn Tennis Association of Australia. John Purdy, aged 19, is Australia's youngest chess champion	At Melbourne Olympic Games Australia wins 13 gold medals; wins all freestyle swimming events, relay and individual, with all three places in men's and women's 100 metres. Lorraine Crapp breaks 18 world swimming records in training. Lew Hoad beats Ken Rosewall in first all-Australian Wimbledon final since 1919	Tulloch is sensationally scratched from Melbourne Cup, for which he was hot favourite. Lew Hoad wins Wimbledon men's singles title from Ashley Cooper in 52 minutes. Australia wins Rugby league World Cup. In cricket match between NSW and South Africa at Johannesburg, Ian Craig, aged 22, is Australia's youngest captain	Marlene Mathews sets world records for running 90 metres and 200 metres. Australia wins Eisenhower Cup for world golf teams championship for first time. Tony Madigan wins world amateur light heavyweight title, International Diamond Belt. Rolly Tasker is world champion yachtsman. Suza Javor is national table tennis champion, first of nine times	Jack Brabham is first Australian to become world Grand Prix champion, pushing his car half a kilometre to end of one race. John Konrads wins all men's freestyle events at Australian swimming championships. Australia is suspended for four years from world soccer for poaching European club players. Alf Dean catches 1208 kg shark on rod and line	At Rome Olympics, Bill Roycroft rides with broken collarbone, enabling equestrian team to win one of Australia's eight gold medals. Twelve world records broken in three nights at Australian swimming championships. Jack Brabham wins world Grand Prix title for second time. West Indies and Australia play only cricket test ever tied
Churchill retires as UK Prime Minister. Bulganin succeeds Malenkov as USSR Premier. Revolt against Peron in Argentina; he goes into exile. Occupation of West Germany ends. Commander Crabbe, frogman, disappears at Portsmouth. State of emergency in Cyprus. Book: Lolita (Nabokov). Film: Rock Around the Clock	Egypt seizes Suez Canal. Anglo-French force attacks Egypt but withdraws when UN force arrives. Khrushchev denounces Stalin. USSR crushes revolution in Hungary. Archbishop Makarios deported from Cyprus. Liner Andrea Doria sinks and 50 die after collision in Atlantic. Grace Kelly marries Prince Rainier of Monaco. Drama: Look Back in Anger (Osborne)	European Common Market comes into being. Russians launch first man-made satellite Sputnik I; later Sputnik II orbits, carrying a dog. The Gold Coast, renamed Ghana, is first independent black African country. Suez Canal reopens. Desegregation riots in Little Rock, Arkansas. Musical: My Fair Lady. Died: Sibelius; Dorothy Sayers; Toscanini; Gigli	States of emergency in Aden and Ceylon. De Gaulle President of France. Pope John XXIII elected. Khrushchev Soviet Prime Minister. Campaign for Nuclear Disarmament march on Aldermaston in England. First US satellite, Explorer I, launched. Beatnik movement spreads. Stereophonic records on sale. Book: Dr Zhivago (Pasternak). Died: Vaughan Williams	Fidel Castro becomes Prime Minister of Cuba. Revolt against Chinese in Tibet; Dalai Lama flees to India. Emergency ends in Cyprus; Archbishop Makarios is first President. Prime Minister Bandaranaike of Ceylon assassinated. Typhoon in Japan kills 5000. USSR launches monkeys into space. Regular colour television in Cuba	End of eight-year emergency in Kenya. South African police fire on unarmed Africans at Sharpeville, killing 67. US U-2 aircraft shot down in Russia. Congo gains independence from Belgium; army mutiny begins civil war and UN sends troops. John Kennedy elected US President. Earthquake at Agadir, Morocco, kills 12,000

The passing years 1961-70

	1961	**1962**	**1963**	**1964**

The Australian scene

1961
Huge iron ore deposits discovered at Pilbara, WA. First commercial oil find at Moonie, Qld. King Street bridge in Melbourne subsides soon after opening. Parkes radio telescope opens. Monash University, Melbourne, opens. University College of Townsville opens. First guided missile base established at Williamtown, NSW. Contraceptive pills begin to be widely used

1962
Standard gauge railway track opens between Brisbane, Sydney and Melbourne. First subscriber trunk dialling—Canberra to Sydney. 'Church of England in Australia' becomes title of Australian Anglican Church. Bank employees awarded five-day week, except in Victoria

1963
Queen and Duke of Edinburgh tour. Ord River project begins. Townsville bulk sugar terminal destroyed in Australia's worst fire, loss £6 million [$30 million]. Large underground water supplies found near Alice Springs. Dr Gilbert Bogle and Mrs Margaret Chandler found mysteriously dead in Sydney. Sir John Eccles awarded Nobel Prize for work in neurophysiology

1964
HMAS *Voyager* sinks after collision with HMAS *Melbourne*; 82 lives lost. Largest bauxite deposit in Australia found at Gove, NT. Laws discriminating against Aborigines in Northern Territory repealed. NSW public servants receive four weeks' annual leave. First flight of Blue Streak rocket, launched from Woomera

Politics and government

1961
Federal Matrimonial Act unifies state laws on divorce. Viscount De L'Isle appointed Governor-General on death of Lord Dunrossil. Tax concessions to exporters begin. Australia sells interest in Tasman Empire Airways to New Zealand

1962
Aborigines get the vote and take part in Northern Territory elections for first time. Tax clearances for Australians going overseas abolished. New defence plan to increase strength of all services at cost of £650 million [$3250 million]. UN Trusteeship Mission talks on New Guinea and Nauru. Australia sends 30 military advisers to Vietnam: first involvement in war

1963
Australia orders four submarines and a guided missile destroyer. Australia grants approval to USA to build communication base at Exmouth, WA, and space tracking station at Tidbinbilla, near Canberra. Robert Menzies knighted

1964
First general election held in Papua New Guinea. Conscription for service at home or abroad announced

Arts and entertainment

1961
El Alamein fountain built at King's Cross, Sydney. *The Bulletin* taken over by Consolidated Press. Power bequest to Sydney University, to set up fine arts faculty and buy art works, announced. Sydney abstract painters form 'Sydney Nine' group. Ken Burstall's film *The Prize* (Music by Dorian Le Gallienne) wins medal at Venice Film Festival. Died: Percy Grainger

1962
Borovansky Ballet becomes Australian Ballet. Australian Ballet School opened. First chair of Australian literature established, at Sydney University. Books: first volume of Manning Clark's *History of Australia; Australian Painting* (Bernard Smith). Died: Dame Mary Gilmore; Frank Hurley. AMP Building (117 m) is first to break 45 m limit in Sydney

1963
Large exhibition of Australian art at Tate Gallery, London. First issue of *Art and Australia*, edited by Mervyn Horton. Sir John Gielgud visits Australia and plays in *Ages of Man*. Alan Seymour's play *The One Day of the Year* first performed. Books: *The Shoes of the Fisherman* (Morris West); *Cooper's Creek* (Alan Moorehead); *In Mine Own Heart* (Alan Marshall)

1964
The Australian, sole national newspaper, begins. First performance at Adelaide Festival, of Helpmann's ballet *The Display*; music by Malcolm Williamson, decor by Sidney Nolan. The Beatles tour. New Fortune Theatre, unique reproduction of Elizabethan theatre, built in Western Australia. Book: *The Lucky Country* (Donald Horne)

Sport

1961
In test series against West Indies, wicketkeeper Wally Grout makes Australian record 23 dismissals; world record crowd of 90,800 watches one day at Melbourne Cricket Ground. Heather Blundell McKay is national squash champion for second of her 14 times. Valerius, at 33 to 1 on the shortest priced winner in Australia, wins Chipping Norton Stakes

1962
At Perth Commonwealth Games Australia wins 17 of 27 gold medals for swimming. *Gretel* challenges for the America's Cup for yachting and loses 4-1. Dawn Fraser is first woman to break 60 sec. for 100 metres freestyle—59.9 sec. Rod Laver wins Wimbledon, US, French and Australian tennis titles. Stewart Mackenzie wins Henley Diamond Sculls for sixth time

1963
Margaret Smith Court is first Australian to win Wimbledon women's singles. Federation Cup for international women's tennis is inaugurated; US beats Australia 2-1. Ken Hiscoe wins all four major world squash titles. D. Mayfield wins world live bird shooting title in Madrid

1964
At Tokyo Olympics, six gold medals are won by Australians, including Bill Northam, 59, in 5.5 metre yacht class; Dawn Fraser wins gold medal for 100 metres freestyle for third successive Olympics. Skier Ross Milne killed training for Winter Olympics in Innsbruck. Donald Campbell sets world land and water speed records in Australia

The outside world

1961
Russian Yuri Gagarin is first man in space. South Africa leaves the Commonwealth. Kennedy meets Khrushchev in Vienna. Berlin Wall built. Population of Tristan da Cunha evacuated to England after volcano erupts on the island. Dag Hammarskjold, UN Secretary-General, killed in air-crash in Congo where heavy fighting continues. US Peace Corps established

1962
Algeria becomes independent after seven-year war with France. Cuban crisis: after US blockade Russians withdraw from the island. Nazi Adolf Eichmann hanged after trial in Israel. John Glenn is first American in space. Thalidomide causes deformities in babies. Live television US to Britain via Telstar. Died: Marilyn Monroe; Kirsten Flagstad

1963
US nuclear submarine *Thresher* lost with 129 crew. Scandal leads to resignation of British War Secretary John Profumo. President Kennedy assassinated. £2.5 million 'Great Train Robbery'. Kremlin-White House hot line opened. Paul VI elected Pope. Rachel Carson writes *The Silent Spring*. Music: War Requiem (Britten). Died: Pope John XXIII; Braque

1964
Khrushchev forced to resign as Soviet Prime Minister; succeeded by Alexei Kosygin. Indonesia at war with Malaysia. Tanganyika and Zanzibar become Tanzania. US planes begin bombing North Vietnam. US campaign against poverty. China explodes atomic bomb. Landslide victory for President Johnson over Barry Goldwater. 'Op' art is popular

1965	1966	1967	1968	1969	1970
First Australia-owned oil refinery opened by Ampol at Lytton, Qld. First mint to be run by Australian Government opened by Prince Philip. Mt Isa miners strike for 101 days. Building of Westgate bridge in Melbourne begins. Churchill Fellowship scheme set up. Jean Shrimpton shocks some Flemington racegoers by wearing miniskirt and no stockings	Decimal currency introduced. Mt Tom Price mine, with highly mechanised systems, starts operation. Important find of nickel at Kambalda, WA. BHP and Esso find oil in Bass Strait. Three Beaumont children disappear from beach in Adelaide; never found. Gurindji tribe occupies 805 kilometres of tribal land. Meter maids employed on Gold Coast	Big demonstration against hanging of Ronald Ryan in Melbourne. 62 die in bushfires in Tasmania. Mt Newman township and mine built. Returned Services League expels two members for opposing Australian involvement in Vietnam. First Australian satellite launched into orbit. Macquarie University, Sydney, opens	Town of Meckering in Western Australia devastated by earthquake. First Australian heart transplant. 20 kilometre fishing limit around Australian territories comes into operation. Courage brewery opens in Melbourne and beer war starts. Mills Cross telescope discovers mysterious radio sources in Milky Way. Viscount airliner crashes near Port Hedland, WA; 26 die	HMAS *Melbourne* collides with USS *Frank E. Evans*, 74 lives lost. Indian-Pacific railway, 3960 kilometres, completed. Bushfire near Lara, Vic., kills 15 and destroys 200 houses. Sydney-Melbourne express train collides with goods train at Violet Town, Vic. Poseidon company announces find of nickel; share prices soar. Natural gas piped to Melbourne	Mineral shares boom; Poseidon shares plummet. Government investigates crown of thorns starfish. Nationwide Moratoriums on Vietnam. Postwar immigration reaches 2.5 million. Cyclone devastates parts of Queensland. Tullamarine airport opens. Pope visits Australia. Westgate bridge, Melbourne, collapses; 33 killed
Australia imposes economic sanctions against Smith regime in Rhodesia. Australian troops serving in South Vietnam total 1350. Sir Thomas Playford defeated as Premier of South Australia after 27 years. Menzies becomes Lord Warden of the Cinque Ports. Lord Casey becomes Governor-General. H. V. Evatt dies	Sir Robert Menzies announces retirement. Harold Holt is Prime Minister. Lyndon Johnson, first US President to visit Australia, meets anti-war demonstrations. Troop strength in Vietnam increased. National minimum wage established. Attempt to assassinate Arthur Calwell. Gough Whitlam becomes leader of Labor Party	Prime Minister Holt disappears in sea off Portsea, Victoria. John McEwen acts as Prime Minister. Anti-war demonstrations during visit of Marshal Ky of South Vietnam. NSW holds referendum on setting up new state of New England; under 60 per cent in favour, so proposal fails. Decision to adopt metric system of weights and measures	John Gorton becomes Prime Minister. Independence granted to Nauru, the world's smallest republic. Australia has 8,000 troops fighting in Vietnam. Northern Territory member of Parliament given full voting rights. Five-year, $1000 million development plan for New Guinea announced	Czechoslovak Consul-General in Sydney defects to Australia. R. J. Hawke elected president of ACTU. Australia Party formed. Sir Paul Hasluck is Governor-General. High Court rules that States have no rights over adjacent waters or the seabed. Arbitration Commission grants equal pay to women for work of equal value	Queen attends celebrations of 200th anniversary of Captain Cook's landing. Phased withdrawal of troops from Vietnam begins. State receipts taxes held by High Court to be illegal. Metric Conversion Board set up. Federal secondary scholarship scheme for Aborigines established
Plans for a national gallery in Canberra announced. First tour by Australian Ballet to Europe and USA; acclaim in London. Peter Sculthorpe's *Sun Music I* also praised in London. First 'op art' exhibition held in Melbourne. Books: *The Slow Natives* (Thea Astley); *The Road to Gundagai* (Graham McInnes)	Utzon resigns from Opera House project after changes forced in his design. Museum of Modern Art of Australia ceases operation. Exhibition *Two Decades of American Painting* causes great interest. William Dobell knighted. Film: *They're A Weird Mob*. Books: *The Fatal Impact* (Alan Moorehead); *The Solid Mandala* (Patrick White)	Circular Australia Square Tower completed in Sydney. Australian Council for the Arts set up to finance arts groups. Play: Jack Hibberd's *White with Wire Wheels*, produced by Australian Performing Group. Music: Richard Meale writes *Images*. *Bellbird* begins on ABC. Book: *Bring Larks and Heroes* (Thomas Keneally)	National Library in Canberra opened. National Gallery of Victoria moves to Melbourne Arts Centre, designed by Roy Grounds. Robert Helpmann knighted. Play: *Norm and Ahmed* by Alexander Buzo. Film: *Age of Consent*. Died: Hans Heysen and Roy de Maistre. 'The Field' exhibition of 'hard edge' paintings in Melbourne	Helpmann returns to dance in Australia, first time for ten years. Norman Lindsay dies. Records of *Hair* banned in Melbourne, also posters by Aubrey Beardsley. Films: *2000 Weeks* by Tim Burstall; *Marinetti* by Albie Thoms, acclaimed overseas and booed here. Bulgarian artist Christo wraps coastline near Sydney in plastic	Film censorship eased. Play: *The Legend Of King O'Malley* by Michael Boddy and Bob Ellis. Sir William Dobell dies. 'Conceptual' and 'lyrical abstraction' art influential. Films: *The Naked Bunyip, Ned Kelly*. Book: *The Female Eunuch* (Germaine Greer)
Linda McGill is the first Australian to swim English Channel. Distance runner Ron Clarke breaks 11 world records in 16 races. Bill Nance sails single-handed round Cape Horn in 7.6 m yacht. Four swimmers suspended for misconduct at Tokyo Olympics. Australian team wins world softball championship. Geoff Hunt, 17, is national squash champion	Jack Brabham wins his third Grand Prix title and is the first to win in a self-designed car. First world lawn bowls championships held at Kyeemagh, Sydney; Australia wins. Bill Moyes sets world record height of 319 metres on a water-ski kite. British Rugby union team defeats Australia 29-0 at Brisbane. The roller game enjoys popularity	Australia wins Admiral's Cup for yachting by record 104 points. *Dame Pattie* loses America's Cup challenge 4-0. On her third crossing, Linda McGill sets women's record for Channel swim of 9 hr 59 min. Manchester United soccer team tours Australia. Australian frog 'Pluto Kangaroo' becomes world jumping champion with hop of 3.2 m in California	At Mexico Olympics Australia wins five gold medals. In first open Wimbledon tournament there is an all-Australian final: Rod Laver beats Tony Roche. Lionel Rose wins world bantamweight title from 'Fighting' Harada, and successfully defends it twice. Rain Lover wins Melbourne Cup in fastest time over two miles of 3 min. 19.1 sec.	Rain Lover wins second successive Melbourne Cup; prize money is $75,000. Johnny Famechon wins world featherweight title from Jose Legra and retains it against 'Fighting' Harada. Lionel Rose retains bantamweight title in fight with Alan Rudkin but loses it to Ruben Olivares. Margaret Court wins US singles tennis title for fourth time	Australia loses third America's Cup challenge: in spite of controversial protest *Gretel* wins only one out of five races. Johnny Famechon retains world featherweight title against 'Fighting' Harada; loses it to Vicente Saldivar of Mexico. Evonne Goolagong first plays tennis overseas. Australia loses cricket Ashes for first time in 12 years
First US marines land in South Vietnam. USSR's Alexei Leonov makes first space walk. Ian Smith declares Rhodesia independent; Britain imposes sanctions. Anti-Communist riots in Indonesia; many thousands die. Red Guard rampage in China in 'cultural revolution'. Short India-Pakistan war. Died: Sir Winston Churchill; Albert Schweitzer; T. S. Eliot	Unmanned Russian spacecraft lands on moon. US finds H-bomb lost off Spain. South African Prime Minister Verwoerd assassinated. Aberfan sludge fall disaster in Wales; 144 die. Unsuccessful meeting on Rhodesia between Harold Wilson and Ian Smith on HMS *Tiger*. Venice and Florence flooded	Six-day war between Israel and Arabs. Suez canal closed. Biafra secedes from Nigeria. Army coup in Greece; King Constantine exiled. Three US astronauts killed at Cape Kennedy. First heart transplant. Francis Chichester reaches Plymouth after 266-day solo voyage round world. Expo 67 held in Canada. Gibraltar votes to stay British	US troops in Vietnam total 560,000. Russians invade Czechoslovakia and suppress liberalisation programme. Papal encyclical *Humanae Vitae* condemns contraception. Tear gas and clubs used against demonstrators at Chicago Democratic convention. Martin Luther King and Robert Kennedy assassinated. Richard Nixon elected US President	Apollo II astronauts Neil Armstrong and Edwin Aldrin are first men to walk on moon. American forces begin withdrawal from Vietnam. Mrs Golda Meir becomes Prime Minister of Israel. Troops sent to Northern Ireland to subdue Catholic-Protestant fighting. Mass starvation threatens blockaded Biafra; world charities airlift supplies	Four jets hijacked by Arab guerillas; three blown up in Jordan desert. Biafra surrenders to Nigeria. Italy legalises divorce. President Nasser dies. Cyclone and tidal wave in East Pakistan kill about 500,000. Swiss women receive vote. Unmanned Soviet spacecraft lands on Venus. Women's liberation movement spreads

The passing years 1971-80

	1971	**1972**	**1973**	**1974**

The Australian scene

1971 The Northern Territory Supreme Court rules that Aboriginal titles to land do not hold good under Australian law. National service is reduced to 18 months. Australia ends fighting role in Vietnam. New South Wales tries daylight saving. Sir Marcus Oliphant is Governor of South Australia. Resale price maintenance is banned. Lake Pedder in Tasmania is flooded. 'Hot pants' are in fashion

1972 There are widespread protests against French nuclear tests in the Pacific; the ACTU places a black ban on French ships and aircraft in Australia. About 1,300,000 women workers receive entitlement to equal pay. Temperature readings are changed to the Celsius scale. Townsville is badly damaged in a cyclone. Wearing seatbelts is now compulsory all over Australia

1973 Albury-Wodonga is declared a growth centre. Journalist Francis James is freed after three years in Chinese prisons. The Wrest Point Hotel-Casino in Hobart opens. Maternity leave is granted to federal public servants. A $50 banknote is introduced. 'Green bans' stop certain development in Sydney. Export of kangaroo products is banned. Wine casks go on sale

1974 Brisbane is badly flooded. Darwin is devastated by Cyclone Tracy. Tertiary education fees are abolished. Strikes reach a record 2809. NSW workers gain four weeks' annual leave and 17½ per cent holiday pay loading. Road speed signs go metric. The Anglo-American telescope at Siding Springs is opened. Bankcard is introduced. TV and radio licences are abolished

Politics and government

1971 Australia joins the Organisation for Economic Co-operation and Development. This year's census includes Aborigines for the first time. South Australia lowers the age of adulthood to 18. William McMahon becomes Prime Minister. John Gorton is dismissed as Minister for Defence. Senator Neville Bonner becomes the first Aboriginal member of Federal Parliament

1972 Diplomatic relations with China and East Germany are established. The Aboriginal tent embassy outside Parliament House in Canberra is closed after several months. Sir Henry Bolte steps down after 18 years as Premier of Victoria. Gough Whitlam becomes Prime Minister in the first Labor Government for 23 years. WEL (Woman's Electoral Lobby) is founded

1973 Eighteen-year-olds get the federal vote. The Prices Justification Tribunal and the Industries Assistance Commission begin operations. The Queen is to be known as Queen of Australia. Environment impact statements now required for projects involving federal funds. Two referenda on federal control of prices and incomes are defeated

1974 Sir John Kerr becomes Governor-General. Trade Practices Commission established to police misleading advertising. Double dissolution follows Opposition challenge in the Senate: Labor returned but fails to gain Senate majority. Gross value of wheat exceeds wool for first time. Fully-elected assemblies set up in the Northern Territory and the Australian Capital Territory

Arts and entertainment

1971 The legally enforceable 'R' film certificate is introduced. James Mollison is director of the Australian National Gallery. The Aboriginal magazine *Identity* begins publication. Film: *Wake in Fright*. Play: *Don's Party* by David Williamson. Book: *A Dutiful Daughter* (Thomas Keneally)

1972 The *National Times* begins publication. The ABC films five Norman Lindsay novels. Rothmans promote a new cigarette using Paul Hogan. Opera: *Garni Sands* by George Dreyfus. Films: *Stork, The Office Picnic, The Adventures of Barry McKenzie*. Books: *The Chant of Jimmy Blacksmith* (Thomas Keneally); *The Americans, Baby* (Frank Moorehouse)

1973 The Sydney Opera House opens. Patrick White wins the Nobel Prize for Literature. Australia pays $1.3 million for *Blue Poles* by Jackson Pollock. The Australia Council is founded. The ABC produces *Seven Little Australians*. Film: *Libido*. Play: *Dimboola* by Jack Hibberd. Book: *The Eye of the Storm* (Patrick White)

1974 *Advance Australia Fair* becomes the national song. Young Russian violinist Georgi Ermolenko asks for political asylum. Construction of the Australian National Gallery begins. The Australian Centre for Photography opens a gallery in Sydney. About 120,000 people in Sydney go to see *Blue Poles*. Opera: *Rites of Passage* by Peter Sculthorpe

Sport

1971 The South African Springbok rugby union team tours Australia; hundreds of anti-apartheid demonstrators are arrested and there is much violence. Wayne Jones is the first Australian to waterski over 100 mph (161 km/h). The women's final at Wimbledon is all-Australian: Evonne Goolagong, aged 19, beats Margaret Court. Orienteering and hanggliding gain popularity

1972 Swimmer Shane Gould, aged 15, wins three gold medals, a silver and a bronze at the Munich Olympic Games. She is the first woman to hold all world freestyle records at once: 100, 200, 400, 800 and 1500 metres. The Melbourne Cup goes metric: it is run over 3200 metres, just short of the former 2 miles. Joe Meissner from Sydney is the first non-Japanese world karate champion

1973 Margaret Court wins her fifth US tennis singles championship. Heather McKay wins her 14th Australian women's squash title. Penrith pays a world record transfer fee of $39,000 for rugby league player Mick Stephenson. The 13th Kangaroos rugby league team tours in England, losing only 2 of 19 games. George Perdon, aged 48, runs from Fremantle to Sydney in 47 days

1974 In Australia's fourth America's Cup challenge, *Southern Cross* loses 4-0. Trifecta betting is introduced. Australia qualifies for the World Soccer Cup finals for the first time. Heather McKay turns professional and does not defend her Australian squash title. Marathon swimmer Des Renford swims the 90 km from Sydney Harbour to North Wollongong in 27½ hours

The outside world

1971 Seven million East Pakistan refugees pour into India after massacres and civil war; India invades; Bangladesh is born. A US table-tennis team plays in China and President Nixon relaxes Chinese trade embargoes. The UN seats China. Britain changes to decimal currency. In Uganda Idi Amin ousts Milton Obote. The microprocessor is invented in the USA

1972 President Nixon goes to China. Palestinian terrorists kill 11 Israelis at the Munich Olympic Games. Britain, Ireland, Denmark and Norway join the EEC. Five men are caught bugging the Democratic National Committee offices in the Watergate Apartments in Washington. Uganda expels its Asian citizens. The US sends its last manned rocket to the moon

1973 President Allende of Chile is killed during a military coup. Vice President Agnew of the USA resigns over tax evasion conviction. Greece abolishes the monarchy. First USA manned space station, Skylab; malfunctions are cleared by astronauts' daring manoeuvres. Cease-fire agreement in Vietnam. Final withdrawal of all US forces

1974 President Nixon resigns; Gerald Ford becomes President and pardons Nixon. The Arab oil-producers increase the price of oil by 400 per cent, causing drastic world-wide inflation. Emperor Haile Selassie of Ethiopia is deposed by a military junta. A miners' strike in Britain provokes political crisis: the Labour Party under Harold Wilson is returned to power

1975	1976	1977	1978	1979	1980
International Women's Year. 'No fault' divorce is introduced. The *Lake Illawarra* collides with the Tasman Bridge in Hobart. Medibank health insurance begins. Jack Lang, former Premier of New South Wales, dies aged 90. Unemployment reaches 5.2 per cent of the labour force. Five Australian journalists are killed in East Timor	The Medibank scheme is modified and the first national strike occurs in protest. Northern Territory Aborigines receive some lands under traditional principles of land tenure. Police raid and raze a hippy community at Cedar Bay, near Cairns. A sealed road across the Nullarbor Plain is completed. Cigarette ads are banned on TV. Backgammon is popular, and CB radio, although illegal	A train is crushed by a bridge at Granville in Sydney: 81 die. Melbourne tramways employee Paul Krutulis is sacked for refusing to join union. Noel Latham is sacked for refusing to pay fine levied by the Barrier Industrial Council. Donald McKay, anti-drug campaigner, disappears in Griffith. The Western Plains Zoo opens. Smoking is banned on Sydney's public transport	Three men are killed by bomb outside the Hilton Hotel in Sydney. The Westgate Bridge in Melbourne opens. Vietnamese refugees come in increasing numbers. The whaling station at Albany is to be closed. A departure tax of $10 for Australians going overseas is introduced. Medibank standard abolished; Medibank private scheme remains. Some cut-price air fares offered	Diamonds are discovered in the Kimberleys. An explosion at Appin in NSW kills 14 miners. Truck-drivers blockade major highways in a protest against road maintenance charges. Low alcohol beer is introduced. Pieces of the Skylab space station shower over Western Australia. Working women can now take 12 months maternity leave.	Justice David Opas is shot dead in Sydney. Baby Azaria Chamberlain disappears from a tent at Ayers Rock. The High Court of Australia building in Canberra opens. The world's fourth 'test tube' baby is born in Melbourne and Australia becomes prominent in in-vitro fertilisation research. The Turkish Consul-General and his bodyguard in Sydney are assassinated.
The loans affair: Rex Connor, unauthorised, tries to raise $8 billion. Connor resigns; Treasurer Cairns is dismissed. The Governor-General dismisses the Whitlam government; Malcolm Fraser leads the Liberal-Country Party coalition to a landslide victory. Papua New Guinea becomes independent. Wage indexation is introduced. Personal tax system is reconstructed	The government offers Australia's second amnesty to illegal migrants. Flexitime is approved for federal public servants. The position of federal Ombudsman is created. Neville Wran becomes Premier of New South Wales. Sir Douglas Nicholls becomes Governor of South Australia. Protests against Sir John Kerr continue	Sir John Kerr resigns. Sir Zelman Cowen becomes Governor-General. Don Chipp founds the Australian Democrats. The Government decides to allow mining and export of uranium. Street marches are banned in Queensland. Of four referenda concerning changes to the constitution, three are carried and one lost	The Northern Territory achieves self-government. Bob Hawke steps down as president of the Labor Party. Sir John Kerr is appointed ambassador to UNESCO but resigns. A points system for selecting immigrants is announced. Australia asks Britain to remove 500 g of plutonium buried at Maralinga. Sir Robert Mark comes from Britain to advise on terrorism	The Minister for Primary Industry, Ian Sinclair, is accused of forgery. The government bans oil drilling on the Great Barrier Reef and creates the first section of the marine national park. Whaling is banned, and whale products will be prohibited imports next year. Don Dunstan resigns as Premier of SA. Australia's fishing zone is increased to 370 kilometres.	The Liberal Party under Malcolm Fraser wins the federal election. The government call to boycott the Olympic Games in Moscow in protest against the Russian invasion of Afghanistan meets with limited success. The premier of NSW, Neville Wran, has permanent voice problems after a throat operation. Death: John McEwen.
Sydney's Seymour Centre theatre complex opens. Colour television, FM radio and ethnic radio are introduced. Verdi's *Aida* is lavishly staged in the Concert Hall of the Sydney Opera House. Films: *Picnic at Hanging Rock*; *The Removalists*; *Sunday Too Far Away*. Books: *Poor Fellow My Country* (Xavier Herbert); *Life in the Cities* (Michael Cannon)	William Bligh's notebook is bought by the National Library for $73,000. Richard Bonynge and Joan Sutherland return to Sydney. Restoration of Elizabeth Bay House in Sydney is finished. The Theatre Royal opens. Films: *Caddie*, *The Devil's Playground*, *Don's Party*, *Storm Boy*. Books: *A Fringe of Leaves* (Patrick White); *The Savage Crows* (Robert Drewe)	Chinese antiquities lent by China go on show. The first Festival of Sydney is held. Malcolm Williamson becomes Master of the Queen's Music. Kim Bonython closes his Sydney gallery and returns to Adelaide. Play: *Big Toys* by Patrick White. Films: *The Last Wave*, *The Picture Show Man*. Book: A new edition of *The Australian Encyclopaedia* is published	Sir Robert Helpmann is made director of the Old Tote Theatre but its closure is announced week later. The 'El Dorado' exhibition of gold objects from Colombia tours Australia. Willem van Otterloo is killed in a car accident. Rock singer Johnny O'Keeffe dies. Films: *The Chant of Jimmy Blacksmith*; *Newsfront*. Play: *The Elocution of Benjamin Franklin* (Steve J. Spears)	Television current affairs programme *60 Minutes* first goes to air. The Sydney Theatre Company is formed. Book: *A Woman of the Future* by David Ireland. Films: *My Brilliant Career*, and *Mad Max* which earns $1 million in its first week of showing.	Ethnic television begins in Sydney and Melbourne. The winning sculpture in a competition for Melbourne's City Square is secretly moved from the square. Newspapers are banned from publishing extracts from a book on defence policy 1968-75. Film: *Breaker Morant*, which becomes an international hit.
Think Big wins the Melbourne Cup for the second year in succession, the fourth horse to win the Cup twice. The world's heaviest fish ever landed on rod and reel is caught by Clive Green at Albany: a 1536.8 kg white pointer shark. Australia comes second in the first World Cricket Cup, the final held at Lords. Skateboard-riding enters a second phase of popularity	Runner Raelene Boyle, strong contender for the 200 metres at the Montreal Olympic Games, is controversially disqualified for two false starts. Apprentice Malcolm Johnston wins the Sydney jockeys' premiership. Chris Wardlaw from Melbourne wins the San Francisco Bay-to-Breakers foot race after missing the starting gun while putting on his shoes	Reckless wins the Sydney, Adelaide and Brisbane Cups and comes second in the Melbourne Cup. World Series Cricket is launched. England and Australia play test in Melbourne to commemorate 100 years of Test cricket. *Australia* loses America's Cup challenge 4-0. Des Renford makes his 11th English Channel swim. Geoff Hunt is again world open squash champion	Bobby Simpson comes out of retirement to captain a young and inexperienced test cricket team affected by World Series enlistments: Australia defeats India 3-2 but fares badly in the West Indies, losing 3-1. Edwina Kennedy of Sydney, aged 19, becomes British woman's amateur golf champion. A record 20,930 people enter the Sydney City-to-Surf foot race	Hot favourite Dulcify breaks down in the Melbourne Cup and has to be destroyed. Controversy over 'commercialised' World Series cricket, and Australia reverts to six-ball overs, having played eight-ball overs since 1928. Robyn Bailey is the first Australian to gain a world ice skating title when she wins the women's professional championship in Spain.	Alan Jones wins the Formula I world drivers' championship. Evonne Cawley becomes the second mother in history to win Wimbledon. Geoff Hunt wins the British, South African and Australian open squash championships all for the seventh time, and is world champion for the fourth time. *Freedom* beats *Australia* in the America's Cup 4-1.
South Vietnam, Cambodia and Laos become communist regimes. Indonesia invades East Timor. King Feisal of Saudi Arabia is assassinated by nephew. General Franco dies and Spain becomes a monarchy under Juan Carlos I. A state of emergency is declared in India. Helsinki Pact on arms and human rights is signed. Portugal has democratic elections	Deaths: Mao Tse-Tung, Chou En-Lai of China. Jimmy Carter is elected US President. There are many earthquakes: in China over 655,000 die in one; the Friuli region of Italy is devastated. Syrian troops enter Lebanon to end the civil war. Israeli commandos free hostages held by Palestinians at Entebbe airport in Uganda. Viking I spaceship lands on Mars and sends back pictures	President Sadat of Egypt visits Israel in peace overture. The 'Gang of Four' is expelled from the Communist Party in China. The world's worst air disaster in the Canary Islands: 582 die. The Silver Jubilee Year of the Queen. German commandos storm a hijacked plane at Mogadisho and free 87 hostages. January is the coldest month ever recorded in the US	Italian statesman Aldo Moro is killed by Red Brigades terrorists. An American religious cult commits mass murder-suicide in Guyana. Pope Paul VI dies; John Paul I dies within 33 days of election; the first non-Italian pope for 456 years is elected and takes name John Paul II. US balloonists cross the Atlantic. The first test-tube baby, Louise Brown, is born in England	The Vietnamese invade Cambodia and set up a puppet government. The Shah of Iran goes into exile and Ayatollah Khomeini becomes ruler; 62 Americans in Teheran are taken hostage. A nuclear accident occurs at Three Mile Island in Pennsylvania. Margaret Thatcher becomes Britain's first woman prime minister. Lord Mountbatten killed by Irish terrorists.	Archbishop Romero of San Salvador is assassinated while he serves Mass. Mt St Helens erupts in the state of Washington. The United States fails in an attempt to rescue the hostages in Teheran. A new nation is born: Vanuatu, once the New Hebrides. A border dispute between Iraq and Iran breaks into war. John Lennon is shot dead.

The passing years 1981-85

	1981	**1982**	**1983**	**1984**

The Australian scene

1981 Former Sydney rugby league player Paul Hayward is sentenced to 20 years jail in Thailand for heroin smuggling. Azaria Chamberlain's parents are committed for trial. Antivenene for funnelweb spider bite becomes available. The Pitjantjatjara people in SA are granted land rights. Australia's first new bank in 50 years, the Australian, established.

1982 The Bank of New South Wales becomes Westpac. 'Bottom of the harbour' tax avoidance schemes are revealed by investigation into the painters and dockers' union. In NSW, the XPT train goes into service, and random breath-testing begins. Entrepreneur Harry Miller goes to jail for fraud. Two Australian tourists in Zimbabwe are murdered.

1983 Fires on Ash Wednesday burn out 359,000 hectares, destroy 2463 homes, claim 76 lives and cause over $500 million worth of damage. Four-year drought in Qld, NSW and Victoria ends with floods. Conservationists win battle to prevent the damning of the Gordon below Franklin River in Tasmania. The security organisation ASIS stages a mock raid on a Melbourne hotel.

1984 Drug fugitive Robert Trimbole is arrested in Dublin; later freed for lack of an extradition treaty. *The Age* publishes extracts from tapes illegally made by NSW police in 1980 that suggest widespread corruption. AIDS epidemic scares Australia. In Sydney 12 heart transplants are performed, and 7 die in a shoot-out between rival bikie gangs.

Politics and government

1981 Wage indexation is abolished and wage demands ensue. In Melbourne, 44 Commonwealth heads of government meet. Australia's strike record the world's worst for the third year in a row. NSW appoints its first woman solicitor-general, Mary Gaudron. Andrew Peacock resigns as Industrial Relations Minister.

1982 Australia and New Zealand lay the grounds for free trans-Tasman trade. The National Country Party drops the 'Country' from its name. John Cain heads Victoria's first Labor government in 27 years. Sir Ninian Stephen is sworn in as Governor-General. Changes to migrant selection aim to reunite families and attract skilled workers.

1983 Malcolm Fraser retires after an election won by Labor with a 25-seat majority. National economic summit meeting establishes a mood of 'national consensus' to lift the country out of recession. The expulsion of Russian diplomat Valery Ivanov leads to ostracising of lobbyist David Combe, and the resignation of Mick Young, Special Minister of State.

1984 The Nuclear Disarmament Party is a powerful force in the federal election but gains only one Senate seat; 6.8% of voters in the election vote informal. A Royal Commission begins investigation into British nuclear tests in Australia in 1950s. Under the Federal Women's Rights Bill discrimination is banned on grounds of sex, marital status or pregnancy.

Arts and entertainment

1981 *Air Supply* is the most successful Australian rock group to tour the US. Rupert Murdoch buys *The Times* of London. E. Smith's painting of Rudy Komon wins the Archibald Prize amid controversy over use of photograph for the portrait. Books: Patrick White's *Flaws in the Glass*; A. B. Facey's *A Fortunate Life*; Peter Carey's *Bliss*.

1982 *The Australian Women's Weekly* becomes a monthly magazine. Thomas Keneally is the first Australian to win the Booker Prize, with *Schindler's Ark*. The Australian National Gallery in Canberra is opened. Film: *The Man from Snowy River*. Book: *Just Relations* by Rodney Hall. Terracotta figures from China are brought for exhibition. Death: Fred Williams.

1983 The ABC becomes a corporation. Writer Alan Moorehead dies, also journalist Wilfred Burchett and author Christina Stead. The Melbourne Concert Hall and Sydney Entertainment Centre open. Films: *Careful, He Might Hear You; Man of Flowers; Phar Lap*. The Sydney Theatre Company stages an 8-hour dramatisation of *Nicholas Nickleby*.

1984 Writers Xavier Herbert and Hal Porter die. The National Film Archive is moved to a permanent home in Canberra. The $5.8 Araluen Arts Centre opens in Alice Springs. Films: *Annie's Coming Out; Silver City; My First Wife*. Television: *Waterfront; The Last Bastion*. Dance: Graeme Murphy's *After Venice*. Books: *The Land Beyond Time*, John Olsen and others.

Sport

1981 Three brothers from the Ella family are included in an international rugby team. Robert de Castella wins the Tokyo marathon. Sue Cook sets a world record in the 5000 metres walk, in 22 minutes 53.2 seconds. Mark Richards wins the world surfing championship for the third year in succession. Vicki Hoffman wins both the British and US open squash championships.

1982 Peter McNamara and Paul McNamee win the Wimbledon doubles. At the Commonwealth Games in Brisbane, Lisa Curry and Neil Brooks each win three gold medals for swimming. Australia takes the world hockey cup, and the women's cricket cup. Mark Richards is four times world surfing champion. The rugby league Kangaroos triumph in England.

1983 Robert de Castella becomes world's top marathon runner after three wins in US, Holland and Finland. NZ horse Kiwi wins the Melbourne Cup in a last-to-first sprint. Australia rejoices as *Australia II* captures the America's Cup, the first yacht from outside the US to win it. The 61-year-old potato farmer Cliff Young wins the 875-km Sydney to Melbourne foot race.

1984 'Ring-in': the horse Bold Personality is substituted for Fine Cotton at Eagle Farm races. At the Disabled Olympics, the Australian team wins 98 medals (33 gold), and at International Paralympics, Australians gain 56 medals (18 gold). Australia win 4 gold medals at Los Angeles Olympics. The Wallabies have a grand slam victory tour of Britain.

The outside world

1981 After 443 days, American hostages in Teheran are freed, half an hour after President Carter leaves office. Chairman Mao's widow Jiang Qing is condemned to death for crimes during China's Cultural Revolution (the sentence becomes life imprisonment). Assassinated: President Sadat of Egypt. Assassination attempts: President Reagan and Pope John Paul II.

1982 NATO officer Brigadier Dozier is rescued after 42 days as captive of Italian terrorists. The Falkland Islands are seized by Argentina; Britain wins the consequent 45-day war but three British warships and an Argentine cruiser are sunk. Israel invades Lebanon; over 700 Palestinians are massacred in a refugee camp. Leonid Brezhnev dies.

1983 Lech Walesa, leader of the outlawed Polish trade union Solidarity, is awarded the Nobel Peace Prize. The recipient of the first artificial heart dies after 3½ months. A Korean passenger plane strays into Russian airspace and is shot down. US troops land in Grenada after Marxist coup. Civilian rule is restored to Argentina. In Beirut 241 US marines die in a terrorist attack.

1984 Yuri Andropov dies and frail Konstantin Chernenko becomes Soviet leader. USSR boycotts the Los Angeles Olympic Games. Prime Minister Indira Gandhi of India is assassinated after a Sikh rebellion is quelled in Amritsar. President Reagan is reelected in a landslide. The world's worst industrial accident occurs in India: over 2000 die.

1985

Three face courts on charges of attempting to pervert the course of justice: High Court Judge Lionel Murphy wins a retrial after conviction; NSW District Court Judge John Foord is acquitted; ex-NSW Chief Magistrate Murray Farquhar is sent to prison. Builders Labourers' Federation leader Norm Gallagher jailed for corruption; later freed to face retrial.

The ANZUS alliance is at risk after New Zealand bans visits of nuclear-armed or -powered ships. The right of appeal to the Privy Council is abolished and the final constitutional ties with Britain thus severed. The Australian dollar reaches a record low of 59.3 US cents. John Howard becomes Liberal leader.

The Sydney Theatre Company finds new home at Wharf Theatre. The ambitious Australian musical, *Jonah Jones*, receives less than critical acclaim. David Williamson's *Sons of Cain* is premiered in Melbourne. Australian Bicentennial Authority chief David Armstrong resigns with settlement package of over $500,000.

Jeff Fenech becomes International Boxing Federation bantamweight champion. Adair Ferguson is first Australian woman to win a world sculling championship. Surfer Tom Carroll becomes only second to win successive world titles. Steven Lee wins World Cup giant slalom in Japan. Dr Geoffrey Edelsten buys Sydney Swans football club.

New Soviet leader Mikhail Gorbachev and President Reagan meet in Geneva. Hijacks: TWA jet in Beirut; cruise liner *Achille Lauro*; Egyptian plane (59 die in commando assault on plane). Greenpeace vessel *Rainbow Warrior* is bombed in Auckland. Soccer fans see 53 die in fire in Britain and 38 die in riot in Brussels. Mexico earthquake kills 10,000.

STONE WAS LAID BY
RABLE KING O'MALLEY. M.P.
F STATE FOR HOME AFFAIRS.
N THE 12TH MARCH 1913.

Part three:
Makers of modern Australia

This part of *Australia's Yesterdays* is a biographical dictionary of men and women who brought colour to life in Australia in the 20th century. Some of the subjects are great Australians whose careers were largely made outside Australia. Many of the others are the subjects of stories in the first part of the book and consequently their entries are restricted to date and place of birth and death. Persons whose names are given in capital letters within entries are themselves the subjects of entries.

King O'Malley (right), minister for Home Affairs, and Andrew Fisher, the Prime Minister, at the ceremony for the founding of Canberra in 1913

Ancher–Bradman

Sydney Ancher
Architect
Born Sydney, 25 February 1904
Died Newcastle, 8 December 1979

See p. 90

Dame Judith Anderson
(Frances Margaret Anderson-Anderson)
Actress
Born Adelaide, 10 February 1898

Stage-struck from childhood, Judith Anderson took lessons in acting and played *ingénue* parts in Sydney amateur productions. Her work attracted the attention of the actor-manager Julius Knight, and she made her professional debut in 1915, playing Stephanie with Knight in *A Royal Divorce*. After a few more appearances on the Australian stage, at the age of 20 she packed her suitcases and dress-baskets and confidently sailed for America.

Success did not come till 1924, when she was acclaimed for her performance in *Cobra*, and given the lead in David Belasco's Broadway production of *The Dove*. When she returned to Australia in 1927, to play the lead in *Cobra*, *Tea for Two* and *The Green Hat*, she was famous and was warmly received.

In 1937, she played Queen Gertrude to John Gielgud's Hamlet and Lilian Gish's Ophelia. In 1940, she was the sinister housekeeper, Mrs Danvers, in the film of Daphne du Maurier's *Rebecca*. But she was 49 when she played her greatest and most demanding role—Medea in Euripides' classic drama.

She returned to Australia in 1955 at the invitation of the newly-founded Elizabethan Theatre Trust to play Medea. Now a Dame

of the British Empire she has retained her Australian citizenship. 'I belong to Australia,' she says. 'I am most grateful to the United States for all it has done for me. But I'll always remain an Australian.'

John Antill
Composer
Born Sydney, 8 April 1904

John Antill began to learn to play the piano when he was about six. At the age of 10, he joined the boys' choir of St Andrew's Cathedral, Sydney, and ultimately became the choir leader and a soloist. But his father, a railways foreman, saw no future for a musician in Australia, and at the age of 16, Antill became an apprentice mechanical draftsman. While journeying by train to work each day, he wrote most of his opera *Endymion*, basing the libretto on Keats' poem.

When his five years' apprenticeship ended, Antill persuaded his father to let him enrol at the New South Wales Conservatorium of Music as a full-time student, where he studied the violin under Gerald Whalen and composition under Alfred Hill.

In 1932 he joined the chorus of the J. C. Williamson Imperial Opera Company as a tenor, so that he could learn stagecraft, and toured Australia and New Zealand for nearly two years, not only singing, but playing bass clarinet in the orchestra, prompting, and doing the backstage conducting.

After his operatic tours, Antill joined the ABC as assistant musical director, and soon afterwards began work on his ballet *Corroboree*, based on snatches of tunes that Antill picked up from Aborigines at La Perouse, Sydney. He was awarded the OBE in 1971 for services to music.

J. F. Archibald
Journalist
Born Kildare, Victoria, 12 January 1856
Died Sydney, 10 September 1919

On 31 January 1880, John Feltham (or as he preferred to be called, Jules François) Archibald founded *The Bulletin* with a fellow-journalist, John Haynes. He edited the magazine from 1886 until he sold it in 1914. Archibald encouraged such authors as HENRY LAWSON and BANJO PATERSON, and black-and-white artists like NORMAN LINDSAY and WILL DYSON. He also founded *The Lone Hand* in 1907. From early 1919 until his death he was literary editor of *Smith's Weekly*.

See p. 151

Harold Desbrowe Annear
Architect
Born Bendigo, Victoria 1866
Died Melbourne, 22 June 1933

See p. 89

Oscar Asche
Actor and playwright
Born Geelong, Victoria, 26 January 1871
Died London, 23 March 1936

John Stanger Heiss Oscar Asche wrote, produced and acted in the famous musical *Chu Chin Chow*, which ran in London for a record time—from August 1916 to July 1921. Asche had left Australia to study theatre in Europe, and had made his stage debut in London in

1893. He became known in England as a Shakespearean actor and producer, and his company toured Australia in 1909-10, and again in 1911-12. He brought *Chu Chin Chow* out in 1921, but after this tour and several theatrical failures he became insolvent. A flamboyant, temperamental man, Asche during the London run of *Chu Chin Chow* used to fortify himself nightly with a dinner of 2 or 3 kg of steak and a bottle of whisky.

See p. 141

Bert Bailey
Actor and producer
Born Auckland, New Zealand, 11 June 1872
Died Sydney, 30 March 1953

See p. 114

Snowy Baker
(Reginald Leslie Baker)
Champion all-round sportsman
Born Sydney, 8 February 1884
Died Hollywood, USA, 2 December 1953

See pp. 186-87

Sir Edmund Barton
Politician and lawyer
Born Sydney, 18 January 1849
Died Medlow Bath, NSW, 7 January 1920

On 31 December 1900, Edmund Barton, a Protectionist, became the first Prime Minister of the Commonwealth of Australia. As a member of the NSW Legislative Assembly since 1879, he had been active in the campaign for federation throughout the 1890s; leader of the Convention on Federation held in Adelaide in 1897; and chairman of the Constitutional Committee. Barton resigned as Prime Minister in September 1903 to take a seat on the Bench of the High Court. He was knighted in 1902.

See pp. 15-16, 19

Daisy Bates
Journalist and humanitarian
Born Ballychrine, Co. Tipperary, Ireland, 1861
Died Adelaide, 18 April 1951

Daisy Bates, whose maiden name was O'Dwyer Hunt, was a well-known wit and beauty in the salons of Dublin and London before she migrated to Australia in 1884, in the hope of curing a spot on her lung.

In New South Wales she married John Bates 'a man of the outback', and bore him a son, but the marriage was not a happy one and in 1894 Daisy returned to London, penniless. She managed to support herself by journalism, and in 1899, when reports of the ill-treatment of Aborigines reached England, *The Times* sent her on an assignment to investigate them.

This was the beginning of her dedicated work among Aborigines. She devoted herself to the study of Aboriginal languages, of which she recorded 188, and Aboriginal legends. For two years, she lived with an ancient tribe in the south-west of Western Australia and for a further two years, travel-

led with them. During World War I, she lived with the Aboriginal tribes near Fowler's Bay, and from 1919 till 1935, she occupied a pitched tent at Ooldea, on the Nullarbor Plain, eating mainly native food. To passengers on the Trans-Continental train she was a familiar sight, an anachronistic figure in her Edwardian ankle-length skirts, high starched collar and voluminous fly-veil.

She believed that contact with Western civilisation was fatal to the Aborigines. They needed their traditional environment. She looked after the very old, the very young, the very sick. Natives journeyed to her from long distances. She clothed them, nursed them, settled their disputes. In return they admitted her to their secret corroborees and initiation ceremonies. A Western Australian tribe gave her the name of 'Kabbarli', the grandmother.

In 1938, her book *The Passing of the Aborigines*, published in London, earned her an international reputation. She explained that the reason why she lived with Aborigines was because she could not bring herself to leave them. 'No one else was willing to live as I have lived,' she said.

When she was more than 80 years of age, she went back again to live with tribal Aborigines, this time at Wynbring, 177 kilometres east of Ooldea. Illness compelled her to return to Adelaide, where she died in 1951.

Octavius Beale
Piano manufacturer and philanthropist
Born Ireland, 23 February 1850
Died Stroud, NSW, 16 December 1930

Beale formed a company to import sewing machines and pianos in 1879. Then in 1893

he established Australia's first piano factory in Sydney; it ceased production in 1975. In 1903 Beale was appointed one of 12 members of a royal commission into the decline of the birth rate in New South Wales (he had 12 children himself). He then asked to be appointed a one-man commission into drugs and patent medicines, and produced a voluminous critical report.
See p. 286

Sir Frank Beaurepaire
Swimmer and businessman
Born Melbourne, 13 May 1891
Died Melbourne, 29 May 1956

See p. 192

George Bell
Painter
Born Melbourne, 1 December 1878
Died Melbourne, 22 October 1966

See pp. 134-5

Francis Birtles
Overlander
Born Melbourne, 7 November 1882
Died Sydney, 1 July 1941

Francis Birtles' life was adventurous and varied. At the age of 16, after running away to sea, he left his ship at Cape Town to fight in the Boer War. On his return to Australia in 1907, he set out by bicycle to Melbourne from Fremantle; later bicycle rides included one from Sydney to Darwin. In 1912, Birtles was the first person to cross Australia by car from Fremantle to Sydney. In 1914, with photographer FRANK HURLEY, he made a 15,000 kilometre tour of tropical Australia and also pioneered the overland route from London to Australia in 1927, although it was not completed until 1955-56.
See p. 215

Charles Blackman
Painter
Born Sydney, 12 August 1928
See pp. 134-5

Edouard Borovansky
Ballet dancer, teacher and director
Born Czechoslovakia, 24 February 1902
Died Sydney, 18 December 1959

In 1939, Edouard Borovansky opened a ballet school in Melbourne; from it grew the Borovansky Ballet, whose dancers formed the nucleus of the Australian Ballet. The Borovansky Ballet gave its first season in Melbourne in 1940, and reached a high professional standard. Borovansky had first come to Australia with Pavlova's company in 1926, and again in 1929. Then in 1938 he toured with Colonel de Basil's Covent Garden Russian Ballet, and this time he remained in the country, becoming an Australian citizen in 1944. He introduced ballets on Australian themes by himself and other choreographers.
See p. 147

Arthur Boyd
Painter
Born Melbourne, 24 July 1920

One of Australia's best-known contemporary painters, Arthur Boyd first made his name with a fine series of paintings of the Wimmera district of Victoria. Prior to this, his paintings had been shown in the early Contemporary Art Society exhibition in Melbourne during the late 1930s. In 1960 he went to London, where he was also successful. After a term as artist-in-residence at the Australian National University, he has made his return to Australia permanent and now lives near Goulburn.
See p. 135

Martin Boyd
Writer
Born Lucerne, Switzerland, 10 June 1893
Died Rome, 3 June 1972

Martin Boyd was a novelist whose best-known books are his four novels about the Langton family. Like *Lucinda Brayford* (1946), which is probably his best work, the Langton tetralogy has an Australian historical background. Martin Boyd's autobiography, *Day of my Delight*, is interesting for the insights it gives into his antecedents.

Robin Boyd
Architect and writer
Born Melbourne, 3 January 1919
Died Melbourne, 15 October 1971

An influential critic up to the time of his death, Robin Boyd was a cousin of ARTHUR BOYD and a nephew of MARTIN BOYD. *The Australian Ugliness*, published in 1960, criticised the Australian aesthetic scene. He designed the Australian displays at Expo 67 in Montreal and Expo 70 in Japan.
See p. 79

Jack Brabham
Racing car driver
Born Sydney, NSW, 2 April 1926

See p. 191

John Bradfield
Civil engineer
Born Brisbane, Queensland,
25 December 1867
Died Sydney, 23 September 1943

In 1912, as an engineer with the Public Works Department of NSW, Bradfield's plans for an underground railway system and a cantilever bridge across Sydney Harbour were approved by State Parliament. After travelling abroad to study the design of underground railways and long-span bridges, he advised the companies tendering for the Sydney Harbour Bridge in 1922.
See pp. 54-5

Sir Donald Bradman
Cricketer
Born Cootamundra, NSW, 27 August 1908

See pp. 176-77

Burnet–Finey

Sir Macfarlane Burnet
Biologist
Born Traralgon, Victoria, 3 September 1899

Frank Macfarlane Burnet, one of the world's great immunologists and virologists, is the son of a bank manager. From Geelong College he went to Melbourne University. He graduated as a doctor in 1921.

His first job was as resident pathologist at the Melbourne Hospital. He was in his mid-twenties when he was awarded a Beit Fellowship for medical research and went to London to work at the Lister Institute. Two years later, he was appointed assistant director of Melbourne's Walter and Eliza Hall Institute, a research establishment specially concerned with virus diseases. His only break with this institute—of which he became director in 1944—until his retirement in 1965 was from 1931 to 1934, when he went back to England and Europe. He was visiting worker at Britain's National Institute of Medical Research at Hampstead on that historic day in 1933 when the ferrets in the laboratory began to sneeze. The sneezing meant that the influenza virus had been isolated.

In 1935, with Jean Macnamara, he did important work on psittacosis, a disease transmitted by birds, after an outbreak in Victoria. In 1937, he isolated and identified the causal agent of Q fever, an acute infectious disease which affects people associated with cattle, sheep or goats. Current work on the problem of making the body tolerate human organ grafts owes much to him but possibly his greatest influence has been in the field of ideas. He believes that fundamental research may solve the most elusive of life's secrets. 'Pure research,' he has said, 'satisfies that almost mystic desire to do something towards seeing the universe all of one piece.'

Burnet was knighted in 1951 and in 1960 he shared the Nobel Prize for Medicine.

Arthur Butler
Aviator
Born Shirley, England, 8th June 1902
Died Sydney, 13 April 1980

In 1930, Arthur Butler designed, built and tested the first all-metal aircraft to be designed and flown in Australia. In October 1931, he clipped two hours off the Englishman C. W. A. Scott's England-Australia record of two days, twenty-three hours set during the 1933 air race. His plane was a 5.4 m long Comper-Swift monoplane.
See p. 239

'Professor' Fred Cavill
Swimmer and teacher
Born London 1839
Died Sydney 1927

See p. 192, for Cavill and his family

Percy Cerutty
Athlete
Born Melbourne, 10 January 1895
Died Portsea, Victoria, 14 August 1975

See p. 184

Andrew 'Boy' Charlton
Swimmer
Born Sydney, 12 August 1907
Died Avalon, NSW, 11 December 1975

See p. 193

Charles Chauvel
Film director
Born Warwick, Queensland, 7 October 1897
Died Sydney, 11 November 1959

See pp. 115, 187

Sir Harold Clapp
Railway engineer
Born Melbourne, 7 May 1875
Died Melbourne, 20 October 1952

See p. 220

Sir Ian Clunies Ross
Scientist and administrator
Born Bathurst, NSW, 22 February 1899
Died Melbourne, 20 June 1959

In 1949, Ian Clunies Ross became the first director of the Commonwealth Scientific and Industrial Research Organisation—the CSIRO. He held this position until his death. A veterinary scientist, Clunies Ross took a leading part in widening the scope of the CSIRO to cover wool, minerals and other topics of industrial concern.

Sidney Cotton
Aviator
Born Goorganga, Queensland, 17 June 1984
Died London, February 1969

When he did his flying training in England in 1916. Cotton flew solo after only a few weeks in the air. He devised the 'Sidcot' flying suit, made in one piece with layers of fur, airproof silk and a waterproof exterior material, when flying bombing raids over Germany. Between the wars Cotton pioneered air services in Newfoundland. In August 1939, when World War II was imminent, he produced an audacious plan to fly Field-Marshal Hermann Goering from Germany to England to meet the British Prime Minister Neville Chamberlain, in order to avert war.
See p. 239

Stan Cross
Cartoonist
Born Los Angeles, USA, 3 December 1888
Died Armidale, NSW, 16 June 1977

See pp. 150-51, 153-54, 164

John Curtin
Politician
Born Creswick, Victoria, 8 January 1885
Died Canberra, 5 July 1945

Curtin became Labor Prime Minister of Australia in 1941, during World War II. In 1942 he introduced conscription without a referendum, although he had vigorously campaigned against conscription during World War I.
See p. 312

Les Darcy
(James Leslie Darcy)
Boxer
Born near Maitland, NSW, 28 October 1895
Died Memphis, Tennessee, 24 May 1917

See p. 181

Jack Davey
Radio personality
Born Auckland, NZ, 8 February 1910
Died Sydney, 14 October 1959

Jack Davey was one of Australia's best-known radio personalities, and virtually changed the Australian concept of radio as a medium of entertainment. He arrived in Sydney in 1931 and joined station 2GB as a singer, but was soon conducting talk and quiz shows. The 'Hi ho everybody!' with which he began the breakfast show was soon known all over the country. In his last year of work Davey made 682 shows.
See p. 122

Peter Dawson
Singer
Born Adelaide, 31 January 1892
Died Sydney, 26 September 1961

See p. 107

Francis Edward De Groot
Soldier and antique dealer
Born Dublin, Ireland, 24 October 1888
Died Dublin, 1 April 1969

De Groot was the horseman who, on 19 March 1932, dashed forward at the opening ceremony for the Sydney Harbour Bridge and cut the ribbon wih his sword before the NSW Premier, JACK LANG, could reach it with his ceremonial scissors. As a member of an extreme right-wing organisation called the New Guard, he was pledged to fight socialism and therefore Lang. De Groot was first charged in the Lunacy Court and was discharged; he was then charged with damaging a ribbon worth £2 [$26.50], and fined £5 [$66] plus £4 [$52.80] costs.
See p. 55

Alfred Deakin
Politician
Born Melbourne, 3 August 1856
Died Melbourne, 7 October 1919

The first Federal Attorney-General of Australia, Deakin was a Protectionist and Prime Minister three times between 1903-10. He started his political career in Victorian politics, where he was responsible for the inauguration of the Murray Valley irrigation scheme in 1885. He played a major role in seeing the new Australian Constitution accepted by the British Parliament.
See pp. 15-16, 25

Roy de Maistre
Painter
Born Bowral, NSW, 27 March 1894
Died England, 2 March 1968

See p. 133

C. J. Dennis
(Clarence Michael James Dennis)
Poet and journalist
Born Auburn, SA, 7 August 1876
Died Melbourne, 22 June 1938

See p. 167

Sir William Dobell
Painter
Born Newcastle, NSW,
24 September 1899
Died Wangi, NSW, 14 May 1970

See p. 133-135

Sir Russell Drysdale
Painter
Born Bognor Regis, England,
7 February 1912
Died Sydney, 29 June 1981

See p. 133-35

John Duigan
Aviator
Born Terang, Victoria, 31 May 1882
Died Ringwood, Victoria, 11 June 1951

See pp. 230-31

Bob Dyer
Radio and television personality
Born Nashville, Tennessee, 22 May 1909
Died Gold Coast, 9 January 1984

Bob Dyer's radio show *Pick a Box* set a record in 1970 as the longest running peak-
hour television show. Through it, Dyer's
slogans—'Howdy customers' and 'Tell them
Bob sent you'—became known throughout
the country. Dyer started in vaudeville and
radio as a hillbilly comedian, making his first
tour of Australia in 1937. He returned in 1940
to appear on the Tivoli circuit, and was first
heard on Australian radio in 1941. In 1957
Pick a Box took him to television. Production of the show ceased in 1971.

Sir John Eccles
Scientist
Born Melbourne, 27 January 1903

John Carew Eccles, one of the world's most
distinguished brain scientists, was educated
at Warrnambool and at Melbourne University. In 1925, he took his master of arts degree, and became a Rhodes Scholar. After
working in England, he returned to Australia
in 1937 to become director of the Kanematsu
Memorial Institute of Pathology at Sydney
Hospital. In 1943, he was appointed professor of physiology at the University of
Otago, New Zealand, and in 1951, professor
of physiology at the John Curtin School of
Medical Research at the Australian National
University. From 1957 to 1961, he was president of the Canberra Academy of Science.

Knighted in 1958, in 1963 he shared the
Nobel Prize for Medicine. The citation said
that he had reached a new level of clarity in
the problem of nervous transmission.

Eccles has contributed greatly to know-

ledge of the way nerves interact in the spinal
cord. By inserting fine micro-electrodes into
single cells in the spinal cord, he has been
able to measure how the very small electrical
potential present in the cell changes when
the cell is excited or inhibited. Combined
with electron microscopic studies, this work
has enormously advanced understanding of
the working of the central nervous system.
He has also investigated the part of the brain
which controls posture and locomotion.

Eccles left the Australian National University in 1966 but he did not retire. He took
up a position as professorial lecturer at a new
Institute of Biomedical Research in Chicago,
but soon moved to the State University of
New York, where he continued his researches. In 1976 he moved to Switzerland.
In spite of his researches into the function
of the brain, he thinks man is a spiritual
being. 'If we are to move into the 21st century
there has to be a radical change in the basic
philosophy of man,' he told an interviewer
in 1973. 'The academic world is betraying
man. They are presuming to know the whole
nature of man and how he should be taught
and how he should behave.

'Our academic institutions will have to become much more open to ideas which go
against the customary materialistic concepts.'

Herb Elliott
Runner
Born Perth, 25 February 1938

See p. 184

Louis Esson
Playwright, author and journalist
Born Edinburgh, 1879
Died Sydney, 27 November 1943

See p. 138

Herbert Vere Evatt
Politician and jurist
Born East Maitland, NSW, 30 April 1894
Died Sydney, 2 November 1965

A brilliant but controversial Labor politician, Evatt came to politics from a successful legal career; and first entered
Federal Parliament in 1940. He led the
Australian delegation to the Paris Peace
Conference in 1946. Evatt took great interest in the formation of the United
Nations and was President of the UN General Assembly in 1948-49. On taking up the
leadership of the Labor Party in 1951, Evatt
found himself bitterly opposed to ROBERT
MENZIES, the leader of the Liberal Party.
After the 1955 Labor Party split Evatt remained leader of the newly-formed ALP
until 1960, when he became Chief Justice
of New South Wales.

See pp. 133-34

Peter Finch
Actor
Born London, 28 September 1916
Died Beverly Hills, California,
14 January, 1977

Peter Finch was the son of Professor George
Ingle-Finch, a scientist and mountaineer. He
was educated by a Buddhist monk in India,
at a school in France, and at the North Sydney Intermediate High School. After leaving
school, he tried his hand as a journalist, a
waiter, a jackaroo, and comedian's stooge.

He joined George Sorlie's famous Tent
Theatre Company, travelling widely
throughout Queensland and the New South
Wales outback. His first straight acting job
was in *While Parents Sleep* in 1935 and he
had a minor role in the Australian film *Dad
and Dave Come to Town*.

After the war, he joined a company which
had its headquarters in the tiny Mercury
Theatre in Phillip Street, Sydney; it presented lunch-hour plays to factory workers.
While he was performing Molière's *Le
Malade Imaginaire* at a factory canteen, he
was spotted by Laurence Olivier and Vivien
Leigh, who suggested he should go to London to further his career.

He made his London debut in 1949, at
Wyndham's Theatre, playing Ernest Piaste
in James Bridie's play *Daphne Laureola*, supporting Dame Edith Evans. Within a few
years, he had played a great variety of roles
in West End theatres and become an established and versatile film star.

See p. 114

George Finey
Cartoonist
Born Auckland, NZ, 15 March 1895

George Finey came to Australia after World
War I to join the staff of *Smith's Weekly*. He
was soon the top caricaturist in Australia.
When *Smith's Weekly* closed down in 1950,
Finey turned to painting; he was possibly
the first Australian painter to exploit the
possibilities of collage.

See p. 151

Fisk–Herbert

Ernest Fisk
Radio pioneer
Born Sunbury-on-Thames, England,
8 August 1886
Died Sydney, 8 July 1965

See pp. 118-19

Doris Fitton
Actress and theatre director
Born Manila, Philippines, 3 November 1897
Died Sydney, 2 April 1985

Doris Fitton played her first part with the Melbourne Repertory Theatre at the age of 18. In August 1930 she opened the Independent Theatre in St James Hall, Phillip Street, Sydney, and was director of the theatre until its closure in 1977. After a few months the Company moved to Bligh Street, and then in 1939 to North Sydney. The Independent Theatre School was started in 1931. In 1974, Doris Fitton returned to the stage temporarily to take a part in *A Little Night Music* for J. C. Williamson's.

See p. 138

Lord Florey
Scientist
Born Adelaide, 24 September 1898
Died Oxford, England, 23 February 1968

Howard Florey, a key figure in the development of penicillin, was the son of a boot manufacturer. He was educated at Kyne College, St Peter's Collegiate School, and the Adelaide University, where he did a medical course, and was awarded a Rhodes Scholarship for 1921. At Oxford he graduated Bachelor of Science, and in 1935 he returned to Oxford to become professor of pathology. Here began the fruitful and famous collaboration with Professor Chain, a refugee from Hitler's Germany.

Together, they organised a systematic study of anti-microbial substances produced by micro-organisms. The first of these antibiotics to be investigated was an unstable mould called penicillin. The Scots-born bacteriologist Alexander Fleming had discov-

ered this in 1928, but it had not been put to clinical use. Florey carried out crucial experiments that demonstrated the great therapeutic value of penicillin. He succeeded in extracting it as a stable powder, and in treating patients with it. The first was a friend who was critically ill with meningitis. Within three days, penicillin effected a cure.

When World War II broke out, Florey went to America to arrange for the mass production of penicillin. In 1943, he was in the Middle East, studying its use for war wounds. In 1944, he lectured on penicillin in Russia, Australia and New Zealand. That year he was knighted, and the Australian Government asked him to plan a school of medical research—the John Curtin School—for the Australian National University. In 1958 he flew from England to Australia to open the £1,250,000 [$6 million] school.

In 1945, Florey shared with Fleming and Chain the Nobel Prize for medicine, and in 1965 became Baron Florey of Adelaide and Marston, and was awarded the rare Order of Merit. Installed as Chancellor of the ANU in 1966 his greatest honour had come in 1960 when he became the first Australian president of the Royal Society.

Florey was buried in Oxford, the city that had cradled his great work.

John Flynn
Founder of the Inland Mission
Born Moliagul, Victoria, 25 November 1880
Died Sydney, 5 May 1951

See pp. 290-91

Errol Flynn
Film actor
Born Hobart, 20 June 1909
Died Vancouver, Canada, 15 October 1959

The adjective 'swashbuckling' fits both the public screen roles played by Errol Flynn and his private life. After being expelled from three schools in Australia, Flynn spent some adventurous years in New Guinea. Offered the film part of Fletcher Christian in CHARLES CHAUVEL's *In the Wake of the*

Bounty in 1934 Warner Brothers offered him a contract in Hollywood. Flynn soon rose to stardom, while scandals in his private life brought him notoriety. From 1953 his career declined. One of his best-known screen performances was in the title role in the 1935 film *Captain Blood. The Adventures of Robin Hood* (1937) brought him further renown.

See p. 115

Sir Hudson Fysh
Aviator and founder of QANTAS
Born Launceston, Tasmania, 7 January 1895
Died Sydney, 6 April 1974

See p. 240

Dame Mary Gilmore
Writer and social worker
Born near Goulburn, NSW, 16 August 1865
Died Sydney, 3 December 1962

Mary Jean Cameron, better known by her married name of Mary Gilmore, began her career as a schoolteacher, and a writer of radical verse. In 1896 she went to Paraguay to take charge of the school at Cosme, the settlement in which a few hundred Australian bushworkers and tradesmen, led by the messianic Willian Lane, hoped to create a brave new world. Lane's utopian dream failed and four years later Mary Gilmore returned to Australia, disenchanted.

For 23 years she edited the women's page of *The Australian Worker*. She was a prolific writer, publishing six books of verse, and a tireless social worker. She championed the cause of underpaid shearers, of brutally treated Aborigines, and of children condemned to what was virtually slave labour in factories. She fought passionately for old age and invalid pensions, for women's electoral rights, for maternity allowances, for child health centres, for a new deal for illegitimate children, and against the retention of capital punishment.

For the last 10 years of her life, she wrote an unpaid weekly column for the Communist Party's newspaper *Tribune*. Despite this,

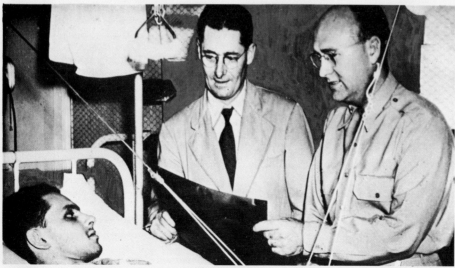

Howard Florey (centre) beside the bed of a wounded American soldier in a New York hospital in 1944

in 1937, she was made a Dame Commander of the Order of the British Empire, and when she died at the age of 97, still a working journalist, she was unquestionably the most distinguished woman in Australia. It was said of her that 'her indomitable mind, spirit and enterprise had a profound effect on Australian social and political organisation'.

James Gleeson

Painter, writer and critic
Born Hornsby, NSW,
21 November 1915

See p. 133

Percy Grainger

Pianist and composer
Born Melbourne, 8 July 1882
Died New York, 22 February 1961

See p. 146

Germaine Greer

Feminist, writer and academic
Born Melbourne, 29 January 1939

Germaine Greer gained world-wide attention in 1970 with her book about the status of women, *The Female Eunuch*. After studying at Melbourne and Sydney Universities, in 1963 she went to Cambridge University, where she became the first woman to be elected to the University Union.

Walter Burley Griffin

Architect
Born Maywood, Illinois, 24 November 1876
Died Lucknow, India, 13 February 1937

See pp. 70-73, 88

Sir Roy Grounds

Architect
Born Melbourne, 18 December 1905
Died Melbourne, 2 March 1981

One of the first Australian architects to design in the new 'international' style in the early 1950s, Roy Grounds is now best known for his Academy of Science building in Canberra (1959) and the National Gallery of Victoria building (1968).

See p. 91

Hal Gye

(Harold Frederick Neville)
Cartoonist,
Born Sydney, 22 May 1888
Died Melbourne, 25 November 1967

See pp. 153, 167

Robert Joseph Haddon

Architect
Born London, 25 February 1866
Died Melbourne, 16 May 1929
See pp. 79, 89

Ken Hall

Film director
Born Sydney, 22 February 1901
See p. 114

Sir Edward Hallstrom

Engineer and zookeeper
Born Coonamble, NSW, 25 September 1886
Died Sydney, 27 February 1970

Hallstrom played a leading part in the development of refrigeration in Australia and thousands of his 'Silent Knights' were dropped into New Guinea during World War II—as unbreakable containers for penicillin. Hallstrom was also interested in aviation and took part in some of the first Australian powered flights. From 1959 to 1967 he was director of Sydney's Taronga Zoological Park.

See pp. 100-01, 228

Don Harkness

Car designer and record breaker
Born Sydney about 1890
Died Sydney, 11 November 1972

See pp. 188, 215

Lawrence Hargrave

Scientist and inventor
Born Greenwich, England, 29 January 1850
Died Sydney, 6 July 1915

See p. 228

Harry George Hawker

Aviator
Born Moorabbin, Victoria, 22 January 1889
Died Hendon, England, 12 July 1921

See p. 233

Sir Robert Helpmann

Dancer, choreographer, actor and producer
Born Mount Gambier 9 April 1909

Robert Helpmann's mother encouraged him to recite poetry almost as soon as he could talk. At the age of five, in Adelaide, he began ballet lessons. He learned the piano while he was at the Prince Alfred Preparatory School, and by the time he was 11, had often danced in public. Dame Nellie Melba was impressed by his solo at a charity concert where he danced in a ballerina's tutu and a blonde wig.

In 1926, when Anna Pavlova visited Australia, he toured with her company as an extra, and took lessons from her leading male dancer, Laurent Novikoff. Pavlova urged him to study overseas, but it proved impossible at that time, and it was not till 1933 that he sailed for London.

Helpmann joined the Sadler's Wells Ballet School as a student and within a short time became the leading dancer of the company, succeeding Anton Dolin. When told he could select his junior lead from a class of young girls, he chose a dark-haired, dark-eyed 16-year-old named Peggy Hookham. With Helpmann as partner, she danced to world fame as the first and greatest British-trained ballerina—Dame Margot Fonteyn.

Helpmann also appeared in films *(Caravan, The Red Shoes, The Tales of Hoffmann)*; played Shakespeare at the Old Vic and at Stratford-on-Avon; did the choreography for many ballets *(Adam Zero, Hamlet, Comus, Miracle in the Gorbals, The Birds)*;

Sir Robert Helpmann with singer Shirley Bassey in Sydney for the opening of *Hair* in 1972

and produced two elegant operas at Covent Garden *(Coq d'Or* and *Madame Butterfly)*.

In 1949, he announced that he would retire. 'A ballet dancer's life is finished at 40,' he said emphatically.

But when he returned to Australia after 24 years, it was to appear in Shakespeare with Katherine Hepburn. And in 1958, after touring Australia and New Zealand in Noel Coward's *Nude with Violin*, he rejoined his old ballet company in Melbourne and danced again.

In 1965, Helpmann became joint artistic director, with Peggy van Praagh, of the Australian Ballet, and was in Sydney for the premiere of his ballet, *The Display*. But in 1974 Peggy van Praagh fell ill, and Helpmann became the sole director, choreographing *The Merry Widow* for the Australian Ballet in 1975. He was hardly prepared, however, for the shock decision to terminate his services which took place in 1976. Even more was to follow, for on his appointment as director of the Old Tote Theatre in 1978, the federal funds supporting it were withdrawn and Helpmann found himself discarded yet again. Resilient as ever, he returned to England, continuing to direct and dance.

See pp. 140, 255

Xavier Herbert

Writer
Born Port Hedland, WA, 15 May 1901
Died Alice Springs, NT, 10 November 1984

Xavier Herbert's novel *Capricornia*, about life in North Queensland and the harsh treatment of Aborigines, is one of the classics of Australian literature. Herbert had a varied early career, working as a stockman, deep-sea diver and sailor, and also as Superintendent of Aborigines at Darwin from 1935 to 1936. In 1975 his most ambitious and long-awaited novel — the 1464 page *Poor Fellow my Country*—was released and became an instant bestseller. Other novels include *Soldiers' Women* (1961) *Disturbing Element* (1963).

Heysen—Lindsay

Sir Hans Heysen
Painter
Born Hamburg, Germany, 8 October 1877
Died Adelaide, 2 July 1968

Hans Heysen's best paintings of the Australian landscape are beautiful and evocative, but unfortunately the popularity of his work has led to many inferior imitations. Heysen came to Australia as a child, and studied painting in Australia and Europe. His watercolours were popular from his first exhibition in 1908, his best-known subjects being the rocks of the Flinders Ranges and gum trees—of which he is an acknowledged master. Heysen won the Wynne Prize for landscape painting nine times.

Bert Hinkler
Aviator
Born Bundaberg, Queensland,
8 December 1892
Died Italy in a plane crash, 7 January 1933

See p. 232

Bland Holt
Actor-manager
Born Norwich, England, 24 March 1853
Died Melbourne, 28 June 1942

Known as the 'Monarch of Melodrama', Joseph Bland Holt astounded Australian audiences with his theatrical productions for three decades until his retirement in 1909. He had come to Australia with his actor father in 1857, making his stage debut at six. Skilful and versatile as both actor and producer, he embellished his productions with titillating effects.
See p. 138

Billy Hughes
Politician
Born London, 25 September 1864
Died Sydney, 28 October 1952

Prime Minister of Australia during World War I, William Morris Hughes split the Labor Party on the question of conscription. He formed the Nationalist Party, retaining the Prime Ministership when his new party was elected to government—though conscription was not introduced. A controversial politician, Hughes had been active in the Labor movement since the early 1890s, when he had organised the Waterside Workers Federation. He reached the peak of his career when he spoke for Australia at the Versailles Peace Conference at the end of World War I and ceased to be Prime Minister in 1923, though he continued in politics.
See pp. 234-36, 298, 303, 306-07

Barry Humphries
Satirist, writer and actor
Born Melbourne, 17 February 1934

Edna Everage, Australian housewife superstar from Moonee Ponds, and now a 'Dame', is Barry Humphries' most profound creation: he invented her and he acts her. But he has also lampooned many other Aus-

tralian types, including Sandy Stone, returned soldier; Les Patterson, diplomat; and pre-eminently, Barry McKenzie, originally created for a cartoon strip in the English magazine, *Private Eye*, and later the hero of a film, *The Adventures of Barry McKenzie* (1972). Humphries, who played Edna Everage and a number of other roles in this film, lives mainly in London.
See pp. 31, 94, 140, 147

Frank Hurley
Photographer
Born Sydney, 15 October 1885
Died Sydney, 16 January 1962

James Francis Hurley received world-wide recognition for the movie films he made when he accompanied four expeditions to Antarctica between 1911 and 1914. Hurley also travelled widely in Australia and in unmapped New Guinea, where he made the brilliant documentary *Pearls and Savages*. Hurley was an official Australian war photographer in both World Wars.

George Johnston
Novelist
Born Melbourne, 20 July 1912
Died Sydney, 22 July 1970

George Johnston began his writing career as a journalist in Melbourne, and during World War II he gained a reputation for his despatches from battle zones for American magazines and Australian newspapers. After the war Johnston became a pacifist, and for 10 years he retired with his wife—the writer Charmian Clift—and family, to live on the Greek island of Hydra. His best-known work is the semi-autobiographical novel of growing up in Australia, *My Brother Jack*, published after he returned to Australia in 1964.
See pp. 31, 266-67

Eileen Joyce
Pianist
Born Zeehan, Tasmania, 21 April 1912

Eileen Joyce, the barefoot girl of the Australian bush who became a great concert pianist, was born in a tent in Tasmania. Her father, an impoverished bushman of Irish descent, moved to the back-blocks of Western Australia, near Kalgoorlie, when she was a baby. With her brothers and sisters, she was brought up in a wooden hut which had no furniture except a table.

The first piano Eileen played was a battered instrument in a miner's pub. At the convent school where she was educated she took sixpence-a-week [33c] piano lessons. Percy Grainger and Wilhelm Backhaus heard her play when they visited the convent and insisted that she should study abroad. A local appeal raised £900 [$12,000] to send her to Leipzig for three years.

After her training in Germany she went to England as a teenager and had a desperate struggle to establish herself. Gramophone companies refused to record her, so she saved £7 10s [about $100] and paid to have

a record made. When Parlophone, the recording company, heard the record they immediately bought it and commissioned her to make more. Her records became immensely popular, she played regularly for the BBC, and made sound tracks for three successful films: *The Seventh Veil, Brief Encounter* and *Wherever She Goes*, the story of her life. By 1950, she had the widest following of any concert pianist in England.

She gave up concerts in the early 1960s. Plagued by muscular trouble when she played long sessions, she returned to London after an exhausting tour of India and Hong Kong, and decided to retire to her home in Chartwell Farm, Kent, where Sir Winston and Lady Churchill were her neighbours and close friends.

In 1967, she staged a highly acclaimed come-back at a charity concert with the Royal Philharmonic Orchestra at the Royal Albert Hall, and in 1971, she received an honorary doctorate from Cambridge University. She had come a long way from the little tent.

Sir James Joynton-Smith
Businessman and entrepreneur
Born London, 1858
Died Sydney, 10 October 1943

See pp. 150-51

Annette Kellerman
Swimmer and film actress
Born Sydney, 1887
Died Gold Coast, 6 November 1975

See p. 193

Thomas Keneally
Writer
Born Sydney, 7 October 1935

Recognised as one of Australia's most important novelists, it was not his plan to become a writer. He spent seven years studying for the Roman Catholic priesthood, but withdrew just two weeks before his ordination. Turning to law, after three years of study, he abandoned this also.

Turning to writing as a profession, his first ventures appeared in *The Bulletin*, to be followed by a prolific list of novels, some like *Three Cheers For The Paraclete* (1968) drawing on his experiences in the seminary; and others like *Bring Larks And Heroes* (1967) turning to Australian history for their theme. Apart from a short stint as Lecturer in Drama at the University of New England, he has continued to make his living by writing.

Sister Kenny
Nurse, innovator
Born Warialda, NSW, 20 September 1886
Died Toowoomba, Queensland,
30 November 1952

Elizabeth Kenny was brought up on a property on the Darling Downs, Queensland. She took up nursing with the aim of becoming a missionary in India, but after graduating in 1911, became a bush nurse in Queensland.

Early in her nursing career she encountered cases of poliomyelitis (infantile paralysis) and devised a method of treating them that was directly opposed to accepted medical practice.

During World War I, she was wounded on active service in France. When she recovered, she served on transports bringing sick and wounded soldiers back to Australia. After the war, and an interlude as matron of a big English military hospital she resumed her bush nursing in Queensland.

She invented and patented a stretcher that allowed patients to be treated for shock while being transported, and in 1933, when there was an epidemic of poliomyelitis, opened a free clinic in a Townsville backyard, meeting some of the costs with royalties earned by her stretcher. Despite the continuing opposition of the medical profession, she achieved remarkable cures, and in 1934 her clinic received government recognition.

In 1940, with references from the Queensland Government, which had always supported her, Sister Kenny went to the United States, where she demonstrated her theories.

She met with initial discouragement, but slowly won recognition and in December 1941, her theories were endorsed by the medical committee of the National Foundation for Infantile Paralysis. She became guest instructor at the University of Minnesota Medical School, and in 1942 the Elizabeth Kenny Institute of Minneapolis was founded.

Several other Kenny clinics were opened, and Sister Kenny received many honours, including the Distinguished Service Gold Key of the American Congress of Physical Therapy, and degrees from New York, Rochester and Rutgers Universities. She lunched with President Roosevelt, himself a poliomyelitis victim, at the White House, was given by special act the right to enter and leave the United States at will, and a feature film was made dealing with the main features of her life and work.

Sir Charles Kingsford Smith
Aviator
Born Brisbane, 9 February 1897
Died Bay of Bengal, 8 November 1935

See pp. 197, 236-37

John and Ilsa Konrads
Swimmers
Born Riga, Latvia, 21 May 1942 (John) and 29 March 1944 (Ilsa)

See p. 193

Jack Lang
Politician
Born Sydney, 21 December 1876
Died Sydney, 27 September 1975

During his second term of office as Labor Premier of NSW (1930-32), John Thomas Lang was dismissed from his position by the NSW Governor, Sir Phillip Game, for unconstitutional action. It was during the De-

pression, and Lang had barricaded the Treasury, proclaimed 'wages before dividends', and refused to honour overseas interest payments. Lang was expelled from the NSW Labor Party in 1943, but he always retained his interest in politics. In 1974 he still edited a weekly newspaper.

See pp. 55, 236, 266, 343

Ray Lawler
Playwright and actor
Born Melbourne, 1921

No Australian play has been seen in as many places as Ray Lawler's *Summer of the Seventeenth Doll*. It was first produced in Melbourne in 1955, and was immediately acclaimed. The following year it was produced in London, backed by Sir Laurence Olivier; then it went to New York. It has been translated into Russian, and also made into a film (1959). Lawler, who played the role of Barney in the first Melbourne and London productions, began his career as a variety artist. He joined the National Theatre in Melbourne as an actor and producer.

See p. 139

Henry Lawson
Writer and journalist
Born Grenfell, NSW, 17 June 1867
Died Sydney, 2 September 1922

Undoubtedly Australia's best-known short story writer, Lawson was also a poet, adept at producing the lilt of the popular ballad. His characters were almost all drawn from life, and the reality of the bush was his fairly constant theme. He tended to a more tragic view of it than some other writers, among them, 'Banjo' Paterson with whom he carried on a running argument in *The Bulletin*.

Lawson's life, begun in a tent on the goldfields, was not always happy. His father was a Norwegian seaman whose attempts at farming failed to provide security for his family; and his mother, Louisa, the most important influence in Lawson's life, encouraged her son's interest in writing, but he failed to matriculate and could not find a suitable job in Sydney. He did, however, become a regular contributor to *The Bulletin*, and his name was soon well-known. Nonetheless, happiness and economic security continued to elude him, and although he married in 1896, he had already begun a battle against alcoholism.

In 1899, he estimated that he had only earned about £700 [$20,000] for 12 years of writing. It depressed him that Australian writers received so little encouragement and he said that his advice 'to any young Australian writer whose talents have been recognised would be to go steerage, stow away, swim, and seek London, Yankee-land or Timbuctoo—rather than stay in Australia till his genius turned to gall, or beer'.

His stories, collected in *While The Billy Boils* (1896), *Joe Wilson's Mates* (1901) and later volumes, are brilliant in their economy and feeling for humanity, but their steady acceptance as true reflections of Australian

life did not save him from dying in poverty; although he did receive a State funeral!

Walter Lindrum
Billiards player
Born Kalgoorlie, WA, 29 August 1898
Died Surfers Paradise, 30 July 1960

See p. 185

Sir Daryl Lindsay
Painter and gallery director
Born Creswick, Victoria, 1 January 1890

See pp. 132, 145, 159, 164, 171

Sir Lionel Lindsay
Painter, illustrator and writer
Born Creswick, Victoria, 18 October 1874
Died Sydney, 22 May 1961

See pp. 132-3, 159, 168, 170-71

Norman Lindsay
Painter, illustrator, cartoonist and writer
Born Creswick, Victoria, 22 February 1879
Died Sydney, 21 November 1969

See pp. 17, 42, 45, 156, 162, 170-71

Percy Lindsay
Painter and illustrator
Born Creswick, Victoria, 17 September 1870
Died Sydney, 21 September 1952

See pp. 159, 168, 170-71

Lindsay–Rafferty

Ruby Lindsay (Ruby Dyson)
Painter
Born Creswick, Victoria, 1887
Died London, March 1919

See pp. 168, 170-71

Sumner Locke-Elliot
Playwright
Born Sydney, 17 October 1917

See p. 139

Raymond Longford
Film producer
Born Sydney, 1875
Died Sydney, 2 April 1959

See pp. 110-11

Lennie Lower
Humorist
Born Dubbo, NSW, 3 September 1903
Died Sydney, 10 July 1947

See p. 169

Lottie Lyall
Film actress
Born Sydney 1891
Died Sydney, 21 December 1925

See pp. 110-11

P. J. McGinness
Aviator
Born Framlingham, Victoria,
4 February 1896
Died Perth, 25 January 1952

See p. 240-41

Hugh Donald McIntosh
Boxing promoter and businessman
Born Sydney, 10 September 1876
Died in England, 2 February 1942

Hugh Donald McIntosh rose from pie-selling to own a prosperous catering business. He owned theatres and newspapers, and promoted the Burns-Johnson fight in 1908, also financing a 1200 m film of the event. McIntosh lived in grandeur in England for some years before his business empire crashed in the Depression.
See p. 180

Claude McKay
Journalist
Born Kilmore, Victoria, 19 July 1878
Died Bowral, NSW, 21 February 1972

In 1919, Claude McKay started the weekly magazine *Smith's Weekly* with JAMES JOYNTON-SMITH and R. C. PACKER. He was editor-in-chief from 1919 to 1927 and from 1939 to 1950, when it closed.
See p. 150

Gregan McMahon
Theatre director
Born Sydney, 2 March 1847
Died Melbourne, 30 August 1941

See p. 138

Daniel Mannix
Roman Catholic Archbishop
Born in Co. Cork, Ireland, 4 March 1864
Died Melbourne, 6 November 1963

Strongly anti-communist, Archbishop Mannix was the driving force behind the Catholic Action group whose activities precipitated the split in the Labor Party in 1955. The outcome of this was the formation of the DLP. He was appointed Coadjutor Archbishop of Melbourne in 1912, and became Archbishop in 1917. His outspoken views influenced the Irish Catholics of Victoria during the campaign against conscription during World War I. His support of the DLP has been seen as a prime reason why the party's influence was greatest in Victoria.
See p. 306

Sir Douglas Mawson
Geologist and Antarctic explorer
Born Bradford, England, 5 May 1882
Died Adelaide, 14 October 1958

Douglas Mawson came to Australia with his parents at the age of four. He was educated at Sydney's Fort Street High School and at the University of Sydney where he graduated bachelor of engineering, and, three years later, bachelor of science. In 1905, he published a report on a geological survey of the New Hebrides and took a poorly paid post as lecturer in mineralogy and petrology at the University of Adelaide.

In Adelaide, he studied glaciation at the Barrier Ranges and located the first radium-bearing ore in Australia. After making a difficult ascent of Mount Kosciusko, he was invited in 1907 to join the scientific team accompanying Ernest Shackleton to Antarctica. It included his former professor, the eminent geologist Edgeworth David.

Mawson played a very active part in Shackleton's expedition. In 1908 Mawson and three companions made the first ascent of Mount Erebus, a 3794 m high volcano. Later the same year, while Shackleton struggled to a spot only 156 km short of the Pole, Mawson, David and MacKay set off to locate the South Magnetic Pole. Their journey of over 2000 km on foot has become an epic of polar exploration.

Back in Australia, Mawson made expeditions to the Flinders Ranges, and did research on radioactive material found there.

In 1911-14, he organised and led the first Australian polar expedition, one of the most efficient and successful ever made. It explored more than 1600 kilometres of coast, made hundreds of readings, took many soundings and collected valuable specimens. Mawson named the land where he established his main base King George V Land, and His Majesty returned the compliment by knighting Mawson. The King was also honouring Mawson's courage, for he had endured an agonising 160 kilometre solo trek across the polar ice.

Mawson had incurred considerable debts which he met by lecturing in America and writing. In 1915, he published *The Home of the Blizzard*, a classic of polar exploration.

During World War I, he worked in England in the explosives section of the Ministry of Munitions, returning to Adelaide in 1920 to become professor of geology. His interest in Antarctic exploration continued. Between 1929 and 1931, he led two summer expeditions to the Antarctic, making important surveys and oceanographic studies, and using a plane to facilitate his work.

His outstanding polar achievements were largely responsible for the British Government agreeing in 1933 to cede to Australia sovereignty in Antarctica between the 45th and 160th eastern meridians.

Mawson was elected a Fellow of the Royal Society in 1933. At the time of his death, he was chairman of the Australian National Committee on Antarctic Research, and adviser to the Australian National Antarctic Research Expedition.

Dame Nellie Melba
Singer
Born Melbourne, 19 May 1861
Died Sydney, 23 February 1931

See pp. 144-5

Max Meldrum
Painter and teacher
Born Edinburgh, 3 December 1875
Died Melbourne, 6 June 1955

A strong influence on the Australian art scene, Max Meldrum aroused controversy in the 1920s and 1930s with his 'tonal' paintings. After 13 years study in Europe, Meldrum had returned to Melbourne in 1913, where his artistic philosophy of using only minimal drawing and colour in paintings and emphasising the 'tonality' instead brought him into conflict with the established Australian Impressionist school.

Sir Robert Menzies
Politician
Born Jeparit, Victoria, 20 December 1894
Died Melbourne, 15 May 1978

Robert Gordon Menzies, Prime Minister of Australia from 1949 to 1963, was a brilliant law graduate of the University of Melbourne. After making a reputation as a barrister, he was elected to the Victorian Legislative Assembly in 1929, and entered Federal Parliament in 1934. He became deputy leader of the United Australia Party and Prime Minister in 1939. He resigned after a disagreement with his Cabinet in 1941. In 1944 Menzies formed the Liberal Party and led the successful Liberal-Country Party coalition until 1963, when he retired and was knighted.
See pp. 132-33, 310-19

Sir John Monash
Soldier
Born Melbourne, 27 June 1865
Died Melbourne, 8 October 1931

General Sir John Monash has been called 'Australia's greatest soldier' for his role in World War I. He commanded the Australian

Army Corps in France in 1918, and broke through the Hindenburg Line, leading to the German surrender. After the war, Monash became chairman of the State Electricity Commission of Victoria.

Gladys Moncrieff
Singer and actress
Born Bundaberg, Queensland, 13 April 1892
Died Gold Coast, 8 February 1976

See p. 141

Albert Namatjira
Painter
Born Hermannsburg Mission, NT,
28 July 1902
Died Alice Springs, 8 August 1959

See p. 132.

Syd Nicholls
Cartoonist
Born Devonport, Tasmania,
20 December 1897
Died Sydney, 3 June 1977

See p. 164

Sir Sidney Nolan
Painter
Born Melbourne, 22 April 1917

Sidney Nolan, perhaps the most distinguished Australian painter of the century, attended a state school till he was 14. During the Depression, he became a professional racing cyclist, and worked in a variety of jobs.

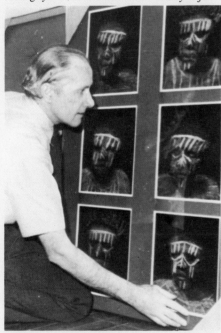

After doing a part-time correspondence art course and studying at Melbourne's National Gallery Art School, he designed advertisements for a hat company and, in 1938, turned to painting.

In 1940, he held his first exhibition in the tiny ramshackle room where he lived but sold nothing.

While stationed at Dimboola, in the Wim-mera district of Victoria, he painted a series of landscapes, raw, barren and startling. But it was not till after the war, when he started work on his famous Ned Kelly paintings that, in the words of art historian Dr Bernard Smith, he 'revealed that it was possible to create a witty, decorative and sophisticated art by turning to local history for his sources of inspiration'. Nolan held his first London one-man show in 1951, but it was not till 1957, when he held a large retrospective exhibition in London, that he was accepted as a major talent.

See pp. 134-35

Johnny O'Keefe
Singer
Born Sydney, 19 January 1935
Died Sydney, 6 October 1978

Johnny O'Keefe, 'The Wild One', was the most successful Australian rock 'n' roll singer of the 1950s and one of the country's first teenage idols. In 1955 changed his style to rock 'n' roll. In 1958 he was given his own national television programme, *Six O'Clock Rock*, which he conducted until it closed in 1961. He returned to television with *The Johnny O'Keefe Show* and *Where the Action Is*, but his later career was marred by ill health.

See p. 125

Sir Marcus Oliphant
Physicist
Born Adelaide, 8 October 1901

Marcus Oliphant, one of the progenitors of the hydrogen bomb, is also a most ardent opponent of nuclear weapons. Educated at the Universities of Adelaide and Cambridge, he worked in the famous Cavendish Laboratory under the eminent New Zealand atomic physicist, Lord Rutherford.

At the age of 34, Oliphant became the laboratory's assistant director of research, and from 1937 to 1950, was Poynting professor of physics and head of the physics department at the University of Birmingham. In 1943, he worked with American scientists on the project that eventually developed the atomic bomb that was used against Japan.

Oliphant was one of the team of scientists who, working with Rutherford, discovered the 'deuterium reaction' that led to the development of the hydrogen bomb, and during World War II, he did important research on radar and atomic energy. After the war, he played a key role in the development of nuclear power in Britain.

He has consistently opposed the use of nuclear weapons. In 1948, he reiterated his belief in the moral responsibility of the scientist. 'Scientific knowledge suffers from the disadvantage that from it spring industies that affect profoundly man's way of life ...' he said. 'So scientific discovery must be studied in relation to its use and misuse by mankind.'

Oliphant was knighted in 1959. From 1971 to 1976 he was Governor of South Australia.

King O'Malley
Federal politician
Believed born in Canada, 4 July 1858
Died Melbourne, 20 December 1953

Chief driving force behind the search for a national capital, King O'Malley arrived in Australia in the 1880s. When elected to the House of Assembly in South Australia in 1896 he soon showed himself to be a political radical. He advocated that children born out of wedlock be legitimised if the parents married, that lavatories be provided on trains, and that barmaids be abolished. In 1901, he was elected to the first Federal Parliament.

See pp. 68-71

Sir Hubert Opperman
Cyclist and businessman
Born Rochester, Victoria, 29 May 1904

See p. 174

Evelyn Ernest Owen
Inventor
Born Wollongong, NSW, 15 May 1915
Died Wollongong, NSW, 1 April 1949

During the 1930s, Owen invented and perfected a revolutionary sub-machine gun. Simple, sturdy, cheap to produce as well as being a reliable weapon, the Owen gun was patented in 1941 and manufactured in large quantities for the Australian army.

'Banjo' Paterson
Poet and journalist
Born near Orange, NSW, 17 February 1864
Died Sydney, 5 February 1941

Andrew Barton Paterson's poems sold tremendously in his lifetime, and are still popular today. The son of a grazing family, he practised as a solicitor in Sydney until about 1900, when he gave up the law to become a journalist and writer. His early ballad verses, written for *The Bulletin* under the name of 'The Banjo', were collected and published as *The Man From Snowy River and Other Verses* in 1895. Paterson was a war correspondent in the Boer War and in the Boxer Rebellion in China, and remained a journalist until his death.

See p. 166

Nat Phillips (Stiffy)
Comedian
Born about 1883
Died Sydney, 21 June 1932

See p. 140

Chips Rafferty
Actor and film producer
Born Broken Hill, NSW, 26 March 1909
Died Sydney, 27 May 1971

An actor whose style and appearance suggested the typical Australian bushman, Chips Rafferty starred in many successful Australian films. Originally named John William Goffage, he did not begin acting until he was 29, one of his first roles being in Cinesound's *Dad Rudd, MP*. Rafferty

Rene—Wright

made his name internationally when he played an Australian soldier in CHARLES CHAUVEL's *Forty Thousand Horsemen*, and he later appeared in several Hollywood films. One of his last films was *They're a Weird Mob* (1965).

See pp. 30, 115

Roy Rene (Mo)
(Henry van der Sluice)
Comedian
Born Adelaide, 15 February 1892
Died Sydney, 22 November 1954

See p. 140

Henry Handel Richardson
(Ethel Florence Robertson)
Writer
Born Melbourne, 3 January 1870
Died Hastings, England, 20 March 1946

Henry Handel Richardson remains one of Australia's most distinguished writers, although most of her life was spent in England. In 1877, at the age of 17, she went to Germany to study piano but abandoned music for writing. She returned to her native country only once, for a few months in 1912, to gather material for her masterpiece, *The Fortunes of Richard Mahony*. This great tragic novel deals with the struggle of a sensitive Irish doctor to adjust himself to the hurly-burly of the 1850s Gold Rush.

Tom Roberts
Painter
Born Dorchester, England, 9 September 1856
Died Kallista, Victoria, 14 September 1931

Sometimes called 'the father of Australian landscape painting', Tom Roberts was one of the initiators of Australian impressionist painting and a founder of the Heidelberg School. He had arrived in Melbourne in 1869, then returned to England to study. On coming back to Melbourne in 1885, he established an artists' camp at Box Hill. In 1901 he was commissioned to paint the first Federal Parliament.

See pp. 132-35

Alfred Cecil Rowlandson
Bookseller and publisher
Born Daylesford, Victoria, 15 June 1865
Died Wellington, NZ, 15 June 1922

See p. 168

Steele Rudd
(Arthur Hoey Davies)
Journalist and writer
Born Emu Creek, Queensland
14 November 1868
Died Brisbane, 11 October 1935

See p. 166

Harry Seidler
Architect
Born Vienna, Austria, 25 June 1923

Harry Seidler was one of the first architects to introduce the 'international' style of architecture to Australia in the late 1940s. He had worked with the famous architects Marcel Breuer in New York and Oscar Neimeyer in Brazil before coming to Sydney in 1948. In 1951 the house he designed for his parents won the Sulman Medal for design, and he won the medal again in 1967 for his circular tower, Australia Square, in Sydney.

See p. 90

Kenneth Slessor
Poet and journalist
Born Orange, NSW, 27 March 1901
Died Sydney, 30 June 1971

Kenneth Slessor took his first job as a reporter at the age of 19. For the rest of his life he was to be connected with newspapers and magazines—including four years as editor of *Smith's Weekly*, a term as an official war correspondent, and many years with the Sydney *Daily Telegraph*. However, he is probably best known as a poet. His major works, both published in the 1930s, are *Five Visions of Captain Cook* and *Five Bells* (the inspiration for John Olsen's large mural in the Sydney Opera House).

See pp. 52, 74, 151, 167, 262

Keith Smith
Aviator
Born Adelaide, 20 december 1890
Died Sydney, 19 December 1955

See pp. 234-35

Ross Smith
Aviator
Born Adelaide, 4 December 1892
Died Brooklands, England, 13 April 1922

See pp. 234-35

Cozens (or Cousens) Spencer
Film producer
Born North America
Died Canada, September 1930

See pp. 109, 110

Nellie Stewart
Actress and singer
Born Sydney, 20 November 1858
Died Sydney, 20 June 1931

See p. 141

Dame Joan Sutherland
Singer
Born Sydney, 7 November 1926

Joan Sutherland received her first singing lessons from her mother. She continued her musical studies while working as a private secretary, and sang in a number of concerts and oratorios.

In 1950, she won the Sydney *Sun Aria* competition. This encouraged her to continue her vocal studies in London at the Royal College of Music. After a year she joined the Royal Opera Company at Covent Garden and made her debut as the First Lady in Mozart's *Die Zauberflöte*.

With only six hours' notice, she sang Amelia in Verdi's *Un Ballo in Maschera* at the Hamburg State Opera.

After her marriage to the Australian pianist Richard Bonynge in 1954, she abandoned heavier roles to concentrate on operas by Donizetti, Bellini, Mozart and Handel.

Her international status was firmly established in 1959, when the Royal Opera Company presented her in Donizetti's *Lucia di Lammermoor* and in her New York debut critics groped for new metaphors to describe her brilliant coloratura technique.

On the establishment of the Australian Opera in 1969, she returned to her homeland and made a number of guest appearances, but in 1974, when she performed the four leading roles in *The Tales of Hoffmann*, she had committed herself to regular participation in the seasons of the company. With her husband, Richard Bonynge, as its musical director, Joan Sutherland, now a Dame of the British Empire, was the company's brightest star.

See p. 143

Tait brothers
Theatrical entrepreneurs, film producers

The Tait brothers, in 1905, made one of Australia's—and the world's—first feature films, *The Story of the Kelly Gang*, with script and direction by Charles Tait and all the family playing roles. Inspired by the film's success, they formed Amalgamated Pictures, which produced *The Mystery of the Hansom Cab*, among other films. In 1908 they formed their theatre management company J. and N. Tait and managed the Australian tours of many famous artists from overseas including MELBA, Paderewski, Chaliapin and Amy Castles. In 1920 the Tait brothers took over the management of the theatrical firm of J. C. WILLIAMSON.

See pp. 109, 138

Harley Tarrant
Car designer and record breaker
Born Clunes, Victoria, 1860
Died Melbourne, 25 February 1949

See pp. 213-14, 216

Arthur Tauchert
Film actor
Born Sydney, 1877
Died Sydney, 27 November 1933

C. J. DENNIS himself chose Arthur Tauchert, a former vaudeville actor, to play the title role in the 1919 silent film of his *The Sentimental Bloke*. His battered, good-natured face seemed to typify The Bloke, and he instantly became popular.

See pp. 110-11, 113

George Augustine Taylor
Painter, journalist, inventor
Born Sydney, 1872
Died Sydney, 20 January 1928

See pp. 118, 228

Frank W. Thring
Film producer
Born Wentworth, NSW, 1883
Died Melbourne, 1 July 1936

See pp. 114-15

Charles Ulm
Aviator
Born Melbourne, 18 October 1897
Disappeared 4 December 1934

See pp. 236-37

George Wallace
Comedian
Born Aberdeen, NSW, about 1894
Died Sydney, 19 October 1960

George Wallace made films for Efftee Studios in the 1930s. *His Royal Highness, Let George Do It* and *Harmony Row* were among his successes. For Cinesound he made *Gone To The Dogs*, which was less successful. However, Wallace did not become a full-time entertainer until 1919, when he became a partner in the comedy team 'Dinks and Onkus'.

See p. 115

Patrick White
Writer
Born London, 28 May 1912

Patrick White, the first Australian to be awarded the Nobel Prize for literature, exemplifies the biblical adage that 'a prophet is not without honour, save in his own country. . .' Acclaimed overseas as one of the greatest of living novelists, he has been savagely denigrated by Australian critics.

The descendant of a colonist who settled in New South Wales in the 1820s, White was born in London when his mother was visiting England. He went to school in Sydney and in England where he spent five years. Back in Australia, he worked as a jackaroo for two years, during which he made his first attempt to write a novel. When he was 20, he went to Cambridge to study modern languages, and continued writing. 'Ironed out in an English public school, and finished off at King's, Cambridge, it was not until 1939, after wandering by myself through most of Western Europe, and finally most of the United States, that I began to grow up and think my own thoughts,' he says.

The fruit of these wanderings was his first published novel, *Happy Valley*, which appeared just before the outbreak of World War II. In 1945 he spent a happy year in Greece where he found, as he puts it, 'not only the perfection of antiquity, but that of nature, and the warmth of human relationships expressed in daily living'.

After demobilisation, he lived in London where, immediately after the war, he wrote *The Aunt's Story*. It was published in 1948, and remains his favourite work. But he felt a persistent longing to return to the scenes of his childhood and in 1948, he returned to Australia setting the pattern of the post-war novel with *The Tree of Man* which deals with

the familiar themes of pioneering, flood, drought and bushfire. But essentially, the book is a psychological study of man's failure to communicate with others.

Yet there is no question that White is Australia's one novelist with an international reputation. In his own land he has received the coveted Miles Franklin award on two occasions, for *Voss* in 1957, and *Riders in the Chariot* in 1962. Many other novels have since appeared, among them *The Eye of the Storm*. He has also established a reputation as playwright, with *The Ham Funeral, Season at Sarsaparilla,* and *Big Toys*, to name only some. Not uncritical of Australia, when awarded the Nobel Prize for Literature in 1973, he set up a trust fund with the $80,000 prize money to assist Australian writers.

Sir Hubert Wilkins
Arctic Explorer
Born Mount Bryan East, SA,
31 October 1888
Died Framingham, Mass., USA,
1 December 1958

At the age of 20, Hubert Wilkins worked his way to England, and served as photographer and second-in-command with Stefansson's Arctic expedition of 1913-16.

In 1917, he was commissioned in the Australian Flying Corps and appointed official photographer to the AIF in France. He was twice mentioned in despatches, and won the Military Cross and Bar.

In 1919, he entered the English-Australia air race but retired after an adventurous flight to Turkey. In 1920-21, he was second-in-command of a British Antarctic expedition. He then served as naturalist and photographer with Shackleton's last expedition, and was in charge of the British Museum natural history expedition to Australia in 1923-25.

In 1928, he flew in a single-engine skiplane from Barrow, the most northerly headland in Alaska, to Spitzbergen, on the Arctic Circle, an achievement for which he was given a big civic welcome in New York, and knighted by King George V.

In 1930, the United States authorities sold him a submarine for one dollar, on condition that he scrap it when the expedition ended. Wilkins agreed, and named the submarine *Nautilus*, after the submarine in Jules Verne's *Twenty Thousand Leagues Under the Sea*. In it, he succeeded in travelling to within 640 kilometres of the North Pole.

J. C. Williamson
Theatrical entrepreneur
Born Mercer, Pennsylvania, 26 August 1845
Died Paris, 6 July 1913

James Cassius Williamson, whose name lives on in the theatrical firm he founded, introduced many famous performers to the Australian public. Among them were Sarah Bernhardt, Emma Albani, MELBA and ADA CROSSLEY.

See pp. 139-41, 142-3, 145, 312

Fred Williams
Painter
Born Richmond, Victoria, 23 January 1927
Died Melbourne, 22 April 1982

See p.135

Judith Wright
Poet and writer
Born Armidale, NSW, 31 May 1915

One of Australia's leading poets, Judith Wright is also the author of books for children, a critic and a conservationist. The daughter of a grazier, she was educated in Armidale and at the University of Sydney. Her first book, *The Moving Image*, was published in 1946. Her other books include *Woman to Man* (1949) and *Collected Poems* (1971), and, for children, *King of the Dingoes* and *Generations of Men*.

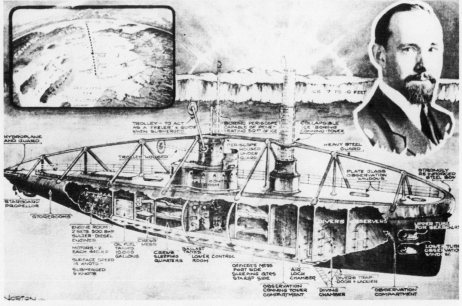

Sir Hubert Wilkins and the submarine in which he travelled beneath the Arctic ice-cap

Index

Page numbers in *italics* refer to
  illustrations

Abalone 36
Abbott, J. H. M. 30-31
Abbott, Sir John *14*
Aborigines 28-29
    land rights 28-29
    mistreatment 132, 341
    population 28
    reserves 28
Adams, Arthur 21, 138
Adams' Marble Bar 38
Adamson, L. A. 31, 229
Adamson, Rev. T. 197
Adelaide 62-63
    Eagle Hotel *63*
    Glenelg *63*
    John Martin's Store *62*
    Rundle Street *63*
    South Australian Hotel *62*
    plan for 62
    satellite development 62
Advertisements 158-61
    billboards 161
    classified 151
    posters 158-9, 160-1
Aerial League 228-9
Aerial Services Ltd. 240
Agache, Professor D. A. *71*
Air races:
    London-Sydney 238-40
Aitken, Jonathan 60, 64, 94, 173-4
Albert Park Ladies' Bowling Club 174
Alice Springs *75*
Allen, Frederick 248
Allen, J. Alex 21
Altmann, Herman 22
Amalgamated Wireless Australia 118,
  120
Americans in Australia 314-5
Amusements 103, 108-9
    at home 104-5
    childhood 130-1
    cruises 126
    magic lantern 104
    picnics 126-7
Ancher, Sydney 79, 90, *91*, 340
Anderson, Professor Francis 294
Anderson, Dame Judith 340
Anderson, Keith 236
Angus and Robertson 156-7, 166-7
Anketell, J. A. 220
Annear, Harold Desbrowe 79, 89, 340
Antill, John 340
Anti-transportation League 20-21
Anzac (racing car) 190
Anzacs 297
Aqua-planing *203*
Aranda artists 132
Archibald, J. F. 151, 158, 170, 340
Archibald Prize 133
Architectural styles 80-91
    California bungalow 83
    Spanish mission 83
    Queen Anne 83
    Tudor 83
Armstrong, Charles 144
Armstrong, Edward 156
Armstrong, Nellie, *see* Melba
Armstrong, Dr W. G. 40
Art:
    contemporary 132-5
    galleries 132-5
    prices for 135
Art Gallery of NSW 132-5
Arthur, Dr 270
Art nouveau 89, 93
Asche, Oscar 141, 340
Ashton, Howard 132
Ashton, Julian 133, 170
Ashton, Queenie *122*
Ashton, Will 132
Aunger, Murray 214-5
Austral, Florence 143
Australasian Motor Cab Company 210
Australasian Science Congress 98

Australian Academy of Art 133
Australian Boomerang Association
  174
Australian Broadcasting Commission
  121-2, 125
Australian Broadcasting Company 121
Australian Federation League 20
Australian flag designs 20, *21*
Australian Freedom League 301
Australian Inland Mission 290-1
Australian National Airways 240
Australian National Defence League
  300
Australian Opera 142
Australian Performing Group 139
Australian Rules, *see* Football
Australian Six 219
Australian Theatre Society 138
Australians:
    attitudes 30-31
    development 30
    typical 30-31
Auto Import Company 216
Automobiles 210-2, 214-9
    see also Motor cars
Aviation 228-39
    commercial 240-1
Avocado 37

Bailey, Bert *114*, 138, 340
Baird, John Logie 124
Baker, Reginald Leslie ('Snowy') 181,
  186-7, 340
Baker, Sidney J. 44
Bancks, J. C. 164
Bank notes 22-23
Bannister, Roger 184
Barlow, Fred 188
Barnet, Nahum 90
Barracluff, Mr J. 247
Barrett, Franklyn 109
Barry, Joan 257
Barton, Sir Edmund 15-16, 19-20, 298,
  340
Basic wage 262
Battarbee, Rex 132
Bates, Daisy 341
Bathurst *75*
Batten, Jean 121, 238
Battista, John 39
Battle of Broken Hill 305
Bayal, W. F. 51
Bayertz, C. N. 56
Beale, Octavius 279, 286, 341
Beale and Co. 104
Bean, C. E. W. 276
Beaurepaire, Sir Frank *192*, 341
Beck, Fred 174
Becke, Louis 168
Beecham's Pills 286
Beer
    consumption 40-41
    varieties 41
    adulteration 36
Bell, George 133
Bellin, Howard 39
Bennett, J. M. 234-5
Bennett, W. C. 54
Bentley, Dick 147
Berlei Ltd 250
Bernadini, Micheline 257
Beynon, Richard 139
Biddle, Albert 295
Bikini 257
Billiards 185
Birtles, Francis 28, *215*, 341
Blackfriars Demonstration School *294*
Blackman, Charles 133, 135
Blaikie, George 151
Bland, F. A. 270
Bloomfield, Professor John 281
Blundell, R. P. 159
Blunden, Godfrey 170-1
Boer War 297-9
Books 166-9
    paperbacks 168

Borgioli, Dino 142
Borovansky Ballet 147, 341
Borovansky, Edouard 147, 341
Boulder *75*
Bowers, Richard 65
Boxing 180-1
    standardisation of rules 186
Boyd, Arthur 341
Boyd, Martin 340
Boyd, Robin 79, 89, 94, 116-7, 340
Brabham, Jack 191, 340
Bradfield, Dr J. J. C. 54, 340
Bradman, Donald 174-5, 340
Brady, E. J. 163, 168
Brassey, Lord 113
Brearley, Major Norman 240
Brent of Bin Bin
    see Franklin, Miles
Brisbane 60-1
    Fire Brigade *60*
    Victoria Building *60*
    Queen Street *61*
    Regent Theatre *116*
British Motor Corporation 219
Brodsky, Leon 138
Brogan, D. W. 33
Brookes, Norman 184
Browne, Coral 138
Brownlee, John 106, 142-3
Bruce, Stanley Melbourne 120, 255
Bubonic plague 51, 282
Buchanan, Alfred 255
Buchdahl, Professor Hans 26
Buckley and Nunn *48*, 275
    tearooms 35
    mail order catalogue *244*
    window display *250*
Bull and Mouth, The 38
Bull, Mr T. W. 285
Bunny, Rupert 133, 136-7
Burdekin House, Sydney 34
Burdon, Alec 179
Burke, William 269
Burke and Wills 206
Burley Griffin, Lake *73*
Burnet, Sir Macfarlane 342
Burns, Tommy *180*, 181
Butler, Arthur *239*, 342
Butt, Dame Clara 145

Café Bohemia, Melbourne 35
Café Denat, Melbourne 35
Cain, Jack 35
Cairns *74*
Caldwell, Felix 218
Caldwell-Vale Company 218
California bungalow 83
Calwell, Arthur 21, 26-7
Camels *206*, 220
Campbell, Donald 190
Campbell, Eric 55
Campbell-Black, T. 238
Camusso, Lorenzo 35
Canberra:
    naming 70
    plan 69-73, 88
Carlton Brewery 160
Carmichael, H. C. 294
Car-Glynn, Neva 140
Carroll, E. J. 110, 186-7
Cartoons 152-5
Castlecrag 88
Castles, Amy 142
Cavill family 192-3, 342
Cazaly, Roy 178
Celott, Welsa 112
Censorship:
    press 303, 315, 318
    theatre 139
    books 156-7
Cerutty, Percy 184, 342
Chain stores 274
Charlton, Andrew 'Boy' *193*, 342
Chauffeurs' Club of Victoria 210
Chauvel, Charles 115, 342
Chemists 272

Chevrolet, Louis 219
Chichester, Francis 238
Chifley, J. B. 219
Chilton, R. 124
Chisholm, Professor A. R. 108, 254,
  292
Chinese:
    market gardeners 75, *273*
    restaurants 35
    settlers 76
    workers 92
Chrysler Corporation of America 219
Cigarette cards 43
Cigarettes 42-3
Cilento, Sir Raphael 284
Cinemas 75, *116-7*
Cinesound *114*
Circuses 128-9
Clabby, Jimmy 181
Clapp, Sir Harold 222, 342
Clarke, Sir William 84
Clarke, Marcus 30
Class distinction 10-11
Clements Tonic 158
Clifton, Tony 29
Close, Robert 157
Clothes:
    ready-made 244, 249
    children's 248
    men's 254-5
    women's 244-53, 256-7
Clunies Ross, Sir Ian 342
Cobb & Co. 206, *207*
Cobb, Freeman 206
Cobra Boot Polish 159
Codognotto, Beppi 35
Coe, Paul 29
Coffee 33
Cole, E. W. 15
Coles, Arthur and George 274
Coles Stores *274*
Collier, Frederick 142-3
Collier, Marie 142
Collins, Lottie 138
Comics 162-5
Commonwealth Arbitration Court 261
Commonwealth Day 16-7
Commonwealth Year Book 30
Conoulty, Bill 189
Conscription 301, 306-7
Constitution Act 15
Contemporary Art Society 133
Cook, Joseph 70, 302
Cooke, J. B. 22
Coombe Cottage 92, 145
Coombs, Dr H. C. 28
Cost of living 260-5
Cotton, Sidney 239, 342
Coulter, Robert 69
Council for Aboriginal Affairs 28
Council for Scientific and Industrial
    Research 342, 351
Counihan, Noel 133
Counter lunches 38
Cowra 318
Cramer, John Francis 295
Cricket 176-7, 199
Crocker, Barry *125*
Crosby, Caresse 246
Cross, Stan 150-51, 153-54, 342
CSIRO, *see* Council for Scientific and
    Industrial Research
Culotta, Nino 166
Curtin, John 35, 312, 314, 317-8, 343
Custance, Fred 229
Customs Department 156
Customs duties 13
Customs House, Jingellic *13*
Cycling 198

Dalgety *68*
Dal Monte, Toti 142-3
Dampier, Alfred 110, 138
Dancing 249

acceptance 104
tango 44
Dani, Carlo 106, 142
Daniel, Helen, see Danieli, Elena
Danieli, Elena 145
Darcy, Les 181, 343
Darwin:
    development 76-77
    bombing 77, 312-3
Davenport, Sir Samuel 92
Davey, Jack 122, 343
David, Edgeworth 349
David Jones' 105, 161, 246, 248, 262, 275
Davis, Arthur Hoey, see Rudd, Steele
Davis Cup 184
Dawson, Peter 107, 137, 147, 343
Daylight Express 222
Deakin, Alfred 15-16, 25, 343
Death, causes 281
Decimal currency 275
De Cisneros, Eleonora 142
De Dion Voiturette 210
Dedman, John Johnstone 316
Defence:
    Defence Act 300-1
    Department of 228
Defries, Colin 229
De Groot, Captain 55, 343
De Gunst, Molly 143
De Maistre, Roy 133
De Mole, Lancelot 304-5
Denat, Calexte 35
Denman, Lord and Lady 70, 220
Dennis, C. J. 21, 55, 110-1, 114, 139, 167, 343
Dent, H. C. 295
Dentistry 279, 288-9
Depression 73, 169, 266-71
Derwent Bridge 66
Desmond, Therese 123
Diabolo 202
Dixon, Les 31
Dobell, Sir William 133-4, 343
Dobson, Agnes 109
Dodds, Robin 98
Dog on the Tuckerbox 147
Domestic staff 80, 96, 97, 98, 317
Donaldson, George 151
Donges, K. 74
Donnellan, Frank 174
Dooley, James 40
Dorman Long and Co. Ltd 54
Dovey, Justice 157
Doyle, Stuart 114
Drake-Brockman, Geoffrey 220
Driffield, Lance 151
Driving tests 211
Drought 319
Drysdale, Sir Russell 133-35, 343
Dudley, Countess of 244
Duffy, Charles Gavan 12
Duggan, Edmund 139
Duigan, John Robertson 230-1, 343
Duke of Cornwall and York 18
Duncan, Alistair 122
Dunlop Rubber Company 211, 276-7
    Reliability Trial 212-3
Dunne, Frank 151
Dunstan, Don 62
Dunstan, Keith 41
Durack, Fanny 198, 256
Dutton, Harry 214
Dyer, Bob 343
Dyson, Edward 30, 138-9, 168
Dyson, Will 168

East, Charlie 188
Eccles, Sir John 343
Edison, Thomas Alva 209
    phonographs 106
Edmond, James 15
Education 279
    demonstration school 294
    great public schools 294
    high schools 294-5

Montessori method 294
primary schools 292-3
travelling teachers 295
Edwards, George 123
Efftee Films 114-5
Elder, Thomas 206
Electricity 49, 100
    electric belt 284
    in hospitals 284
    lighting 216
Electrolytic Zinc Company of Australasia 67
Elizabethan Theatre Trust 139
    Opera Company 143
Ellery, Reg 293
Elliot, J. W. C. 210
Elliot, Madge 120, 140
Elliott, Herb 184, 344
Elliott, Tom 124
Emancipation of women 264-5
Employment 10-11, 264
    women 263-4
    children 263
Emu Wine 40
Enterprise, The 215
Esplin, Donald 90
Esson, Louis 34, 138, 344
Eton-Harrow Travelling School 295
Evans, Ivor 20
Evans, Norman 291
Evatt, Dr H. V. 133-34, 151, 344
Everage, Edna 140
Everett, G. F. 34

Fadden, Arthur 310, 312
Fane, Maude 120
Farmer and Co. 121, 246, 275
Farming 276-7
Fashions, clothing 11
    children's 130, 245, 248
    Dior's 'new look' 252
    Edwardian 244-5
    men's 254-5
    mini skirt 253
    motoring 211
    shopping 63
    sporting 198-9
    swimming 193-5, 256, 257
    thirties 250-1
    underwear 246, 248-9
    wartime 302, 316
'Fashions for Victory' 252
Fasoli, Vincent 34-35
Fasoli's, Melbourne 34-35
Featherston, Grant 94
Federal capital, search for 68-69
Federal Match Company 43
Federal Parliament 137
    opening 18-19
Federation 9, 12-17
Ferguson, Sir Ronald Munro 67, 234-5
Ferguson, S. R. 215
Fields, W. C. 140
Finch, Peter 114, 344
Finey, George 151, 344
Finlayson, W. F. 76
Fish:
    consumption 36
    scallops 38
Fisher, Andrew 70, 73, 302-3, 310
Fisk, Ernest 118-9, 124, 344
Fitchett, Reverend W. H. 44
Fitton, Doris 138-9, 344
Fitzpatrick, Brian 25
Flats 84
Florentino Restaurant, Melbourne 35
Florey, Lord Howard 344
Flying boats 241
Flying doctor 291
Flynn, Errol 115, 345
Flynn, John 290, 291, 344
Flynn, Percy 197
Foll, Senator Hattil Spencer 158
Food 38-9
    adulterated 36
    Australian dishes 33, 36, 38

Australian diet 32-34, 37
    Chinese 35
    consumption of 32, 36-37
    deep frozen 39
    Eskimo Pie 39
    European influence 37
    Italian 35
    pizzas 39
    prices in 1901 260
    pure food regulations 36
    restaurants 34-35, 262
    sundaes 39
    take-away dispensers 39
Football 178-9
    Australian Rules 178-9
    Rugby League 178-9
    Rugby Union 178-9
    Soccer 178
Ford, Model-T 216, 240
Ford Motor Company 219
Fort Street Boys' High School 295
Foster, A. W. 306
Fox, E. Phillips 133
Frazer, C. E. 22
Freeland, Professor J. M. 84, 93
Freshman, Ivor 121
Friend, Donald 134
Frith, Alfred 120
Fry, C. B. 178
Fulford, Charles 287
Fuller, Lord and Lady 244
Fuller-Gonsalez Opera Company 142
Fuller's Royal Grand Opera 143
Fullwood, Sid 197
Furniture:
    Victorian 92
    modern 94-95
Fysh, Sir Hudson 77, 240, 345

Gallipoli 302
Game, Sir Philip 269
Games:
    children's 130-1
    indoor 104-5
Gane, Douglas 126
Garland, Nicholas 31
Garlick, Phil 188
Garner, Madge 251
Garvan, J. P. 14
Gas lights 49, 75, 93
Gas producer 219
General Motors-Holden's 219
George Robertson 156
Georgian House 157
Gilbert, Ernest 287
Gillies, Duncan 14
Gilmore, Dame Mary 345
Glassop, Lawson 156-7
Gleeson, James 133
Goble, Stanley 238
Gocher, William 194
Gold 64
Gold Coast 61
Golden Gate Soda Fountain 39
Golf 174, 198
    midget 203
Gonsalez Opera Company 142
Gordon, F. H. 219
Grace Bros 42, 104, 246, 264, 275
Grainger, Percy 146, 345
Grainger Museum 146
Gramophone 104
Granforte, Apollo 142
Grant, Julius 139
Grapes, G. Hamilton 219
Grattan, C. Hartley 255
Greenway, C. A. 38
Greenway, Francis 54
Greer, Germaine 345
Gregg, Norman 280
Gregoire, J. A. 215
Grey, Earl 12
Grice, James 80

Grieg, Eduard 146
Griffin, David 38
Griffin, Walter Burley 70-72, 79, 88, 90, 116-7, 345
Grime, Billy 129
Grocers 272-3
Grounds, Sir Roy 79, 91 345
Guillaux, Maurice 232
Gundagai 147
    songs about 147
    railway station 222
Gunn, Jack 35
Gunther, John 60, 62
Gurner, Sir George 15
Gurney, Alex 31
Gye, Hal 167, 345

Haddon, Robert Joseph 79, 89, 345
Hall, Bernard 22
Hall, Frederick 107
Hall, Ken 114, 340, 345
Hallett, Charles 151
Hallstrom, Sir Edward 228, 345
Ham, Dr Burnett 284
Hammond, Joan 143
Hancock, Hubert 15
Hannan, Jimmy 125
Hansom cabs 209, 211
Hargrave, Lawrence 228, 346
Harkness, Don 188, 215, 346
Harper, Robert 260
Harris, Max 38, 157
Harris, R. Keith 56
Harrison, E. J. 156
Harrison, R. A. 23
Hart, Fritz 142
Hart, W. E. 233
Hartnell, Lawrence 219
Hartt, Cecil 150
Hasluck, Sir Paul 314, 316
Hats:
    bowler 254
    cabbage tree 255
    men's 254
    women's 244, 248, 250
Hawker, Harry George 233, 346
Hawkesbury Agricultural College 247
Haynes, John 340
Hazon, Roberto 142
Headache powders 284
Heagney, Muriel 271
Health 278-91
Heenzo 158
Heidelberg School 134, 351-2
Helpmann, Sir Robert 140, 255, 346
Henderson, Admiral 301
Henderson, Peter 54
Herbert, A. P. 72
Herbert, Harold 133, 164
Herbert, Xavier 346
Herman, Sali 133
Hertz, Carl 108
Hesling, Bernard 34
Hetherington, John 27, 255, 272, 292-3
Heysen, Sir Hans 132, 346
Higgins, Arthur 111
Higgins, Henry Bourne 260-1, 298
Hill, Alfred 146, 340
Hill, Ernestine 290-1
Hill, F. J. 301
Hills, G. J. 90
Hill Top Station 222
Hinkler, Bert 232, 346
His Master's Voice 107
Hitchcock, Bobby 237
Hobart 66, 67
    All Nations Hotel 67
    Derwent River 66, 183
    floating bridge 66
    Hadleys Hotel 38
    hydro-electricity 67
    Imperial Hotel dining room 34
    Mount Wellington 66
    Theatre Royal 66
    viaduct bridge 66

Wrest Point Casino 66
Hobart Town Bazaar 67
Hodge, Harry 128, 277
Hogan, James 30
Hogan, Paul 30
Holbrook, David 295
Holden 219
Holland, Fritz 181
Holman, William 44, 298
Holmes, Dr Mervyn 76
Holt, Joseph Bland 138, 346
Home guards 12
Hood, Dr A. Jarvie 280
Hopetoun, Lord 9, 16, 18, 209, 260
Hordern, Lebbeus 232
Horne, Richard Henry 'Orion' 173
Horning, H. W. and Co. 50
Horses 208-9
    care of 208
    farming 277
    horse troughs 209
    racing 175
    horse-drawn vehicles 208, 209
Hosiery 249, 51
Houdini, Harry 229
Housing:
    architectural style 82-83, 90-91
    flats 84
    interior design 11, 92-93, 98-99
    mansions 80, 81
    slums 58, 282
    terraces 85
    war service homes 86-87
    workers' homes 260
Housing of the People Committee 58
Howell, Madelaine 123
Howell, Ted 123
Hughes, Billy 47, 68, 70, 72, 107, 118,
    150-51, 180, 234-6, 282, 298, 303,
    306, 314, 346
Humphries, Barry 31, 94, 140, 147,
    346-7
Hunt, H. A. 90
Hurley, Frank 235, 339, 347
Hutchison, R. C. 39
Hutton, J. C. Pty Ltd 160

Ice chests 100
Ice-skating 203
Immigrants 25-27, 86
    discrimination against 27
    housing 86
    life-style 26
Immigration 25-27
    assisted 26
    restrictions 35
Imperial Airways 241
Income tax 11
Indian-Pacific route 221
Infant mortality 281
Influenza 282-3
Inglis's Billy Tea 161
International Grand Opera
    Company 143

Jackson, W. F. 52
Jardine, D. R. 175
Jenkyns, H. 37
Jenvey, H. V. 118
Jerome, Daisy 140
Jervois, Major-General Sir William 300
John, Cecilia 307
Johns, W. E. 122
Johnson, Amy 238-9
Johnson, Gertrude 141-2
Johnson, Jack 180-1
Johnston, George 31, 160, 266-7, 347
Jolliffe, Eric 31
Jones, F. H. 229
Jonsson, Joe 151
Joyce, Eileen 347
Joynton-Smith, Sir James 347

Kahanamoku, Duke 196
Kean, Ellen 56
Kellaway, Alec 114
Kellerman, Annette 193, 347
Kelly, Dr Michael 45
Kelly, W. H. 70
Kelly, W. T. 219
Kenneally, Thomas 347
Kennedy, Alexander 240, 241
Kennedy, Graham 125
Kenningham, Charles 18
Kenny, Sister Elizabeth 347
Kerry, Charles 200
Keesing, Nancy 266
Kincaid, Dr Hilda 270
Kingsford Smith, Sir Charles 107, 197,
    219, 236-7, 347
Kipling, Rudyard 15, 30, 150-51, 166
Kisch, Egon 27
Kitchener, Lord 298, 299, 301
Kitchens 99
Kiwi Shoe Polish 160
Knibbs, G. H. 30
Konrads, Ilsa and John 174, 193, 347
Korody, George 94

Labour Day 261
Ladd, Pearl 141
Lambert, George 133
Lamond, Hector 163
Lamplighter 49, 75
Landy, John 184
Lane, William 345
Lang, Jack T. 55, 236, 266, 343, 348
Larwood, Harold 175
Lauder, Harry 121, 140, 158
Laver, James 248
Lawler, Ray 137, 348
Lawlor, Adrian 133
Lawrence, D. H. 52
Lawson, Henry 10, 158, 163, 338,
    345, 348
Lay-by system 275
Leason, Percy 160
Lee, Alfred 18, 210
Leslie, Fred 140
Lewis, Howard 218
Lewis, Thomas Essington 348
Lievain, Gaston 34
Life expectancy 281
Light, Colonel William 62
Lilley, Norman 163
Lilydale Express 145
Lind, Ruby, see Lindsay, Ruby
Lindbergh, Charles 237
Lindrum, Walter 185, 348
Lindsay, Sir Daryl 133, 145, 159, 164,
    171, 348
Lindsay, Jack 38, 41, 52
Lindsay, Joan 145
Lindsay, Sir Lionel 44, 49, 133,
    159, 168, 170-1, 180, 348
Lindsay, Mary 170
Lindsay, Norman 17, 42, 45, 50, 58,
    156, 162, 166, 168, 170, 171, 180,
    292, 300, 348
Lindsay, Pearl 170
Lindsay, Percy 159, 168, 170, 171, 348
Lindsay, Reginald 170
Lindsay, Rose 49, 171, 246
Lindsay, Ruby 168, 170, 171, 348
Lindsay, Vane 164
Lisson, Jack 291
Litchfield, H. A. 237
Lloyd, Reginald, 240
Locke-Elliot, Sumner 139, 348
Lockwood, Douglas 253, 312
London, Charmain and Jack 180
Long, Sydney 45, 132-3
Longford, Raymond 110-1, 186, 348
Longstaff, John 133, 134, 157
Loveday, J. F. 280
Low, David 166-7, 171
Lowe, Mr Justice 313
Lower, Lennie 169, 269, 348

Lucas, E. V. 167
Luffman, Mrs Bogue 98
Lumière, Louis and August 108
Lunn, Lionel 123
Lyall, Lottie 110, 111, 349
Lyne, Sir William 16, 69
Lyon, Harry H. 196
Lyons, Joseph A. 147, 167, 310

Macartney, Frederic 272
MacArthur, General Douglas 314
McAuley, James 157
McCormack, John 142
McCormick, Peter Dods 21
McCubbin, Fred 133-4
MacDonald, J. S. 133
Macdougall, Pakie 34, 138
McDowall, Dr Val 124
McDowell, Betty 123
McGowen, 'Big Jim' 110
McGregor, Craig 31, 60
McGinness, P. J. 240-1, 349
McInnes, Graham 127
McIntosh, Hugh D. 39, 44, 180-1, 186,
    349
McIntosh, John 238
McIntyre, Iver 238
McKay, Claude 150, 349
MacKenzie, Jeanne 56
McKimmin, S. M. 39
McLay, Roger 94-5
Maclurcan, Charles 120
Maclurcan, Mrs Hannah 32-3
Maclurcan, Robert 91
McMahon, Gregan 138, 349
McMahon, William 38
McMaster, Fergus 241
McMillan, William 14
McMurtie and Co. 126
MacRobertson-Miller Airlines 240
McWilliams, T. H. 237
Maddocks, Cyril 236
Madelaine, Mademoiselle 251
Madigan, Dr C. T. 206
Magazines:
    Adam & Eve 151
    Art in Australia 151
    The Bulletin 150, 340
    Chums 162
    The Home 151
    The Lone Hand 151, 162, 338
    Smith's Weekly 150, 338
    The Triad 151
Magic lantern 104
Magnet, Mona 147
Mah Jong 105
Mahony, Frank 132
Mailey, Arthur 174
Mann, Leonard 171
Mannix, Dr Daniel 306, 349
Marconi, Guglielmo 118, 120, 259
Marconi Wireless Telegraph Company
    118
Mark Foy's 210, 248
Marks Motor Construction Company
    219
Marquet, Claude 162
Marshall, Alan 267
Marshall, Jock 134
Martin, Justice 157
Massoni, Rindaldo 35
Mattinson, Lance 151
Mawson, Sir Douglas 349
Meat pies 38
Medicine 280-1
Meekin, Dave 128
Melba, Dame Nellie 72, 75, 92, 106,
    136, 137, 142, 144-5, 170-1, 307-8,
    349
Melbourne 56-59
    aquarium 193
    Australian building 52
    Bourke Street 59
    Buckley & Nunn 35, 48, 275
    Café Bohemia 35
    Café Denat 35

Capitol Theatre 116, 117
Cole's Book Arcade 49
Collins Street 56, 57, 59
Eastern Markets Building 59
Elizabeth Street 59
Fasoli's 34-35
Fitzroy 58
Florentino Restaurant 35
Menzies Hotel 58
Mockbell coffee shops 34
Regent Theatre 117
rivalry with Sydney 56-57
Melbourne Cricket Ground 178
Melbourne Cup 175
Melbourne Repertory 138
Meldrum, Max 133, 349
Melrose, Jimmy 239
Menzies, Sir Robert Gordon 133, 255,
    262, 275, 310, 312, 314, 316, 319,
    350
Menzies Hotel, Melbourne 58
Meyers, Lilian 110
Milk bars 39
Millar, Grace 141
Miller, Mrs Keith 192
Miller, Monty 306
Miller, Syd 151
Mills, James 122
Miniature golf 203
Miranda, Lalla 142
Mitchell, Helen Porter, see Melba
'Mo', see Rene, Roy
Mockbell coffee shops 34
Mockridge, A. T. 160
Molina, Ernesto 35
Moll, J. J. 238-9
Mollison, James 238
Monash, Sir John 350
Moncrieff, Gladys 107, 137, 140, 141,
    308, 316, 350
Monkey brand soap 160
Montagu, Pansy 42, 43
Moore, Carrie 140
Moore, William 35, 133, 263
Moran, Cardinal 44
Moran, F. P. 56
Moran, Dr Herbert 302
Moratorium 266
Moree 74
Morris, Edward Ellis 156
Morris, Reverend Hugh 45
Morris, James 57
Morrison, George Ernest 247
Moses, Charles 121
Moses, Jack 147
Mosman Musical Society Ballet 147
Motion pictures 103, 108-9, 112-3,
    116-7
Motor Cars 210, 212, 214-9
    all-Australian 218-9
    Austin 219
    Australian Six 219
    Bean 217
    Brush 215
    Coventry Humber 210
    Darracq 212
    De Dion Buton 211
    De Dion Voiturette 210
    Eco 219
    Essex 215
    Excelsior 217
    Hartnett 219
    Holden 219
    Minerva 215
    Model-T Ford 216
    Morris 219
    Napier 215
    racing 188-9
    registration of 210
    Southern Cross 219
    Summit 218
    Talbot 214
    Tarrant 218
    Thomson 218
Motor Cycles 210
    racing 189
Motoring records 212-5
Motor racing 188-9

tracks 188-9
Motor Traffic Act 211
Movietone 112-3
Mudgee *74*
Muggeridge, Malcolm 295
Mummery, Browning *142*, 143
Mundy, Lieutenant-Colonel 126
Munro-Ferguson, Lady Helen 304
Murdoch, J. S. 71
Murdoch, Rupert 151
Murphy, Lynn 122
Murray, Jack 191
Murray Valley Irrigation Scheme 343
Musgrove, George 138, 142
Musical Association of NSW 21
Muskett, Dr Phillip 32
Mutch, Tom 163
Myer, Sir Sidney 48

Namatjira, Albert 132, 350
Napier Cabs 210-1
Nathan, Lady 253
National Anthem 21
National Council of Clothing Styles 252
National Institute of Dramatic Art 139
National Opera of NSW 143
National Theatre Movement 143
Naval Defence Act 301
Navy 301
Neate, Kenneth 143
Nelson, Leonard 107
Newlands, S. F. 100
Newspapers:
    The Australian 151
    Smith's Weekly 150
NSW Bookstall Company 168
NSW Central Labour Exchange *261*
Niblo, Fred 138
Nicholls, Syd 164, 350
Nichols, Beverley 170-1
Nolan, Sir Sidney 134-5, 350
Nuttall, Charles 163

O'Connell, Michael 94
O'Connor, Patrick *129*
O'Farrell, Ernest 159
Ogilvie, Will 298
Ogilvy, Frances 140
O'Grady, John 166
O'Hagan, Jack 145, 147
O'Keefe, Johnny *125*, 350
Oldfield, W. A. 175
Oliphant, Sir Marcus 350
Olympia Speedway 188
O'Malley, King 68-71, 73, 88, 220, *336*, 350
Omnibuses 224-5
Opera 137, 142-3
Opperman, Sir Hubert 174, 351
Orange 68
Ormsby, Lyster 197
Ostrich feathers 247
Owen, Evelyn Ernest 351
Owen, P. T. 70

Packer, Robert Clyde 150
Paddle steamers *227*
Page, Sir Earle 120, 310
Pakerinen, Tuija 257
Pakie's Club 34
Palmer, Ambrose 179
Palmer, Nettie 268
Palmer, Vance 138
Palotta, Grace 138, 140, *141*
Parer, Raymond 238
Paris House, Sydney *34*
Parkes, Sir Henry 14, 50
Parliament House *72*, *73*
    opening of 137, 145
Parmentier, K. D. 238-9
Parry, Mervyn 91

Pate, Michael 115
Paterson, A. B. ('Banjo') 10, *166*, 200, 212-3, 338, 351
Paul, Mick 150
Payne, Arthur 282
Pearl Harbour 312
Peasley, Sam 130
Peel, Clifford 291
Pelaco 160
Penfold, Dr Christopher Rawson *40*
Perfume 245
Perry, Major 108
Perth 64-65
    Barrack Street *65*
    Esplanade Hotel *65*
    Hay Street *64*
    Murray Street *64*
    Queen's Hall *116*
Pethybridge, Tommy 237
Phar Lap *175*
Phillips, Nat ('Stiffy') 140, 351
Phonographs *106-7*
Photography 105
Pianos *104*
Picnics 126-7
Pike, Jim *175*
Ping-pong 202
Pioneer Players 138
Pitt, Marie E. J. 96-7
Plague 282
Pollard, Bob *123*
Ponder, Winifred 145
Population:
    capital cities 47
    country towns 47
    distribution 10, 25, 50, 60
    growth 47, 64
    towns 74
Porter, Hal 92, 293
Port Pirie 272
Post, Joseph 143
Postage stamps *22-23*
Postal rates, introduction 22
Prichard, Katharine Susannah 267,
Pringle, John Douglas 85, 135
Pringle, Lempriere 142
Prisoners-of-war *305*, *318*
Proctor, W. J. 211
Prohibition 73
Provan, Norm *179*
Pure Food Act 36

Qantas 241
Quacks 284-7
Queanbeyan 73-4
Queen Anne style 82
Quick, Dr 14
Quinlan Opera Company 142

Radio 103, 118-9
    introduction 104
    licences 120, 122
    serials 122-3
    stations 120-1
Radok, Uwe 26
Rafferty, Chips *30*, 115, 351
Railways 205-6, 220, *221*, 227
Rand, Professor M. J. 281
Rationing *316*, 317-9
Ravogli, Giulia 142
Rayon 250
Reard, Louis 257
Records 145
Recreation, outdoor 74-5
Redex trials 191
Reed, John 157
Reeve, Ada 140
Refrigerators 100
Reid, George 18
Reilly, Vergil 151
Renard, Doctor 211
Rendle, Val 236
Rene, Roy ('Mo') 114, *140*, 351

Rennie, Dr George 286
Restaurants 34-35, 262
    Amendola's, Sydney 34
    Café de Boheme, Sydney 34
    Café Denat, Melbourne 35
    Chinese 35
    'Ethnic' 35
    Fasoli's Melbourne 34-35
    Florentino, Melbourne 35
    Mockbell coffee shops 34
    Pakie's Club, Sydney 34
    Paris House, Sydney 34
    Pelligrini's, Sydney *34*
    Pfahlert's Grill, Sydney 34
    Metropolitan, Sydney 34
    Walker's Sydney 34
Returned Services League 21
Revue 140
Richards Industries 219
Richardson, Henry Handel 351
Arthur Rickard and Co. 50
Rickard, Harry 138
Rignold, George 138
Rigo Opera Company 142
Ritchard, Cyril 120, 175
River boats 205, *226*
Roberts, Lord 298
Roberts, Tom 18, 134, 351
Roberts Tracklayer *221*
Robertson, Ethel Florence, *see*
    Richardson, Henry Handel
Robertson, George 167
Robertson, Sir John 14
Robertson, Sir Macpherson 238
Robinson, Sir Hercules 159
Robinson, Ray *175*
Robson, L. L. 305
Robur Tea 126-7
Rocks, The 54
Roller Skating 203
Roper, Mr Justice 134
Roughley, T. C. 36
Rowing 183
Rowlandson, Alfred Cecil 168, 351
Royal Australian Navy 301
Royal Easter Show 129
Royal Flying Doctor Service 291
Royal Grand Opera Company 142
Ruark, Robert 124
Rubbo, Datillo 49, 133
Rudd, Steele 110, 139, 166, 168, 339
Rugby, *see* Football
Russell, Ella 142
Russell, Jim 164
Rylah, Arthur 156

Saarinen, Eliel *71*
Sachse, Bert 33
Sailing 182
Sailing ships 226-7
Sanche, Dr Hercules 284
Sass, Alex 150
Scaddan, John 44
Schilling, Ivy *140*
Schlink, Herbert 200
School 292-5
Schweppes 159
Scorfield, Ted 49
Scott, C. W. A. 238, 342
Scott, Peter 38
Scratchley, Lieutenant-Colonel Peter 300
Scullin, J. H. 113
Sculling championships 183
Scully, W. A. 316
Secession 271
See, Sir John 68
Seidler, Harry 79, *90*, 91, 351
Servants
    see Domestic staff
Service, James 12, 14
Sestier, Maurice 108
Seymour, Alan 139
Shackleton, Ernest 349
Sharman, Jimmy *129*

Shaw, John 143
Shaw, Mrs Percival 246
Shearer, David 210
Shiers, W. H. 234-5
Shrimpton, Jean 253
'Sidcot' flying suit 239
Silver Star Starch 260
Silvester's Butchery *273*
Simmons, David 260
Simond, P. L. G. 282
Simpson, Colin 61
Simpson, Dr George *291*
Simpson, Miss M. M. 294
Simpson, Norah 133
Sinclair, G. M. 160
Six o'clock closing 41, 44-45
Size, John and William 301
Skating 203
Skiing 200-1
Slapoffski, Gustav 142-3
Slessor, Kenneth 52, 74, 151, 167, 262, 351
Sloper, Ally 42
Smith, B. Barr 215
Smith, Bernard 133
Smith, Fanny Cochrane 28
Smith, Sir Harold Gengoult 238
Smith, Joshua 134
Smith, Sir Joynton 150
Smith, Keith and Ross 234-5, 352
Smith, Dr L. L. 285
Smith, Norman 'Wizard' 190, *215*
Smoking 42-43
Snelling, Douglas 94, *95*
Snowy Mountains Hydro Electric Authority 346
Snowy River 68
Soccer, *see* Football
Social life:
    at home 104-5
    in country towns 74-75
Soda fountains *39*
Souter, D. H. 164
Southern Cross 236-7
    Junior 237
    Lady 237
    Miss 237
Sovereign purses 244
Spanish mission style 83
Speedway Royale 189
Spencer, Cozens 109-10, 352
Spirit of Progress 222-3
Sport:
    aqua-planing *203*
    bowls 174
    boxing 180-1, 186
    cricket 176-7, 199
    cycling 200-1
    diabolo 202
    female fashions for 198-9, *200*, *201*
    female participation in 198
    football 178-9
    golf 174, 198
    indigenous 174
    miniature golf 203
    ping pong 202
    rowing 183
    sailing 182
    skating 203
    skiing 200-1
    water skiing 203
    sphairee 174
    speedway racing 174
    squash 174
    surfboard riding 174
    surfing 194-7
    swimming 192-7
    table tennis 202
    tennis 174, 184
Spurr, Mel B. 160
Squires, Bill 180
Stampfl, Franz 26
Steamroller and Traction Engine Act 211
Steamships 226
Steam trains 222-3
Steinbeck, Muriel *123*

Stephens, A. G. 49
Stephenson, George 54
Stern, Hans Otto 37
Stevens, H. L. *212*
Stevens, Horace 143
Stewart, Sir Frederick 156
Stewart, Gerald 37
Stewart, Harold 157
Stewart, Nellie 18, 31, 137-9, 141, 352
Stone, 'Wizard' 232-3
Stovehaven, Lord 113, 116
Strachan, David 133
Streeton, Sir Arthur 134, 160
Strikes:
    coal industry 318
    police 262
Sullivan, Walter *122*
Sulman, John 98
Summit, The *218*, 219
Summons, Arthur *179*
Sunbathing 195-7, 256
Supermarkets 274-5
Surf Life Saving Clubs 196-7
Surfers Paradise 61
Surfing 194-7
    Life-saving clubs 196-7
Sustenance 270
Sutherland, Joan 143, 352
Swagmen *24, 30*
Swimming 192-7
    fashions for 193-5, 198, *256, 257*
    laws against 194, *257*
    mixed bathing 196-7, 256
    strokes 192
Swimsuits 193-5, 198, *256, 257*
Sydney 50-5, 65
    Adams' Marble Bar 38
    Amendola's 34
    Anthony Horderns *51*
    Australia Hotel 50
    Bridge Street *53*
    Burdekin House 34
    Café de Boheme 34
    Circular Quay *50, 53*
    Culwulla Chambers *52*
    David Jones 275
    Farmers Ltd 275
    Grace Bros 275
    Grosvenor Hotel 51
    Manchester Unity Building *53*
    Mark Foy's 210
    Metropolitan Hotel 34
    Pakie's Club 34
    Paris House 34
    Pelligrini's 34
    Pfahlert's Grill 34
    rivalry with Melbourne 56-7
    Rowe Street 49
    State Theatre *117*
    Walkers 34
    Wexford Street *10*
    Wynyard Park *53*
Sydney Harbour Bridge *46*
    opening of 55
    plan for 54-55
Sydney Repertory Theatre Society
    136

Table tennis 202
Tait brothers 109, 138, 352
Tait, J. and N. 109, 138, 339, 352
Talbot car 212, *214*
Tango:
    introduction of 44
Tanna, Tommy 196
Tariff duties 14
Tarrant, Colonel Harley *213*, 214, 216
    352
Tauchert, Arthur 110, *111, 113*, 187,
    352
Taxation 262
Taxis 210-11
Taylor, George 118, *228*, 352
Taylor, Gordon 237
Taylor, Grant 115
Tea and Sugar train *221*

Teale, Leonard *123*
Television 103, 124
Temperance drinks 36
Tennis 184, 198
Tennyson, Lord 18, *19*
Tent Theatre Company 344
Terrace houses 85
Theatres:
    Independent 138
    live 138-9
    movie 116-7
    Playbox 136
Theatrical entertainment 137-9
The Firm 139
Thomas, Harry 110
Thompson, Mrs Ben 212, *213*
Thomson Motor-Phaeton *218*
Thring, Frank W. 114-15, 352
Tiles:
    Marseilles 11, 86
    Roman *86*
Tilley, E. J. 231
Tin Lizzie 216
Tobacco 42
Tomato sauce 32
Toowoomba 74-5
Torrey, Reverend Dr 44
Towns, George 183, 290
Toys 130-1
Trackson, James 211
Traeger, Alfred *290*, 291
Trains:
    electric 56-57, 202
Trams *51*, 224-5
    cable 224-5
    electric *51*, 60, 224-5
    steam 224-5
Transcontinental Railway 205, 220-1
    building of 220-1
Transport 202-3, 205
    camels 202
    coaches 202-3
    electric trolley buses *221, 225*
    motor cars 210-19
    ships 222-3
    trams 51, 60, 224-5
    trains 56-7, 202
Tressider, Richard 183
Triaca, Camillo 35
Trickett, Edward 183
Troedel, Walter 160
Troedel & Cooper 159-60
Trolley buses *225*
Tropical fruit, introduction of 37
Trumble, Hugh and Florence 247
Tucker, Albert 133
Tumut 69
Tunney, Gene 181
Turner, Roscoe 238
Turton, 'Petrov' 151

Ulm, Charles Thomas 236-7, 352
Ulm, Phillip 196
Underwear, women's 246
    corsets *246*
    sports 248-9
Unemployment 267-71
Uranium, discovery of 77
Ure Smith Pty Ltd 166
Ure Smith, Sydney 49, 151

Vacuum cleaners 101
Van der Sluice, Henry, *see* Rene, Roy
Vaudeville 137, 140
Vaughan, H. M. 56
Vickers, Dr Allan 291
Victoria Park Racecourse 150
Vigano, Mario 35
Wages 260-5
Wakelin, Roland 133
Walker, Lennox 347
Wall Street crash 266
Wallace, George 114, *115*, 140, 352-3

Wallace-Crabbe, Chris 178
Wallis, Reverend H. E. 45
War:
    Boer 297-9
    World War I 65, 297, 302-5, 308-9
    World War II 73, 297, 310-16
    Armistice 308
    austerity measures 316-18
    bombing of Darwin 312-3
    Japanese submarine attacks 313
    pensions 309
    rationing 316-9
    war service homes 87
Ward, Frederick 94, *95*
Ward, Hugh J. 141
Ward, Russel 62
Warner, Jim 196, 236
War Service Homes Commission 87
Washing machines *98*, 101
Water heater 98
Water speed record 190
Watkins, R. G. 195
Watson, J. C. 180
Wattle Path Palais de Danse,
    Melbourne 39
Waugh, Alfred 238-9
Wayda, Janina 142
Webb, Beatrice and Sidney 30
Weddings 247
Wege, William 218
Weingott, Owen *123*
Welch, Dr K. H. Vincent 291
Wells, H. G. 156, 167, 310
Werder, Felix 26
West, Claude *196*
Western Australian Airways Ltd 240
Wheat production 64, 74
Wheeler, Charles 132, 160
Whelan, A. S. A. 22
White, Alan *123*
White Australia Policy 27
White, G. H. 215
White, Patrick 353
White, Colonel T. W. 154
Wickham, Captain 76
Wilding, Anthony 184
Wilkins, Sir Hubert 196
Wilkinson, Leslie 83
Wilkinson, W. Percy 36
Williams, Fred *135*
Williams, Freddie *196*
Williams, J. D. 109
Williamson, J. C. 139-41, 142-3, 145,
    312, 353
Williamson-Melba Opera Company
    143
Wilson, Batty *199*
Wilson, Hardy 22, 70, 86, 99
Wine:
    adulteration 36
    consumption 40
Wireless Institute of Australia 118
Wirth Bros 128
Wise, Bernhard Ringrose 294
Withers, Walter 133
Wolfsohn, Professor Hugo 26
Wood, Professor Arnold 298
Wood, Dr Thomas 33
Woodfull, W. M. 175
Woolworths *275*
World Radio Convention 124
World Record (Aust.) Pty Ltd 107
Worrall, John 175
Wowsers 44-5
Wright, Arthur 168
Wright, Judith 353
Wright, Orville and Wilbur 228, 230
Wynn, Samuel 35

'Yellow peril' 300
Young, Blamire 22-23, 138, 158

Acknowledgements

Many people and organisations helped in the preparation of this book. The publishers would like to thank them all, particularly:

The Advertiser; The Advocate; The Age; Albury and District Historical Society; Amalgamated Wireless (Australasia) Ltd; Ampol Public Relations; Sydney Ancher; Angus & Robertson Ltd; Archives Office of New South Wales; Art Gallery of New South Wales; ATN Channel 7, Sydney; ATV Channel 0, Melbourne; Australian Bureau of Statistics; The Australian Government Department of Education; Australian Government Department of Health, Nutrition Section; Australian Information Service; Australian Inland Mission Frontier Services; The Australian Post Office, Historical Section; Australian War Memorial; AWA Recording Department; Bank of New South Wales; the Barr Smith Library, University of Adelaide; Beryl Barker; Alf Beashel; Richard Beckett; Beecham (Australia) Pty Ltd; Bondi Surf Bathers Life Saving Club; Jack Brabham; Nancye Bridges; Broken Hill Proprietary Ltd; Buckley and Nunn Ltd, especially D. W. Dobson; the late Keast Burke; Camera Supply Co. Pty Ltd; Michael Cannon; Richard Cardew; Margaret Carlyle; Frank Cayley; M. O. Chalmers; Arthur Cheney; Jim Christie; L. G. Clark; WO1 C. F. Clayton, NSW Army Records Office; R. W. Cleland; J. Donges, Cobb & Co.; M. C. Cohen & Co.; G. J. Coles & Co. Ltd; Bill Collins; Commonwealth Railways; Confederation of Australian Motor Sport; The Council of the City of Sydney, City Planning and Building Department; Philip Cox; *The Courier-Mail*; E. M. Crawford; New South Wales Cricket Association; Stan Cross; The Cunard Steam-Ship Co. Ltd; Dairy Farmers Co-operative Ltd; Dr and Mrs H. J. Daly; David Jones Ltd., especially the archivists; Pedr Davis, S. Rawson Deans; Vere Dodds; Drummoyne & District Presbyterian Home; J. D. Duigan; Geoffrey Dutton; Walter Dye; The Echuca Historical Society; Education Department of Victoria; Electricity Trust of South Australia; The Examiner Newspaper Pty Ltd; W. M. Farley; Farmer and Company, especially Harry Woodward; Federal Match Company; Fisher Library, University of Sydney; Jim Fogarty; Sandra Forbes; R. H. Fowler; Professor J. M. Freeland; Geelong Historical Society; General Motors-Holden's Pty Ltd; The General Reference Library of New South Wales; Ron Gibson; Dr Lionel Gilbert; Golden Fleece Petroleum; Government Printing Office of Western Australia; Grace Bros Pty Ltd; Grace Gibson Radio Productions; The Trustees of the Grainger Museum, University of Melbourne; John Hallstrom; Les R. Harrison; Sir Laurence Hartnett; The Herald and Weekly Times Ltd; Hollander & Govett Pty Ltd; J. H. Horn; J. C. Hutton Pty Ltd; Department of Immigration; Industrial Information Bureau, Department of Labour and Industry; Nadine Kahanamoku; M. J. Kelly; Australian Broadcasting Commission, especially Pat Kelly; Patricia Kennedy; Sir Eric Langker; Harold Larwood; Dr J. R. Laverty; Marshall Lindenburg; Sir Daryl Lindsay; Peter H. Lindsay; Joan Long; Geoff McCabe; Roger McLay; Robert Maclurcan; Manly Life Saving Club; Manly-Warringah & Pittwater Historical Society; Jack Mannix; Maritime Services Board of NSW; Mark Foy's Ltd; Marrickville Holdings Ltd; E. A. Marshall; Meat & Allied Trades Federation of Australia (NSW Division); Beryl Meekin; *The Mercury*; Ray Mitchell; The Mitchell Library; Modern Magazines (Holdings) Ltd; V. H. Mulvany; Jack Murray; The Museum of Applied Arts and Sciences; NSW Amateur Swimming Association; National Capital Development Commission; National Film Theatre of Australia; National Gallery of Victoria; National Heart Foundation; National Library of Australia; National Parks and Wildlife Service of NSW; National Trust of Australia (Victoria); National Trust of Australia (WA); New South Wales Department of Education; New South Wales Government Printer; New South Wales Police Department; Peter Newell; Stanley Nicholls; C. W. Nielson; Northern Regional Library, State Library of Tasmania, Launceston; Keith Oatley; Hugh O'Neill; Sir Hubert Opperman; The Oxley Memorial Library, Queensland; Parke Davis & Co.; Samuel Peasley; Pelaco Ltd; W. C. Penfold & Co. Pty Ltd; P.M.U. Products; Jack Pollard; Lynette Postle; Presto Smallgoods Pty Ltd; Jean Pulsford; Public Transport Commission of New South Wales, Rail Division Archives; Qantas Airways; Queen Victoria Museum and Art Gallery, Launceston; Queensland Department of Education; Queensland Museum; Randwick Historical Society; The Reserve Bank of Australia; Royal Australian Air Force; Royal Australian Historical Society; Royal Australian Institute of Architects (NSW Chapter); Royal Australian Institute of Architects (Victorian Chapter); Royal Flying Doctor Service of Australia (NSW Section); Royal Historical Society of Victoria; Royal Society of Tasmania; Science Museum of Victoria, especially F. J. Kendall; Harry Seidler; Department of Services and Property; Jimmy Sharman; John Sherwood; Showmen's Guild of Australasia; Silvesters Butchery (F. J. Walker Ltd); Slazengers (Australia) Pty Ltd; A. H. Smith Bequest Fund, Art Gallery of New South Wales; The Smith Family; Douglas Snelling; Dr R. J. Solomon; Vic Solomons, Sydney Tramway Museum; Doris Stallman; The State Electricity Commission of Queensland; State Electricity Commission of Victoria; State Electricity Commission of Western Australia; State Library of Queensland; State Library of South Australia, especially J. H. Love; State Library of Tasmania, Hobart; The State Library of Victoria, especially Patricia Reynolds and the staff of the La Trobe Collection; Steam Tram and Railway Preservation Society; Douglas Stewart; Walter W. Stone; F. R. Strange Pty Ltd; Surf Life Saving Association of Australia; A. F. Sutton; The *Sydney Morning Herald*; The Sydney Olympic Office; Howard Tanner; Tasmanian Museum and Art Gallery; TCN Channel 9, Sydney; Professor Ross H. Thorne; George Tibbits; Tooth & Co. Ltd; W. Tyrrell; University of Adelaide; University of Melbourne; University of Sydney, Architecture Library; University of Tasmania; M. Ure; The Veteran Car Club of Australia (NSW); Nevin Walker, The Vintage Record Shop; A. M. Ward; West Australian Newspapers Ltd; Bert Weston; Maxwell Whiting; David Wilkinson; Dr E. A. Williams; J. C. Williamson Theatres Ltd; Peter Willis; W. D. & H. O. Wills (Australia) Ltd; The Librarian, Windsor Castle, Berkshire, U.K.; Woman's Day; Brian Woodward; Jack Woodward; Woolworths Ltd; Wunderlich Ltd

Sources of reference

The publishers also acknowledge their indebtedness to the following books which were consulted for reference:

Aboriginal Policy and Practice, Vols I-III C. D. Rowley (Penguin); *Adelaide* M. Williams (Longman); *Alfred Deakin* J. A. La Nauze (Melbourne University Press); *Ampol's Australian Sporting Records* Jack Pollard (Jack Pollard Pty Ltd); *Architecture in Australia* J. M. Freeland (Cheshire); *Australasian Dental Jurisprudence* H. B. Bignold (Law Book Company of Australasia); *An Australasian Wander-Year* H. M. Vaughan (Seeker); *Australia and Australians in Civil Aviation* Ron J. Gibson (Qantas); *Australia During the War* Ernest Scott (Angus & Robertson); *Australia Since Federation* Fred Alexander (Nelson); *Australian Accent* J. D. Pringle (Chatto & Windus); *Australian Architecture* Robert Haddon (Geo. Robertson); *Australian Aviator* Norman Brearley with Ted Mayman (Rigby); *The Australian Ballet* Ian F. Brown (Longman); *Australian Bank Notes 1817-1963* G. W. Tomlinson (Hawthorn Press); *The Australian Encyclopaedia* (Grolier); *Australian Facts and Prospects* Richard Henry 'Orion' Horne (Smith, Elder); *Australian Father and Son* R. G. Casey (Collins); *The Australian Language* Sidney J. Baker (Angus & Robertson); *The Australian Legend* Russel Ward (Oxford); *Australian Music and Musicians* James Glennon (Rigby); *Australian Painting* Bernard Smith (Oxford); *Australian Silent Films* Eric Reade (Lansdowne); *The Australian Ugliness* Robin Boyd (Cheshire); *Australia's Heritage* (Hamlyn); *Australia's Home* Robin Boyd (Penguin); *Australia's Music* Roger Covell (Sun); *Australia's Pearl Harbour* Douglas Lockwood (Cassell); *The Aviators* William Joy (Shakespeare Head); *Aviator Extraordinary: The Sidney Cotton Story* R. Barker (Chatto & Windus); *By-Ways of Romance* W. F. Jackson (E. A. Vidler); *James Howard Catts* Dorothy M. Catts (Ure Smith); *Chronology of the Modern World* Neville Williams (David McKay); *City Sketches* William Moore (Fitchett Bros); *Cobbers* Dr Thomas Wood (Oxford); *Crusts and Crusades* W. M. Hughes (Angus & Robertson); *Dental Hygiene* H. Hayes Norman (W. K. Thomas); *Digging Stick to Rotary Hoe* Frances Wheelhouse (Cassell); *The Dreadnought of the Darling* C. E. W. Bean (Alston Rivers); *Duck and Cabbage Tree* Cedric Flower (Angus & Robertson); *Earlier Days* Douglas Miller (Angus & Robertson); *Echuca: a Centenary History* Susan Priestley (Jacaranda); *The Education of Young Donald* Donald Horne (Angus & Robertson); *Encyclopaedia of Australia* A. T. A. & A. M. Learmonth (Frederick Warne); *Encyclopaedia of Australian Art* Alan McCulloch (Hutchinson); *The Fabulous Phonograph* Roland Gelatt (Cassell); *Fact'ry 'Ands* Edward Dyson (Geo. Robertson); *A Family of Brothers* Viola Tait (Heinemann); *Federated Australia* ed. J. A. La Nauze (Melbourne University Press); *The First A.I.F.* L. L. Robson (Melbourne University Press); *Fish and Fisheries in Australia* T. C. Roughley (Angus & Robertson); *Flag of Stars* Frank Cayley (Rigby); *Flying Doctor Calling* Ernestine Hill (Angus & Robertson); *Flying Matilda: Early Days in Australian Aviation* Norman Ellison (Angus & Robertson); *Food for the People of Australia* R. C. Hutchinson (Angus & Robertson); *The Fortunes of Samuel Wynn* Allan Wynn (Cassell); *The Front Door* Douglas Lockwood (Rigby); *Genesis of a Gallery I and II* (The National Gallery of Australia); *The Government and the People 1939-1941* Paul Hasluck (Australian War Memorial); *The Government and the People 1942-45* Paul Hasluck (Australian War Memorial); *Le Grandi Voci* ed. Rodolfo Celletti (Istituto per la Collaborazione Culturale); *The Great Bust* J. T. Lang (Angus & Robertson); *The Hill End Story Volume III* Harry Hodge; *An Historical Geography of New South Wales to 1901* D. N. Jeans (Reed); *History of Australia* Marjorie Barnard (Angus & Robertson); *The History of Australian Aviation* Stanley Brogden (Hawthorn); *A History of Australian Literature* H. M. Green (Angus & Robertson); *History of Dentistry in South Australia 1836-1936* ed. Arthur Chapman (Australian Dental Association); *History of Magazine Publishing in Australia* Frank S. Greenop (K. G. Murray); *Homes in the Sun* Walter Bunning (Nesbit); *William Morris Hughes* A. Farmer Whyte (Angus & Robertson); *An Illustrated History of Australian Cricket* R. S. Whitington (Lansdowne); *The Inked-In Image* Vane Lindesay (Heinemann); *In Mine Own Heart* Alan Marshall (Cheshire); *Journey Among Men* Jock Marshall (Angus & Robertson); *Land of Fortune, a Study of the new Australia* Jonathan Aitken (Atheneum); *The Last Grain Race* Eric Newby (Secker & Warburg); *The Leafy Tree* Sir Daryl Lindsay (Cheshire); *Life in the Country* Michael Cannon (Nelson); *The Long View* Lionel Wigmore (Cheshire); *The Making of Australian Drama* Leslie Rees (Angus & Robertson); *Melba* John Hetherington (Faber); *The Melbourne Album* ed. Clive Turnbull (Georgian House); *Melodies and Memories* Dame Nellie Melba (Butterworth); *Men Were My Milestones* A. R. Chisholm (Melbourne University Press); *The Morning Was Shining* John Hetherington (Faber); *Music on Record* Frederick W. Gaisberg (Robert Hale); *My Brother Jack* George Johnston (Collins); *My Life with Charles Chauvel* Elsa Chauvel (Shakespeare Head Press); *My Life's Story* Nellie Stewart (John Sands); *My Mask* Norman Lindsay (Angus & Robertson); *No Memory for Pain* Sir Kingsley Norris (Heinemann); *Official History of Australia in the War of 1914-18* C. E. W. Bean (Angus & Robertson); *Official Year Books of the Commonwealth of Australia*, 1900-1972 (Commonwealth Bureau of Statistics); *Official Year Books of New South Wales*; *On the Wool Track* C. E. W. Bean (Angus & Robertson); *One for the Road* Jack Pollard (Angus & Robertson); *100 Australian Lives* (Hamlyn); *Painter's Journal* Donald Friend (Georgian House); *Paper and Gold* Geoffrey Blainey (Georgian House); *The Pattern of Australian Culture* ed. A. L. McLeod (Cornell University Press); *A Pictorial History of Australian Railways 1854-1970* Ron Testro (Lansdowne); *Russell Drysdale* Geoffrey Dutton (Thames & Hudson); *A Pictorial History of Surfing* Frank Margan & Ben R. Finney (Hamlyn); *Pioneers and Painters* ed. Alan Marshall (Nelson); *Policies and Potentates* W. M. Hughes (Angus & Robertson); *Profile of Australia* Craig McGregor (Hodder & Stoughton); *Proof Against Failure* Frederick Macartney (Angus & Robertson); *Queanbeyan, District and People* Errol Lea-Scarlett (Queanbeyan Municipal Council); *Reminiscences* Douglas MacArthur (McGraw-Hill); *The Rising Sun* Richard James Webb (North West Champion for the Moree Centenary Celebrations Committee); *River Boat Days* Peter Phillips (Lansdowne); *The Road to Gundagai* Graham McInnes (Hamish Hamilton); *The Roaring Twenties* Jack Lindsay (Bodley Head); *Sands' Sydney & Suburban Directories 1900-1931* (John Sands); *Singers of Australia* E. & F. Mackenzie (Lansdowne); *Solidarity Forever* Bertha Walker (National Press); *Stars of Australian Stage and Screen* Hal Porter (Rigby); *Story of Australian Art* William Moore (Angus & Robertson); *The Story of Australian Motoring* K. Winser (Motor Manual); *The Sunburnt Country* ed. I. Bevan (Collins); *The Tale of a City: Geelong 1850-1950* David Wild (Cheshire); *The Talkies Era* Eric Reade (Lansdowne); *Taming the North* Hudson Fysh (Angus & Robertson); *A Thousand Miles Away* G. C. Bolton (Jacaranda Press in association with the Australian National University); *The Turning Wheel* Geoffrey Drake-Brockman (Paterson Brokensha); *Twenty-Five* Beverley Nichols (Cape); *Two Centuries of Opera at Covent Garden* Harold Rosenthal (Putnam); *Uncommon Men* John Hetherington (Cheshire); *Victorian Year Books*; *Voices of the Past* John R. Bennett (Oakwood Press); *The Way It Was* T. J. Barker (NSW Government Printer); *Who's Master? Who's Man?* Michael Cannon (Nelson); *William Dobell* James Gleeson (Thames & Hudson); *Wowsers* Keith Dunstan (Cassell)

Artists, designers, photographers

The following did work for this book: W. R. Astley; Bill Bryant; David Carroll; Russell Coulson; Norman Danvers; Derek Dennis; Kerry Dundas; Mike Elton; Doug Holleley; Penelope Lee; David Naseby; Des O'Brien; Chris Reardon; Barbara Tilzey; Barry Weller

Manufacture

Original typesetting by The Dova Type Shop, Melbourne, Vic.; 1986 typesetting by Adtype Photocomposition, Ultimo, NSW. Reproduction by Litho Platemakers Pty Ltd, Netley, SA. Printing and binding by Dai Nippon Printing Co (HK) Ltd, Hong Kong.

Photographs

The publishers wish to thank the following people and organisations who provided photographs and gave permission for their use. The numbers indicate the page on which each is reproduced, and the letters, the position on the page: t–top, c–centre, b–bottom, r–right, l–left.

Front cover, NSW Government Printer. Back cover, NSW Government Printer. Endpapers, NSW Government Printer. Pages 2-3: NSW Government Printer. 4: Tyrrell's Book Shop. 6: NSW Government Printer. 8: NSW Government Printer. 10: Mitchell Library, Sydney. 11: The Feitel Collection, The National Gallery of Victoria. 13: b, W. W. Fielder. 14: cl, Australian Information Service. 15: tl, National Library of Australia;b, Australian Information Service. 16: NSW Government Printer. 17: tcl, NSW Government Printer;tcr, Mitchell Library, Sydney; bcl, Mitchell Library, Sydney; bcc, NSW Government Printer; bcr, copyright Janet Glad C/o Curtis Brown (Aust) Pty Ltd; bl, Mitchell Library, Sydney; br, NSW Government Printer. 18: c, Australian Information Service; b, Mitchell Library, Sydney. 19: t, La Trobe Collection, State Library of Victoria; cl, La Trobe Collection, State Library of Victoria; tcr. La Trobe Collection State Library of Victoria; bcr, The South Australian Archives; bl, Australian Information Service; br, La Trobe Collection, State Library of Victoria. 20: r, La Trobe Collection, State Library of Victoria. 21: tr, Ausflag 88; b, Mitchell Library, Sydney. 23: Australian notes reproduced by authority of Reserve Bank of Australia. 24: NSW Government Printer. 26: bl, West Australian Newspapers Ltd; br, The South Australian Archives. 27: br, Mitchell Library, Sydney. 28: Tasmanian Museum and Art Gallery. 29: t, The South Australian Archives; c. The South Australian Archives bl, Tyrrell's Book Shop; br, Tyrrell's Book Shop. 30: t,A. C. Butcher Collection, National Library of Australia; bl, ATN Channel 7, Sydney; br, TCN Channel 9, Sydney. 31: bl, E. Jolliffe; bc, The Herald and Weekly Times Ltd; br, Nicholas Garland and Barry Humphries. 32: Sydney Morning Herald. 34: cr, br, Mitchell Library, Sydney 35: Buckley and Nunn Ltd. 36: Charles Troedel Collection, State Library of Victoria. 38: t, Paul Popper Ltd; b, Sydney Morning Herald. 39: c, Courier-Mail. 40: l, Paul Popper Ltd. 41: Tooth and Co Ltd. 42: bc, br, Charles Troedel Collection, State Library of Victoria. 43: l, W. D. and H. O. Wills (Australia) Ltd; tr, Charles Troedel Collection, State Library of Victoria. 44: t,copyright Janet Glad C/o Curtis Brown (Aust) Ltd; bl, Peter Lindsay. 45: t, The News; bl, Art Gallery of New South Wales, Sydney. 46: NSW Government Printer. 48: t, Buckley and Nunn Ltd; b, Herald and Weekly Times Ltd. 50: Tyrrell's Book Shop. 51: t, Tyrrell's Book Shop; cl, Mitchell Library, Sydney; b, NSW Government Printer. 52: maps based on original by Dr D. N. Jeans and Professor M. I. Logan, originally reproduced in The Australian Geographer. 53: t, cl, NSW Government Printer; tcr, bcr, Public Transport Commission of New South Wales; b, National Library of Australia. 54: t, Foster Collection, National Library of Australia; bl, br, Commissioner for Main Roads, New South Wales. 55: tl, NSW Government Printer; bl, Public Transport Commission of New South Wales; bc, The Sydney Morning Herald; br, photo by John A. Carnemolla. 56: photo by Mark Strizic. 57: t, photo by Mark Strizic; b, Herald ad Weekly Times Ltd. 58: t, Herald and Weekly Times Ltd; br, Australian Information Service. 59: t, National Library of Australia; c, La Trobe Collection, State Library of Victoria; b, photo by Mark Strizic. 60: t, Tyrrell's Book Shop; bl, Courier-Mail; br, Paul Popper Ltd. 61: c, b, Paul Popper Ltd. 62: The South Australian Archives. 63: t, Paul Popper Ltd; cl, bl, The South Australian Archives; r, Advertiser Newspapers Ltd. 64: tl, tr, West Australian Newspapers Ltd; bl, Government Printing Office of Western Australia. 65: tr, West Australian Newspapers Ltd; b, Government Printing Office of Western Australia. 66: Beatties Studios; c, Benjamin A. Sheppard; b, Don Stephens and Associates. 67: t, Archives Office of Tasmania; b, The Mercury. 68: c, b, National Library of Australia. 69: t, c, National Library of Australia; b, Mitchell Library, Sydney. 71: t, Australian Information Service; c, NSW Government Printer; b, National Library of Australia. 72: t, Australian Information Service; bl, National Library of Australia.73:tl, Photographic Library of Australia; tr, The Age; b, Qantas; br, Parliament House Construction Authority. 74: t, Paul Popper Ltd. 75: tl, reproduced from the original in the Battye Library; tr, Special Services Division, Education Department of Victoria; c, b, Paul Popper Ltd. 76: Australian Information Service. 77: t, c, Australian Information Service; b, The South Australian Archives. 80: t, Australian Information Service; b, Herald and Weekly Times Ltd. 81: t, The South Australian Archives. 82: b, NSW Government Printer. 84: NSW Government Printer. 85: tl, NSW Government Printer. 86: cl, Victorian Chapter, Royal Australian Institute of Architects; cr, Australian Information Service. 87: NSW Government Printer. 88: t, National Library of Australia. 89: t, Hugh O'Neill; b, Victorian Chapter, Royal Australian Institute of Architects. 90: bl, r, Harry Seidler and Associates. 91: b, Peter Newell. 92: t, The South Australian Archives; b, La Trobe Collection, State Library of Victoria. 95: b, Roger McLay. 96: Geoffrey Dutton. 97: tl, Mitchell Library, Sydney; tcr, Charles Troedel Collection. State Library of Victoria. 100: cr. r, John Hallstrom. 101: tl, washing machine in Museum of Applied Arts and Sciences, Sydney; b, John Hallstrom. 102: The South Australian Archives. 104: bl, magic lantern in Museum of Applied Arts and Sciences, Sydney. 105: bl, Walter Dye; br, V. H. Mulvany. 106: t, National Library of Australia; b, gramophones in Australian Broadcasting Commission museum, Sydney. 107: t, Charles Troedel Colection, State Library of Victoria; b, Sydney Morning Herald. 108: bl, Dorothy M. Tayler; br, Sydney Morning Herald. 109: National Library of Australia. 110: Emilie Longford. 111: National Library of Australia. 112: United Artists Television. 113: t, J. Tauchert, Cinema International Corporation Pty Ltd; bl, Cinesound Movietone Productions Pty Ltd; br, National Library of Australia. 114: National Library of Australia. 115: t, Sydney Morning Herald; b, National Library of Australia. 116: tl, West Australian Newspapers Ltd; cr, br, Adrian Crothers Pty Ltd; bl, Professor Ross H. Thorne. 117: b, Adrian Crothers Pty Ltd. 118: AWA. 119: radios in Australian Broadcasting Commission museum, Sydney. 120: br, Herald and Weekly Times Ltd. 121: Australian Broadcasting Commission. 122: tl, AWA Recording Department; tr, Grace Gibson Radio Productions; b, Australian Broadcasting Commission. 123: t, AWA Recording Department; cr, AWA Recording Department; bl, Grace Gibson Radio Productions. 124: l, Courier-Mail; r, Sydney Morning Herald. 125: tl, TCN Channel 9, Melbourne; tr, ATV Channel 0, Melbourne; br, television set in Museum of Applied Arts and Sciences, Sydney; b, Australian Broadcasting Commission. 126: Archives Office of Tasmania. 127:t, The Mercury; c. Archives Office of Tasmainia; bl Northern Regional Library, State Library of Tasmania, Launceston; br,

David Jones Ltd. 128: Jim Fogarty. 129: b, Jimmy Sharmon. 130: t, br, Archives Office of Tasmania, bl, Mitchell Library, Sydney. 131: t, br, Jean Pulsford; c, bl, Museum of Applied Arts and Sciences, Sydney. 132: Art Gallery of New South Wales, Sydney. 133: tl, Art Gallery of New South Wales, Sydney; tr, NSW Government Printer. 134: Art Gallery of New South Wales, Sydney. 135: tr, A. H. Smith Bequest, Art Gallery of New South Wales, Sydney; b, Art Gallery of New South Wales, Sydney. 136: J. C. Williamson Theatres Ltd. 138: Mitchell Library, Sydney. 139: J. C. Williamson Theatres Ltd. 140: bl. United Press International. br. Mirror-Australian-Telegraph Publications. 141: tl, tc, La Trobe Collection, State Library of Victoria; tr, Mitchell Library, Sydney; b, Harold Casneaux. 142: b, Herald and Weekly Times Ltd. 143: J. C. Williamson Theatres Ltd. 144: t,Sydney Morning Herald; b, Mitchell Library, Sydney. 145: b, Herald and Weekly Times Ltd. 146: bl, W. H. Paling Pty Ltd. 147: t, Allan Studios; cl, Battye Library, Perth; cr, Mitchell Library, Sydney. 150: c, Stan Cross. 152: lc, Stewart McCrae. 153: b, Stan Cross. 154: tr, Stan Cross. 155: tr, 'Unk' White; b, Ken Maynard. 156: copyright Janet Glad C/o Curtis Brown (Aust) Pty Ltd. 157: tl, Angus and Robertson (Publishers) Pty Ltd; tc, Georgian House Pty Ltd; tr, Max Harris. 159: t, Charles Troedel Collection, State Library of Victoria. 160: tr, J. C. Hutton Pty Ltd; b, Pelaco Ltd. 161: t, Mitchell Library, Sydney; lc, David Jones Ltd; rc, Inglis (Pty) Ltd; b, Hollander and Govett Pty Ltd. 162: tl, copyright Janet Glad C/o Curtis Brown (Aust) Pty Ltd; b, Stanley Nicholls. 164: bl, Stanley Nicholls. 165: t, John Fairfax Ltd; b, Syd Nicholls. 166: t, National Library of Australia; b, E. D. Davis. 167: bl, Angus and Robertson (Publishers) Pty Ltd. 168: Fisher Library, University of Sydney. 169: t,Sydney Morning Herald. 170: Peter H. Lindsay. 171: tl,Harold Casneaux; tcl, tcr, Walter Stone; tr, Faber and Faber Ltd; br, Sir Daryl Lindsay. 172: NSW Government Printer. 174: Australian Information Service. 175: t, M. Lindenberg; c. Charles Troedel Collection, State Library of Victoria; bl, Jack Woodward; br, Herald and Weekly Times Ltd. 176: bl, Mirror-Australian-Telegraph Publications; tr, The South Australian Archives; br, Mirror-Australian-Telegraph Publications. 177: tr, Australian Broadcasting Commission; b, Sydney Morning Herald. 178: tl, Charles Troedel Collection, State Library of Victoria; tr, Herald and Weekly Times Ltd. 179: tl, The Age, tr, Sydney Morning Herald; b, Mr Jack Pollard. 180: t, Mitchell Library, Sydney. 181: tr, Ern McQuillan. 182: Alf Beashell. 183: t, Alf Beashell; c, Mitchell Library, Sydney; b, Archives Office of Tasmania. 184: t, Mitchell Library, Sydney; b, The Herald and Weekly Times Ltd. 185: t, Barry Weller; b, Central Press Photos Ltd. 187: National Library of Australia. 188: t, Laurie Richards; b, Pedr Davis Pty Ltd. 189: tl, Pedr Davis Pty Ltd.; tr, James Flood Trust; b, Pedr Davis Pty Ltd. 190:tr, Ampol Petroleum Ltd. b. The Sydney Morning Herald 191: t, Sydney Morning Herald. 192: b, Sydney Olympic Office. 193: tr, E. Konrads; br, Sydney Morning Herald. 194: t, Manly Life Saving Club; b, NSW Government Printer; b, West Australian Newspapers Ltd. 196: t, Northern Regional Library. State Library of Tasmania, Launceston; b, Nadine Kahanamoku. 197: c, Battye Library, Perth; b, Bondi Surf Bathers Life Saving Club. 198: t, The South Australian Archives; bl, A. C. Butcher Collection, National Library of Australia. 199: t, Central Press Photos Ltd. 200: Tyrrell's Book Shop. 201: tl, b, NSW Government Printer. 204: Public Transport Commission of New South Wales. 206: t, NSW Government Printer. 207: c, The South Australian Archives; b, Australian Post Office. 208: t, Courier-Mail; b, Tyrrell's Book Shop. 209: t, Mitchell Library, Sydney. 210: t, Archives Office of Tasmania: c, The South Australian Archives. 211: tl, The South Australian Archives; c,Courier-Mail; tr, The South Australian Archives; bl, NSW Government Printer. 212: b, Laurie Richards. 213: t, Laurie Richards; b, James Flood Charity Trust. 214: The South Australian Archives. 215: t, Michael Terry; bl, Pedr Davis Pty Ltd; br, New Zealand Herald and Weekly News. 216: l, Courier-Mail r, Petroleum Information Bureau (Australia). 217: t, NSW Government Printer; b, James Flood Charity Trust. 218: t, James Flood Charity Trust. 219: t, General Motors-Holden's; b, Wheels magazine. 220: t, National Library of Australia ; c, Commonwealth Railways. 221: tl, tr, bl, Commonwealth Railways; bc, br, Public Transport Commission of New South Wales. 222: t, A. C. Butcher Collection, National Library of Australia; c, b, Public Transport Commission of New South Wales. 223: t, br, Public Transport Commission of New South Wales. 224: t, Courier-Mail; bl, Mitchell Library, Sydney; br, The South Australia Archives. 225: tl, The South Australian Archives; tc, Tyrrell's Book Shop; tr, Mitchell Library, Sydney ; cl, Archives Office of Tasmania; cr, bl, NSW Government Printer; br, Herald and Weekly Times Ltd. 226: t, Paul Popper Ltd; b. The South Australian Archives. 227: t, La Trobe Collection, State Library of Victoria, b. NSW Government Printer. 228: t, Science Museum, London; b, Qantas Airways. 229: tl, The Age; tr, National Library of Australia. 230: b, Science Museum of Victoria, by permission of J. D. Duigan. 231: Science Museum of Victoria, by permission of J. D. Duigan. 232: c, Sydney Morning Herald; b, Mirror-Australian-Telegraph Publications. 233: t, Mirror-Australian-Telegraph Publications; c, Qantas Airways; bl, Hawker De Havilland Aust. Pty Ltd. 234: t, Courier-Mail; b, National Library of Australia. 235: tc, Courier Mail; bl, Mitchell Library, Sydney. 237: t, National Library of Australia; c, The Christchurch Star. 238: Royal Australian Air Force. 239: t, Australian Information Service; c, AWA; b, Qantas Airways. 240: Qantas Airways. 241: t, Courier-Mail; bl, Qantas Airways. 244: l, Buckley and Nunn Ltd; cr, La Trobe Collection, State Library of Victoria; br, Mitchell Library, Sydney.247: tl, The South Australian Achives. 248: t, br, Mark Foys Ltd. 249: cr, Holeproof Hoseiry; bl, Sandra Forbes; br, Archives Office of Tasmania. 250: t, Buckley and Nunn Ltd; bl, The Advertiser; bc, br, The South Australian Archives. 251: bl, Courier-Mail; br, The Age. 252: Advertiser Newspapers Ltd; br, Press Association; br, David Jones Ltd. 253: tl, David Jones Ltd; tr, Sydney Morning Herald; bl, Herald and Weekly Times Ltd; bc, bl, Sydney Morning Herald. 255: t, Courier-Mail; b, Royal Australian Historical Society. 256: bl, Herald and Weekly Times Ltd. 257: t, Mirror-Australian-Telegraph Publications; bl, NSW Government Printer. 258: NSW Government Printer. 261: t, c, NSW Government Printer; b, Herald and Weekly Times Ltd. 262: b, La Trobe Collection, State Library of Victoria. 263: t, NSW Government Printer; b, James Flood Charity Trust. 266: l, Sydney Morning Herald. 267: b, West Australian Newspapers Ltd. 268: Sydney Morning Herald. 269: Sydney Morning Herald. 270: NSW Government Printer. 271: t, Sydney Morning Herald; b, NSW Government Printer. 272: The South Australian Archives. 273: t, c, Mitchell Library, Sydney; b, F. J. Walker Ltd. 274: t, G. J. Coles & Coy Ltd; b, J. C. Hutton Pty Ltd. 275: t, Woolworths Ltd; b, Australian Information Service. 276: t, Paul Popper Ltd; cl, Tyrrell's Book Shop; bl, Mitchell Library, Sydney; br, Tyrrell's Book Shop. 277: t, NSW Government Printer. c. Tyrrell's Book Shop; b, Paul Popper Ltd. 278: NSW Government

Printer. 280: t, b, NSW Government Printer. 281: t, NSW Government Printer. 282: Mitchell Library, Sydney. 283: t, NSW Government Printer; bl, Mitchell Library, Sydney; br, The South Australian Archives. 285: Charles Troedel Collection, State Library of Victoria. 288: NSW Government Printer. 290: t, Australian Inland Mission; bl, National Library of Australia; br, The News. 291: t, Royal Flying Doctor Service; b, Australian Inland Mission. 292: c, Archives Office of New South Wales; b, NSW Government Printer. 293: t, copyright Janet Glad C/o Curtis Brown (Aust) Pty Ltd; c, br, NSW Government Printer; bl, Museum of Education, Teachers' College, Armidale, NSW. 294: NSW Government Printer. 295: t, Division of Planning, NSW Department of Education; b, NSW Government. 296: La Trobe Collection, State Library of Victoria. 298: NSW Government Printer. 299: tr, br, The South Australian Archives; cl, W. H. Paling Pty Ltd; cr, National Library of Australia; bl, Royal Society of Tasmania. 300: tr, br, copyright Janet Glad C/o Curtis Brown (Aust) Pty Ltd. 302: l, Australian War Memorial; r, Errol Lea-Scarlett. 303: tl, b, Australian War Memorial. 304: tl, b, Australian War Memorial; tr, Buckley and Nunn Ltd. 305: t, bl, Australian War Memorial; br, relics held by NSW Police Department. 306: t, Australian War Memorial; bl, National Library of Australia. 307: l, Australian War Memorial; r, La Trobe Collection, State Library of Victoria. 308: Australian War Memorial. 309: Australian War Memorial. 310: Australian War Memorial. 311: bl, La Trobe Collection, State Library of Victoria; r, Australian War Memorial. 312: tl, Australian War Memorial; tr, Sydney Morning Herald. 313: tl, West Australian Newspapers Ltd; tr, b, Australian War Memorial. 314: bl, United States Information Service. 315: tr, br, Courier-Mail. 316: Australian War Memorial. 317: tl, Australian War Memorial; tr, The Advertiser; br, West Australian Newspapers Ltd. 318: Australian War Memorial. 319: tr, Sydney Morning Herald; b, West Australian Newspapers Ltd. 320: NSW Government Printer. 322: (top to bottom) Archives Office of Tasmania; Australian Information Service; Sydney Morning Herald; Launceston Weekly Courier; Ford Motor Company of Australia Ltd. 324: (top to bottom) Mirror-Australian-Telegraph Publications; NSW Government Printer; National Library of Australia; Battye Library, Perth; Australian War Memorial. 326: (top to bottom) Sydney Morning Herald; The Australian; Mirror-Australian-Telegraph Publications; Herald and Weekly Times Ltd; Australasian Record Company Ltd. 328: (top to bottom) Commissioner for Main Roads, New South Wales; Sydney Morning Herald; National Library of Australia; Geoff McCabe; Central Press Photos Ltd. 330: (top to bottom) General Motors-Holden's; Australian War Memorial; AWA Recording Department; Sydney Morning Herald; ACME. 332: (top to bottom) Mirror-Australian Telegraph Publications; Syney Morning Herald; United Press International; Slazengers (Australia) Pty Ltd; New Era News and Information Service. 334: (top to bottom) Mirror-Australian-Telegraph Publications; Sydney Morning Herald; Australian Broadcasting Commission; Ansett Airlines of Australia; United Press International. 336: News Ltd.; World Series Cricket; News Ltd. 338: NSW Government Printer. 339: Australian Broadcasting Commission. 340: The South Australian Archives; b, Australian Broadcasting Commission. 341: The South Australian Archives. 343: Australian Broadcasting Commission. 345: Sydney Morning Herald. 346: Sydney Morning Herald. 348: The Mitchell Library. 349: The Australian Broadcasting Commission. 350: Mirror-Australian-Telegraph Publications.